Encyclopedia of Romance Fiction

Kristin Ramsdell, Editor

 GREENWOOD™

An Imprint of ABC-CLIO, LLC
Santa Barbara, California • Denver, Colorado

Library of Congress Cataloging-in-Publication Data

Names: Ramsdell, Kristin, 1940- editor.
Title: Encyclopedia of romance fiction / Kristin Ramsdell, editor.
Description: Santa Barbara, California : Greenwood, an imprint of
    ABC-CLIO, LLC, [2018] | Includes bibliographical references and index.
Identifiers: LCCN 2018016499 (print) | LCCN 2018036761 (ebook) |
    ISBN 9780313054051 (ebook) | ISBN 9780313335723 (alk. paper)
Subjects: LCSH: Romance fiction—Encyclopedias.
Classification: LCC PN3448.L67 (ebook) | LCC PN3448.L67 E53 2018 (print) |
    DDC 808.3/8503—dc23
LC record available at https://lccn.loc.gov/2018016499

ISBN: 978-0-313-33572-3 (print)
        978-0-313-05405-1 (ebook)

22 21 20 19 18   1 2 3 4 5

This book is also available as an eBook.

Greenwood
An Imprint of ABC-CLIO, LLC

ABC-CLIO, LLC
130 Cremona Drive, P.O. Box 1911
Santa Barbara, California 93116-1911
www.abc-clio.com

This book is printed on acid-free paper ∞

Manufactured in the United States of America

Contents

List of Entries

Guide to Related Topics

Cultural and Social Aspects of Romance

Cultural Influences on the Popular
Romance Genre
Empowerment of Women
Feminism and Popular Romance Fiction
Rape in Romance

History

American Romance Comic Book
(1947–1977)
Domestic Sentimentalists
Harlequin Books: Cupid's Publisher;
A Brief History of Romance
Publishing
Historical Perspectives on Changes
within the Genre
Mills & Boon

Organizations, Groups, Awards, and Publications

Affaire de Coeur: The Publisher's Voice
Critique Groups and Partners
Daphne Du Maurier Awards
International Association for the Study
of Popular Romance (IASPR)
Journal of Popular Romance Studies
(JPRS)
Prism and On the Far Side Awards
Romance Writers of America (RWA)
Romance Writers of Australia
Romance Writers Report (RWR)
Romantic Novelists' Association
(RNA)
Royal Ascot Awards
RT (Romantic Times) Book Reviews:
The Founder's Voice
RT (Romantic Times) Booklovers
Convention
RUSA-CODES Reading List Awards

Other Genres and Forms and Romance

Genreblending
Mystery/Suspense/Thriller and
Romance
Shoujo Manga in Romance
Soap Opera and Romance
Westerns and Romance
Women's Fiction and Romance

Plot Patterns and Themes

Arranged (or Forced) Marriage Plot
Beauty and the Beast Plot Pattern
Cinderella Plot Pattern
Mail-Order Bride Plot
Marriage of Convenience Plot
Pygmalion/Plot Pattern
Second Chance at Love/Reunion Plot
Secret Baby Plot
Themes in Popular Romance Fiction

Sharing the Genre: Access and Education

Libraries and Popular Romance
Fiction
The Popular Romance Project and
Love between the Covers (2015)
Reviews and Reviewing
Romance Readers
Romance Research Collections
Teaching Popular Romance
Translations (English to Other
Languages)

Technology and Romance

Audiobooks and Romance
Fanfiction and Online Community
Fiction in the Romance Genre
Romance Blogs, Wikis, and
Websites

Preface

Purpose and Scope

Encyclopedia of Romance Fiction attempts to provide basic, relevant information on the popular Romance fiction genre in an accessible format for students and general readers who wish to know more about the topic. Subjects included cover the proverbial waterfront, ranging from detailed discussions of the various Romance subgenres and all that they entail to the nitty-gritty of the publishing and professional environment that is part of the genre—and everything in between. Each entry also includes a list of references and recommended resources for further research. Although this is not a biographical resource per se, it does include entries on a few classic or otherwise important authors and, in some cases, their iconic works. Readers interested in more information on authors will find appropriate resources listed in the bibliography at the end of the encyclopedia.

Organization

The entries that comprise the main body of this encyclopedia are arranged alphabetically by title. These entries are preceded by an introduction that briefly discusses the importance of the Romance genre and a Guide to Related Topics. The volume concludes with a list of Rita Award winners, a core reading list of suggested romance titles, a bibliography, and subject index.

Suggestions for Use

The basic arrangement of this resource is alphabetical and, therefore, straightforward, and many readers will be able to go directly to the entry they want. However, the following information may be helpful:

- Readers looking for information on romance by broad theme (for example, romance authors, cultural and social aspects, technology issues) should consult the Guide to Related Topics.
- Not all topics will have a separate entry but may be included in other articles. The index at the end of the volume will help readers find embedded topics, as will the "see also" references provided at the end of some entries.
- Readers interested in sampling the various romance subgenres may find Appendix 2: Testing the Waters, a list of suggested titles arranged by Romance subgenre, useful. Appendix 1: Rita Award Winners may be helpful as well, although some older titles may no longer be in print or available in libraries.
- Each article includes relevant references and sources for readers who want more information. Students, in particular, may find these good sources for further research and study. Note: Using the bibliographies of books and articles as a guide to other sources is a time-honored method for finding more information—although retrospective information—about a topic.
- For a brief list of more general online and print resources, consult the bibliography at the end of the encyclopedia.

Acknowledgments

An endeavor like this is never a solitary effort, and it was only with the help and advice of many people that it was accomplished. I would like to thank all the contributors for their advice, cooperation, and hard work; my several editors for their patience and help in shepherding this work through to completion; my colleagues and friends in the library, academic, and Romance worlds for their advice and encouragement; and my family.

Introduction

It's been more than 20 years since best-selling romance author Jayne Ann Krentz boldly announced, "Romance has arrived!" to a crowd of 700 stunned, but thrilled, librarians at the 1996 Public Library Association Conference in Portland, Oregon—and that remark is still as true today as it was then, if not more so. According to the latest statistics from Romance Writers of America (www.rwa.org/p/cm/ld/fid=580), the popular Romance genre accounted for at least 34 percent of the popular fiction market in 2015 and brought in over $1 billion in sales in 2013. The genre is definitely holding its own, and considering that much of the data collected doesn't include large segments of the burgeoning indie and self-published market, it's likely doing even better than reported.

Romance is one of the most popular and widely read of all the fiction genres; but for years (actually decades), it has quietly bubbled along under the literary radar, pleasing its numerous readers and often attracting attention only when it becomes the object of ridicule or scorn. There are any number of reasons, or at least opinions, as to why Romance is the most easily dismissed and maligned of the popular fiction genres, but one thing is almost certainly true—of all the fiction genres, it is the least understood by the majority of people.

At its heart, the Romance is a story of a romantic relationship, and while there is obviously much more to it, it is a relationship that has its roots in one of the most basic human drives—the survival of the species. This pair bond and the related courtship and family-structure themes are key to many romances, and while the genre has evolved in recent times to become much more inclusive, a nurturing, loving relationship between the protagonists is still a foundation of the genre. (This successful relationship is as necessary to a romance as the solution of the crime is to a murder mystery.)

According to the Romance Writers of America, a romance must have "a central love story and an emotionally satisfying and optimistic ending," but that doesn't mean that all romances are alike. There are as many different romances as there are writers, and the variety of subgenres under its broad umbrella arguably makes Romance one of the most inclusive, diverse, and flexible of all the popular fiction genres. A glance at its history shows how it has evolved over the years, changing with the times to meet the needs of readers.

Romances and love stories are as old as time, passed down through the ages, first by means of the oral tradition and then codified in written form. While literary forms that influenced the genre can be found much earlier, most scholars credit Samuel Richardson's epistolary *Pamela: Or Virtue Rewarded* (1740) with being the first romance novel. Works published between 1811 and 1818 by Jane Austen, as well as popular sensational authors of the day, such as Ann Radcliffe, soon followed suit, and later in the century the Brontës added their eerie Gothic touch as the Domestic Sentimentalists annoyed writers like Nathaniel Hawthorne, who famously referred to them as a "damn'd mob of scribbling women," with their overwhelming popularity.

By the end of the century, interest in these novels that largely focused on the details of domesticity and the relationships important to women had declined, but the issues they raised had laid the groundwork for the romances to come. During the early decades of the 20th century, writers like Elinor Glyn (*Three Weeks,* 1907) and Edith M. Hull (*The Sheik,* 1919) gave romance a daring, exotic touch, while the 1930s provided both the modern-day prototype for the Gothic romance with Daphne du Maurier's *Rebecca* (1938) and the independent, take-charge, not-always-good heroine of Margaret Mitchell's *Gone with the Wind* (1936). The next decade gave us another bad-girl heroine, but of a totally different kind, with Kathleen Winsor's racy-for-the-times *Forever Amber* (1944). In 1957, Canada-based Harlequin began publishing reprints of Mills & Boon romances, a decision that had lasting effects on the genre and led to Harlequin's prominent place in the market today. The 1960s ushered in the modern Gothic romance with the release of Victoria Holt's *Mistress of Mellyn* (1960), and the 1970s set the genre on its puritanical ear when Kathleen E. Woodiwiss's *The Flame and the Flower* (1972) and Rosemary Rogers's *Sweet Savage Love* (1974) sent the sensuality levels in historical romance spiking. Contemporary romance took the hint, and as the decade rolled over, sweet contemporary series lines were joined by their new, sexier sisters, and a romance boom was on.

The 1990s brought with it both diversity and change as a long-simmering interest in ethnic and multicultural romances resulted in the launch of Pinnacle's Arabesque line of African American romances in 1994, and fans began to look at the various Alternative Reality groups (Fantasy, Futuristic, Paranormal, Time Travel, and so on) with new eyes. Technology was also beginning to have an effect as romance writers and readers, often early tech adopters, took advantage of the Internet and then the Web to connect with one another for social and professional reasons. By the end of the 1990s, romances were becoming increasingly sexy, and the turn of the century witnessed the launch of a number of steamier imprints and lines. At the same time, inspirational romances (thanks to a boom in Christian fiction), a wide range of paranormal romances, and multicultural romances, along with trilogies or other groups of books linked in various ways, all grew in popularity. However, it is technology, enabling the rise of the independently or self-published author, that has had one of the greatest impacts on the genre and the industry in the new century, causing everyone to rethink their strategies and possibly consider new options.

Recently, Romance has found itself in the limelight with the blazing success of E. L. James's erotic Fifty Shades trilogy, which had its birth as a fan-fiction riff on the Twilight Saga. Despite the fact that it's more erotica than romance and bears little resemblance to the majority of romances published, the fact that many women are now feeling free to read what they consider Romance openly is a plus in most romance fans' books.

Although Romance fiction has been studied by scholars for years, until recently it has been approached in a negative, sometimes even pejorative way. Lately, this has changed. Realizing the importance of having valid scholarly research that resulted in publications, the Romance Writers of America, in 2005, established the Academic Research Grant, to be awarded to scholars who are pursuing "academic research devoted to genre romance novels, writers, and readers." More than 20 grants have been awarded since the inauguration of this grant. Two years later, the International Association for the Study of Popular Romance (IASPR) was formed, and in 2010 the *Journal of Popular Romance Studies,* an open-access, peer-reviewed, online publication of the association, was born.

Clearly, times are changing, and the Romance genre is finally getting some of the academic attention it deserves. But while the number of scholarly and professional articles and books is growing, general readers still need available resources. It is the hope that *Encyclopedia of Romance Fiction* will provide basic, authoritative information in a single place for the nonspecialist reader on this popular, most enduring subject that has too long been ignored.

A

Affaire de Coeur: The Publisher's Voice

Affaire de Coeur (AdeC) is a bimonthly publication that reviews Romance fiction, as well as a number of other popular fiction and, occasionally, nonfiction genres. The magazine was established in 1981 by bookstore owner Barbara Keenan. In 1994, I assumed the publisher and senior editor responsibilities when I became *AdeC*'s sole proprietor. The corporate offices are located in Oakland, California.

In addition to book reviews, *AdeC* includes author interviews, contest and conference information, relevant articles, trivia, and other news of interest to readers. *AdeC* maintains a vibrant, content-rich website, as well as The *AdeC Scratching Post Blog*. The magazine is available by subscription in print and online formats, both having the same content.

Affaire de Coeur (AdeC) was born out of frustration and desperation. The literary world tried to ignore the new emerging genre known as Romance, labeling it as "trash" unworthy of reviewing and its authors as unimaginative and almost illiterate.

After attending the first Romance Writers of America (RWA) conference in 1981 in Houston, Barbara Keenan came home with inspiration, a vision, and a plan. Since the Sci-fi genre had established a trade magazine for its readers, why shouldn't Romance have the same thing? This magazine would contain all the information other literary media ignored—romance author interviews, reviews of romance books, and articles about the genre itself. No stranger to the business side of Romance, as she was a bookstore employee and ultimately an owner, Keenan contacted some of the editors and authors she had met at that first RWA and put her plan into motion.

Barbara Keenan, Karen Johnson (because she had a computer—a rarity in those days), and four women, whose passion for the Romance genre prompted them to volunteer as reviewers, created *Affaire de Coeur*. Doing the layout was a challenging feat since everything had to be done by the two aforementioned neo-phytes without a mentor—and it was done by hand. The end result was a newslet-ter that was only four pages long and that consisted of reviews of romance novels, an article, and interviews of two romance authors.

When *Affaire de Coeur* hit the market, it was the first magazine of its kind. *Romantic Times* (now *RT Book Reviews*) followed months thereafter and was based in New York, while *Affaire de Coeur* continued from its West Coast ori-gins. *Affaire* became a solid force and a voice for the Romance market, thereby helping to bring respect to a genre that had been a pariah before then. Interviews with such notable authors as Kathleen Woodiwiss, Nora Roberts, Catherine Coulter, and Rosemary Rogers graced the pages of *Affaire* frequently, while topics such as book covers (bodice rippers or flowers?) were discussed by fans. Some of *AdeC*'s reviewers became famous, too, like best-selling author Sherrilyn Kenyon. *Affaire* provided a forum for everyone interested in Romance literature.

Shortly after the launch of the magazine, *Affaire de Coeur* began to organize conferences. Called Rom-Con (Romance Conference), the *Affaire de Coeur* con-ference focused on awards. From the outset, *Affaire de Coeur* has believed that readers play an integral part in the success of this genre, and because of this, the magazine has allowed reader participation in the selection of the award winners. Each year, *Affaire* conducts the "Reader/Writer Poll" wherein authors and readers vote. All votes carry the same weight—authors', editors', and/or publishers' votes are the same as readers' votes. Categories include everything from Best Contemporary Romance to Best Hero to Best Book Cover. Creative twists on sub-genres, such as Paranormal, Fantasy, and Steampunk, send the poll creators back to the drawing board every so often.

The focus of the 1991 Rom-Con conference in San Antonio, Texas, was to facilitate the publishing of romance novels with minorities as heroes and/or heroines, as well as the publication of romance novels written by minority au-thors. Kensington, always progressive in business, was the first publisher to commit to the goals of the conference, and with its Dafina imprint, the publisher continues to follow through. In 1994, Pinnacle (a Kensington imprint) launched its Arabesque line, which featured African American characters. Eventually, Arabesque was sold to BET and later to Harlequin, where it became part of its Kimani series line.

Louise Snead

Further Reading

Affaire de Coeur. http://affairedecoeur.com/. Accessed March 20, 2017.

Agent

A literary agent is an agent who represents novelists in the sale of their work to publishers. Agents present or "pitch" the novel to one or more publishing houses and, if an offer is made to publish the work, negotiate the terms of the contract between the publisher and the author. Depending on the terms of each publishing contract, the agent may also work with subagents to negotiate subsidiary rights to their clients' work; for example, these may include foreign and translation rights, audio rights, or film and television adaptation rights.

Some agents may require clients to sign an agency contract specifying the terms of the agreement between the author and the agent, while others operate under a "handshake deal" wherein the author and agent verbally agree upon the agent's terms of representation. Most legitimate agents will not require that any fees be paid to them up front by the author. Current industry standard indicates that the agent receives a 10–15 percent commission from the author's advances and royalties.

With the recent proliferation of self-publishing, several agencies have begun to launch e-book self-publishing endeavors, which offer an additional set of services to their clients. These services can include editorial consultation, manuscript formatting and file conversion, cover art, distribution/upload to e-book retailers, copyright registration and ISBN (International Standard Book Number) assignment, subsidiary-rights management, and marketing and promotion. Notable romance agencies that have opened self-publishing programs include BookEnds Literary Agency and The Knight Agency.

The Publishers Marketplace and Predators & Editors: Literary Agents websites listed below are excellent information sources for literary agents. The Publishers Marketplace website provides information on agents and agencies, including profiles of what genre of manuscripts an agent is looking for as well as books the agent has sold to publishers in the past. Additionally, it offers a daily electronic report called "Publishers Lunch," which lists recent book deals. The Predators & Editors: Literary Agents website provides information on various agencies, including a rating system of how reputable the agents are in their business practices.

Crystal Goldman

Further Reading

Beyond the Page Publishing. "About Us." http://www.beyondthepagepub.com/about_us.html. Accessed March 8, 2017.

Gayles, Jia. "Our Digital Letter to Clients." *The Knight Agency Blog,* July 29, 2011. http://knightagency.blogspot.com/2011/07/our-digital-letter-to-clients.html. Accessed March 8, 2017.

Herman, Jeff. *Jeff Herman's Guide to Book Publishers, Editors, and Literary Agents: Who They Are, What They Want, How to Win Them Over,* rev. and updated ed. Novato, CA: New World Library, 2014.

Predators & Editors: Literary Agents. http://pred-ed.com/pubagent.htm. Accessed March 8, 2017.

Publishers Marketplace. http://www.publishersmarketplace.com/. Accessed March 8, 2017.

Sambuchino, Chuck, ed. *The Guide to Literary Agents 2017: The Most Trusted Guide to Getting Published,* 26th ed. Cincinnati: Writer's Digest Books, 2017.

Strauss, Victoria. "Writer Beware: Literary Agents." *Science Fiction and Fantasy Writers of America,* September 24, 2011. http://www.sfwa.org/for-authors/writer-beware/agents/. Accessed March 8, 2017.

Alternative Reality Romance Subgenres

An alternative reality romance is just what the title suggests: a story that is set in a world or reality that is different from the one we know and understand. Generally, this means that almost any story not based on history or contemporary times can be considered a type of alternative reality. More specifically, these types of genres are, according to one definition, "one of many possible space-time continua, having a different history or physical laws than our own space-time continuum" (Prucher, 6). With this definition in mind, the Alternative Reality Romance sub-genre is one that encompasses many different genres including Paranormal, Fantasy, Futuristic, and Time Travel, to name a few. One description for the Alternative Reality subgenre is to define it as a type of multiple-subgenres collective with the similar theme of "unreality" (Ramsdell, 211).

Alternative reality romances can include multiple genres, making it hard to classify as a single Alternative Reality subgenre. Veronica Roth's Divergent series is one example of an alternative reality romance that combines several genre categories. The series starts with the book *Insurgent,* in which readers are introduced to a world in which everyone has a predetermined path in life that is decided through an aptitude test. This series falls under the futuristic and science fiction categories in addition to its Romance classification. Although there can certainly be some argument for the Divergent series to be specifically categorized as dystopian science fiction, the broader categories for the series would be that of Romance, futuristic fiction, and science fiction. Another series with multiple genres would be Gail Carriger's Parasol Protectorate series. This particular alternate world is a

Victorian England that is inhabited by werewolves, vampires, and all kinds of other supernatural beings and has undergone a steampunk revolution. The Alternative Reality categories for the Parasol Protectorate series include Romance, Fantasy, and Steampunk (fiction heavily featuring steam-powered machines in lieu of the traditional advanced machinery of the 19th century).

However, alternative reality romances do not have to have a new or imaginary basis of reality. That is, not all alternative realities have the additional element of magic, time displacement, or advanced science. Another type of Alternative Reality is one in which history has changed. Alternate-history romances are different from time-travel novels. In the Time Travel genre, the basic premise must be that there is a character being displaced either backward or forward in time. The Alternative History genre's premise is that there is something that changed in how history has recorded events. The Alternative History genre is more common in fanfiction (see "Fanfiction and Online Community Fiction"). In Alternative History fanfiction, more often called AU (alternate universe) or AR (alternate reality), fanfiction authors play with the idea of "what if this happened instead of _____." Taking the Star Wars series as an example, possible alternative histories would be what would have happened if (1) Darth Vader never turned to the Dark side, (2) Qui-Gon Jinn (Obi-Wan Kenobi's master) survived and became Anakin Skywalker's master, or (3) Jar Jar Binks was never a character in *Episode I: The Phantom Menace.* However, the genre can also include historically based plots such as Colin Falconer's *Anastasia,* which has a woman who could possibly be Princess Anastasia Romanov falling in love with the man trying to uncover her past.

While the world in which the Alternative Reality Romance genre may change, as the saying goes, "the more things change, the more they stay the same." The appeal of reading alternative reality romances is that there is the possibility to explore worlds so different from the ones that we inhabit. These are the worlds filled with creatures only in our imaginations or filled with technologies beyond our reach. Despite (or perhaps because of) all of the strangeness that comes along with an alternative reality, whatever that reality may be, the differences that the reader encounters make the universal similarities of the romantic elements all the more clear and relatable. No matter what the time, the location, or the environment may be, whether the story takes place in the farthest corners of an uncharted galaxy or in a time filled with magic, at the core of the story there will always be the simple relationship between two beings.

Hannah Lee

Further Reading

Prucher, Jeffrey, ed. *The Oxford Dictionary of Science Fiction.* Oxford and New York: Oxford University Press, 2009.

Ramsdell, Kristin. *Romance Fiction: A Guide to the Genre*. Santa Barbara, CA: Libraries Unlimited, 1999.

Saricks, Joyce G. *The Readers' Advisory Guide to Genre Fiction*. Chicago: American Library Association, 2001.

American Romance Comic Book (1947–1977)

Emergence of the Romance Genre (1947–1948)

Since the 1938 debut of Superman, the emerging American comic book industry had been dominated by colorfully costumed superheroes. But with the end of World War II in 1945, the popularity of the superheroes began to fade, and readers were ready to try something different. Most other story genres that rose in popularity to fill the gap—Westerns, Science Fiction, Horror, Crime, and War/Espionage—appealed primarily to the same young male audience that had been the main devotees of superhero fare. But 1947 also brought something new: a genre that featured stories set in "down-to-earth" surroundings, with the added novelty of appealing primarily to female rather than male comics readers. That genre was, of course, Romance.

The first comic book completely devoted to the Romance genre, Prize Comics's *Young Romance* #1 (September 1947 cover date), was the product of Joe Simon and Jack Kirby, the legendary writer/artist duo best known as the creators of Captain America. Simon and Kirby had begun moving in the direction of producing romance comics earlier in the year in the pages of Hillman Comics's *My Date Comics*. *My Date* was primarily a Teen Humor comic, another genre growing in popularity as the superhero craze waned. But each issue of this book's short run reportedly also contained a more-or-less serious romance story.

It could be argued that romance comics emerged from a tweaking of various tropes and conventions of the teen humor book (best exemplified by the Archie Comics line). The primary changes were (a) omitting the continuing characters such as the aforementioned Archie Andrews, who served as the backbone of the teen humor books, (b) making the standard story protagonist a teen or young adult female rather than a teenaged male, (c) dealing with the protagonist's problems and challenges in a serious (if not wholly realistic) manner, and (d) resolving the heroine's romantic dilemma by story's end, rather than recycling it story after story, issue after issue.

Also supporting the case for the teen humor/romance connection is the existence of a subgenre closely akin to both—the "career girl" book, starring the likes of Millie the Model and Tessie the Typist, which had its heyday at the same time romance comics were coming into prominence. However, since the career girl and romance story types by and large maintained their separate identities throughout the 1950s and on into the 1960s, career girl comics (a classification that could at various times arguably include both Marvel/Atlas's *Venus* and DC's *Superman's Girl Friend, Lois Lane*) are generally not considered romance comics.

But examining the lineage of the romance comic requires looking outside the comics industry as well as within. In 1947, various types of magazines shared newsstand space with comic books—among them the so-called true-confessions magazine. Just as the heroic pulps can be seen as a precursor to superhero comic books, so too can the true-confessions (or tell-all) magazine, put out by companies such as Macfadden Publications, be considered a "parent" of the romance comic.

Heyday of the Romance Comic Book (1949–1958)

Young Romance proved to be a rousing success. The 500,000-copy print run of issue #1 sold out, and circulation for the book was soon up to 1 million copies per issue (an unheard-of number these days, but far from unprecedented then). Attracted by this success, other publishers soon entered the fray, and by 1949 newsstands were awash with romance comics. Bill Boichel, in his introductory essay for a recent anthology of modern-day romance stories, *Project: Romantic*, wrote, "In the second half of 1949, a mere two years after the genre's inception, 99 new romance titles were introduced—more than the total number of superhero titles published at the apex of the golden age market in 1942" (Boichel, 8).

The speedy success of romance comics even caught the attention of *Time*, which reported in its August 22, 1949, issue: ". . . At 10 cents a throw, America's boys and girls, ages 8 to 80 [had] their pick of 100 love & romance books, published by two dozen different concerns, with an average press run of 500,000 copies" ("Love on a Dime," 41).

Time's story also reported on a sharp downturn in the financial fortunes of Macfadden Publications, the leading publisher of true-confessions magazines, which strongly suggests that romance/true-confessions magazines were losing readers to their comic book "offspring."

The romance comic book clearly owed much of its success to the fact that it tapped into the underserved market of female comics readers. Although girls certainly enjoyed some of the same types of comics as boys, until the arrival of romance comics there really wasn't any type of comic geared primarily to girls' interests and sensibilities. Dealing nonhumorously with issues being faced by young adult (or older teen) females, romance comics also appealed to a somewhat older readership. Indeed, the cover of *Young Romance* #1 proclaimed it to be "For the ADULT Readers of Comics." The target audience was not a hypothetical average 10–12-year-old boy but, rather, his older sister.

Also of importance to the success of the romance comics was that the values they portrayed reflected those of the society as a whole:

> During WW II, women tasted independence and freedom as a result of their being asked to assume many masculine roles and responsibilities. . . . These same women were subsequently displaced in the workplace by the millions of returning soldiers, at which point they were strongly encouraged . . . to begin leading domestic lives centered on being wives and mothers. (Boichel, 8)

With their husbands, fathers, sons, and brothers returning from the war, women were expected to surrender their recent independence and reintegrate themselves into the traditional nuclear family of husband/breadwinner, wife/mother/homemaker, and children. In *Comic Book Nation,* author Bradford Wright places this trend into the context of the Cold War:

> Romance and anticommunism were two of the most common and successful themes exploited by comic book makers during the early Cold war years. . . . [B]oth served common cultural objectives. . . . For boys, there were he-man adventure tales of U.S. soldiers and secret agents. . . . For the girls, there were romance comic books, which were instructional in the virtues of domesticity and offered the means for securing the vital home front by starting with the American home. Comic books offered up soldiers and housewives as heroic role models for a generation coming of age in a time of both affluence and anxiety. (Wright, 110)

Romance Comic Book Publishers and Their Output: An Overview

Data compiled by Dan Stevenson as posted at the site All the Romance Comics Ever Published (?) provide a measure of the changes in the American comics industry's output of romance comics during the period of 1947 to 1977 (and slightly beyond). Stevenson shows that nearly 6,000 romance comics were issued by mainstream American comic book publishers—primarily between 1947 and 1977, with a very small smattering of romance comics (often reprints) published in the late 1970s and on into the early 1980s. John Benson's article "Romance Comics" in *The Encyclopedia of American Comics from 1897 to the Present* states that over 60 percent of these books (some 3,700 plus) were published in the period of 1949–1959 (311). More than 500 issues of romance comic books appeared in 1952, which Bill Boichel identified as the genre's peak year (Boichel, 8).

Well over 300 different romance comic titles were published. While many of these lasted for only a few issues, some 30 titles ran for 50 or more issues, with the longest-running romance title being *Young Romance,* which lasted over 200 issues. Publishers involved in producing romance comics run the gamut from "A" (Avon et al.) to "Z" (Ziff-Davis). Ten companies stand out both in quantity and/or quality of the romance comics produced: Ace, ACG, DC, Charlton, Fawcett, Harvey, Marvel, Prize, Quality, and St. John.

Charlton

Charlton (1946–1986) was the only publisher to produce over 1,000 romance comics and was the last to leave the field. (The short-lived *Soap Opera Love* and *Soap Opera Romance* were launched in 1982.) But while tops in quantity, Charlton was well back in the pack in terms of quality and was certainly not considered the "premiere" publisher of romance comics.

DC Comics

Claiming that spot—with over 900 romance comics published—was powerhouse DC Comics (1935–present). While its first romance-related title, the western/romance-hybrid *Romance Trail* (one of many crossgenre books that saw print in the late 1940s and early 1950s), lasted a mere six issues, the company's next three efforts—*Secret Hearts, Girls Love Stories,* and *Girls Romance*—firmly established DC in the field. Solidifying its dominance in the genre, DC inherited one of its best-remembered romance books, *Heart Throbs,* from Quality Comics when that company shut down in 1956. Seven years later DC added *Young Romance* and its sister book *Young Love,* taking over from Prize Comics when that publisher closed up shop in 1963. DC's last regularly published romance comic was *Young Love* #126 (July 1977).

Marvel Comics

Already the leading publisher of "career girl" comics, Marvel Comics (1939–present) enthusiastically embraced the Romance genre in the late 1940s and stayed active in romance until 1963, producing over 600 romance comics during that time. Under editor/chief writer Stan Lee, Marvel tended to integrate more concepts from other genres into its romance stories than did most publishers, resulting in romance tales that had larger dollops of adventure, crime, or suspense than was usually found elsewhere. Marvel also came close to effecting a merger between the Career Girl and Romance genres: "By the sixties, even *Patsy Walker* and *Millie the Model* had become soap opera, and the two heroines spent much of the decade in tears" (Robbins, 66).

Marvel is unique in being the only major publisher that tried to reenter the romance field after having abandoned it. But the handful of books published during its abortive romance relaunch in 1969, while offering art that was often top drawer, failed to provide stories that were innovative enough to attract a readership beyond the shrinking core of dedicated romance comics fans.

Others

Prize (1940–1963), Ace (1940–1956), Quality (1939–1956), ACG (1943–1967), Fawcett (1940–1953), St. John (1948–1957), and Harvey (1939–1990s) each published in the range of 175–400 romance comics during their time in the field. Most of these companies (Prize, Quality, Ace, St. John, and Fawcett) were active in the genre right up to the time they left the comics field and almost certainly would have published many more competently produced romance comics had they not left the industry when they did. (Indeed, some romance titles begun by Fawcett, Quality, and Prize survived their original publishers being taken over by either DC or Charlton.) ACG, for its part, survived only three more years after canceling its last romance title in 1964. Harvey Comics's departure from the Romance genre is notable in that this was a still-viable major publisher (which survived into the early 1990s) that decided to drop its romance line, rather than a company exiting romance because it was leaving the comics industry completely. This shows that even as early as 1958, not every comics publisher felt obliged to offer one or more romance titles.

Decline of the Mainstream Romance Comic Book

Riding high during the 1950s and still successful into the early 1960s, romance comics were for all intents and purposes gone as a distinct genre by the later 1970s. No single "extinction event" can explain its disappearance. Rather, the genre's demise resulted from the cumulative effects of a variety of interrelated factors.

Imposition of the Comics Code

In response to the anti–comic book crusade of the early 1950s, desperate comic-book publishers banded together to create the self-censoring Comics Code. Life under the code meant limits. Addressing romance, the code decreed, "The treatment of love-romance stories shall emphasize the value of the home and the sanctity of marriage." Basically, this meant that the only safe conclusion for a romance story (and certainly the only one that could be presented as "happy") was for the protagonist to assume the role of supportive housewife by story's end. Admittedly, this was the way most romance stories ended anyway (although publishers such as

St. John offered romance stories that were often more celebratory of a woman's independence). Nevertheless, adherence to the code meant that the genre became even more formula-bound and less open to experimentation.

The Rise of Television

The growing popularity of television undoubtedly helped to lead to a permanent downsizing of the comics-reading population. It does not seem that romance comics were hit harder than the industry in general, but the successful move of soap operas from radio to television gave the potential audience for romance comics a handy alternative. Additionally, while television initially probably helped reinforce the cultural climate in which romance comics thrived, its ubiquitous presence served over time to affect both the nature of societal change and the speed at which it has occurred.

Return of the Superheroes

The Silver Age of (Superhero) Comics is generally agreed to have started by 1956. With romance comics hitting their peak in the early 1950s, some have suggested the reemergence of superheroes was the primary cause for the decline of romance comics.

This is almost certainly an overstatement, but clearly Marvel's exit from the Romance genre had a lot to do with the company's concentrating its resources on its superhero line. Others (Harvey Comics in 1958 and American Comics Group in 1964) may have canceled their romance titles in part to concentrate on doing more superhero books and related titles.

Loss of Publishers

As already indicated, many romance comics disappeared when the company publishing them left the comics industry altogether. By and large, the loss of publishers was not a genre-specific issue but was related to the dynamics of the industry as a whole. Still, fewer publishers meant fewer romance titles—and, perhaps more important, less competition meant less incentive to push the boundaries of the genre to carve out a unique market niche.

Failure to Adapt and Evolve

The final and most important factor in the decline of the romance comics was the genre's failure to adapt and evolve sufficiently to remain relevant to the comic book readers of later decades. In hindsight, the genre probably needed the interplay and competition among several publishers—each offering its own take on the romance story—to survive and evolve. Lacking sufficient competition, romance comics failed to reflect societal changes and fell into irrelevance.

At DC Comics, for instance, editors tightly controlled story plots and structure and seemed bound and determined to stay with their time-tested story approach, even when it should have been clear that significant changes were needed to keep the genre relevant to the readers of the day. "DC had always adhered to rigid formulas, and the formulas became more restrictive as time passed. . . . [C]ommented one writer who worked for them in Fifties, 'They paid very well, but they were namby-pamby books'" (Benson, 313)

While times were changing, the Romance genre—under the watchful eye of the still-powerful Comics Code—didn't (and perhaps couldn't) change along with them. The world of 1977 was a substantially different one from that of 1947, when the romance comic was born. The ground rules for romance and other types of male/female relationships had changed significantly, and the companies still publishing romance comics simply didn't know how to incorporate such changes into their stories:

> The entire country had changed drastically by the mid-sixties, and the surviving love comics tried to keep up with the change. Their heroines moved up in the world; they evolved from waitresses and housewives into college students, stewardesses and rock stars. . . . Unfortunately the stories, no matter how well drawn read as though they were written by clueless 45-year old men—which they were. (Robbins, 70)

Conclusion: Legacy of the Mainstream American Romance Comic Book

While the mainstream American Romance Comic Book genre seems unlikely to return in anything resembling its original form, romance comic books are not entirely gone. In Japan, the romance comic is alive and well. In America, stories from "classic" romance comic books are available to a new generation of readers thanks to various paperback and hardcover collections and anthologies (see "Further Reading" for a partial list of such books), while 2007 saw the publications of the previously cited *Project: Romance* anthology of all-new "modern" tales of romance.

The Romance genre has clearly left its mark on the American comics publishing scene. The focus on "adult" interpersonal relationships once found only in romance comics has been incorporated into other types of comics storytelling. From the outset, the romance influence was clear in virtually all Marvel superhero comics, such as the book starring the company's most popular hero, *The Amazing Spider-Man*:

> Romantic entanglements played such a central part in the foundation and success of the entire Marvel mythos that it is not unreasonable to conclude that adding reality-based romance to fantasy-based superhero action was Marvel's greatest single innovation, differentiating it from other publishers (notably DC) and appealing to a more diverse and sophisticated readership. (Boichel, 12)

While this may be overstating the case a bit, romance comics clearly did help point the way toward a more mature approach to depicting interpersonal relationships, both at Marvel and at other companies.

Having helped contribute to the maturation of interpersonal relationships in superhero comics, the Romance genre itself has found new expressions elsewhere—albeit generally in successor works that are much more aptly labeled "relationship comics" rather than romance comics per se. The modern-day relationship comic is often but not always autobiographical in nature and creator-owned rather than done as work-for-hire. Published (often self-published) free from the constraints of the Comics Code, the modern relationship comic often melds together many of the same themes found in the classic romance comic with the freedom of expression and storytelling sensibilities first brought to the comics medium by the so-called underground comics of the 1960s.

Two notable examples of long-running relationship comics are *Love & Rockets* by brothers Gilbert and Jaime Hernandez, which Trina Robbins described as "a new kind of love comics for grown-up girls" (107–8), and *Strangers in Paradise* by Terry Moore, which Robbins hailed as "probably the best 1990s *[sic]* successor to *Love and Rockets . . .*" (139). Both are worthy successors to the mainstream romance comic—not so much updating the genre conventions as evolving from them, while avoiding the genre's most significant narrative limitations and pitfalls.

It is clear, then, that while the Romance Comics genre may have always been destined to exist in a "moment in time" (albeit a "moment" of some 30 years' duration), its influence is still being felt. To coin a cliché (or mix a metaphor), the song may be over for the mainstream American Romance Comic genre, but the melody lingers on.

Doug Highsmith

Further Reading

Bailey, Bruce. "An Inquiry into Love Comic Books: The Token Evolution of a Popular Genre." *Journal of Popular Culture* 10, 1 (Summer 1976): 245–48.

Benson, John. *Confessions, Romances, Secrets, and Temptations.* Seattle: Fantagraphic Books, 2007.

Benson, John. "Romance Comics." In *The Encyclopedia of American Comics from 1897 to the Present,* edited by Ron Goulart. New York: Facts on File, 1990.

Benson, John, ed. *Romance without Tears.* Seattle: Fantagraphics, 2003; London: Turnaround, 2003.

Benton, Mike. *The Comic Book in America: An Illustrated History.* Dallas: Taylor Publishing, 1989.

Boichel, John, with Jim Rugg. "Romance Comics: A History." In *Project: Romantic—An Anthology Dedicated to Love and Love Stuff,* 6–13. Richmond, VA: AdHouse, 2006. Also available at http://isotopecomics.com/communique/projectromantic.pdf#search =%22%22romance%20comics%22%20OR%20%22romance%20comic%20 books%22%22.

Comics Code Authority. *The Comics Code.* Lambiek.net. http://lambiek.net/comics/code .htm. Accessed March 8, 2017.

"Love on a Dime." *Time,* August 22, 1949, 41. http://www.time.com/time/magazine /article/0,9171,800653,00.html. Accessed March 8, 2017.

Mansfield, Stephanie. "Requiem for Romance: The Last Days of Love Comics." *Washington Post Magazine,* November 27, 1977, 18+ (3 p). LEXIS/NEXIS Academic Universe Database. Accessed March 8, 2017.

Perebinossoff, Phillippe. "What Does a Kiss Mean?: The Love Comic Formula and the Creation of the Ideal Teen-Age Girl." *Journal of Popular Culture* 8, 4 (Spring 1975): 825–35.

Robbins, Trina. *From Girls to Grrrlz: A History of [Women's] Comics from Teens to Zines.* San Francisco: Chronicle Books, 1999.

Stevenson, Dan. *All the Romance Comics Ever Published (?).* 1998. http://www .matt-thorn.com/comicology/romance/stevenson.html. Accessed March 8, 2017.

Wright, Bradford W. *Comic Book Nation: The Transformation of Youth Culture in America.* Baltimore and London: Johns Hopkins University Press, 2001.

Romance Comics Collections and Anthologies

Barson, Michael. *Agonizing Love: The Golden Era of Romance Comics.* New York: Harper Design, 2011.

Drake, Arnold, et al. *It Rhymes with Lust.* Facsimile Reprint Edition. Milwaukie, OR: Dark Horse Books, 2007.

Lee, Stan, et al. *Marvel Masterworks: Atlas Era Venus,* vol. 1. New York: Marvel Comics, 2011.

Lee, Stan, et al. *Marvel Romance.* New York: Marvel Comics, 2006.

Martinet, Jean. *Truer Than True Romance: Classic Love Comics Retold.* New York: Watson-Guptill Publications, 2001.

Parker, Jeff, et al. *Marvel Romance Redux: Another Kind of Love.* New York: Marvel Comics, 2007.

Pilcher, Tim. *Little Book of Vintage Romance*. London: Ilex Gift, 2012.

Showcase Presents: The Secrets of Sinister House. New York: DC Comics, 2010.

Showcase Presents: Young Love. New York: DC Comics, 2012.

Simon, Joe, and Jack Kirby. *Real Love: The Best of Simon and Kirby Romance Comics, 1940s—1950s*. Forestville, CA: Eclipse Books, 1988.

Simon, Joe, and Jack Kirby. *Young Romance: The Best of Simon & Kirby's Romance Comics*. Seattle: Fantagraphic Books, 2012.

Amish Romances

In 1985, *Witness,* a crime thriller starring Harrison Ford and Kelly McGillis, featured the forbidden love between an Amish widow and a man outside her faith and culture. Audiences had a taste of how powerful such a love story could be, but it wasn't until 1997, when Beverly Lewis published *The Shunning,* that a whole subgenre of romance skyrocketed to popularity.

Author Beverly Lewis's grandmother was shunned by her father and their Old Order Mennonite community. This inspired Lewis to write *The Shunning,* the first book in Lewis's The Heritage of Lancaster County trilogy, which paved the way for Amish romances. Some of the many books by Lewis include *The Witness, The Sacrifice, The Englisher, The Revelation,* and *The Reckoning.*

Fear and distrust of outsiders is an aspect of Amish culture, yet the most common theme of the Amish romance is forbidden love. This occurs when an Amish person falls for an Englisher (non-Amish person) or vice versa. There's also non-forbidden love in Amish romances, such as Beth Wiseman's *The Wonder of Your Love* (2011), in which an Amish widow meets an Amish widower. There are stories about Amish men and women who meet each other when one of them moves to the other's community. The tone of Amish romances is "sweet," meaning there are no sex scenes and no steamy sensuality. However, one of the aspects of forbidden love is heightened tension.

Other themes in Amish romances include family, faith, and community. These books extol the virtues of a simple life, devoid of modern technology. The expectation of absolute obedience to the dictates of the community as well as to the faith is one of the underlying foundations in Amish stories. The return of the prodigal son, another common theme, can be seen in Amy Clipston's *A Simple Prayer* (2015) and Mary Ellis's *A Plain Man* (2014). The tone of the Amish romance is usually serious. If there is humor, it's mild and subtle, such as Kelly Long's *The Amish Bride of Ice Mountain* (2014) or Tina Runge's *Treasures of the Heart* (1999).

Settings are usually small towns and semicloistered communities. Most are in Pennsylvania, especially Lancaster County. Mindy Starns Clark's two series, Men of Lancaster County and Women of Lancaster County, and Suzanne Woods Fisher's Lancaster County Secrets series are examples of this location. There are other places featured in Amish romances. Shelley Shepard Gray's Sugarcreek, Karen Harper's Maplecreek, and Cindy Woodsmall's Berlin are all in Ohio. Amish romances can be set in other places too, such as Shelley Shepard Gray's Crittenden, Kentucky; Amy Lillard's Well's Landing, Oklahoma; Wanda E. Brunstetter's Arthur, Illinois; and Linda Byler's Montana.

Sometimes known as "bonnet and buggy" books, Amish romances are also sarcastically referred to as "bonnet rippers." The requisite bonnet represents a woman's purity and adherence to her religious faith. The protruding sides keep her eyes straight ahead and prevent distractions.

The finely crafted quilts, for which the Amish are famous, appear in many of these romances. Quilts are featured in single titles such as *The Christmas Quilt* by Patricia David (2011) and *A Wedding Quilt for Ella* by Jerry S. Eicher (2011). Quilts can also be themes for series: Cindy Woodsmall's Sisters of the Quilt series; Wanda E. Brunstetter's Half-Stitched Amish Quilting Club series; Barbara Cameron's Quilts of Lancaster County series; and Adina Senft's Amish Quilt series. There are also quilt anthologies, such as *An Amish Christmas Quilt* by Charlotte Hubbard, Kelly Long, and Jennifer Beckstrand (2004).

Amish romances appear as single titles, such as Leslie Gould's *Amish Promises* (2015); series, such as Amy Clipston's Kauffman Amish Bakery (2012); and anthologies, such as *The Amish Christmas Sleigh* (2015). There are also literature-inspired Amish romances, including Sarah Price's *The Matchmaker: An Amish Retelling of Jane Austen's Emma* (2015) and Leslie Gould's *Courting Cate* (2013), which is a retelling of Shakespeare's *The Taming of the Shrew*.

Amish romances can feature mystery and danger. One of the most prolific authors of Amish romantic suspense is Marta Perry, whose many titles include *Where Secrets Sleep* (2015), *Search the Dark* (2013), and *Hide in Plain Sight* (2007). Other Amish romantic suspense titles include *Plain Threats* by Alison Stone (2015), *The Witnesses* by Linda Byler (2015), and *Sworn to Silence* by Linda Castillo (2009). Since the Amish eschew such modern conveniences as automobiles, the horse-drawn buggy can play a pivotal part in some Amish romances. These include Karen Harper's *Dark Road Home* (1996) and Nancy Mehl's *Unbreakable* (2013), both romantic suspense.

Amish romances are often seen as a subset of inspirational romances. However, if the emphasis is on the Amish culture, faith, and religious beliefs, and there is no romantic relationship, the book doesn't fall in the Inspirational Romance category. The first book in Linda Byler's Colonial American Hester's Hunt for Home series,

Hester on the Run, is one example. Byler grew up Amish and continues to practice the faith. Her novels are filled with vivid details only a true insider would know.

Amish romances continue to be a favorite subset of the Romance genre. In the hustle and bustle of our technology-laden modern life, Amish romances provide an escape to a simpler life, and perhaps this alone ensures them a very promising future.

Shelley Mosley

See also: Inspirational Romance

Further Reading

Goodman, Leah McGrath. "Fifty Shades of Amish: A Strange Genre of the Romance Novel." *Newsweek,* April 26, 2015. http://www.newsweek.com/2015/05/08/fifty-shades -amish-strange-genre-romance-novel-324940.html. Accessed March 9, 2017.

Arranged (or Forced) Marriage Plot

The arranged (or forced) marriage plot is a trope found most often in works of historical romance, although scattered examples can be found in contemporary works. In an arranged or forced marriage story, the hero and heroine rarely have a choice over whether or not to wed; the decision is made for them, either by the ruler of their country or clan, by their parents, or by the dictates of social respectability or convention. The trope thus allows romance authors to draw on the inevitable tension that arises when two people who know little about each other are thrown together without choice. Unlike spouses in marriages of convenience stories, husbands and wives in fictional arranged marriages typically engage in sex. When the forced or arranged wedding occurs at the beginning of a novel, the sanction of marriage allows writers to include more explicit sex scenes far earlier in the plot than one might expect in the more traditional romance that concludes with marriage.

Before the Early Modern Period, arranged marriage was a historical fact of life for most Europeans. Tribes cemented diplomatic and trading relationships through marriage. After the rise of feudalism, with its differentiation of wealth, marriages could also symbolize social status: no longer content to marry a child off to just anyone in a neighboring group, parents would demand a partner from a family of equal power or wealth. During the Middle Ages, marriages among the nobility were frequently arranged by a country's ruler for strategic purposes: to solidify alliances, to reward political supporters, to reinforce military conquests, or to reap financial rewards.

Historical accuracy, as well as narrative possibilities, thus accounts for the presence of the trope in medieval romance fiction. Despite the lack of agency such protagonists are granted, the heroes and heroines of these romances gradually come to know, respect, and inevitably love each other by their novels' ends. The lovers may be figures from actual history, such as William Marshall and Isabelle de Clare, the Earl and Countess of Pembroke, in Elizabeth Chadwick's *The Scarlet Lion* (2006), or completely fictional, such as the couples in Julie Garwood's *The Bride* (1989) and Madeline Hunter's *By Arrangement* (2000).

If a sovereign did not exercise the power to command nobles to wed, parents certainly could, and did. Although by the 18th century companionate love increasingly became valued in a choice of marriage partner, many parents, particularly those of the aristocracy, continued to insist on their right to choose their children's spouses. Many Regency romances, such as Catherine Coulter's *Lord Deverill's Bride* (1980) and Jo Beverley's *An Unwilling Bride* (1992), depict marriages forced on children by their parents. More rarely, the trope can be found in contemporary romances, such as Susan Elizabeth Phillips's *Kiss an Angel* (1996).

By the 19th century, love, not financial or family advancement, became the socially accepted reason to marry. But the forced marriage trope continued in the form of the "shotgun" or "compromising positions" marriage. Rather than being forced to wed by a sovereign or a parent, compromised couples wed to avoid social stigma. The unwritten social codes of different time periods forbade different acts; couples who were caught performing them (or even only *appeared* to be performing them) had to marry to prevent shame from unfairly falling on their families, or to save their own reputations or honor. In one of the most humorous versions of the shotgun wedding, Anthony Bridgerton, in Julia Quinn's *The Viscount Who Loved Me* (2000), is mistakenly believed to be kissing the breast of his intended bride's sister, Kate Sheffield, when in fact he is only trying to suck out venom from a bee sting.

The social and economic changes wrought by the Industrial Revolution led to many financially straightened landowners, forcing English aristocrats to marry well-dowered heiresses to support estates run into the ground by fiscally irresponsible previous holders of their titles. Many romances set during the 19th century reflect this necessity. The heroes in Rose Lerner's *In for a Penny* (2010), Meredith Duran's *A Lady's Lessons in Scandal* (2011), and Sherry Thomas's *Ravaging the Heiress* (2012) all pursue brides for financial reasons, but discover to readers' delight that love, too, is part of the bargain.

Arranged marriages occur in American-set historicals as well as in English ones, most frequently in the mail-order bride story. Throw together a woman who needs to escape her past and a man who thinks he needs a woman only to keep his home or take care of his orphaned children, and you have the makings of a compelling mail-order bride romance, such as Johanna Lindsey's *Tender Is the Storm* (1985), Linda Lael Miller's *High Country Bride* (2002), and Deanne Gist's *A Bride in the Bargain* (2009). Debbie Macomber's *Morning Comes Softly* (1993) takes the trope into the present, recasting the mail-order as the personal-ad bride.

By drawing on the cultural traditions of the past or inventing traditions specific to their own imaginary worlds, fantasy novels can also deploy the arranged or forced marriage plot. The concept of "destiny" or "soul mates" is particularly prevalent, for example, in fantasies such as Sharon Shinn's *Archangel* (1996) and Patricia Briggs's Alpha and Omega series (2008–2012).

Though most modern Americans consider arranged marriage woefully outdated, the practice is still valued in many other countries, such as India, Pakistan, Nepal, and other countries of Southeast Asia, as well as in many countries in Africa and the Middle East. Positive depictions of arranged marriages are rare in today's English-language contemporary romance, but with the emergence of a global Romance genre in the coming decades, the arranged marriage plot might witness yet another incarnation.

Jackie Horne

See also: Marriage of Convenience Plot

Further Reading

All About Romance: "Arranged Marriages." https://allaboutromance.com/?s=arranged +marriages. Accessed May 12, 2018.

All About Romance: "Shotgun Weddings." https://allaboutromance.com/?s=shotgun +weddings. Accessed May 12, 2018.

Coontz, Stephanie. *Marriage, A History: How Love Conquered Marriage.* New York: Viking, 2005.

Litte, Jane. "What's Wrong with the Arranged Marriage Trope?" *Dear Author.* http://dear author.com/features/letters-of-opinion/whats-wrong-with-the-arranged-marriage -trope/. Accessed March 8, 2017.

Ramsdell, Kristin. *Romance Fiction: A Guide to the Genre.* Santa Barbara, CA: Libraries Unlimited, 2012.

Arthurian Romance

As popular today as it was in the Middle Ages, Arthurian romance is rife with tales of magic, incest, adultery, revenge, warfare, deception, and, yes, courtly love and brotherhood. What started as a sixth-century poem, recounting one man's extraordinary military prowess, has become one of the most beloved and enduring romances of all time: the story of King Arthur of Camelot, his beautiful wife, Guinevere, and her lover, Lancelot, the greatest knight in the realm and Arthur's best friend.

The basic story involves King Arthur and his unswaying love for Guinevere, the queen. Proud of his elite band of Knights of the Round Table, the king holds tournaments, encourages the pursuit of wondrous adventures, and generally oversees peace in the land. But this idyll is unexpectedly disrupted when Guinevere is savagely abducted by the lecherous lord Maleagant. Lancelot, Arthur's favorite knight, risks his life to rescue the queen, ultimately leading to his becoming Guinevere's champion and lover. Arthur, however, refuses to acknowledge the affair until he is forced to do so, many years later, by his illegitimate son, Mordred, who wants to assume the throne. War ensues, Arthur is mortally wounded, and Camelot is destroyed.

Although evidence of a real King Arthur remains elusive, storytellers have been fascinated by his legendary exploits since the Dark Ages. He is mentioned in a ninth-century history of Britain called the *Historia Brittonum* and appears as a major character in the *Historia Regnum Britanniae,* Geoffrey of Monmouth's 12th-century chronicle of Britain's royal lineage. Even Chrétien de Troyes, a medieval French author, wrote extensively of Arthur's court and the illicit love affair between Lancelot and Guinevere.

Perhaps the single most influential Arthurian romance is Sir Thomas Malory's *Le Morte d'Arthur (The Death of Arthur).* First published in 1485, *Le Morte* epitomizes the romantic literature of the period and sets the standard of Arthurian storytelling for many centuries to come. Malory's masterpiece presents the legendary tale of Camelot's noble king as well as the individual stories of the Knights of the Round Table. In the end, Arthur and his kingdom are destroyed by his best friend's disloyalty and his wife's infidelity. Still, Malory speculates that Arthur will continue to live on and may one day come again. As his tombstone is supposed to have read: *Hic facet Arthurus, Rex quondam, Rexque futurus* ("Here lies Arthur, the once and future king").

Arthur's story indeed lives on today in many forms: comic books, movies, theatrical plays, games, television series, and hundreds of novels written since the turn of the 20th century. Among the best-known fiction is T. H. White's *The Once and Future King* (1958), on which both the musical play and movie *Camelot* are based. Inspired largely by Malory, *The Once and Future King* opens with the childhood of young Arthur, who reluctantly becomes king when he accidentally pulls the sword Excalibur from its stone. Other key characters include Arthur's tutor, the magician Merlin, and, of course, Queen Guinevere and her lover, Lancelot, who is, interestingly, depicted here as a misshapen, "ill-made knight." The book's antagonist is Morgause, Arthur's evil half-sister with whom he innocently has a one-night stand, resulting in the birth of his bastard son Mordred and the eventual downfall of Camelot. Other more recent novels inspired by *Le Morte d'Arthur* include Thomas Berger's *Arthur Rex* (1978), Mary Stewart's *The Last Enchantment* (1979) (narrated by Merlin), Persia Woolley's Guinevere trilogy (1987–1991), Rosalind Miles's Guenevere novels (1998–2001), and Nancy MacKenzie's *Queen of Camelot* (2002). In addition, there are a handful of novels in which, in an interesting twist, Arthur finds happiness in the arms of another woman. These include Barbara Ferry Johnson's *Lionors* (1975), in which Arthur secretly weds his childhood sweetheart, Lionors, and Joan Wolf's *The Road to Avalon* (1988), in which the king's cousin Morgan is actually his one true love.

The Arthurian saga is so universal that many novelists have used the basic plot to create their own updated versions of the romance. In Peter David's *Knight Life* (1987, 2002), for instance, a resurrected Arthur decides to run for mayor of present-day New York City—he is, after all, the once and *future* king! Helping him is Gwendolyn DeVere, a modern 20th-century woman who strongly reminds Arthur of his long-lost love. Likewise, in Dennis Lee Anderson's *Arthur, King* (1995), the title character is transported forward in time to World War II, where he is sent to help Great Britain fight the Nazis. Along the way, he falls happily in love with Jenny Hamilton, a doctor who is attracted to his old-world charm. Meg Cabot reimagines Camelot as a 21st-century high school in *Avalon High* (2006), in which a contemporary version of Arthur is class president and captain of the football team. Two authors have even set Arthurian-inspired stories in the Old West: James C. Work's Keystone Ranch series (1999–2005), which features rancher Art Pendragon, his wife, Gwen, and her lover and ranch hand, Link Lochlin; and Aaron Latham's *Code of the West* (2001), the story of Jimmy Goodnight, a cattleman who gains attention after pulling an ax out of an anvil at the county fair. On the other end of the spectrum is Patricia Kennealy-Morrison's trilogy *The Tales of Arthur* (1990–1996), an excellent science-fiction retelling that takes place on the planet Keltia.

If Arthur really existed, scholars believe he would have been a fifth-century Roman warlord. Not surprising, then, that a subgenre of Arthurian fiction has emerged situating Arthur and his cohort in a more historically accurate period. Usually set in the Dark Ages, either during or directly after the abandonment of Briton by the Roman Empire, these novels tend to focus on Arthur's fight to protect the land from marauding barbarians. Although Arthur (also called Artos, Artorius, Arturo), Guinevere (Gwenhwyfar, Gwenhumara), and Bedwyr (replacing Lancelot) are stripped of their royal garb and medieval trappings, the underlying love story nevertheless remains intact. By far, the greatest of these historical novels is Rosemary Sutcliff's brilliant *Sword at Sunset* (1963)—a personal favorite of bookwoman extraordinaire Nancy Pearl. Narrated by Arthur as he lies dying on the battlefield, the story looks back at his life and how he regretfully sacrificed love in the name of duty. Other outstanding examples of historically based Arthurian fiction include Henry Treece's *The Great Captains* (1956), Parke Godwin's *Firelord* (1980), Bernard Cornwall's *The Warlord Chronicles* (1996–1997), and Jack Whyte's multivolume *The Camulod Chronicles* (1996–2005).

A refreshingly recent trend in Arthurian storytelling is the appearance of several novels told from a woman's perspective. Vera Chapman's *The Green Knight* (1975), Sharan Newman's *Guinevere* (1981), and Gillian Bradshaw's *In Winter's Shadow* (1982) are among the first novels to examine Camelot from a female point of view. In fact, until the 1970s, Arthurian romance was conveyed almost exclusively through a male lens. Then, in 1983, Marion Zimmer Bradley released the groundbreaking *The Mists of Avalon,* her decidedly feminist take on the Arthur-Guinevere-Lancelot story. *Mists* quickly became one of the most important Arthurian novels of all time. Told primarily through Morgan's eyes, Bradley's sweeping narrative also includes the stories of Arthur's mother, Igraine; the Lady of the Lake, Vivian; and Guinevere, Arthur's very Christian queen. Although the traditional love story remains an underlying theme here, the main conflict is between the feminine "old ways" of Avalon and the male-dominated confines of Christianity. Bradley's influence can be seen in many subsequent Arthurian novels, including Mary J. Jones's lesbian love story *Avalon* (1991), Courtway Jones's *The Witch of the North* (1992), Kim Headlee's *Dawnflight* (1999), Diana Paxson's The Hallowed Isle series (1999–2000), and Nancy Springer's *I Am Morgan le Fay* (2001).

A parallel, and perhaps even more tragic, Arthurian love story is that of Tristan and Isolde, who have inspired their own body of romance fiction as well as a world-famous opera by Richard Wagner. A renowned knight of the Round Table, Tristan is sent by his uncle, King Mark, to fetch the king's betrothed, Isolde, from Ireland. But on the voyage home, the ill-fated couple accidentally drinks a love potion meant for the newlyweds. Much like Lancelot and Guinevere, the lovers continue their affair long after Isolde marries Mark. Unlike Arthur, however, Mark is a vengeful cuckold and so eventually exiles his nephew and the queen from the kingdom. When Isolde reluctantly returns to Mark, Tristan is forced to flee to France, where he weds the unfortunately named Isolde of the White Hands. In the end, Tristan dies of a broken heart, longing to see his true love one last time. Among the best of the Tristan-Isolde novels are Hannah Closs's *Tristan* (1967), Dee Morrison Meaney's *Iseult: Dreams That Are Done* (1985), Diana L. Paxson's *The White Raven* (1988), Kate Hawks's *The Lovers: The Legend of Trystan and Yseult* (1999), Rosalind Miles's Tristan and Isolde trilogy (2002–2003), and Nancy McKenzie's *Prince of Dreams* (2004).

Cindy Mediavilla

See also: Medieval Romance, Classic

Further Reading

Lacy, Norris J., ed. *The New Arthurian Encyclopedia*. New York: Garland Publishing, Inc., 1996.

Lupack, Alan. *The Oxford Guide to Arthurian Literature and Legend*. Oxford: Oxford University Press, 2007.

Mediavilla, Cindy. *Arthurian Fiction: An Annotated Bibliography*. Lanham, MD: The Scarecrow Press, Inc. 1999.

Thompson, Raymond M. *The Return from Avalon: A Study of Arthurian Legend in Modern Fiction*. Westport, CT: Greenwood Press, 1985.

Audiobooks and Romance

An audiobook is a recording of a text being read aloud. The narrator of the text is a storyteller, performing the material rather than taking a basic text-to-speech approach. Audiobooks may appeal to the vision-impaired, readers who struggle with comprehending the written word, or people who enjoy being read to.

Since the 1960s, audiobooks have become available in a growing number of formats. At first, books on tape were offered on vinyl and then cassette, followed by books on disc (CD). Beginning in 2004 and mounting in popularity ever since, audiobooks have become available as downloadable MP3 files.

Popular online audiobook services with large Romance genre offerings include the following:

www.amazon.com
www.audible.com (owned by Amazon)
www.audiobooks.com
www.simplyaudiobooks.com

The accessibility of the Internet allows users to take advantage of instantly downloading MP3 audiobooks from the comfort of their homes. However, the price of audiobooks is often higher than that of the print version due to the materials and production time involved. Audiobooks are read by a narrator and also involve a producer, sound engineer, and production team. As one can assume, the narrator can make or break the success of the audiobook. Most often the entire book is narrated by a single voice actor. If budgets allow, there may be a male and female narrator, or a small cast, depending on the character demands of the material.

With romance audiobooks, the narrators are not exclusively male or female. However, there are listeners who prefer one over the other, unable to endure either a male narrator portraying the heroine in an effeminate voice or a female narrator attempting the male dialogue in her deepest voice. Yet this is often the way in which romance audiobooks are performed.

For that reason, well-received voice actors are highly sought after for romance audiobooks. The AudioFile website (http://www.audiofilemagazine.com/audies/) provides an extensive list of voice actors recognized for outstanding audiobook narration, complete with the option to listen to the actors read brief passages. Phil Gigante, Susan Ericksen, Rosalyn Landor, Isabel Keating, Max Bellmore, Susan Duerden, and Katherine Kellgren are among the more popular narrators.

Goodreads.com, the largest free online community where people create reading lists and review books, offers a user-generated "Listopia—Best Romance Audiobooks." Users can access the website to see the 100 Best Romance Audiobooks as currently ranked by Goodreads users.

Joanna Schreck

Further Reading

AudioFile. "The Audies Award Finalists 2017." http://www.theaudies.com/. Accessed March 8, 2017.

Goodreads. "Best Romance Audiobooks." http://www.goodreads.com/list/show/11039.Best_Romance_Audiobooks. Accessed March 8, 2017.

Austen, Jane (1775–1817)

Jane Austen was an English novelist noted for her engaging, insightful novels that focused on the life of the English gentry during the years just before and after the turn of the 19th century. Drawing on her quiet rural life as the daughter of a country rector and her keen powers of observation, Austen penned stories that brought the everyday life of the British middle class, primarily landed gentry and clergy, into sharp relief, cleverly depicting and often subtly poking fun at the very society of which she was a part. Characterized by sly wit, wry humor, and a focus on ordinary contemporary people, Austen's works were considered examples of a modern, more realistic novel, something that earned her favorable comments from many influential sources, including Sir Walter Scott, the Countess of Morley, and Princess Charlotte, among others. She also had a gift for parody, as *Northanger Abbey,* her novel that satirized the conventions of the sentimental Gothics so popular at the time, clearly shows. Austen's works are considered the inspiration for what was later to become known as the Traditional Regency Romance, and in the hands of Georgette Heyer more than a century later, it spawned a romance subgenre that is still revered to this day.

Austen was born on December 16, 1775, in the village of Steventon, Hampshire, England, into a large, agreeable family—six brothers, one sister—with parents who encouraged their literary and academic pursuits. She began writing at an early age, experimenting with a variety of forms and styles, some of them parodies of current popular forms. Written between 1787 and 1793, these writings have survived, along with a serious short story, "Lady Susan," written at the end of this period but not published until 1971.

Jane Austen never married, but she did accept one proposal, only to rescind it the next day. Although there were rumors of a tragic love, the details of Austen's personal life are shadowy, partly because her letters to her sister and confidante, Cassandra, were carefully censored by Cassandra, who fiercely guarded Jane's privacy.

Austen wrote drafts of what would become *Sense and Sensibility, Pride and Prejudice,* and *Northanger Abbey* before the end of the century, but her father's retirement in 1801 resulted in a move to Bath and years of moves and disruptions that weren't conducive to writing. That changed in 1809 when Austen moved with her mother and sister (her father had died in 1805) to a cottage on her brother Edward's Hampshire estate. She began polishing *Sense and Sensibility* and *Pride and Prejudice,* which were published anonymously in 1811 and 1813, respectively, with much success. *Mansfield Park* appeared in 1814 and was followed by *Emma* in 1815. Austen began work on *Persuasion* in 1815, but in early 1816 her health began a downward spiral, and in 1817 she died of what was later diagnosed as Addison's Disease. *Persuasion* and *Northanger Abbey* were published posthumously in 1817, the year that her brother Henry revealed her as the author who had gone unrecognized for so long. In addition to these completed works, Austen also left a number of partial or draft stories, including *Sanditon,* a novel that has been the subject of a number of "completions" by talented authors.

Austen's books are essentially comedies, or novels, of manners and focus almost exclusively on the interactions between the characters and how they dealt with the constraints of both family's and society's expectations. Like the rules of behavior and etiquette, the social structure of the period was fairly rigid, and many people took their place in it seriously. Social consequence was important—and for some, self-defining. Love and marriage are topics of great concern: it was important to marry because women had few rights of their own and were dependent upon the men in their lives (usually father, then husband or brother, then son) for their support. It was also important to marry well, preferably to someone of a higher (or equal) social standing and with a decent income. Love and affection were of secondary concern; although these, like the paramount importance of one's social rank, were things that Austen often took issue with in her work, believing one should not marry without affection.

Austen is primarily known for six novels, all of which were well received when they were published and are still read and studied today. Her stories have also been retold by contemporary authors in print and in film—for example, the film *Clueless,* a retelling of *Emma*—and have spawned books based on her characters—consider all the "Mr. Darcy" books—and she, herself, has been reimagined in a number of ways, including as a solver of mysteries. Written more than 200 years ago, Austen's works have become literary classics that still speak to readers today—a remarkable accomplishment for someone who began her career as an anonymous writer of stories that while certainly much more, were at their core contemporary romances.

Kristin Ramsdell

See also: Regency Romance, Traditional

Further Reading

Boyle, Laura. "Jane Austen's Fame and Fortune, Now and Then." *Jane Austen: Celebrating Bath's Most Famous Resident*. July 16, 2015. http://www.janeausten.co.uk/jane-austens -fame-and-fortune-now-and-then/. Accessed August 22, 2017.

Boyle, Laura. "Sir Walter Scott: Author and Critic." *Jane Austen: Celebrating Bath's Most Famous Resident*. July 15, 2011. http://www.janeausten.co.uk/sir-walter-scott-author -critic/. Accessed August 22, 2017.

Bradbourne, Edward Lord, ed. *Letters of Jane Austen*. https://archive.org/details/letter sofjaneaus01aust. Accessed August 22, 2017.

"Jane Austen." *Encyclopedia Britannica*. https://www.britannica.com/biography/Jane -Austen. Accessed August 21, 2017.

"Jane Austen." https://www.janeausten.org. Accessed August 21, 2017.

Jane Austen's Fiction Manuscripts. http://www.janeausten.ac.uk/index.html. Accessed August 22, 2017. Digitized collection of some of Austen's handwritten works.

Regis, Pamela. "The Best Romance Novel Ever Written: *Pride and Prejudice,* 1813." In *A Natural History of the Romance Novel,* 75–91. Philadelphia: University of Pennsylvania Press, 2003.

Tomalin, Claire. *Jane Austen: A Life*. New York: Knopf, 1997.

B

Backlist

An author's backlist is the titles or editions that she or he has previously published that are still available for sale or are considered "in print." Backlists are very valuable to publishers as the popularity of the Romance genre continues to grow. A 1990 article published in the *New York Times* stressed that the "backlist is the financial backbone of the book industry." Every time a writer publishes a new book, new readers may then decide to purchase an author's previously published titles, thus increasing sales for both the author and the publisher.

For the reader, having the backlist available provides an opportunity to explore a previous series or fill in a missed volume. One caveat about the backlist—many authors and publishers will reissue their previous materials with new covers. Prolific authors especially may have one book republished many times. Authors that may have started in the Harlequin or Silhouette category publishing lines and then moved into single-title works may have their category novels repackaged years later and sold as new. Publishers also repackage books in a series, making a multivolume set look like a new publication. A word of caution to readers is to check the publication date of the title to make sure the title is a new publication and not a repackaged book from the backlist.

Sarah Sheehan

Further Reading

McDowell, E. "The Media Business: Publishing's Backbone: Older Books." *New York Times,* March 26, 1990. http://www.nytimes.com/1990/03/26/business/the-media-business-publishing-s-backbone-older-books.html. Accessed March 8, 2017.

Beauty and the Beast Plot Pattern

The scarred, wounded, or otherwise damaged hero (or heroine) redeemed by love is a staple of the Romance genre. The roots of this story are ancient, and while most of today's readers think of this story in terms of the Disney films and stage play, the story has evolved from age-old legends and customs with darker cultural, and sometimes political, roots. Although the oral traditions of the story are likely older, in written form the early roots of this story can be traced back to the Greek myth (or legend) of "Cupid and Psyche" (also "Eros and Psyche") in *The Golden Ass (Metamorphoses),* a second-century CE bawdy satirical work by the Roman writer Apuleius (aka "Lucius" Apuleius Madaurensis). This work, as well as "Reo Porco" ("The Pig King") by 15th-century writer Straporola, influenced Charles Perrault's "Ricky of the Tuft" ("Riquet a al Houppe" in *Histoires ou Contes du Tempes Passé,* 1697). Perrault's work, along with the fairy tales of Mme. d'Aulnoy, gave rise to the publication in 1740 of what is considered to be the earliest known version of the tale, "La Belle et la Bête" by Mme. Gabrielle-Suzanne Barbot de Villeneuve. This was followed in 1757 by Mme. Jeanne-Marie Leprince de Beaumont's much shorter—and somewhat changed—version of the story that has become the basis for most of the popular versions known today. In addition to the traditional reworking of the classic children's versions, versions intended for older audiences have surfaced. Of these, two of the more important are Robin McKinley's *Beauty: A Retelling of Beauty and the Beast* (1978) and *Rose Daughter* (1997).

Although magic and enchantment play important parts in these fairy-tale versions, it is the rare romance that leaves the path to true love in the hands of a wicked fairy or jealous goddess today. This is not to say, however, that supernatural elements aren't to be found. Paranormal romance is the perfect arena for the Beauty/Beast plot with stories such as Sherrilyn Kenyon's *Unleash the Night* (2006), featuring a human heroine and a shunned were-tigard hero; Kristen Callihan's *Firelight* (2012), in which a dangerously gifted heroine weds—and saves—a cursed, physically and emotionally damaged hero; and Christina Dodd's *Wilder* (2012), a dark tale of betrayal and redemption set in the treacherous, demon-haunted tunnels under New York City, being only a few of the many examples.

However, the majority of romances that make use of the classic Beauty and the Beast plot pattern aren't magically inclined, and while a number are contemporary, most fall within the traditional historical romance boundaries. This makes sense because of the social strictures of past times and the fact that women were often forced into unwanted marriages for family or financial reasons and had little to say about whom they would marry. The following are only a few examples of the ways in which this plot pattern has been used in the historical arena: Tessa

Dare's humorous Regency *The Duchess Deal* (2017), Eloisa James's clever riff on the classic plot *When Beauty Tamed the Beast* (2011), Georgina Gentry's Western version *Diablo* (2010), Mary Balogh's poignant *Simply Love* (2006), Judith Ivory's turn-of-the-century tale *Beast* (1997), Mary Lennox's engaging Victorian *My Lord Beast* (2005), Karen Hawkins's sensual romp *How to Entice an Enchantress* (2013), and Cathy Maxwell's spirited, Scotland-infused *The Bride Says Maybe* (2014).

While fewer in number, there are contemporary romances that make use of this plot to good advantage as well. Susan Wilson's heart-wrenching *Beauty: A Novel* (1996), Maya Banks's high-stakes thriller *When Day Breaks* (2014), and Sara Price's touching *Belle: An Amish Retelling of Beauty and the Beast* (2017) are only a few examples.

Although most romances of this type hold true to form, it's not always the hero who is the "beast" in this plot pattern; sometimes it's the heroine. The "Loathly Lady" is the feminine counterpart of the "Beast," with a heroine who has flaws and issues similar to those of the "Beast." For example, Deborah Smith's insightful contemporary *The Crossroads Café* (2006) tells the story of a beautiful woman coming to terms with her tragic loss of physical beauty and the hero who helps her regain her perspective; in Edith Layton's engaging Regency *The Cad* (1998), an infamous rake offers marriage to a facially scarred, penniless lady; and a legal secretary jilted because of her scars leaves her job to become a cook on an Oklahoma ranch and finds healing and love in *Always a Lady* by Sharon Sala (1993).

The Beauty and the Beast plot pattern is a standard in the Romance fiction genre, and its variations are endless—and its long-standing popularity and proven ability to adapt to the times guarantee that it's likely to stay in favor for the foreseeable future.

Kristin Ramsdell

Further Reading

Bettelheim, Bruno. *The Uses of Enchantment: The Meaning and Importance of Fairy Tales*. New York: Knopf, 1976.

Evans, Ivor H., ed. *Brewer's Dictionary of Phrase and Fable,* rev. ed. New York: Harper and Row, 1981.

Warner, Marina. *From the Beast to the Blonde: On Fairy Tales and Their Tellers*. New York: Noonday Press, 1995.

Zipes, Jack. *Breaking the Magic Spell: Radical Theories of Folk and Fairy Tales,* rev. and exp. ed. Lexington: University Press of Kentucky, 2002. Original ed. published by Heinemann Educational Books, Ltd., in 1979.

Zipes, Jack. "The Dark Side of Beauty and the Beast: The Origins of the Literary Fairy Tale for Children." *Proceedings of the Eighth Annual Conference of the Children's Literature Association, University of Minnesota, March 1981.* (1982): 119–25. https://www.scribd.com/doc/50978372/The-Dark-Side-of-Beauty-and-the-Beast-The-Origins-of-the-Literary-Fairy-Tale. Accessed August 13, 2017.

Blogs, Romance

See Romance Blogs, Wikis, and Websites

Brontë, Charlotte (1816–1855)

Charlotte Brontë is most recognized for her novel *Jane Eyre*. She is part of a literary trio of sisters whose works are still studied today. Brontë is important to the study of the romance novel because her novel *Jane Eyre* has many romantic elements in it, including the brooding, bad-boy hero that many romance novels are famous for.

Charlotte Brontë was born on April 21, 1816, at Thornton in Yorkshire, England. She was the third of six children, but her two older sisters died in 1825 of tuberculosis. Brontë spent about a year at the Clergy Daughter's School in Cowan Bridge before being brought home after her eldest sister, Maria, had died. She was supervised at home by her aunt Elizabeth Branwell, who was a stern woman and ill equipped to take care of the children. It is said that Brontë wrote around 180 poems and 120 stories, most of which were set in the fictitious land Angria that she and her siblings had created. She was then sent to Roe Head for her schooling and became a teacher there as well. Both Emily and Anne attended as well. Brontë and her brother and sisters were said to have begun writing stories as soon as they could read and write. Only four of the Brontë children survived to adulthood: Charlotte's brother Branwell and the three literary Brontë sisters, Charlotte, Anne, and Emily. Brontë and her sisters, Anne and Emily, took up the pseudonym of Bell: Currer, Acton, and Ellis, respectively. Charlotte, Anne, and Emily published a book of poems entitled *Poems by Currer, Ellis, and Acton Bell* in 1846; this work sold only two copies, but the following year each of them had a novel published.

The first novel Brontë wrote, *The Professor,* was not accepted for publication. It was, however, the encouragement and constructive criticism of one of the rejection notices from this novel that gave her the courage to keep on writing. *The Professor* had been inspired by Brontë's interest in one of her teachers, Heger, a married man.

It was *Jane Eyre* (1847) that put her on the literary map. It had immediate success and went through many editions; it is still the most successful and most popular of her works. Many modern romance novels have been based on or influenced by the tantalizing characters of Jane and Rochester. Rochester, the brooding Byronic hero, is still the model for many heroes in modern romance novels, and Jane allows the reader to take the journey with her and share in her experiences as she navigates the world of love and life on her own—and on her own terms.

A year later Brontë suffered the loss of her brother, Branwell. Her sister Emily died three months later, and her last surviving sister, Anne, died five months after that. *Shirley* was published in 1849, mere months after Anne's death. Brontë had used the work on this novel as a distraction from her loss. This novel was about the industry and the times about which other authors such as Dickens and Gaskell were writing, but it did not have their same degree of sharpness. *Villette* was published in 1852 and pulled some material from the failed manuscript of *The Professor,* which had been rejected again. *Villette* came at a time in Brontë's life when she had felt the burden of the loss of her sisters. She brought the Gothic elements and a little of the supernatural into this novel to portray the loneliness and the exploration of religion and the relationships she had through the male characters and Lucy's self exploration.

Brontë married in June 1854 to Arthur Nicholls, the curate of her father's parish. Her father disapproved and chose not to attend the ceremony. Brontë had several marriage proposals in her life, but she did not believe that a woman needed to be married and tended to respect women who turned down marriages of convenience.

Brontë wrote in a time when women were becoming prominent writers. Although she felt she had to publish with a pseudonym, she and other women writers of the time paved the way for the number of women writers that followed.

Brontë died on March 31, 1855, at the age of 38 from consumption, the same disease that killed most of her family, along with her unborn child. She was working on a novel, *Emma,* of which only a fragment exists. After her death, her first novel, *The Professor,* was finally published in 1857. Elizabeth Gaskell, a contemporary and friend of Brontë's, wrote the first official biography. Gaskell's biography is limited by her decisions of what to reveal and what not to reveal. Brontë's work is still being read and studied, and her influence on the romance novel lives on.

Lisa Jass

See also: Brontë, Emily; Gothic Romance; *Jane Eyre.*

Further Reading

Gaskell, Elizabeth. *Life of Charlotte Brontë,* vol. 1. London: ElecBook, 2000. ProQuest ebrary. Accessed February 6, 2017.

Stoneman, Patsy. *Writers and Their Work: Charlotte Brontë*. Tavistock, UK: Writers and Their Work, 2013. ProQuest ebrary. Accessed February 19, 2017.

Brontë, Emily (1818–1848)

Emily Brontë was a Victorian novelist and poet best known for her novel *Wuthering Heights*. The portrait of Emily drawn both during her lifetime and after her death is in many ways a chimera. When Emily died in 1848, at the age of 30, she left behind very few personal documents. These include three workaday letters, two diary entries, and two birthday papers. As a result, biographers have been left to search for clues to Emily's life and attitudes in her literary work, while analyzing the contradictory testimony of her contemporaries. Despite this fact, or perhaps because of it, her life has tantalized biographers who hope that by moving the puzzle pieces about and reexamining them from a variety of perspectives, they may finally assemble a fuller picture of the woman who has remained so teasingly elusive. What *is* certain is that she left behind an extraordinary novel, *Wuthering Heights,* whose place in the canon is firmly established.

Born on July 30, 1818, in Thornton, Yorkshire, England, Emily Jane Brontë was the fifth child of Reverend Patrick Brontë and Maria Branwell. She had three older sisters, Maria, Elizabeth, and Charlotte, an elder brother, Branwell, and a younger sister, Anne. It is difficult to speak of Emily Brontë without mentioning her siblings because her life and literary achievements are so entangled with theirs—like Emily, both Charlotte and Anne became authors. In 1820 the family moved to Haworth, where Patrick became perpetual curate. Shortly after this move, when Emily was only three years old, Mrs. Brontë died. This loss marked the beginning of an unfortunate sequence of deaths in the Brontë family. In 1824 Emily's older sisters entered The Clergy Daughters' School at Cowan Bridge. Emily joined them in November of the same year, but this stint of education was short lived. By 1825 both Maria and Elizabeth had fallen gravely ill and returned to Haworth within three months of each other. By June both sisters were dead. Fearing for Charlotte's and Emily's health, their father withdrew them from the school, and they returned to Haworth.

To occupy themselves in the parsonage upon the moors, the remaining Brontë children invented imaginary worlds inspired by contemporary social and political affairs (Barker, 149–66). The first of these fantasy worlds, "Glasstown" and

"Angria," were primarily fashioned by Branwell and Charlotte. Presently, Emily and Anne—to whom Emily was closest—detached themselves from this saga and created their own fictional world: Gondal. It is estimated that the two sisters were writing about Gondal as early as 1831 (Gérin, 23). As scholars have noted, the key characters in the tales of Gondal are strong, emancipated women, with men occupying subordinate roles in the narratives (Gérin, 26; Barker, 273; Vine, 25–26). Emily's engagement with Gondal continued throughout her life and was the source of many of her poems. Winifred Gérin has speculated that Gondal may have acted as a façade to conceal Emily's true feelings about her life and the lives of those around her (99).

Throughout her life, Emily demonstrated an intense attachment to Haworth and the moors; indeed, she became overwhelmingly homesick when she was separated from them. After her time at Cowan Bridge, her next significant departure came in July 1835 when she attended Roe Head School. However, by October it was decided that Emily would return to Haworth, owing to a marked decline in her well-being. It is notable that in 1850, several years after Emily's death, Charlotte suggested that Emily resented the restrictions of the school environment. As Gérin notes, the change in circumstances would have been a shock to Emily's strong sense of autonomy, which had been facilitated by life at Haworth and the freedom of the moors (29, 52–55). Indeed, Gérin presents Emily's faith in nature as her principal conviction (148–49, 255).

In September 1838, Emily left Haworth to commence a teaching position at Law Hill School near Halifax. As with her earlier departures from Haworth, Emily's sojourn overwhelmed her, although she wrote numerous poems during this time. In a letter to their friend Ellen Nussey, Charlotte described the Law Hill position as one of "slavery" and predicted that Emily would not withstand it (Barker, 294). Unsurprisingly, Emily returned to the parsonage in March in ill health. Once home, she continued writing poetry, as well as a number of Gondalian prose pieces—these, unfortunately, have vanished.

By 1841, Emily and her sisters were discussing the prospect of starting a school at Haworth. Emily and Charlotte traveled to Brussels in February 1842 with the intention of improving their language skills under the instruction of M. Heger. During this time, Emily penned a series of essays as exercises in French composition. This was a task she did not enjoy, as she disliked Heger's teaching method, fearing that it would interfere with the originality of her artistic thought (Gaskell, 197). Following their Aunt Branwell's death, the sisters returned to Haworth, arriving at the parsonage by early November 1842. This time spent in Brussels was Emily's last significant absence from the parsonage.

On her return to Haworth, the sisters' plans for the school continued but were later abandoned. During this time, Emily began transcribing her poems into two notebooks, which were later discovered by Charlotte. By 1846, Charlotte had begun negotiations with a publisher with the intention of producing a compilation of the sisters' poetry. The Brontë sisters, Emily in particular, felt compelled to hide their authorial identities. The first publication in May 1846, entitled *Poems by Currer, Ellis, and Acton Bell,* included 21 of Emily's poems. This volume garnered mixed reviews and sold poorly. Reportedly, Emily was furious when Charlotte revealed to an outsider that Ellis Bell was in fact Emily Brontë (Barker, 563).

Emily's secretive nature and tendency toward silence (Vine, 2–4, 16), coupled with the fact that there is no evidence to suggest that she ever had, or was interested in, any type of romantic attachment, has led some biographers to surmise that she directed all her passion into her art (Gérin, 254; Spark, 315). Certainly this romantic abstinence throws an interesting light on the fact that Emily produced arguably one of the most astonishing Gothic romances in the history of romantic fiction. Emily appears to have written *Wuthering Heights* from 1845 to 1846. When it was published, under her pseudonym Ellis Bell in December 1847, its content shocked and divided reviewers. The critic in *Douglas Jerrold's Weekly Newspaper* stated, "In *Wuthering Heights* the reader is shocked, disgusted, almost sickened by details of cruelty, inhumanity, and the most diabolical hate and vengeance, and anon come passages of powerful testimony to the supreme power of love—even over demons in the human form" (quoted in Dunn, 285).

In 1848, Emily contracted tuberculosis. Intractable to the end, Emily stubbornly refused medical treatment, and, thus, her physical decline was a protracted one. She died, allegedly lying on a horsehair sofa, at Haworth on December 19, 1848 (Gérin, 259). In 1850 Charlotte wrote a preface to the second edition of *Wuthering Heights* that spurred the romantic legend of Emily. Although there is evidence that Emily was writing a second novel prior to her death (Barker, 533–34), nothing remains of this manuscript, and there has been speculation that Charlotte destroyed it (Barker, 579). Regardless of the fact that many details of her existence still elude us, *Wuthering Heights* attests to Emily Brontë's significance as a writer and continues to beguile contemporary readers.

Emily Direen

See also: Brontë, Charlotte; Gothic Romance *Wuthering Heights.*

Further Reading

Barker, Juliet. *The Brontës*. London: Weidenfeld and Nicholson, 1994.

Dunn, Richard J., ed. *Wuthering Heights: The 1847 Text, Backgrounds and Contexts, Criticism*, 4th ed. New York: Norton, 2003.

Gaskell, Elizabeth. *The Life of Charlotte Brontë*. London: Smith, Elder, and Co., 1857. Edited with an introduction by Winifred Gérin. London: Folio Society, 1971.

Gérin, Winifred. *Emily Brontë: A Biography*. Oxford: Clarendon Press, 1971.

Spark, Muriel. *The Essence of the Brontë's: A Compilation with Essays*. London: Peter Owen, 1993.

Vine, Steve. *Emily Brontë*. Twayne's English Author Series 550. New York: Twayne, 1998.

C

Carr, Philippa

See Hibbert, Eleanor Burford

Cartland, Barbara (1901–2000)

Often dubbed the "Queen of Romance," Dame Barbara Cartland was truly a legend in her own time. Popular and incredibly prolific, she wrote more than 700 novels (723 by most accounts) that were published during her lifetime and left 160 manuscripts to be published after her death. These latter titles are being published as The Barbara Cartland Pink Collection in e-book format by her son, Ian McCorquodale.

Born Mary Barbara Hamilton Cartland on July 9, 1901, in Edgbaston, Birmingham, England, to British Army Officer Major Bertram Cartland and Mary ("Polly") Hamilton Scobell, Barbara was educated at the Alice Ottley School, the Malvern Girls' College, and Abbey House, Netley Abbey, Hampshire. The family's circumstances changed when her father was killed during World War I, and her ever-resourceful mother opened a dress shop in London. Vivacious and outgoing, the young Barbara made her way into London society and was soon writing about the social scene for *Daily Express*. She was also putting her keen interest and experience in upper-class society to use in another way, and in 1925 Duckworth published her first novel, *Jig-Saw,* the somewhat racy story of a young woman's first foray into the grown-up social world. The reviews were mixed, but this, as well as the titles that followed, were popular with readers.

In 1927 she married Alexander George McCorquodale, but the marriage didn't last, and in 1933 they separated in a highly publicized divorce. Three years later she married her first husband's cousin Hugh McCorquodale in a union that lasted until his death in 1963. She had one daughter by her first husband and two sons by her second.

Throughout her domestic ups and downs and the tumultuous World War II years—which included work for the war effort—she continued to write, but not at the speed, nor in the style, she was so famous for later in her career. Her earlier books and other writings were most often contemporary and generally considered edgy and risqué; but then in her mid-forties she tried something new, and in 1949 she published *A Hazard of Hearts,* the Victorian historical that was the first of the classic, Cinderella-type stories that would become her trademark for the rest of her career. Filled with strong, manly, aristocratic heroes, virtuous, feminine heroines, assorted crafty villains, and fast-paced plots that kept readers engaged, these passionate, emotion-rich romantic adventures were, nonetheless, sweet and chaste when it came to sexuality. They also echoed her deeply held moral values and optimistic feelings about marriage, family, love, and romance. She was a fast writer, and at times, especially later in her career, was noted for turning out a book every two weeks. Her books were famously dictated to her secretarial staff as she reclined on a sofa while often clad in her trademark pink.

Her personal style was flamboyant, outgoing, and elegant, and in addition to being an astute businesswoman and having a keen instinct for what women wanted, she was also a fierce advocate for a number of charitable causes, in particular those related to health and education. She also had a slight claim to royalty when she became the step-grandmother to Diana, Princess of Wales, when her daughter, Raine, married John Althop, the 8th Earl Spencer, in 1976.

Over her long career, she won a number of acknowledgments and honors, and in 1991 she was made a Dame of the British Empire (DBE) by the Queen.

She died on May 21, 2000, just shy of her 99th birthday and was laid to rest at her estate, Camfield Place, in Hatfield, Hertfordshire.

Kristin Ramsdell

Further Reading

Cadogan, Mary. "Cartland, (Mary) Barbara (Hamilton)." In *Twentieth-Century Romance & Historical Writers,* edited by Aruna Vasudevan, 114–20. London: St. James Press, 1994.

Cartland, Barbara. *I Reach for the Stars: An Autobiography*. London: Robson, 1994.

Gilbert, Elizabeth. "She Spoke Volumes." *New York Times Magazine,* January 7, 2001, 6.21.

Robyns, Gwen. *Barbara Cartland: An Authorized Biography*. London: Sidgwick & Jackson, 1984.

"Romance Novelist's Frothy Façade Hid a Steely Character: Wrote 700 Novels, in Later Years at Rate of One Every Two Weeks." *National Post,* May 22, 2000, A15.

"Romance Queen Barbara Cartland Dies." *The Washington Post,* May 22, 2000. https://www.washingtonpost.com/archive/local/2000/05/22/romance-queen-barbara-cartland-dies/29bb942a-2472-4f7c-a1d9-71d431500d62/?utm_term=.e2d197baa1eb. Accessed July 5, 2017.

Category Romance

Category romance, or series romance, is a separate classification within the Romance genre to describe those novels published in clear, defined categories on a monthly basis. Category romances tend to have shorter word counts than single-title releases, ranging anywhere from 50,000 to 85,000 words. Each line, or category, of releases features its own unique style, ranging in sensuality from sweet to spicy, with a new, set number of releases being offered up every month. Over the years, category romance has also been known as series romance, a name derived from the publishers' practice of numbering the new releases sequentially on the spine label of each book.

The publisher that has become synonymous with category romance in North America is Harlequin, which launched the Harlequin Romance line in 1949. By the middle of 2017, this particular line of category romances tallied well over 4,500 titles. However, it was not until the 1950s, when Harlequin acquired rights to distribute Mills & Boon's U.K.-published romances in North America, that Harlequin made the decision to focus solely on the Romance genre.

Over the years, category romance lines have come and gone, with a variety of publishers exploring the format. This led to the "Romance Wars" of the 1980s after Harlequin severed its distribution ties with Simon & Schuster. Ultimately, that publisher launched its own line of category romance titles, which were under the Silhouette name. What made Silhouette titles unique was that unlike Harlequin's focus on European and British locales, Silhouette focused on North American settings and characters, which were popular with American readers. Harlequin eventually acquired Silhouette from Simon & Schuster in 1984 and continued to publish titles under that name until 2011, when it was dropped entirely and all remaining Silhouette lines took the Harlequin name.

The practice of categorizing books in specific lines has had both positive and negative effects on the format. From a marketing standpoint, it has been a shrewd move, a financial boon that allows readers to focus their energies and dollars on the types of stories they know they will enjoy. However, the very marketing savvy that allows these books to find their readers also makes for detractors. Because books are published in specific lines and each line has different requirements and its own set of branding, some readers have the misconception that within each line all the stories are interchangeable—feeding the belief that the stories are not created by writers who work hard on their craft but, rather, by hacks who simply fill in templates provided by a publishing juggernaut. The reality of the format and the authors who build their careers on it could not be further from this stereotype that, unfortunately, persists to this day.

Category romance is believed to be, by many admirers, the Romance genre in its purest form. While fans of the genre love it for a variety of reasons, at the end of the day what ultimately they all come back to is the central love story. Category romance needs to deliver everything that a longer single-title release does, only in a shorter word count. Because of these shorter word counts, authors need to have a strong, intense focus on the relationship building between the couple to make the romance believable. This means fewer secondary characters and subplots in exchange for an intensely focused love story that pulls readers immediately in.

This intense focus on the romantic couple plays well into the shorter category format largely because writers have fewer pages to introduce external plot-driven conflict. Many category romance lines, although not all of them, primarily feature internal, character-driven conflict. This further lends to the intensity of the read and is an immediate draw for readers who like to identify with, and root for, romantic couples.

Category romance lines have evolved over the years to the point where they now include a wide array and selection of stories. Early traditional lines, like Harlequin Romance, were built around innocent heroines and a sweeter tone. The launch of a new line, Harlequin Presents, in 1973 brought about a shift. This line promised exotic locales and powerful, sophisticated alpha heroes to sweep the heroines off their feet. This line was such a success, and developed into such a worldwide phenomenon, that the argument can be made that the Presents line is the face of all category romance.

The sensuality envelope was pushed further by the launch of Harlequin Temptation in 1984. A response by Harlequin to the North American success of Simon & Schuster's Silhouette, Temptation had a completely different feel and look from other Harlequin lines at that time. Unlike the exotic locales and larger-than-life characters that dominated the Presents line, Temptation featured strong, often down-to-earth heroes and heroines who were comfortable and in touch with their sexuality. No longer was category romance the playground for innocent ingénues only; the Temptation heroine could be so bold as to be college-educated, a successful businesswoman, and even divorced. Many authors who went on to major single-title success wrote within the Temptation line, including Barbara Delinsky, LaVyrle Spencer, Judith McNaught, and Jayne Ann Krentz.

Harlequin Temptation was discontinued in 2005 in large part because of the success of Harlequin Blaze, a line that actually started out as a Temptation promotion.

Blaze was advertised as "red hot reads" and proved to be so successful that it led to one Blaze title's being released within the Temptation line every month. Then, in 2001, Blaze became its own separate category line, severing ties with Temptation.

Within category romance, Blaze continued to be the most explicit and sensual of the lines. These stories have a contemporary feel, and the physical relationship of the couple is more central to the story. While Blaze had built its reputation on sexy, the tone of the stories ran the gamut from fun and flirtatious to dark and brooding. There have even been paranormal stories published within the Blaze line over the years. The Blaze line was discontinued in 2017, and Harlequin Dare, a new sizzling series featuring "riveting, irresistible romance stories featuring highly explicit sexual encounters, making it the publisher's sexiest series ever," was launched in February 2018 (The Reading Café).

Not all category romance lines are defined by their sensuality content. Over the years, lines that have a strong focus on family and community have been quite successful with readers. Lines like Harlequin American Romance, Harlequin Special Edition, Harlequin SuperRomance, and the newer Harlequin Heartwarming are built around characters who feel like everyday people and conflicts that feel authentic. These types of category romances appeal to readers who enjoy reading about characters who could possibly exist in the real world. These are life-affirming category lines that show readers that one does not have to be a sheikh or a billionaire or have exotic good looks to fall in love and find a happy ending.

Category lines can also be highly specialized, targeting very specific readers and markets. Harlequin Intrigue and Harlequin Romantic Suspense are both romantic suspense lines, yet with very subtle differences. Harlequin Intrigue, while featuring a romance, tends to focus slightly more on the suspense and danger of the conflict. Harlequin Romantic Suspense turns a slightly stronger focus on the budding romance, with the suspense angle serving more of a subplot focus.

With the popularity and demand for faith-based fiction, Love Inspired currently features three inspirational lines. Love Inspired features contemporary settings; Love Inspired Historical features historical stories in a variety of settings and eras; and Love Inspired Suspense delivers a faith-oriented story against the backdrop of danger.

Even with the addition of feel-good, family-oriented, and more-specialized lines, category romance still has plenty of glamour. Over the years, Harlequin Desire has evolved to feature sexy, wealthy alpha heroes who have everything but the right woman in their lives. Harlequin Kimani Romance features characters of color, predominantly African American, and highlights both glamour and passion but also strong family and community ties in the stories. Harlequin Nocturne was launched in 2006 in response to the growth and insatiable reading appetites of the paranormal romance market and features dark, sensual stories.

Over the years, category lines and publishers have come and gone, a testament to the lucrative and loyal marketplace. Both Harlequin and Mills & Boon have seen lines come and go. Some lines, like Harlequin Flipside, a romantic-comedy line, and Silhouette Bombshell, an action-adventure line, lasted only a few years before sales figures and lack of public interest led to their demise. Then there are lines like Harlequin Temptation that enjoy a 20-year run before their success is cut by one of their own spin-offs.

Other publishers have entered the category marketplace with varying levels of success. Simon & Schuster's Silhouette made a big splash, in part because it was providing North American romance fans with something they were not getting from other category publishers—stories that featured characters like them. Again, in response to the Romance Wars of the 1980s, Bantam launched its own category line called Loveswept, which, while discontinued in 1999, continued to be a fan favorite among romance readers. Loveswept published a veritable who's who within the genre, including authors like Janet Evanovich, Sandra Brown, Suzanne Brockmann, Tami Hoag, Iris Johansen, and Kay Hooper. This impressive backlist, and the growth of digital publishing, ultimately led to the revival of Loveswept in 2011 as a digital imprint by Random House.

Despite the long, interesting, and diverse history of category romance, the subgenre continues to have detractors. There is also the perceived notion that because of the number of former category writers who eventually went on to mainstream, single-title success, the format is nothing more than a training ground for new writers to graduate from. However, at the heart of category romance are many writers and readers devoted to the subgenre. Authors such as Carole Mortimer and the late Penny Jordan have delivered a prolific output in the format to the delight of their many fans. Even the most successful romance author to ever come out of the category world, Nora Roberts, continued to work within the format until 2001, when her last title for Silhouette, *Considering Kate,* was published.

While the continually changing landscape of publishing and the rise of digital have narrowed the gap somewhat, category romance is still unique to the romance landscape thanks to its prodigious output and shorter publishing timelines. Because of the volume of titles published every month in a variety of lines, it is a fertile ground not only for new, emerging writers, but also for timely story lines. Category romance succeeds when it has the pulse of popular culture and what is going on in the real world. While escapist stories featuring billionaires and sheikhs have always been popular and will likely never go out of fashion, the more family-oriented, internal-angst lines thrive on real-life characters and conflict and are likely to appeal for years to come.

With the events of 9/11 and the U.S. involvement in two simultaneous wars in Afghanistan and Iraq, the military hero, and now heroine, enjoyed a rebirth within the realm of category romance. Not only did Navy SEALs and Army Rangers continue to flex their muscles in the romantic suspense lines, but they also found their way into the gentler Harlequin Romance and SuperRomance lines, where their personal baggage and experiences provided plenty of conflict.

As recession and economic downturn has affected many readers in the 2010s, category romance has also reflected those real-life struggles—single mothers, or fathers, struggling to raise their children and make ends meet, or heroines who have been laid off from their jobs, or fired, and move back to their hometowns to lick their wounds. Certainly, while Romance, and particularly category romance, can provide an escape from everyday trials and ordeals, it can also reaffirm and reinforce hope in the reader. That "life is full of bumps in the road, and bad things do happen to good people, but it is never hopeless as long as you have hope" is a core message of the Romance. "Work hard, believe, and things will get better" is a theme that is at the heart of many contemporary romances.

Often maligned and misunderstood, category romance is, at its heart, the purest form of romantic fiction. It strips away the noise that can pollute and dilute a love story and polishes everything to a bright sheen. It takes the two most important parts of any romance novel, the hero and the heroine, and puts an intense, bright spotlight on their falling in love. It not only gives readers this intensity, it provides it against a variety of backdrops with varying tones. Fun, flirty, serious, brooding, sexy, or gently sweet, category romance is not one size fits all.

Wendy Crutcher

See also: Forms and Formats Common to Popular Romance Fiction

Further Reference

Harlequin. http://www.harlequin.com/store.html. Accessed March 20, 2017.

"Harlequin to Publish Its Most Explicit Romance Line Yet." Toronto, March 15, 2017. http://finance.yahoo.com/news/harlequin-publish-most-explicit-romance-130000432.html. Accessed March 20, 2017.

The Reading Café. http://www.thereadingcafe.com/the-february-launch-of-dare-from-harlequin-reviews-excerpt-giveaway/. Accessed May 12, 2018.

Cinderella Plot Pattern

The story of a young girl cruelly treated by her stepmother and stepsisters and then rescued by and happily married to a handsome prince is one of the oldest and most popular of romance plot patterns. To be sure, in today's romances the pattern is not usually that obvious, nor does it normally involve princes or wicked stepmothers; but the appeal of a worthy but often poor and sometimes badly used heroine who ends up with the man of her dreams—preferably, strong, rich, handsome, and capable of keeping her safe—cannot be denied. This does not mean, however, that today's heroines are simply sitting by, waiting to be rescued. These are not the passive, helpless women so often associated with the classic Cinderella myth; and while they may be constrained by social custom, economics, or a domineering relative or other controlling force, they are usually trying to figure out ways to solve their problems on their own and are not waiting around for an errant prince (or other heroic type) to do it for them. They may need help, of course, and that often comes from the hero; but the heroine is always part of the solution and in some cases may even rescue the hero, as well as herself.

Examples of stories using this plot pattern can be found in romances of all kinds. However, they are more common in the Historical subgenre, in part because of the cultural values and customs during certain eras and the fact that women often had little official power of their own and were expected to marry a man who would take care of them. For example, in Julia Quinn's pure play on the Cinderella theme *An Offer from a Gentleman* (Avon, 2001), the orphaned heroine is banished from her home by her stepmother and stepsisters after she secretly attends a ball and attracts one of the most eligible bachelors of the *ton*, only to be rescued—and eventually recognized—by the hero. Magic slippers and a fairy godmother play a part in Olivia Drake's *Stroke of Midnight* (St. Martin's Paperbacks, 2013); a village girl dons a special dress, crashes the duke's masquerade ball, and attracts his attention in Sophie Barnes's *The Trouble with Being a Duke* (Avon, 2013); and an overworked heroine is forced by her stepmother to attend a ball as her indisposed stepsister and ends up attracting the prince in Eloisa James's *Once Upon a Kiss* (Avon, 2010). These are just a few of the many historical versions of the Cinderella story that exist. Of course, it's not just historicals that make use of this plot idea, and Luanne McLane's *Redneck Cinderella* (Signet, 2009), in which a Southern country girl gains social skills (à la the *Pygmalion* plot style) and ends up winning the love of a prince at a ball, is only one example.

Old and flawed though it is, the Cinderella plot pattern is a staple of the Romance genre, and as it continues to prove its adaptability, it is likely to retain its popularity.

Kristin Ramsdell

Further Reading

Dutheil de la Rochère, Martine Hennard, Gillian Lathey, and Monika Wozniak, eds. *Cinderella across Cultures: New Directions and Interdisciplinary Perspectives*. Detroit: Wayne State University Press, 2016.

Evans, Ivor H., ed. *Brewer's Dictionary of Phrase and Fable,* rev. ed. New York: Harper and Row, 1981.

Northrup, Mary. "Multicultural Cinderella Stories." *Book Links* 9.5. May 2000. ALA: American Library Association. http://www.ala.org/offices/resources/multicultural. Accessed July 8, 2017.

Contemporary Romance

Strictly speaking, contemporary romances are romances that are set in the times in which they are written. Usually this means romances set in the present day, although anything set after World War II is currently considered contemporary for romance classification purposes. However, just as it has in the past, this time window will change as the years go by, turning stories that were once "contemporaries" into "historicals" for their current readers. Consider for a moment the many classics we read today as historicals that were actually contemporaries when they were written—for example, the works of Samuel Richardson, especially *Pamela: Or Virtue Rewarded;* Jane Austen; the Brontë sisters; and even most of Charles Dickens, to name only a few.

Contemporary Romance is the largest of all the Romance subgenres; it is also the subgenre that most people have in mind when they are talking about the popular romance, in general. Broad and inclusive, the Contemporary Romance umbrella covers everything from tightly crafted stories that focus solely on one couple and their romantic relationship to wide-ranging stories with so many characters and subplots that charts and legends are needed to keep things straight—however, most fall somewhere in between.

The subgenre can be broken down roughly into two broad groups—category, or series, romance; and traditional contemporary romance. (Category romances—dedicated series lines with specific guidelines, now published primarily by Harlequin/Mills & Boon—are discussed in another entry in this work and will not be included in any detail here.) Traditional contemporaries are primarily single-title romances and are not part of a category line. They are usually longer than most category romances and can either be stand-alone titles or parts of the many, increasingly popular linked-books series, such as trilogies or other family/community-based series.

The settings can range from edgy city streets and sleek corporate offices to idyllic seaside villages, bucolic small towns, and realistic western ranches, with characters just as diverse. As expected, contemporary romance will reflect the current cultural values, and a wide variety of social issues—for example, abuse, illness, addiction, infidelity, divorce, PTSD, incarceration, disabilities—are often part of these stories. The characters are also products of the current culture, and many of today's contemporaries feature smart, savvy heroines who take control of their own lives and equally smart, alpha-to-the-core-but-caring heroes who learn to appreciate and value having a strong, equal partner at their side. Except for New Adult romances—which focus on characters 18 to 30 years old, either in college or making their way in the world for the first time—many stories now feature protagonists who are in their thirties, forties, and even older, reflecting the current trends toward later relationship, marriage, and family establishment. The style and tone of these stories will vary widely and include everything from funny, fast-paced romps and child- and family-centered heartwarmers to intense, angst-driven dramas filled with conflicted characters and sometimes a dash of danger. The sensuality levels run the gamut as well, rising from sweet, kisses-only chaste to incendiary, page-singeing sexy, with most falling somewhere in between.

Contemporary Romance has elements in common with a number of the other larger popular fiction genres, but it is particularly closely aligned to Women's Fiction. While these two genres are not the same, they have much in common, and there is a great deal of crossover readership between the two. Usually, it's easy to distinguish one from the other; however, at times, the romance line is so strong that the story could fall into either camp. This probably makes little difference to the readers—all they want is a good story—but it's worth noting that this happens often enough so that the Romance Writers of America has established a separate category in its Rita Awards for books like these—Mainstream Fiction with a Central Romance.

Contemporary Romance—love stories with modern-day settings—continues to be the backbone of the genre. Sweet or steamy, rural or urban, intense or laid back, and filled with angst or light-hearted humor, the Contemporary Romance subgenre is as diverse and varied as the readers are themselves, providing something for every contemporary romance fan's taste.

Kristin Ramsdell

See also: Category Romance; Linked Books; Women's Fiction and Romance

Further Reading

Ramsdell, Kristin. "Contemporary Romance." In *Romance Fiction: A Guide to the Genre,* 47–130. Santa Barbara, CA: Libraries Unlimited, 2012.

Romance Writers of America. "Romance Subgenres." https://www.rwa.org/p/cm/ld /fid=579. Accessed August 13, 2017.

Critique Groups and Partners

Romance writers join or establish critique groups and critique partnerships to improve and develop their fiction writing. The focus is the critique, an analysis of the manuscript to uncover both potential flaws and recognize where the document works. Although mixed-genre critique groups are common, a romance-fiction group can help the writer with genre-specific conventions.

Critique groups consist of two or more members. The ideal size for a group is often recommended as between 6 and 10 participants (Barry), although larger groups of more than 30 people also exist (Lofty). Group members tend to meet either in-person or online, at a regular time, such as once every two weeks. Critique partners tend to liaise between two and four people but not necessarily meet at predetermined times. However, at times those in critique groups will also refer to one another as partners. Organizations such as the Romance Writers of America often provide access to critique partners and groups.

In groups, there are two main methods of delivering a critique if the critique is presented in a face-to-face situation. The first occurs when the writers read their pieces aloud and are given immediate feedback by the other group members. While the responses to the work are given, the writer remains silent. The other approach is for stories or chapters to be distributed before the meeting. The group participants critique the fiction before the meetings in written form and deliver their perceptions and the written report on the day of the meeting.

Generally, the critiques benefit not only the writer who receives them but the person who produces them. The process of engaging in criticism of a piece uses dual reader and writer roles, teachable moments, and a state of metacognition (Cleary). The process can also be likened to peer-assisted learning, in which members learn cooperatively as they engage in critiquing (Barry). In her thesis, Lisa Barry notes that there are few in-depth writing courses available to learn specifically about the Romance genre; therefore, the critique group helps the writer to develop through constructive feedback. The ultimate decision on whether to change the text in response to the critique lies with the author.

The benefits of getting involved with critique groups and partners include built-in deadlines and audiences, and camaraderie. The drawbacks include "writing by committee," in which individual voices become generic; unconstructive negative feedback, in which the participant is derided; or too much deference given to a now-published author, so that she or he no longer receives useful feedback (Lofty). Participants may outgrow a group, but for as many who do so, others grow with their partners throughout their romance-publishing careers.

Doreen Sullivan

Further Reading

Barry, Lisa. "Critique Groups: A Technique for the Author's Toolbox?" Masters by Research Thesis, Queensland University of Technology, 2009. http://eprints.qut.edu .au/32148/1/Lisa_Barry_Thesis.pdf. Accessed March 20, 2017.

Cleary, Anna. "Critiquing and Why It Works." *Hearts Talk: The Official Journal of Romance Writers of Australia* 205 (2010): 8.

Lofty, Carrie. "Writing by Committee? Exploring the Unsavoury Side of Critique Groups." *Romance Writers Report* 29, 12 (2009): 18–21.

Cultural Influences on the Popular Romance Genre

Literary formulas, like popular romances (or mysteries) that last centuries, experience considerable changes as they adapt and are adapted to the evolving needs, interests, and values of new generations and various cultures. Despite the universality of the romance plot, the romance novel will reflect trends and issues that pervade the culture and incorporate cultural, political, and economic concerns. For example, while the narrative reflects and perpetuates current models of gender expectations, it will reveal and reflect women's frustrations, even potentially subversive responses to those expectations. Romances, then, across time and geography will reveal cultural adaptations and differences. Attitudes about and valuations of love, courting, marriage, sex, and race often shift, sometimes drastically, according to the time and place of the story's production. The inclusion of socially conscious issues like domestic violence, sexual abuse, tobacco use, even the presence of technology, illustrates the cultural responsiveness of the popular Romance.

Types of Cultural Influence

There are two general ways in which popular romance is culturally influenced, chronological and geographical.

Chronological

The international popularity of the genre reveals how romance writers have found ways to vary and adapt genre conventions, reworking and adapting standards to meet readers' expectations. The Romance genre is universal, but romances are not identical. The dominant culture influences the popular romance through value shifts or dramatic events.

England and the European tradition are able to trace romance literature back centuries to the medieval, courtly love tradition of Sir Gawain. U.S. history is much shorter, loosely traceable to the "romance" of the early 19th century—which is more of a misnomer because of the distinction between the literary Romantic Movement and the popular, more sentimental romance. Jane Austen is perhaps the most significant British romance writer and considered by many to be the progenitor of the genre. Austen's novels, which set the formula and tone for the English romance, were contemporary comedies of manners when written. There is no such tradition in the United States; Austen's novels did not become popular there until the 1970s.

The most visible shifts in the Romance are the incorporation of sex and the overt exploration of women's sexuality. During the 1950s, popular romance reinforced marriage and helpmate concerns. If the heroine were working, once she married, she gave up outside employment; her job was to be a "good wife." *The Flame and the Flower* (1972) signaled a shift, resulting from the sexual revolution of the 1960s–1970s. Succeeding romances included category lines like Candlelight Ecstasy, Temptation, Desire, Blaze, and Ecstasy Supreme, which contained enhanced depictions of sensuality and set the stage for an explosion of explicit sexuality. Since the 1970s, the openness of women's awareness and practice of sexuality in the popular romance has been an integral part of the narrative. Earlier romances suggested sex or perhaps allowed only some heavy petting.

During the 1980s, as the topic of sexuality became more open and socially acceptable, romances also became more erotic. The discussion of birth control and condom use became commonplace. The vocabulary and descriptions of sex became much more explicit—so much so that the popular romance has become a common vehicle for the exploration of a woman's sexuality, sexual activities, and erotic fantasies. As women put off marriage, heroines became older—they are no longer only 18–20 but in their later twenties and early thirties. Heroines are no longer required to be virginal but may be sexually active, may have been married, widowed, or divorced, or may be a single parent.

Harlequin romances of the 1950s featured heroines working as nurses or secretaries, and they would have had to forego their careers to become housewives in support of the heroes. Over the next half century, the careers for heroines ranged from entrepreneur to chef to doctor to businesswoman to first responder. Nor is the heroine any longer required to forfeit her career in the interests of marriage and husband. Romances like *Trust in Advertising* (Victoria Michaels, 2010) and *Weekends Required* (Sydney Langdon, 2012) feature heroines who navigate the overlapping fields of work and home to find a balance that leads to success and happiness in both realms. These shifts in the construction of the heroine result from the shifts in society.

The early 1990s marked the emergence of contemporary romances featuring ambitious working heroines with significant economic power. Heroines possess economic and social power equal to that of their heroes and can enter (and exit) a romantic relationship on their own terms. Corporate heroes are not misogynistic cavemen; they recognize a lucrative partnership—in business and in love—when they see it. Both hero and heroine are faced with the challenge of balancing the demands of home and work, as in *The Law of Attraction* (N. M. Silber, 2014).

Cultural shifts toward behaviors and issues are reflected in romance novels. The mid–1990s witnessed a series of serious challenges and lawsuits in the United States, England, and Australia against large tobacco companies. These antismoking campaigns altered cultural behavior regarding smoking practices. Popular romance reflects that shift: novels written and published prior to the mid-to-late 1990s, like Kathleen Korbel's *The Princess and the Pea* (1988) and Nora Roberts's *Sweet Revenge* (1996), feature heroes who light up, blue smoke swirling around their heads, and crush out butts in frustration.

Several romances incorporate socially conscious issues like homelessness, domestic violence, sexual abuse, and drug addiction. Writers may not offer conclusive methods of curing or eliminating these problems, but they may suggest how they could or should be treated. Lisa Kleypas's *Blue-Eyed Devil* (2002) and Laura Kinsale's *The Shadow and the Star* (1991) feature survivors of sexual abuse and rape. In Jo Beverly's *To Rescue a Rogue* (2006), the protagonists must confront the hero's opium addiction resulting from treating war wounds—a contemporary problem with a historical setting.

Political conflicts also influence popular romance. The suspense plot in Korbel's *The Princess and the Pea* (1988) is built on Cold War tensions, spies, and militant liberation groups. By the mid-1990s, in the middle of the Clinton administration, Janet Dailey critiques the attitude of the Clinton administration's "Compromise, appease, give in, give up, that's the new American way" in *Notorious* (1996).

The attack on the World Trade Towers in September 2001 sparked a surge in romances featuring heroes (and heroines) as first responders, particularly firefighters and EMTs: for example, Kathryn Shay's *After the Fire* (2003) and *Nothing More to Lose* (2005) or Jennifer Bernard's *The Fireman Who Loved Me* (2012). This trend involved all the subgenres: Bella Andre's *Wild Heat* (2009) is more erotic; Radclyffe's *Trauma Alert* (2010) and Damon Suede's *Hot Head* (2011) feature same-sex couples; and Karen Kingsbury's *Every Now and Then* (2008) is inspirational. Some post-9/11 romances feature plotlines in which protagonists have lost partners in the World Trade Center attack: Kathleen O'Reilly's *Sex, Straight Up* (2008) and Karen Kingsbury's *One Tuesday Morning* (2003).

Another post-9/11 trend was the increased popularity of sheikh and desert romances. The Arab male/sheikh stereotype provided an apparently diabolical male protagonist who could be humanized and healed by love, as in Susan Mallery's *The Sheik and the Virgin Princess* (2002), Lucy Monroe's *The Sheikh's Bartered Bride* (2005), or Olivia Gates's *The Sheikh's Redemption* (2012). The incorporation of a terrorist plotline or a handsome Arab man is a technique that may normalize a warrior nation by incorporating women into it. In the end, the heroine embraces the family-oriented culture of the Arab world even as the sheikh adopts the liberal feminism of his Western lover. Amira Jarmakani argues that driving this subgenre is the premise that romance provides a platform "for investigating how desire functions, particularly in relation to potent sociopolitical realities" (2). The subgenre has been around since E. M. Hull's *The Sheik* (1919) but spiked in popularity after 2001.

As the United States struggled through wars, more and more soldiers or wounded warriors occur as heroes. Some novels take on the military environment. As the United States experienced a surge in militarism, more military and aggressive themes appeared. A common trope in many category romances is the Navy SEAL, a modern equivalent to the medieval knight, as in Carol Ericson's *Navy SEAL Security* (2011) and Tawny Weber's *A SEAL's Surrender* (2013).

Harlequin's intrigue/suspense lines featured spy and espionage themes. The United States's military activity, earlier in Vietnam and more recently in Iraq (2002–2010) and Afghanistan (2002–2014), has created a plethora of heroes who suffer from military injuries. Kathleen Korbel's *A Soldier's Heart* (1994) features a Vietnam nurse who suffers from PTSD and Kira Sinclair's *Handle Me* (2014) an Afghani War veteran. In historical and Regency romances, the heroes may have served at Waterloo or in the Peninsular Wars. Alistair Carsington, the hero of Loretta Chase's *Miss Wonderful* (2004), suffers from both physical and emotional injuries incurred at the Battle of Waterloo. Mary Balogh explores several physical and psychological injuries sustained during the Napoleonic wars in her Survivor series (2012–2016).

Other cultural shifts include a growing interest in and involvement of females in professional sports. Susan Elizabeth Phillips incorporates professional football into a loose series revolving around the Chicago Stars that began with *It Had to Be You* (1994). Deidre Martin has written several novels, including *The Penalty Box* (2006) and *Chasing Stanley* (2007), involving hockey. In 2006, Harlequin launched its NASCAR Library Collection category romances, designed to appeal specifically to the growing number of female racing fans, with Gina Wilkins's *Hearts under Caution* (2007). While most of the athletes are still the heroes, females are allowed to exercise or run or bicycle. Most heroines as athletes tend to be amateurs, like the Olympic hopefuls in Cindi Myers's *The Right Mr. Wrong* (2008, skiing) or Rachel Ruddick's *Rapid Hearts* (2012, kayaking), or the bicyclist Lexie Marshall in Ruthie Knox's *Ride with Me* (2012). The heroine in Sarah Mayberry's *Below the Belt* (2008) is a boxer.

It was not until the 1980s that category romances with African American characters emerged as a distinct genre. *Entwined Destinies,* published by Dell Candlelight, came out in 1980, the first contemporary commercial romance written by an African American, Rosalind Welles. Harlequin published its first "multicultural" romance in 1985: *Adam and Eva* by Sandra Kitt. Both reflect the growing awareness, influence, and readership of African Americans. This subgenre has expanded exponentially, propelled by writers like Beverly Jenkins, Brenda Jackson, and Zane.

Gay and lesbian romance novels existed in the margins for the latter part of the 20th century. They received a tremendous boost when the U.S. Supreme Court cut down same-sex marriage bans. Since then, the subgenre has moved out of the underground. Novels like Alex Beecroft's *False Colours* (2009), Radclyffe's *Fated Love* (2005), and Heidi Cullinan's *Fever Pitch* (2014) project the possibility of a happily-ever-after ending.

Geographical

Sociopolitical and cultural factors are often geographical and national in origin. Values and traditions, even for something as universal as love and romance—those items about which the romance plotline operates—also vary among disparate societies, languages, and locations.

The Western European romance tradition is derived from the medieval courtly love and chivalry traditions. Medieval romances are fantasies containing heroic knights, adventurous quests, and damsels being rescued. Included in this tradition are legends and fairy tales that may include magic, fairies, wizards, and dragons. They emphasize themes like courtly love and faithfulness in adversity, made popular in Chrétien de Troyes's *The Knight of the Cart*. Inherent in this European tradition is the heroic knight with superhuman abilities on a quest, usually fighting and defeating giants and monsters, adhering to chivalry's strict codes of honor and demeanor and thereby winning the love and favor of his lady. Later romances drew freely upon royal pageantry, which heightened sentiment and exoticism.

The United States values individual happiness and freedom above everything else; therefore, it is ripe for romantic-love beliefs. The elevated standard of living resulting from the Industrial Revolution and the growth of capitalism allowed Americans to view marriage as an act of individual happiness rather than one of economic necessity. Because Americans are "free to marry for love," the arranged-marriage trope has less validity. Arranged marriage and marriage as a socioeconomic tool to advance family status, auger incomes, or merge estates are Western European traditions. The United States places almost exclusive reliance on romantic love as the basis for marriage. Over the 20th century, American culture—males especially—moved away from an etherealized, spiritual ideal of love.

The western Romance, set in a particular region of the United States, is distinctly American. In the United States and Canada, the cowboy and western settings are very popular. Both motifs are integral parts of the cultural heritages of these countries. The western is specifically American in its setting, themes, and characteristics. The hero is the westerner, the individual who can negotiate the demands of the harsh landscape; he is the uncivilized savage who must be tamed by the heroine. The heroine, frequently an easterner, is the symbol of civilization. She may learn the ways of the West, but she will also tame the hero. The western features lots of nature, land, and horses. There is nothing positive about cities or urban areas; perhaps there is a local small town, but the raw, western landscape is always the attraction. Harlequin's first American writer was Janet Dailey, whose *No Quarter Asked* (1976) is set at a Texas ranch.

Even though Australia has a comparable geographic setting in its Outback, the treatment of it is dramatically different. The Outback may be rustic and difficult, even harsh, but it is not the uncivilized landscape of the American frontier. The stations may be every bit as isolated as the western ranch, but travel is by plane. The Australian hero moves easily between Outback and city. But he's not a "cowboy"; he's a landowner and businessman. These romances set in the Outback are colloquially referred to as RuRo or "chook lit," as in Rachel Treasure's *Jillaroo* (2002).

One aspect of the "wilderness" that has been modified, especially in historical westerns set in the United States, is the romanticization of the Native American, the noble uncivilized warrior male who needs to be civilized. In England, this trope plays out against the Scottish Highlands, whose warrior males can be "tamed," as in Teresa Medeiros's *The Bride and the Beast* (2001). This role of the Other is particularly important in paranormal romances featuring aliens and shape-shifters, as in Karen Marie Moning's Highlander series (1999–2004).

However, cowboys, ranching, and the accompanying slang tend not to translate well into Italian or Polish. In continental Europe, the cowboy is not at all popular. European romantic heroes can be sheikhs or business tycoons; both of those stereotypes are uncommon in the United States. Military uniforms, metaphors, and idioms are also difficult to translate.

George Paizis discusses how the translations of Harlequin Mills & Boon publications treat what may be politically or sexually offensive material. Sex scenes may be completely omitted, or the amount of sexual enjoyment suppressed. Likewise, romantic idioms and euphemisms and various cultural myths pose problems for translation. And while the novel may be translated, the settings, values, and characters remain essentially English or American.

The writers for Harlequin Mills & Boon have been overwhelmingly English, Canadian, or American; so their romances have a decidedly Anglo-Saxon spin in terms of cultural values and sensibilities. Harlequin's availability in expanded numbers of translations has resulted in some international uniformity in the Popular Romance genre; however, the company's publishing partnerships have also resulted in increasing numbers of indigenous writers from various countries. In the late 20th century, Harlequin extended its reach with romances, notably with Mondadori Libri, Italy's leading publisher, to produce the Harmony line.

In Côte d'Ivoire, NEI-CEDA developed the Adoras line. In these French-language West African romances, the plot and setting are affected by colonialism, postcolonialism, color, and class; and black Africans are celebrated. While novels like Joëlle Anskey's *Opération séduction* (2014) and Fibla Koné's *Cache-Cache d'Amour* (1998) are commercially successful, they receive no respect from critics because they've stepped outside the highbrow "literary" model inherited from colonialism.

In the mid-1980s, the Sanrio Company of Tokyo began New Romances, a line written by Japanese women. The protagonists are both dark haired and dark eyed; the heroine displays no reluctance or guilt about sexual aggressiveness and tends to exhibit a stronger sense of self-esteem than the standard Harlequin heroine. The impediments to the romance tend not to be related to the heroine's or hero's personal traits but rather to the concern for family status or other in-group issues.

As a form of popular literature, the Popular Romance is responsive to the practices, values, and concerns of the culture that produces it. The changes in attitudes, behaviors, and characterizations are visible and recorded in the body of the romance novel. Because the Popular Romance functions as a document of the morals and standards of the culture that produces and consumes it, the Popular Romance genre will also reflect and reveal the ethos of its time and place.

Maryan Wherry

Further Reading

Balducci, Federica. "When Chic Lit Meets Romanzo Rosa: Intertextual Narratives in Stefania Bertola's Romantic Fiction." *Journal of Popular Romance Studies* 2, 1 (December 2011). Available online at http://www.jprstudies.org. Accessed May 12, 2018.

Flesch, Juliet. *From Australia with Love: A History of Modern Australian Popular Romance Novels*. Fremantle, West Australia: Curtin University Press, 2004.

Jarmakani, Amira. *An Imperialist Love Story: Desert Romances and the War on Terror*. New York: New York University Press, 2015.

Moudileno, Lydie. "The Troubling Popularity of West African Romance Novels." *Research in African Literatures* 39, 4 (Winter 2008): 120–32.

Mulhern, Chieko Irie. "Japanese Harlequin Romances as Transcultural Women's Fiction." *The Journal of Asian Studies* 48, 1 (February 1989): 50–70.

Paizis, George. "Category Romances: Translation, Realism and Myth." *The Translator* 4, 1 (1998): 1–24.

Current Publishing Environment

The current publishing environment for romance fiction is a varied ecology, in which large multinational publishers, independent publishers, self-publishers, re-tailers, and consumers interact. The relationships between these agents have been radically altered by the increasing market for digitally published romance fiction. As a result of digitization, the formats and distribution channels for romance fic-tion have dramatically multiplied and diversified. Such upheaval creates new opportunities as well as challenges for publishers of romance fiction.

Romance-fiction publishing comprises a significant share of the publishing industry. Industry statistics from the Business of Consumer Book Publishing indi-cate that in 2012 the Romance genre represented 16.7 percent of the U.S. book-publishing market and generated $1.439 billion in sales ("2012 ROMStat Report," 11). According to BookStats, in 2013 Romance accounted for $1.08 billion in sales, and in 2015 Nielsen BookScan/PubTrack Digital put the romance share of the total fiction market at 34 percent (Romance Writers of America, 2017). Romance-fiction publishing is also at the forefront of the industry in the area of digital publishing. The highest sales for e-books come from genre fiction, suggest-ing that e-books are for many readers a replacement for mass-market paperbacks. Romance fiction has had a particularly successful uptake among e-book readers. For example, e-book sales of romance books proportionally doubled between the first quarter of 2011 and the first quarter of 2012, from 22 percent to 44 percent ("2012 ROMStat Report," 9). With sales of e-books increasing, publishers of ro-mance fiction face the challenge of ensuring their profitability given the lower average price point of e-books compared to print books. Digital publishing has had a profound influence on the current activities all major types of romance-fic-tion publishers: Harlequin, large multinational publishers, independent publishers, self-publishers, and the more recent retailer-publisher Amazon.

Harlequin

The most iconic romance publisher is Harlequin, which now wholly owns its for-mer competitor Mills & Boon. Harlequin, in turn, is owned by the independent Canadian media company Torstar, which also publishes *The Toronto Star* newspa-per. Harlequin is the largest romance publisher in the world, releasing more than 1,320 titles each year in 34 languages across 110 international markets. Ninety-five percent of its sales comes from outside Canada, with 48 percent in the United States (*Publishers Weekly* "Global Publishing Leaders 2013: Harlequin," 2013). Harlequin is well known for its series or category romances, shorter books that are released each month in lines such as Harlequin Blaze and Harlequin Medical.

Harlequin also publishes single romance titles through its imprints Mira Books, HQN, Luna (romantic fantasy), and Spice (erotica). Its digital-only imprints include Carina Press and Escape (Australia). Harlequin publishes romance across a range of formats, including mass-market paperback, trade paperback, hardcover, and e-book, and sells these through multiple channels, including retail outlets, mail order to consumer, and e-commerce.

Harlequin's digital sales are increasing. In 2013, 24.1 percent of its global sales was digital, compared with 20.7 percent in 2012, 15.5 percent in 2011, and 7.7 percent in 2010. However, Harlequin's overall net profits have declined every year for the past four years. In 2013, its revenue was C$397.7 million, a fall of 6.7 percent from that of 2012 (Milliot, "Sales Earnings," 2014). This suggests that the transition to digital publishing, which has been accompanied by declining print sales and lower cover prices for e-books, has had some impact on Harlequin's profitability. In 2014 Harlequin was acquired by HarperCollins in an arrangement that is so far beneficial to them both (Milliot, "HarperCollins," 2014).

Romance Imprints of Large Multinational Publishers

Similar circumstances are impacting other major publishers. Much romance fiction is published by large multinational trade-fiction publishers. Colloquially known as "the big five," the major international publishing houses are Penguin Random House, Hachette, Macmillan, HarperCollins, and Simon & Schuster. Each publisher owns several imprints, which are generally editorially independent units. In many cases, imprints bear the names of formerly independent presses that were acquired by a larger publisher. Some imprints exclusively publish romance fiction, while others may publish romance fiction, or fiction that has elements of the Romance genre, as part of broader lists. Large publishers are acutely aware of the need to adapt to a changing digital-publishing landscape. The success of romance-fiction titles in e-book sales means that romance publishing is an area where publishers experiment with digital initiatives. The current romance-publishing activities of large multinational publishers are thus embedded in complex organizational structures and are at the cutting edge of technological development.

Penguin Random House became the largest publishing company in the world following the merger in 2013 of Penguin and Random House. The parent company of Random House, Bertelsmann, owns 53 percent of the new company, while Penguin's parent company, Pearson, owns 47 percent. Penguin Random House comprises nearly 250 imprints and publishes over 15,000 new titles annually.

Penguin Random House publishes romance in a wide range of subgenres through multiple imprints. It owns NAL (New American Library), a mass-market publishing group that includes the romance imprint Signet, as well as the Berkley

Publishing Group, which includes romance imprints Jove, Berkley, Berkley Heat/ Sensation, Berkley Jam, and Amy Einhorn Books. In 2012, Berkley and NAL launched InterMix to publish e-book originals and reprints in a range of genres. As one component of InterMix, the Signet Regency imprint was revived to publish Regency romance in digital form. Another example of a digital-only imprint owned by Penguin is Destiny, which features Australian authors of romance fiction. In 2013, Penguin relaunched Book Country, an online writing and publishing community for readers and writers of genre fiction, including Romance. In mid-2015, Penguin announced its intention to combine NAL and Berkley into a single unit, the Berkley Publishing Group, with the purpose of expanding the number of hardcover and trade-paperback titles it publishes, and combining the various editorial and production functions of the individual imprints as single departments under Berkley (Milliot, "Penguin," 2015). Fall 2016 was set as the date when NAL would begin publishing the nonfiction titles and Berkley Books would publish the fiction. Although the mass-market-paperback lines were not mentioned specifically, according to spokesperson Craig Burke, specifics "are still evolving," but those lines "will continue to be an important component of the Berkley Publishing Group mix" (Weinman).

Penguin Random House also owns Random House's romance imprints. One such imprint, Ballantine, combined with Bantam Dell in 2010 and now incorporates the imprints Ivy, Delacorte (YA), Dell, and Bantam Press. Random House's division Cornerstone Publishing includes the imprints Century and Arrow, which publish some romance. Bantam's Loveswept imprint was one of the most popular romance imprints in the 1980s and 1990s and was revived in 2011 as an e-book-only line featuring both original works and repackaged previously released titles. In 2014, Loveswept partnered with the online writing site Wattpad to debut a new novel, encouraging readers to interact with the author and help choose the cover.

Hachette Livre is another large multinational publisher, owned by French media company Lagardere. Hachette publishes nearly 15,000 new titles each year. It recorded profits of €223 million in 2012, which is on par with 2011 (*Publishers Weekly,* "Global Publishing Leaders 2013: Hachette Livre," 2013). Hachette owns Little, Brown and its romance imprints Piatkus and the digital-only Piatkus Entice. In addition, Hachette owns Grand Central Publishing Group and its romance imprints Forever, 5 Spot, and Poppy (YA). Its imprint Hodder & Stoughton has published some contemporary and historical romance, and in 2013 Hachette acquired Disney-Hyperion, which publishes some young adult romance. Hachette also has a partnership with Phoenix Publishing & Media Group in China, a large company with diverse publishing interests that include romance fiction.

Macmillan Publishers is owned by German company The Holtzbrink Publishing Group. Because it is a privately owned company, its profit figures are not made public. Macmillan publishes romance through the St. Martin's Press, St. Martin's Paperbacks, and St. Martin's Griffin imprints. St. Martin's Press is based in New York City and publishes around 700 titles a year across a range of genres. Some romance fiction is also published through Macmillan's imprints Picador (literary fiction) and Tor/Forge and Orb Books (science fiction, fantasy, and paranormal romance). In 2013, Macmillan children's imprint Feiwal and Friends launched Swoon Reads, a crowdsourced teen-romance imprint and online community. Romance authors submit manuscripts online, where readers can rate and comment on the submissions. Highly rated manuscripts are reviewed by editors from Macmillan, with some securing traditional publishing contracts for their authors.

HarperCollins Publishing is owned by Rupert Murdoch's News Corporation, a media company that has holdings in television and newspapers as well as book publishing. Until it acquired Harlequin Books in 2014, HarperCollins's primary romance imprint was Avon, which was originally founded in 1941 by the American News Corporation and acquired by HarperCollins in 2010. In 2012, while HarperCollins had a slight fall in profits, the Avon imprint saw a 72 percent increase in revenues, mainly in the e-book market (*Publishers Weekly,* "Global Publishing Leaders 2013: HarperCollins," 2013). Avon's imprint Impulse publishes original e-book romance fiction at the rate of two titles per week. Other HarperCollins imprints that publish romance fiction include William Morrow, Zondervan (Christian), and Eos (science fiction and fantasy).

Simon & Schuster is the publishing division of the CBS Corporation. In 2012, its revenue remained stable, with growth in e-books offsetting the decline in print sales. Simon & Schuster publishes romance through the Gallery Publishing imprint, which also houses the Pocket Books and Pocket Star imprints. Pocket Star was relaunched in 2012 as an e-book-only imprint. Simon & Schuster also owns the Atria Publishing Group, which publishes some romance fiction through the imprints Atria Books, Washington Square Press, Emily Bestler Books, Strebor Books International (erotica), and Howard Books (Christian).

Independent Romance Publishers

There are a number of independent romance publishers which publish multiple authors but are not associated with one of the large multinational publishing groups. This is an area of the publishing industry that experiences a great deal of change, with small publishers sold to larger companies and new start-ups emerging on a regular basis. One of the most significant and long-lived independent romance publishers is Kensington Publishing Corporation, which releases more than 500 books each year and accounts for around 7 percent of mass-market-paperback sales in the United States. Kensington Publishing Corporation's romance imprints include

Zebra, Brava, Aphrodisia (erotic), Dafina (African American), KTeen, eKensington, and the digital-first Lyrical Press, which Kensington acquired in 2014.

The large independent publisher Scholastic publishes some young adult romance. Other independent romance publishers also target particular markets or subgenres of romance. For example, Torquere Press, Intaglio Publications, Medallion Press, Cleis Press, Firebrand Books, Alyson Books, New Victoria, and Bold Strokes Books publish lesbian, gay, bisexual, queer, or transgender romance. Tyndale House Publishers, Harvest House Publishers, Barbour, and Baker Publishing Group publish Christian romance, while Red Sage Publishing publishes erotica. Independent romance publishers working across a variety of subgenres include All Romance Ebooks, ImaJinn Books, Seal Press, Samhain, Spinsters Ink, and BelleBooks, to name a few.

A number of the newest independent romance publishers focus exclusively on digital publishing. Some of these include Ravenous Romance, which publishes erotica; Totally Bound, which releases up to 11 erotic romances each week; and Liquid Silver, which is the romance imprint of e-publisher Atlantic Bridge. One of the most prominent romance e-book publishers has been Ellora's Cave, founded by Tina Engler in 2000 as a website selling her unpublished romantic erotica manuscripts in digital format. This very early digital-publishing initiative involved payment through PayPal and distribution of romance fiction as PDFs via e-mail. Ellora's Cave was incorporated in 2002 and distributed its e-books through online and print-on-demand retailers as well as its own website. It published books in four different lines, each with a slightly different focus or heat level: Romantica, Blush, Exotika, and EC for Men. In 2012, Ellora's Cave estimated that it sold 200,000 books per month. In 2013, the company grossed $15 million (Pilon). That same year revenues declined, and in 2014 the firm cut expenses and downsized its staff, blaming a sudden drop in Amazon sales (Reid 2014). The downward slide continued, and after a round of non-royalty-payment accusations, bankruptcy rumors, vitriolic threats, and lawsuits, Ellora's Cave closed its doors on December 31, 2016 (Nelson).

However, Ellora's Cave was not the only publisher to hit hard times. A number of smaller presses have gone defunct in the past few years; among the most recent as of this writing are All Romance Ebooks and Torquere Press, which shut down at the end of 2016, and Samhain, which did the same in early 2017.

Self-Publishing

The growth of Ellora's Cave, which began as a self-publishing venture for Engler, illustrates the new opportunities open to romance authors in the area of self-publishing. Self-publishing, sometimes described as indie publishing, is the most significant innovation in the current romance-publishing industry, and an increasing number of romance writers have embraced this route to market in recent years. The processes involved in self-publishing vary, particularly in cost. An author who is prepared to work on her own manuscript is able to release a title very cheaply; alternatively, authors can purchase individual services such as editing, cover design, or technical help or pay more significant fees for a package of services.

A growing industry of web-based companies facilitates the process of self-publishing. Author Solutions Inc., which was acquired by Penguin in 2013 and was later sold to Najafi Companies, a private equity firm, at the end of 2015, has partnered with a number of publishers to create different sites offering packages to authors, including Harlequin's DellArte Press (which severed connections and shut down in early 2015) and Simon & Schuster's Archway Publishing. Author Solutions Inc. also has a partnership with the print-on-demand site Lulu. One popular independent-author service company, Smashwords, distributes self-published e-books and charges authors a percentage of the profits rather than an initial payment. The online retailer Amazon owns Kindle Direct Publishing, which does not charge authors a fee to publish but retains a percentage of the royalties. A spokesperson for Amazon has stated that a quarter of its top-selling e-books in the United States in 2012 were published through Kindle Direct Publishing, indicating a strong growth in self-publishing. Amazon also owns the print-on-demand service CreateSpace, which registered 131,460 ISBNs in 2012, an increase of 123 percent over 2011, and of 3,300 percent over 2007 (Bury). Other websites, such as WattPad, support self-publishing by enabling authors to post work in installments and receive progressive feedback from readers.

Industry interest in self-publishing has been galvanized by a number of high-profile bestsellers, many of which are romance fiction. Erika Leonard (E. L. James) wrote an early version of her novel *Fifty Shades of Grey* as fanfiction based on Stephanie Meyers's Twilight series. It was published online in installments as *Masters of the Universe* in 2009. A small Australian company, The Writer's Coffee Shop, published the Fifty Shades of Grey trilogy as e-books and print-on-demand in 2011, selling around 250,000 copies. James then secured a contract with Random House, and the first trade paperback was released in June 2012. The trilogy has been translated into 51 languages and has sold more than 100 million copies worldwide.

Amanda Hocking is another prominent author who has self-published romance fiction. Hocking sold more than a million copies of the 17 paranormal-romance e-books she self-published. In 2011, she secured a contract with St. Martin's Press for the rights to her first three books, the Trylle trilogy, as well as a new four-book series. Other romance-fiction self-publishing successes include Barbara Freethy, who sold more than three million e-books about the Callaway family, and Bella

Andre, who sold over a million copies of her self-published novels about the Sullivan family. Andre has now signed a contract with Harlequin's Mira Books for print versions of some of her e-book titles. In 2013, Beth Reeks, who publishes romance fiction under the name Beth Reekles, was named as one of *Time* magazine's most influential teenagers in the world. She has a contract with Random House after building a following of 19 million readers on WattPad for her first romance, *The Kissing Booth*.

Self-publishing has qualities that appeal to some authors. Self-publishing offers authors a high degree of control over their own work, including the typesetting, cover design, and price point. Self-publishing can offer higher-than-average royalty rates: for example, authors earn 70 percent royalties on titles published with Amazon's Kindle Direct Publishing. Self-publishing allows authors to publish much more quickly than traditional publishing and can also be an effective way of reviving backlist titles that are out of print. As part of *The Guardian* newspaper's self-publishing showcase, romance author Talli Roland commented that she "had a very satisfactory experience working with a traditional publisher for my first two novels, but with hardly any distribution in print and 99% of my sales in ebooks, it made more sense for me to pay a one-off fee to an editor and cover designer, and keep the remainder of the profits for myself" (Roland). Self-publishing can support publication in multiple formats and outlets and can be used to release a variety of content, including short stories and novellas.

For all the opportunities it presents, self-publishing can also pose challenges to authors. A self-published author may need to source and pay for services including copy editing, typesetting, and design. A self-published author is entirely responsible for marketing, which can be time consuming and laborious. The trend for successful self-published authors to enter contracts with major publishing houses suggests that traditional publishers still offer considerable strength in the publishing industry. These strengths can include editorial expertise, access to distribution channels, experience in and networks for selling foreign translation or adaptation rights, and the marketing value of their reputation. A pattern has emerged, in that publishers look to successful self-published authors to find future best sellers, and self-published authors look to traditional publishers to increase their sales and reach.

Retail Publisher: Amazon

The blurring of the boundary between author and publisher caused by self-publishing is one feature of the current romance-publishing industry; another blurred boundary is that between retailer and publisher. Amazon is the largest online retailer of books in the world and launched its own publishing operation, Amazon Publishing, in 2009. It publishes in multiple formats including print, e-book, and audio. In 2011, Amazon Publishing created the imprint Montlake Romance. Montlake Romance approaches self-publishers with high sales as well as accepting agents' submissions. According to Jeff Belle, vice president of Amazon Publishing, "romance is one of our biggest and fastest growing categories, particularly among Kindle customers" (Business Wire). Amazon Publishing bought rights to the backlists of a number of independent romance publishers, including Dorchester Publishing and Avalon Books in 2012.

Conclusion

The current romance-publishing environment is marked by increasing diversity and radical change. A globalized economy continues to drive mergers and acquisitions for large publishers, so that many formerly independent romance publishers are now owned by multinational corporations that publish romance fiction across an array of imprints. At the same time, the low cost and ease of digital publication has opened up new opportunities for small publishers and for authors who want to self-publish romance fiction. The changes that digital self-publishing have wrought in the romance-fiction industry are profound, ranging from the increasing legitimacy of fan-fiction, to the growing significance of online romance-reading communities, to the strengthening of markets for subgenres and formats that appear to be well suited to e-reading, such as erotica and novellas and short stories. Traditional publishers have responded to this changed environment by creating digital imprints and crowdsourcing communities, by occasionally entering into partnerships with self-publishing service providers, and by carefully watching the self-publishing market for successful authors to acquire. The online bookseller Amazon has also emerged as a major force in romance publishing.

The boundaries between publishers, authors, retailers, and readers are becoming more permeable, and this is particularly noticeable in the field of romance publishing where authors and readers have for many years been actively engaged in communities. In the current publishing environment, works of romance fiction can find multiple routes to market: serial publication on an online forum, self-publication digitally or as print-on-demand, or publication by an independent or large multinational publisher. These channels can be combined to create diverse publishing trajectories for romance works, and many romance authors are choosing the hybrid route and are both traditionally and self-published. As organizations and individuals respond to the opportunities and challenges of digital publishing, they create a diversified, dynamic environment for the publication of romance fiction.

Beth Driscoll

See also: Harlequin Books

Further Reading

"2011 ROMStat Report." *RWR: Romance Writers Report* 32, 11 (November 2012): 8–11.

"2012 ROMStat Report." *RWR: Romance Writers Report* 31, 11 (November 2012): 10–12.

"Author Solutions Partner Imprint Bites the Dust with the Closure of Harlequin's DellArte Press." *The Independent Publishing Magazine,* February 9, 2015. http://www.theinde pendentpublishingmagazine.com/2015/02/author-solutions-partner-imprint-bites-the -dust-with-the-closure-of-harlequins-dellarte-press.html. Accessed April 24, 2017.

Bury, Liz. "Amazon Reveals Quarter of Kindle Ebook Sales in US Were for Indie Publishers." *The Guardian,* December 5, 2013. http://www.theguardian.com/books/2013 /dec/04/amazon-kindle-ebook-sales-indiepublishers. Accessed March 29, 2017.

Business Wire. "Amazon Launches New Publishing Imprint, Montlake Romance." May 4, 2011. http://www.businesswire.com/news/home/20110504007299/en/Amazon-Launches Publishing-Imprint-Montlake-Romance. Accessed March 29, 2017.

Milliot, Jim. "HarperCollins to Buy Harlequin." *Publishers Weekly,* May 2, 2014. http:// www.publishersweekly.com/pw/by-topic/industry-news/publisher-news/article/62097 -harpercollins-to-buy-harlequin.html. Accessed April 13, 2017.

Milliot, Jim. "Penguin Merges Berkley, NAL." *Publisher's Weekly,* June 3, 2015. http:// www.publishersweekly.com/pw/by-topic/industry-news/publisher-news/article/67234 -penguin-merges-berkley-nal.html. Accessed April 21, 2017.

Milliot, Jim. "Sales Earnings Fell at Harlequin in 2013." *Publisher's Weekly,* March 5, 2014. http://www.publishersweekly.com/pw/by-topic/industry-news/financialreporting /article/61299-sales-earnings-fell-at-harlequin-in-2013.html. Accessed March 29, 2017.

Nelson, Virginia. "The Great EC Books—Ellora's Cave Debacle—My Story." October 4, 2016. http://virginianelson.blogspot.com/2016/10/the-great-ec-bookselloras-cave-debacle .html. Accessed April 21, 2017.

Pilon, Annie. "Entrepreneur Creates Publishing Powerhouse with Niche Romance Novels." June 8, 2013. http://smallbiztrends.com/2013/06/elloras-caveentrepreneur-romance -novels.html. Accessed March 29, 2017.

Publishers Weekly. "Global Publishing Leaders 2013: Hachette Livre." July 19, 2013. http://www.publishersweekly.com/pw/by-topic/industry-news/financialreporting /article/58281-global-publishing-leaders-2013-hachette-livre.html. Accessed March 20, 2017.

Publishers Weekly. "Global Publishing Leaders 2013: Harlequin." July 19, 2013. http:// www.publishersweekly.com/pw/by-topic/industry-news/financialreporting/article/58291 -global-publishing-leaders-2013-harlequin.html. Accessed March 29, 2017.

Publishers Weekly. "Global Publishing Leaders 2013: HarperCollins. July 19, 2013. http:// www.publishersweekly.com/pw/by-topic/industry-news/financialreporting/article /58292-global-publishing-leaders-2013-harpercollins.html. Accessed March 29, 2017.

Reid, Calvin. "Ellora's Cave Cuts Staff, Blames Big Amazon Sales Drop." *Publishers Weekly,* August 22, 2014.

Reid, Calvin. "Samhain Publishing to Shut Down Operations." *Publishers Weekly,* February 26, 2016. http://www.publishersweekly.com/pw/bytopic/digital/contentand

-e-books/article/69517-samhain publishing-to-shut-down-operations.html. Accessed April 21, 2017.

Roland, Talli. "As Wonderful as Self-Publishing Is, It Does Have Its Limits." *The Guardian,* August 13, 2013. http://www.theguardian.com/books/2013/aug/13/talli-roland -selfpublishing. Accessed March 29, 2017.

Romance Writers of America. "Romance Genre." 2017. http://www.rwa.org/p/cm/ld /fid=580. Accessed March 29, 2017.

Strauss, Victoria. "Torquere Press Is Closing." *Writer Beware,* December 13, 2016. http:// www.victoriastrauss.com/2016/12/13/torquere-press-is-closing/. Accessed April 21, 2017.

Weinman, Sarah. "NAL IS Merged into Realigned Berkley Publishing Group." *Publishers Lunch,* June 23, 2015. https://lunch.publishersmarketplace.com/2015/06/people-nal-is -merged-into-realigned-berkley-publishing-group/. Accessed April 21, 2017.

D

Dailey, Janet (1944–2013)

Janet Dailey was a romance novelist who began her career with Harlequin Enterprises and has written almost 100 romance novels that have earned over $300 million. She was instrumental in Harlequin's expansion into the American romance novel market in the 1970s and pioneered the contemporary American romance novel.

Born in Storm Lake, Iowa, in 1944, Dailey moved to Omaha, Nebraska, where she worked as a secretary and eventually married Bill Dailey, the owner of the company where she worked. By 1974, Dailey and her husband decided to retire from the business and travel the United States in a camper. Shortly after, Dailey began writing her first romance novel with encouragement from her husband, who became her business manager and researcher. They later settled in Branson, Missouri, where Dailey lived until she died on December 14, 2013. Her husband, Bill, had died earlier in 2005.

Dailey sold her first romance novel, *No Quarter Asked*, to Harlequin in 1975 and became the first American author to write for Harlequin. Until Harlequin signed Dailey to a contract, it had published only British authors, a consequence of its distribution relationship with and eventual purchase of Mills & Boon, a British publisher of romance novels.

No Quarter Asked blended elements of the already established Western genre with the Romance novel, introducing romance readers to the love story of a rancher and a woman from the city, set in the iconic landscape of the American West. But unlike the traditional western, the cowboy hero in the western romance, despite his initial disdain for the heroine's feminine, citified ways, is tamed and domesticated by his love for the heroine.

Dailey's early romances frequently featured a western setting, and for many Harlequin readers, these settings likely appealed to their curiosity about foreign locations. British authors for Mills & Boon had frequently set their novels outside of Great Britain, in countries such as France, Spain, Italy, and Greece, as well as in former or current British colonies, such as Australia, South Africa, and the Caribbean countries. The American West was all the more attractive because of the uniqueness of both the landscape and the iconic cowboy hero.

However, Dailey went further in her exploration of the American landscape. A prolific author, as well as a seasoned traveler, Dailey did not confine her novels to western settings. Instead, she wrote about America in all its geographic variety, an America that was accessible and interesting to a broader American audience. In a series of books for the Harlequin Presents line, Dailey wrote a book set in each of the 50 states. Now known as her Americana series, it accomplished the goal of identifying America not as an exotic British colony but as a separate nation filled with multiple settings and multiple opportunities for other novelists to follow her lead. She was, therefore, the ideal author to spearhead Harlequin's expansion into the American publishing market. Her use of American settings appealed to American readers.

Dailey is also known for several innovations in the Romance genre. She was one of the first writers to write romance novels featuring recurring characters in an established world. Today, a familiar feature of a romance novelist's oeuvre is the series of novels linked by a common setting, family, or group of friends. But in the 1970s, it was unusual for an author to revisit a character or characters from a previous book. When the book ended, so did the lives of the characters in it.

For Dailey, her characters existed past the happy endings prescribed by the Romance genre, particularly secondary characters. Cord, from *No Quarter Asked*, appears in *Fiesta San Antonio* as the best friend of the hero. LaRaine Evans, the spoiled antagonist of *Sonora Sundown*, is redeemed and given her own romance in *A Land Called Deseret*. The characters in these novels live in the same universe.

For Bitter or Worse, in particular, pushes the boundaries of the Romance genre. In this novel, Dailey takes the unusual step of revisiting the hero and heroine, Cord and Stacy, from *No Quarter Asked* after they have been married for several years. A plane crash has left Cord with severe injuries, and in *For Bitter or Worse*, his marriage to Stacy is tested by his depression and anger as he fights to recover. The novel stands on its own, but the readers' knowledge of Cord and Stacy's previous courtship makes the love story of *For Bitter or Worse* all the more poignant.

Dailey's popularity enabled her to make the transition from the category romances of Harlequin and later, Silhouette, to more mainstream success as a single-title, mass-market novelist. Dailey was not the first to write for a single-title mass-market audience (that was Kathleen Woodiwiss in 1972), but she entered the single-title market only seven years later with *Touch the Wind*, published by Pocket Books, a division of Simon & Schuster.

Dailey's Calder series, a series of single-title novels written for Pocket Books, is another example of the ways she broke new ground in the Romance genre. Published in 1981, the first novel in the series, *This Calder Sky*, told the story of how Chase Calder and Maggie O'Rourke found love in the grasslands of Montana. Nine novels followed, recounting the love stories of various members of the Calder family, crossing generations. This kind of series was a marketing boon, drawing in readers not just by the name of the author but for the promise of finding out more about beloved characters.

Dailey's involvement in a high-profile plagiarism scandal was also a first for the contemporary-romance-novel industry. In 1997, Dailey was accused of plagiarizing from the works of equally prolific novelist Nora Roberts. Dailey admitted to the act, claiming that personal stress and a previously undiagnosed psychological disorder had led her to plagiarize. The two authors settled the case in 1998, but Dailey's reputation was tarnished as a result. In 2001, she signed a contract with Kensington Books and continued writing until her death in December 2013, but not with the same level of readership she had enjoyed before.

Wendy Wagner

Further Reading

Colker, David. "Janet Dailey Dies at 69; Romance Novelist Overcame Plagiarism Scandal." *Los Angeles Times*, December 23, 2013. http://articles.latimes.com/2013/dec/23/local /la-me-janet-dailey-20131224. Accessed April 4, 2017.

Regis, Pamela. *A Natural History of the Romance Novel*. Philadelphia: University of Pennsylvania Press, 2003, 155–68.

Daphne du Maurier Awards

The Daphne du Maurier Award for Excellence in Mystery/Suspense is presented by the Mystery/Romantic Suspense Chapter (also known as the Kiss of Death [KOD] Chapter) of the Romance Writers of America (RWA). Named for Du Maurier, the author of *Rebecca*, a suspenseful, now-classic tale featuring Gothic and romantic elements that have since become standard in contemporary Gothic and romantic suspense novels, this award is presented at the chapter's annual Daphne Awards/Death by Chocolate Party usually held during RWA's annual conference in July. Finalists are announced in the late spring, but the winners are not named until the awards ceremony.

The competition includes two separate tracks and is open to published and unpublished writers of "romantic suspense, mystery, suspense and thrillers with romantic subplots and mainstream mystery, suspense and thrillers." In the case of published authors, only works published during the previous year are eligible for consideration. Separate awards are given for published and unpublished manuscripts in each category. Current categories include Category (series) Romantic Mystery/Suspense, Historical Romantic Mystery/Suspense, Inspirational Romantic Mystery/Suspense, Mainstream Romantic Mystery/Suspense, Paranormal/Time Travel/Futuristic Romantic Mystery/Suspense, and Single Title Romantic Mystery/Suspense.

Kristin Ramsdell

Further Reading

Daphne du Maurier Award for Excellence in Mystery/Suspense. http://www.rwamystery suspense.org/daphne. Accessed March 20, 2017.

Dell, Ethel M. (1881–1939)

Ethel M.(May/Mary) Dell was a British author of more than 30 exotically set, action-packed romantic novels and a larger number of short stories—most of which have been published as collections—popular during the first half of the 20th century. Her improbable, wildly entertaining stories were filled with adventure, drama, and passion; often employed semireligious/spiritual themes and metaphors; and exuded an infectious vitality that appealed to her large, loyal readership. Elinor Glyn, E.(Edith) M.(Maude) Hull, and Marie Corelli were among her contemporaries who also wrote popular romances in a similar vein.

Dell was born in Streatham, a district in south London, on August 2, 1881, to a middle-class family and was the youngest of three children. Reserved and painfully shy, Dell let her imagination take full reign in her bold, colorful, racy stories. She began writing early and published some short stories. (Many of the stories in her collections were first published individually in magazines.) Dell's first novel, *The Way of the Eagle*, was published in 1911 to unexpected success, and she maintained a steady output of novels, approximately one each year, until her death. Her novels were popular and many were best sellers, allowing her to be so financially successful that when she married Lieutenant-Colonel Gerald Savage in 1922, he was able to retire from the service while Dell continued to write and support the family.

Although her subsequent novels were obviously popular, *The Way of an Eagle* is one of her more memorable. Set against the violence of unrest in colonial India, Dell's is a tale of passion, treachery, and danger as young Muriel Roscoe, the general's daughter, is saved from disaster by Captain Nick Ratcliffe, when he spirits her away at her dying father's request, promising to care for her. Their resulting engagement is soon broken by spiteful lies and Muriel's insecurity and fears, and it isn't until the very end—after another broken engagement, a betrayal, and much soul-searching and introspection—that she understands what love really is and realizes they are meant to be together. The story's fast-paced, sometimes violent action, exotic setting, and emotional angst are typical of Dell's work, and while this early romance is less overtly passionate than some, the adventure, excitement, and dramatic plot draw readers in. Tame by today's standards, Dell's stories were daring and edgy for their day, and although derided by literary and social critics, their approval was not Dell's goal. She was a storyteller writing for her readers, and as long as they were satisfied, that was all she cared about.

Her works, and those of her contemporaries, are the focus of some academic study today. Many are still available in libraries, and a selection of her titles can be downloaded from Project Gutenberg.

Dell died of cancer on September 19, 1939.

Kristin Ramsdell

Further Reading

Anderson, Rachel. "Dell, Ethel M(ary)." In *Twentieth-Century Romance and Historical Writers*, edited by Aruna Vasudevan, 180–81. London: St. James Press, 1994.

Dell, Ethel M. "Books by Ethel M. Dell (Ethel May)." Project Gutenberg. http://www.gutenberg.org/ebooks/author/3564. Accessed April 4, 2017.

Dell, Penelope. *Nettie and Sissie: The Biography of Ethel M. Dell and Her Sister Ella*. London: Hamish Hamilton, 1977.

Domestic Sentimentalists

If Samuel Johnson is sometimes said to be the grandfather of the modern romance novel, the women who penned 19th-century domestic fictions might well be regarded as its great aunts. Domestic sentimentalists wrote about the quotidian details of life in the domestic sphere, particularly about relationships within that sphere, and validated the importance of the emotional lives of women, all qualities that would prove central to the later development of 20th-century Romance.

Romance would also be tainted by the scholarly disdain of domestic sentimentalism, a disdain first expressed by F. O. Matthiessen in *American Renaissance* (1941), the earliest academic study of 19th-century American literature. To justify the study of previously maligned works by early male American writers such as Hawthorne, Melville, and Whitman, Matthiessen set them in opposition to lesser, low 19th-century sentimental fiction by women authors such as Catharine Maria Sedgwick, Susan Warner, and E.D.E.N. Southworth. That such women-authored volumes far outsold those by their male contemporaries only justified Matthiessen's denigration.

Ironically, the roots of domestic sentimental fiction lie in works written largely by men: the 18th-century novel of sentiment (or novel of sensibility). Sentimental novels such as Henry Mackenzie's *The Man of Feeling* (1771) and Oliver Goldsmith's *The Vicar of Wakefield* (1766) relied on an emotional response, from both their readers and their characters. Scenes in which characters experience distress and tenderness work not to advance the actions of the plot but to display emotions. Characters thus serve as a model for the reader not only in how to feel but how to feel *correctly*, in a refined, sensitive manner. The ability to display feelings was thought to show character and experience and to shape social life and relations, demonstrating who truly belonged to the genteel class, whether female or male, and who did not.

As beliefs about what constituted masculinity began to shift during the opening decades of the 19th century, however, the novel of sentiment quickly fell out of style. But women writers did not abandon emotion entirely. By the 1820s, the desire to evoke feelings through literature began to emerge in a new genre, which critics variously refer to as sentimental fiction, women's fiction, domestic fiction, or, in its American incarnation, domestic sentimentalism. Whatever it is called, such fiction would prove immensely popular throughout the following century in both England and the United States.

While not feminist in the contemporary sense of the word, domestic sentimentalism stemmed, critic Lora Romero argues, from an antipatriarchal critique of the way in which women functioned as commodities in the aristocratic patriarchal family, a function that demanded that women be educated only in the ornamental graces needed to attract a spouse and create an advantageous familial alliance through marriage. Both the radical Mary Wollstonecraft and the conservative Hannah More argued that such treatment of women made them little more than commodities to be bought and sold. The domestic ideology that developed in particular from More's critique, and the domestic fiction that helped construct and promulgate said ideology, argued that women should be educated not just to be attractive to the male gaze but, more important, to prepare them for their role as household managers and moral guides for their children and husbands.

Domestic ideology, and the novels that embraced it, took for granted that men and women were inherently different. But this difference did not mean that women were lesser; in fact, domesticity suggested that women were in many ways greater than their male counterparts. Women in patriarchal aristocratic systems suffered a loss of authenticity due to their need to perform for the male gaze; in contrast, domestic ideology offered women, as representatives of the domestic interior life, the chance to cultivate principle to preserve the authenticity of the self. Under domestic ideology, internal character rather than external performance became the standard against which women would be judged. Domestic ideology also idealized love as an agent of spiritual and moral regeneration, with woman as the conduit through which such regeneration took place. While men participated in the public sphere for the good of the family, such participation could be corrupting; such corruption could be mitigated through the influence of the domestic wife or mother. Because domestic ideology insisted on the moral difference between men and women, though, it always contained the possibility of reducing women to little more than the conduits through which men would be saved.

According to Nina Baym, who analyzes the 19th-century American sentimental novel in *Woman's Fiction* (1978), the basic sentimental plot features "a young girl who is deprived of the supports she had rightly or wrongly depended on to sustain her throughout life and is faced with the necessity of winning her own way in the world" (11). At the start of each story, this girl expects little of herself, depending on those around her to nurture and sustain her. But over the course of the novel, such expectations are dashed, and the heroine awakens to her own power to fulfill her own expectations. By story's end, because she herself has changed, the world around her changes, too, "so much that was formerly denied her now comes unsought" (19). Though the heroine's initial poor self-image may be the result of how she was raised, educated, or socialized, ultimately these novels argue that the most damaging factor is the heroine's false perception of her own abilities. In America, each woman has not only the opportunity but also the responsibility to change.

In some versions of the story, such as Maria Cummins's *The Lamplighter* (1854), the heroine is an orphan, or believes herself one, and is typically impoverished and without friends. In others, the heroine is a pampered heiress who, through the death or financial failure of her legal protectors, becomes reduced to the same threatened state as the orphan. Whether an actual or metaphorical orphan, the heroine must struggle for self-mastery, learning the pain of conquering her own passions. She must also learn to balance society's demands for self-denial with her own desire for autonomy, a struggle often addressed in terms of religion. Before she can recreate a new family for herself, she often suffers at the hands of abusers; as Cindy Weinstein notes, in sentimental fiction, "women are the primary sufferers and weepers" (213). The ultimate goal is to make the reader cry, to engage in an act of sympathy via literature. For with tears comes relief for the sufferer, both inside and outside the book.

Ironically, though, the plots of these novels "repeatedly identify immersion in feeling as one of the great temptations and dangers for a developing woman. They show that feeling must be controlled" (Baym, 25). Women who *only* feel will be at the mercy of those feelings, and at the mercy of the feelings of others. But women who connect their feelings to wisdom, responsibility, rationality, and self-command will never be content to remain passive victims, no matter how much abuse they suffer; instead, they will work to become active agents of moral good.

Domestic sentimental novels almost always end with a happy marriage. Yet they also explore the myriad ways in which marriage can be a real problem for women. By law in 19th-century America and England, women who married became *femes covert*, their legal identities subsumed within those of their husbands. A good marriage constitutes a joyous fulfillment of the domestic woman's destiny, but a bad marriage, which many American domestic novels depict in excruciating detail, can lead to myriad atrocities: abandonment; poverty; the loss of property; the loss of a child; or emotional, physical, or sexual abuse. Domestic ideology promises women a more authentic sense of selfhood, yet the boon it holds out as its highest reward—marriage—also has the potential to erase the very selfhood that lies at its heart, as novels such as Mary Jane Holmes's *Ethelyn's Mistake* (1869) and E.D.E.N. Southworth's *The Fatal Marriage* (1863) demonstrate.

The good marriages that end each novel can result either from reforming the bad or too-wild male, as in Augusta Evans's *St. Elmo* (1867) and Southworth's *Miriam the Avenger* (1854), or in marrying a man good from the start, one who admires feminine moral integrity more than feminine scheming and display, such as in Caroline Lee Hentz's *Helen and Arthur* (1853) and Susan Warner's *The Wide, Wide World* (1850).

Sentimental domestic fiction flourished during the first half of the 19th century, particularly during and just after the Civil War years. Warner's *The Wide, Wide World* sold more than one million copies worldwide; Cummins's *The Lamplighter* sold 70,000 copies in its first year (Showalter, 83). But by the end of the 19th century, sentimental literature faced complaints about the abundance of "cheap sentiment" and its excessive bodily display. Critics, and eventually the public, began to believe that sentimentalism could lead to unhealthy physical symptoms such as nervousness and oversensitivity. As a result, the genre began declining sharply in popularity. By arguing that sentimentalism by its nature made for flawed, unpolished, and inferior fiction hardly worthy of the name "literature," 20th-century literary scholars contributed to the erasure of the memory of these once-popular works.

Recent work by feminist literary scholars has only just begun to reclaim 19th-century American women writers from nearly a century of critical disapprobation.

Scholars have shown that domestic sentimentalism's investment is not in the flight from society, as in many male-authored books of the times, but rather in the desire for sympathy and for connection. Critics have also begun to explore sentimental fiction's cultural critique of very public issues such as education reform, women's rights, social and racial inequality, and the construction of American citizens. Authors of domestic fiction might evoke empathetic feeling for conservative or subversive purposes; they might also deploy it to express ambiguities or contradictions. As critic Cindy Weinstein concludes, "Art and expression in the age of antebellum women's fiction is complicated and diverse, both constituted by the limiting experiences of women at the time and invigorated by a commitment to represent as fully as possible those limitations and to move beyond them" (219).

Jackie Horne

Further Reading

Baym, Nina. *Women's Fiction*: *A Guide to Novels By and About Women in America, 1820–1870*. Ithaca, NY: Cornell University Press, 1978.

Brown, Gillian. *Domestic Individualism: Imagining Self in Nineteenth-Century America*. Berkeley: University of California Press, 1990.

Doolen, Andy. "Women Writers and the Early U.S. Novel." In *The Cambridge History of American Women's Literature*, edited by Dale M. Bauer, 119–38. Cambridge: Cambridge University Press, 2012.

Langland, Elizabeth. "Women's Writing and the Domestic Sphere." In *Women and Literature in Britain 1800–1900*, edited by Joanne Shattock, 119–41. Cambridge, UK: Cambridge University Press, 2001.

Romero, Lora. "Domesticity and Fiction." In *The Columbia History of the American Novel*, edited by Emory Elliott, 110–29. New York: Columbia University Press, 1991.

Showalter, Elaine. *A Jury of Her Peers: American Women Writers from Anne Bradstreet to Annie Proulx*. New York: Knopf, 2009.

Todd, Janet M. *Sensibility: An Introduction*. London and New York: Methuen, 1986.

Tompkins, Jane. *Sensational Designs: The Cultural Work of American Fiction, 1790–1860*. New York: Oxford University Press, 1985.

Weinstein, Cindy. "Sentimentalism." In *The Cambridge History of the American Novel*, edited by Leonard Cassuto, 209–20. Cambridge, UK: Cambridge University Press, 2011.

Du Maurier, Daphne (1907–1989)

Writing was Daphne du Maurier's raison d'etre, and for more than 50 years she turned out novels, biographies, plays, essays, and short stories. Du Maurier's literary efforts regularly hit the best-seller lists on both sides of the Atlantic, and several of her novels and stories became the inspiration for an assortment of critically acclaimed and commercially successful movies (including three directed by the legendary Alfred Hitchcock). With the publication of her novel *Rebecca*, du Maurier not only gifted readers with a spellbinding tour de force of romance and suspense, she created one of the iconic masterpieces of the Romance genre.

Born on May 3, 1907, in London, England, to Gerald and Muriel (Beaumont) du Maurier, Daphne du Maurier grew up in England and attended schools in London before completing her education at a finishing school in Paris. Du Maurier married Major Frederick Arthur Montague Browning on July 9, 1932, and the couple eventually had three children: Tessa, Flavia, and Christian. Du Maurier's husband's job with the British Army took the couple away from England, but they eventually returned home and settled down in Cornwall. After a long and productive literary career, du Maurier died in her beloved Cornwall on April 19, 1989.

Du Maurier's first novel, *The Loving Spirit*, was published in 1931. Inspired by du Maurier's obsession with family and place, the book is a tale of three generations of the Slade family, who live in Cornwall. Du Maurier followed *The Loving Spirit* up with several other novels, as well as *Gerald: A Portrait*, a biography of her father, actor and theatrical manager Gerald du Maurier, before *Jamaica Inn*, her first great contribution to the Romance genre, was published in 1934.

Jamaica Inn is the story of Mary Yellan, who after the death of her mother goes off to live with her aunt Patience and her husband, Joss Merlyn, at Jamaica Inn. Richly imbued with an abundance of danger and desire, *Jamaica Inn* is the quintessential Gothic romance as Mary stumbles across evidence that not only is Joss trading in smuggled goods, but he is also part of a group of murderous locals who lure ships and their sailors to their doom. Even the local vicar, Francis Davey, seems to be keeping secrets, and Mary soon finds herself entangled in a web of deceit. The one man who can help her escape is the one man she doesn't think she can trust: Joss's younger brother Jem.

Du Maurier takes full advantage of the bleak landscape of the British moors as the splendidly realized setting for *Jamaica Inn*, isolating the novel's heroine from any potential source of help and leaving her stranded at the atmospherically evil inn. The almost Brontë-esque flavor of *Jamaica Inn* is not really surprising since du Maurier not only held the Brontë family in high literary regard, she also later wrote her own critical analysis of the family, *The Infernal World of Branwell Brontë*. In addition to creating a wonderfully evocative sense of place, du Maurier also makes effective use of the standard Gothic convention of one "good" male character and one "dangerous" male character in the persons of Francis Davey and Jem Merlyn as Mary struggles to find someone whom she can trust.

Du Maurier followed *Jamaica Inn* up with *Rebecca* in 1938, which is not only her own greatest literary achievement but also one of the classics of the Romance genre. The novel's unnamed heroine meets the story's hero, wealthy, mysterious Maxim de Winter, while working in the south of France. After a whirlwind courtship, the protagonist marries Maxim, and the couple returns to Manderley, the de Winter family estate in Cornwall. Once there, the heroine finds herself locked in a figurative battle of wills with Maxim's deceased first wife, Rebecca, for her new home and her new husband.

With *Rebecca*, du Maurier created a timeless tale of love and danger that has enthralled generations of readers. The novel's perfectly realized setting, its subtle mix of suspense and romance, and its engaging heroine (whose triumph over the "other woman" in the book becomes the reader's triumph as well) come together brilliantly in one spellbinding story. *Rebecca* is the epitome of everything readers have come to expect from the Gothic and Romantic Suspense subgenre and has yet to be equaled, let alone surpassed.

Du Maurier's third great gift to the Romance genre is *My Cousin Rachel*, which was published in 1951. The novel's protagonist, Philip Ashley, finds himself falling in love with his late cousin Ambrose's wife, the enigmatic Rachel. Ambrose had met Rachel while staying in Italy for his health, and the last letter Philip receives from Ambrose is one in which his cousin begs him to come to Italy because he is tormented by his new wife. When Philip arrives in Italy, he is too late as Ambrose has died under rather mysterious circumstances and Rachel is nowhere to be found. Philip returns home to England; and when he discovers Rachel is also in the country, he invites her to stay at Ambrose's estate. Philip gradually finds himself bewitched by Rachel; but when he falls ill, Philip begins to wonder if he might be the latest victim of Rachel and her mysterious herbs.

With *My Cousin Rachel*, du Maurier successfully turned one of the major conventions of the Gothic romance on its head. The Gothic novel's requisite young, naïve "heroine" is really its narrator: Philip Ashley. Additionally, the traditional role of the older, enigmatic hero is now taken on by the mysterious, seductive Rachel. Du Maurier slowly and successfully builds the tension in the novel to the breaking point as Philip (as well as readers themselves) begins to wonder if Rachel is either an innocent woman or a scheming murderess. *My Cousin Rachel* just misses being another classic Gothic romance because of its ending, which moves the novel out of the Romance genre and into the world of suspense fiction.

After the publication of *My Cousin Rachel*, du Maurier went on to write more novels, assorted nonfiction titles, and a score of short stories. Family had always played an important role in du Maurier's life, but it also provided a rich source of literary fodder for the author as well. Not only did Du Maurier complete several biographies about her family, including one on her actor father, Gerald du Maurier, but she based her book *The Glassblowers* on family history. In addition, *Mary Anne* was inspired by the life of her great-great-grandmother, Mary Anne Clarke, who was mistress to the Duke of York.

Another plot idea that intrigued du Maurier was the idea of a person's having a double or a twin. Du Maurier used this theme not only in *The Scapegoat*, a story that centers on a university professor named John who discovers his exact twin, a nobleman named Jean, living in the French countryside, but also in *The Flight of the Falcon*, the tale of two brothers living in 20th-century Italy, whose lives are connected to those of two brothers who lived in the 15th century. Du Maurier also continued to be fascinated by the supernatural, using it as inspiration not only for many of her short stories, including the infamous "The Birds" and "Don't Look Back," but also for her novel *The House on the Strand*, in which the protagonist time-travels back to the 14th century.

Du Maurier's gift for creating captivating female characters, sweeping romantic plots, and richly realized settings have kept readers enthralled for decades. Her novels *Jamaica Inn*, *My Cousin Rachel*, and, most important of all, *Rebecca* helped define and refine the Romantic Suspense and Gothic subgenres of romance fiction for every writer who has since followed in du Maurier's literary footsteps.

John Charles

See also: Daphne Du Maurier Awards

Further Reading

Auerbach, Nina. *Daphne du Maurier: Haunted Heiress*. Philadelphia: University of Pennsylvania Press, 1999.

Du Maurier, Daphne. *Myself When Young*. New York: Doubleday, 1977.

Du Maurier, Daphne. *The Rebecca Notebook and Other Memories*. New York: Doubleday, 1980.

Du Maurier, Daphne. *Vanishing Cornwall*. London: Gollancz, 1967.

Forster, Margaret. *Daphne du Maurier: The Secret Life of the Renowned Storyteller*. New York: Doubleday, 1993.

Kelly, Richard Michael. *Daphne du Maurier*. Boston: Twayne, 1987.

E

Editor

An editor, broadly speaking, is a person with responsibilities for the selection, revision, and preparation of material for publication. Editors may also have managerial and/or policy-establishing duties, especially if they work for a publishing company. They may also write for publication themselves, as, for example, when an editor writes an editorial for the newspaper he or she works for. Editors perform a variety of duties, and publishing houses of all kinds may have editors-in-chief, executive editors, and managing editors, as well as editors with varying titles in charge of various departments and divisions, and those who work in them. Although the organizational structures are not the same for all publishers, all houses have people who perform these editorial functions, whatever their titles.

Acquisitions editors do exactly what their name implies: they acquire books to be published. Their responsibilities include studying and analyzing the current fiction-market conditions, spotting new trends, and signing authors of books that will meet these demands. Many houses will consider only agented proposals, but in the case of romance, many editors make it a point to attend a number of professional conferences each year (for example, the annual Romance Writers of America's [RWA] conference, RT Booklovers Convention, and selected regional or local RWA chapter conferences and workshops) to hear in-person pitches from authors. These editors are often the first contact an author has with the publishing house. In many cases, the acquiring editor will continue to work with the author during the developmental stage of the publishing process, essentially becoming the content or development editor; in other instances, the author may be handed off to another editor.

It is the job of the development editor (sometimes considered the main or general editor) to provide feedback to the author, suggesting revisions that will result in a better book. These editors will usually offer both big-picture/storywide suggestions concerning the overarching flow of the narrative, as well as line-editing suggestions that deal with issues of language use, writing style, pacing, content, tone, transitions, and any number of other concerns at the sentence, paragraph, or scene level. A book may go through any number of revisions during this process, but once it has been satisfactorily edited, it will be passed on for copy editing.

Copy editors, most of whom are freelance contractors, are responsible for making sure that grammar, spelling, punctuation, capitalization, syntax, usage, and style elements are correct and consistent with the publisher's chosen style. They will also make a note of anything that is unclear or wrong and will highlight any internal inconsistencies (for example, unexplained names or description changes and the like). Copy editing is always done after the final developmental and line edits have been completed and is one of the last steps before the book goes into production.

However, not all editors work within the traditional publishing structure. With the rise of the self-publishing and indie markets, there has been a growing need for freelance editors to serve that clientele. As a result, the number of freelance editors willing to perform those services has increased, and they are playing an important part in the romance-publishing arena.

Kristin Ramsdell

Further Reading

Bay Area Editors' Forum. www.editorsforum.org/what_do.php. Accessed March 20, 2017.
Jeffries, Sabrina. "A Writer's Guide to How Traditional Publishers Work." www.rwa.org/p
/cm/ld/fid=572. Accessed March 20, 2017.

Empowerment of Women

There are not many literary genres as loved and loathed as Romance fiction. For all its millions of readers for hundreds of years, it has been dismissed as sentimental, sappy, and trashy, as well as mad, bad, and dangerous to read. Yet Romance fiction, predominantly written by women, published by women, and read by women, remains one of the most popular and powerful genres on the planet.

Romance has been called the first form of feminism. When it began in medieval times around the 12th century, the word *romance* originally referred to the language *romanz* linked to the French, Italian, and Spanish languages in which love stories, songs, and ballads were written. Stories written in this language were called "romances" to separate them from more serious literature. Romance spread like wildfire through the courts of Europe. It flourished in "courts of love," female-dominated courts in France like those of Eleanor of Aquitaine and Marie of Champagne. Romance revolutionized gender relationships and radically changed the way society viewed love.

In the 20th century, the second wave of feminism during the 1960s and 1970s ushered in massive change in many areas of women's lives. Popular romantic fiction was particularly unpopular with second-wave feminists, seen as reflecting the stereotypes of the patriarchal status quo. Some early feminists were vehement in their attacks. Romance was viewed as a form of deception that deliberately prevented women from recognizing their oppressed and subordinate roles in patriarchal society. Literary criticism bemoaned it, and whether to include it as part of women's writing canon became hotly debated. Romance represented a dilemma. Was it poetry, pop, or porn for women? Romance fiction was argued to be a form of subliterature: sentimental, slushy, lush, and unforgivable. As women remade the world, the role of romance was reduced to pulp.

Postmodernism presented a new perspective. Postmodernism exceeds the limits of modernism, as romance those of realism, and in so doing both embody a counterdiscourse that resists, without transgressing, the certainties and boundaries that modernism/realism establish and upon which they depend (Elam). In postmodernist terms, Romance fiction could be considered powerfully subversive. Further feminist criticism of Romance fiction probed deeper. This included Tania Modleski's seminal reading of Harlequin romances and soap operas through feminist and psychoanalytic theory. She used a psychoanalytic approach to explain the value of the imaginative experience that Romance provides for women. Her critique made some pointed jabs at the genre and the women who read it, arguing that it aided women in their own objectification and trapped women in fantasy instead of assisting them to remake their reality. But Modleski did not overlook the possibilities for female empowerment inherent in utopian dreaming (Modleski).

Romance readerships became particularly active and vocal in demanding the kind of novels they wanted to read, including self-actualized heroines. Thurston considered that Romance fiction offered women a plurality of pleasures: a form of private relaxation, a shared reading experience, a site of playfulness, experimentation, and exploration, as well as female erotica that also provides insights into human relationships and behavior. It has been argued that romance fiction narratives go further, by actively challenging traditional patriarchy, to both empower and entertain (Crusie). In romance fiction, women are the primary characters, not in supporting roles, equal to men in power, intelligence, and ability. They have their own desires, including—and especially—for sex (Crusie). Above all, in romance, love is powerful and important.

Romance fiction shifted and changed as women actively reshaped the genre. No longer could romances be dismissed as "bodice rippers." From the 1980s onward, rigid gender roles and rules were broken as plotlines featuring strong women became blockbusters. Subgenres expanded to include contemporary, historical, speculative, fantasy, paranormal, science fiction, erotica, sexy, sweet, inspirational, steampunk, and more. The publishing field remained female dominated. The 21st-century self-publishing boom has further increased the agency of romance authors.

Not only has the genre exploded, there has also been a concurrent rise of Romance studies in cultural and gender studies, including a revaluing and deeper understanding of the complexity and sophistication of love and its place as a form of women's ways of being and knowing. The conventions of romantic fiction began to be explored though critics condemned such a romantic revival as revisionist and as a form of rose-colored false consciousness-raising. Modleski warned of the conflation of feminization with feminist. Women's dominance in the genre did not necessarily equal empowerment. Yet situating romance readers and writers as cultural dupes became increasingly problematized. Romance fiction is not a monolithic and unchanging entity but a discourse constantly being remade and reconstituted for and by women. Scholarship evolved beyond defending the genre to discussing its values and complexities.

In the 21st century, Romance fiction is being embraced as a form of female empowerment offering opportunities for consciousness-raising, awareness, and activism. This can be contextualized amid third-wave or lifestyle feminism. Love and romance is also being explored in the academy beyond popular cultural and gender studies, in philosophy, law, politics, social science, and psychology. This emerging interdisciplinary field, wryly dubbed "Love Studies," includes such topics as love, desire, and intimate relationships and an interest in gender and power while retaining a critical wariness about the costs of love to women (Selinger).

Romance fiction is a woman-powered genre from which novel ideas come. Women continue to lead the way in a revaluing and deeper understanding of romance and recognition of the lasting power of its philosophy. Romance is at heart a language, and languages, like love, are eternally being recreated.

Elizabeth Reid Boyd

Further Reading

Crusie, Jennifer. "Defeating the Critics: What We Can Do About the Anti-Romance Bias." http://www.jennycrusie.com/for-writers/essays/defeating-the-critics-what-we-can-do-about-the-anti-romance-bias/. Accessed March 30, 2017.

Elam, Diane. *Romancing the Postmodern*. London: Routledge, 1992.

Modleski, Tania. *Loving with a Vengeance: Mass-Produced Fantasies for Women*. New York: Routledge, 2008.

Selinger, Eric Murphy. "Editor's Note." *Journal of Popular Romance Studies* 4, 1 (2014): 1–2.

Thurston, Carol. *The Romance Revolution. Erotic Novels for Women and the Quest for a New Sexual Identity*. Urbana: University of Illinois Press, 1987.

Erotic Romance

While erotica has a long history in the publishing and reading world, the subgenre of Erotic Romance is a fairly new addition to the Romance genre. As a genre, Erotica focuses heavily on the sexual natures and relationships of the characters. Since the focus is on sex as a catalyst to further the plot and character development, erotica is often blended with other genres, such as Erotic Thrillers.

Erotica as an emerging force within the Romance genre can be traced back to the early 1990s when Virgin Books launched Black Lace, an erotica line advertised as being written by women, for women. While Black Lace did not have strict authorial guidelines to include romantic elements in its stories, many authors, such as Emma Holly and Portia Da Costa, did include romances, albeit sometimes untraditional ones, in their novels.

However, the availability of Black Lace titles in the United States was spotty at best, in part because Virgin Books was based out of the United Kingdom. Romance readers looking for more sexually explicit stories featuring frank, provocative female characters turned to a handful of pioneers who were melding erotica with Romance. Trailblazers like Bertrice Small, Thea Devine, Susan Johnson, and, later, Robin Schone were strongly pushing the envelope, although by current standards some of their sexual content may be considered tame. There were also a number of other historical writers who were increasing the sensuality levels in their books, while not entirely crossing over into erotica territory. Some of the earlier Avon releases by Nicole Jordan and Lisa Kleypas featured spicier love scenes, although the characters' sexual natures and appetites did not necessarily factor directly into the conflict of the story. This made for more sexually explicit love scenes but kept their books from completely leaving romance territory for erotica.

Another early adopter of more erotic content in Romance was publisher Red Sage, whose first Secrets anthology was released in 1995. This anthology series continues to be a staple for the publisher, and early volumes featured many now-recognizable names within the genre, including Angela Knight, Emma Holly, and MaryJanice Davidson.

Even with the successes of Black Lace and Red Sage, what ultimately paved the way for Erotic Romance becoming its own subgenre within Romance was the founding of digital publisher Ellora's Cave in 2000. An early adopter of e-books,

Ellora's Cave looked to the idea of melding both erotica and romance together and marketing the stories directly to romance readers. These books would have explicit content, while straying away from the current industry practice of euphemisms and purple prose during love scenes, and would promise the one thing to readers that erotica could not always provide, that is, an emotionally satisfying happy ending. Erotic Romance, in the vein of what Ellora's Cave would publish, would give readers the traditional happy ending that all romances have but, like erotica, would place a strong importance on the characters' sexual relationships.

The success of Ellora's Cave led to mainstream success for many of its writers, including Jaid Black, Lora Leigh, Sarah McCarty, and Angela Knight. As Ellora's Cave's success grew, the company trademarked the word "romantica" to describe the types of stories they were actively publishing: those books that would meld both romance and erotica. Also, as success grew, traditional New York publishing houses took notice. Many authors who got their start writing for Ellora's Cave received contracts with traditional publishers, and many of those publishers formed their own erotic imprints, such as Avon Red, Kensington Brava, and Harlequin Blaze. This adoption of more-explicit sexual content by traditional publishers brought up fierce debates among romance readers, some of them welcoming the inclusion while others were worried it would denigrate the genre to what detractors had long accused it of being, that is, merely porn for women.

Now that it was reaching a wider audience, how this new subgenre would be defined within the romance reading and publishing community took center stage. "Romantica" was an early-adopted term, created and trademarked by Ellora's Cave. Today, the preferred term tends to be "Erotic Romance," although how that is defined continues to be a ripe subject for debate. Confusion between Erotica and Erotic Romance continues to take place, even among those within the romance-reading community.

The simplistic definition of Erotic Romance is that it is Erotica but that it stays within the conventions that the Romance genre traditionally features: that is to say, a central love story and an emotionally satisfying, positive ending. However, that definition opens up the debate about what makes a romance an erotic romance. Is it the inclusion of more sex scenes, more than one sexual partner, or perceived kinky sex?

The simplest answer is that the sex in an erotic romance plays an integral part in the story. The explicit scenes serve a catalyst function in spurring forth not only the plot of the story but character development and growth as well. Remove the erotic elements of an erotic romance and the story would be drastically altered, not necessarily for the better.

Erotic Romance has its roots in small, independent, oftentimes digital publishing, and the subgenre thrives in that arena to this day. No longer relegated to seedy adult bookstores, these stories made it easy for women to access them in the privacy of their own homes. Long before personal e-reading devices, such as the Amazon Kindle and Barnes & Noble Nook, existed, readers were downloading stories, both novella and single-title length, to their home computers to read. The existence of this market, when one was believed to not exist before, led the way for the mainstreaming of Erotic Romance.

Kensington Brava launched quickly on the heels of Ellora's Cave's success and did so by bringing together early pioneers of the Erotic Romance subgenre. Bertrice Small, Thea Devine, Susan Johnson, and Robin Schone quickly found themselves issuing new stories and novels with Brava, and Brava also reissued a number of titles from these authors' backlists. Brava was also an early adopter of the trade-paperback format, a format later adopted by other erotic romance imprints, such as Avon Red and Berkley Heat.

Not to be outdone, category romance juggernaut Harlequin kicked open the door for erotic romance in 2001 by making Harlequin Blaze its own line. Originally a promotion within the Harlequin Temptation line, the steamier offerings proved to be so popular with readers that Harlequin was issuing a Blaze story every month under the Temptation banner. With that success, along with other publishers' success in the marketplace, making Blaze its own imprint was a natural progression, one that ultimately led to the demise, after 20 years, of Harlequin Temptation. And the evolution is set to continue as Harlequin ceased publication of Blaze in 2017, and a new line, Harlequin Dare, released its first titles in January 2018. Billed as "the publisher's sexiest series ever," it will deliver "riveting, irresistible romance stories featuring highly explicit sexual encounters."

As Erotic Romance has emerged as a force within the Romance genre as a whole, it has grown to include many diverse themes, elements, and authorial writing styles. Erotic romance continues to have success in shorter formats, such as short stories, novellas, and grouped anthologies, and yet full-length single titles have also found a home. Though it was once believed to be merely a regular romance with spicier and more frequent love scenes, its writers now explore themes that were once considered taboo for romance readers and publishers. Ménage, BDSM (consensual adult sexual activities involving bondage, discipline, dominance, submission, and sadomasochism), and gay and lesbian relationships are now, in many instances, staples of the subgenre, no longer seen as off limits.

However, despite the openness and inclusiveness of Erotic Romance and the publishers and writers who work within the subgenre, some themes are still considered taboo. Pedophilia, incest, and bestiality continue to be frowned upon, although the emergence of paranormal elements in Erotic Romance has certainly created a fine line for shape-shifting characters and love scenes. Just as the Romance genre predominantly has a female readership, so too does Erotic Romance. While elements such as ménage and BDSM may have once been wrongly perceived as being unappealing to a female readership, it seems highly unlikely and absurd that pedophilia will ever gain a foothold in a mainstream female-dominated marketplace.

Even though traditional New York print publishing eventually realized there was a market for Erotic Romance and sought to capitalize on it, until recently that had not led to the demise of Erotic Romance for digital publishing or smaller presses. With flagging sales and other issues, Ellora's Cave closed its doors at the end of 2016, and Samhain ceased publication on March 1, 2017. As of this writing, several other small erotic romance publishers, such as Loose Id, continue to hold their own. While many of these publishers have diversified their offerings for readers, erotic romance continues to be a staple for all of them.

Debate surrounding the Erotic Romance subgenre is unlikely to ever wane. What and how the subgenre is defined continues to vary depending on whom you are asking; the saturation of certain themes, like BDSM, within stories, and how far the envelope can be pushed before it's no longer acceptable to the reading masses continue to provide plenty of fodder for discussion. One thing is for certain, however, and that is that the subgenre has been embraced, accepted, and continues to excite readers. While all erotic romances utilize sex as a catalyst for the conflict and story, it opens up a wide playing field on which writers can work. Stories can have varying themes, feature a number of different elements, and range in tones from sexy fun to emotionally draining angst.

This broad canvas on which the subgenre exists, and which writers can explore, goes against the idea that was believed by many in the early days of Erotic Romance: that the stories were nothing more than sex and porn for women. The success of the genre, the emotional depth of the story lines, and the safe, accepted sexual exploration of female characters has empowered an entire generation of readers. Female sexuality, no longer taboo, is completely at the forefront of erotic romance. Without that exploration, without that acceptance, the subgenre does not work or exist. The very existence of Erotic Romance, the acceptance of it by readers who were desperate for it, means that it is acceptable for women to be in touch with their own sexual natures. It is the foundation on which Erotic Romance was built, and the very foundation on which the subgenre continues to thrive to this day.

Wendy Crutcher

Further Reading

"Goodbye from Team Samhain." Samhain Publishing. http://smhn.com/. Accessed March 31, 2017.

"Harlequin to Publish Its Most Explicit Romance Line, Yet." Harlequin Press. March 15, 2017. http://www.harlequin.com/store.html?cid=623868. Accessed March 31, 2017.

"What Is Erotic Romance?" *Passionate Ink.* http://www.passionateink.org/faq/. Accessed March 31, 2017.

Ethnic/Multicultural Romance

Ethnic and multicultural romances are romances in which the ethnic, racial, or cultural backgrounds of the characters are key aspects of the story and are important to the development of the protagonists' romantic relationship. In theory, this definition is broad enough to include romances that focus not only on ethnic and racial differences but on novels that deal with a wide range of cultural, religious, and even national origin or political differences as well. For example, a case for inclusion might be made for Amish romances or even stories with a strong, say, Italian, Irish, or Finnish American focus. However, in practice this is rarely the case, and this category generally focuses primarily on romances with a racial or ethnic component. In addition, the ethnic, racial, or cultural component must play an integral part in the story. In other words, the story would not be the same without it, nor could the story be told in a different setting and still ring true.

Multicultural romances can be found in of all the typical Romance subgenres—Contemporary, Historical, Paranormal, Inspirational, Romantic Suspense, and so on—and there is a growing consensus that these romances should not be considered as a separate subgenre—or even separate sub-subgenres—but instead take their rightful places in the main romance groups. The trend is definitely in this direction; nevertheless, while Ethnic and Multicultural Romance may not be considered a strict subgenre, it deals with some unique issues, is important in its own right, and deserves a separate discussion.

Love stories featuring characters of different races and cultures have been around for centuries and, in themselves, are nothing new. Myths, legends, the Bible, and the classics all have their share, although not all of these would qualify as romances by today's definition. American fiction of the 19th and early 20th centuries sometimes included multicultural characters—usually African American, Native American, or Latino, and most often in supporting roles—and occasionally they had romantic themes (for example, *Ramona* [1884] by Helen Hunt Jackson and *Showboat* [1926] by Edna Ferber).

The late 1950s saw the rise of the violent, sexy plantation romances that often featured African American or Caribbean characters—Kyle Onstott's *Mandingo* (1957) is a classic—but it wasn't until the late 1970s and 1980s that multicultural characters began to slowly work their way into the broader popular romance market. Celeste De Blasis's *The Proud Breed* (1978) featured a Latino heroine in a three-generational saga, and Rosalind Welles's *Entwined Destinies*, published by

Dell Candelight in 1980, was one of the earliest category romances to feature an African American hero and heroine. Native American cultures were often part of romances set in the American West, and Janelle Taylor's Gray Eagle/Alisha series and Susan Johnson's Braddock-Black Absarokee series are two classic examples.

The 1990s proved to be a decade of change as several small presses emerged to focus on romances with African American heroes and heroines; Odyssey Books, launched in 1990, and Genesis Press, established in 1993 with its first Indigo Romance title released in 1995, were two of the most important. Then in 1994 Kensington Publishing set things on fire with its launch of Pinnacle's Arabesque Romance, a line of multicultural romances, with Sandra Kitt's *Serenade* and Francis Ray's *Forever Yours*, two African American romances. The line was a success and in 1998 was bought by BET (Black Entertainment Television). Arabesque changed hands once again in 2005 when it was acquired by Harlequin as part of Kimani Press, its new program that featured several lines of African American romances. In the meantime, in 2005, Kensington launched its own African American imprint, Dafina.

But the publishing landscape is changing; and while at the moment there are still a few presses and/or imprints that focus exclusively on culturally specific romances (for example, Genesis Press's Indigo, Indigo After Dark, and Love Spectrum; Kensington's Dafina; and Harlequin's Kimani, all featuring African American romances), more and more romances with culturally diverse characters are being released as part of mainstream publishers' traditional romance lines. While it's worth noting that Harlequin (now part of HarperCollins) is discontinuing the Kimani line at the end of 2018, this is part of the inevitable social change. In short, the Romance genre is beginning to look like the country as a whole, reflecting its great diversity and using it to full advantage.

In addition to those mentioned above, these are a few authors who have been or are influential in Multicultural Romance: Rochelle Alers, Alyssa Cole, Kathleen Eagle, Shirley Hailstock, Brenda Jackson, Beverly Jenkins (2017 Nora Roberts Lifetime Achievement Award winner), Jeannie Lin, and Candice Poarch.

Kristin Ramsdell

Further Reading

Cultural, Interracial, Multicultural Special Interest Chapter of Romance Writers of America. http://www.cimrwa.org/. Accessed August 23, 2017.

Naughton, Julie. "In Loving Color." *Publishers Weekly*, November 10, 2014, 28–36.

Romance in Color. http://romanceincolor.com/. Accessed August 23, 2017.

The State of Racial Diversity in Romance Publishing. 2016. http://smartbitchestrashy books.com/WP/wp-content/uploads/2017/10/RippedBodiceReport2016-FINAL.pdf. Accessed October 5, 2017.

F

Fanfiction and Online Community Fiction in the Romance Genre

The term *fanfiction* (also known as Fanfic) describes fiction authored by fans, using pre-established characters of popular media. Fanfiction, in itself, is a world of user-generated literature, with most falling into the Romance genre. In fanfiction, authors adopt their beloved characters from well-known existing fiction and create their own story lines.

Fanfiction includes, but is not limited to, anime/manga, books, cartoons, comics, video games, movies, plays/musicals, and TV shows. By using characters from published material, fanfiction creates a sense of familiarity for other readers and allows Fanfic authors to reach an audience that already has an interest in, and basic understanding of, the characters. In some instances, Fanfic authors write crossovers, a single work of fiction combining characters from multiple popular works.

On the whole, fanfiction works are produced by fans for the enjoyment of other fans and are currently limited to the Internet. To reach its intended audience, fanfiction is organized by the original work on which the story is based. Therefore, searching for fanfiction is a relatively easy process.

One free online community catering to fanfiction and crossovers is www .fanfiction.net, established in 1998 and self-proclaimed as the world's largest fanfiction archive and forum with 2.2 million users. The Romance genre makes up a majority of fanfiction works available at the popular website; the number of stories that fall under romance total three times more than the second-most-written-for genre, Humor.

As of November 2016, the following 20 original works have the most fanfiction stories available on Fanfiction.net in descending order:

1. *Harry Potter* (757,000)
2. *Naruto* (409,000)

3. *Twilight* (218,000)
4. *Hetalia: Axis Powers* (119,000)
5. *Supernatural* (117,000)
6. *Inuyasha* (116,000)
7. *Glee* (108,000)
8. *Pokémon* (90,000)
9. *Bleach* (84,000)
10. *Kingdom Hearts* (73,200)
11. *Doctor Who* (73,000)
12. *Percy Jackson and the Olympians* (70,000)
13. *Yu-Gi-Oh!* (67,000)
14. *Fairy Tail* (60,000)
15. *Sherlock* (57,000)
16. *Lord of the Rings* (55,000)
17. *Buffy, the Vampire Slayer* (50,000)
18. *Dragon Ball Z* (49,000)
19. *Fullmetal Alchemist* (48,000)
20. *Once Upon a Time* (46,000)

The lure of fanfiction and user-generated online community fiction is its inter-active nature. Online communities catering to fanfiction encourage reviews and discussion forums. Unlike published fiction, online community fiction is often released incrementally with chapters posted as soon as the author has prepared them. With no publishing dates to adhere to, users post regularly, and readers have the option to subscribe to notifications and alerts to follow the in-progress stories. Also, unlike published fiction, authors of online community fiction may opt to take readers' suggestions into consideration in the next installment, allowing fol-lowers to have input on the plot.

A unique characteristic of fanfiction is that most often the romantic pairings are identified in a story's summary. Establishing the intended couples up front al-lows the reader to determine if they want to continue reading. Stating this informa-tion allows the reader a chance to consider the well-known characters as a pair and make a decision about whether or not to invest time in reading the Fanfic.

Other times the characters themselves may not be disclosed, but instead the sexual orientation of the pair is clearly noted. The common terms used to denote the pairings are "slash," "femslash," and "general." Slash romance fiction refers to same-sex pairings, usually two men as the main romantic couple, while femslash refers to two women. The term "general" typically refers to heterosexual pairings.

In fanfiction and online community fiction, homosexual couples are not the minority. In fact, slash and femslash fiction dominate the romance category and receive more hits and reviews overall. As the purpose of fanfiction and online community fiction is for fans to fulfill their own story lines using preestablished characters, Fanfic authors typically write relationships between characters who were not romantically involved in the original author's story.

In 2000, Fanfiction.net experienced such rapid growth of original fiction that any non-Fanfic content was relocated to a new site, www.fictionpress.com, which houses over one million stories, poems, and plays.

Similar to the features of its sister site, Fictionpress.com is free to join and offers members the ability to create communities and forums. The more communities a story is added to, the more visible it is to users. The online communities of Fictionpress.com and Fanfiction.net often consist of user-compiled lists of favorites or themed fiction. Popular communities feature one-shots (short stories), highly reviewed stories, completed fiction versus ongoing fiction, and, of course, slash and femslash.

Meanwhile, discussion forums mostly cater to online RolePlay (RP). As in most RP forums, there is an open invitation for users to develop a fictional character and write themselves into an ongoing plot. Using forum threads, users take turns moving the plot forward. They contribute to the story by manipulating their character and base their turn on the content contributed previously. Like fanfiction, a majority of online community fiction and RP forum plots are romantic in nature.

As fanfiction writing utilizes other creators' characters, legality is called into question. Therefore, fanfiction has not, nor will it ever, see commercial publication. However, in a way, fanfiction has managed to transition into the publishing world, most notably with the Fifty Shades of Grey series by E. L. James. James's *Fifty Shades of Grey* story was originally a fanfic of the popular Twilight series by Stephanie Meyer. On FanFiction.net under the pen name "snowsqueen icedragon," James posted a fanfic titled *Master of the Universe*, one of 202,045 Twilight fanfiction works available on the site. However, changing Meyers's identifiable character names and replacing them with original names, James moved forward with publishing her novels without consequence.

Note that fanfic works are not approved, nor do they require approval, by the original creator. Fanfiction writing is done without consent and typically contains a disclaimer stating that the characters and certain plot points are not the authors' own and that the story is instead a work of fanfiction. Most often, the original work and author are credited in this disclaimer, but as fanfiction is not created for monetary gain or widespread use, stating these facts is at the discretion of the Fanfic author.

That being said, there are authors and publishers who have contacted fanfiction websites and requested that fanfiction based on their original works not be hosted by the site. Fanfiction.net is one such site that has respected these requests and features a short list of authors and publishers in their guidelines, stating that any stories posted based on original works by these individuals will be removed and could result in suspension of the fanfic author's account.

Joanna Schreck

Further Reading

FanFiction.Net. http://www.fanfiction.net/. Accessed April 2, 2017.

FanFiction.Net. "50 Shades of Grey, Formerly Master of the Universe." http://www.fanfiction.net/forum/50-Shades-of-Grey-Formerly-Master-of-the-Universe/112030/. Accessed April 2, 2017.

FanFiction.Net. "Guidelines." http://www.fanfiction.net/guidelines/. Accessed April 2, 2017.

FictionPress.com. http://fictionpress.com/fiction/Romance. Accessed April 2, 2017.

W3snoop. "fictionpress.com whois information." http://fictionpress.com.w3snoop.com/. Accessed April 2, 2017.

Fantasy Romance

A blend of fantasy and romance, these stories are Romance's nod to the larger Fantasy genre. Drawing heavily on legend, myth, fairy tales, and folklore, these inventive tales send their characters out into strange, often magically infused worlds to fulfill a quest, do battle with any number of dark forces, slay a dragon (unless it's a good one), undo a curse, save the realm, or accomplish any number of similar, heroic objectives, all the while keeping the romantic relationship between the two main characters at the center of the story. Fairies, sorcerers, witches, dragons, elves, goblins, and all kinds of fantastic beings play their parts in stories that can be serious and intense, light-hearted and humorous, or anywhere in between. While strange new worlds are common, it is not unusual for these romances to use the everyday, real world as a setting for either all or part of the story.

As with other Romance subgenres, Fantasy Romance can trace its origins back to antiquity and the myriad magical tales passed on through time. Although Fantasy's exact roots remain murky and are often in dispute, many consider Edmund Spenser's epic poem *The Faerie Queen* (1590–1596) to be the first fantasy written in English (Spivak). Fantasy themes appeared sporadically, surfacing in the 18th century in Jonathan Swift's social/political satire *Gulliver's Travels* (1726), and in the next century in works such as those by George MacDonald (for example, *Phantases* [1858]; *The Princess and the Goblin* [1872]) and Lewis

Carroll (*Alice's Adventures in Wonderland* [1865]). However, it wasn't until the 20th century when works by J. R. R. Tolkien (*The Lord of the Rings* [1954–1955]), T. H. White (*The Once and Future King* [1958]), and C. S. Lewis (the classic theologically inspired children's series *The Chronicles of Narnia* [1950–1956]) that fantasy began to be taken more seriously.

None of these works, of course, would be considered fantasy romance by today's definition, but the seeds had been planted and took root, beginning to bud several decades later in works by Robin McKinley (for example, *Beauty: A Retelling of the Story of Beauty and the Beast* [1978]), the fantasy spoof *The Princess Bride* (1973), and even Anne McCaffrey's Dragonriders series (1968–), which were actually science fiction novels but read like fantasy.

Like many of the "otherworldly, supernatural" romance types, Fantasy Romance is a niche market with a loyal following; and while its popularity has waxed and waned over the years, like most fiction genres, it continues to hold its own, attracting new readers and writers and even casting its magical spell on Romance subgenres outside the traditional Fantasy realm. Lynn Kurland's Nine Kingdoms series and Nora Roberts's Circle, Cousins O'Dwyer, and Guardians trilogies, classic good-versus-evil/quest stories; Barbara Bretton's Sugar Maple books, community centered and sweetly magical; Kristine Grayson's Charming series, whimsical and fairy-tale based; Christine Feehan's Sea Haven series, grounded in elemental magic and danger; Susan Krinard's Fane tales, historical and rich with unicorn lore; and Kristen Callihan's Darkest London series, historical, mysterious, and dark enough to please many Paranormal fans, are only a few examples of the wide variety of romances that are part of this subgenre.

The subgenre continues to attract readers, but in the past decade, the Romance genre, as a whole, has attracted the interest of scholars as well. Currently, the Futuristic and Fantasy subgenres, in particular, are topics of recent interest as the call (January 1, 2017, submission deadline) for papers from the *Journal of Popular Romance Studies* for a special issue on "The Romance of Science Fiction/ Fantasy" (http://jprstudies.org/submissions/special-issue-call-for-papers/) clearly shows.

Kristin Ramsdell

See also: Alternative Reality Romance Subgenres

Further Reading

Fantasy, Futuristic, and Paranormal Romance Writers. http://romance-ffp.com/.

Ramsdell, Kristin. *Romance Fiction: A Guide to the Genre*. Santa Barbara, CA: Libraries Unlimited, 2012.

"Special Issue Call for Papers: The Romance of Science Fiction/Fantasy." *Journal of Popular Romance Studies*. http://jprstudies.org/submissions/special-issue-call-for-papers/. Accessed April 9, 2017.

Spivack, Charlotte. *Merlin's Daughters: Contemporary Women Writers of Fantasy*. New York: Greenwood Press, 1987.

Feminism and Popular Romance Fiction

Out of all genres of fiction, Popular Romance is tailor made for writers and readers with feminist ideals. After all, it is the rare genre written (for the most part) by women and for women. And within the myriad variations, at heart romances are stories *about* women—stories in which women are central to the plot, triumph over any obstacles, and are guaranteed a happy ending. That is not to say that every romance novel is feminist in nature, or that feminist critics who have been tough on the genre (particularly during the 1970s) have never been wrong. As in any great love/hate relationship, both sides have understandable reasons for their points of view.

One way of examining the dynamic relationship between feminism and Popular Romance is to imagine a congenial relationship between the two philosophies, delve into the origins of their sometimes contentious connection, and take a look at examples in various subgenres that prove that romance novels can not only happily coexist with feminism, but that as in any great love story, the two are often at their best when married to each other.

In many ways, Nora Ephron is an example of the ideal relationship between Romance Fiction and feminism. Before starting her second or third career as a filmmaker, Ephron was a journalist, essayist, and novelist. She was also an outspoken and pragmatic feminist. As an artist, she was a great example of showing how a funny, romantic, and uplifting story can absolutely be told within a feminist framework. Feminism isn't something that a woman does some of the time. If an artist is a feminist, her ideals will filter into whatever it is she is creating. Now not every romance novelist has declared herself an advocate for the rights of women the way that Ephron did throughout her life and career, but the message can be found on the pages of the stories the writers create for their predominantly female readership.

Perhaps before feminist critics and romance novelists and lovers can get on the same page about the potential inherent within the genre, it is important to deal with the (often ugly) past. Let's start with the biggest point of contention—rape. When paperback romances experienced their first huge boom in the 1970s (often in the form of swashbucklers and other historical romances), it was normal for the heroine of any of these books to experience a painful rape. Even worse, the hero of the story was often the one who raped the heroine, and it was after the assault that the two would fall in love.

While this setup denigrates women (and is difficult for the modern reader to put into any sort of understandable or forgivable context), romance novels were not alone in telling this sort of story. One of the most popular romances of any genre is that of Luke and Laura on the soap opera *General Hospital*. That couple ended up falling in love and marrying after he had violently raped her. At the time, the rape was explained away as an aggressive seduction, something along the lines of "it wasn't really rape if she secretly wanted him (even if he had no way of knowing that, especially as she was fighting him off)." This manner of excusing rapists for their crimes goes back a long way and exists beyond the Romance genre. Novelist Ayn Rand used it in her novel *The Fountainhead* back in 1943. So while romance novelists were guilty of using rape as a stepping-stone on the path to true love, they were not doing so in a vacuum.

It makes perfect sense, however, that any feminist would take issue with a genre that told this sort of story regularly. Readers are engaged on an intellectual and emotional level with what they read (or what's the point?), and using rape as the meet-cute in a love story is not something that should ever be normalized or romanticized.

It is also of note that marital rape was only brought into the public sphere in the 1970s with Diana Russell's book *The Politics of Rape* (Rosen, 18) and the first cases in America of men being tried for that crime (Stansell, 344). Before then, it wasn't acknowledged that a husband *could* rape his wife—that even in the context of this legal relationship a woman had sole ownership of her body and the right to say no to sex. So at the same time as some women were fighting for their right to bodily autonomy, others were writing romances like *The Flame and the Flower* in which the heroine is almost raped, mistaken for a prostitute, raped, becomes pregnant from that rape, forced to marry her rapist, falls in love with him, is almost raped again, and then lives happily ever after with her rapist husband.

Fortunately, women readers quickly grew tired of rape in their romances. Perhaps they always had been but were able to show their preferences only when they had more choices to choose from as publishers paid attention to buying habits and rape romances went away.

Many have tried to explain away the rape in those romances by positing that at the time the only way to get sex into such a book was if the heroine was forced into it first—it was okay to be a victim but not a "slut." She may have had to get raped first, but eventually she would get all of the pleasure and none of the guilt! However, the truth may be much simpler. Women had been treated like property and second-class citizens for so long that women's pain (at the hands of rapists and abusive husbands) was not taken seriously. The feminist movement was crucial in challenging these beliefs, and that is why things began to change—in society, in law, and in popular culture such as romance novels.

So when Popular Romance and feminism first met, they were not on the same page. Along with the rape stories, feminists had other problems with romance novels. Many argued that these books perpetuated patriarchal systems and beliefs: that monogamy and marriage are the foremost goals that women should strive for, that men have the upper hand/experience in sexual relationships, and that women have to subvert or change themselves to find happiness through a man (Regis, 4).

However, beginning in the 1980s, romance novels began to evolve with the women's movement. As a genre, Romance became more and more feminist, and some critics' issues seemed to be based more on what romance novels had been and not what they were becoming. There is also a condescending trend of critics being dismissive of romance readers and their ability to think critically and to differentiate between fantasy and reality. This is especially troubling as the "fantasy" became that a woman could have a fulfilling career, friends, and family, overcome all sorts of adversity, find love with someone who respects her and treats her well, and have many orgasms. Are such ideas fantastical or aspirational?

There are many examples of romance fiction from the 1980s, 1990s, and 2000s that support and even use feminist ideals as part of storytelling. By taking a close look at various subgenres of Romance, we can see that feminism is now everywhere. A reader is more likely than not to stumble upon a romance in the library or bookstore or e-library that has feminist protagonists and stories. Most of these books were published in the 1990s and 2000s. Few of them end in an actual marriage, and some don't even have a proposal.

In each subgenre, feminism is dealt with in various arenas, such as interpersonal relationships (with love interests, family, and other women), sex (what's acceptable, issues of slut-shaming, power balance), careers, intersection with other issues (race, class, homosexuality), ageism, and gender roles.

Contemporary Series Romance

Contemporary series romance is what most people mean when they mention Popular Romance Fiction. They are those numbered romances known more for the publisher or the line than the author. Harlequin, for instance, has many different lines that promise different sorts of stories. Blaze and the newly announced Dare offer steamy stories; Nocturne, paranormal; Kimani, African American/multicultural; and so on.

Series romances are considered the most disposable of romances. They are the shortest (the story is usually pared down to just the love story). Nevertheless, it is easy to find feminist ideology supported in their pages.

In Like Flynn by Dorien Kelly is number 27 of Harlequin's Flipside imprint. Inspired by the popularity of so-called Chick Lit (*Bridget Jones's Diary, Confessions of a Shopaholic,* and so forth), the stories have a humorous twist. Annie, the heroine, begins the book wanting to earn a promotion at her job. She is thrown together with a handsome Irishman, whom she takes to be an obstacle to that goal but later becomes an ally (as well as her love interest). From the beginning, she is shown to be capable, if a touch insecure (although her insecurity never holds her back). She is fond of control in both her personal and professional lives, and although part of her character arc is learning to have a more open mind, her enjoyment of power is never portrayed as a negative or something that the love of a sexy man will cure her of.

After she expresses remorse the morning after a close romantic encounter, her man Flynn declares that next time he wants proof in writing that she actually wants him before they get busy. While refusing to admit the likelihood of ending up in another clinch, she mulls his proposal in her head: "A written demand for sex. . . .Weird, but the thought appealed to her. In fact it was just kinky enough to make her toes curl, and in a good holding-all-power way, too" (132).

Not only is Annie's sex drive portrayed as a positive, but the sex also happens on her timetable and her terms. She has complete autonomy of her body, and that is portrayed as a normal, healthy, and sexy fact.

Contemporary Single-Title Romance

Unlike series romance, contemporary single-title romances are known more for their authors. Many of these authors began as series novelists for Harlequin or other publishers and moved on once they developed a following. Because of this, there is more blending of genres as many of the authors like to play in different sandboxes. These books are longer than series romances and often have more involved plots with minor characters.

Nora Roberts, who started out writing series novels, is the most popular romance author around. Her books sell like hotcakes, so the feminist beliefs that are littered throughout all her work reach the widest range of readers (perhaps her obvious feminism is even a reason why her books are so widely read and loved by women). One of the standouts of her work is that her heroines have relationships with other women that are just as interesting, dynamic, and important to the plot as the ones they have with their love interests.

In *Carolina Moon*, Tory returns to the town in which her best friend was murdered when they were children. Aside from a few easily jumped hurdles, her love story with the dead girl's brother goes along fairly easily. However, Tory's relationship with her friend's twin sister, Faith, is much more dynamic and unpredictable.

The women begin as opponents, and after a few fights, battles in which they are on the same side, and heart-to-hearts, they end up friends. At one point, Tory even punches out a lecherous creep who threatens Faith, and the two women often save themselves and each other before the all-male cavalry has a chance to show up.

In *The Villa*, Roberts also tackles the issue of ageism. Pilar, the main heroine's mother, gets a complicated romance of her own. Separated for years from a philandering husband, she rediscovers her joie de vivre and self-confidence through a new job and a new relationship with a younger man. Debunking the myth of the happily-ever-after, Roberts instead gives an example of a second chance. In a fun scene, three generations of women (Pilar, her daughter, and her mother) stumble upon one another in the kitchen after they have each had sex. There aren't many genres in which one will find a grandmother having and enjoying sex without it being made a joke.

While Pilar deals with and overcomes stereotypes around age, her daughter, Sophia, confronts her own love interest when he attempts to slut-shame her (to deny his own attraction to her). Sophia enjoys sex and propositions Ty. When he uses her sexual past and forthrightness as an excuse to reject her, she defends herself: "I'm a whore, in your opinion, because I think of sex the way a man does. . . . It would be alright, wouldn't it, if I pretended reluctance, if I let you seduce me. But because I'm honest, I'm cheap" (113).

Ty, to his credit, is already apologizing before she can finish reaming him out. He knew that he was wrong and, more important, never believed what he was saying. A man who didn't respect her would never be an appropriate match for Sophia in the world presented in this novel.

Historical Romance

Historical romances generally include any story that takes place before 1945. They have been called anachronistic—characters may speak or behave in a way that is not historically accurate. However, this only makes historical romances more relevant when considering feminism since the beliefs supported in the texts represent not those of the times during which they are set, but those of the time in which they are written. A reader will find a lot more freedoms (sexual and otherwise), reversed gender roles, and equality than if they were reading a novel actually written in those times.

A Fifth Avenue Affair by Tracy Cozzens is a historical romance set in New York just before the turn of the previous century. The protagonist, Clara, has no desire to marry. She spends her time doing volunteer work—it is her dream and goal to keep doing this work for the rest of her life. When she does eventually fall in love, it is with a man who has come to support and contribute to this work (this in a world in which every other man from her father to a determined suitor thinks that her work is a passing fancy that will end when she marries). Aware of her position, she explains to the man she loves: "If I married him [the practical match], I fear that I would be pushed into a corset tighter than the one I wore for the ball. Forced to abandon all my projects and resort to basket charity. Allowed to do only what my husband deemed proper and appropriate. . . . I can't imagine Mr. Burnby ever thinking of ways to improve my efforts as you did" (274).

Although Clara is moderately feminist, her sister pushes even further. Meryl is attending Bryn Mawr. She prides herself on being the only one of her sisters to graduate from more than a finishing school and plans to take over her father's business someday. The sisters are close, and Meryl encourages Clara to indulge her newly discovered lustiness. Clara follows the advice and goes so far as to have premarital sex. This being a romance novel, Clara is not punished for her actions (not even with an unplanned pregnancy). A heroine would never get away with that in a Henry James or Edith Wharton novel. If it's an unreal fantasy, then at least it is a feminist one! Romance is one genre in which heroines are never punished for desiring or indulging in sex, even if it seems like an anachronism.

Inspirational Romance

In inspirational romances, religious (most often Christian) beliefs are an important part of the story. In *Cinderella Heart* by Ruth Scofield, religion is the center of the heroine's life and the one connection between her and her love interest. After years of looking after her father and living life the way he wanted, Cassie is given a chance to make her own choices after he dies. Within the boundaries of a chaste love story, this book is also about a passive woman learning how to take power back in her life and make her own choices.

A schoolteacher, Cassie decides to join a more progressive, social church. For the first time in her life she connects with people—making friends and having her first experience with a man. At 39, Cassie is a virgin. When the hero (who has been around the block several times) tries to make a move, she explains that she won't have sex before marriage. Just as the character in the Nora Roberts novel refused to be shamed for having a lot of experience, Cassie is allowed to make the opposite choice without judgment.

Paranormal Romance

Paranormal romances have supernatural elements such as vampires, ghosts, werewolves, and the like. They can be series or single titles and vary greatly in tone from the very serious to the completely comic.

Undead and Unappreciated by Mary Janice Davidson falls into the more comic end of the paranormal spectrum (though it also has a few scares). It is the third book in a series about Betsy, a twenty-something heroine who is turned into a vampire and destined to become the queen of the dead. A modern girl, she never wanted such a life (no matter how sexy it might be at times), and she does her best to keep her normal life and friends.

There is a clever scene involving three vampires and two humans that shows how sometimes in modern life issues like race, sexuality, and gender can intersect. Marc (who is white and gay) is debating with Jessica (who is black and a woman) about the use of the *N* word. He posits that since it is the 20th century, the word has lost all meaning and there is no reason why he shouldn't be allowed to use it. Tina (who is white, a woman, and a vampire) was alive during slavery and doesn't want to have that conversation. Listening to her friends' debate, Betsy describes it in the following passage:

> "No, no, no," Jessica said, and I curled my fingers around the door handle, just in case. I knew that tone. "In this day and age, there are quite a few more important things to worry about. It *is* just a word. It's totally lost its meaning." Sinclair was looking up at her in the rearview, and Tina was edging away. Only Marc, who couldn't smell emotions, was oblivious. "Now go ahead, " she continued calmly. "You just call me that *once*. " (57)

Even though this is a paranormal romance, the author adds depth to the universe and the characters by letting them have conversations about important issues (albeit in a funny scene). Since the third wave of feminism (when minority women took more of a voice and the movement expanded beyond the interests of middle-class white women), these are the sorts of things women think about. It is also an example of a human woman demonstrating power in a scene in which she is surrounded by powerful beings. This moment gives words a moment to have supremacy over physical power (although a few pages later, Jessica also gets to hit a vampire across the head with a silver tray).

Regency Romance

Regency romances are historical romances that are set against the Regency Period of the British Empire (the early 19th century). Jane Austen is the ultimate inspiration for this sort of romance, and the most well-known author of this style is Georgette Heyer. Heyer's romances didn't have love scenes because she was writing in an earlier time—from the 1920s to the early 1970s.

As with historical romances, Regency heroines often behave like modern women. In *A Matter of Class* by popular writer Mary Balogh, the heroine climbs up trees as a child and has spontaneous, premarital sex by the side of a river as an adult. The two young people eventually get married, but Anna is never attached to her virtue and tosses it aside easily and without fear. The biggest issue is one of class, as her desired beau has money but no title. In fact, she pretends to run away with a lower-class man so that her father will force her to marry someone better right away. She is never as concerned with being "ruined" as a woman of that period would have been.

African American and Interracial Romance

By taking a close look at both African American romances and romances by mainstream authors that feature interracial relationships, we can see how race intersects with gender in popular romance fiction.

Rochelle Alers's *Stand-in Bride* features two generations of love stories (one interracial and one intraracial). The story begins with a teacher going home to Georgia to tell her father that she is getting married to a Frenchman. At first, her father is shocked and possibly angry at the fact that she is marrying someone outside of her culture (both in terms of race and nationality), but any objections are bowled over by his daughter's enthusiasm and steely resolve. Later in the novel he has a romance with her bridal coordinator (a beautiful black woman about his age). This book gives positive examples of both romances in different age groups and different cultures.

Learning to Love by Gwynne Forster is another African American romance depicting a culture clash, though this one has a more overtly feminist story. The heroine, a distinguished college professor, falls in love with a Nigerian prince. She was already visiting his homeland for work, and although she is more than willing to get to know his culture and respect its people, she is unwilling to conform to its patriarchal system to be with him. If she were to marry him according to his culture, then she would be subservient to him. Love is shown to be important in this novel, but it is also shown as something that a woman should never compromise her ideals and self-respect for. And since it is a romance after all, she gets her happy ending anyway.

In Nora Roberts's *Black Hills* there is a secondary romance between the protagonist's best friend and surrogate brother. Tansy, a black woman in her thirties, is aware of how society would view her relationship with a younger white man. Her fear of their difference and the judgment of the outside world are the obstacles to their burgeoning romance. She talks the issues out with the primary heroine, Lil, who is Tansy's best friend, and their relationship is an important one in the novel. For example, they also have many conversations that are not about men but about other important things, such as work.

Lil is a "love rules" type of person and tells her buddy to forget race and age and to follow her heart. Both women have a point, and both are shown to be right in the end. Tansy and her man are good together in spite of and because of their differences, but they will face challenges that an intracial couple would not because the idea that we are in a postracial America is a bigger fantasy than any romance.

In the past, feminism in Romance has been inspired by developments in the evolving politics and beliefs of the real-world feminist movement. Some critics deride Romance fiction as a disposable genre because the books are written and published so quickly. However, this gives writers the opportunity to be topical and on track with (and sometimes even ahead of) the zeitgeist. At best, romance novels can take feminist ideas that are discussed in academia and politics and share them with their readers. In the end, love (with happy endings) and feminism (in the form of female empowerment) form a couple that is made for each other.

Natalie McCall

Further Reading

Alers, Rochelle. "Stand-in Bride." In *Going to the Chapel*. New York: St. Martin's Paperbacks, 2001.

Balogh, Mary. *A Matter of Class*. New York: Vanguard Press, 2010.

Bouricius, Ann. *The Romance Readers' Advisory: The Librarian's Guide to Love in the Stacks*. Chicago: American Library Association, 2000.

Cozzens, Tracy. *A 5th Avenue Affair*. New York: Kensington Publishing Corp., 2003.

Crusie, Jennifer. *Strange Bedpersons*. Don Mills, Ontario: MIRA, 1994.

Davidson, MaryJanice. *Undead and Unappreciated*. New York: Berkley Sensation, 2005.

Forster, Gwynne. "Learning to Love." In *Going to the Chapel*. New York: St. Martin's Paperbacks, 2001.

Heyer, Georgette. *Arabella*. Thorndike, ME: Thorndike Press, 1992. (First edition published in 1949.)

Kelly, Dorien. *In Like Flynn*. Toronto: Harlequin, 2004.

Regis, Pamela. *A Natural History of the Romance Novel*. Philadelphia: University of Pennsylvania Press, 2003.

Roberts, Nora. *Black Hills*. New York: G. P. Putnam's Sons, 2009.

Roberts, Nora. *Carolina Moon*. New York: G. P. Putnam's Sons, 2000.

Roberts, Nora. *The Villa*. New York: G. P. Putnam's Sons, 2001.

Rosen, Ruth. *The World Split Open: How the Modern Women's Movement Changed America*. New York: Viking, 2000.

Scofield, Ruth. *Her Cinderella Heart*. New York: Steeple Hill Books, 2006.

Stansell, Christine. *The Feminist Promise: 1792 to the Present*. New York: Modern Library, 2010.

Wendell, Sarah. *Everything I Know about Love I Learned from Romance Novels.* Naperville, IL: Sourcebooks Casablanca, 2011.

Wendell, Sarah, and Candy Tan. *Beyond Heaving Bosoms: The Smart Bitches' Guide to Romance Novels.* New York: Simon & Schuster, 2009.

Forced Marriage Plot

See Arranged (or Forced) Marriage Plot

Forms and Formats Common to Popular Romance Fiction

The novel, which is defined by *Webster's Third New International Dictionary* as "an invented prose narrative of considerable length," is the most common form for the popular romance to take; however, short stories and novellas have their place as well. These shorter forms have gained popularity in recent years; and while often published in anthologies (works by various authors) or collections (several works by the same author), with the advent of e-books, they may also be available digitally as stand-alone titles. These stories may have links to existing series by the same author, perhaps serving as prequels or stories about minor characters in the series world, or they may be completely independent tales. However, with the ongoing popularity of series and related books in the Romance genre as a whole, short stories and novellas linked to larger series are far more common than those of the solitary variety. Often, authors will release these shorter, series-linked stories as e-books in between publication of the novel-length books in the series to keep fan interest ongoing, sometimes even offering them at no cost to attract new readers.

Opinions vary on the length requirements of these forms, but it is generally agreed that novels are at least 40,000 words, but usually more; novellas are anywhere between 20,000 and 40,000 words; and short stories are less than 20,000 words in length.

Romances are published in all of the traditional formats: print—which includes hardcover, trade paperback, and mass-market paperback—e-books, and audiobooks in both physical and downloadable formats. Although for years print dominated the romance market, according to 2015 statistics from the Romance Writers of America, e-books have surged and accounted for 61 percent of popular romance sales in 2015, not including self-published or Amazon-published e-books. However, print is holding its own, with mass-market paperbacks (26 percent) the clear winner over trade paperbacks (11 percent) and hardcovers (1.4 percent) (Romance Writers of America). This survey did not cover romance audiobooks; but overall market statistics reported by the Association of American Publishers (AAP) for the same period found that audiobook download sales had increased 38.1 percent over the year before. It is logical to assume that romance audiobooks shared in the increase (Graham).

As mentioned earlier, self-published and Amazon e-books were not covered in the statistics above. However, this is not because the numbers are negligible. They are, in fact, enormous. According to a 2016 RWA Conference presentation by Data Guy of AuthorEarnings.com, 89 percent of all romances sold in the United States are digital, and more than 50 percent are self-published, but because more than 67 percent of romance fiction sales are not tracked by traditional industry data gatherers (for example, Nielsen, AAP), a huge part of the sales of the Romance genre, largely in e-book format, goes unreported.

Kristin Ramsdell

Further Reading

Graham, Luke. "Book Sales Are in Decline but Audio Books Are Thriving." CNBC, March 3, 2016. http://www.cnbc.com/2016/03/03/book-sales-are-in-decline-but-audio-books-are-thriving.html. Accessed March 20, 2017.

Romance Writers of America. Romance Statistics. https://www.rwa.org/p/cm/ld/fid=580. Accessed March 20, 2017.

Romance Writers of America RWA PAN Presentation 2016. "Romancing the Data: A Comprehensive Look at Amazon Author Earnings for Romance" by Data Guy. http://authorearnings.com/2016-rwa-pan-presentation/. Accessed March 20, 2017.

Futuristic (or Science Fiction) Romance

Futuristic Romance is essentially Romance with a science-fiction setting. Usually taking place at some time in the future, these stories employ a variety of scientifically possible (though not necessarily probable) settings and scenarios that may include, but are not limited to, intergalactic space travel and exploration; colonial life on far-flung planets; interactions with alien cultures and civilizations; interplanetary battles and conflicts; and future, often dystopian or postapocalyptic, versions of life on Earth. Futuristic or Science Fiction Romance varies from Fantasy Romance in the same way that the larger Science Fiction genre differs from

Fantasy in that Science Fiction builds on what is currently known as scientific fact and extrapolates to create potential logical versions of the future, while Fantasy allows for the building of completely imaginary worlds and situations, often making use of magic, sorcery, and other supernatural elements, and limited only by the necessity of remaining true to the rules of the world established by the author. The romantic relationship between the two main characters is always the prime focus, but in the best works of this type, the futuristic setting and related elements are so integral to the plot and the relationship that the romance wouldn't be the same in another setting.

Although the larger Science Fiction genre can trace its roots back centuries (for example, David Russen's *Iter Lunare: or A Voyage to the Moon* [1703] and before), Futuristics came on the scene much later. In 1986, with *Sweet Starfire* and *Crystal Flame*, Jayne Ann Krentz is credited with being one of the first romance authors to venture into this realm, and others quickly got on board. Lori Copeland's *Out of This World* (1986) joined the fray, and although not a romance writer per se, Lois McMaster Bujold, with her memorable *Shards of Honor* (1986), contributed a work that had enough romance to qualify it as a Futuristic and a modern classic in the field. (Anne McCaffrey's sci-fi Dragon Riders of Pern Saga, begun with *Dragonflight* [1968], also has a romantic element. and some might consider it well within this Romance subgenre.) Although a definite niche market, Futuristics continued to attract both loyal fans and writers, and as a number of sci-fi authors realized the importance of the Romance genre and the suitability of their own works, many of them crossed over and joined the growing the subgenre.

The subgenre is holding its own as both traditionally and independently published authors continue to produce ever more innovative stories. Robin D. Owens's Celta HeartMate series and Jayne Castle's Harmony series, both involving psychically gifted cultures that began as colonies from Earth; Linnea Sinclair's edgy, intergalactic space adventures; Joss Ware's postapocalyptic Awakening Heroes series; and J. D. Robb's (aka Nora Roberts) Eve Duncan (. . . in Death) near-future, romantic, hard-hitting detective series are only a few examples of the diversity that currently exists within the subgenre.

The subgenre continues to attract readers, but in the past decade, the Romance genre, as a whole, has attracted the interest of scholars as well. As of this writing, the Futuristic and Fantasy subgenres, in particular, are topics of recent interest as the call (January 1, 2017, submission deadline) for papers from the *Journal of Popular Romance Studies* for a special issue on "The Romance of Science Fiction/Fantasy" (http://jprstudies.org/submissions/special-issue-call-for-papers/) clearly shows.

Kristin Ramsdell

See also: Alternative Reality Romance Subgenres

Further Reading

Fantasy, Futuristic, and Paranormal Romance Writers. http://romance-ffp.com/. Accessed April 13, 2017.

"The Galaxy Express: Adventures in Science Fiction Romance." http://www.thegalaxy express.net/. Accessed April 9, 2017.

Massey, Heather. *A Brief History of Science Fiction Romance.* Smashwords ed., 2015. https://www.smashwords.com/books/view/548258. Accessed April 9, 2017.

"Special Issue Call for Papers: The Romance of Science Fiction/Fantasy." *Journal of Popular Romance Studies.* http://jprstudies.org/submissions/special-issue-call-for -papers/. Accessed April 9, 2017.

G

Gay (M/M or Male/Male) Romance

See M/M (Male/Male) Romances

Genreblending

Genreblending, or genre-blurring as it is sometimes known, is the tendency of distinctive elements from one fiction genre to migrate into another. Sometimes this simply adds a creative twist, something a bit unexpected, to a story that remains happily grounded in its original genre. For example, many contemporary, historical, and even inspirational romances include mysteries that need to be solved, secrets that eventually are revealed, or even hints of the paranormal that add interest but are merely tangential to the main story and don't send it into another genre or subgenre. On the other hand, if the blend of elements is especially effective and turns out to be popular, it may, in time, end up becoming a fiction genre of its own.

Genreblending is common to most fiction genres, but the Romance genre has been particularly fertile ground for this trend. Many of what are now considered Romance subgenres are intersections between Romance and the other broad fiction genres. Romantic Suspense is a classic example, borrowing equally from Romance and mystery/suspense; Gothic Romance is another, infusing romance with the early Gothics' sense of brooding isolation; and Stuart Voytilla makes a more recent case for the Adventure Romance from the film point of view. Science Fiction, Fantasy, and even Horror to some degree have impacted Romance, as well, and the supernatural and "other worldly" romance subgenres (for example, Futuristic Romance, Fantasy Romance, Paranormal Romance, Time Travel Romance, Urban Fantasy Romance) are several established examples.

Like all of literature, Romance is a dynamic genre, growing and evolving as tastes and interests change. What is popular now may not be in fashion 20 years— or even five years—from now. However, paying attention to what is happening in the genreblending arena has provided some early clues in the past and is likely to do so in the future.

Kristin Ramsdell

Further Reading

Ehrenkranz, Penny Lockwood. "Mixing It Up: Writing Across Genres." *Writing-World .com*. http://www.writing-world.com/fiction/crossgenre.shtml. Accessed June 9, 2017.
"Genreblending." *Fantasy-Faction*. September 2, 2012. http://fantasy-faction.com/2012 /genre-blending. Accessed June 9, 2017.
Voytilla, Stuart. "Genre Blending: The Romance of Adventure, and the Adventure of Romance." *The Writer's Store*. https://www.writersstore.com/genre-blending-the -romance-of-adventure-and-the-adventure-of-romance. Accessed June 9, 2017.

Glyn, Elinor (1864–1943)

Elinor Glyn was a British author, scriptwriter, filmmaker, and journalist who established herself as an expert on romantic love and female sexuality in the first decades of the 20th century. Her most famous novel, *Three Weeks*, in which an older, glamorous woman and a younger man engage in an adulterous relationship, challenged prevailing moral standards and introduced a degree of eroticism hitherto lacking in romantic novels for women. Subsequently, her talent for self-promotion and her controversial personal observations about love and sex pushed the boundaries of 20th-century censorship and established a new public conversation about love, sex, and female experience.

She was born in Jersey in 1864 to a Scots engineer and a Canadian mother. Her father's early death and her mother's return to Canada saw her heavily influenced by her maternal grandmother, whose emphasis on the family's aristocratic French ancestry and disciplined training had a profound effect on the young Elinor. After her mother's remarriage and the family's return to England, both Elinor and her sister, Lucy, who later became the fashion designer Lucile, Lady Duff Gordon, were introduced to upper-class social circles. In 1892, Elinor married Clayton Glyn. Though the marriage proved both a financial and emotional disappointment, it gave Elinor the entrance to the aristocratic circles she admired. She began to write society novels, the first of which, *The Visits of Elizabeth*, was published in

1900. While amusing and sometimes unconventional, these novels did not elicit the notoriety that *Three Weeks* brought her. It was published in 1907; its frank sexuality and sympathetic portrayal of adultery outraged public opinion, and it became an international best seller.

In a controversial role reversal, it is the heroine, a nameless Balkan royal, who is the sexual aggressor, seducing the much younger virginal English hero. The image of the lady reclining on a tiger skin with a rose between her teeth as she waits for her young lover became embedded in the popular culture of the day and was copied and parodied in both novel and film. However, the novel is remarkable for its sympathetic portrayal of a sexually confident heroine, its elevation of sex as a spiritual act, and its condemnation of loveless marriage.

Despite the fact that the novel was condemned and, in some parts of the United States, banned for decades, Glyn defended its integrity as a moral tale. She also capitalized on its popularity, traveling to America to promote it and move in New York's high society. *Three Weeks* transformed her from a mildly popular writer of society novels into an international celebrity. Glyn exploited this fact, revealing herself to be a modern businesswoman who not only understood the power of celebrity but knew how to use it to her advantage. Since she had become the sole breadwinner for an improvident husband and two daughters, there was a practical aspect to her quest for celebrity and self-promotion.

Widely traveled, Glyn became a war correspondent in 1914, adding journalism to her list of writing credits. However, it was the postwar world that brought Glyn increasing fame. While she continued to write popular romances, Glyn's reinvention of herself as the flamboyant arbiter of all things romantic eventually led to Hollywood, where she worked as a scriptwriter, turning her novels into vehicles for Gloria Swanson and Rudolph Valentino. Her first film, *The Great Moment*, was a financial success, but she reached the pinnacle of Hollywood fame with the actress Clara Bow and the 1927 film *"It."* Glyn's creation of the term, as a pseudonym for sex appeal, immediately caught the imagination of the general public. Female sexuality had never been celebrated so publicly, and its embodiment in Clara Bow's feisty shopgirl in search of love epitomized the new sexual frankness of the 1920s.

Elinor Glyn continued to pioneer as a female in the early film industry, financing and directing her own films in England, which, however, proved to be financial disasters. Glyn continued to write into the late 1930s, but her public persona as the incarnation of her *Three Weeks* heroine and her output of courtly romantic fantasies soon seemed old-fashioned. She wrote her autobiography, *Romantic Adventure*, in 1936, affirming her philosophy of love as a spiritual ideal. She died in 1943.

Elinor Glyn, through her focus on the sexual politics of her era, was an important element in the shift from Victorian to modern values in the early 20th century.

Reviled for the excesses of her prose and the erotic content of her work, she nevertheless opened an early conversation about love, sex, and marriage in the modern era.

Heather Cleary

Further Reading

Etherington-Smith, Meredith, and Jeremy Pilcher. *The 'It' Girls: Lucy, Lady Duff Gordon, the Couturiere "Lucille," and Elinor Glyn, Romantic Novelist.* London: Hamish Hamilton, 1986.

Glyn, Anthony. *Elinor Glyn: A Biography.* London: Hutchinson, 1955.

Glyn, Elinor. *Romantic Adventure.* London: Nicholson and Watson, 1936.

Glyn, Elinor. *Three Weeks.* 1907. London: Virago, 1996, reprint ed.

Hardwick, Joan. *Addicted to Romance: The Life and Adventures of Elinor Glyn.* London: Andre Deutsch, 1994.

Gone with the Wind (1936)

Gone with the Wind is a novel written by Margaret Mitchell, published in 1936. Set in America's Deep South in the 19th century in the years during the American Civil War and Reconstruction, it captures the demise of the privileged lifestyle of white plantation owners, a civilization "gone with the wind." It has been described as an historical saga, an epic, a romance novel, and a coming-of-age story. While critiqued for its historical revisionism, white planter–class perspective, and stereotypical representations of slavery and African Americans, it remains one of the most popular and beloved novels of all time. Made into an award-winning film in 1939, it set box-office records and became embedded in popular culture. *Gone with the Wind* has a unique place in the Romance canon.

The sprawling narrative follows the adventures of its willful and spirited heroine, black haired, pansy-eyed Scarlett O'Hara, Southern belle and femme fatale. Scarlett comes of age during the tumultuous era of war and reconstruction in Georgia, such as the burning of Atlanta and Sherman's march to the sea. It also follows her personal challenges and tribulations, including the deaths of her parents.

Scarlett believes herself in love with the boy from the plantation next door, honorable and handsome Ashley Wilkes, who is betrothed to gentle, ladylike Melanie Hamilton. While declaring her love for Ashley, Scarlett comes to the attention of quintessential sexy rogue Rhett Butler. The love triangle between Scarlett,

Rhett, and Ashley is the three-sided cornerstone of the plot. In this it follows the traditions of courtly love and the *romanz* legends of the Middle Ages, from which all Romance Fiction is descended.

Scarlett O'Hara is a difficult and not always lovable heroine; it is her determination to overcome adversity that inspires readers. Following the devastation of war, she declares she will never be hungry again, nor any of her kin. Scarlett alone demonstrates the courage to save her family and her home, the cotton plantation Tara, albeit through some unscrupulous and flirtatious means, including marrying men she doesn't love. When she eventually marries Rhett Butler and makes her true love match, the tragedy of the story is that Scarlett doesn't recognize she passionately loves Rhett, not Ashley, until it is too late; and by that time Rhett frankly (my dear) no longer gives a damn.

Gone with the Wind subverts the traditional romantic ending. There is no happy ever after for Scarlett or Rhett, nor even for Scarlett and Ashley. *Gone with the Wind* reveals that romance is not based on love but hope. It is hope that promises happiness for Scarlett O'Hara and for all true romantics. After all, tomorrow is another day.

Elizabeth Reid Boyd

Further Reading

Crank, James A., ed. *New Approaches to* Gone with the Wind. Baton Rouge: Louisiana State University Press, 2015.

Harwell, Richard, ed. Gone with the Wind *as Book and Film*. Columbia: University of South Carolina Press, 1983.

Mitchell, Margaret. *Gone with the Wind*. New York: Macmillan, 1936.

Gothic Romance

The Gothic Romance is part of the larger romantic mystery group, with occasional horror or paranormal influences, and is essentially a suspenseful romance defined by mood, atmosphere, and setting. Isolated settings—often cliff-top castles, estates on windswept moors, or other similarly remote places—mysterious secrets, ghostly legends, and sometimes supernatural events; closed, almost claustrophobic environments with limited casts of characters, primarily family members and servants; brooding, taciturn heroes; threatened, vulnerable, and unprotected heroines; and an overall sense of impending doom are classic elements in the subgenre. Another signature characteristic, and perhaps one of the most critical, is that the house is also a major character in the story, exuding its own influence on the plot, and is just as important, if not more so, than the protagonists. Manderley, the mansion in Daphne du Maurier's *Rebecca*, is a classic example. While often set in the past—the Victorian Period is a particular favorite—Gothic romances set in the present are not uncommon, and the works of Phyllis Whitney and Barbara Michaels (aka Barbara Mertz) are classic examples.

Gothic romances often trace their origins from the late 18th century and the popular novels of Ann Radcliffe and her contemporaries. Influenced by Horace Walpole's terrifying, supernatural Gothic *The Castle of Otranto* (1764) and possibly the works of Clara Reeve, who used the unfamiliarity of the past to chilling effect, Radcliffe spun sentimental, romantic, thrilling tales of threatened heroines, valiant heroes, and wicked villains that were exceptionally popular with the readers of her day. *The Mysteries of Udolpho* (1794) is one of her most memorable. Her works influenced a number of other writers, as well as Jane Austen, whose *Northanger Abbey* (written earlier but published in 1817) satirized the genre's conventions and is considered to be a Gothic parody of the type.

In the middle of the 19th century, the works of Charlotte and Emily Brontë made their mark on the subgenre as well, providing not only the lonely, isolated setting, complete with its secrets, and several classic character types (for example, the poor-orphaned-governess-who-marries-the-master-of-the-house; the enigmatic, brooding hero; and the mad-woman-in-the-attic) but also the requisite eerie, mysterious, often dangerous, and sometimes supernatural atmosphere that pervades these stories—and in many ways defines the subgenre. However, it wasn't until Daphne du Maurier published *Rebecca* in 1938 that the prototype of the modern-day Gothic was born. With its newly married heroine fighting the ghostly memory of her predecessor, the drowned Rebecca, for her husband's affections and the resentful, malicious housekeeper for control of the house, plus the menacing atmosphere and the forbidding, isolated mansion, Manderley, *Rebecca* was a best seller and remains a popular classic to this day.

Two decades later, with the 1960 publication of *Mistress of Mellyn*, a Victorian Gothic by Victoria Holt (aka Eleanor Hibbert), interest in Gothic romances exploded, and the "Decade of the Gothic" flourished, expanding the careers of established romantic-mystery authors such as Mary Stewart and Phyllis Whitney, as well as adding new authors to the fold. Interest waned after the middle of the next decade as other Romance subgenres came to the fore; but it took on new life when Signet launched a new line of sexier Gothics in 1986 and reached a high point in 1993 with the Silhouette Shadows line of Gothically infused contemporary romances. However, by the middle of the 1990s, interest had once again declined, giving way to its sister subgenre, Romantic Suspense, which continues increasingly strong.

In recent decades, while the Gothic Romance has never regained its former popularity as a separate subgenre (although there are still some being written), its elements have gradually migrated into a number of other romance categories as the lines separating the various groups continue to blur. Romantic Suspense is the obvious beneficiary of this cross-pollination—and in some cases, books that once would have been categorized as Gothics have simply been relabeled as Romantic Suspense. Paranormal Romance, especially in some of its darker subsets, has benefited as well. Clearly, the Gothic Romance has not disappeared. Its key elements remain and continue to appeal—the reader just might have to look harder to find them.

Kristin Ramsdell

See also: Brontë, Charlotte; Brontë, Emily; Du Maurier, Daphne; Hibbert, Eleanor Burford; *Jane Eyre; Rebecca; Wuthering Heights*

Further Reading

Gothic Romance Forum. http://www.gothicromanceforum.com/. Accessed August 15, 2017.

Norton, Rictor. *Mistress of Udolpho: The Life of Ann Radcliffe*. London: Leicester University Press, 1999.

Ramsdell, Kristin. "Romantic Mysteries." In *Romance Fiction: A Guide to the Genre*, 81–110. Englewood, CO: Libraries Unlimited, 1999.

Vasudevan, Aruna, ed. *Twentieth-Century Romance and Historical Writers*, 3rd ed. London: St. James Press, 1994.

H

Harlequin Books: Cupid's Publisher; A Brief History of Romance Publishing

It was pure happenstance that Harlequin became the dominant publisher of Romance Fiction throughout the world, but once it established its presence in the field, it worked hard to maintain its hegemony. The firm was among the early mass-market publishing houses that began to form in North America after World War II. Mass-market publishing had been introduced some years before the war by Sir Allen Lane when he formed Penguin Books (1936) in the United Kingdom. The books were six-penny paperbacks in red-and-white jackets. The initial line sold poorly until Lane arranged for distribution with Clifford Prescott, the buyer for Woolworth's five-and-ten-cent stores. When the line launched, it was estimated that 2 million volumes a year would ensure success. By 1938, sales totaled 25 million. The success of Penguin did not go unnoticed and led Robert Fair de Graff to develop a 25-cent American version of the paperback in 1938. Initial printings were modestly planned at 10,000 copies per title. To make sure the reader did not feel cheated with the small-sized reprints of their hardbound counterparts, the jacket cover guaranteed that the book was "complete and unabridged." The new Pocket Books took New York by storm, and the rest is publishing history.

The paperback revolution was stalled with the advent of World War II. The paper shortage of the war years ended not long after the war did, but this was offset by a rapid rise in manufacturing costs. Paperback reprints thus "offered the best chance to keep a wide range of books available to the public at prices that large numbers of people could afford to pay" (Tebbel, 348). The result was a boom in mass-market publishing between 1948 and 1955. Among the new paperback houses were New American Library (1948), Harlequin (1949), Pyramid (1949–1977), Fawcett (1950), Ace (1952), Ballantine (1952), and Berkley (1955). Many of these houses continue to be dominant mass-market publishers today, though some, like Penguin, have shifted their emphasis to "quality" paperbacks and others, such as

Berkley, Jove, Fawcett, and, more recently, Harlequin (2014), have merged with other firms but continue to publish paperback books under their original names.

In the Beginning: 1949–1969

Harlequin Enterprises Limited was founded in 1949 by the former mayor of Winnipeg, Richard Gardyn Bonnycastle. Prior to launching Harlequin Enterprises— a name chosen to convey light entertainment—Bonnycastle owned a company that produced American paperbacks for distribution in Canada. This company provided the base for Bonnycastle's publishing venture.

Harlequin was not much different from other paperback houses of the day. Between 1950 and 1959, Harlequin published an average of 50 books per year: some years it offered as few as 25 (1955) to 28 (1956) titles, and some years as many as 61 (1953) to 65 (1950). Most of these titles were reprints of westerns, mysteries, and thrillers and included books by such authors as W. Somerset Maugham, Arthur Conan Doyle, and Edgar Wallace. The list was lightly peppered with romances. The first decade was unmarked by any notable success.

The romance stage of Harlequin's enterprise began in late 1957 when it published its first British romance, a Mills & Boon reprint entitled *Hospital in Buwamba*. This transcontinental arrangement and the consequent domination of Mills & Boon romances among Harlequin's titles was prompted by Mary Bonnycastle, then editor of the house and the publisher's wife, who considered the Mills & Boon romances to be "fiction of good taste" (Guiley, 84). That Mary Bonnycastle would decide to focus increasingly on Romance because she enjoyed the books should not be considered unusual: editors tend to select novels they personally enjoy, assuming that their enjoyment will be reflected in the consumer's taste.

Mary Bonnycastle's personal preference for the genre may have been one reason for Harlequin's decision to increase its romance line, but it is not the only one. The arrangement with Mills & Boon was also financially sound for both publishers. For Mills & Boon, it provided an outlet for its hardcover romances that had traditionally been marketed to libraries, at a time when that market was drying up in the United Kingdom. For Harlequin, the reprint agreement would provide a steady stream of fiction titles that would already have established themselves as proven sellers in Britain. The decision must have proved satisfactory because between 1957 and 1963 Harlequin's list of Mills & Boon romance titles increased steadily from 33 to 78. Yearly romance production rose to 96 titles in 1964, the year Harlequin began publishing Mills & Boon romances exclusively; it remained at this level until 1973, when Harlequin debuted Presents and added another 48 Mills & Boon titles to its list.

Glory Years: 1970–1979

Harlequin vastly expanded its market when it entered into an arrangement with Pocket Books in 1970 to have its books distributed in the United States. The only real thematic difference between Harlequin's product and that being released by American mass-market houses was that Harlequin's novels were all set in the contemporary world while American romances were predominantly historical romances. They were otherwise very much alike: sweet, with stereotyped "1950s" heroes and heroines and no overt sexual nuances. To compete in the American marketplace, and to set its product apart from American-based romance publishers, Harlequin had to do something unique, and it did.

The first major decision Harlequin made was to appoint W. Lawrence Heisey as president in 1971. Heisey must have seemed an unusual choice in the publishing world since he had no background in publishing: he was a marketing executive at Proctor & Gamble. His marketing background would prove significant because he didn't try to sell each novel as it rolled off the presses; instead, he focused on selling the overall product—romance novels. He was able to do this because unlike most publishers of the day, Harlequin did not have a range of fiction and nonfiction to promote. Heisey reasoned that if a publisher could arouse interest in one book, they could arouse interest in the series, a point, Heisey says, that "seems terribly obvious today, but it wasn't then" (Heisey). It was this insight that led Harlequin to emphasize its romance line, while most publishers were attempting to arouse interest in particular authors or titles.

To "hook" the consumer on its romance line, Harlequin employed numerous giveaways, which Heisey readily acknowledged as gimmicks. One of these was to distribute 2 million copies of the book *Dark Star* to dealers at no cost in 1973. The book was sold to consumers for 15 cents. By giving the books to dealers and allowing them to sell each book, dealers were assured a quick, straight-up profit on every paperback. In other introductory offers for readers who might be reluctant to spend even 15 cents, Harlequin gave away millions of other books outright, among them 5 million copies of Violet Winspear's *Honey Is Bitter*. These books were targeted to the audience Harlequin wished to attract, the housewife. One such targeted product was arranged with Heisey's old company, Proctor & Gamble: inside each box of P&G Bio-Ad laundry detergent was a free Harlequin novel. The success of these giveaways can be judged by the firm footing Harlequin established by 1976, when Heisey abandoned the gimmicks for the more traditional promotion of advertising. "We finally built a big enough business base," Heisey said, "that we were able to [begin] formal advertising" (Heisey). The formal advertising campaign was also strongly focused: over 80 percent of an unprecedented $1.3 million was spent on daytime (Monday through Friday) television. Clearly, Harlequin was gearing its ads to a specific audience: the high female soap-opera viewership.

By the mid 1970s, Harlequin had been acceded organizational domain by publishers of romance in the United States. The domain of an organization is the claim it stakes out for itself with respect to the range of products offered, the market served, and the services rendered. Domain consensus exists when an organization's claim to a niche is recognized as legitimate by both the public and other producers. By failing to challenge Harlequin, American producers acknowledged the Canadian publisher's domain of the romance market. Domain worked both ways because Harlequin never published historical novels in the United States during this time, even though they were being published in Britain under the Mills & Boon imprint. Harlequin seemed to have been perfectly content with its contemporary niche and left the "thin" (and increasingly sensual) historical field to American publishers.

Harlequin was perceived as dominating the sweet contemporary romance market throughout the 1970s. American publishers made no attempt to compete with Harlequin in this market, instead providing an alternative product, notably historical romances. Even after Avon introduced changes in the sensual content of historical romances in 1972 (Kathleen E. Woodiwiss's *The Flame and the* Flower [1972] was the first of these new, hot historicals, sometimes disparaged in the press as "bodice-rippers."), American romance publishers continued to view Harlequin as maintaining domain of the contemporary romance field. They saw the overall contemporary market as nearly saturated, with Harlequin providing whatever novels were necessary to cater to a small audience. Thus, rather than invest the amounts required to compete with Harlequin, American publishers were satisfied with their small but cozy niche in historical romances.

Harlequin's presence in the North American market was not due solely to marketing and distribution strategies. One thing it did shortly after Heisey arrived was to purchase Mills & Boon. The purchase did not affect the basic organizational structure of either publishing firm; however, it did guarantee Harlequin an undisturbed flow of Mills & Boon romances. The purchase also provided the opportunity for international expansion.

Despite Mills & Boon's international presence, it never really made much headway beyond reprinting books in Australia and New Zealand. Paul Grescoe reports Heisey's assessment of Mills & Boon's European sophistication: "[T]hey never really had a sense of what they could do. . . . Alan [Boon] thought about being in other countries, but he didn't know enough about business to figure [out] how it could be done" (Gresco, 80). Mills & Boon simply licensed the rights to its books to local publishers who reprinted them under their own logos, which explains why Mills & Boon reaped only 1–2 percent of the cover price of the novels when the industry standard was 10–15 percent. Harlequin soon ended this licensing arrangement and began publishing the books itself. By the late 1970s, Harlequin had started its true international expansion, mostly by setting up joint ventures with local publishers. These alliances—mainly in France, Germany, and the Netherlands—allowed Harlequin to quickly expand its product in the global arena. These alliances are now looked at as a key means by which an organization can expand its market. Harlequin was ahead of the curve when it embarked on these ventures in the 1970s.

Harlequin also made some innovative content changes during the 1970s. Its typically sweet romances were "notched up" a degree with the introduction of Presents in 1973. These books, though still sweet, did at least acknowledge that individuals in a committed relationship engaged in sexual activity before marriage, even if the novel did not venture into the bedroom. It also introduced Janet Dailey in 1976. Dailey was Harlequin's first non–Mills & Boon author, and being American, she situated her romances in the United States instead of in the United Kingdom, Australia, or the "continent." Dailey quickly became one of Harlequin's most successful authors. Harlequin did not take advantage of this by building on her success and debuting more American novelists because by the late 1970s it was distracted from its primary product as it expanded into unrelated ventures: for example, Miles Kimball of Oshkosh, Wisconsin, a mail-order business for gifts, household goods, books, and assorted products; as well as the Lauffer Company, a North American publishing group that put out entertainment and teen magazines, among a host of others.

The broad-based diversification effort Harlequin undertook in the late 1970s was recognized as a mistake in the 1980s by Harlequin's new president, Dave Galloway (1983–1988), who felt that the house "lost touch with its readers." To sharpen the back-to-basics focus under his presidency, Galloway distributed a case of the best-selling business book *In Search of Excellence* to his staff, reminding them, as Thomas Peters and Robert Waterman put it in their book,

> Acquisitions, even little ones, suck up an ordinate amount of top management's time, time taken away from the main-line business. . . . The typical diversification strategy dilutes the guiding qualitative theme. . . . Organizations that branch out but stick very close to their knitting outperform the others. . . . The least successful, as a general rule, are those companies that diversify into a wide variety of fields. Acquisitions, especially among this group, tend to wither on the vine. . . . [A]ny "back to basics" move is, according to the studies we have reviewed and the excellent companies' message, good news indeed. (Peters and Waterman, 293–94)

On Shaky Ground, 1980–1989

In early 1976, top executives at Harlequin were engaged in regular and serious deliberations over the Pocket Books distribution contract. These sessions, which often ran long into the night, eventually resulted in the decision to terminate the agreement. Fred Kerner, the newest member of management's executive team, dissented; however, his objection was less to the decision than the method. He felt that Harlequin should not forewarn Pocket of its intention and give the company only the required three-month termination notice. Kerner's advice went unheeded, and senior management informed Dick Snyder at Simon & Schuster of Harlequin's intention. Snyder was furious and argued that they had a gentleman's agreement to stay with Pocket Books. Heisey called from Kennedy Airport on his way back to Toronto and said, "We are men of honor and will honor our agreement with you." (All this was verified by interviews with Heisey and Snyder.) Four years later, Harlequin's break was anticipated, and Silhouette Books, a line Simon & Schuster specifically designed to go head-to-head with Harlequin in the sweet contemporary market, was already in the pipeline.

Simon & Schuster's decision to compete with Harlequin was exclusively managerial, based on (1) knowledge of the Harlequin product; (2) Pocket's extensive distribution system; and (3) an astute awareness of just how much income was generated by these slim volumes of love and marriage. The decision was reinforced by research between 1977 and 1979 that clearly showed that the romance-reader consumption rate in America was below the norm: Canadian consumption was 1,500 books per 1,000 women, but in the United States it was only 800. Simon & Schuster also found growth potential among loyal Harlequin readers.

One of the few in the industry to have knowledge of Harlequin's closely guarded sales figures, Simon & Schuster pumped millions into starting Silhouette Books. Management directed its staff to emulate Harlequin, to use it as their "role model." This strategy was clearly visible on Silhouette's prelaunch promotional material aimed at book retailers, which carried the bold-print logo "When It Comes to Romance, Experience Is the Best Teacher." It was also seen in Silhouette's early postlaunch retail advertising, which simply stated, "The only other line you need is Harlequin."

Simon & Schuster did four other things to make the new line Harlequin competitive. First, it hired P. J. Fennell, Harlequin's vice president of Marketing and Sales in North America, as the president of Silhouette Books. Second, it secured the services of Janet Dailey, who had become one of Harlequin's best-selling authors, and used her name to help promote the new line, which even subsequent CEO of Harlequin David Galloway admitted was a "good strategy" to attract new readers, even if she was a loss leader (Galloway). Third, Simon & Schuster had a one-year inventory of novels ready to go when Silhouette launched because it was open to all those American women who had written contemporary romances set in the United States but had no outlet for their manuscripts. And fourth, Silhouette debuted in 1980 with a $3 million advertising campaign, spending $1.1 million for airtime from mid-May to mid-June, when the line premiered. Another $1 million was spent on other forms of advertising; this burgeoned to $22 million by 1982—a figure comparable to Harlequin's increased advertising expenditure and more than the entire U.S. publishing industry spent in domestic advertising.

The battle for market share between Harlequin and Silhouette raged until 1984 when Silhouette threw in the towel and sold to Harlequin. The battle had simply become too expensive for generalist publisher Simon & Schuster, which had other ventures to shore up its bottom line, which Silhouette was draining. Harlequin, being a specialist publisher, was fighting for its very survival. Just purchasing Silhouette was insufficient, however, to regain market share. Harlequin was behind the curve because Dell Publishing in the United States had introduced Ecstasy, a line with radically updated contemporary sensual content that was shaking up the American market. Harlequin would spend the rest of the decade trying to update its overly sweet romances and bring them into the latter part of the 20th century. In addition, the new president spent much of the second half of the 1980s instituting a variety of organizational tactics to rein in Harlequin's spending and return the company to prominence.

Galloway turned Harlequin around, and in the four years after his arrival at Harlequin he moved sales from a low point of $11 million to $52 million. When Galloway moved upstairs to run Torstar in 1988, he had accomplished his formidable task and returned Harlequin to supremacy in the romance market. His last task before leaving Torstar in 2002 was to appoint Donna Hayes as the new president of Harlequin (2002–2013). Hayes was the first president of Harlequin to come from a literary rather than a marketing background, and under her watchful eye, Harlequin introduced an array of new products that kept it in the catbird seat.

Transitioning to the New Millennium

Brian Hickey took the reins from Galloway when Galloway moved to Torstar. He came from the international division at Harlequin, and international sales was one of his strong suits. Forays into Eastern Europe after the fall of the Berlin Wall in 1992 did not pan out, but that was due largely to infrastructure issues and an antiquated distribution system. Harlequin's entry into Japan, however, was quite significant. Strategies to gain a foothold there, while rocky at first, soon worked out, and Japan today is among Harlequin's top foreign markets.

During Hickey's tenure, Harlequin also introduced MIRA (1994), which was not Harlequin's first venture into noncategory mainstream fiction but would be its most successful. MIRA would make Harlequin competitive with other mainstream houses that release women's fiction, not just category romance fiction. Its success is in the numbers: as early as 2001, just six years after launching

MIRA, single-title sales represented 25.6 percent of Harlequin's revenue (Milliot, "Harlequin," 16).

Red Dress Ink was also introduced under Hickey. The line was positioned to take advantage of the chick-lit craze that followed the publication of *Bridget Jones's Diary* in 1996. Most major publishing firms jumped aboard this bandwagon and rushed to publish chick-lit novels as part of their mainstream press; a few even had dedicated chick-lit imprints, such as Kensington (Strapless) and Simon & Schuster (Downtown). Harlequin, whose expertise was in category fiction, was the only house to develop chick-lit as a category line, which means that while most houses were releasing a few novels every year in the chick-lit format as part of their overall program, Harlequin was publishing a new title every month. It was a contentious in-house issue because it didn't fit snugly into the Harlequin oeuvre, which explains why the line didn't launch until late in 2001. It had a good run, however, and lasted until January 2013 when it simply ran out of steam. It is noteworthy that Donna Hayes led both of these very successful product developments, a factor that Galloway mentioned when he announced her accession to the throne.

During Hayes's tenure, Harlequin stayed product competitive. Kimani Arabesque was purchased from BET Books and debuted as Harlequin's African American line in December 2005; it has since introduced two offshoots: Kimani Romance and Kimani TRU. At this same time, Steeple Hill Books was born, and the Christian Love Inspired line (1997–present) was expanded into Love Inspired Suspense (2005–present) and Love Inspired Historical (2008–present). Some of the other lines that were shepherded to fruition on Hayes's watch were Blaze (2001–present), Everlasting Love (2005–2008), NEXT (2005–2012), Spice (2006–2011), Nocturne (2006–present), NASCAR (2007–2010), Teen (2009–present), and Heartwarming (2011–present).

It was one of the most active product-development periods in Harlequin's history and has managed to keep the company atop the romance field. This, along with Harlequin's strong international presence, was what attracted HarperCollins as a suitor. The deal was announced by the new CEO of Harlequin, Craig Swinwood, in May 2014 and quickly finalized in August of that year. Harlequin became a freestanding house within HarperCollins, with headquarters remaining in Toronto.

HarperCollins had a strong presence in the romance field with its Avon lines. It recently increased its romance position by purchasing two Christian houses that were known for their romances, Zondervan and Thomas Nelson, and folding them under the umbrella of HarperCollins Christian. Harlequin simply became the jewel in the crown and made HarperCollins, practically overnight, the dominant romance publisher in the world.

John Markert

Further Reading

Berg, A. S. *Max Perkins: Editor of Genius*. New York: Washington Square Press, 1978.

Coser, Lewis. "Publishers as Gatekeepers of Ideas." *The Annals of the American Association of Political and Social Sciences* 421 (1975): 14–22.

Coser, Lewis, Charles Kadushin, and Walter W. Powell. *Books: The Culture and Commerce of Publishing*. New York: Basic Books, 1982.

Galloway, David. Interview.

Gresco, Paul. *The Merchants of Venus: Inside Harlequin and the Empire of Romance*. Vancouver, Canada: Raincoast Books, 1986.

Guiley, Rosemary. *Love Lines: A Romance Reader's Guide to Printed Pleasure*. New York: Facts on File Publications, 1983.

Heisey, W. Lawrence. Interview.

Johnson, Arthur. "Heartbreak at Harlequin: New Entries Distorting Blissful Profit Picture at Romance Fiction Firm." *The Glove and Mail*, October 28, 1983.

Markert, John. *Publishing Romance: The History of an Industry, 1940s to the Present*. Jefferson, NC: McFarland, 2016.

Milliot, Jim. "Harlequin Pushes to Boost Single-Title Sales." *Publishers Weekly* 249, no. 5 (February 4, 2002), 16.

Milliot, Jim. "HarperCollins to Buy Harlequin." *Publishers Weekly*, May 2, 2014. http://www.publishersweekly.com/pw/by-topic/industry-news/publisher-news/article/62097-harpercollins-to-buy-harlequin.html. Accessed April 13, 2017.

Peters, Thomas J., and Robert H. Waterman, Jr. *In Search of Excellence: Lessons from America's Best-Run Companies*. New York: Harper & Row, 1982.

Simon, R., and J. Fyfe. *Editors as Gatekeepers: Getting Published in the Social Sciences*. Lanham, MD: Rowman & Littlefield, 1992.

Snyder, Dick. Interview.

Tebbel, John. *A History of Book Publishing in the United States, Vol. 4: The Great Change, 1940–1980*. New York: R. Bowker, 1981.

White, David Manning. "The Gatekeeper: A Case Study in the Selection of News." *Journalism Quarterly* 27 (1950): 383–90.

Heyer, Georgette (1902–1974)

Novelist Georgette Heyer (Rougier) was born on August 16, 1902, at 103 Woodside, Wimbledon, England, to George and Sylvia Heyer (née Watkins). In 1919, when she was 17, Heyer made up *The Black Moth* as a serial story for her convalescing younger brother, Boris. It was published just after her 19th birthday in September 1921 and is still in print. Between 1921 and her death in 1974, Heyer published 55 novels and one anthology of short stories. Her last novel, *My Lord John*, was published posthumously in 1975. She wrote across several different genres, including contemporary and detective fiction, as well as historical fiction set in the medieval, 16th, 17th, 18th, and early 19th centuries. It is these latter two eras that were her particular forte, and it is with the English Regency Period of 1811–1820 that her name has become synonymous. She remains notable for her stylish prose, witty dialogue, and ironic humor; and her historical novels are frequently lauded for their meticulous historical detail. Her 26 novels set within the Regency Period established her as the creator of the enduringly popular Regency subgenre of historical fiction. Since her death, Heyer has remained a perennial best seller, with 51 books continuously in print. The remaining five were the four contemporary novels and her 17th-century book, *The Great Roxhythe* (1922), which she herself suppressed after 1939.

Apart from several months spent in Paris in 1914, Heyer grew up in Wimbledon and enjoyed a tranquil childhood. Her parents took an active interest in her education, and before the age of 13 she was educated at home. Her father, George Heyer (1869–1925), was a Classics graduate of Cambridge and a minor poet with works published in *Granta*, *Punch*, and the *Pall Mall Gazette*. His translation of François Villon's poems (Oxford University Press, 1924) was well received. A charismatic man, he had a great love of literature, especially the works of Shakespeare, Dickens, and the biblical and Renaissance poets, which he instilled in his daughter. They were very close, and her father was a vital influence on Heyer's early writing life. Her mother, Sylvia Watkins (1875–1962), was a graduate of the Royal Academy of Music, where she studied piano, cello, and singing. She gave up her aspirations for a musical career when she married George Heyer in 1901. Georgette was the eldest of their three children with two younger brothers, (George) Boris Heyer (1907–1973) and Frank Dmitri Heyer (1912–2002).

In 1915, when Heyer was 13, her father enlisted in the army and went to serve in France. Consequently, Heyer was sent to school at Wimbledon's Oakhill Academy. In 1918 she spent a term at The Study school before giving up formal education altogether. By 1925 Heyer had published a number of short stories and five novels, including her first contemporary novel, *Instead of the Thorn* (1923), and her only pseudonymous book, *The Transformation of Philip Jettan* (Mills & Boon, 1923), written under the name Stella Martin. She had not yet settled on any single genre and had aspirations to write biography and serious literature as well as popular fiction. Her father was her most enthusiastic supporter, and his sudden death from a heart attack on June 16, 1925, was a personal cataclysm for his daughter that marked the beginning of the lifelong reticence and passion for privacy for which she would become famous. On August 18, 1925, two months after George Heyer's passing, Georgette married (George) Ronald Rougier at St. Mary's Parish Church, Wimbledon.

Rougier was a mining engineer, and in 1926 Heyer followed him to Tanganyika (Tanzania) where he was prospecting for tin. For 18 months she lived in an elephant-grass hut in a small compound in a remote corner of Kyerwe, the only white woman for 150 miles. Both *Helen* (1928) and *The Masqueraders* (1928) were written in East Africa. After returning to England in 1928, Heyer wrote *Pastel* (1929), her third contemporary novel, which drew on her experiences as a newly married woman and which she thought would please her mother "since it contains so much that is Really and Truly her" (Kloester, 96). Later that year, Heyer followed Rougier to Macedonia, where she wrote a swashbuckling 16th-century novel, *Beauvallet* (1929), and her last contemporary novel, *Barren Corn* (1930), with its theme of the clash of class in post–World War I England. The Rougiers lived in Kratovo until early 1930, when they returned to England to start a family.

In 1931, Heyer moved to Colgate near Horsham in Sussex, where her husband had taken a lease on a sports store. The following year, their only child, Richard, was born on February 12, the same day that Heyer's first detective novel, *Footsteps in the Dark* (1932), was published by Longmans. Between 1932 and 1942, Heyer averaged two books a year, writing both detective and historical fiction with such remarkable facility that her first drafts were often her final drafts. In 1933, the family moved to Blackthorns, a large house set on 15 acres and, in keeping with Heyer's penchant for privacy, invisible from the road. It was here that she wrote her first Regency novel, *Regency Buck* (1935), followed two years later by her acclaimed "Waterloo book," *An Infamous Army* (1937), which later became recommended reading at the Royal Military Academy Sandhurst for its vivid account of the Battle of Waterloo.

In 1936, Rougier gave up the sports store and began reading for the bar. He was admitted to the Inner Temple in 1939. Through these years, Heyer's writing was their primary source of income, and she often felt the strain of being the main family breadwinner. She and Rougier were a devoted couple. He was always her first reader and a valued critic. With the exception of her 1935 mystery, *Death in the Stocks*, he collaborated with her on her murder mysteries by providing the "how" of each crime, including an ingenious and complicated shooting in *No Wind of Blame* (1939), which caught the interest of the War Office. Between 1933 and 1939, Heyer wrote seven detective novels, five of which feature either Superintendent (later Chief Inspector) Hannayside or his humorous subordinate, Sergeant (later Inspector) Hemingway. Heyer's mysteries were very popular in the 1930s, 1940s, and 1950s, and novels such as *The Unfinished Clue* (1934), *Behold, Here's Poison* (1936), *A Blunt Instrument* (1938), and *Envious Casca* (1941) are counted as belonging to the Golden Age of detective fiction.

In 1939, Heyer revisited the Napoleonic Wars and wrote *The Spanish Bride* (1940), based on Peninsular War veteran Harry Smith's diaries. After World War II broke out in 1939, the carnage across the English Channel made it difficult for

Heyer to write modern fiction. In the months following the evacuation of Allied troops from Dunkirk, she chose to write another period novel, *The Corinthian* (1940), telling her agent, L. P. Moore, that "it would be a comforting book to write, all about a very different age" (Kloester, 209). This was quickly followed by *Faro's Daughter* (1941) and her most unusual detective novel, *Penhallow* (1942), a book that she hoped would be a tour de force. In 1942, the Rougiers left Sussex and moved into chambers in F3 Albany in central London. Rougier's legal practice was based in London, which made the move to the capital expedient despite the challenges of wartime and the danger of air raids. They lived at Albany until 1966, and Heyer wrote several of her finest novels there. It was in the 1940s that her "gift for the farcical" came to fruition in novels such as *Friday's Child* (1944), *The Foundling* (1948), *Arabella* (1949), and *The Grand Sophy* (1950). She also continued to satisfy her penchant for detective fiction by occasionally incorporating a mystery into her historical fiction, as in *The Reluctant Widow* (1946), *The Quiet Gentleman* (1951), and *The Toll-Gate* (1954).

By the 1950s, Heyer had achieved an international reputation and instant bestseller status in Britain and several Commonwealth countries, including Australia and New Zealand. After the instant success of her 1944 book, *Friday's Child* (which sold 250,000 in its first two years despite the severe wartime paper shortage), and with just two exceptions, Heyer wrote only Regency novels until her death in 1974. In 1951 and 1953 she published her last two detective stories (*Duplicate Death* and *Detection Unlimited*) to help pay her tax bill. Despite her enormous success, for much of her adult life Heyer worried about money. From the time of her father's death in 1925 until her financial situation was secured in 1968 by selling 18 of her copyrights to the Booker company, Heyer was largely responsible for her family's (including her mother and one brother) financial well-being.

Writing originally for the generations affected by two horrific world wars, Heyer aimed to transport her audience to another time and place; and her novels proved an excellent escape from the horror and tragedy of war, sending readers into a world of elegance, civility, good manners, and humor. This was what Heyer herself confessed to enjoying while writing period romances, and although at times she could be self-deprecating, she genuinely valued her work. Her son, Richard (later Sir Richard Rougier, a QC and a High Court judge), always said that his mother was "a compulsive weaver of stories" and that it was "just talk to say she had to write another Regency to pay tax."

Heyer wrote as much because she loved writing and storytelling as for the money. Through the 1950s and 1960s she wrote some of her finest novels, including *Cotillion* (1953), *Sylvester* (1957), *Venetia* (1958), *The Unknown Ajax* (1959), *A Civil Contract* (1961), *Frederica* (1965), and *Black Sheep* (1966). Despite some repetition among her novels and a cast of characters that she enjoyed reusing from time to time, Heyer brought something new to each of her 55 novels. She was a superb plotter, and her evocation of Regency language, culled from a wide range of primary sources, remains unmatched. Jane Austen was her favorite author and an acknowledged inspiration in Heyer's writing, which abounds in subtle moments of homage to the writer Heyer considered a genius.

Contrary to the belief that Heyer rarely received critical acclaim, her novels were in fact regularly reviewed in the major periodicals in both the United Kingdom and the United States, with 40 reviews in the *Times Literary Supplement* alone. She is cited 80 times in the *Oxford English Dictionary*, and despite her fear that most of her works would die with her, her novels continue to sell in large numbers around the world with approximately 30 million books sold since 1921. Heyer's achievement lies partly in her mastery of the historical detail that she used to bring the past to life, but it is also her brilliance in creating memorable characters (sometimes in just a few sentences), her masterful plots, and her wit and insight into human nature that set her novels apart. Like P. G. Wodehouse, Heyer was a world-builder; she created the ever-popular Regency genre, and unlike many of her literary generation, her novels have remained popular into the 21st century.

Heyer's last novel, *Lady of Quality* (1972), was written after a long period of ill health. In May of 1974, she was diagnosed with lung cancer, and on July 4, 1974, she died at Guy's Hospital, London. In 1975, The Bodley Head published her unfinished medieval manuscript as *My Lord John*. Heyer had always maintained a strong fascination for the medieval period, but it is the English Regency Period that proved her forte, and it is her novels set in this period for which she will be remembered.

Jennifer Kloester

Further Reading

Flood, Alison. "Forgotten Georgette Heyer Stories to Be Republished." *The Guardian*, September 20, 2016.
Hodge, Jane Aiken. *The Private World of Georgette Heyer*. London: Bodley Head, 1984.
Kloester, Jennifer. *Georgette Heyer*. London: William Heinemann, 2011.

Hibbert, Eleanor Burford (1906–1993)

Eleanor Burford Hibbert was a prolific writer of romance novels as well as of works in other genres, such as crime novels and murder mysteries. She wrote under numerous pseudonyms, including Jean Plaidy for fictionalized history of

European nobility, Victoria Holt for Gothic romances, and Philippa Carr for multigenerational family sagas.

In many ways, Hibbert's life was like a plot from one of her own books. She was born Eleanor Alice Burford in London on September 1, 1906. Her father was a dockworker, and her mother stayed at home to raise their family. When financial circumstances put an end to Eleanor's formal education, she attended a business college and then entered the labor force, where she held various jobs, including working for a jeweler. In the 1920s, she met and fell in love with George P. Hibbert, a wholesale leather merchant and a married man, who subsequently left his own wife and family and moved in with her. The two lived together for several years before they finally married in 1935.

Hibbert started writing "serious" fiction, but after several years of submitting novels to various publishers, she had yet to see any of her work in print. Hibbert subsequently turned to writing short stories, and based on the advice she received from an editor at *The Daily Mail* (one of the newspapers to which she had been submitting stories), she switched literary gears and wrote a romance. *Daughter of Anna* was accepted for publication and appeared in print in 1941. Hibbert sold several more novels as Eleanor Burford before she adopted her first pseudonym, Jean Plaidy, for her book *Together They Ride* published in 1945. She continued to use her Plaidy pseudonym for her historical novels (essentially fictionalized history) and is especially noted for her many popular series about European nobility. Typically, her Plaidy titles centered on the lives of real women, important either in their own right or because of their connections to powerful men, and told the story from the heroine's point of view. The Norman Trilogy (three titles), The Georgian Saga (10 titles), and The Plantagenet Saga (15 titles) are three of her more popular series.

The 1950s were busy times for Hibbert, who expanded her writing output by taking on several new pseudonyms including Elbur Ford, Ellalice Tate, and Kathleen Kellow. In 1960, she wrote her first Gothic romance, the *Mistress of Mellyn*, under the name Victoria Holt. She added another pen name to her list in the 1970s when she began writing her Daughters of England series as Philippa Carr. Hibbert wrote seven days a week, averaging 5,000 words per day. Her total literary output included 200 books, which have sold more than a million copies around the world. In addition, she consistently hit the *New York Times* best-seller list during the last three decades of her writing life. Hibbert died while cruising the Mediterranean on the ship *Sea Princess* on January 18, 1993.

When *Mistress of Mellyn* was published in 1960, the book inspired a new literary craze that eventually earned her the sobriquet "Queen of the Gothic Romance." In *Mistress of Mellyn*, the heroine, Martha Leigh, travels to Mount Mellyn in Cornwall to begin work as a governess for Connan TreMellyn's young daughter

Alvean. While trying to forge a bond with Alvean, Martha investigates the mysterious death of Alvean's mother. Martha finds herself falling for the dark and brooding Connan, who according to local rumor had something to do with his wife's death. Technically, the Gothic novel's roots go all the way back to the 18th- and 19th-century novels of Anne Radcliffe and Mathew Lewis, but with *Mistress of Mellyn*, Hibbert cleverly refashioned many of the elements—an enigmatic and seemingly dangerous hero, an isolated, atmospheric setting, and a generous soupçon of intrigue—of these classic Gothics into a love story that readers in the 1960s found irresistible.

Over the next three decades more Gothic romances followed as Hibbert, writing as Victoria Holt, spun different variations on *Mistress of Mellyn*. At the heart of every Holt Gothic romance is its heroine: a young woman who, while never a great beauty, does possess a certain unique charm as well as an independent (occasionally stubborn) sense of spirit. This heroine is almost always alone in the world, either orphaned or dependent on the financial whims of some relative for her survival. To support themselves, Victoria Holt's heroines usually take on one of the two traditional occupations of the well-bred but penniless Victorian woman: governess or companion. Other Holt heroines consider themselves fortunate when they land an unexpected proposal of marriage. Either because of her new job or her new position as a married woman, the Holt heroine soon finds herself living with the enigmatic hero in some isolated locale, such as a gloomy estate or an ancestral castle. Of course, the hero seems to be keeping secrets—possibly dangerous ones—from the Holt heroine, who can't resist investigating.

Another key component of the Victoria Holt Gothics are their settings. Almost all of the Holt novels take place in the mid- to late 19th century and are set in some part of the British Empire. England—and in particular Cornwall—was a favorite geographic locale. A perfect example of this is *Bride of Pendorric*, in which Favel Farrington's whirlwind marriage to Roc Pendorric takes Favel to her husband's ancestral home in Cornwall. Once there, Favel discovers that several previous Pendorric brides—including Roc's mother—all tragically died soon after they married.

While England may have held a special place in Hibbert's literary toolkit, she also set romances in such exotic locales as Hong Kong, Australia, and Ceylon. For example, in *House of a Thousand Lanterns*, Jane Lindsay's marriage to Sylvester Milner eventually takes her to Hong Kong, where she must face off against a determined murderer in the "House of a Thousand Lanterns." In *The Road to Paradise Island*, Annalice Mallory's discovery of her ancestor Ann Alice's journal in a sealed-off room in her home will ultimately send her on a dangerous search for lost treasure on Paradise Island off the coast of Australia. After her father's death, Sarah Ashington, the heroine of *The Spring of the Tiger*, travels to his tea plantation in Ceylon, where she becomes caught up in a deadly legend involving a pearl necklace.

"Never regret," Hibbert once said. "If it's good, it's wonderful. If it is bad, it's experience" (Motivational Quotes). Eleanor Hibbert lived her own life with no regrets, leaving behind a literary legacy consisting of contemporary romances, children's books, nonfiction, historical novels, and Gothic romances. Her ability to seamlessly fuse passion and peril into one thrilling story line garnered her a world-wide audience of readers, whose only regret is that this legendary author didn't write more books.

John Charles

Further Reading

"Eleanor Alice Burford Hibbert." *Contemporary Authors Online*. Detroit: Gale, 2003. Literature Resource Center. http://morelibrary.org/resource/contemporary-authors-online. Accessed April 19, 2017.

Fowler, Christopher. "Forgotten Authors: No 7: Victoria Holt." *The Independent*, September 28, 2008.

Hinckley, Karen. "Victoria Holt." In *St. James Guide to Crime and Mystery Writers*, 4th ed., edited by Jay P. Pederson, 529–32. Detroit: St. James Press, 1996.

Marks, Jeffrey. "Victoria Holt." *Guide to Literary Masters and their Works* (January 2007): 1–6.

Motivational Quotes for the Day. December 8, 2015. https://motivationfortheday.word press.com/2015/12/08/never-regret-if-its-good-its-wonderful-if-its-bad-its-experience -victoria-holt/. Accessed April 19, 2017.

Mussell, Kay. "Jean Plaidy." In *Twentieth Century Romance and Historical Writers*, edited by Aruna Vasudevan, 521–24. London: St. James Press, 1994.

Historical Perspectives on Changes within the Genre

Romance fiction as we now know it came into prominence with the founding of Canadian publishing company Harlequin in 1949. Indeed, for many, the two words "romance" and "Harlequin" are synonymous. Though the company published all kinds of books at the start, Harlequin began purchasing romances from British publisher Mills & Boon in the late 1950s. But even though Harlequin was a Canadian company selling British books, the majority of readers were American women. Finally, in the mid-1970s, Harlequin acquired its first American author, Janet Dailey, who wrote several stories set in the West.

The early Harlequin romances were sweet and relatively chaste, much like the short romances that were published in magazines at the time. The heroines were young (usually 18 or so) and sexually inexperienced. If they had jobs, they were stereotypically gendered female (nurses, teachers, and so on). The heroines fell in love and experienced their first feelings of lust at the same time. Male love interests, on the other hand, were older and more experienced, usually having slept with many women without falling in love with them first. The implication was that for women as represented by "good girl" heroines, love creates sexual desire, but that for men, desire can exist on its own, although love is shown to ultimately give sex meaning. (Note that not much consideration was given to the thoughts or feelings of the "bad girls" these men must have been having this sex with.)

By the beginning of the 1980s, readers were beginning to like their romances steamier and more explicit. As Harlequin was slow to adapt to changing tastes, other publishers began moving in on the market. Silhouette started publishing its own lines and signed its own American authors. Wanting to differentiate itself from Harlequin, Silhouette encouraged writers to experiment with the genres. Dell also launched a sexier series line with Candlelight Ecstasy.

With more publishers getting into the game, the options in Popular Romance Fiction became more diverse. Naiad press was founded in 1973. It published exclusively lesbian fiction. One of its most famous and prolific writers, Katherine V. Forrest, wrote the seminal lesbian romance *Curious Wine* (1983). However, the 1970s was not the first decade that had lesbian fiction or romances. Beginning in the 1950s, many lesbian pulp-fiction novels had been published. While some of the stories, which were written by both men and women, had positive depictions, most featured lesbians as predators and ended with the heroines returning to men after a scintillating, yet ultimately negative, detour to the land of Sappho. Naiad republished some of the better out-of-print books from that time but also had a mission to publish more positive lesbian and feminist fiction.

In the 1990s and beyond, creating special presses or imprints to appeal to a growing diverse readership became a trend. It is now easy to find paperback romances geared toward Spanish speakers, African Americans, lesbians, Christians, and more. There are also various imprints that offer different levels of steaminess, so that readers can enjoy everything from romances that leave what happens after a few innocent kisses to the imagination, to stories with sex scenes that are graphic and explicit and go into great detail in describing how the heroine (and sometimes the hero) feels about it all. The perspective in today's era seems to be that anything goes, and that every woman should be able to find the kind of romance she likes. One commonality is that women are written as equals in relation to their male love interests, which reflects shifting perspectives about femininity, masculinity, and gender roles.

Because there is now greater diversity in Romance Fiction, the books are often segregated by racial or gender elements and shelved in different sections in the bookstore. This erroneously implies that white women wouldn't be interested in romance featuring black heroines, that black women would not be interested in reading about Hispanic women, and that only lesbians would read stories about two women in love. One area in which this is not the case is teen, or young adult, romance fiction. In most bookstores and libraries, titles such as *Perfect Chemistry* (interracial romance), *Annie on My Mind* (lesbian romance), *Manifest* (African American and paranormal romance), and *Wither* (paranormal romance) will all be found on the same shelf. Hopefully, adult romance will follow this lead, and publishers, authors, and readers will become used to not only diverse titles but also the idea of diverse reading habits. After all, there is nothing more universal than a good romance.

We can get an even clearer idea about how heroines, leading men, and gender roles have changed since romance's first big boom in the 1970s by analyzing the evolution of its most popular novelist. Nora Roberts has been writing romances steadily since her first was published in 1981. Over the course of several decades, her heroines have become older, more experienced, and more complex. Her love interests have become less aggressive, poorer, and more open-minded. She began including more nuanced and forward-thinking depictions of race, female sexuality, and the many different ways that a woman can be powerful. While many of these changes reflect the author as an individual, they didn't happen in a vacuum. A deeper look at these issues in five novels written over the course of over four decades also reveals changes in the genre as a whole, and on a greater level, the shifting identities of women in American culture over the course of this time.

Nora Roberts's first published novel is called *Irish Thoroughbred*, and the title could refer to both the heroine and the prize horses with which she works. While the story reflects the limited possibilities for heroines in romance novels during the time it was published, there are also small hints of the ways the author would challenge those very limitations in her later work.

The heroine, Adelia Cunnane, is inexperienced in almost every way imaginable. At the start of the story, she is on a plane to America after having been sequestered on a farm in Ireland with her aunt until the older woman's death. She's young, has never traveled, has a limited education, is sexually inexperienced, and is generally naïve. Moreover, the men she encounters tend to find her wide-eyed lack of real-world experience charming—even though it continually puts her at a disadvantage. An early example of this is her shock at modern kitchen devices:

> The stove, she decided, had more to do with magic than technology. And a machine that washed and dried the dishes at a touch of a button—marvels! Hearing about such things and reading about them was one matter, but seeing them with your own eyes . . . it was easier to believe in the Pooka and the little people.

When, with a sigh, she said as much to her uncle, he threw back his head and laughed until tears flowed down his cheeks, then enveloped her in a hug as crushing as the one he had greeted her with at the airport. (Roberts, *Irish Hearts*, 21)

In stark contrast, her love interest is an experienced man of the world. He's about a decade older, wealthy (and actually employs both Adelia and her uncle), has been around the block several times over, and makes all of the moves in their relationship (tricking her into dates, kissing her aggressively, and pushing her into marriage). The fact that Adelia is spunky, hardworking, and can swallow whiskey like a pro doesn't make up for the fact that she is rarely in control of the relationship. Her moments of standing up for herself are superficial and perfunctory—especially since men keep thinking she's adorable while she's doing it, which takes the power out of it. It's as if she's a child pretending to be a strong woman.

However, there are flashes in this first novel of the direction that Roberts would move in. Even though Adelia is sexually inexperienced, she gives in to her desires without any qualms. Yes, she is carried off to the bed in his big, strong arms, but she is not shown to need a careful or tentative initiation. And unlike most other virginal heroines in romances at this time, she doesn't experience any pain. She takes her pleasure as her right, something that is a hallmark of Roberts's heroines.

In *Sweet Revenge*, published only seven years later, things have changed a great deal in Roberts's storytelling. As much as it is a romance, it is also a story about a world-class thief stealing jewels and power (that is rightfully hers) from the clutches of a patriarchal society that used and destroyed her mother. Both women struggle against sexism and misogyny in two separate cultures. Adrianne is the princess of a Muslim country called Jaquir. In a dark twist on a Grace Kelly–type tale, her mother, Phoebe, had been a beautiful movie star that married royalty. Once worshipped, she eventually became the disgraced first wife in a harem because she had a daughter and no sons.

In an early chapter, a very young Adrianne overhears as her father rapes her mother. However, this isn't a story of a victimized white woman being oppressed by a foreign culture. Soon mother and daughter escape to America, only to find more of the same. As a teen, Adrianne is almost raped by a sleazy Hollywood agent, but she is saved by her mother: "Phoebe was on him like a tiger, fists pounding, sinking in teeth and nails. She ripped at him, tearing clothes and flesh. They were nearly even when it came to height and weight, but she was driven by a rage so hot, so deep, only murder would quench it" (Roberts, *Sweet Revenge*, 100).

Phoebe is able to protect her daughter when she hadn't been able to save herself. There is actually a scene in *Irish Thoroughbred* in which the hero saves Adelia from being raped and bloodies her attacker. However, in those circumstances, it seemed like another opportunity to showcase his strength, her weakness, and her need to have a man to protect her. In *Sweet Revenge*, there are many examples of women protecting and supporting one another. Adrianne becomes a cat burglar but also spends a great deal of her stolen money on building a shelter for battered women.

Of course, a proactive heroine who has seen the worst of men would need a different kind of love interest. She would despise a brute and would be too clever to believe that a cad can be reformed through love. Philip Chamberlain is a reformed thief working for Interpol. He starts out trying to catch Adrianne but falls in love and gains respect for her—and changes his mind. So when he can't talk her out of her big job (a plan of revenge against her father), he decides to be her backup instead. The fact that he is a good man who respects women is an important part of Adrianne's character arc. While a novel about her getting revenge on misogynistic men might have been fun, the fact that romance heals some of the pain from her childhood is more to the point, highlighting that the one unchanging theme in romance novels is that love rules.

Published in 1991, *Carnal Innocence* is notable as one of Nora Roberts's early attempts at attacking the issue of racism. The story is about a well-traveled violinist named Caroline who has moved to a small Southern town. She is white, as is her love interest, but race plays an important part in the plot as well as in revealing important information about the quality of several players' characters.

The message portrayed in this book is positive yet relatively simple—black people are human beings, white people are not superior in any way, and racism is bad. However, more complicated issues, such as the fact that the wealthy love interest lives on a plantation that was built on the backs of slaves, that the town is still segregated, that the social order implemented during slavery still exists, and that the main characters benefit financially and socially from institutionalized racism, are not addressed.

At one point in the story the heroine and hero save an African American family from a gang of racist thugs. If they hadn't arrived in the nick of time, the husband would have been lynched, the wife raped, and the children left to witness the terror. There are a lot of complicated layers to the scene (for example, enlightened, upper-class white characters save decent middle-class black characters from poor, ignorant white racists) that are not really processed the way they need to be. In later books, Roberts would have black characters who were not victims and who had more of a voice, but this book is an early and important step on that road.

Again set in the South, *Midnight Bayou* (2001) deals with race and particularly "whiteness" in a more modern and nuanced way. Race isn't outright mentioned in this book, but the story makes more sense if it is indeed coded in those terms, because even if the author didn't intend for it to be, it is there.

Midnight Bayou is a ghost story, and our modern lovers seem to be repeating in some way the love story of a tragic married couple from 1899. The story is set in New Orleans, a city that has many different races and ethnicities and a long history of miscegenation. The 1899 romance is described as both a Cinderella story and a scandal. A Cajun servant married the dashing young master of the house. Although she is never explicitly described as mixed-race, the following passage, when she examines the differences between her newborn baby and herself, implies that she is: "Oh, she had such hope those eyes would stay blue, like Lucien's. The baby's hair was dark like her own. Dark and curling, but her skin was milk white—again like papa's rather than the deeper tone, the dusky gold of her Cajun mama's" (Roberts, *Midnight Bayou*, 7).

Relationships and even marriages between white men and light-skinned black or mixed-race women were not at all uncommon in that location and time (Walker). Abby's pleasure in her child's more white features was sadly not uncommon for mothers of mixed-raced children at the time, either. In a racially stratified society, it would have as much impact as issues like social status or wealth on how easy or difficult a child's life would turn out to be. (Mark Twain's *The Tragedy of Pudd'nhead Wilson* deals with this issue, as well.)

In the current story line, Lena is also coded as something other than white (likely the result of generations of racial mixing): "Her hair was midnight black, a gypsy mane that spilled wild curls over her shoulders. . . . Her skin was dusky, her eyes, when they flicked to his, the deep, rich brown of bitter chocolate" (Roberts, *Midnight Bayou*, 51). But more interesting than the exact racial makeup and percentages of either of these characters is the way that their "otherness" factors into their experience of womanhood.

Both women are viewed as extremely desirable and exotic in a way that proves to be damaging. Abby snags the most desirable bachelor, but then is coveted and eventually killed by his brother. Lena attracts men easily, but to most she is primarily an object of lust, and their interest is superficial. However, the novel also shows the difference that a hundred years or so can make. Lena, a successful business owner, has more choices than Abby did—to be a lower-class servant or to marry up. In many ways, Lena's story retells and "fixes" Abby's story, even though the society she lives in is still dealing with the crimes of the past.

In direct contrast to *Carolina Moon*, these issues are not explicitly addressed and therefore cannot be fixed. In the first novel, the racists are easily spotted and carted off to jail. In *Midnight Bayou*, race is part of the characters but it doesn't define them. It is an unspoken element in the way people interact with one another—just as in real life—but it does not define their characters or limit their stories.

In many ways *The Witness*, published in April 2012, circles back to Roberts's first novel and updates the heroine, the love interest, and the power dynamics in their relationship. Like Adelia in *Irish Thoroughbred*, the heroine of *The Witness* starts out quite sheltered and inexperienced. However, as a genius and a member of the Internet generation, she has read widely and thought about nearly everything. The first chance she gets, she goes out clubbing with a new friend. The two have a powwow in the bathroom, and she is supportive of the other girl's plan to have sex with a man she just met and is considering doing the same herself. She explains her thoughts on sex in the following passage:

> Sex is a natural and necessary act, not only for procreation but also, certainly in humans, for pleasure and the release of stress. . . . It's an unfortunate by-product of a patriarchal society that women are deemed sluttish or cheap for engaging in sex for pleasure while men are considered vital. Virginity shouldn't be a prize, or withheld. The hymen has no rewarding properties, grants no powers. Women should—no, must—be allowed to pursue their own sexual gratification, whether or not procreation is the goal or the relationship a monogamous one, just as a man is free to do so. (Roberts, *The Witness*, 39)

The virginal heroine has come a long way, and the message Roberts is sending is loud and clear. Underscoring this point, the heroine has been around the block several times by the time she meets her love interest 12 years (and over 50 pages) later. Such a heroine could handle any type of man, but she falls for one who is decent and funny and enjoys the fact that she says what's on her mind. And unlike in *Irish Thoroughbred*, there isn't a clear imbalance of power—they take turns.

The idea of emotional, intellectual, and sexual equality as romantic and sexy has been a change in perspective in both Roberts's novels and the entire genre of Romance Fiction that is hopefully here to stay.

Natalie McCall

Further Reading

Arthur, Artist C. *Manifest*. New York: Kimani Tru, 2010.

Elkeles, Simone. *Perfect Chemistry*. New York: Walker, 2009.

Forrest, Katherine V. *Curious Wine*, 10th anniversary ed. Tallahassee, FL: Naiad Press, 1993.

Frankenberg, Ruth. *Displacing Whiteness: Essays in Social and Cultural Criticism*. Durham, NC: Duke University Press, 1997.

Goren, Lilly J. *You've Come a Long Way, Baby: Women, Politics, and Popular Culture*. Lexington: University Press of Kentucky, 2009.

Lipsitz, George. *The Possessive Investment in Whiteness: How White People Profit from Identity Politics*. Philadelphia: Temple University Press, 1998.

"Reader Statistics." *Romance Writers of America.* https://www.rwa.org/p/cm/ld/fid=582. Accessed April 19, 2017.

Regis, Pamela. *A Natural History of the Romance Novel.* Philadelphia: University of Pennsylvania Press, 2003.

Roberts, Nora. *Carnal Innocence.* New York: Bantam Books, 1991.

Roberts, Nora. *Irish Hearts.* New York: Silhouette Books, 2000. (Contains *Irish Thoroughbred* [1981] and *Irish Rose* [1988]).

Roberts, Nora. *Midnight Bayou.* New York: G. P. Putnam's Sons, 2001.

Roberts, Nora. *The Witness.* New York: G. P. Putnam's Sons, 2012.

Roediger, David R. *The Wages of Whiteness: Race and the Making of the American Working Class.* London: Verso, 1991.

Twain, Mark. *The Tragedy of Pudd'nhead Wilson.* Champaign, IL: Project Gutenberg, 1999.

Walker, Clarence Earl. *Mongrel Nation: The America Begotten by Thomas Jefferson and Sally Hemings.* Charlottesville: University of Virginia Press, 2009.

Historical Romance

Of all the Romance subgenres, Historical Romance is perhaps the most expansive and diverse. The borders between subgenres are blurred by incorporating suspense, inspirational elements, and multiculturalism in an almost infinite variety of ways based on chronology, location, and level of sensuality. The label "historical romance" is itself problematic because it is inherently anachronistic: intrinsic in the term "history" is the sense of reality about the past, whereas "romance" suggests a sense of fantasy of somewhere else. There exists a basic binary opposition beneath the term: fact/fiction, reality/fantasy, then/now. Furthermore, writers must achieve a balance between historical information, the romance plotline, and the contemporary reader. The historical romance and romance formula allow for a sort of "doubleness" in which readers may know the outcome of the story from the past but still immerse themselves in it.

The historical setting allows for the mingling of distance and reality; however, the period should be self-contained with no overt link to the present and should be distant enough to separate the reader and the period to allow for unfamiliarity. Therefore, historical romances tend to be slightly more escapist than contemporary romances. There is an element of world-building in all historical-fiction writing in that the novel structure imposes an unnatural beginning and ending. The result is a world apprehended rather than a world defined; yet any historical fiction can say more about the era in which it was written than the era it is depicting.

It is possible to make a distinction between romantic historicals, Historical romances, and historical Romances, determined mostly by the level and amount of historical accuracy and authenticity and the prominence of the love story. Romantic historicals feature actual historical figures as essential elements of the plot. Because of the emphasis on history over romance, these romances can blur the line with historical fiction, so the level of historical accuracy tends to be higher and more exact. They frequently include a grand romance that is shaped by historical events but may not be the primary story line. This fiction as history operates in the realm of "truth" if it doesn't compromise known "fact," but this type of history and historical fiction tends to be discounted by traditional historians even as it is often taken as reality by its readers. Sara Donati's *Into the Wilderness* (1998) begins the saga of Elizabeth Middleton and Nathanial Bonner in a sort of Jane-Austen-meets-James-Fenimore-Cooper romance on the American frontier. *The Virgin Queen's Daughter* (2009), by Kimberly Cates, weaves a romantic plot through the reign of Elizabeth I.

The most basic Historical romance is the love story in a historical setting, in which the writer must balance believability and authenticity. However, there is a paradox in the retrospective methodology. The writer sets the priorities about what historical issues and details get emphasized. Thus, as the historical world and events may be familiar, they are intensified and edited by the writer's imagination (Hughes, 1993). The history, filtered through the values of the writer and the needs of the genre, tends to omit the ordinary and uncomfortable realities of the period and focus on the romantic mythology. History, then, functions as a site for the construction of, consideration of, and struggle over cultural meanings and values.

The use of exotic and historical settings adds to a sense of escape; more important, it "functions as a mirror for the present," as the writer can examine the ideas and practices of the present and offer at least an implied resolution (Hughes, 8). Embedding a problem in a different, yet reasonably familiar, setting provides enough distance to defamiliarize problems, which encourages closer (stricter) scrutiny. Laura Kinsale's *Flowers from the Storm* (1992; 2003) considers disability, madness, and faith—timeless issues—and their human influences and social manipulations against a late-Georgian backdrop.

Even as the romance narrative is imposed upon a historical setting, a well-written historical romance still must have accurate historical details (fashion, atmosphere, food, customs, houses, behavior, and so forth). These details breathe life into the historical setting, but they cannot be so overwhelming as to distract from the basic plot. They may include actual events like wars or political events that do not generally affect the basic plot. The historical detail should enrich the story rather than distract from it. However, the setting is an important element in structuring the plotline. In many cases, the historical setting becomes a character itself in how it adds romance, drama, and conflict to the plotline as frequently the protagonists challenge the social norms of the period.

The essential difference between the Historical romance and the historical Romance (sometimes referred to as Period Romance) is the burden and level of authenticity and accuracy. In historical Romances, the history provides more of a background and context for the romance formula. These worlds may be more "imagineered" than either a romantic historical or a Historical romance (Lin). At times, they may be regarded more as "wallpaper" or costume historicals or even "mysticals." Frequently, accuracy is sacrificed in favor of the emotion and romantic plotline; historical inaccuracies and anachronisms are rather easy to identify, resulting in questionable validity. More than with the Historical romance, the task of the historical Romance is one of world-building. The setting is not really a fantasy world, as it must contain details that are as authentic as possible and still must immerse the readers in the historical environment. The general historical facts are correct, but the emphasis is on the characters. For example, Eloisa James places her fairy-tale adaptations in a loose Regency setting, and Ann Herendeen's *Phyllida and the Brotherhood of Philander* (2009) romps across the Regency stage. Although there is great variation, the majority of popular historical romances, including most of those discussed below, fall into the historical Romance or Period Romance category.

The world-building ability and historical distance allow for a broad range of sensuality and ethnicity. The most influential books in the turning point of popular romance and sensuality are both historicals: *The Flame and the Flower* (Kathleen Woodiwiss, 1972) and *Sweet Savage Love* (Rosemary Rogers, 1974). The amount of sensuality ranges from Barbara Cartland's (1901–2000) several hundred soft or sweet historical romances to Madeline Hunter's lusty *Ravishing in Red* (2010) to Alex Beecroft's m/m romance *False Colors* (2009). There are abundant opportunities for a variety of ethnicities in historical romance, including Mary Jo Putney's *The China Bride* (2000), Madeline Baker's *Lakota Love Song* (2002), and Beverly Jenkin's classic, *Indigo* (2000).

The level of optimism required by the genre determines historical limitations and settings, but theoretically, the romance can be adapted to any location, place, and nationality. The medieval years, England during the Napoleonic Wars, and the American West are the most popular. Because of the vastness of the subgenre, historical romances are generally simply discussed by their chronological, or historical, era.

The Celtic tradition of mythology, folktale, and legend is a particularly attractive period for romance novels. The Norse, Scot, or Irish warrior provides ample context for an alpha hero warrior who needs to be tamed or civilized. Mythology is also excellent for paranormal elements such as shape-shifting, Valkyries, heroes, rituals, and beliefs that create a multidimensional world with greater risks and secret machinations that threaten the very human nature of the characters.

Both Scottish and Irish histories pose the same sort of attraction as romance settings because both cultures have a heritage of folktales and legends and a strong warrior tradition coupled with the fantasy of mythology. A number of writers are drawn to medieval Scotland and the legendary Scottish and Norse warrior hero traditions; Irish history is also popular, but while mythically heroic, it also tends to be rather tragic.

The tradition of courtly love, knights, and chivalry in medieval mythology is steeped in folklore and legends about heroic knights who rescue ladies and perform noble deeds motivated by love for their ladies. Courtly love as an ennobling force is a natural sort of setting for the historical romance novel. Another appeal of the medieval setting is the role that the power of honor played. Adding to the sense of romance are the troubadours and minstrels and the medieval romances like *The Knight of the Cart* or *Sir Gawain*.

Nearly every historical romance writer has dabbled with Vikings and Celts. Johanna Lindsey's *Fires of Winter* (1980) results from a Viking raid into Celtic England. Sandra Hill has two multiple-book series, beginning with *The Reluctant Viking* (1994). Kinley MacGregor's *Master of Desire* (2001) begins with a conflict resolved by King Henry II in an arranged marriage. Bertrice Small's *A Dangerous Love* (1991), the first of her Border Chronicles, immediately follows England's Wars of the Roses (1485) and features a crossborder raid and kidnapping by Scots. Betina Krahn's *The Husband Test* (2001) is set in an alternative reality roughly based on the plumbing, transportation, and superstitions of the Middle Ages. Medieval worlds are not necessarily limited to Western Europe. Jeannie Lin sets *The Dragon and the Pearl* (2011) in the Tang Dynasty in early medieval China.

Another exotic setting is provided by the world of piracy, which reached romantic proportions during the 16th and 17th centuries. As another untamed warrior figure, pirates are popular romance heroes, more savages to be civilized. Romance pirates are often dashing off to adventure on the sea, their daring exploits conjuring up images of swordfights, sea-swept quarterdecks, and billowy shirts. Bertrice Small's *Skye O'Malley* (1980), set in 16th-century Elizabethan England, features a female pirate swashbuckling her way across the ocean. The pirate or buccaneer is still a popular character during the Regency Period, as in Karen Robards's *Island Flame* (1981).

The Georgian Period was a time when England became a world empire despite its conflict with Napoleon and France. It also saw the development of its colonies in America, India, and the Far East. The expansion witnessed a shift in domestic life and political attitudes. Elizabeth Hoyt's *Wicked Intentions* (2010), set in 1730s London, includes a rich contrast between the very wealthy and the very poor. Patricia Veryan has written several romances (beginning with *Practice to Deceive* [1983]) revolving around the failure of the Jacobite rebellion at Culloden (1746).

The Georgian Period culminates with the Regency, the most popular historical romance period (see Regency Romance, Traditional).

The Victorian Era offers a vast array of settings because of the length of Victoria's reign (1837–1901). In that century, there were tremendous shifts in social and political institutions, literary and artistic styles, reform and ferment. Her early reign, the 1840s–1850s, was much different from that of her later years, after the death of Albert.

A popular trope in Edwardian or Belle Epoque novels is an American heiress marrying an English title such as in Judith Ivory's *Beast* (1997) or Victoria Alexander's *The Princess and the Pea* (1996), which show the interaction between the two nations. This sort of migration theme also provides a plotline with inherent conflict and complications both cultural and ethnic. For example, Jade Lee's Tigress series (*White Tigress*, 2005), set in fin-de-siècle China, rather starkly contrasts the differences between the cultures of the English heroine and the Taoist hero. Sherry Thomas's *Not Quite a Husband* (2009) is set in the Northwest Frontier of British India. Meredith Duran's *Duke of Shadows* (2008), set in 1850s British India, features a biracial hero and the conflicts of British colonialism. Christine Monson's *Rangoon* (1985) sends an American heroine into colonial Burma. The use of exotic and historical settings adds to the sense of escapism.

The most mythologized periods of American history are those of the Antebellum South and the American Cowboy West (see Western Romance). Despite the presence of slavery, the American Old South and New Orleans/Creole cultures remain romantic, providing the settings for Woodiwiss's *The Flame and the Flower* (1972), set in colonial Virginia; Shirlee Busbee's *At Long Last* (2000), set in French colonial Natchez; and Rogers's *Sweet Savage Love* (1974), set in New Orleans and Spanish Texas. Even in Civil War–era romances, the South receives the most attention, as in Nan Ryan's *Dearest Enemy* (2006).

Colonial and Revolutionary America have some popularity as settings. Pamela Clare has set her MacKinnon's Rangers series during the tension and drama of the French and Indian War (1755–1763) and in 1760s Virginia. This period saw great social and political change for the colonies as they grew to view themselves as Americans rather than English. The American Revolution provides a dramatic setting for novels like Patricia Potter's *Star Keeper* (1999), Laura Lee Guhrke's *The Charade* (2000), and Rita Gerlach's *Before the Scarlet Dawn* (2012).

While historical romance writers tend to specialize in one historical era, nearly every one has produced at least one novel set in nearly every era. Romance novels are intended to entertain, so the historical material will be culturally adapted to the genre requirements and the values of the contemporary reading audience. Some historical periods or eras are more popular because they add to the overall sense of romance. The subgenre of Historical Romances will undoubtedly expand. Currently, it is defined as any story set prior to 1945 (World War II), when cultural shifts occurred to create the "modern" generations. As societies expand and cultures shift, the distance necessary to separate the historical period from the contemporary reader will also shift, only increasing the infinite combinations and adaptations made possible by the historical romance.

Maryan Wherry

See also: Regency Romance, Traditional

Further Reading

Fletcher, Lisa. *Historical Romance Fiction: Heterosexuality and Performativity.* Burlington, VT: Ashgate, 2008.

Hughes, Helen. *The Historical Romance.* London: Routledge, 1993.

Lin, Jeannie. "History and Alternative History." Jeannie Lin Website. http://www.jeannielin.com/extras/history-and-alternative-history/. Accessed April 11, 2017.

Strehle, Susan, and Mary Paniccia Carden, eds. *Doubled Plots: Romance and History.* Jackson: University of Mississippi Press, 2003.

Holt, Victoria

See Hibbert, Eleanor Burford

Hull, E. M. (1880–1947)

E. M. Hull was the creator of the "desert romance" in which a European woman and an Arab, or a presumed Arab, lover play out a passionately sadomasochistic relationship in an exotic desert location. Published in England in 1919, her first novel, *The Sheik*, caused a sensation in the post–World War I world with its combination of frank sexuality and implied interracial romance. While she was the author of several desert romances, *The Sheik* remains her most famous novel. Its translation onto the screen with Rudolph Valentino in the title role successfully imprinted the alpha male lover into the romantic fantasies of a generation of women.

Born Edith Maud Henderson in London on August 16, 1880, she was the second child of James Henderson, a wealthy shipowner, and Katie Thorne, his Canadian wife. She traveled extensively as a child, and her marriage at the age of 19 to engineer Percy Winstanley Hull saw the couple eventually established in The Knowle, in Hazelwood, Derbyshire, England. Edith Maude would spend the rest of her life there as the wife of a gentleman farmer and the mother of her only child, a daughter, Cecil. While nothing in her upbringing or her life of domesticity prepared anyone for the eventual publication of *The Sheik*, she began to write it during her husband's absence in World War I. Its mixture of erotic fantasy and sexual yearning quickly found an audience in the postwar world, where the social changes wrought by global conflict saw an emerging market catering to female desire. The fact that this market reacted so strongly to enforced female captivity and rape—and the very real possibility of miscegenation involving an Englishwoman and an "uncivilized" Arab—brought condemnation from literary reviewers and social commentators. This did little to deter the reading public, and the story of the strong-willed Lady Diana Mayo, abducted on horseback by Ahmed, the Arab sheik, and kept as his sexual prisoner, offered the female reader both powerful erotic fantasy and a narrative that focuses on the heroine's sexual and emotional experience.

An intensely private person, E. M. Hull did not actively promote her novel, nor engage in the entrepreneurial activities of many other best-selling female authors of the 1920s. The novel's transformation into a film in 1921, the same year as the first U.S. edition was published, saw little, if any, input from the author. Due to concerns about censorship, the novel's rape themes were softened by the film, although the central image of the barbarian lover brutalizing the imperious heroine but eventually civilized by love, remained intact. Rudolph Valentino's performance catapulted him into immediate stardom, and the word "sheik" entered the lexicon as another word for "lover," celebrated in both film and song.

Hull continued to write desert romances and novels set in the outposts of the British Empire, exploring both the emotional and geographical boundaries confronting her heroes and heroines. While colonialism and race are issues implicit in these novels, Hull was conservative in her attitudes to interracial marriage, a fact reflected in the European background of her sheiks.

In 1925, Hull published the sequel to *The Sheik*, *The Sons of the Sheik*, which was successful as both a novel and as a film, again starring Rudolph Valentino in the dual role of father and son. Her subsequent novels *The Shadow of the East* (1921), *The Desert Healer* (1923), *The Lion Tamer* (1928), and *The Captive of the Sahara* (1931) continued to explore both the North African desert and the edge of empire as an emotionally and sexually fulfilling setting for the European heroine. However, none of her subsequent novels emulated the success of *The Sheik*. Her last novel, *The Forest of Terrible Things*, was published in 1939.

In 1926, she published an account of the two journeys she made to Algeria in 1923 and 1925, accompanied by her daughter, Cecil. In *Camping in the Sahara*, she describes the desert and its people with great lyricism. Her brief reference to a visit to Algeria as a child suggests that the memory was the motivation for choosing the desert as the emotional landscape in which she explored both passion and female desire.

E. M. Hull continued to live a quiet life, largely forgotten as an author. She died on February 11, 1947, at her home in Derbyshire, aged 66.

Heather Cleary

Further Reading

Hull, E. M. *Camping in the Sahara.* New York: Dodd Mead and Company, 1927.

Hull, E. M. *The Sheik* (1921). Project Gutenberg. Project Gutenberg, #7031, http://www.gutenberg.org/ebooks/7031. Accessed April 6, 2017.

Leider, Emily. *Dark Lover: The Life and Death of Rudolph Valentino.* London: Faber and Faber, 2004.

Melman, Billie. *Women and the Popular Imagination in the Twenties: Flappers and Nymphs.* New York: St. Martin's Press, 1988.

Papers of Edith Maud Hull. The National Archives. London: London University, London School of Economics, The Women's Library. http://discovery.nationalarchives.gov.uk/details/rd/610f43d4-bf92-4aca-99ed-6869447e9068. Accessed April 6, 2017.

Humor in Romance

Love and laughter are a perfect mix for romance novels. Although most romantic comedies are single titles written by individual authors, some publishers have released lines devoted to humorous romances. In 1996, Harlequin premiered its Love and Laughter line with JoAnn Ross's *I Do, I Do for Now.* The Love and Laughter line reappeared in 2011 under the Harlequin Treasury imprint with such titles as *Too Stubborn to Marry* by Cathie Linz and *Wife Is a 4-Letter Word* by Stephanie Bond. In 1998, Waterbrook Press published the humorous Time for Laughter series. These books even came with a "giggle guarantee." Titles included *Love on the Run* by Shari MacDonald (Salinger Sisters #1) and *Say Uncle* by Suzy Pizzuti (Halo Hattie's Boarding House #1).

Humorous Devices

Humorous devices are what the author uses to make the reader laugh. Different devices appeal to different readers. Some of the more common humorous devices used in the Romance genre include matchmakers, irony, humorous dialogue, hidden identity, mistaken identity, running jokes, quirky primary and secondary characters, unexpected twists, slapstick, and fish-out-of-water.

Matchmakers

Matchmakers can be very funny, whether they work in secret or are outwardly aggressive in their efforts. There are examples of matchmaking shenanigans in all subgenres and time periods. Debbie Macomber features determined—but sometimes bumbling—angel matchmakers in *Shirley, Goodness and Mercy* (1999). In Lisa Plumley's *The Matchmaker* (2003), a humorous historical romance set in the American West, a secret, albeit successful, matchmaker makes the entire bachelor population of Morrow Creek incredibly nervous. The matchmaker in Elizabeth Bevarly's *Undercover with the Mob* (2004) is a landlady who will stop at nothing to get the hero and heroine together. In Day LeClaire's *The Nine-Dollar Daddy* (1999), the matchmaker is a boy genius. A grandmother arranges for an eccentric single mom to win her grandson in a bachelor auction in Kasey Michael's *Raffling Ryan* (2000). Laurelin McGee's *Miss Match* (2015) has a down-on-her-luck heroine playing matchmaker to Boston's most eligible bachelor. Rachel Gibson's *Truly Madly Yours* (1999) features accidental matchmaking when her father's will forces the heroine to stay in town a year—but stay away from the town bad boy during that period.

Irony

The form of irony most used in romantic comedies occurs when one result is expected, and another one occurs. In Jayne Ann Krentz's *Family Man* (1992), the hero, who has no use for his family, is the one who ends up saving the family business. In *Mystique* (1995), written under Krentz's nom de plume, Amanda Quick, a princess makes a list of attributes for the perfect husband—but the hero has none of them. The heroine in Deborah Shelley's *Marriage 101* (2008) is a relationship expert who's never had one of her own. In Kristan Higgins's *Too Good to Be True* (2009), an advice columnist has to make up her own boyfriend. When the hero in Jill Barnett's *Wicked* (1999) puts his feisty bride-to-be in a convent while he's gone, he has no idea it's the home of warrior nuns, and she's more than ready to be trained. In Stephanie Laurens's *An Unwilling Conquest* (2006), the hero leaves town to escape matchmaking women, only to step right into the trap set by one of them.

Humorous Dialogue

Humorous dialogue covers a lot of territory. It can contain malapropisms, word plays, double entendres, witty repartee, sarcasm, verbal sparring, and so on.

The heroine of Jen Turano's *In Good Company* (2015) carries a small dictionary in her pocket but still fractures many words. Teresa Medeiros's heroine in *The Devil Wears Plaid* (2010) can stop the hero dead in his tracks with her caustic wit. When an Irish food critic pans a woman's new Italian restaurant in Millie Criswell's *The Trouble with Mary* (2000), a battle of words begins. The sassy heroine of MaryJanice Davidson's *Yours, Mine, and Ours* (2012) can speak seven languages and can wisecrack in all of them.

Hidden Identity

Books using hidden identity as the comedic device have characters that deliberately disguise themselves to avoid detection. In *To Tame a Texan* by Georgina Gentry (2003), the teenaged boy hired on for a cattle drive is actually a suffragist who's run out of options to get to an important women's rights meeting. Jen Turano debuted in 2012 with *Change of Fortune*, a story in which an heiress masquerades as a governess to get revenge on the man she believes stole her fortune. In Isabel Sharpe's *Beauty and the Bet* (2000), a gorgeous woman disguises herself as a plain Jane. The heroine in *Surprising Lord Jack* by Sally MacKenzie (2013) dresses like a man, so she ends up reluctantly bunking with Jack Valentine at a traveler's inn. In Christie Ridgway's *Take My Breath Away* (2014), a Hollywood star goes incognito.

Mistaken Identity

Unlike characters who deliberately hide their identities, characters with mistaken identities are incorrectly assumed to be someone else. In Lisa Kleypas's *Suddenly You* (2001), a writer tired of being a virgin at her "advanced" age greets a man she assumes is her hired lover at the door and proceeds with her plans, not realizing the man is actually a publisher and not the person she expected. A rich businessman is mistaken for a butler in Christina Dodd's *Just the Way You Are* (2003). The hero arrests the heroine of Julia Quinn's *To Catch an Heiress* (1998), believing her to be an infamous spy.

Running Jokes

A running joke is a comedic device that takes a humorous joke or concept and repeats it throughout the story. The paper-thin walls in the heroine's apartment and the sounds of passion that come through them are a running joke in Alice Clayton's *Wallbanger* (2013). The knight disguised as a monk who's taken a vow of silence really wants to say something in Tori Phillips's *Silent Knight* (1996). An ancient Egyptian curse makes the most eligible bachelor in town the most undesirable nobleman in the *ton* in Jacquie D'Alessandro's *Who Will Take This Man?* (2003).

Quirky Characters (Primary)

When either the hero or the heroine—or both—has quirky characteristics, hilarity is sure to ensue. The romance in Susan Elizabeth Phillips's *Heroes Are My Weakness* (2014) is between a ventriloquist heroine who turns to puppetry after failing at acting and a hero who writes horror novels. In Phillips's *Heaven, Texas* (1995), a wallflower who works at a nursing home is hired to babysit a bad-boy sports hero and keep him out of trouble until the big game. In Deidre Martin's *Power Play* (2008), a soap-opera actress hires a hockey player to pose as her boyfriend. *Get a Hold on You* by Pat White (2003) has a puritanical accountant who has to become the wrestler Tatianna the Tigress to save her family's finances. In Kieran Kramer's *When Harry Met Molly* (2010), the hero is dubbed "Impossible Bachelor" by the Prince Regent. Lori Wilde's uncertain heroine in *There Goes the Bride* (2007) hires a man to kidnap her.

Quirky Characters (Secondary)

Zany secondary characters can enhance the humor in a romantic comedy or provide comic relief in a more serious romance. From their look-alike goofy haircuts to their crushes on the heroine, the baseball players in Kate Angell's *No One Like You* (2015) lend a lively tone to the book. In *The Charm School* by Susan Wiggs (1999), the heroine's etiquette teachers are pirates. Sue Civil-Brown's *Catching Kelly* (2000) features an offbeat family. In Suzann Ledbetter's *East of Peculiar* (2000), the heroine becomes the manager of a retirement home full of idiosyncratic seniors. The heroine of Deeanne Gist's *Tiffany Girl* (2015) fills her Chicago boardinghouse with oddball characters. Patience Griffin's *Some Like It Scottish* (2015) has an entire island of quirky people. In Kasey Michaels's *Everything's Coming Up Rosie* (2007), secondary characters create a chaotic preamble to a society wedding. *Must Love Dragons* by Stephanie Rowe (2006) includes a sassy, shape-shifting goblet among its supernatural characters.

Quirky Characters (Children)

Dealing with incorrigible children is one way to add humorous conflict to the story. The children in Jen Turano's *In Good Company* (2015) have run off every nanny except one—a nanny with a string of terminations. In *An Uncommon Governess* by Monique Ellis (1998), the children are so horrible they're delivered to the governess tied up. Janet Dailey's *Scrooge Wore Spurs* (2002) features a grouchy hero who learns the true meaning of chaos when he unexpectedly inherits his four orphaned nieces and nephews.

Quirky Characters (Animals)

It's not hard for an animal to add lots of humor to romantic comedies. In Kate Angell's *No One Like You* (2015), a goofy Great Dane with an entourage of other dogs is a scene-stealer. Jen Turano's cranky peacocks (*In Good Company*, 2015) wreak havoc on a society event. Jennifer Crusie's beagle in *Anyone But You* (1996) has mood swings.

Unexpected Plot Twists

In romantic suspense, an unexpected plot twist enhances the tension. In romantic comedies, a plot twist makes the humorous moments even funnier. In Vicki Lewis Thompson's *The Nerd Who Loves Me* (2004), an uptight accountant's Las Vegas showgirl mother helps save the day. The heroine in Julie Garwood's *Guardian Angel* (1990), a seemingly helpless young woman, is really the dread pirate Pagan. When she meets her new boss, the veterinary intern in Jill Shalvis's *Then Came You* (2014) realizes he was her anonymous one-night stand. Suzanne Enoch's *Flirting with Danger* (2005) features a wealthy man who falls for the thief who's robbing his house. In Katie MacAlister's *The Truth about Leo* (2014), an impoverished princess marries a nearly dead British officer, figuring, dead or alive, he's her ticket to England; then he wakes up and discovers he's a husband.

Slapstick Humor

Slapstick humor was the mainstay of American vaudeville. Tripping, falling, crashing into people—slapstick humor tends to be physical. Although there are those who prefer a more "intellectual" approach to their humor, many find this comedic device a side-splitting addition to any book. Angie Fox's *The Dangerous Book for Demonslayers* (2009) has a heroine whose grandmother is part of a fearless bikers' coven that leaves chaos in its wake. Kathleen Bacus's heroine *Calamity Jayne* (2006) comes by her name naturally—she literally stumbles over her own two feet. In Jojo Moyes's *One Plus One* (2014), a rich computer nerd, a high-IQed daughter, a gigantic dog, and a Goth stepson are jammed into the car a single-mother heroine drives to Scotland.

Fish-Out-of-Water

The fish-out-of-water device puts characters in situations that are completely foreign to them. Sandra Hill's Viking series features Vikings time-traveling to the present and contemporary characters finding themselves flung back in time into the midst of Scandinavian warriors. Both Jill Marie Landis's *The Orchid Hunter* (2000) and Suzanne Enoch's *Reforming a Rake* (2000) involve learning how to fit into proper society the hard way. In the western historical romance *A Wanted Man* by Nancy J. Parra (2002), a librarian decides to become a bounty hunter. In Jayne Ann Krentz's *Perfect Partners* (1992), the CEO of a sporting-goods business is forced to teach a librarian the ropes after she inherits the company from her uncle.

Humorous Inspirational Romances

The inspirational romance market, also known as "Christian" or "faith-based" romances, has a wide range of amusing novels. In *Tried and True* by Mary Connealy (2014), the heroine disguises herself as a man so she can leave the Wild West behind. The pastor in *Heavens to Betsy* by Beth Pattillo (2005) has to deal with her capricious congregation. In *Always the Baker, Never the Bride* by Sandra D. Bricker (2010), the pastry-chef heroine deals with a wedding business that suddenly becomes personal. Humorous inspirational series include Jen Turano's The Ladies of Distinction, Tracy Victoria Bateman's Drama Queens, and Cathy Marie Hake's Only in Gooding. Several authors have rewritten their secular romantic comedies as humorous faith-based books. Robin Lee Hatcher's suffragist book, *Kiss Me, Katie* (1996), was rewritten for the inspirational market as *Catching Katie* (2003). Lori Copeland's *Sisters of Mercy Flats* (2013) is a rewrite of a series of historical western romances about three swindling sisters—*Promise Me Today* (1992), *Promise Me Tomorrow* (1993), and *Promise Me Forever* (1994).

Titles That Let You Know the Book Is Funny

Sometimes, a reader doesn't have to open a book to know whether or not it's funny—the title gives it away. A few examples of these cleverly named books are Mary Jane Hathaway's *Pride, Prejudice and Cheese Grits* (Jane Austen Takes the South series, 2014); Kieran Kramer's Impossible Bachelor series, which includes *Dukes to the Right of Me, Princes to the Left* (2010) and *Cloudy with a Chance of Marriage* (2011); Shirley Jump's *The Bride Wore Chocolate* (2004) and *The Devil Served Tortellini* (2005); and Leslie Langtry's *Guns Will Keep Us Together* (2008).

Range of Humor

Although humor abounds in the Romance genre, there is no one "type," and no two romantic comedies are alike. A sense of humor is highly individual and very subjective. Some readers might find one book hilarious, while others think that same book is "dull" or even "silly." Humorous romance novels span time periods and subgenres: Historical, Paranormal, Contemporary, Romantic Suspense, and Inspirational. The varieties of humor go from subtle to laugh-out-loud, knee-slapping funny. The comedic element may be whimsical, witty, or slapstick, and the amount of humor in a book ranges from little or no humor to cover-to-cover comedy. However, the popularity of humor in the romance novel endures, and the reader who laughs last, laughs best.

Shelley Mosley

Further Reading

Seaman, Donna. "The 101 Best Romance Novels of the Past Ten Years." *The Booklist Reader*, September 9, 2015. http://www.booklistreader.com/2015/09/09/book-lists/the -101-best-romance-novels-of-the-last-10-years/. Accessed April 20, 2017.

Snow, Shayne. "A Quest to Understand What Makes Things Funny." *The New Yorker*, April 1, 2014. http://www.newyorker.com/tech/elements/a-quest-to-understand-what -makes-things-funny. Accessed April 20, 2017.

XOXO After Dark. "Best Romance Reads: 10 Great Books That Combine Laughter and Romance." *The Huffington Post*, September 11, 2014 (updated November 11, 2014). http:// www.huffingtonpost.com/xoxo-after-dark/best-romance-reads-10-gre_1_b_5800356 .html. Accessed April 20, 2017.

I

Inspirational Romance

Inspirational or "Christian" romances feature a hero or heroine, or both, who have faith in God. This faith is, or becomes, an intrinsic part of their lives. Sometimes the faith has been lost, and the story tells about the journey back to belief. Common themes in faith-based romances are love (romantic and *agape*), forgiveness, mercy, healing, redemption, hope, courage, justice, and a moral life. Inspirational romance authors consider themselves Christians and write with what is referred to in the Christy Awards as a "Christian worldview." In the past, inspirational romances were marketed mainly to evangelical Protestants. Today, however, the readership base has become much broader.

Inspirational romances are "sweet" romances. Love is often innocent, and physical contact doesn't go much beyond handholding and chaste kissing. These romances are less sensual than secular romances, and there are almost no sexual encounters or love scenes. There usually aren't even references to sex. As in secular romances, the relationship between the hero and heroine is monogamous, and there is a happily—or hopefully—ever-after ending. Inspirational romances don't include alcohol or drugs (unless someone is a villain of the piece, or is being rehabilitated), swear words (some publishers also discourage euphemisms for these, including "darn," "geez," and "heck"), or nudity.

The best inspirational romances do just what their name implies—they inspire. Their message is subtly integrated into the story. The worst inspirational romances lack subtlety and tend to be preachy, dogmatic, or didactic and exhibit an exclusivity that doesn't include other faiths or even other Christian denominations. In spite of the stricter protocols, there are many varieties of inspirational romances, and they come in most of the same subgenres as the secular romances: Historical, Contemporary, and Romantic Suspense. Many of them are written in series.

Historical Inspirational Romances

Biblical Times

Biblical inspirational romances take place during either the Old Testament or New Testament eras. Romantic elements in biblical fiction are a tradition dating back to *Quo Vadis* by Henryk Sienkiewicz (1895); *The Robe* by Lloyd C. Douglas (1942); and *The Silver Chalice* by Thomas B. Costain (1952). Popular titles set during this era include *Bathsheba* by Jill Eileen Smith (2011), *The Damascus Way* by Janet Oke and Davis Bunn (2011), *The Gladiator* by Carla Capshaw (2009), *Martha* by Diana Wallis Taylor (2011), and *Pilate's Wife* by Antoinette May (2006). Series, such the Mark of the Lion trilogy by Francine Rivers, are also popular with fans of inspirational romance.

19th-Century America

Inspirational romances, like other romances, are considered historical if the setting is 50 years or more before the present. The Old West (historical American westerns usually set from the mid- to late 1800s) is a common backdrop for historical inspirational romances. These books have the same themes as secular westerns: mail-order brides, a sheriff trying to clean up a town, an outlaw who changes his ways, vigilantes, and range wars. The difference is the faith-based message. Titles set in the Old West include *The Outlaw Takes a Bride* by Susan Page Davis (2015), *The Heart's Pursuit* by Robin Lee Hatcher (2014), and *A River to Cross* by Yvonne Harris (2011). The American Civil War and the years that immediately followed are also popular time periods for inspirational romances. These include *Hearts Made Whole* by Judy Hedlund (2015), *A Beauty So Rare* by Tamera Alexander (2014), and *Sixteen Brides* by Stephanie Grace Whitson (2010). An example of the end of the era is Deeanne Gist's *Fair Play* (2014), which takes place during the 1893 Chicago World's Fair. Examples of inspirational romance series set in the 19th century are Mary Connealy's Wild at Heart series, Laura Frantz's Ballantyne Legacy books, and Tracie Peterson's Lone Star Brides.

Regencies

Inspirational Regency romances, which take place between 1811 and 1820, when George Augustus Frederick, Prince of Wales, ruled England as regent in place of his mentally ill father, King George III, are becoming more common. This is the time of Jane Austen. Regency-era romances include such elements as the Napoleonic Wars; social class and financial issues, such as poor or nonaristocratic heroes falling for rich, titled heroines, and vice versa; young girls having their

Season; landed gentry and the workers on their estates; proper manners; vicars; and the *ton* (*le bon ton,* or British high society). Traditional Regency romances (noninspirational) by such authors as Georgette Heyer are almost always "sweet" sensually and have a stricter adherence to the minute details of history than other historical genres. Inspirational Regencies add a faith-based message to the Regency tradition. Examples of inspirational Regencies include *A Heart's Rebellion* by Ruth Axtell (2014), *The Honorable Heir* by Laura Alice Eakes (2014), *The Silent Governess* by Julie Klassen (2009), *The Courting Campaign* by Regina Scott (2013), and *The Baron's Honourable Daughter* by Lynn Morris (2014).

20th Century

There are also inspirational romances set in the 20th century, but to be considered historical, they have to meet the criteria of having a setting at least 50 years before current times. The year 1906 is when Lauraine Snelling's *Valley of Dreams* (2011) takes place. Julie Lessman's *A Hope Undaunted* (2010) is set during the 1920s. Karen Halvorsen Schreck's interracial story, *Sing for Me* (2014), is a Depression-era romance, as is *Wonderland Creek* by Lynn Austin (2011). World War II novels (1939–1945) include *Thief of Glory* by Sigmund Brouwer (2014), which begins when Japan invades Java, and *In Perfect Time* by Sarah Sundin (2014), which takes place on the European front.

Contemporary Inspirational Romances

Contemporary inspirational romances take place during the present day. Events and issues are modern: PTSD, disabilities, illness, death, poverty, homelessness, divorce, and runaways. Characters have a wide range of occupations and might be military personnel, librarians, ranchers, firefighters, police officers, doctors, attorneys, chefs, artists, writers, athletes, homemakers, or actors. Examples of contemporary inspirational romances are *Take a Chance on Me* by Susan May Warren (2013), *Found* by Karen Kingsbury (2006), *Sand Castles* by Nancy Gotter Gates (2009), *Fall from Grace* by Kristi Gold (2007), *Together with You* by Victoria Bylin (2015), and *Larkspur Cove* by Lisa Wingate (2011). Series include Becky Wade's Porter Family novels.

Inspirational Romantic Suspense

Some inspirational romantic suspense novels can be historical, like Elizabeth Camden's 2012 *Against the Tide,* in which a female translator for the U.S. Navy is recruited to fight the opium trade, or Jill Marie Landis's 2011 *Heart of Lies,* which takes place in 1870s New Orleans. However, contemporary inspirational romantic suspense titles far outnumber the historical. Contemporary inspirational suspense titles include *Home by Dark* by Marta Perry (2012), *Deceived* by Irene Hannon (2014), *Remember to Forget* by Deborah Raney (2007), *Hostage in Havana* by Noel Hynd (2011), *Lie for Me* by Karen Young (2011), *Dangerous Passage* by Lisa Harris (2013), and *The Promise* by Beth Wiseman (2014). Inspirational romantic suspense series include Valerie Hansen's Capitol K-9 Unit series, DiAnn Mills's FBI: Houston series, and Colleen Coble's Sunset Cove novels.

Amish Romances

One of the popular subsets of inspirational romances is the Amish romance, which can be either contemporary or historical. Common themes are a simple life, forbidden love, family, and obedience to religious and community dictates. Amish novels, jokingly referred to as "bonnet rippers" or "bonnet and buggy books," are considered inspirational romance only if the element of romantic love is stronger than that of community and culture. The beginning of the popular trend of Amish romances is attributed to Beverly Lewis's novel *The Shunning*, published in 1997. Amish romances include *His Love Endures Forever* by Beth Wiseman (2012), *Sarah's Son* by Jerry S. Eicher (2008), *Never Far from Home* by Mary Ellis (2010), *The Healing* by Wanda E. Brunstetter (2011), *Blessings* by Kim Vogel Sawyer (2008), *Anna's Crossing* by Suzanne Wood Fisher (2015), *The Witnesses* by Linda Byler (2014), and *When the Soul Mends* by Cindy Woodsmall (2009). Amish romances are also in series: Adina Senft's Amish Quilt novels, Sarah Price's Amish Retellings of Jane Austen, and Shelley Shepard Gray's Sisters of the Heart.

Humor in Inspirational Romances

There are humorous books as well as serious books in the inspirational romance market. In 1998, Waterbrook Press published the humorous Time for Laughter series. These books came with a "giggle guarantee." Titles included *Love on the Run* by Shari MacDonald (Salinger Sisters #1) and *Say Uncle* by Suzy Pizzuti (Halo Hattie's Boarding House #1). Humorous faith-based books can be found in both contemporary and historical varieties. *Married 'Til Monday* by Denise Hunter (2015), *The Accidental Bride* by Jen Turano (2012), *Tried and True* by Mary Connealy (2014), *Heavens to Betsy* by Beth Pattillo (2005), and *Always the Baker, Never the Bride* by Sandra D. Bricker (2010) are a few recent examples. Humorous series include Tracy Victoria Bateman's Drama Queens, Cathy Marie Hake's Only in Gooding, and Mary Ann Hathaway's Jane Austen Takes the South.

Switchover Authors

Some authors in the secular romance market decided to begin writing for the inspirational market instead. One example is Jill Marie Landis, a popular historical romance writer, who moved to the inspirational market with her historical Irish Angel series—*Heart of Stone* (2010), *Heart of Lies* (2011), and *Heart of Glass* (2011). Another is Margaret Brownley, who wrote western historical romances, such as *Rawhide and Lace* (1994), as well as steamy contemporary romances like Harlequin Temptation's *Body Language* (1998), Harlequin Blaze's *Pure Temptation* (1998), and *Private Lessons* (1998). Brownley now writes historical titles for the inspirational market, such as her Undercover Ladies series, which began with *Petticoat Detective* (2014), the story of a female Pinkerton agent in the 19th century. Other writers of secular romances not only switched to writing for the inspirational market but also rewrote their back titles to be faith-based stories. For example, Lori Copeland wrote a humorous series of historical western romances about three con-artist sisters who end up with three vastly different husbands—*Promise Me Today* (1992), *Promise Me Tomorrow* (1993), and *Promise Me Forever* (1994). In 2013, she rewrote these titles for the inspirational market and combined them into one book, *Sisters of Mercy Flats*. Robin Lee Hatcher's suffragist book, *Kiss Me, Katie* (American series, book #4, 1996), was rewritten for the inspirational market as *Catching Katie* (2004).

Publishers of Inspirational Romances

In 1998, Harlequin published three titles a month in its inspirational romance line, Steeple Hill. By 2015, Harlequin was releasing at least a dozen inspirational romance titles every month, and the market shows no sign of slowing down. Inspirational romances are one of the few Romance genres to be published in a trade-paperback format (approximately 8" × 5", with production values superior to those of the mass-market paperback, such as glossy covers and higher quality paper). There are also titles in standard mass-market paperback format (approximately 4" × 7"), as well as e-books, hardcover books, and large-print versions of titles. The popularity of inspirational romances can be seen by the number of publishers in this area. The following list includes a recent title:

- Abingdon Press (*The Road to Paradise* by Karen Barnett, 2017)
- Baker Publishing Group
    - Bethany House (*Treasured Grace* by Tracie Peterson, 2017)
    - Revell (*To Follow Her Heart* by Rebecca DeMarino, 2016)
- Barbour Publishing
    - Shiloh Run Press (*The Blessing* by Wanda E. Brunstetter, 2017)

- Hachette Book Group/Hachette Nashville
  - FaithWords (*Someday Home* by Lauraine Snelling, 2015)
- Harlequin
  - Love Inspired (*The Dad Next Door* by Stephanie Dees, 2017)
  - Love Inspired Historical (*An Unlikely Mother* by Danica Favorite, 2017)
  - Love Inspired Suspense (*Amish Rescue* by Debby Giusti, 2017)
- HarperCollins
  - Avon Inspire (*Her Secret* by Shelley Shepard Gray, 2017)
  - Thomas Nelson (*Whenever You Come Around* by Robin Lee Hatcher, 2015)
- Harvest House Publishers (*A Goose Creek Christmas* by Virginia Smith, 2016)
- Howard Books (*Tiffany Girl* by Deeanne Gist, 2015)
- New Hope Publishers (*Restoring Love* by Jennifer Slattery, 2017)
- Tyndale House Publishers (*Crisis Shot* by Janet Cantore, 2017)
- WaterBrook Multnomah Publishing Group (*Grace and the Preacher* by Kim Vogel Sawyer, 2017)
- Whitaker House (*The Cautious Maiden* by Dawn Crandall, 2016)
- Zebra (*Marrying Jonah* by Amy Lillard, 2017)
- Zondervan (*The Writing Desk* by Rachel Hauck, 2017)

Awards for Inspirational Romance

The top award for romance novels is the Romance Writers of America's RITA, which recognizes "excellence in romance fiction." Until 1990, the RITA was called The Golden Medallion. The first Golden Medallion was awarded in 1982. The first Golden Medallion awarded for an inspirational romance wasn't until 1985, with Charlotte Nichol's *For the Love of Mike*. In 1986, this was followed by *From This Day Forward* by Kathleen Karr. However, from 1987 to 1994, the Romance Writers of America gave no awards in the inspirational romance category. This run was broken in 1995, when Francine Rivers won best inspirational romance for *An Echo in the Darkness*. Rivers won the next two RITAs for inspirational romance: *As Sure as the Dawn* (1996) and *The Scarlet Thread* (1997). RITAs awarded for the last decade and a half in the inspirational romance category are:

2016 *A Noble Masquerade* by Kristi Ann Hunter
2015 *Deceived* by Irene Hannon
2014 *Five Days in Skye* by Carla Laureano
2013 *Against the Tide* by Elizabeth Camden

2012   *The Measure of Katie Calloway* by Serena Miller
2011   *In Harm's Way* by Irene Hannon
2010   *The Inheritance* by Tamera Alexander
2009   *Finding Stefanie* by Susan May Warren
2008   *A Touch of Grace* by Linda Goodnight
2007   *Revealed* by Tamera Alexander
2006   *Heavens to Betsy* by Beth Pattillo
2005   *Grounds to Believe* by Shelley Bates
2004   *Autumn Dreams* by Gayle Roper
2003   *Never Say Goodbye* by Irene Hannon
2002   *Beneath a Southern Sky* by Deborah Ranney
2001   *The Shepherd's Voice* by Robin Lee Hatcher
2000   *Danger in the Shadows* by Dee Henderson

The Christy Awards, "Honoring and Promoting Excellence in Christian Fiction," are also important honors for the writers of inspirational romance.

Shelley Mosley

See also: Amish Romances

Further Reading

Faith, Hope, and Love, a Special Interest Chapter of Romance Writers of America. http://www.faithhopelove-rwa.org/. Accessed April 24, 2017.

Reffner, Julia M. "Crossing Over: Christian Fiction Genre Spotlight." *Library Journal,* November 24, 2014. http://reviews.libraryjournal.com/2014/11/books/genre-fiction/christian-fiction/crossing-over-christian-fiction-genre-spotlight/. Accessed April 24, 2017.

International Association for the Study of Popular Romance (IASPR)

The International Association for the Study of Popular Romance (IASPR) is a global organization of students, scholars, readers, authors, and industry professionals dedicated to fostering and promoting the scholarly exploration of Popular Romance Fiction and, more broadly, the logics, institutions, and social practices of romantic love in global popular culture. IASPR is committed to building a community of scholars through open, digital access to all scholarly work published by the Association, by organizing or sponsoring international conferences on popular romance studies and by encouraging the teaching of popular romance at all levels of higher education.

Founded in 2009 by Sarah (Frantz) Lyons and Eric Murphy Selinger, IASPR was born out of the realization that scholars of Popular Romance Fiction and other media often worked not only in isolation but in surprising ignorance of the range of academic work being done around the world on popular romance. The seeds of the organization were planted at the 2007 national conference of the Popular Culture Association/American Culture Association (PCA/ACA), whose Romance area, quiescent for several years, had undergone a quick revival after the establishment of the RomanceScholar listserv, the Romance Scholarship Wiki Bibliography, and Teach Me Tonight, a collaborative blog offering "Musings on Romance Fiction from an Academic Perspective." The presence of scholars from Australia and Europe at the PCA conference, in particular, inspired Lyons and Selinger to plan a new international association—one that would keep this scattered group of academics in touch and would provide an enduring foundation for what promised to be a "third wave" of work on the genre. (In academic circles, the "first wave" of romance scholarship is generally taken to be the foundational work by academics in the 1970s and 1980s; the "second wave," in the 1990s, was marked by contributions from romance authors writing as scholars in their own right, notably in the University of Pennsylvania Press anthology *Dangerous Men, Adventurous Women,* edited by Jayne Anne Krentz.)

Rolled out at the Spring 2009 Princeton Conference on Romance Fiction and American Culture, IASPR held its own First International Conference later that summer in Brisbane, Australia. Five conferences have followed, in Brussels (2010), New York City (2011), York (2012), Thessaloniki (2014), and Salt Lake City (2016), and as of this writing, the seventh conference is planned for Sydney, Australia, in the summer of 2018. Each has gathered up to 60 students, scholars, and industry professionals, sometimes from more than a dozen countries. Financial support for these conferences has come primarily from host universities, but over the years the Romance Writers of America (RWA) has also provided sustained and substantial help as part of that organization's commitment to, as its website explains, "develop and support academic research devoted to genre romance novels, writers, and readers." There are also less visible ties between the two organizations; notably, several members of the IASPR leadership team, including its successive presidents (first Lyons, then Pamela Regis, then Selinger) and its vice presidents (Jayashree Kamble and Belgian scholar An Goris), have also been recipients of a separate, competitive grant from the RWA: the organization's annual Academic Research Grant.

In 2016, IASPR announced its own monetary award: this one not to support new work (as the RWA grant aims to do) but to give recognition to as-yet-unpublished scholarship on popular romance media and/or the logics, institutions, and social practices of romantic love in global popular culture, including the culture of real-world courtship, dating, and relationships. Named in honor and memory of Conseula Francis, an emerging scholar of African American romance and Black love, the award prioritizes essays that address the diversity of, and diversities within, Popular Romance and romantic love culture: for example, diversity of race, ethnicity, gender, religion, class, sexuality, disability, or age. Winners are promised a cash prize (the initial figure is US$250) and publication in IASPR's peer reviewed *Journal of Popular Romance Studies*.

Eric Murphy Selinger

Further Reading

International Association for the Study of Popular Romance (IASPR). http://iaspr.org/. Accessed April 24, 2017.

Ivanhoe (1819)

Sir Walter Scott wrote *Ivanhoe* in 1819, at a time when he had already enjoyed considerable success as the anonymous author of *Waverley* and eight subsequent historical novels with Scottish settings. *Ivanhoe* was a new venture for Scott. It featured an English medieval setting and its subtitle, "A Romance," signaled its alignment with the genre of chivalric romance. The experiment was an immediate success: the first 8,000 copies quickly sold out, and two more editions followed in 1820. *Ivanhoe* became Scott's most popular work. It was regarded for many years as a foundational text for younger readers, and it has engendered numerous theatrical, operatic, and screen adaptations. Over the last century, Scott's digressive prose style has lost currency, and *Ivanhoe*'s popularity has waned, yet many of the novel's dramatic elements still permeate popular culture. Its version of the Robin Hood legend through the figure of the yeoman outlaw, Locksley, has been hugely influential, and its representation of the knightly tournament has been revived in various contexts, including George R. R. Martin's *A Game of Thrones*.

Ivanhoe is set in the 1190s—more than a century after the Norman conquest—but it compresses events of a much wider time frame and depicts a world in which tensions between Normans and Saxons shape English political and social life. The Crusader King, Richard I, is absent from England when the novel begins, and his brother John plots for the throne and allows his Norman nobles to oppress the country. The hero of the novel, Wilfred of Ivanhoe, returns from the

Crusades in disguise, and the central plot concerns his quest to obtain his father's forgiveness for deserting the Saxon cause, while battling his nemesis, the Templar knight Brian de Bois-Guilbert. Eventually, Ivanhoe regains his inheritance, his honor, and the hand of the Saxon Lady Rowena, thanks in large part to the assistance of a Jewish moneylender, Isaac, and his beautiful, heroic daughter, Rebecca.

Once the plot of *Ivanhoe* gathers momentum, it delivers a lively tale of romantic adventure. Its episodes of high drama and sexual tension feature chivalric combats, a besieged castle, disguised identities, and numerous abductions and rescues. The two heroines—fair and dark—are relentlessly pursued by amorous and conflicted Norman knights yet remain steadfastly attached to the hero. The more fanciful aspects of the narrative are balanced, nevertheless, by Scott's incisive social observation and his comedic treatment of key characters, such as Ivanhoe's father Cedric, the Saxon chief Athelstane, and even King Richard himself. At its broadest level, *Ivanhoe* is about the origins of English cultural identity and the resolution of Norman-Saxon conflict as symbolized by the union of Ivanhoe and Rowena. Scott complicates his vision of a chivalric past, however, by allowing lowly commoners and persecuted Jews to feature prominently as heroic actors, while his ostensible hero is rendered passive through injury for much of the tale. The novel critiques Christian hypocrisy and religious oppression, and the happy ending is tempered by the exclusion of Rebecca, whose faith precludes her from marriage with the hero and from a life within England itself.

Rosemary Gaby

Further Reading

Cooper, Joan Garden. "The Rebel Scott and the Soul of a Nation." *Scottish Literary Review* 2, 2 (Autumn–Winter 2010): 45–63.

Lumsden, Allison. "Walter Scott." In *The Cambridge Companion to English Novelists*, edited by Adrian Poole, 116–131. Cambridge, UK: Cambridge University Press, 2010.

J

Jane Eyre (1847)

Written by Charlotte Brontë under the pseudonym Currer Bell, *Jane Eyre: An Autobiography* was first published in 1847 in London by Smith, Elder, & Co. It was not Charlotte Brontë's only novel, but it was one of her most successful, and remains her most famous. Essentially, it is the story of a young woman's journey as she moves from a singularly cruel, loveless childhood to blissfully wedded, self-assured adulthood, growing in understanding and compassion as she matures. Issues of class and gender bias, educational value, and religious hypocrisy permeate this gently supernatural Victorian story that features a smart, determined heroine who manages to come out on top, despite the odds. The bare bones of the story are as follows:

Orphaned as a baby, Jane is taken in by her Aunt and Uncle Reed and raised with her three cousins until she is 10. But as she is constantly reminded that she is just a poor, undeserving relative, her life is anything but happy, especially after her kindly uncle dies. So when a fight with her bullying cousin John results in her being sent to Lowood, a school for charity girls, she hopes for the best. But the minister who runs the school is cruel and miserly, and when his penury results in a typhus epidemic—and the death of a dear friend of Jane's—he is replaced, and the situation improves. Over the years Jane excels in her academics—and also drawing ability—and eventually becomes a teacher at the school.

After teaching for several years, Jane longs for a new challenge, which she finds at Thornfield Hall as governess to 10-year-old Adèle Varens. Thornfield's grim, somewhat gruff owner, Edward Rochester, is a challenge, as well, although from their first, inauspicious meeting when Rochester falls from his horse, there is a connection between them that continues to grow and eventually results in their engagement. However, from the first, Jane has been troubled by deranged laughter and noises from the upper floors, supposedly caused by a strange servant, Grace Poole. But when it turns out that Grace is actually the caretaker for Rochester's violent, mad wife—the source of the laughter—and that Rochester is still married, Jane flees, angry, disillusioned, and broken-hearted.

Jane finds refuge at Marsh End (Moor House), the home of clergyman St. John Rivers and his sisters—who turn out to be her cousins—and gradually puts her life back on track. St. John plans to become a missionary to India and wants capable, sensible Jane as his wife. She almost agrees—and then she "hears" Rochester calling her and leaves Moor House and goes to find him.

Thornfield has burned to the ground, a result of Rochester's mad wife's actions, and Rochester has lost a hand and an eye in trying to save her—a futile effort because she commits suicide by jumping from the roof. Jane finds him living at Ferndean, and after they have made their peace, they soon marry.

Ten years later, as Jane writes this account, she relates that Rochester has partially regained his sight, they are still happily married, and they have a new son.

Together with Ann Radcliffe's *The Mysteries of Udolpho* and, more recently, Daphne du Maurier's *Rebecca*, *Jane Eyre* is a precursor of the modern historical Gothic—those stories that authors like Victoria Holt, with her chilling, suspenseful *Mistress of Mellyn,* made so popular during the 1960s. Although there are many differences—one being that *Jane Eyre* was actually written as a contemporary, while Holt and other 20th-century authors using Victorian settings were writing historicals—many of the elements found in *Jane Eyre* are also common to a number of modern Gothics. The vulnerable, orphaned heroine supporting herself as a governess; the brooding, troubled Byronic hero; the bleak, isolated setting on the windswept moors; the dark, foreboding atmosphere with hints of the paranormal; the first-person narrative from the heroine's point of view; and, of course, the mad woman in the attic are only a few examples.

Jane Eyre is a compelling, complex story that can be read on many levels and has contributed much to literature in general and to the Gothic romance in particular. Although surely a woman's journey, this story is also a romance, complete with the protagonists' romantic arc and the requisite happy ending. Should there be any doubt, the first line in the last chapter of the book, "Reader, I married him," pithy and memorable, says it all.

Kristin Ramsdell

Further Reading

Berg, Maggie. *Jane Eyre: Portrait of a Life*. Boston: Twayne Publishers, 1987.

Jane Eyre: An Autobiography. http://www.gutenberg.org/files/1260/1260-h/1260-h.htm. Accessed August 4, 2017.

Pfordresher, John. *The Secret History of Jane Eyre*. New York: Norton, 2017.

Journal of Popular Romance Studies (JPRS)

The *Journal of Popular Romance Studies* is a peer-reviewed interdisciplinary journal dedicated to exploring Popular Romance Fiction and, more broadly, the logics, institutions, and social practices of romantic love in global popular culture. Founded in 2010, *JPRS* (pronounced "Jeepers" in the Romance Studies community) is the official publication of the International Association for the Study of Popular Romance (IASPR), a scholarly organization dedicated to fostering the study and teaching of popular romance media at all levels of higher education.

Like other IASPR projects, the journal has aimed to bridge the gap between academic and general audiences for scholarship on romantic fiction, film, TV, music, comics, and advice literature, as well as studies of courtship, dating, relationships, and the consumer culture of love. To reach this mix of audiences, *JPRS* has been made available without subscription as an "open access" journal, published online at http://jprstudies.org.

Even as it aims for a general readership, however, *JPRS* aspires to a level of rigor that has often been lacking in academic accounts of popular romance media, especially popular romance fiction. As Pamela Regis (*A Natural History of the Romance Novel*) argued in an early issue of the journal, academic discussions of the genre have often relied on overgeneralizations, with unsubstantiated claims and factual errors cropping up in scholarly journals and books from university presses. All essays in *JPRS* are, therefore, subject to at least two double-blind evaluations (that is, neither the author nor the reviewer knows the other's identity) and to the close evaluation of the journal's editors. A lineup of the *JPRS* editorial board includes most of the 21st century's most important popular romance scholars, including academics from the United States, the United Kingdom, Europe, and Australia.

Many of the most important recent monographs on popular romance fiction appeared in some early form in *JPRS,* including work by Catherine Roach (*Happily Ever After: The Romance Story in Popular Culture*), Hsu-Ming Teo (*Desert Passions: Orientalism and Romance Novels*), and Jin Feng (*Romancing the Internet: Producing and Consuming Chinese Web Romance*). The journal has also included special issues on thematic topics like "Romancing the Library" and "Queering Popular Romance," on regional traditions ("The Popular Culture of Romantic Love in Australia"; "Love in Latin American Popular Culture"), and on individual authors ("Nothing but Good Times Ahead: A Special Forum on Jennifer Crusie").

In keeping with its mission to support the teaching of popular romance, the "Teaching and Learning" section of *JPRS* has offered peer-reviewed articles on teaching popular romance in a variety of contexts: American courses on women's literature; German courses on British Regency and desert romances; Australian courses on authorship, genre, and textual analysis in popular fiction; and so on. Also of use to students are the journal's substantial interviews with authors in and around the Romance genre, including Beverly Jenkins, Susan Elizabeth Phillips, Anne Gracie, and French romance reviewer/journalist Agnès Caubet, founder of the important webzine *Les Romantiques*.

Scholarship on popular romance fiction dates back to the 1970s and 1980s, but until *JPRS* was established, this work had no dedicated home in the academy. The publication of this journal thus marks a turning point in the maturation and institutionalization of such scholarship as a legitimate and lively academic field.

Eric Murphy Selinger

Further Reading

International Association for the Study of Popular Romance. http://iaspr.org/. Accessed April 21, 2017.

JPRS: Journal of Popular Romance Studies. http://jprstudies.org/. Accessed April 21, 2017.

JPRS

See Journal of Popular Romance Studies (JPRS)

L

Language in Romance

Romance constitutes a heterogeneous genre that has greatly evolved and changed over the centuries. As Regis stresses, "the term 'romance' is confusingly inclusive, meaning one thing in a survey of medieval literature, and another, not entirely distinct, in a contemporary bookstore" (19). The explanation behind this heterogeneity lies in the fact that Romance, like most genres, is closely connected to its cultural and historical context, taking the form of an unofficial "contract" (Radford, 9) between the romance author and his/her readers. Radford's choice of legal terminology to describe the author-reader relationship successfully captures the obligations that bind both sides: the author has to satisfy the expectations of the readership by following the dominant norms of the genre (for example, in popular romance by providing a happy ending), while the readership is expected to buy the book and help build the author's reputation. This author-reader cultural contract "changes over the centuries, adapting itself to the contemporary needs of both writers and readerships and evolving into the expectations of twenty-first century [. . .] romance readers" (Lamprinou, "Translated Romances," online).

Focusing on 20th- and 21st-century popular romances, this article will present some of the linguistic elements that authors employ to enable their readers to identify with the literary characters, experience intense emotions, and escape their insecurities and ambiguities, with the authors' ultimate aim being the fulfillment of readers' expectations. However, before continuing, it has to be stressed that although escapism plays a considerable role nowadays in the experience and study of popular romances, this is not the sole contribution of this subgenre: as Saunders (540) explains, the idealized world of romances is created out of stereotypes, patterns, and motifs; however, it is enriched with realistic details, and it is often used as a form of social comment, exactly through the contrast of the real and the ideal element. In other words, romances may allow their readers to temporarily reside in a more ideal "reality," but the story and plot often reflect the sociocultural changes occurring within a given community, providing scholars with a more comprehensive picture of the context in which these texts were created. This infusion of romances with realistic elements is what Carter and Nash call "realistic unrealism" (99–100), a technique based on the employment of, first, easily recognizable cultural norms and literary traditions that give the reader a sense of familiarity, and, second, realistic details that convince the reader that this version of events could occur in real life. Besides, as Shumway (43) explains, if a book were understood as not carrying any truth, then it would be difficult for the readers to accept its version of love and human relationships.

Starting with a brief discussion of the clichés that may be found in popular romances, Goris (59) mentions that such texts are full of narrative conventions, with Paizis (36) explaining that conventions can be identified in both the narrative structure and the organization of characters. Focusing on the language of narration, Badr Al-Bataineh (30) maintains that in popular romances, and popular fiction in general, the vocabulary used is "marked" and "unordinary" (30). For instance, "instead of the simple, straightforward 'go' or 'run,' in Mills & Boon we have: *dash, rush, fly, hurry, scuttle*" (Badr Al-Bataineh, 32, emphasis by author). Moreover, romance authors tend to use many adjectives and adverbs, especially combined with less-marked lexical units, to indicate emotions, increase the intensity of certain passages, and maintain the reader's interest even when there is practically nothing happening in the text.

The linguistic construction of romance characters also efficiently reflects the careful use of language and the adoption of conventions, as previously mentioned. As Paizis (39) argues, characters are constructed around binary oppositions to communicate symbolic meaning to the reader, a point that can be better understood through Fowler's (56–62) "Madonna"–"whore" opposition: borrowing the idea from the Christian context, Fowler explains that the author always portrays the heroine as the ethical one who works hard and cares for her family, while the female foil is basically the villain who tries to create obstacles to romantic love and leads a parasitic life.

Nevertheless, the qualities of the heroes and heroines are not only stressed through their differentiation from the secondary characters but also through their reaction to serious social issues such as alcoholism, racism, or rape. Following Pearce (535), the various sociocultural changes have led to the evolution of the socioeconomic profile of the heroines, with Talbot adding that it is exactly these changes that have led to the gradual appearance of "tormented," imperfect protagonists (109). The employment of language to construct less-ideal characters together with the mention of everyday social issues and the occasional enrichment of the texts with measurements, technical specifications, and even the names of existing companies, helps the authors construct a semirealistic world where, however, things happen as they ought to happen.

Another important element in the construction of this unrealistically real world is dialogue, which plays a dual role: first, as Badr Al-Bataineh (38) explains, dialogue makes the interaction between the characters more realistic because it is closer to what Rimmon-Kenan describes as "showing" (107), meaning, providing a direct account of events that renders the existence of a narrator less apparent. Moreover, especially in the case of dialogues, many authors go to great lengths to compensate for the loss of suprasegmental elements (for example, pitch of voice, stress) in their texts, often adopting different typographical means such as italics or capital letters to stress certain words and/or phrases and help their readers reconstruct the dialogue in their heads. The second role that dialogue fulfills, according to Paizis, is related to the power differential between the hero and heroine. Dialogue is perceived as a "site of struggle" (34) but also, toward the end of romances, as a sign of the heroine's victory since the man is finally forced to talk and declare, not just show, his love.

An important element that helps the readers' identification with the characters and their escapism is the stirring of emotions, meaning the skillful manipulation of language to reveal the characters' emotions, which in their turn will affect readers' participation in the story. It would be a mistake to reduce the emotional variety that is apparent in romances to just different expressions of love. Love may seem to dominate, but Baker (63) argues that negative emotions like frustration and anxiety are crucial to the plot. Otherwise, if the protagonists do not suffer, there will be no suspense, and the readers will not be satisfied to the same extent in the end, when everything is resolved. This point is, arguably, verified by Bigey's (online) study on several aspects of the vocabulary of French romantic novels: as she explains, the verbs revealing negative emotions (for example, trahir, désoler) are usually more frequent than those expressing positive ones.

Romance writers employ an entire arsenal of linguistic strategies to describe, or let their characters reveal, emotions. These strategies vary greatly, including the employment of simple nouns or adjectives that may either directly express the emotional situation of a character (for example, he felt angry) or have some connotative meaning that the readers can easily decode. For instance, Bigey (online) argues that different parts of the human body, such as the hands or mouth, may carry such connotations and allow the readers to infer the emotions that the author is trying to convey. While the employment of lexical units is perhaps the simplest linguistic strategy for the verbalization of emotions, romance authors additionally employ a variety of figures of speech ranging from stereotypical metaphors to personifications, rhetorical questions, allusions, alliterations, and parallelisms, just to mention a few. Moreover, as the construction of emotions is ultimately a complicated task, even the length of sentences may be of significance in the communication of emotions, while, depending on the author's skills and the limitations of each language (and culture), an author may masterfully use verb tense and aspect, diminutives and augmentatives, as well as offensive language, to ensure that the readers understand and even co-suffer with the protagonists. To this end, the author must also not ignore the importance of emotional intensity, which is crucial in the reader's experience of the text.

A final point that connects emotions with narrative conventions is Radway's notion of "repetition" (196). As in the case of narration, whereby a number of motifs are often repeated, romance authors have the habit of producing different sentences that communicate the same emotion, possibly through different linguistic strategies. The reason behind that, according to Radway, is that romance authors do not take for granted that their readers will immediately comprehend the emotion that they are trying to convey, and, consequently, even when a passage clearly evokes a certain emotion, they feel the need to add a sentence that unmistakably expresses or describes that emotion. This technique, in accordance with genre norms and reader expectations, minimizes the readers' interpretative efforts to ensure that the readers will experience reading as pleasure and not work. However, even if popular romances are created so as to be easily decoded, this does not mean that popular romance readers are passive: "as they imagine the characters and events described and invest in them emotionally, romance readers actively participate in constructing the story" (Lamprinou, "Translated Romances," online), collaborating, thus, with the authors.

Having discussed some basic linguistic aspects of the romance text, the last part of this article will briefly focus on the language of the paratext, most important, the front cover. Following both Paizis (51) and Goris (59), studying the case of category romances, the cover plays a considerable part in the publisher's effort to produce an easily recognizable product. As the front cover is usually the first thing that a potential reader and buyer of the book encounters, the packaging and, of course, the title have to advertise within seconds the text that follows and identify it as a certain type of novel; besides, as Vanderbilt stresses, "so much of a book's fate depen[ds] on everything but what is between its covers" (91). The linguistic message of the title has to capture the essence of the book but still communicate a promise of excitement and a feeling, be memorable, and spark the reader's curiosity. What would have happened, for instance, to Margaret Mitchell's *Gone with the Wind* had she elected to call it "Ba! Ba! Black Sheep," a title that was indeed on her list of possibilities? Following Vanderbilt (97), in today's market, a poorly titled book could easily vanish, taking into consideration that "the average shelf life of a book is between milk and yogurt" (Trillin, 87).

These are the linguistic aspects of romance novels that greatly contribute to the "honoring" of the author-reader contract and reflect reader expectations. It is important to remember that so much depends upon the author's skillful manipulation of the language to communicate familiar motifs or raise emotions and, finally, lead the reader step by step to a universe where the ideal harmoniously coexists with reality.

Artemis Lamprinou

Further Reading

Badr Al-Bataineh, Afaf. "The Modern Arabic Novel: A Literary and Linguistic Analysis of the Genre of Popular Fiction, with Special Reference to Translation from English." PhD diss., Heriot-Watt University, 1998.

Baker, Donna. *Writing a Romantic Novel and Getting Published.* London: Teach Yourself, 1998.

Bigey, Magali. "Stratégies Narratives et Mises en Scène Lexicales du Roman Sentimental Sériel Contemporain : l'Auteure, le Corps et les Sentiments [Narrative Strategies and Lexical Choices in Contemporary Category Romance: the Author, the Body and the Feelings]." *Belphégor* 7, 2 (2008). http://etc.dal.ca/belphegor/vol7_no2/articles/07_02_bigey_strate_fr.html. Accessed April 25, 2017.

Carter, Ronald, and Walter Nash. *Seeing through Language: A Guide to Styles of English Writing.* Oxford: Basil Blackwell, 1990.

Cawelti, John G. *Adventure, Mystery and Romance: Formula Stories as Art and Popular Culture.* Chicago: The University of Chicago Press, 1976.

Fowler, Bridget. *The Alienated Reader: Women and Popular Romantic Literature in the Twentieth Century.* London: Harvester Wheatsheaf, 1991.

Goris, An. "Romance the World Over". In *Global Cultures,* edited by F. A. Salamone, 59–72. Newcastle upon Tyne, UK: Cambridge Scholars, 2009.

Lamprinou, Artemis. "A Study on the Cultural Variations in the Verbalisation of Near-Universal Emotions: Translating Emotions from British English into Greek in Popular Bestseller Romances." PhD diss., University of Surrey, 2012.

Lamprinou, Artemis. "Translated Romances: The Effect of Cultural Textual Norms on the Communication of Emotions." *Journal of Popular Romance Studies* 2 (2011). http://jprstudies.org/2011/10/%e2%80%9ctranslated-romances-the-effect-of-cultural-textual-norms-on-the-communication-of-emotions%e2%80%9d-by-artemis-lamprinou/. Accessed April 27, 2017.

Paizis, George. *Love and the Novel: The Poetics and Politics of Romantic Fiction.* Basingstoke, UK: Macmillan, 1998.

Pearce, Lynne. *Romance Writing.* Cambridge, UK: Polity, 2007.

Radford, Janice. "Introduction." In *The Progress of Romance. The Politics of Popular Fiction,* edited by Janice Radford, 1–20. London: Routledge and Kegan Paul, 1986.

Radway, Janice A. *Reading the Romance: Women, Patriarchy and Popular Literature.* London: Verso, 1987.

Regis, Pamela. *A Natural History of the Romance Novel.* Philadelphia: University of Pennsylvania Press, 2003.

Rimmon-Kenan, Shlomith. *Narrative Fiction: Contemporary Poetics*. London: Routledge, 1983.

Saunders, Corinne. "Epilogue: Into the Twenty-first Century." In *A Companion to Romance: From Classical to Contemporary,* edited by C. Saunders, 539–41. Oxford: Blackwell Publishing, 2004.

Shumway, David R. *Modern Love: Romance, Intimacy, and the Marriage Crisis*. New York: New York University Press, 2003.

Talbot, Mary M. "'An Explosion Deep Inside Her'. Women's Desire and Popular Romance Fiction." In *Language and Desire: Encoding Sex, Romance and Intimacy,* edited by K. Harvey, 106–22. London: Routledge, 1997.

Trillin, Calvin. *Quite Enough of Calvin Trillin: Forty Years of Funny Stuff*. New York: Random House, 2011.

Vanderbilt, Arthur T. *The Making of a Bestseller: From Author to Reader*. Jefferson, NC: McFarland and Company, 1999.

Lesbian, Gay, Bisexual, Transgender, and Queer/Questioning (LGBTQ) Romance

Lesbian, gay, bisexual, transgender, and queer/questioning (LGBTQ) Romance is a subtype of romance literature. It is a general umbrella term for romance fiction that includes characters that identify as LGBTQ, and in which the plot or themes are related to issues of gender or sexual identity and sexual orientation. LGBTQ Romance is also often referred to as GLBTQ Romance, placing "gay" at the front of the acronym. "A" for alternative is sometimes added, and the subtype as a whole may be referred to as Queer or Alternative Romance. Aside from involving issues of gender and sexuality, LGBTQ romances do not usually differ markedly from heterosexual romance fiction. LGBTQ Romance spans many subgenres, such as Historical, Young Adult, Erotic, Science Fiction, Paranormal, and Suspense. A contentious aspect of defining romance is the assertion made by some that it requires heterosexual characters. In 2006, there was debate in the world of Romance Fiction after a letter to the editor of Romance Writers of America's (RWA) *Romance Writers Report* suggested that Romance be defined as being between a man and a woman (Lynch, Sternglantz, and Barot). However, such contestations are limited, and generally Romance containing LGBTQ characters and themes is considered a legitimate subtype of the genre. Note: RWA's definition of Romance remains inclusive, requiring only "a central love story and an emotionally satisfying and optimistic ending" (Romance Writers of America).

Like other romance subtypes, the main caveat for defining works in this area is a predominant focus on love between the protagonists, rather than a focus on the erotic or other issues such as social problems or inequality. Though often concerned with issues of sexual attraction, levels of sexually explicit content vary throughout different works of LGBTQ romance as in other areas of romance fiction. Narratives that focus specifically on romance between gay male characters are often referred to in the industry as "m/m." Similarly, stories focusing on lesbian female characters are known as "f/f." Romance between more than two characters, for example, when a love triangle is occurring or when three or more characters are in a relationship together, is referred to as "ménage" or polyamorous romance. Ménages may or may not qualify as LGBTQ Romance, depending on the nature of the romantic connections depicted and whether these are related to same-sex attraction or transgender themes.

The acronym LGBTQ (and similar derivations) and grouping of the terms *gay, lesbian, bisexual, transgender,* and *queer* has its historical foundation in the emergence of Western gay and lesbian activism in the 1960s and 1970s. Following the Stonewall riots of 1969, a social movement involving both gay and lesbian communities arose, and these terms came to be used in greater conjunction with one another. Over time, as the language around sexual and gender identity diversified, *bisexual* and *transgender* were also conceptually grouped with *gay* and *lesbian,* predominately in terms of challenging society's heterosexual norms and expectations. While there are distinct and contrasting identities included under this acronym, LGBTQ is used broadly to describe sexuality and gender that is alternative to heterosexual partnership or identification. For example, the definition of *transgender* and its grouping with *gay, lesbian,* and *bisexual* is often contested, though most commonly used to refer to persons who identify as a gender different from that which they were given at birth.

In relation to Romance Fiction, LGBTQ has come to describe stories focusing on characters that have same-sex attraction (be that gay, lesbian, or bisexual) and/or identify as transgender, or novels that revolve around issues of sexual orientation or gender identification. The coming-out process, of understanding and acknowledging one's sexual orientation or identity, may be a major part of the plotline as seen in *Shining in the Sun* by Alex Beecroft (2011), in which the main character, Alec, struggles with his same-sex attraction throughout the novel. Alternatively, coming out may not be a key issue, and the characters' sexual orientation may be assumed and is not a source of central drama as seen in Radclyffe's (2008) *The Lonely Hearts Club,* which focuses on a group of lesbian friends and their various relationships. Similar to the issue of coming out, the transition for transgender characters identifying or appearing as one gender and then identifying and embodying another may be a key part of the romance story, as in *Hawk's Landing* by Carol Lynne (2011) or C. C. St. Clair's (2004) *Morgan in the Mirror.* There are few examples of transgender romance narratives in which the characters identify as transgender without a focus on a transition period or on issues of transition. However, some novels in this category may involve transgender characters who have already transitioned, and tension focuses on revealing this transition to their romantic interest. This is seen in novels such as Brian Katcher's *Almost Perfect* (2009), in which the protagonist Logan struggles to come to terms with his romance for Sage when she comes out to him as a transgender woman. Coming out as transgender, or coming out with a particular sexual identity in relation to this transition, is often central to transgender romance as in other gay, lesbian, and bisexual stories. "Gay for You" (often abbreviated as GFY) LGBTQ Romance refers to plotlines in which one or both of the characters did not previously identify as gay, lesbian, or bisexual but in which same-sex attraction occurs when they fall in love. This is seen, for example, in the plot of *Promises* by Marie Sexton (2010), in which the main character Jared is gay and develops a friendship with straight man Matt, which leads into a deeper romantic relationship. Characters in GFY stories may or may not identify as bisexual. An example of a bisexual romance story is the historical LGBTQ romance *Phyllida and the Brotherhood of Philander: A Bisexual Regency Romance* by Ann Herendeen (2005), which involves a couple who have an open marriage such that the male protagonist has both a wife and a boyfriend. Though polyamorous relations are not essential to defining bisexual romance, such triangles within LGBTQ Romance often suggest complex attractions and romantic feelings across sexes. However, such triangles may also be exclusively gay or lesbian, as seen, for example, in Tessa Cárdenas's *The Strongest Shape* (2009), which follows a romance between three male characters, Scott, Caleb, and Chris.

Though love stories containing gay and lesbian characters and themes have appeared since the early 20th century, earlier works often ended in tragedy and, therefore, have not often been considered part of the Romance genre. One notable example of an early work containing LGBTQ themes is Radclyffe Hall's *The Well of Loneliness* published in Britain in 1928. The novel was highly controversial at the time, for depicting both lesbian and gender-questioning characters and presenting these identities as God-given. Hall's novel ends unhappily, and she pleads to God for greater acceptance of same-sex attraction. Despite this ending, *The Well of Loneliness* has had a large impact on LGBTQ romance writers, activists, and academics alike. However, it was not until the 1950s that LGBTQ themes reached the mainstream, with pulp fiction that included gay and lesbian characters. These often depicted young homosexual lovers whose stories ended in tragedy, violence, and/or heterosexual pairings. Some categorize these pulp novels as romance fiction; however, it may also be argued that LGBTQ Romance did not come fully to fruition until the activism of the 1960s and 1970s.

Often regarded as the first lesbian pulp, Tereska Torres's (1950) *Women's Barracks* is about French female soldiers in World War II. Marijane Meaker's

Spring Fire, which followed in 1952, focused more specifically on a romantic lesbian pairing between characters Mitch and Leda. However, like the majority of LGBTQ pulp of the era, *Spring Fire* had a tragic ending. During this time, pulp involving gay male protagonists also rose in popularity, but often these would also end unhappily. As Sara Ahmed (1) discusses, in the 1950s authors of pulp fiction involving LGBTQ romance were often forced by their publishers to include tragic endings to avoid homosexuality's appearing socially acceptable. But as Ahmed argues, this requirement inadvertently opened up a social arena, albeit limited, for stories to involve gay and lesbian characters. Phyllis Marie Betz (2) similarly contends in *Lesbian Romance Novels: A History and Critical Analysis* that early lesbian romance novels allowed a space for lesbian protagonists to exist, noting that the large body of lesbian novels printed since the days of pulp covers vast territory exploring the lesbian experience. It is sometimes noted that one exception to the unhappy-ending rule for LGBTQ pulp in this era is Patricia Highsmith's (published under the name Claire Morgan) 1952 *The Price of Salt.* However, though it is hinted at the end that the lesbian protagonists Carol and Therese may stay together, this involves Carol's losing custody of her children. Following the limited acceptability of LGBTQ Romance in the 1950s, the 1960s brought a renewed hope for happy endings. In 1962, Ann Bannon published *Beebo Brinker* from her series of the same name, which follows the life of Betty Jean Brinker and her various romantic pursuits with women. Published in 1971, Gordon Merrick's *The Lord Won't Mind* is also a notable example of a gay novel with a more positive ending, a hint at the beginnings of more explicitly romantic (rather than tragic) LGBTQ fiction.

As activism and interest in gay and lesbian identity increased into the 1970s and beyond, greater and more diverse LGBTQ romances were published. However, LGBTQ Romance was confined mainly to smaller publishing houses rather than major ones that did not wish to risk investing in the niche area (Ramsdell, 372). Since the 1980s, LGBTQ romance has increased in scope, with works now extending into many subgenres of Romance fiction. A key source for LGBTQ Romance continues to be independent publishers, particularly those that specialize in feminist and queer interests. Despite the possibility of appeal to wider audiences, LGBTQ Romance remains a niche area. In particular, LGBTQ Romance that includes transgender elements is particularly limited in comparison to a larger body of work that explores gay, lesbian, and bisexual characters and themes. Arguably, the emergence of online publishing has increased the feasibility and capacity to publish diverse subtypes of the Romance genre such as LGBTQ Romance, and there may be an enhanced capacity for transgender story lines to gain greater traction.

Notwithstanding limitations, LGBTQ Romance continues to increase in popularity. The audience for LGBTQ Romance extends beyond those identifying as

LGBTQ, and some works have found mass appeal. For example, although it doesn't have the requisite happy ending, Annie Proulx's (1999) *Brokeback Mountain,* about two cowboys who fall in love (included in her collection of short stories *Close Range: Wyoming Stories*), received high acclaim and popularity after being adapted for screen in 2005. Like its audience, not all authors of LGBTQ Romance are lesbian, gay, transgender, or bisexual. Authors of LGBTQ fiction may or may not identify with a similar gender or sexual orientation to their protagonists. Along with increasing demand for LGBTQ Romance, there are many LGBTQ Romance writers as groups at national, state, and local levels. Formed in 2009, Rainbow Romance Writers is a chapter group of the Romance Writers of America that specifically aims to connect and foster authors of LGBTQ Romance fiction in the United States. The Rainbow Romance Writers also hold the annual Elisa Rolle Rainbow Awards for work in LGBTQ Romance. Other awards exist for LGBTQ writing, notably the annual Lambda Literary Awards, run by the Lambda Literary Foundation, instituted in 1988. These awards have faced some controversy with regard to the Romance genre, however, awarding only lesbian and gay romance awards as well as citing author identification as LGBTQ as important to the awards. Such controversies allude to the difficulties of defining LGBTQ Romance and its various subcategories. Despite its difficult history, LGBTQ Romance remains a burgeoning subtype of Romance fiction.

Hannah McCann

Further Reading

Ahmed, Sara. "Happiness and Queer Politics." *World Picture* 3 (2009): 1–20.

Betz, Phyllis Marie. *Lesbian Romance Novels: A History and Critical Analysis.* Jefferson, NC: McFarland & Company Inc. Publishers, 2009.

Love, Heather. "Transgender Fiction and Politics." In *The Cambridge Companion to Gay and Lesbian Writing,* edited by Hugh Stevens, 148–64. Cambridge, UK: Cambridge University Press, 2010.

Lynch, Katherine E., Ruth E. Sternglantz, and Len Barot. "Queering the Romantic Heroine: Where Her Power Lies." *Journal of Popular Romance Studies* 3, 1 (2012).

Mitchell, Kaye. "Gender and Sexuality in Popular Fiction." In *The Cambridge Companion to Popular Fiction,* edited by David Glover and Scott McCracken, 122–40. Cambridge, UK: Cambridge University Press, 2012.

Naughton, Julie. "Anything Goes: Focus on Romance: Fall 2012." *Publishers Weekly* 259, 46 (2012): 27ff.

Rainbow Romance Writers. A Special Interest Chapter of the Romance Writers of America. http://www.rainbowromancewriters.com/. Accessed April 3, 2017.

Ramsdell, Kristin. *Romance Fiction: A Guide to the Genre,* 2nd ed. Santa Barbara, CA: ABC-CLIO, 2012.

Romance Writers of America. "About the Romance Genre." https://www.rwa.org/p/cm/ld/fid=578. Accessed April 3, 2017.

Weise, Don. "The Hard-Core in Gay & Lesbian Publishing." *Publishers Weekly* 256, 22 (2009): 17ff.

Libraries and Popular Romance Fiction

One of the roles of a public library is to loan popular materials to customers. In the pursuit of loaning materials to customers, libraries must consider what types of materials to include in their collections, how to acquire those collections, and how to make the items findable by customers. Each of these considerations plays a role in how public libraries treat the fiction genre of Romance.

The Romance genre is an over $1 billion industry, and in 2015 romance book sales made up approximately 29 percent of all fiction titles sold, according to Nielsen's "Romance Reader's by the Numbers." Given the large readership, it is no wonder that public libraries that carry romance novels see high circulation numbers for the genre; however, it is also important to remember that there are library systems that have collection-development policies that impact the purchase of romance titles.

Formats

One factor in the purchase of romance fiction for public libraries is the collection and/or material types a library will purchase. For instance, there are library systems that do not purchase mass-market paperback materials as they are considered an ephemeral collection type. With many romance titles published only in mass-market paperback, this means that these titles are not being purchased as often by libraries that purchase hardcover fiction only. By not having the romance titles available for customers to check out, the library will not show high romance-fiction circulation.

Though some library systems will not purchase mass-market paperback titles using their collection budgets, most will accept and add donations of mass-market paperback items. By relying solely on donations, libraries that do not purchase mass-market paperback titles are unable to ensure all titles of a particular romance series are available for checkout to customers. Also, reliance on donations for popular romance titles means titles are coming available well after they are published. In this case, libraries have to rely on customers' purchasing and reading the title prior to donating it to the library collection. This means, often, that the titles are outdated and not as current as what is being sold by booksellers.

By not having many of the popular romance titles available, the relevance of the entire romance collection is limited. Customers who are routinely unable to find the titles they are looking for at the library start going other places for titles. With the low cost of mass-market paperback titles, romance readers are able to purchase titles they are looking for without undue hardship; therefore, once a reader stops using the library for their romance fiction needs, they are unlikely to come back.

Another area where mass-market paperback titles and thus romance titles are treated differently from hardcover materials is in the cataloging. Since mass-market paperbacks are often deemed ephemeral and often are donated rather than purchased, less staff time is spent on the cataloging of these materials. Often, these titles are added haphazardly and without detailed catalog information. Detailed catalog information is used by librarians to inform future purchasing decisions, and without that information for romance titles, they are often overlooked when compared to genres that have detailed catalog information. Additionally, by not adding much (if any) catalog information, libraries prevent customers from determining which mass-market paperback romance titles a library has available. This limits the circulation numbers for the genre as customers who are unable to find what they are looking for will not borrow these items from the library.

Romance fiction is not published only in the mass-market paperback format; it is also published in hardcover, large print, audiobook, and trade paperback. In these formats, libraries do typically purchase romance titles; however, these formats represent a limited number of the titles published each year in the Romance genre. Looking only at the Romance Writers of America's statistics of those romance fiction titles sold, hardcover titles make up only 1.4 percent, and trade paperbacks make up 11 percent; the remainder are sold as e-books and mass-market paperbacks. In addition, when these titles in these formats are purchased for library collections, they are done so with the full catalog records, and they are not treated differently from other fiction titles.

Shelving Locations

Where romance titles are physically shelved is another factor in public-library collections. There are a number of ways to organize fiction titles, either as a large group, in distinct genre subcategories, or with all mass-market paperback titles separate from the regular fiction collections. If a library shelves its romance fiction titles separately from other fiction, it is easier for the customer to find the materials they are looking for on the shelf. Additionally, it makes it easier for library systems to determine usage of the genre; therefore, these systems are better able to indicate how much should be spent on Romance Fiction based on circulation statistics.

If a system does not separate out the romance collection from other fiction titles, librarians still have the option of using genre labels on a print book or audiobook spines to indicate classification. Again, adding the Romance genre label can make it easier for customers to identify books in the Romance genre that they might want to read. However, unless the cataloging specifically indicates these titles are romance fiction, circulation statistics may not be able to show the percentage circulation of romance fiction in both the print collection and the audio collection.

Shelving mass-market paperback fiction separate from hardcover and trade-paperback fiction can also make it more difficult for customers to find the romance titles they want to check out. Libraries can choose to use the genre labels to help identify romance titles in these separate sections, but unless these are specifically cataloged to indicate they are romance fiction titles, the usage statistics may not be useful when looking at what genres to purchase.

E-books

E-books are another format in which libraries purchase romance titles. This format is purchased at much the same rate as other fiction titles. All of the large publishers are represented in the e-book market for libraries. Though they all offer different price points, checkout limits, and purchase options, these publishers are making their titles available to librarians that purchase titles in Overdrive, CloudLibrary, and/or Axis 360. With the expansion of e-book collection dollars in many library jurisdictions, collection-development librarians are able to purchase more romance titles than they may be allowed to in their other collections (due to collection-development policies that restrict purchases of mass-market paperbacks). Most mass-market paperback titles are published as e-books; therefore, these titles are accessible to libraries in this format.

In the catalog entries for the e-book platforms, detailed information is available that indicates genre information so libraries are able to keep track of usage of the Romance genre. Most libraries also put e-book information in their online public-access catalogs, and circulation statistics are also tracked there, which allows for romance usage to be determined.

E-book romance titles also do not have the same limitations in shelving that print materials do. Libraries are able to set up special collections on the e-book platforms highlighting specific collections. Additionally, all three platforms offer read-a-like recommendations that show customers similar books to the one they are looking at, which can further showcase the Romance genre and increase accessibility of these titles.

Self-Publishing

With the uptick in self-publishing by authors of all genres, including Romance Fiction, libraries have to determine which self-published titles should be purchased. Many library collection-development policies indicate that titles purchased for the library collection will have positive peer reviews. For titles that are self-published, this requirement can make inclusion in a library collection difficult as the review sources for self-publishing are not as great as for traditionally published titles. In addition, the ease of purchase of self-published books can present difficulty for libraries, as many have contracts with Brodart, Ingram, or Baker & Taylor, which do not necessarily carry self-published titles. For those self-published titles that are available in e-book format only, it is dependent upon what the e-book platforms have available for purchase. These considerations all make it difficult for self-published romance fiction to be carried in libraries.

Erin Christmas

Further Reading

"Romance Readers by the Numbers." Nielsen.com. http://www.nielsen.com/us/en/insights /news/2016/romance-readers-by-the-numbers.html Accessed May 25, 2018.

"Romance Statistics." Romance Writers of America RWA.org. https://www.rwa.org/p/cm /ld/fid=580. Accessed February 24, 2017.

Linked Books

Linking books into duets, trilogies, and longer series has become a popular practice in the Romance genre. Individual romances connected by characters, setting, themes, or artifacts are written, promoted, and marketed as a group. Although linked in some way, the novels are not necessarily written in fixed chronological order, nor are they necessarily contiguous or interdependent by plot. Also, a series may or may not have an extended plotline (for example, mystery, secret, or something that needs resolution) that will be coherent across multiple books, providing intermediate conclusions in each volume but saving the ultimate solution for the final book in the series. Some series are tightly connected; others are more loosely related. While these trilogies, quartets, or octets are essentially self-contained miniseries, each volume must also stand alone to tell a separate, usually romantic, story. Linked romances are found in all the Romance subgenres—Historical, Contemporary, Romantic Suspense, Paranormal, and Inspirational.

Single-title linked romances are discrete stories rather than episodic chapters of a soap opera: "each is a separate window into the same largely fictional world" (Laurens, 1). Linked series tend to be written by a single writer, which allows for connectivity and continuity in style and tone. The first in the series usually introduces the tone and metastory for the whole series. For example, Mariah Stewart's Dead series, beginning with *Dead Wrong* (2004), is connected by its subplot: the first heroine's daughter was kidnapped by an ex-husband. The backstory is expanded in each volume, but that primary plotline is not resolved until the final installment.

Janet Dailey's Calder series, beginning with *This Calder Sky* (1981), is generally considered one of the first series of this type. Dailey's "story about a large ranching family" revolves around the comings and goings of the occupants and visitors at the Calder ranch in Montana and reaches saga proportions through its span of generations (Dailey, para. 1). On the other hand, the editors of *The Official Nora Roberts Companion* claim that Roberts "essentially pioneered the idea of doing linked series" in romance (319), with the duet for Silhouette, *Reflections* and *Dance of Dreams* (1983).

There are three basic ways to create series: spin-offs, serials, and sequels. A spin-off takes an existing character, setting, or concept from one novel and creates a new plot or situation. Cathy Maxwell begins her Cameron Sisters series with *The Temptation of a Proper Governess* (2004); the Camerons are not introduced until the second book, *Price of Indiscretion* (2005), as secondary characters. Each succeeding book is spun from a minor character of the previous one, and earlier primary figures remain as supporting characters. The final installment of the Cameron Sisters series, *In the Highlander's Bed* (2008), introduces the heroine of the first book in the Maxwell's Scandals and Seductions series, *A Seduction at Christmas* (2008).

A serial follows one particular character through several different, mostly unconnected, self-contained episodes. Lauren Willig's Pink Carnation series (2005–2015) is connected by a modern-day historian who continues to research the activities of the Regency Era Pink Carnation and friends. Eve and Rourke in Nora Roberts's In Death series (1995–) are serial characters whose relationship develops over installments. Suzanne Enoch's Samantha Jellicoe series (*Flirting with Danger* [2005–2007]) is more episodic. They are, in essence, continuous narratives released in successive installments.

Sequels involve one continuing story, usually in a finite number of volumes. While each is a self-contained story, the ultimate climax and resolution comes in the last volume. The main plot must be introduced in the first episode to give meaning to the rest. This type of series is best read in sequence for full understanding. Tracie Peterson and Judith Pella's Ribbons West trilogy (1998–-2000) continues their Ribbons of Steel trilogy (1997–1998); both should be read in sequence to truly understand the entire story line.

The most prevalent method of linking novels is through recurring characters. Book-hopping characters in Romance are not new. Georgette Heyer didn't write "series," but *These Old Shades* (1926) is the story of Alastair and Léonie; *Devil's Cub* (1932) is the story of their son, Dominic, and his eventual wife, Mary, who are the grandparents of Lady Barbara in *An Infamous Army* (1937). *An Infamous Army* also features characters from Heyer's first Regency romance, *Regency Buck* (1936). Heyer's linked books also illustrate one of the dangers of concatenation: pacing chronological time. The action of *These Old Shades* occurred in 1755; based on age, *Devil's Cub* couldn't be earlier than 1779, and *An Infamous Army*, concerning the Battle of Waterloo, is 1814. Not enough time has elapsed for the stated ages of Heyer's characters and the years to make sense.

Frequently, the connecting characters comprise large families, so the series develops the stories of siblings. Julia Quinn follows the eight children of Edmund and Violet Bridgerton in her Bridgerton series (2000–). Each child gets her/his own story, but the series as a whole tells the story of the whole family. Unmarried siblings appear as supporting characters, but once married, they have only cameos. A series based upon a family may concern one generation, like the Bridgertons (although Quinn has recently begun writing prequels to this series), or may include several generations. Johanna Lindsey's Malory-Anderson family chronicles (1983–) follows the siblings and cousins of an extended generation. These kinds of connections allow writers to explore a variety of multiple and overlapping relationships.

Less frequently, there is a continuing character who moves through several books like a serial character. The significance of a recurring character like Violet Bridgerton, or Wulfric Bedwyn of Mary Balogh's Slightly series (2003–2004), is determined by whether or not it develops over time. *Emily Goes to Exeter* (1990–1992) begins Marion Chesney's Travelling Matchmaker series, featuring spinster Hannah Pym.

Characters may also be associated through groups and organizations. Jo Beverly's Company of Rogues (beginning with *An Arranged Marriage,* [1999]) is a dozen boys who met at school and formed a brotherhood of protection; Lisa Kleypas's Wallflower series (2004–2008) is a group of friends; Kleypas further signifies the connection through thematic titles incorporating the seasons. Susan Elizabeth Phillips follows several members of a professional football team, the Chicago Stars. The Arcane Society is a secret society devoted to paranormal research, which connects a dozen novels by Jayne Ann Krentz and both of her pseudonyms, Amanda Quick and Jayne Castle, spanning historical, contemporary, and futuristic subgenres. Each novel adds more information about the past, present, and future of the society.

Perhaps the second most common linking device is setting or location. These places tend to feature transient, multiple-occupancy settings: shops, hotels, ranches, small towns, or schools. Robyn Carr's Virgin River series (2007–2014) revolves around individuals living in and moving through a small town. Linda Lael Miller's McKettrick family series (2002–2012) follows an overarching story line on an Arizona ranch but also features several closed trilogies within the whole series. Christine Feehan's Dark series (2005–) involves a race of telepathic "vampires" located in the Carpathian Mountain region. Debbie Macomber's Blossom Street (2004–2014) series is connected through the characters' interactions at the yarn store and other shops on the street. Susan Wiggs's Lakeshore Chronicles series (2006–) revolves around the inhabitants of Avalon, a small town in the Catskills; the prominent Bellamy family also serves to connect individual books. In this sort of shared world, the main characters differ from book to book; previous and future characters make brief or extended appearances. The emphasis is on the location and community.

Books may also be linked through theme or artifact. Eloisa James's Fairy Tales series has no connecting characters; rather, the series is linked by the connotations of the line "once upon a time." However, James has also written three related e-book novellas that develop secondary characters in other fairy-tale archetypes. Artifacts that link stories tend to be associated with magic or superstition. Karen Hawkins's St. John series (2002–2005) is connected by a talisman ring: the one with the ring will be the next to be married. Hawkins also has a more complex series beginning with a curse and revolving around an Egyptian amulet, the McLean-Hurst series (2007). The common thread of Kat Martin's Necklace trilogy (2004–2006) is the mystique attached to a pearl-and-diamond necklace.

The number of books in any series may vary. The individual writer determines whether the series is open or closed. A closed series is a specific number of books, planned from beginning to end (for example, Mary Balogh's Bedwyn series), and acts as a sort of TV miniseries. An open series allows for any number of books to be spun off or for the development of secondary or location-determined characters (for example, Stephanie Laurens's multigenerational Cynster family saga or Jo Beverly's Malloren series). Trilogies and quartets are the most popular, but series can range anywhere from duets to well over 20 titles. Often, one trilogy will function as a prequel to another, as in Joan Johnston's Frontier trilogy, which acts as a prequel to her more contemporary Bitter Creek series.

Some series have become so extensive and have achieved such a level of complexity that they result in the development of family trees, maps, character profiles, and "companions." Diana Gabaldon wrote *The Outlandish Companion* (1999), illustrating and augmenting her Outlander series, which features time travel and contemporary and historical themes, as a "quick reference" and "source of information and insight" into the world and characters (xxix). *The Official Nora Roberts Companion* (2003) is a guide to and compendium of Roberts's work and career, including essays about Roberts and her books. A sort of combination of both is Stephanie Laurens's *The World of Stephanie Laurens* (2011), which acts as a guide to the Cynster and the Bastion Club series. Most romance writers who write series have information on their websites discussing the creation and development of their series.

The practice of linking romances allows romance writers to design worlds involving multiple books and "a virtual web of connections" that extends the fictional world beyond the covers to explore what happens happily-ever-after (James). Readers are drawn into a community and are allowed to get to know a group of characters who are friends, family, enemies, and neighbors and to become invested in the complexities of a world different from or similar to their own. The result is a broader, more consuming experience for the reader.

Maryan Wherry

Further Reading

Dailey, Janet. "Calder Series." Janet Dailey: The Official Website-Books List. http://www .janetdailey.com/books-list/. Accessed April 25, 2017.

Gabaldon, Diana. *The Outlandish Companion*. New York: Delacorte, 1999.

James, Eloisa. "Much Ado about You." Eloisa James Website. http://www.eloisajames .com/bookshelf/ado.php. Accessed April 25, 2017.

Laurens, Stephanie. *The World of Stephanie Laurens*. New York: HarperCollins, 2011.

Little, Denise, and Laura Hayden, eds. *The Official Nora Roberts Companion*. New York: Berkley, 2003.

Listservs

See Romance Listservs

Literary Agent

See Agent

M

Mail-Order Bride Plot

A common convention in the Romance genre is that of the romantic couple being forced into close proximity and learning to care for each other. One of the more popular themes that employs this method is that of the mail-order bride, a practice that gained acceptance during American western expansion in the 19th century.

People traveled west for a variety of reasons, and given the harsh environment and unpredictability of the land, many of those people were single men. They may have been tempted westward by the promise of large tracts of land, by various gold rushes, or simply by the appeal of starting over and making a new life in a post–Civil War time.

Even as the West continued to become more settled, dangers still existed. Various Native American tribes were still a threat to many settlers, as were nature's elements. For instance, a harsh winter could doom whole, healthy families. For that reason, many women would have been hesitant to travel west, especially since it meant giving up the comforts that the eastern half of the country could and did provide. Prior to the completion of the Transcontinental Railroad after the Civil War, this travel would have been particularly perilous for anyone heading west, but especially for women. Travel would have meant stagecoaches and wagons on various trails and exposure to outlaws, unfriendly Natives, and the elements.

Once men settled the West, carving out a piece of land to ranch or farm, or perhaps setting up a business, the drive to pass that legacy on to children would be of importance. Also, the loneliness that western settlers must have experienced, being isolated with no close neighbors for miles, would have been a strong determining factor. With few single women, men took to writing back East, sometimes to family or their church. The use of advertisements in local newspapers and magazines was also employed. Interested women would then write letters to the men, and a courtship correspondence would develop. Sometimes photographs were exchanged, and eventually, if both parties were agreeable, the woman would travel west to marry a man she had never met in person.

Women entered into these arrangements for a variety of reasons, and the aftermath of the Civil War would have certainly escalated the need to escape present circumstances. Many women entered into mail-order marriages because they themselves were adventurous and wanted to see what the West had to offer. Still more, much like men traveling west, may have wanted to escape unpleasant memories in the East and start over.

Certainly, marrying a man with nothing to reinforce that decision other than a few letters would have been a risky proposition. However, women who felt they had no other course of action, whether because of undesirable home situations or Civil War rebuilding difficulties, saw these marriages as a way to start over, build a new life, have children, and hopefully live in harmonious marriages.

The bravery and desperation from which such arrangements must have developed are what has led romance writers, particularly historical western romance writers, to return to the mail-order bride theme time and again. Given that novels, and romance novels in particular, need conflict to drive the plot and romantic relationship forward, authors tend to avoid simple, straightforward stories that simply feature man and woman corresponding, woman arriving out West, and the couple getting married and living, hopefully, happily ever after. There is always some sort of wrench thrown into the works that the romantic couple must navigate.

A popular variation that authors have employed in the past is the hero who does not realize he has a mail-order bride arriving—until, of course, she steps off the train or stagecoach. This is usually the work of a well-meaning family member or neighbor who feels the hero needs to, or should, settle down. This naturally forces our couple into close proximity, and in turn, they must deal with the fallout of being duped.

Other popular turns include either hero's or heroine's not being what the other expected. The hero is expecting a genteel Southern belle, and instead he gets a rough-around-the-edges tomboy. Perhaps someone other than the heroine wrote the letters that spurred forth the hero's marriage proposal.

Another way this theme has been adapted by romance writers is by having the expected groom be unavailable. The heroine arrives out West only to discover that the man she had intended to marry is now dead, or perhaps while traveling west to meet her prospective husband, she finds herself falling in love with another man, the hero.

While certainly a staple among historical western romance writers, the mail-order bride plot is a natural offshoot of the marriage of convenience, which has a long, rich history within contemporary romance stories. Variations on these themes in contemporary settings include a romantic couple meeting online or through home-swap style vacations, or perhaps marrying out of response to some other circumstance, such as the terms of a will or to secure custody of a child.

The continued popularity of mail-order bride stories continues to intrigue romance readers in part because of the amazing possibilities and questions those stories raise. What must a woman's life be like for her to make so desperate a choice? Why would she choose to marry a man she has never met and settle in territories with little to no modern conveniences, where danger is a very real threat?

The answer is that she must be either incredibly desperate or incredibly brave. The history of the Romance genre is built on the backs of strong, brave, and interesting heroines—extraordinary women who do what needs to be done to secure the life and happiness that they deserve, and that all women want in their lives. While the idea of becoming a mail-order bride would be extreme for many women, a lack of options and the desire for something more is what tends to drive historical romance heroines—which, in turn, makes for fascinating writing and reading.

Wendy Crutcher

Further Reading

Enss, Chris. "Getting Personal on the Frontier." *Wild West* 27, 5 (February 2015): 44–51.

Enss, Chris. *Hearts West: True Stories of Mail Order Brides on the Frontier*. Guilford, CT: TwoDot, 2005.

Zug, Marcia A. *Buying a Bride: An Engaging History of Mail-Order Matches*. New York: NYU Press, 2016.

Marriage of Convenience Plot

Marriage of Convenience (MOC) plots in Romance Fiction all start and end the same way. Readers typically find out at the beginning of MOC romance plots that the hero and heroine get married early on in the story rather than at the end as in many romance stories. Couples in MOC plots get married because of the legal and/or social status that comes with becoming husband and wife rather than because they have fallen in love. At the end of MOC stories, the hero and heroine, once legally wedded to fulfill some other motive or obligation, remain married because they have fallen in love and end up living "happily ever after" (HEA). The predictability of the beginning and end of the romance novel is also what makes these stories so appealing to readers. "Although fiction genres, especially the romance, are often criticized because they follow a type of pattern and adhere to certain conventions, it is this very predictability that is so attractive to most genre readers, including romance readers" (Ramsdell).

MOC stories have been written across various periods from Regency to contemporary. From Georgette Heyer, writing MOC romance stories during the mid-20th century, to more modern writers, such as Miranda Neville in the 21st century, the MOC plot has remained a popular plotline that romance writers continue to revisit and create new stories for. As the plot title implies, the characters get married because it is convenient. The marriages in these stories are formed based on some sort of mutual benefit gained from the partnership rather than romantic compatibility. The goal of marriages of convenience is for the characters to gain some sort of benefit, whether that entails an inheritance, social status, or something else, rather than falling in love.

The reasons why the hero and heroine get married vary based on a few common tropes: inheritance and avoiding scandal. Marriages of convenience to gain inheritance are perhaps one of the most popular MOC plotlines. Mary Balogh, Mary Jo Putney, Lisa Kleypas, and Julia Quinn are just a few of a number of romance writers who have written MOC stories based on this plotline. This is a popular theme found in many historical romance novels in which either the hero or the heroine find themselves in the predicament of needing to be married to gain access to their inheritance (Putney, Quinn). Contemporary versions of this MOC plot typically include the hero and heroine's getting married primarily for the social status that marriage brings. In *The Cinderella Deal* by Jennifer Crusie, the hero, Lincoln Blaise, is a history professor who is trying to find a job at a college where they prefer their faculty members to be married. To impress his potential employer, he bribes his neighbor, Daisy Flattery, to enter into a fake engagement with him. What starts out as one weekend of a fake engagement ends up becoming a marriage of convenience, which then ends with both Lincoln and Daisy falling in love and living "happily ever after."

The marriage of convenience to avoid scandal occurs typically when the hero and heroine are found in a compromising position at the beginning of the story and are usually forced to marry each other to avoid the scandal in society. Several historical romance novels employ this version of the MOC plot in which one of the protagonists (typically the hero) is a member of the peerage and ends up marrying the heroine to avoid scandal within their society (*An Arranged Marriage* by Miranda Neville, *The Last Rogue* by Deborah Simmons, *Silver Linings* by Maggie Osborne). Contemporary romances also employ this type of MOC plot (*It Had to Be You* by Susan Elizabeth Phillips, *Tall Tales and Wedding Veils* by Jane Graves), and the hero and heroine end up getting married to avoid scandal and scrutiny from their family and/or society. In both historical and contemporary examples, an element of peer pressure is involved from either the hero or the heroine, or characters from outside the relationship.

Regardless of how the couple ends up married in the first place, the end result of marriage of convenience stories is that the couple lives happily ever after. The "satisfactory ending" is a necessary component defining Romance Fiction (Ramsdell). This satisfactory ending is what keeps readers of Romance Fiction engaged. Readers remain interested in reading MOC stories because they anticipate the HEA, and similarly like other romance fiction plots, they enjoy reading how the protagonists reconcile any differences they may have toward each other and eventually fall in love. To this end, although a number of romance fiction stories end with the two protagonists deciding to get married, MOC plots all eventually end with the hero and heroine deciding to remain married after falling in love with each other and living their own happily ever afters.

Suggested Reading List

Historical

Dancing with Clara (1995) by Mary Balogh
The Temporary Wife (1997) by Mary Balogh
The Convenient Marriage (1952) by Georgette Heyer
A Civil Contract (1961) by Georgette Heyer
Devil in Winter (2006) by Lisa Kleypas
In for a Penny (2011) by Rose Lerner
Confessions of an Arranged Marriage (2012) by Miranda Neville
Silver Lining (2000) by Maggie Osborne
The Bargain (2011) by Mary Jo Putney
Brighter than the Sun (2004) by Julia Quinn
The Last Rogue (1998) by Deborah Simmons

Contemporary

The Cinderella Deal (1996) by Jennifer Crusie
Tall Tales and Wedding Veils (2008) by Jane Graves
Duncan's Bride (1998) by Linda Howard
It Had to Be You (1994) by Susan Elizabeth Phillips

Tammi Kim

Further Reading

Marriages of Convenience. All About Romance, last modified February 2010. http://likes books.com/moc.html. Accessed April 27, 2017.

Mussell, Kay, and Johanna Tuñón. *North American Romance Writers*. Lanham, MD: Scarecrow Press, 1999.

Ramsdell, Kristin. *Romance Fiction: A Guide to the Genre*. Englewood, CO: Libraries Unlimited, 1999.

Medieval Romance, Classic

Medieval romance, as the term is understood today, refers to the body of vernacular verse and prose adventure literature that was popular throughout Western Europe from the mid-12th century to the 17th century. Featuring knightly adventure, fantasy settings, and a quest undertaken to win the hand of a woman, the genre is both expansive and enduring, with its themes reworked and imitated throughout the Middle Ages and beyond.

The word *romance* derives from the Old French phrase "mettre en romanz," meaning to translate into the vernacular. The earliest vernacular romances were composed at the French-speaking English court of Henry II and Eleanor of Aquitaine in the mid-12th century. These early French romances circulated in the countries of Western Europe and were translated and imitated in different languages. Romances in Middle High German began to emerge in the late 12th century, Spanish romances in the first half of the 13th century, Middle English romance in the mid-13th century, and romances in Italian from the late 13th century. More than 500 romances survive, drawn from almost every medieval European language, including Middle English, Old French, Anglo-Norman, Italian, German, Occitan, Dutch, and Spanish (Kreuger, 4). While these linguistically distinct romances continued to use common characters and stories, as the genre developed, these universal themes and motifs were reworked and refined in accordance with national and social settings.

The subject matter of medieval romance ranges widely, from the legends of classical antiquity to the Crusades or the chivalric court of Arthur and his Knights of the Round Table. The key central theme of romance is the narrative journey of human life, from birth to death, exile and return, accusation and forgiveness, abandonment and restoration. Romances are the stories of long-suffering mothers, rebellious daughters, desperate fathers, and daring sons, and the relationships between them. Filled with the imagery of daily life—clothing, feasts, dancing, songs, war, travel, prayer, sex—medieval romances offer an unparalleled insight into medieval culture and society. Romances end happily, concluding tumultuous narrative events with the reconciling of estranged family members, the return of the long-lost son, the marriage of two lovers, the birth of heirs, the conversion to

Christianity, the conquering of lands, or the resumption of heritage. The subject matter of medieval romance resonates with that of the modern popular romance.

In the 12th century, a French cleric called Jean Bodel categorized the emerging genre of Romance into three subject groupings that are still used today, although numerous romances resist such simple classification. These are: the Matter of France, or the Carolingian cycle, which centers on Charlemagne and his military exploits; the Matter of Britain, or the Arthurian cycle, consisting of the romances of Arthur and his court; and the Matter of Rome, or the Cycle of Rome, which retold stories of Roman antiquity. Later 20th-century critics added the "Matter of England" as a fourth category, denoting those romances with English heroes or derived from English legend.

Romances often feature fantastic and sometimes monstrous creatures, such as giants, fairies, demons, wild animals, and magical intervention or supernatural characters, such as the Green Knight in the famous English romance *Sir Gawain and the Green Knight* (c. 1350–1400). Romance narratives are often hyperbolic, featuring solo knights decimating armies 10,000-strong or riding vast distances with no apparent difficulty or fatigue. The language and emotion of romance is often similarly exaggerated, as characters profess deep and instant desire for each other with no apparent courtship or contact having occurred (the medieval equivalent of love at first sight).

The questing nature of many romances meant that their geographical span was impressive, encompassing both real and imagined geographies and peoples. Romances move from local villages, fields, and gardens to the national geographies of cities and the routes traveled to reach them and beyond, to international and imaginative geographies of deserts, oceans, forests, and mountains. Romances made use of the exoticism of contemporary travel literature; John Mandeville's *Travels*, a fantastic and largely fictionalized travelogue first published in the mid-14th century, was arguably the most popular travel narrative of the later Middle Ages. Many parallels can be drawn between Mandeville's narrative and the content of many romances. In fact, as has been argued elsewhere, it is possible that romance itself could have functioned as imaginative travel literature, in the same way that modern romances act as armchair travel for some readers today.

A significant proportion of European romances features violent confrontations between Christians and Muslims, and a smaller number feature romantic relationships between different religious groups. For example, the Middle English romance *The King of Tars* (early 14th century)—a popular medieval romance that appears, in different forms, in many European languages—deals with the monstrous issue of a sexual union between a Christian princess and a Muslim sultan. It has been suggested that medieval romances featuring crossreligious relationships are precursors to the modern sheikh romance (Burge; Teo).

Some romances have didactic or penitential themes, for example, the 13th-century Spanish romance *Libro de Alexandre* (c. 1220–1240), about the life of Alexander the Great, or the popular Middle English romance *Sir Isumbras* (early 1300s), which tells the story of a knight who is offered either happiness in old age or in youth, and who must work to restore his wealth and heritage after choosing the first option. Other romances, particularly those of the later Middle Ages, focus on the family, exploring inheritance and lineage, representations of different kinds of families, and their crises. Such romances reveal the modification of subject matter in accordance with contemporary concerns. Romances also gently satirized the very chivalric values they appeared to uphold, exposing their contradictions and indicating the tension between such aristocratic ideals and medieval social reality. Romance can thus be subversive, commenting on and reworking formulas, in the same way that modern romances have often been considered to do.

Medieval romance was, as modern romance is often taken to be, a genre of tribute, imitation, and innovation. Medieval romance authors regularly drew on other romances and their themes, either translating and modifying existing texts or reusing their characters, placing them in new situations and settings. One of the most influential romance authors was Chrétien de Troyes, the creator of the Arthurian romance, whose influence on the romance genre is difficult to overstate. It was Chrétien who first introduced the love affair between Lancelot and Guinevere in his romance *Lancelot, Le Chevalier de la Charrette* (c. 1170–1177), and his unfinished romance *Le Conte du Grail* (c. 1179–1191) hints at what was to become, in later romances, the Quest for the Holy Grail.

Another influential French romance, one of the most widely read texts in the Middle Ages, was the *Roman de la Rose*, an allegorical romance started by the court poet Guillaume de Lorris between 1125 and 1145 and completed by Jean de Meun between 1268 and 1285. At almost 22,000 lines, the poem is an extended rumination on the art of courtly love and contains several motifs that were to become common in romance and love poetry, including dreams and idealized springtime settings. Almost 300 extant manuscripts of the poem survive: an astonishing number, indicating the popularity of the work. The *Roman de la Rose* was translated into English as the *Romaunt of the Rose* in part by Chaucer in the 14th century and was widely influential on the Romance genre in England.

Medieval romance also draws its source material from other literary genres, including *chanson de geste:* epic poetry; saints' lives; chronicles; and fabliaux—bawdy, sexually explicit stories that originated in mid-12th-century France. Indeed, it is possible to categorize the same texts as simultaneously belonging to several different genres. The *Roman de la Rose* is a good example of the genre blurring that occurs in so many medieval romances. Containing a range of themes and styles, Lorris and Meun's text can be classified as a romance, even as it also contains elements of the dream vision and the allegorical verse, revealing how genre boundaries and literary categories that, to modern eyes appear fixed, were more fluid in the Middle Ages. Romance also relies heavily on adaptation and imitation, as many romances reuse familiar characters (such as Arthur's knights) and survive in different versions and languages, indicating the transnational migration of romance stories and the tenacity of their appeal.

The majority of surviving medieval romances are found in manuscript collections, although a number of late-medieval romances survive only in print. These manuscripts were often expensive and served for the education and entertainment of the whole family, often containing historical accounts, recipes, saints' lives, and religious narratives alongside romances. While the medieval romances we know today are those that have survived in manuscripts and printed books, it is likely that many more romances have been lost forever due to the poor survival rate of manuscripts and the oral transmission of romances.

A longstanding debate has considered the nature of romance consumption, and most current thought agrees that romance was both an oral and a written tradition, intended to be read aloud in some places at some times and set down by scribes at others, or in early print books, which paved the way for mass dissemination of such narratives. Of course, the oral tradition of romance is largely lost to us today, although evidence for such a culture can be seen in manuscript variations between different versions of romances, and in textual references to minstrels and performance. Similarly, while the cast of romance is generally chivalrous, featuring knights and ladies, kings and queens, and attendant stewards and squires, its readership encompassed all levels of medieval society; the vibrant and diverse themes of romance would have appealed to both the lowest servant at a feast and the most senior members of the royal court. Indeed, it was the growth of the newly literate mercantile and gentry classes that contributed to the popularity and longevity of the Romance genre.

In many ways, the connections between medieval and modern romance are not obvious. Featuring an aristocratic male protagonist, focusing on his adventures, and having romantic encounters usually incidental to the overall plot, surviving medieval romances seem to correspond more to adventure fiction rather than romance as we understand it today. Nevertheless, medieval romance stands as the literary antecedent of today's popular romance novel and has been widely influential on postmedieval literature: Miguel de Cervantes satirized chivalric romance in *Don Quixote* (1605/1615), claimed as the first modern novel; William Shakespeare's late romance plays share generic features of medieval romance; and Tennyson's *Idylls of the King* (1842) retold the popular story of King Arthur's court. Medieval romance has done more to shape modern ideas of the "medieval" than any other medieval genre, conjuring images of questing knights, dragons, maidens, and adventure that were widely appropriated by 18th- and 19th-century Romantic artists and authors, introducing us to such characters as Tristan and Isolde, and Arthur and the Knights of the Round Table. Indeed, it is to this long tradition of reworking, revisiting, and revaluing the medieval romance that modern popular Romance owes its origins.

Amy Burge

See also: Arthurian Romance

Further Reading

Burge, Amy. "Desiring the East: A Comparative Study of Middle English Romance and Modern Popular Romance." PhD diss., University of York, 2012.

Cooper, Helen. *The English Romance in Time: Transforming Motifs from Geoffrey of Monmouth to the Death of Shakespeare*. Oxford: Oxford University Press, 2004. Identifies key motifs of the medieval romance and traces the development of romances through the Middle Ages and beyond.

Database of Middle English Romance. http://www.middleenglishromance.org.uk. Accessed April 26, 2017. Online resource created by the University of York with plot summaries, manuscript, and date information for most Middle English romances.

Fuchs, Barbara. *Romancei*. New York: Routledge, 2004. Offers a brief, accessible overview of the Romance genre and its transformations from classical antiquity to the present day.

Goodman, Jennifer R. *Chivalry and Exploration, 1298–1630*. Woodbridge, UK: Boydell Press, 1998.

Heffernan, Carol Falvo. *The Orient in Chaucer and Medieval Romance*. Woodbridge, UK: D. S. Brewer, 2003.

Krueger, Roberta L., ed. *The Cambridge Companion to Medieval Romance*. Cambridge, UK: Cambridge University Press, 2000. Provides a chronological list of European romances and chapters on the genre.

Mencal, Maria Rose. *The Arabic Role in Medieval Literary History: A Forgotten Heritage*. Philadelphia: University of Pennsylvania Press, 1987.

Rouse, Robert. "Walking (Between) the Lines: Romance as an Itinerary/Map." In *Medieval Romance, Medieval Contexts*, edited by Rhiannon Purdie and Michael Cichon, 135–47. Cambridge, UK: D. S. Brewer, 2011.

TEAMS Middle English Texts Series. http://d.lib.rochester.edu/teams. Accessed April 26, 2017. Online resource by the University of Rochester providing free online access to many medieval romance texts.

Teo, Hsu-Ming. *Desert Passions: Orientalism and Romance Novels*. Austin: University of Texas Press, 2013.

Metalious, Grace (1924–1964)

Grace Metalious neé DeRepentigny was an American author made famous by her racy exposé of life in small-town New England, *Peyton Place* (1956). Born on September 8, 1924, to struggling French Canadian parents in the mill town of Manchester, New Hampshire, the young DeRepentigny married her childhood sweetheart George Metalious at the age of 18. The couple had three children. After years of working low-paid jobs to support her family, Metalious began writing her first novel while her husband was attending the University of New Hampshire.

Peyton Place was published by small New York publisher Julian Messner in 1956 and was to go on to overtake *Gone with the Wind* (1936) as one of the best-selling novels of the 20th century. The novel follows "the lives of three women who, in different ways and for different reasons, come to terms with their identity as women and as sexual persons in the repressive atmosphere of small-town America" (Cameron, xi). *Peyton Place* was biting in its exposure of the hypocrisy upon which small towns thrive. It was also unusually earthy in its depiction of sex, a feature of the novel that led to its banning in Indiana, Canada, Italy, and Australia (xvi–xvii).

Peyton Place was made into a film in 1957 and from there into an extraordinarily popular TV show that ran from 1964 to 1969. It was followed by a handful of other books—*Return to Peyton Place* (1959), *The Tight White Collar* (1961), and *No Adam in Eden* (1963). However, none of these books was to replicate the success of Metalious's first novel.

Grace Metalious's personal life was turbulent, marked by an ongoing struggle with alcoholism and a propensity toward excess that was compounded by the success of her novel. After the publication of *Peyton Place*, the author embarked on an affair with disk jockey T. J. Martin, whom she married in 1958, three days after her divorce from Metalious was finalized. In 1960 she divorced Martin and remarried Metalious. Happiness with her first husband proved to be elusive, and by the end of her life, Metalious had taken up with an Englishman, John Rees. She died on February 25, 1964, at age 39 in Beth Israel Hospital, Boston, from cirrhosis of the liver.

Claire Knowles

See also: *Peyton Place*

Further Reading

Brier, Evan. "The Accidental Blockbuster: *Peyton Place* in Literary and Institutional Context." *Women's Studies Quarterly* 33, 3/4 (2005): 48–65.

Callahan, Michael. "*Peyton Place's* Real Victim." *Vanity Fair*, January 22, 2007. http://www.vanityfair.com/news/2006/03/peytonplace200603. Accessed April 26, 2017.

Cameron, Ardis. "Open Secrets: Rereading *Peyton Place*." In *Peyton Place*, by Grace Metalious, vii–xxxvi. London: Virago Press, 1999.

Miner, Madonne. *Insatiable Appetites: Twentieth Century American Women's Bestsellers.* Westport, CT: Greenwood Press, 1984.

Toth, Emily. *Inside* Peyton Place*: The Life of Grace Metalious.* Jackson: University Press of Mississippi, 1991.

Mills & Boon

In 1908, Gerald Mills, Educational Manager at Methuen, and Charles Boon, General Manager also at Methuen, decided to set up their own imprint. They moved into an office at 29 Whitcomb Street, Covent Garden, London, and in 1909 began what Charles Boon called their "adventure." In a harbinger of things to come, their first publication was the romance *Arrows from the Dark* by Sophie Cole, who was to write 65 novels for them over three decades. But their list in the early years offered all genres of fiction and also included school textbooks, travel guides, art books, memoirs, plays, and politics, child care, crafts, and cookery books. Their authors included P. G. Wodehouse, Jack London, E. F. Benson, and Denise Robins. From the start, Mills & Boon was to give many women authors the opportunity to earn a considerable amount of money, and made stars of some of them. In the 1930s, Sophie Cole bought a fur coat, which she referred to as her "Woolworths' coat," as it had been bought on the earnings from her sales in that store.

By the outbreak of World War I, Mills & Boon was well established and showing a respectable profit. But in 1916 Jack London, who was a mainstay of the firm's earnings, died, and both Gerald Mills and Charles Boon were called to war. This left the firm in the hands of Margaret Boon, and they returned after the war to a firm that, in effect, had to be built up again. In 1928 Mills died and the firm faced bankruptcy, since a considerable portion of the company rested in his estate. It was rescued by the company secretary, Joseph W. Henley, who had inherited money from his father and who now bought 750 shares, becoming a director three days after Mills's death.

With Henley at the helm and Charles Boon's ability to find excellent authors, by 1935 profits had doubled. Authors reaped the benefit of Charles Boon's decision to concentrate on Romance Fiction for the circulating libraries, with print runs averaging seven thousand per title. That period saw some quite sexy novels, often set in an exotic foreign location, dealing with such topics as adultery, pre-marital sex, and a woman's need to earn her own living. During this period, Mills & Boon, as well as selling in the United Kingdom, sold in Australia, New Zealand, South Africa, Singapore, and Canada in English, and in translation in Norway, Germany, and Holland. Charles Boon also negotiated serial rights in magazines and newspapers for his authors, a policy the firm continued throughout the 20th century. Indeed, Alan Boon was to base the firm's recovery after World War II on a mutually beneficial arrangement with women's magazines.

Alan Boon joined the firm in 1931, with his brothers, Charles (Carol) and John, joining in 1938. "Mr Alan," as he was known by the staff, read manuscripts; Carol was in production; and "Mr John" developed a direct-mail operation, the precursor of the successful Reader Service operations, which was started in 1965.

In 1937, Joan Blair wrote *Sister of Nelson Ward*, one of the first doctor-nurse romances, although the very first of this type was Louise Gerard's *Days of Probation*, published in 1917. Medical romances were popular, and Harlequin chose two for its first Mills & Boon publications in Canada and the United States: Anne Vinton's *Hospital in Buwambo* and Mary Burchell's *Hospital Corridors*. However, the star of the line was to be Betty Neels who, between 1968 and her death in 2001, wrote over 134 novels for both the medical and contemporary lines.

In 1943, Charles Boon died and Henley was elected chairman "until further notice," as all three sons were away on war duty. This was a difficult time for Mills & Boon, with rising costs and print runs limited to four thousand by government decree. On the credit side, readership rose, and everything produced sold, including the backlist, so there was a small profit; but the growth of the firm was stopped.

On returning from the war, Alan Boon, an editorial genius, came into his own. He and John Boon, in finances and sales, formed an unbeatable partnership that took Mills & Boon onto the world stage. In the 1950s Alan Boon signed many women writers who were to become prolific and well-known Mills & Boon authors.

The books of this period are often domestic, with many of the heroines being contented housewives. However, Pamela Kent shattered that standard as she blew away the cobwebs of domesticity with her novels of heroines who did not sacrifice their careers for marriage. Kent was one of the pseudonyms of Ida Pollock, third wife of Enid Blyton's first husband; and in 1964 she published under the Pollock name a successful historical novel, *The Gentle Masquerade*, which was to give the name of "Masquerade" to Mills & Boon's historical line. Mills & Boon's first historical, *My Lady Wentworth* by Allan Fea, set in the time of the Monmouth rebellion, had been published in 1909, and the company had continued to publish the occasional historical title ever since; but it was not until 1977 that the decision was taken to divide the different subgenres into contemporary, historical, and medical.

By the mid-1960s profits were steadily increasing, thanks to the start of the paperback editions. This was an exciting decade for the company. By 1969, it was publishing annually 144 hardbacks at 13s 6d, and 72 paperbacks at 3s 6d. Authors were earning undreamed-of sums. When Betty Beaty received a royalty cheque for £9,000 in the late 1960s, she phoned Mills & Boon, thinking it was a mistake! And it seemed as though Alan's policy of becoming friends with the authors, answering all letters sent to him personally, was paying off. He was often to be seen at the Ritz or L'Etoile, wining and dining authors and their agents as the champagne flowed.

A new name to the list in 1961 was Violet Winspear with her first book, *Lucifer's Angel*. Winspear based all her heroes on Humphrey Bogart, working with his photograph stuck above her typewriter. Another popular author signed in the 1960s, very different in style from Winspear, was Essie Summers, a New Zealand Presbyterian pastor's wife who wrote warm, family-oriented stories.

In 1966 Henley resigned and John Boon became Managing Editor, receiving in 1968 a CBE (Commander of the Most Excellent Order of the British Empire) for his services to the publishing industry. In 1972, after long discussions, came the merger with Harlequin. Both Boon brothers came to regret this, in effect, take-over, but at the time it seemed to be the right thing to do. For nearly a decade editorial continued undisturbed, with two new editors, Frances Whitehead and Jacqui Bianchi, joining the team, and the prolific authors Carole Mortimer and Janet Dailey being signed.

In 1969 Winspear published *Blue Jasmine*, her homage to E. M. Hull's *The Sheik* (1919), and in doing so opened the way to a subgenre of "sheik" books, which took off in the 1970s and is still going strong. Nearly all the new authors of the 1970s and 1980s wrote at least one "sheik" novel, including Penny Jordan and Charlotte Lamb. Partly under their influence, and partly as the mores of the times changed, the novels became more sexually explicit. Always attuned to the times, the romances now explored the problems the "sexual revolution" held for women, along with their fight for equal working conditions.

By the mid-1980s, having bought out Silhouette, Mills & Boon's main rival, the company was selling 250 million books worldwide. And by 1990 the three editorial offices in London, Toronto, and New York had more than 600 authors among them. In the same year, 750,000 books were given away to East German women when the Berlin Wall came down. Today Mills & Boon sells 130 million books worldwide, in 26 languages and 109 countries.

In 1994, Karen Stoecker became U.K. Editorial Director. Upon her retirement in 2011, Tessa Shapcott replaced her in the position of Executive Editor. Currently (2018), Bryony Green is Executive Editor, and Joanie Grant is Editorial Director. In 2008 Mills & Boon celebrated its centenary. Sadly, neither John nor Alan were alive to see this anniversary, John having died in 1996 and Alan in 2000. Without them and their father, Charles Boon, the world of Romance would look very different, and millions of women worldwide owe them a debt of gratitude for their dedication to a genre that has given readers such a lot of pleasure.

jay Dixon

Further Reading

Dixon, jay. *The Romance Fiction of Mills & Boon 1909–1990s*. London: UCL Press, 1999.

Hull, E. M. *The Sheik*. London: E. Nast & Grayson, 1919.

McAleer, Joseph. *Passion's Fortune: The Story of Mills & Boon*. Oxford: Oxford University Press, 1999.

Vivanco, Laura. *For Love and Money: The Literary Art of the Harlequin Mills & Boon Romance*. Penrith, CA: Humanities-Ebooks LLP, 2011.

Mitchell, Margaret (1900–1949)

Margaret Mitchell was an American novelist who won the Pulitzer Prize for fiction for her best-selling novel *Gone with the Wind* (1936). A tale of the old South, *Gone with the Wind* became one of the most popular novels of all time and was made into an award-winning and record-breaking film (1939).

Mitchell was born in Atlanta, Georgia, daughter of attorney Eugene Mitchell and suffragist "Maybelle" Stephens; they were a privileged and prominent family with Irish Catholic roots. Mitchell's early life was filled with stories of faded Southern grandeur and the Civil War, recounted by her maternal grandmother. A tomboy, Mitchell wore male clothes until her teens, rode horses, and read adventure stories. Mitchell attended Smith College, writing poetry during this time under the name "Peg," inspired by the winged horse Pegasus, symbolic muse of poets. She left college following the death of her mother in 1918.

Making her society debut into Georgia's high society in the 1920s, Mitchell was a self-described flirt and Southern belle, if not a femme fatale, with many beaux. She created a society scandal with her daring dancing. In 1922 she married Berrien "Red" Upshaw against her family's wishes. It has been speculated that Red Upshaw was the model for Rhett Butler in *Gone with the Wind*. Following alleged violence and physical and emotional abuse by Upshaw, the couple were divorced. In 1925, Mitchell married John Marsh, who had been best man at her first wedding. The couple had no children. Their home in Atlanta is now the Margaret Mitchell House and Museum.

From 1922 to 1925, Mitchell was a journalist for *The Atlanta Journal*. During the 1920s she became a collector of women's erotica and wrote a stage play, *Oh! Lady Godiva!* (1926). Between 1926 and 1929 (purportedly dressed in men's trousers), she wrote the novel *Gone with the Wind*.

Gone with the Wind is an historical romance set in America's Deep South during the last half of the 19th century. It tells the story of headstrong heroine Scarlett O'Hara, against the backdrop of Civil War and Reconstruction in the South. Both widely beloved and critiqued, it pivots on Scarlett's determination to keep her family plantation, Tara, following the tumult of war. Its love triangle, with Scarlett torn between honorable Ashley Wilkes and dashing Rhett Butler, has become a romance classic, and phrases from the novel are part of the love lexicon.

Mitchell became celebrated as a writer, but when she found fame following the publication and movie release of *Gone with the Wind* overwhelming, she became reclusive. She died in 1945 after being hit by a car at the age of 49.

Elizabeth Reid Boyd

Further Reading

Edwards, Anne. *The Road to Tara: The Life of Margaret Mitchell.* New York: Dell, 1983.

Walker, Marianne. *Margaret Mitchell and John Marsh: The Love Story behind "Gone with the Wind."* Atlanta: Peachtree Publishers, 1983.

M/M (Male/Male) Romances

Books and videos that feature two men in a relationship have traditionally been written for other gay men and have historically been distributed from retail outlets that were proximate to gay clubs. The advent of the Internet has changed this and has also expanded the audience for m/m romances. Heterosexual females have long been a peripheral audience for m/m romances, but they were not a core group since they were not likely to frequent gay clubs and might be put off by the covers of these novels, not because they personally had an issue with the illustrations but because the covers would define their reading choice. The Internet obviates the first obstacle, with e-books counting for 30 percent of all books sold, and the use of iPads and other reading devices mitigates others' identifying the reader's choice of "trashy" novels.

Most mainstream houses today release a smattering of LGBTQQ novels, almost all in digital form. The primary outlet for m/m novels, beside those published by traditional LGBTQQ publishers (for example, Riptide, Bold Strokes Books, Torquere, Cleis Press, Wilde City, Amber Quill, Less Than Three, Rocky Road) and released both online and in bookstores, are those houses that specialize in romantic digital books, such as Siren and Ellora's Cave, though their m/m books are more likely ménage m/f/m novels (more so than f/m/f). The growing popularity of ménage and m/m novels among heterosexual women is based on the idea that two are better than one. This has long been the rationale for f/f action enjoyed by heterosexual males. "Why not?" says Constance Penley, who teaches a course in pornography at the University of California, Santa Barbara. "We take it for granted that guys love their girl-on-girl. Why shouldn't women have an appreciation for guy-on-guy?" (Alimurung). Linda Williams, who wrote the seminal study on pornography *Hard Core*, agrees: if the women are heterosexual and they desire men, "then you doubled the pleasure" (Alimurung). It also, Williams argues, solves the problem of who's on top. In this sense, you have the standard alpha male (top) but also the sweet, subservient beta male (bottom). This means the female reader gets to pick which one she identifies with, which allows her in one scene to identify with the "top" and in another with the "bottom." In any event, most people in the industry, both traditional and digital publishers of erotica, agree that books about m/m relationships are about men only superficially. In other words, the books are romance novels because the focus is on finding a soulmate and, thus can be enjoyed by heterosexual females even if the plot revolves around two men in love.

Dreamspinner Press: Male/Male Romances for Gay Men

Elizabeth North started Dreamspinner in 2006 for two reasons. One was that an author friend had been taken advantage of by a now-defunct, unscrupulous publisher. This is not an uncommon complaint in the digital world, but it is not sufficient to be considered motivation to launch a publishing venture. Perhaps a more germane reason for launching the business was that her gay brother-in-law complained of not being able to find gay books with a happy ending; he was getting married at the time and wanted to read books that reflected where he was in his life. This indicated to North that there might be a market for gay romance novels since the very crux of a romance novel is the requisite happy-ever-after ending, even if that has been somewhat modified today to a happy-at-the-moment ending. North's rationale is similar to that of Riptide and other LGBTQQ publishers. Riptide, for example, was cofounded by Rachael Haimowitz and Alexsandr Voinov. They were less than satisfied with their relationship with other houses and felt there were a lot of other writers in their situation who were looking for more quality work in the LGBTQQ genre.

Every publishing house tries to find its special niche. Dreamspinner's is gay men, with women m/m devotees a strong secondary market. The company has most of the traditional romance categories, including New Adult (NA), which has long been a mainstay of gay fiction. In fact, LGBTQQ publishers had New Adult before New Adult became all the rage (c. 2012) in mainstream fiction. New Adult mainstream novels focus on a young 20-something-year-old coming to terms with his or her sexual awakening—this may explain the popularity of these novels in both Young Adult (YA) and NA romantic fiction since many younger-than-20-year-olds grapple with their sexual orientation today. Coming-of-age stories in gay fiction parallel the New Adult genre. Coming-of-age novels in LGBTQQ fiction revolve around coming to terms with one's "different" sexuality. But while coming-of-age novels are part of any LGBTQQ house's list, Bittersweet Dreams at Dreamspinner is rather unique, especially given the primary reason for starting the press. The name itself suggests that even happy-at-the-moment endings are not a given. Arile Tachna, of Dreamspinner Press, says that's because "not all great love stories have a happy ending, and we got tired of not publishing these books because they weren't traditional romances" (Tachna).

Dreamspinner is similar to but also different from other houses in its international presence. Many publishers, both LGBTQQ and even small mainstream ones, as well as many self-published authors, have some international presence today, especially in English-speaking countries. The international presence today has been facilitated by Amazon Europe. But few LGBTQQ publishers have the Dreamspinner European presence: its books are translated in-house into French, Spanish, Italian, and German. The reason for such an extraordinary move, Tachna says, is because the publisher saw how well its books were selling in English-speaking markets, such as the United Kingdom and Australia. By translating the books in-house, the publisher ensures quality control. Dreamspinner also strongly markets its translations: "We have a media coordinator in each language who runs our social media accounts and works with reviewers and media outlets in the respective language to publicize the books" (Tachna). Few other publishers outside the larger mainstream houses take such steps.

In a similar vein, Dreamspinner is also seeking to extend its focus to increase readership. This is becoming increasingly common, even if it is still a small part of what LGBTQQ houses do. This was seen with the move to snag heterosexual readers of male/male romances. This expansion was also explored with Cleis Press, which is moving into mainstream heterosexual romance publishing to capture a wider slice of the romance pie. Dreamspinner is approaching its brand expansion in a more conventional way by adding subgenres. Dreamspinner will remain a gay publisher of m/m novels, but it is moving beyond its initial and limited romance focus by launching a line of sci-fi books. Sci-fi books were already part of the offerings at Dreamspinner, but the books were overlooked because of the house's strong romance brand.

DSP Publications was launched in the fall of 2014 to promote and market the non-romance line. The new press will have a strong presence at sci-fi and fantasy conferences, which are heavily populated by men, and then will be expanded into the Horror genre, an area also well known for its heavy male readership. The books will continue to feature gay characters, but they are now secondary to the primary sci-fi and horror themes. It is felt that the DSP designation, though it obviously stands for Dreamspinner Press, will avoid any offputting association among potential readers. The DSP designation is meant to appeal to gay men who are not romance readers. The publisher also hopes to tap the heterosexual romance market by relegating gay characters to a less prominent role. "We are attempting," says Tachna, "to make the non-gay market realize our books aren't any different than theirs. . . . Our goal is to have the idea of 'gay' become a non-issue" (Tachna). This is a lofty goal. It remains to be seen how successful the company will be when a heterosexual male is reading one of its sci-fi or horror books and encounters a scene that depicts intimacy between two men.

ManLoveRomance Press: Male/Male Romances for Heterosexual Women

While many LGBTQQ publishers are attempting to reach a wider audience by extending their books to tap a heterosexual audience, ManLoveRomance Press is going after those women who read m/m romances. Because it is the only house that specializes in gay novels for female romance readers, it has a greater chance of reaching its intended audience, both in terms of the number of books released yearly and in its focused marketing strategy, which is similar to the strategy used by traditional romance publishers.

Like many publishers, Laura Baumbach started as a writer. She began writing in 2010. She took up this "hobby" when she found herself at home taking care of a toddler. She focused on same-sex, typically male/male (m/m), because she saw it as a neglected area, "so I jumped in." Timing was good because soon "slash" (m/m) fiction was gaining ground, if not respectability. Her early works appeared on the LGBTQ lists of erotic publishers; she was published by Samhain and Loose Id, among others. She was cheated by one digital publisher who didn't pay her for three books of hers that it had published, besides doing "poor quality [work] when they did publish them." The next logical step, taken by many, especially then, before self-publishing gained momentum, was to start her own publishing house: "I felt if they could do it, I can do it, and I can do it better"—the driving reason why so many romance authors pick up the pen or, in this case, start publishing ventures.

"So I got together with some best-selling authors within the genre that I was friends with who contributed stories and I opened my first press—there were three of us, now there's 210 of us" (Baumbach).

Had she focused on gay men and published with an LGBTQQ press, she would have experienced little resistance to her m/m romance tales. Baumbach experienced resistance within the industry, however, because she was publishing romances for female romance readers before the subgenre became a staple within the mainstream romance industry. The resistance was similar to that which was encountered by erotic e-book publishers when they first started publishing romances outside the mainstream tradition. For example, *Romantic Times*, a popular fan magazine, refused to review her books, and Romance Writers of America resisted her entry into the organization. Once the subject matter, as with erotica, was seen as a staple within the industry and not just a fad, these organizations adapted. This is the biggest change she's seen in the male/male fiction industry: acceptance. But that's now because m/m love has become mainstream, and every publisher of romances dabbles in the subgenre.

Most mainstream publishers address m/m romance for women today, though it took them a while to get around to doing it. ManLoveRomance, like Ellora's Cave in erotic publishing, was first out of the chute and established a clear, early identity—*Rolling Stone*, in a feature article, called Baumbach one of the pioneers of the m/m genre. ManLoveRomance has a full-time editorial staff of six content editors and publishes between two and three books a week, around 130 novels a year. It has, like its erotic counterparts, started a traditional romance line, but it is mainly to keep its authors happy: "Some of our authors write traditional romance and wanted to say with me. Probably shouldn't have bothered but we're family." The m/m books were popular from the get-go, she says, because women "would tell me that they've been reading m/m romances for years," and since they couldn't get m/m romantic fiction, "they were settling for gay fiction" (Baumbach). Now they don't have to.

John Markert

Further Reading

"About Riptide Publishing." http://www.riptidepublishing.com/Home. Accessed April 7, 2017.

Alimurung, Gendy. "Man on Man: The New Gay Romance . . . Written By and For Straight Women." *L. A. Weekly*, December 16, 2009. http://www.laweekly.com/arts/man-on-man-the-new-gay-romance-2162963. Accessed April 7, 2017.

Baumbach, Laura. Publisher, ManLoveRomance Press. Interviews.

Greenfield, Jeremy. "Ebook Growth Slows to Single Digit in U.S. in 2013." *Digital Book World*, April 1, 2014.

Knight, Brenda. Publisher, Cleis Press. Interviews.

Markert, John. *Publishing Romance: The History of an Industry, 1940s to the Present.* Jefferson, NC: McFarland, 2016, 231–41.

Milliot, Jim. "Ebooks Still Outsold by Hardcover and Paperbacks." *Publishers Weekly,* September 26, 2014.

Tachna, Ariel. Translations Coordinator, Dreamspinner Press. Interviews.

Williams, Linda. *Hard Core: Power, Pleasure, and the "Frenzy of the Visible."* Berkeley: University of California Press, 1989.

The Mysteries of Udolpho (1794)

The Mysteries of Udolpho (1794) is a three-volume Gothic novel widely recognized as the masterwork of its author, "the first poetess of romantic fiction," Ann Radcliffe (1764–1823). A best seller in its day, *The Mysteries of Udolpho* began a trend for the Gothic that persisted until well into the 19th century. The book also helped to establish many of the conventions of the Gothic novel: from the dark and mysterious castle whose chambers lock only on the outside; to the trembling and compassionate heroine of sensibility, bereft of the protection of a mother and father; and to the dark, brooding, dangerous villain.

The Mysteries of Udolpho was Radcliffe's fourth novel. The success of her previous book, *The Romance of the Forest* (1791), led Radcliffe's publisher George Robinson to offer her "what was then considered as an unprecedented sum of £500" (Scott, 216) for the copyright to her next novel. *The Mysteries of Udolpho* soon eclipsed *The Romance of the Forest* in popularity, becoming something of a sensation. Writing some 30 years after its publication, Sir Walter Scott remembers the excitement with which the novel was greeted: "the very name was fascinating," he observed, "and the public, who rushed upon it with all the eagerness of curiosity, rose from it with unsated appetite" (216). No less than 10 editions of *The Mysteries of Udolpho* were published "in its first decade, including those published in Dublin, Boston and Philadelphia" (Ellis, *History of Gothic Fiction*, 51), with the book receiving wide coverage in the periodical press.

Radcliffe's long novel centers upon the experiences of Emily St. Aubert, a young Frenchwoman of deep emotional susceptibility, who is left to fend for herself upon the death of her parents. Emily's physical attractiveness is coupled with an enquiring mind and, perhaps most important, with a poetic sensibility that pervades the novel. After the death of Emily's mother, her father is urged for his health to travel from their hometown of Gascony to Languedoc and Provence. It is on this journey that Emily and her father meet Valancourt, the hero of their novel, with whom Emily falls in love.

Her father dies soon afterward, and Emily is sent to live with her aunt, the unsympathetic Madame Cheron. Madame Cheron then marries the villain of the novel, Montoni, and takes Emily to live in the castle of Udolpho, situated high in the Italian Alps. When Madame Montoni dies as a result of neglect at the hands of her new husband, she leaves Emily the sole heir of her estate and all of the lands belonging to it. As a number of critics have noted, "property looms larger than love in *The Mysteries of Udolpho*, and the last half of the novel is mainly concerned with the consolidation of her [Emily's] property rights" (Norton, 102). Montoni attempts to force Emily to sign over her inheritance to him (which she eventually does, with much regret) and to forget Valancourt and instead marry his friend, Count Morano. When things become unbearable for her at Udolpho, Emily finds a way to escape from the castle with another young man, Du Pont. By the end of the novel, Montoni has died, and Emily finds herself the owner once more of all of her aunt's property. Emily now has the ability to relieve the financial burdens of her former and current tenants, and she and Valancourt marry.

The Mysteries of Udolpho is famous for its deployment of terror. Terror is predicated on the idea that rationality can always overcome the threat posed by the forces of irrationality. Throughout the novel, Emily learns that she must "learn to command her tendency to respond with terror and supernatural explanations to unusual 'surrounding circumstances'" (Ellis, *Contested Castle*, 113) that prove, in the end, to have a rational explanation. There is much to suggest that Radcliffe's novels served a didactic function by advocating to young women the importance of tempering deeply emotional responses to the world (sensibility) with rationality. In fact, Markman Ellis goes further than this, noting "rather than mere entertainments, her [Radcliffe's] novels direct her readers to consider one of the central issues of the 1790s: the status of women" (50).

By the time of its author's death, *The Mysteries of Udolpho* had cemented its claim as one of the most influential novels of the 1790s. It had been published in numerous editions and "could be found in virtually every private library" (Norton, 104). Radcliffe remains the most important novelist of her era, and although *The Mysteries of Udolpho* is not as widely read as it was in her heyday, Radcliffe's innovations in the ever-popular genre of Gothic Romance should not be overlooked.

Claire Knowles

Further Reading

Ellis, Kate Ferguson. *The Contested Castle: Gothic Novels and the Subversion of Domestic Ideology*. Urbana and Chicago: University of Chicago Press, 1989.

Ellis, Markman. *The History of Gothic Fiction*. Edinburgh: Edinburgh University Press, 2000.

Norton, Rictor. *The Mistress of Udolpho*. London and New York: Leicester University Press, 1999.

Radcliffe, Ann. *The Mysteries of Udolpho*. Oxford: Oxford University Press, 2008.

Scott, Walter. "Mrs. Radcliffe." *Lives of the Novelists*, vol 1. Paris: A. and W. Galignani, 1825.

Mystery/Suspense/Thriller and Romance

While Mystery, Suspense, and Thriller are all full-fledged fiction genres on their own, the Romance genre is greatly enhanced when elements or devices of the other three are interjected into its realm.

Briefly, consider a few definitions. A mystery is defined as a fictional piece in which there is a puzzle (some sort of secret or crime) that needs to be solved; it tends to be thought of as rationally based. A suspense novel works more on an emotional or psychological level and generally involves an individual who is a victim and needs to escape from danger. A thriller ratchets up the suspense novel and also plays upon a reader's emotions and fears through suspenseful encounters, cliffhangers, and fast-paced action. In thrillers, the heroes are often fighting against a larger force such as a corrupt law firm, a medical emergency, or a natural disaster.

While a mystery must have something to be solved, there does not have to be a murder, although that is the most common crime in the Mystery genre. "Detective fiction" is the label usually associated with the Mystery genre; sleuths may be police officers, private detectives, or any number of amateurs. Conventional mystery plots will solve the puzzle (secret or crime), and justice will be served. A mystery often has a more logical and rational tone to it, a methodical pace perhaps, which sounds counter to something that would work for a romance novel. But keep in mind that the resolution and search for justice often bring a decidedly emotional and moral tone to any mystery. Like romance readers, mystery fans anticipate a positive resolution to the story.

Suspense novels, in contrast to mysteries, appeal to the reader's emotions—like Romance—and are laden with tension and fear. There is some sort of threat out there, be it serial killer or blackmailer, and the main characters are in danger. The reader will know this through the author's use of alternating narrators—for example, the villain and the hero. Suspense novels are known for their rapid pace, unsettling environments, and heroines who will probably make bad choices. Suspense is such an important and emotional complement to the Romance genre that it has its own subgenre, Romantic Suspense, which is described more fully in its own entry.

Beyond that, the thriller is a more amplified version of the suspense novel, and clearly it has its roots in the adventure novel. The thriller will keep a reader involved because there is abundant action from the very beginning, the time span of the novel is usually short, and a more collective threat (with a deadline, no less) may hang over the protagonists. Typically plot-driven rather than character-centered, the Thriller genre has numerous subgenres—Legal, Medical, Military, and so on—that give the reader somewhat of an insider's point of view. The proliferation of such specialized thrillers has spawned numerous movies and television series as well. Thrillers are often mentioned in the same breath as espionage or spy novels. Violence is implied if not actually happening, and a hero's personal code of ethics may necessitate working outside the rules of authority.

Credit for the first detective protagonist—C. August Dupin—goes to Edgar Allan Poe with his famous short story, published in 1841, "The Murders in the Rue Morgue." Further, his "The Purloined Letter" (1844) can be called an early spy thriller. Poe's detective has influenced countless other authors and really established certain formulaic devices that are easily recognizable: the loner detective who's a genius at solving puzzles being a prime example. Jumping ahead to the end of the 19th century, one finds the other mainstay of detective fiction: Sherlock Holmes, the creation of Sir Arthur Conan Doyle. Doyle's collections of short stories, beginning with *A Study in Scarlet* in 1887, represent a type of literary shorthand for all detective fiction. Doyle's works showcase the ever-important sidekick character, too.

In the 1860s, between the fictional detectives mentioned above, came the "sensation novels," or what one might call suspense novels or thrillers today. Sensation novels, most notably two works by Wilkie Collins, *The Woman in White* (1860) and *The Moonstone* (1868), were a delicious blending of detective, Gothic, and melodrama. Collins, a friend of Charles Dickens, was a major force in the Detective genre, and he is commonly labeled as the father of the English detective novel. Collins's novels were serialized first—a popular Victorian style of publishing—in Dickens's publications. This author's talent for generating suspense might be partially attributed to serialization publication. He had to master the art of the cliffhanger so that readers would clamor for more.

Collins's suspenseful writing influenced a whole host of other authors, and two notable examples are Mary Roberts Rinehart and Mignon G. Eberhart. Rinehart's 1908 novel, *The Circular Staircase*, comes directly out of the sensation novel tradition; along the way this came to be known as the "Had-I-But-Known (HIBK)" school. HIBK certainly has a patronizing or pejorative ring to it, but it's a well-used and quite popular plot element. Rinehart's title is considered a classic in early romantic suspense.

Agatha Christie ushered in the "Golden Age" of mystery writing—broadly encompassing the period between the two world wars—and women mystery authors dominated this time. While not necessarily romantic, the "cozy" frame of villages and genteel folks solving puzzles flourished.

Across the pond, Nebraskan Mignon G. Eberhart, whose novels were published beginning in 1929, also subscribed to the HIBK school of suspense. Eberhart experimented with detection (mixing the rational with the intuitive), and her tone is more suspenseful than puzzle solving. She is one of the first mystery writers to use the weather to heighten the drama of her stories. For example, one of her best-known protagonists was a traveling nurse, Sarah Keate (*While the Patient Slept*, 1930), who worked at spooky places, such as old mansion, on a regular basis. Mix in a good storm, add a mysterious stranger, and suspense builds.

So, by the 1920s, the detective, the sidekick, the closed-room drama, cozy puzzles, and bad weather are all in place. A little bit of Gothic mixed in with rational detecting is in play. All that's missing is some humor.

An early master of wit and humor was Georgette Heyer, a prolific writer who defied easy categorization since she freely experimented with both mystery and romance and produced works over several decades. Heyer is an excellent example of a writer's incorporating mystery elements into her romance writings. *Behold, Here's Poison* (1936) is a prime example of a romantic suspense novel that interjects a lighter tone than that of a typical Gothic (Smith, 1188). Her lightening up of the mood served as an inspiration to authors who have tried their hands at the romantic caper or romp, while still solving a mystery.

Up until World War II, this Golden Age of mysteries flourished with well-known names such as Agatha Christie, Dorothy Sayers, and Josephine Tey. While fictional couples show up as characters (for example, Dorothy Sayers's Lord Wimsey and Harriet Vane), the books still remain grounded in mystery—but it does indicate a humanizing trend in the rational genre. Also, in the midst of this period, the Gothic influence reemerged, most obviously with Daphne du Maurier's enormously successful *Rebecca*.

Way ahead of the post–World War II curve in terms of espionage and spy thrillers, Helen MacInnes, aka "Queen of the Spy Novel," published *Above Suspicion* in 1941. She, too, has her roots in the sensation novel. She merits mention because of her unique place as a woman writing spy fiction and continuing to succeed in that specialized area of the Thriller genre for several decades.

Another notable 20th-century writer, Mary Stewart, is considered the icon of traditional romantic suspense. But she also ventured into the thriller realm occasionally, and her *Airs above the Ground* (1965) is considered to be a thriller.

Among the legions influenced by Stewart came Elizabeth Peters (aka Barbara Mertz). She's best known for her Victorian Era amateur sleuth, Amelia Peabody, an adventurous woman who traveled the world and encountered mystery cases in assorted exotic locales. While her Amelia Peabody series (starting with *Crocodile on the Sandbank*, 1975) is classed as a mystery, one could argue that the series ventures into romantic suspense.

Along the same lines, Dorothy Gilman created an endearing spy with her Mrs. Pollifax character (*The Unexpected Mrs. Pollifax*, 1966), the grandmother who decided she needed some adventure. Later in the series, she also finds new love, but it is not the dominant element of the work.

Suspense became tremendously popular in the 1980s, and interest hasn't abated since. Mary Higgins Clark—while not a romantic—is a best-selling suspense writer (*Where Are the Children?*, 1992) whose works converted a whole host of romantic suspense authors into suspense writers. Interestingly, while Clark's works are topical (endangered children, violence against women), they are not as graphic or violent as what new authors are generating. Two examples of harder-hitting suspense writers include Lisa Gardner (*The Perfect Husband*, 1998) and Iris Johansen (*Face of Deception*, 1998).

Two major romance authors, Nora Roberts (also writes as J. D. Robb) and Jayne Ann Krentz (Amanda Quick, Jayne Castle), have both pioneered new styles as their writing careers continue over the decades. Both write under different pen names, write about different historical periods, and experiment with subgenres, including Romantic Suspense. These romance masters manage to please a wide range of readers who either cherry-pick the types of reads they like—or jump in and try a subgenre they never knew they might like.

A modern thriller-infused romance will probably involve technical details, and there are myriad subgenre possibilities. Examples would include the military romance of Suzanne Brockmann and Cherry Adair, and Tess Gerritsen's medical thrillers (*The Surgeon*, 2001).

Certainly, one would be remiss not to comment on law enforcement (the FBI has done well) as being a tremendous draw for contemporary thriller-infused romance. A startling number of authors use the folks in uniform for their jumping-off point: Allison Brennan, Carla Neggers, Karen Robards, J. D. Robb (aka Nora Roberts), and Christy Reece, with her mercenaries, to name just a few. And it's not just the men who are in uniform—plenty of heroines are enforcers too! Consider Tami Hoag's *Ashes to Ashes* (1999), whose heroine is a former FBI agent.

And so the 20th century went, generating ever-expanding horizons for the Mystery, Suspense, Thriller, and Romance genres. Cawelti theorizes that formula fiction gives us a chance to absorb some of the changes going on in the culture around us in a risk-free manner (36). Reading gives us permission to experience exciting worlds vicariously with characters for whom we care.

Mysteries being written at the beginning of the 21st century demonstrate more character development and emotional elements, rather than a rigid adherence to plot and puzzle. While the field has seen growth in historical mysteries with their strong sense of place and romantic overtones, the mystery element still dominates. Anne Perry, Tasha Alexander, Robin Paige, and Rhys Bowen all write emotionally rich historical mysteries, but with varying degrees of romantic entanglement.

In summary, the elements of mystery, suspense, and thriller can all be used—and have been used—by romance writers to great effect. In the context of the romance novel, however, the expected outcome of an optimistic ending and a satisfying love story must prevail. If the other elements dominate, then the work has most probably shifted into either a different genre or might be considered a genreblended work.

Teresa L. Jacobsen

See also: DuMaurier, Daphne; Heyer, Georgette; Radcliffe, Ann; *Rebecca;* Roberts, Nora; Romantic Suspense; Stewart, Mary; Whitney, Phyllis A.

Further Reading

Cawelti, John G. *Adventure, Mystery, and Romance: Formula Stories as Art and Popular Culture*. Chicago: University of Chicago Press, 1976.

Charles, John, Candace Clark, Joanne Hamilton-Selway, and Joanna Morrison. *The Readers' Advisory Guide to Mystery*, 2nd ed. Chicago: American Library Association, 2012.

Niebuhr, Gary Warren. *Make Mine a Mystery: A Reader's Guide to Mystery and Detective Fiction*. Westport, CT: Libraries Unlimited, 2003.

Panek, LeRoy Lad. "Mignon Good Eberhart." In *Mystery and Suspense Writers: The Literature of Crime, Detection, and Espionage*, edited by Robin W. Winks and Maureen Corrigan, 345–56. New York: Scribner's, 1998.

Saricks, Joyce G. *The Readers' Advisory Guide to Genre Fiction*. Chicago: American Library Association, 2001.

Smith, Jennifer Crusie. "The Romantic Suspense Mystery." In *Mystery and Suspense Writers: The Literature of Crime, Detection, and Espionage*, edited by Robin W. Winks and Maureen Corrigan, 1183–97. New York: Scribner's, 1998.

Walton, Priscilla L. "Helen MacInnes." In *Mystery and Suspense Writers: The Literature of Crime, Detection, and Espionage*, edited by Robin W. Winks and Maureen Corrigan, 651–64. New York: Scribner's, 1998.

O

On the Far Side Awards

See Prism and On the Far Side Awards

P

Pamela (1740)

First published in 1740, Samuel Richardson's *Pamela, or Virtue Rewarded* is often regarded as the first English novel. Pamela Regis argues that Richardson's tale of a maidservant sexually importuned by, kidnapped by, and ultimately married by her employer should also be viewed as a key progenitor of contemporary romance. With his bestselling *Pamela*, Regis suggests, "Richardson brings the courtship plot, which is to say the romance novel, into more than prominence. He makes it famous" (63).

Richardson's novel, told through letters between 15-year-old Pamela Andrews, a maidservant, and her parents, opens with the death of Pamela's mistress. Before dying, Lady B recommends her servants to her son, who promises to keep them, including Pamela, employed. But Mr. B, a lecherous libertine, has more in mind for the innocent girl than simply washing his linen. Pamela's letters document Mr. B's increasingly bold sexual offers and her consistently adamant refusals. In his frustration, Mr. B kidnaps Pamela and finally attempts rape. When Pamela faints, he fears she is dying and ceases his assault. Eventually reformed by the girl's beauty, morals, and noble resistance, Mr. B finally offers marriage. Pamela refuses; defeated, Mr. B allows Pamela to return to her parents. But when he falls sick and requests that she return to him, Pamela, who has fallen in love with Mr. B's gentlemanly qualities, accepts, taking on the role of docile, proper wife.

What roots of the contemporary romance can first be found in Richardson's novel? *Pamela*'s epistolary format allows the reader immediate access into Pamela's thoughts and feelings as the story of her seduction/courtship unfolds, an immediacy and interiority rarely seen in earlier prose fiction. The novel's telling of a single courtship, rather than a series of loosely related episodes, also differs from previous prose fiction. Unlike the amatory fiction popular during the 17th and early 18th centuries, tales of passion and seduction, *Pamela* ends happily, not with its heroine's ruin. Finally, as Regis suggests, *Pamela* differs from comedy in its treatment of the declaration of love: "When declaration and betrothal follow mechanically upon the removal of the barrier, the romance novel's debt to comedy is evident. When it probes the motivation for declaration and betrothal, it concerns itself with matters typical of the newer form [romance]" (69).

With its sexually demanding hero, virginally virtuous heroine, titillating threats of sexual violence, and Cinderella-like crossing of class boundaries, Richardson's novel finds its echo in much 20th-century category romance, as well as in many early historical single-title works of the 1970s and 1980s.

Jackie Horne

See also: Richardson, Samuel

Further Reading

Ballaster, Ros. *Seductive Forms: Women's Amatory Fiction from 1684 to 1740*. Oxford: Clarendon Press, 1998.

Doody, Margaret Ann. *A Natural Passion: A Study of the Novels of Samuel Richardson*. Oxford: Clarendon Press, 1974.

Regis, Pamela. *A Natural History of the Romance Novel*. Philadelphia: University of Pennsylvania Press, 2003, 63–74.

Rivero, Albert J. "Introduction." In *Pamela, or Virtue Rewarded*, by Samuel Richardson, xxxi–lxxvi. Cambridge, UK: Cambridge University Press, 2011.

Paranormal Romance

The Paranormal Romance genre is defined by the Romance Writers of America as "Romance novels in which the future, a fantasy world, or paranormal happenings are an integral part of the plot" (RWA, "Romance Subgenres"). This definition opens this subgenre up for any romance novel that has elements that are paranormal in nature. This includes but is not limited to vampires, faeries, werewolves, ghosts, time travel, locations on other planets, and so forth. With such broad parameters, the field is wide open. With other entries focusing on some of these things more specifically, this article will have a more focused definition that centers more specifically on a conflict between a paranormal and human hero and heroine located on Earth at some point. These paranormals have very fast and loose rules, so there are always exceptions to the rules.

The Paranormal Romance has roots in early literature with works such as Bram Stoker's *Dracula* and other Gothic novels, but the Paranormal Romance usually makes the vampire or other paranormal entity the hero or heroine rather than the villain. The first woman to write a Gothic novel was Anne Radcliff; her novel *The Mysteries of Udolfo* (1789) opened the door for the Brontë's Gothics. These novels consisted of the paranormal in the form of ghosts or a spooky atmosphere rather than the array of paranormal elements we see today.

The modern Paranormal Romance started in the 1970s with novels by Victoria Holt and Phyllis A. Whitney and continued with authors such as Jayne Castle (aka Jayne Anne Krentz), Jude Deveraux, and Johanna Lindsey. They declined a bit until the 1990s when they saw a resurgence as Silhouette launched its Silhouette Shadows line, marketed as romances "from the Dark Side of Love" (1993–1996); but it was a young, niche market and hard for authors to find other publishers willing to risk it. It wasn't until 2000 that publishers began to take a chance on the varying types of Paranormal Romance and launched it into the mainstream category that it is today. Silhouette Nocturne did not launch until 2006 (becoming Harlequin Nocturne in 2008). Today's list of paranormal authors is exhaustive, but some of the most popular are Sherrilyn Kenyon, Christine Feehan, J. R. Ward, Nalini Singh, and Kresley Cole. Many authors are crossing Romance subgenres and are contributing to the paranormal world; Nora Roberts is one such example.

J. R. Ward's Black Dagger Brotherhood series has vampires that feed on vampires of the opposite sex for their strength instead of on humans. They do not get their vampire strength until they go through their transition around the age of 25, and not all of them survive this. Prior to the transition, they are very weak. They cannot be out in the sunlight. They have the ability to dematerialize and travel from one place to another. They live for hundreds of years, but reproducing is very difficult and dangerous. This shows one way the authors of these paranormal romances are able to create otherworldly beings that are similar enough to those paranormal species that are familiar to readers but romanticize them in ways that are only imagined.

Part of the allure of this genre is its wide variety and the ability of the reader not only to escape into the romance elements of the story but also to find themselves encountering different worlds and different species. The most popular of the paranormal species is the vampire; however, the vampire has changed much from the Bram Stoker days. While the erotic use of the blood sucking remains, most of the evil has been done away with unless the hero is fighting other vampires. The paranormal has branched out to include werewolves, faeries, mermaids and mermen, dinosaurs, dragons, shapeshifters, and gods and goddesses; even ghosts make an occasional return. It seems that if there is existing legend or lore, or if an author can create it, then it is up for grabs in the world of the paranormal. The paranormal does not have to be just dark and brooding either; humor also plays a role in the Paranormal Romance world. Authors such as Vicki Lewis

Thompson, Nina Bangs, and Molly Harper have successfully created comedic paranormal romances.

The young adult audience clamors for these paranormal romances. Obviously, Stephenie Meyer's Twilight series has had a major impact on this genre, but other authors such as Gena Showalter, Kelley Armstrong, P. C. Cast, Sherrilyn Kenyon, Melissa De La Cruz, Lauren Kate, and Tera Lynn Childs, to name only a few, have also tapped into this market. Young adults love the idea that these teenagers experience their everyday social issues with supernatural beings. It is hard enough to love a regular teenage boy or girl, so add to this the factor that this boy or girl has fangs or fins, and these adolescents get lost in reading about what will happen next. It seems to free them in some ways from having to deal with the real underlying issue. The young adult section of the bookstore is filled with these paranormal romances, and many of these books are being optioned for television and film as well.

While readers explore other possibilities within the realm of the supernatural, the Paranormal Romance also allows for a subversion of the traditional conventions of gender roles (sometimes by emboldening them), a heightened sexuality, an exploration of cultural and political issues, and whatever else an author wants to explore because there are no rules in these worlds but what the author creates. By definition, the paranormal is otherworldly even if existing here on Earth. The romance author is bound in some ways by the two components that the RWA says define a romance novel: "a central love story with an emotionally satisfying or optimistic ending" (RWA, "About the Romance Genre"). Especially in terms of the paranormal, the ways in which these components are reached are limitless, and an author can give her (or his) readers the type of men and women she (or he) has been looking for. Many of the men in these paranormal romance novels are hyper-masculine and/or hypersexual while also being sensitive to his woman's needs. He may struggle with her need for independence, but ultimately he will understand. It may drive the conflict in the plot, and it may be a part of his growth. Sometimes the struggle for the paranormal species is due to longevity of life. Many of these paranormal entities can live for hundreds of years. This gives them the advantage or disadvantage of having lived through many eras and having seen many different social periods. An author might also use the political unrest of the species as a parallel to what is going on in contemporary societal culture. In some novels it will be part of the backdrop, and in others it will be more direct, but because it is ultimately indirect due to the supernatural nature of the paranormal, it allows the reader to choose to engage in its political consciousness when one is present. Many paranormal romances deal with all sorts of issues such as body image, rape (both male and female), slavery, gender equality, homosexuality, contemporary politics, and so on. As authors continue to push these boundaries into the 21st century, this realm of the paranormal continues to be a perfect arena to explore these and many other issues. Readers feel a sense of safety, or are able to convince themselves they feel safe, because of the distance the "otherness" provides through the paranormal element in the book. The issues are there and can be dealt with and even processed without some of the harshness that the "real world" provides; but the message is still being delivered, whether it is being given on purpose or sometimes even unintentionally. Sometimes, however, the story is just a romance, grounded in good, old-fashioned emotional conflict, only with a paranormal and a human as the protagonists.

Lisa Jass

See also: Alternative Reality Romance Subgenres

Further Reading

Crawford, Joseph. *The Twilight of the Gothic?: Vampire Fiction and the Rise of the Paranormal Romance*. Cardiff: University of Wales Press, 2014. eBook Academic Collection (EBSCOhost), EBSCOhost. Accessed February 19, 2017.

Davis, Nina. "Spellbound: The Magic of Paranormal Romance." *Booklist* 100, 2 (September 15, 2003): 222.

Mukherjee, Ananya. "My Vampire Boyfriend: Postfeminism, 'Perfect' Masculinity, and the Contemporary Appeal of Paranormal Romance." *Studies in Popular Culture* 33, no. 2 (2011): 1–20. http://www.jstor.org/stable/23416381. Accessed April 12, 2017.

Regis, Pamela. *A Natural History of the Romance Novel*. Philadelphia: University of Pennsylvania Press, 2003.

RWA: Romance Writers of America. "About the Romance Genre." https://www.rwa.org/p/cm/ld/fid=578. Accessed April 12, 2017.

RWA: Romance Writers of America. "Romance Subgenres." https://www.rwa.org/p/cm/ld/fid=579. Accessed April 12, 2017.

Tobin-McClain, Lee. "Paranormal Romance: Secrets of the Female Fantastic." *Journal of the Fantastic in the Arts* 11, no. 2 (2001): 294–306.

Peyton Place (1956)

Peyton Place (1956) is a best-selling novel written by American author Grace Metalious and published by Julian Messner, a small New York publishing house. Described by its publisher Kitty Messner as a "product of genius" (quoted in Cameron, xxii), *Peyton Place* is an earthy and occasionally salacious exposé of life in small-town New England. The novel spent "a total of 59 weeks at the top of the *New York Times* best-seller list" (Brier, 51) and was to go on to overtake *Gone with the Wind* (1936) as one of the best-selling American novels of the 20th century.

Peyton Place was a controversial book, infamous for challenging conservative 1950s attitudes toward sexuality. The novel features depictions of various sexual acts, some of which were still outlawed between consenting adults in the United States; a sympathetic account of an abortion; and a scene in which a young woman kills her sexually abusive stepfather with an axe. These aspects of the book led to its banning in Indiana, Canada, Italy, and Australia.

Set in the picturesque New Hampshire mill town of Peyton Place, Metalious's novel focuses on the lives of three women: Constance Mackenzie, a single mother who runs her own dress shop; Connie's teenaged daughter, Allison, who aspires to be a writer; and Allison's friend Selena Cross, a girl from the wrong side of the tracks who finds work at Connie's shop. All three women face considerable obstacles in their quests to find fulfillment in life and work. Connie eventually finds happiness and sexual satisfaction in her marriage to schoolteacher Thomas Makris. Allison escapes the repressiveness of small-town life to become a writer in New York City, and Selena triumphs over the sexual abuse she suffers at the hands of her stepfather to become a respected member of Peyton Place society.

As a result of its immense popularity, only one year after its publication *Peyton Place* was made into a film. It also became an extraordinarily popular TV show in the 1960s that ran from 1964 to 1969 and launched the careers of Mia Farrow and Ryan O'Neal. According to Ardis Cameron, "both the film and the television series based on *Peyton Place* substantially altered the book and its meaning" (xx). It seems that *Peyton Place* was too risqué to be adapted faithfully by post–McCarthy-era Hollywood. As a result, the film changed the focus from the novel's female protagonists to its male ones, while the television series adopted a conservative and moralistic tone that was almost diametrically opposed to Metalious's original approach.

Both Jerry Wald, producer of the film of *Peyton Place*, and Kitty Messner were keen to capitalize on the success of Metalious's first novel. As a result, the author was convinced to write a sequel to the book, *Return to Peyton Place*, in 1959. The novel was produced quickly and written at a time when Metalious was drinking heavily (the author was to die of cirrhosis of the liver in 1964). *Return to Peyton Place* needed to be significantly rewritten and was panned upon publication.

The first decades of the 21st century have witnessed a resurgence of interest in *Peyton Place*, particularly from feminist critics who applaud its unflinching portrayal of the difficulties facing women in the conservative atmosphere of the postwar period. In 1999, some 40 years after the first publication of the novel, Virago Press published an edition of the book featuring a scholarly introduction by Ardis Cameron.

Claire Knowles

See also: Metalious, Grace

Further Reading

Brier, Evan. "The Accidental Blockbuster: *Peyton Place* in Literary and Institutional Context." *Women's Studies Quarterly* 33, 3/4 (2005): 48–65.

Cameron, Ardis. "Open Secrets: Rereading *Peyton Place*." In *Peyton Place*, by Grace Metalious, vii–xxxvi. London: Virago Press, 1999.

Miner, Madonne. *Insatiable Appetites: Twentieth Century American Women's Bestsellers*. Westport, CT: Greenwood Press, 1984.

Toth, Emily. *Inside* Peyton Place*: The Life of Grace Metalious*. Jackson: University Press of Mississippi, 1991.

Plaidy, Jean

See Hibbert, Eleanor Burford

The Popular Romance Project and *Love between the Covers* (2015): The Creator's Voice

Love between the Covers is an award-winning documentary film (completed in 2015) about the billion-dollar romance fiction business and the global community that romance authors and readers have built. The film is one part of the ground-breaking, multiplatform Popular Romance Project, which also includes a nation-wide library program featuring more than 100 screenings of *Love between the Covers* plus panel discussions and a broad range of events, a large website about popular romance across time and across cultures (PopularRomanceProject.org), and a February 2015 conference at the Library of Congress, *What Is Love? Romance Fiction in the Digital Age*, which brought scholars and industry insiders together to explore the deep roots of Romance Fiction and its future in the digital age.

I attended my first romance conference in 2009. Having made two ground-breaking films about women's communities (*A Midwife's Tale* and *Tupperware!*), I was intrigued by the romance community, which is a major powerhouse in the publishing world—and is also predominantly female. When I discovered that the National Endowment for the Humanities was interested in funding ambitious crossplatform projects, I put together a coalition of first-rate institutions: the International Association for the Study of Popular Romance (IASPR) to advise the project (headed by Sarah Frantz and Eric Murphy Selinger), The Roy Rosenzweig Center for History and New Media (CHNM) at George Mason University to build the website PopularRomanceProject.org (Kelly Schrum oversaw the website creation), the Library of Congress (LoC) Center for the Book to organize and host a conference focused on romance fiction (overseen by the center's director, John Cole), and Blueberry Hill Productions (BHP), my own film-production company, to make the documentary film *Love between the Covers*. At every step of the way, the Popular Romance Project's partners coordinated our efforts, shared resources, and built upon one another's efforts.

After shooting began in 2011, PopularRomanceProject.org was launched in 2012. The website features two-to-four minute video excerpts from interviews with romance scholars, romance authors, editors, cover designers, booksellers, and readers—all shot by BHP. In addition, the website features blogs by scholars from history, literature, psychology, popular culture studies, sociology, and business, plus blogs by romance authors, industry insiders, and romance readers. The topics covered in these blogs range from medieval troubadour songs to Jane Austen, to Korean soaps, to Mrs. Robinson's role in *The Graduate*. The blogs explore popular romance in different cultures, time periods, and media—books, films, comic books, television, and songs.

Filming continued until 2014. I and my crew filmed at numerous writer and reader romance conferences. We shot long interviews with romance scholars and more than 50 romance authors and industry insiders. This footage was used in the film, at the website, at the conference, and at library screenings. (Excerpts from these interviews can be seen at PopularRomanceProject.org and facebook.com /LoveBTCFilm.) The film crew also followed the lives of five accomplished romance authors—Mary Bly/Eloisa James, Beverly Jenkins, Celeste Bradley, Susan Donovan, and Len Barot/Radclyffe—capturing the close relationships they've built with their readers.

As the film was being edited by William A. Anderson in 2014, planning for the conference went into high gear, with Pamela Regis, president of IASPR, working closely with me and John Cole of the LoC. The conference *What Is Love? Romance Fiction in the Digital Age* took place at the Library of Congress on February 10–11, 2015. It opened with a standing-room-only gala sneak preview of *Love between the Covers*, followed by Q&A with the film's creators and its main characters. The following day there were four panels. The subjects of the panels were: I. What Belongs in the Romance Canon? II. What Do the Science and History of Love Reveal? III. Community and the Romance Genre. IV. Trending Now: Where Is Romance Fiction Heading in the Digital Age? These panel discussions and the Q&A with the audience can be viewed at either lovebetweenthecovers.com/loc-con or Popular RomanceProject.org/library-congress-conference. The conference also featured interactive stations where attendees could explore PopularRomanceProject.org with help from those who designed it.

Hot Docs International Film Festival in Toronto hosted the international premiere of *Love between the Covers* in April 2015, and the film's U.S. premiere took place at the Los Angeles Film Festival in June 2015. *Love between the Covers* won Best Documentary Film at La Femme International Film Festival and Best Feature Film at the Newburyport Documentary Film Festival, and the American Library Association's *Booklist* named *Love between the Covers* 2015's Best Video.

The library program of the Popular Romance Project was launched while the film was traveling to film and book festivals in 2015. More than 100 screenings have taken place at public libraries and university libraries. These screenings are typically coupled with panels, discussion groups, book signings, and romance-themed parties. (Lovebetweenthecovers.com/screenings/ lists all of the screenings.)

Romance groups, bloggers, students, university professors, librarians, and readers now watch the film at public events, in their homes, and at their schools and universities. (Lovebetweenthecovers.com/film-release-news provides news about the film's release with links.) *Love between the Covers* is distributed by Women Make Movies (North American educational use), The Orchard (North American consumer use), and Java Films (overseas sales).

The reach of The Popular Romance Project is global, and it has exceeded the expectations of its founders. PopularRomanceProject.org, the Library of Congress conference, *Love between the Covers*, and the library program have all stimulated lively crossdisciplinary discussions about popular romance. And what could be more basic to human society than the stories we tell about love?

Funding to develop the Popular Romance Project came from Mass Humanities, a scholar's grant from the Romance Writers of America, and the National Endowment for the Humanities. Production funding came from the National Endowment for the Humanities, the Nora Roberts Foundation, Amazon.com's Literacy Fund, and more than 300 individuals who responded to the project's Kickstarter campaign.

Laurie Kahn

Further Reading

Blueberry Hill Productions. http://www.blueberryhillproductions.com/ and http://www.lovebetweenthecovers.com/. Accessed April 30, 2017.

Center for History and New Media, George Mason University. http://PopularRomance Project.org/. Accessed April 30, 2017.

International Association for the Study of Popular Romance. http://iaspr.org. Accessed April 30, 2017.

Library of Congress Center for the Book. http://www.read.gov/cfb/. Accessed April 30, 2017.

Prism and On the Far Side Awards

The Prism Awards for published authors and the On the Far Side Awards for unpublished authors are presented by the Fantasy, Futuristic, and Paranormal Chapter (FFP) of the Romance Writers of America (RWA). Entries may be novels or novellas that feature a story with a central romantic relationship that has a satisfactory or optimistic ending and include fantasy, futuristic, or paranormal elements that are integral to the plot. Submissions for the Prism Awards must have been published during the previous year. Finalists for the Prisms are announced in late spring, and the winners are usually announced at the Prism Awards Ceremony during the annual RWA conference in July. Finalists for the On the Far Side Awards are announced in early July, and the winners are posted in August. The On the Far Side contest is handled completely online.

Writers may submit work in a number of categories that currently include Dark Paranormal, Light Paranormal, Science Fiction/Futuristic, Fantasy, Urban Fantasy, Steampunk, Erotic, Historical, Young Adult, and New Adult.

Kristin Ramsdell

See also: Romance Writers of America

Further Reading

On the Far Side Awards. www.romance-ffp.com/on-the-far-side-unpublished/. Accessed April 30, 2017.
Prism Awards. www.romance-ffp.com/prism-contest-published/. Accessed April 30, 2017.

Pseudonyms

Authors may use pseudonyms, pen names, or noms de plume when they wish to publish under a different name than their own. There are several reasons an author may choose to use a different name: (1) to keep his/her personal privacy; (2) to avoid confusing readers when he/she writes in a different genre; (3) to space out works when the writer is very prolific.

In the not-so-distant past, most female authors had to use a male name or no name at all to have their works published. Rarely were women educated or sent to school, and so a literary career was not even possible for most. Poor, working women may have worked outside the home in taverns or similar establishments as seamstresses or maids. Women who were middle class either married and became the property of their husbands or remained spinsters as the unpaid caregivers and companions for relatives for the rest of their lives. During the 17th, 18th, and 19th centuries, society dictated that women were intellectually inferior or that somehow their earning a living was against the natural order. However, by the Victorian Era there were a few women embarking on writing careers without censure or criticism.

One of the most well-known examples of a woman's not using her name was Mary Shelly's *Frankenstein*, which was initially published by the author *Anonymous*. Another is Jane Austen's *Sense and Sensibility*, which was published using the name "By A Lady." In fact, very few people knew that Jane Austen herself wrote fiction, let alone published it. In turn, all three Brontë sisters used male pseudonyms to have their works published; Emily using the name Ellis Bell; Charlotte, the name Currer Bell; and Anne, the name Acton Bell. The Brontës used the male pseudonyms because, as Charlotte stated, "we had a vague impression that authoresses are liable to be looked on with prejudice" (Thormahlen). One of the leading writers of the Victorian Period, Mary Anne Evans, is still known mainly by her pen name George Eliot. Evans explained that she used a male pen name so that her writing would be taken seriously, and because she was living with a married man at the time of publication of her novels. Society would not be so forgiving of a female author of dubious morals.

Although it is now possible for female writers to publish under their own names, many continue to use pseudonyms. One reason is the marginalization of the Romance novel genre, the most disregarded genre in fiction. Accordingly, many romance authors have used pseudonyms to protect their nonauthor identities. For instance, Mary Bly used her pen name "Eloisa James" for over 20 years due to her career in academia. Bly wrote her first romance novel to pay off her student loans and found that she enjoyed writing them. When *People* magazine wanted to write a profile about her, the chair of her English department at Fordham University said, "You can't do that. You won't get tenure" (Sachs). Bly had been told that if her romance-writing career was exposed, her academic career would be over. In the current Internet age, personal privacy takes on a very significant role for some authors, and for their own privacy they will use a pseudonym.

Oftentimes, an author uses a pseudonym when she writes in more than one subgenre within the larger Romance genre. For instance, an author who has published several contemporary romances might decide to publish a historical Regency romance. However, some romance readers read only a specific subgenre of romance. Were that author to publish the historical Regency romance under the same name that she used for the contemporary romance, many of her readers might be confused and disappointed since historical Regency romances have very different elements than contemporary romances. By using a pseudonym, the author can avoid that confusion. One example is Eileen Dreyer, who writes mystery and suspense novels under her own name but uses the name Kathleen Korbel for her earlier romances. Under the name Korbel, Dreyer writes category novels that are shorter and have a contemporary or paranormal setting. For her grittier suspense novels, which include serial killers and other unromantic elements, Dreyer uses her own name. More recently, Dreyer has moved into historical romance with the publication of her Drake Rakes series using her own name. By keeping the Dreyer and Korbel names separate, she is able to please all her readers because when they pick up a Korbel novel or a Dreyer novel, they know exactly what type of story they will get. Nora Roberts has taken a similar path, using the pseudonym J. D. Robb for her gritty, futuristic Eve Dallas mystery suspense series and writing her contemporary romances and romantic suspense novels as Nora Roberts.

Another reason an author could use a pseudonym is to prevent market saturation. Many authors are wildly prolific; for example, Nora Roberts writes over 1,500 words a day. With multiple avenues of publication—shorter category novels, longer contemporary and historical novels, novellas, and so on—an author could easily have multiple books available to her readers in a short amount of time. To avoid this saturation, an author could use a pseudonym so she doesn't seem to overwhelm her readers. Jayne Ann Krentz began writing contemporary and category novels under several names, but in the early 1990s she began publishing historical romance novels using the name Amanda Quick. Later, she again turned to a pseudonym for her futuristic, paranormal novels published under the name Jayne Castle. At one point, Krentz experimented with combining all her pseudonyms within the Arcane Society series, allowing readers to follow the society's developmental arc from the past to the present and into the future. Each year Krentz publishes a contemporary novel under the name Krentz, a historical novel under the name Quick, and a futuristic novel under the name Castle, all standalone romances but some with an occasional reference to events or characters in books written under one of the author's other names. By using different names, Krentz allows herself the multiple publishing opportunities of a successful author without overwhelming the market, and at the same time she lets the reader know just what kind of romance to expect.

Below are some examples of pseudonyms used by romance authors:

- Sandra Brown writes contemporary, historical, romantic suspense, and category romance novels. Writing as Rachel Ryan or Erin St. Claire, she writes category romance novels.
- Eileen Dreyer writes romantic suspense, historical, and mystery novels. Writing as Kathleen Korbel, she writes contemporary category novels.
- Heather Graham writes historical romance, romantic suspense, paranormal romance, and category novels. Writing as Heather Graham Pozzessere, she

writes historical romance, romantic suspense, and category novels; and writing as Shannon Drake, she writes historical romance and paranormal novels.

- Eleanor Alice Burford Hibbert wrote Gothic romances as Victoria Holt, her centuries-spanning Daughters of England series as Philippa Carr, and biographical historical fiction as Jeanne Plaidy.
- Mary Bly writes historical romances as Eloisa James.
- Jayne Ann Krentz writes contemporary and romantic suspense romance novels, historical romances as Amanda Quick, and futuristic/paranormal romances under her maiden name, Jayne Castle.
- Ann Maxwell writes science fiction and romantic suspense novels. As Elizabeth Lowell, she writes contemporary, historical, and category romance; she writes mystery and historical romances novels as A. E. Maxwell. Some of her books are written in collaboration with her husband, Evan.
- Nora Roberts writes contemporary romantic suspense, paranormal, and fantasy novels; she writes futuristic mystery suspense as J. D. Robb.
- Sharon Sala writes contemporary and category romance novels. Writing as Dinah McCall, she writes romantic suspense and paranormal romance novels.

Sarah Sheehan

Further Reading

Rosengarten, Herbert J. "Charlotte Bronte." In *Victorian Novelists before 1885*: *Dictionary of Literary Biography*, vol. 21, edited by Ira Bruce Nadel and William E. Fredeman. Detroit: Gale Research, 1983.

Sachs, Andrea. "Mary Bly a.k.a. Eloisa James Talks to TIME about Her Literary Double Life." *Time*, May 18, 2012. http://entertainment.time.com/2012/05/18/mary-bly-aka -eloisa-james-talks-to-time-about-her-literary-double-life/. Accessed May 1, 2017.

Thormahlen, Marianne. "The Brontë Pseudonyms: A Woman's Image—The Writer and Her Public." *The Victorian Web: Literature, History, & Culture in the Age of Victoria.* 1992. http://www.victorianweb.org/authors/bronte/cbronte/thormahlen.html. Accessed May 1, 2017.

Pygmalion Plot Pattern

Based on the classical Greek myth of Pygmalion, a sculptor and King of Cyprus, who fell in love with the ivory statue of the "ideal woman" he had created and married her after the goddess Aphrodite answered his prayer and brought the statue to life, this plot pattern is one of the oldest and most fascinating that has found its way into the Popular Romance genre. George Bernard Shaw used this myth as the basis for his eponymous play in 1912—the story of linguist Henry Higgins's remarkable transformation of Cockney flower girl Eliza Doolittle into a society miss—and in 1964 the play became the basis for the hit musical *My Fair Lady*, at the hands of Lerner and Lowe.

Although today's romance heroes or heroines rarely fall in love with statues, they often go in the George Bernard Shaw or *My Fair Lady* direction, falling for the very ones they have set out to change and generally being surprised when that happens. Because of the importance of class and social status, and because the way in which one speaks and behaves defines this status, the Pygmalion plot is especially well suited to historical romances. Sometimes the plot will involve a wager, and there may be a time limit placed on the "transformation" process, though not always. For example, a 16th-century knight rescues a penniless woman from the auction block and bets he can turn her into a lady in a scant fortnight in Tori Phillips's *Lady of the Knight* (Harlequin Historical, 1999); a bookish noble-man accepts a wager that he can turn the mousiest girl in an acting troupe into a star on the London stage in Isabella Bradford's steamy Georgian romance *A Reckless Desire* (Ballantine Books, 2016); and a young singer caring for a small band of orphans agrees to help a nobleman win a wager by turning her into an aristocrat in Lydia Joyce's Victorian romance *Voices of the Night* (Signet Eclipse, 2007). Tessa Dare's light-hearted Regency *Any Duchess Will Do* (Avon, 2013) adds a new wrinkle to the pattern when a marriage-averse duke sets out to prove his mother wrong in her insistence that she can turn any girl into a duchess and ends up choosing a well-read serving girl who just wants to own her own book-store and has no intention of being a duchess; and Judith Ivory's *The Proposition* (Avon, 1999) flips the pattern (and Victorian society) on its head when the linguistics-expert heroine accepts a wager that she can turn a Cornish rat-catcher into a society-worthy "nobleman" in just six weeks.

Of course, wagers or dares aren't always involved; often it's simply a matter of necessity. For example, in Nancy Campbell Allen's sweet Regency *My Fair Gentleman* (Shadow Mountain, 2016), the merchant seaman hero inherits a title and wealth and must learn how to navigate the *ton* for the sake of his sister and mother with the help of a proper, but independent, young lady; and a Chinese no-bleman of the Tang dynasty, who must come up with a replacement bride for his superior, chooses the young housemaid and falls for her in the process in Jeannie Lin's *My Fair Concubine* (Harlequin Historical, 2012).

Although most romances that use the Pygmalion plot pattern are historical, a few are set in the present. The social and cultural issues are a bit different, but the goal is still for either the hero or the heroine to get up to speed and fit into the current version of society's expectations. Luanne McLane's *Redneck Cinderella* (Signet, 2009) is the classic story of a country girl who is thrust into society when her dad sells his tobacco farm for a fortune and is encouraged to take speech and etiquette lessons to fit into society by the developer who falls in love with her in the process; and in a reverse-Pygmalion plot, a reclusive model-train painter who wants to marry and settle down is aided by a diner waitress who notices that his social skills need honing in Shannon Stacey's *Falling for Max* (Carina, 2016), a funny, memorable romp.

Historically grounded and popular for years, Pygmalion is a well-used plot pattern that has many guises and variations, and in capable hands it never fails to entertain.

Kristin Ramsdell

Further Reading

Evans, Ivor H., ed. *Brewer's Dictionary of Phrase and Fable*, rev. ed. New York: Harper and Row, 1981.

R

Radcliffe, Ann (1764–1823)

Ann Radcliffe née Ward is an English author widely regarded as the "mother" of Gothic fiction. Her dreamlike and poetic novels, the most famous of which is *The Mysteries of Udolpho* (1794), established many of the conventions of the genre. Radcliffe's influence can be seen in the work of a diverse group of authors, from the scribblers of William Lane's Minerva Press to some of the most important figures in canonical Romanticism. Jane Austen, for example, affectionately parodied Radcliffe's novels in *Northanger Abbey* (1818), while Matthew Lewis's salacious and violent book *The Monk* (1796) was explicitly presented as a reaction to the more decorous work of his female contemporary.

Radcliffe was a retiring woman, and very few of her letters, journals, and papers have survived. As a result, little is known about the events of the author's life. Sir Walter Scott noted, "The life of Mrs Ann Radcliffe, spent in the quiet shade of domestic privacy, and in the interchange of familiar affections and sympathies, appears to have been as retired and sequestered, as the fame of her writings was brilliant and universal" (207). The author was born in London on July 9, 1764, the only child of Ann Oates and William Ward. Although her father was "in trade" (he was a haberdasher), the Wards were a respectable, well-connected family who moved in dissenting circles. In 1772, the Wards moved to the fashionable resort town of Bath, and it was in Bath that the young Ann Ward married William Radcliffe in 1787. Her new husband was an Oxford graduate trained in the law, who was later to become the editor of the *English Chronicle*.

With her husband's encouragement, Radcliffe began writing shortly after her marriage. Her first novel, *The Castles of Athelin and Dunbayne*, was published in 1789 when the writer was 24. It was not widely reviewed (Norton, 57). *A Sicilian Romance* (1790) appeared soon after and was followed by *The Romance of the Forest* (1791); *The Mysteries of Udolpho* (1794); the travel narrative *A Journey made in the Summer of 1794 through Holland and the Western frontier of Germany*

(1795); and *The Italian, or the Confessional of the Black Penitents* (1797). Radcliffe's final novel, *Gaston de Blondeville, or The Court of Henry III Keeping Festival in Ardenne* (1826), was the only one of her books to be set in England and was published posthumously.

Radcliffe's novels are famous for their deployment of terror, a key hallmark of the "feminine" form of Gothic fiction that she pioneered. Whereas horror is designed to shock the reader by shattering everyday reality, terror is predicated on the idea that rationality can always overcome the threat posed by the forces of irrationality. In Radcliffe's own words, "terror and horror are so far opposite, that the first expands the soul, and awakens the faculties to a high degree of life; the other contracts, freezes and nearly annihilates them" ("On the Supernatural in Poetry," 168). In the Radcliffian Gothic novel, that which produces terror is typically deflated at the end of the narrative—the heroine's irrational fears of ghosts, skeletons, and supposed murders are given rational explanation, and order is restored.

Despite the great success of *The Italian* (the author was paid the extraordinary sum of £800 for the book by her publisher Thomas Cadell), it was the final novel to be published in Radcliffe's lifetime. Radcliffe retired from public life at the height of her fame. This decision, the motive for which remains unclear, led some to speculate that she had gone mad: "It was conjectured that her wild imagination had preyed upon itself, that her effort to create visions of horror had finally driven her into a lunatic asylum" (Norton, 203).

After many years of ill health, Ann Radcliffe died in London on February 7, 1823, of what her biographer believes was "bronchial infection, leading to pneumonia, high fever, delirium and death" (Norton, 243). She was buried in a vault in the church of Saint George's, Hanover Square.

Claire Knowles

See also: *The Mysteries of Udolpho*

Further Reading

Norton, Rictor. *The Mistress of Udolpho*. London and New York: Leicester University Press, 1999.

Radcliffe, Ann. "On the Supernatural in Poetry." In *Gothic Documents: A Sourcebook, 1700–1820*, edited by E. J. Clery and Robert Miles, 163–72. Manchester and New York: Manchester University Press, 2000.

Scott, Walter. "Mrs Radcliffe." *Lives of the Novelists*, vol 1. Paris: A. and W. Galignani, 1825, 207–68.

Rape in Romance

Rape seems the very antithesis of romance: violence, violation, and total disregard of a woman's wishes. Yet from Zeus's rape of Leda in Greek myth to "Sheik" Rudolph Valentino's rape of Lady Diana Mayo in American cinema, the trope of men forcing sex upon women has figured largely in Western narrative, and particularly so in the genre of Romance Fiction. We can begin to account for this apparent paradox by noting that while 99 percent of women state they do not want to be raped in reality, between 31 percent and 57 percent of women report having sexual fantasies about being raped (Critelli and Bivona). Given such statistics, if Romance Fiction is defined as a woman's erotic fantasy set down in words, the appearance of rape as a theme in the genre should not be surprising.

Rape, or the threat of rape, has been present in Romance Fiction since its beginnings. The eponymous heroine of Samuel Richardson's 18th-century novel *Pamela* continually escapes Mr. B's forceful seduction attempts, but his earlier violent behavior does not stand in the way of their eventual marriage. In contrast, Clarissa, the heroine of Richardson's later novel by the same name, is actually raped by the novel's purported hero, a fate that leads not to marriage but to her death.

By the 20th century, romance heroines could be sexually taken without consent by the heroes in their novels and not meet an untimely death. Heroines could even be presumed to like being so taken, a trope known as "forced" or "aggressive seduction." As author Jayne Ann Krentz argues, "The fantasy of being aggressively seduced within the safe, controlled environment of a work of fiction is a popular one shared by men and women alike" (110).

In early 20th-century romance, however, scenes of aggressive seduction typically took place offstage, or were merely implied (see, for example, Edith Maude Hull's *The Sheik*, published in 1919). Not until the advent of the so-called bodice ripper, or sexually explicit historical romance of the 1970s and 1980s, were readers invited into the bedroom to witness the heroine's seduction (or violation, depending on the reader's interpretation). Rosemary Rogers's *Sweet Savage Love* (1974) and Judith McNaught's *Whitney, My Love* (1985) both contain some version of the forced-seduction/rape trope, as do myriad other romance novels published in paperback during the feminist second wave.

At the time of their publication, such novels proved immensely popular among women readers. Today, however, with changes in the laws about rape and the public's greater awareness of, and sympathy for, rape victims, reader opinion is decidedly mixed. Debates at popular romance review websites such as Dear Author and Smart Bitches, Trashy Books testify to the mixed feelings readers have toward older books that insist that rape is really only aggressive seduction.

"Rapey" books have been far less common since the 1990s, although the trope can still be found in romances being published today. Christina Dodd's *A Well-Pleasured Lady* (1997), Anne Stuart's *Black Ice* (2005), Anna Campbell's *Claiming the Courtesan* (2007), and Sara Craven's *The Innocent's Surrender* (2009) have all inspired reader debates over whether their heroines have been aggressively seduced (acceptable) or raped (unacceptable).

Not all romance novelists depict rape in the form of a positive seduction. Even as early as 1980, Harlequin writers such as Daphne Clair, in *The Loving Trap*, and Charlotte Lamb, in *Stranger in the Night*, tackled the difficulties of recovering from rape to develop healthy sexual and love relationships (although date rape was termed "rough lovemaking" on the back cover of Lamb's book). Historical romance writers began to explore rape trauma during the subsequent decade, with the theme occurring with regularity in the works of authors such as Catherine Coulter (*Night Fire*, 1989) and Catherine Anderson (*Comanche Heart*, 1991; *Annie's Song*, 1996). Radway and other critics, however, argue that such depictions of rape are still complicit with patriarchal values, for they dangerously minimize the trauma of rape and suggest that all a victim needs is a good man to help her manage her feelings and fears.

More realistic depictions of the trauma of rape are found in recent historical romances, such as Mary Balogh's *One Night for Love* (1999) and *Simply Love* (2006) and Mary Jo Putney's *The Bartered Bride* (2002). Nora Roberts, writing contemporary romance under her own name and suspense under her pseudonym, J. D. Robb, seems particularly invested in exploring the impact of rape; nearly one quarter of her published books include representations of rape, according to An Goris.

Though statistically unusual in real life, forced seduction of an adult male by an adult woman can also be found in Romance Fiction: Susan Elizabeth Phillips's *This Heart of Mine* (2001) and Jo Beverley's *Forbidden* (2003), to name two examples. A more common recent trend is the hero who has experienced sexual abuse as a child, either at the hands of an older woman or, more often, an adult male, and who must come to terms with his experience to develop a healthy adult romantic relationship. Liz Carlyle's *The Devil You Know* (2003) and *Never Deceive a Duke* (2007) explore this trope in a historical romance setting, as do Dinah McCall's *Jackson Rule* (1996) and Nora Roberts's *Rising Tides* (1998).

Jackie Horne

Further Reading

Critelli, Joseph, and Jenny Bivona. "The Nature of Women's Rape Fantasies: An Analysis of Prevalence, Frequency, and Contents." *Journal of Sex Research* 46, 1 (2009): 33–45.

Critelli, Joseph W., and Jenny K. Bivona. "Women's Erotic Rape Fantasies: An Evaluation of Theory and Research." *Journal of Sex Research* 45, 1 (2008): 57–70.

Goris, An. "Rape as Trope in Nora Roberts' Romance Fiction." Unpublished talk, *IASPR* conference 2011.

Krentz, Jayne Ann. "Trying to Tame the Romance: Critics and Correctness." In *Dangerous Men and Adventurous Women: Romance Writers on the Appeal of the Romance*, edited by Jayne Ann Krentz, 107–14. Philadelphia: University of Pennsylvania Press, 1992.

Ménard, A. Dana, and Christine Cabrera. "'Whatever the Approach, Tab B Still Fits into Slot A': Twenty Years of Sex Scripts in Romance Novels." *Sexuality and Culture* 15 (2001): 240–55.

Radway, Janice. *Reading the Romance: Women, Patriarchy, and Popular Culture*. Chapel Hill: University of North Carolina Press, 1984.

"Sexual Force and Reader Consent in Romance." Dear Author blog. September 28, 2010. http://dearauthor.com/features/letters-of-opinion/sexual-force-and-reader-consent-in-romance/. Accessed May 1, 2017.

Tan, Candy. "Talking about the R Word." Smart Bitches, Trashy Books. September 14, 2005. http://smartbitchestrashybooks.com/blog/talking_about_the_r_word/. Accessed May 1, 2017.

Toscano, Angela. "A Parody of Love: The Narrative Uses of Rape in Popular Romance." *Journal of Popular Romance Studies* (April 2012).

Rebecca (1938)

"Last night I dreamt I went to Manderley again." The opening sentence of *Rebecca* is perhaps one of the most famous in all of English literature; and with these mesmerizing words, Daphne du Maurier sweeps readers up in an unforgettable journey of romance and suspense. First published in England in 1938, *Rebecca* not only went on to become a best seller, it also served as the literary source for an Academy Award–winning movie directed by Alfred Hitchcock, as well as two different PBS adaptations, a play, and, most recently, a musical.

The heroine of *Rebecca* first meets Maximillian (Maxim) de Winter while working in the south of France as a paid companion to a wealthy American. After a whirlwind courtship, the heroine marries Maxim, and the two travel to Manderley, the de Winter family estate in England's West Country. There, the heroine finds herself continually battling the lingering memory of Rebecca, Maxim's beautiful first wife, for her husband's affections. Not only does the heroine of *Rebecca* have to deal with her husband's late first wife, she must also engage in an ongoing battle of wits with the estate's housekeeper, Mrs. Danvers, who is determined that no woman will every replace Rebecca as mistress of Manderley.

While there may be the occasional quibble from some critics as to *Rebecca*'s merits as a love story, there is really no disputing the novel's place in the Romance canon. *Rebecca* has all of the quintessential elements of the classic Gothic romance: a subtly chilling and quite sophisticated blend of danger and desire, a beautifully realized and wonderfully atmospheric setting, and a heroine, who after being isolated from all outside forms of support, must rely on her own wits to win the love of the book's aristocratic, enigmatic hero.

With the heroine of *Rebecca*, du Maurier created a woman with whom readers can readily relate, in part because she remains nameless throughout the novel. While du Maurier coyly refers to the heroine's name several times throughout the book, at no point does the reader actually discover what her name is. Thus, the heroine in *Rebecca* becomes an "everywoman" protagonist, and readers quickly find themselves invested in her fight for her marriage (and perhaps even her mind) against the cruelly beautiful Rebecca.

Du Maurier created some wonderfully memorable characters in Rebecca—including the housekeeper to end all housekeepers, Mrs. Danvers—but perhaps her greatest achievement in terms of a character is the story's magnificent setting: Manderley. Du Maurier based Manderley not only on the house of a friend she had visited in her childhood but also on her own home of Menabilly, an Elizabethan estate that she discovered and later bought in Cornwall.

Throughout *Rebecca*, du Maurier provides a richly detailed account of the house and its grounds, giving readers the perfect setting for her bewitching tale of passion and peril. While she was alive, Rebecca put her own indelible stamp on the mansion. Now the book's nameless heroine is constantly striving to fit in as the elegant home's new mistress, but Mrs. Danvers will stop at nothing to protect her late mistress's legacy at Manderley. So well described is Manderley and so vital to the book's plot, the setting itself essentially becomes an important character in its own right.

While literary critics may have chosen to ignore *Rebecca* (or damn it with faint praise), the book became an instant best seller when it was published in England, and its success quickly spread across the Atlantic. *Rebecca* became such a commercially lucrative novel that it not only attracted two different charges of plagiarism (both later found to be unsubstantiated), but it also prompted several authorized sequels after du Maurier's death in 1989. Award-winning British author Susan Hill wrote the first sequel, *Mrs. DeWinter*, in 1993, which picks up the narrative thread 10 years after the events in *Rebecca*. Sally Beauman then offered her own follow-up to *Rebecca* with *Rebecca's Tale* in 2001, in which four different characters try to sort out Rebecca's life and demise. In 1996, Maureen Freely wrote an unauthorized version of *Rebecca*, aptly titled *The Other Rebecca*, in which events of du Maurier's novel are transposed to the present day.

accomplished horsemen, curricle racers, marksmen, or even boxers, these are not stories that are driven by physical action or adventure. Instead, the real action in these books is verbal and usually takes place during a seemingly unending stream of social events that require the characters' attendance, allowing them to engage in the lively banter and rapier-like repartee that often drives the plot and is one of the hallmarks of this subgenre. Quick wit and a cleverly turned phrase are much admired and are skills to be cultivated in a world where a well-done verbal "set down" is as effective as a punch to the jaw in putting someone in his or her place.

Abundant descriptions of the settings, clothing, entertainments, activities, and food are common to this subgenre and are almost always highly detailed. They are also usually accurate to a fault because the Traditional Regency fan takes the subgenre seriously and is sure to notice any mistakes—and the authors know this.

As mentioned above, the classic Regency usually uses some version of the marriage plot. It often begins with the heroine's "coming out," her various adventures and experiences, and her ultimate engagement/marriage to the hero. Although many of these heroines are quite young—women of the period often married in their late teens, soon after their first or second season, and were considered firmly "on the shelf" if unwed by their early twenties—this is not always the case. Governesses, widows, chaperones, writers, bluestockings, and self-confirmed spinsters have all had their turn in the "heroine limelight" in a variety of scenarios with delightful results. Typically, Regency heroes are older, as socially elite men rarely married as young as women did, with many either in school or the military or simply enjoying their bachelorhood before settling down. However, once it becomes necessary to marry either to provide an heir or to shore up the family finances, marriage is definitely in the offing, and the hero steps up to the plate. Whoever the protagonists are, a vast assortment of problems arise to keep them apart, including scandal, parental objections, an embittered other man/woman, an unexpected villain, class differences, and often their own initial dislike of each other. It all works out in the end, of course, in classic happily-ever-after fashion.

The Traditional Regency romance traces its origins from the works of Jane Austen and her insightful contemporary comedies of manners (1811–1818) that brilliantly, and often with scathing wit, depicted the current social situation. Over a century later, British author Georgette Heyer continued Austen's legacy, penning historical novels set during both the Georgian (for example, *These Old Shades*) and, primarily, the Regency Periods. Heyer's books sparked an interest in Regency romance, and a number of romance publishers began publishing them in mass-market format, often as part of Regency-specific lines (for example, Signet Regency Romance, Zebra Regency). However, changing tastes and financial realities led to the eventual closing of the Regency-specific lines, sending a number of Traditional Regency authors in the Regency-set historical romance direction. Jo

Beverley, Mary Jo Putney, Mary Balogh, Kate Moore, Candice Hern, and Loretta Chase are only a few of the many examples of authors who successfully made the transition.

As of this writing, the Regency Period remains one of the most popular settings for historical romance. While most of these current books are Regency-set historicals and not Traditional Regencies, there is access to some of these earlier titles. A number of public libraries still have them in their collections; publishers are occasionally republishing some backlist titles they still have the rights to; and, finally, a growing number of authors are now releasing their backlists independently, either as e-books or in print, making titles available that have been out of print for years.

Kristin Ramsdell

See also: Heyer, Georgette; Historical Romance

Further Reading

Kloester, Jennifer. *Georgette Heyer's Regency World*. London: Heinemann, 2005.

Moore, Kate. "From Regency to Historical." *All about Romance*, December 9, 1997. http://allaboutromance.com/kate-moore-from-regency-to-historical/. Accessed May 11, 2017.

Ramsdell, Kristin. "Traditional Regency Romance." In *Romance Fiction: A Guide to the Genre*, 2nd ed. Santa Barbara, CA: Libraries Unlimited, 2012, 277–311.

Regency Reader. http://www.regrom.com/. Accessed May 11, 2017.

Regency World at candicehern.com. http://candicehern.com/regency-world/. Accessed May 11, 2017.

Reunion Plot

See Second Chance at Love/Reunion Plot

Reviews and Reviewing

It's all about marketing. Flashy packaging, like a sexy cover on a romance novel, can't make up for an inferior product on the inside. It doesn't take long for word to get around when a novel fails to deliver. This is why reviews and reviewers are such important marketing tools for the publishing industry. They validate the product between the covers.

A publishing industry study conducted in 2011 by Bowker revealed word-of-mouth is the number one means of introducing readers to new authors, and it's an effective means of finding the best new releases or an exciting new series. This is what reviewers do. A glowing endorsement by a well-known author or a favorable write-up in a respected industry journal helps boost sales and attract new readers to an author's books. If readers like this current release, they are likely to check out the author's previous books and scan the horizon for the next new release. This type of grassroots publicity can be instrumental in launching a debut author's career or revitalizing a veteran's. Rave reviews, like word-of-mouth recommendations, encourage browsers to buy. Conversely, a negative review cautioning browsers about a book's flaws saves them the disappointment of wasting their money.

So who are these reviewers? What makes them experts? How did they get started and why? Reviewers are professional readers and journalists who have extensive experience with the genres they review. Many are librarians and fellow authors who are accomplished writers themselves. Their expertise to recognize quality writing and engaging plots, and then write entertaining reviews about them, makes these reviewers essential to the publishing industry.

The process of professional reading and reviewing involves more than recreational reading. To say romance reviewers have read hundreds, if not thousands, of novels is not an exaggeration. They know the genre through and through and are credible experts on well-written romance fiction. They read each novel with a critical eye and usually have knowledge of the writing craft as well. Is the dialogue natural? Are the characters realistic? Does the plot lag or rush the reader along at a breakneck pace? Is the story fresh and original or a remake of some worn-out old plotline? Reviewers take note of such things to include in their write-ups.

Often, new releases by rising stars, or even long-established authors, are compared to their previous books. Is this new book a worthy successor to the last? Is this their best ever? Readers deserve to know what to expect in the book they're buying. Tepid reviews can be very motivating to authors anxious to keep their momentum going. Of course, reviewers' observations come from personal perspectives. Their preferences and biases influence their reviews. While one reviewer raves about a book, another pans it.

To solicit credible professional reviews, publishers issue advanced reading copies, known as ARCs, to established booksellers and book-industry periodicals. The ARCs, which are usually uncorrected proofs, are passed along to staff writers or freelance review-writing associates. The resulting reviews are shared with publishers and authors who often select a few snippets to print inside their new releases. These brief teasers pique the interest of potential buyers. Plus, they're gratifying to see for the reviewers who wrote them.

Not all reviewers use publishers' ARCs. Some national publications, like the *New York Times*, invite writers to submit their unpublished books to be considered for their *Sunday Book Review* Section. Staff journalists read and review the books and then select titles to feature in upcoming issues. Library publications such as *Booklist* and *Library Journal* will also consider unpublished manuscripts that are not mainstream publishers' ARCs for review; however, they should be easily available for acquisition by libraries, usually through suppliers such as Ingram or Baker & Taylor.

Book reviews vary in length and content, depending on the publication. *RTBook Reviews* includes feature articles about authors and short write-ups, normally a paragraph or two, on the new releases in each subgenre. Other publications offer more detailed reviews of 200 to 500 words. A typical review presents a plot teaser without divulging too much, introduces the hero and the heroine, and establishes the main conflict they must overcome. It closes with a short, candid assessment of the book and entices the reader into wanting to know the rest of the story. An effective review has value both in *what* is said and in *how* it is said.

This sample review profiles Pamela Clare's contemporary romantic suspense *Breaking Point* (Berkley: New York, 2011. Review originally published by Reader to Reader; used by permission.).

> While Denver investigative reporter Natalie Benoit is traveling to a professional journalism conference in Mexico, the Zeta Cartel attacks her chartered bus inside Ciudad Juarez. She watches in horror as several of her Mexican-born associates are singled out and shot. The gunmen abduct Natalie and throw her into the trunk of a car. Terrified, she's taken to a dilapidated compound deep in the Mexican jungle and locked in a crude, cramped holding cell where she awaits her uncertain fate. She's not alone.
>
> Working undercover, Chief Deputy U.S. Marshal Zach McBride is also imprisoned at this same compound. He's been tortured and questioned repeatedly about the location of a stolen cocaine shipment. From his cell, fresh from another brutal interrogation, Zach hears a woman's trembling voice chanting American nursery rhymes in an adjoining cell. Zach knows that in addition to drug smuggling, this cartel is involved in prostitution and this woman is likely their next unwilling *puta*. The sound of her desperate chanting touches Zach and he calls to her, setting in motion a blockbuster ordeal that binds them together, heart and soul.
>
> Book five of Clare's I-Team series is a spectacular barrage of non-stop, white-knuckle suspense that strikes hard from the opening scene. The realism of Clare's stark, gritty details and in-your-face dialog ratchets up the intensity. Yet at the heart of the unrelenting pace and peril lies a deeply tender love story. Zach

and his fellow I-Team operatives are an unstoppable force intent on protecting Natalie while taking down the ruthless Mexican Zetas. Clare delivers heart-stopping action, cover to cover.

Major Review Sources

There are dozens of book review websites, online booksellers and small presses, reader and writer blogs, and industry journals. So where do you find reliable reviews? A sampling of the major sites is profiled here.

The New York Times Sunday Book Review (NYTSBR)

The New York Times Sunday Book Review (*NYTSBR*), published each Sunday, accepts galleys directly from authors, three to four months prior to the book's publication date. The *NYTSBR* accepts only titles scheduled to be published in the United States and to be sold through bookstores. Because *The New York Times* is such a widely circulated newspaper, its book reviews and endorsements are coveted. However, due to the sheer number of galleys the *NYTSBR* receives, only a small percentage of submittals ever make it into the weekly Sunday edition.

Romantic Times (RT) Book Reviews

Romantic Times (RT) Book Reviews focuses largely, although no longer exclusively, on the Romance genre, which is statistically the best-selling genre of all adult fiction. From 1981 until August 2016, *RT* was published in print; after that it operated exclusively as an online resource. New releases in each subgenre regularly are reviewed and rated. Their overall quality is rated from Phenomenal (Five Star Gold) to Severely Flawed (One Star), and sensuality levels for Contemporary, Historical, and Paranormal Romance and Romantic Suspense are also included with designations ranging from Scorcher to Hot to Mild. Additional defining information is also provided for Erotica and some of the other genres, allowing readers to narrow down their searches more effectively.

Titles are grouped by genre: Romance, Mystery, Paranormal, Young Adult, Inspirational, Mainstream, Sci-Fi/Fantasy, and Erotica. Romance is broken down further into Contemporary Romance, Historical Romance, Romantic Suspense, and Series Romance. The reviews are succinct and candid, reporting both the positives and the negatives. Mainstream fiction is reviewed if the story has an element of romance in the plot.

In May 2018 *RT Book Reviews* announced that it was ceasing publication. The website is secheduled to remain available for a year, although no new content would be added; after that, the website will go dark.

Kirkus Reviews

Kirkus Reviews has been discovering and reviewing new books for 80 years. It is a top authority for both publishing professionals and consumers. In addition to providing the industry with previews of noteworthy, upcoming releases, it provides consumers with reviews and recommendations in weekly e-mail newsletters and on the Kirkus website.

Kirkus receives from 100 to 200 titles for review every day. To manage such a high volume of submittals, Kirkus limits its reviews to unpublished manuscripts, three to four months before their scheduled release date. Kirkus is quite exclusive about the types of books they accept for review. It's easier to list the types of books that are *not* Kirkus material. They are as follows: already published titles, reprints, mass-market titles, self-published titles, print-on-demand titles, poetry (adult), textbooks, specialized technical or professional works, academic titles, reference books, instruction manuals, screenplays or dramatic scripts, computer and technology handbooks, and books of regional interest.

However, many of these books and their authors are eligible for other Kirkus services. Kirkus Indie provides reviews of self-published titles. Kirkus Editorial offers editing services. Kirkus Marketing assists authors by introducing them to consumers and making key contacts with agents, industry officials, and even film executives.

Publishers Weekly (PW)

Publishers Weekly is an American weekly trade magazine serving the publishing industry, booksellers, and libraries with news and reviews of upcoming releases. *PW* has been in continuous publication since 1872, evolving into a premier source of publishing information worldwide.

PW reviews a whopping 7,000 new titles each year, or roughly 130–40 per issue. The anonymous reviews are brief but take up a considerable amount space in each issue. In response to the growing popularity of self-publishing, *PW* began reviewing "vanity press" books in 2010 with its new *PW Select* program. Approximately one fourth of the self-published titles received are included in the *PW Select* quarterly supplement to the *PW* magazine. Publication in a digital edition and a listing in an online database are also available for a nominal registration fee.

Booklist Magazine and Booklist Online

Booklist Magazine, a twice-monthly publication of the American Library Association, provides 8,000 recommended-only reviews on books and other media each year. It is another well-respected source of new-book information, dating back to 1905. Its reviews are also posted on its website, Booklistonline.com. *Booklist* targets librarians and collection developers, but anyone with an interest in its reviews can visit the website, or subscribe to the *Booklist* newsletter to find book information not available on the website.

Library Journal

Library Journal selects books based on the title's potential appeal to all types of libraries. It reviews forthcoming new, first releases, as well as titles previously published in foreign markets being released in the United States for the first time through a U.S. distributor. However, textbooks, children's books, books of a highly technical nature, and foreign-language books are outside *Library Journal*'s area of interest. (*School Library Journal* handles children's and young adult materials.)

A three-to-four–month prepublication lead time is preferred to allow the review to precede the book's release. But there are certain types of books that may be reviewed up to three months after publication, including reference books, coffee-table books, art books, graphic novels, crafts and do-it-yourself books, library-science books, and poetry.

Library Journal offers a free *Review Alert* service for subscribers that e-mails lists of the books to be reviewed in upcoming issues of the magazine. If an item hasn't appeared in the *Alerts* or on the website by its publication date, it probably isn't being reviewed. Hardcover-graphic-novel reviews are published six times per year in *Library Journal* but appear weekly on the website's *Xpress Reviews* section.

Adapting to the new normal of the publishing industry, *Library Journal* recently began reviewing e-book romances, though there are limitations. Books must be first-run, novel-length romances only, but not simultaneous print/e-book titles. However, original romances that will later spin off print editions are accepted. Romance e-book reviews appear six times per year in *Library Journal*. There are plans for other genre fiction e-books to be added to the review rotation in the future.

In addition to print versions, *Library Journal* uses NetGalley, an online digital galley service, to provide its reviewers with prerelease reading copies. Through NetGalley, prequalified professional reader/reviewers download digital books to various e-readers, mobile devices, and computers.

NetGalley

NetGalley is a relatively new publishing-industry service. It launched in 2008 to capitalize on the growing digital-galley market. NetGalley uses e-book downloads to distribute galleys to approved reviewers. This service appeals to publishers because it eliminates the expense of printing and shipping paper galleys and advanced-reading copies. The roster of publishers participating in NetGalley is growing and includes a number of major romance publishers.

NetGalley is not a book-review site but a service to connect publishers with qualified reviewers, providing a clearinghouse for their galleys. Professional readers/reviewers browse through titles on the NetGalley book list and request the ones they would like to review. After the publisher approves their requests, reviewers are able to download their requested titles and start reading. The resulting reviews are posted on the reviewers' associated websites or publications and submitted to NetGalley, where they are available to the publishers.

Other Review Sources

Some major online booksellers, such as Amazon, often include reviews from respected sources like Kirkus, *Booklist*, and *Publishers Weekly* to promote their new romance releases. These reviews are in contrast to the often irreverent freelance comments posted by readers. Combined, these sources present browsers with the full spectrum of reader observations, from professional to profane.

Smaller online booksellers have their own cadres of reviewers to promote the titles they carry on their websites. Many of these sites use a combination of ARCs and NetGalley to distribute their titles. The reviews on these sites are usually upbeat and focused on the story's and the writer's strengths. After all, the objective is to sell books not chase customers away. Still, some sites do point out their books' weaknesses as well as strengths. Many readers prefer this gloves-off approach to book reviewing, but it's important to note that a flawed book isn't necessarily a bad book. Ultimately, it is up to the readers to decide.

Sometimes the way a review is written reveals more about a book than the review itself. A glowing review speaks volumes about a book. A polite review says even more. Writing favorable reviews on mediocre titles can be challenging. Of course, none of this matters if the website has little or no readership. A review matters only if it's read.

A sampling of popular online review sites whose positive comments have appeared on the covers or internal "review pages" of new romances includes *Affaire de Coeur;* Coffee Time Romance; Fresh Fiction; Goodreads; Midwest Book Review; Night Owl Romance; Reader to Reader; Romance Junkies; Romance Reviews Today; Smart Bitches, Trashy Books; The Romance Reader; and The Romance Reviews.

Reader blogs are other popular sources for book reviews, recommendations, and commentary. The casual, conversational tone is appealing to readers, and the bloggers' comments and recommendations express the candid opinions of one reader to another. No one is trying to sell anything. Bloggers tend to be frank, telling it as they see it. This grassroots feel and delivery make book blogs fun to read.

With all this information on book reviews, one question remains—how much of an effect do positive or negative reviews have on book sales? An article by Gabe Habash, "How Much Does the Times Book Review Matter?" in *Publishers Weekly*, explores this very question.

The first phase of the *Publishers Weekly* study involved three nonfiction titles about motherhood and family life, featured on the cover of the May 13, 2012, issue of the *New York Times Sunday Book Review* (*NYTSBR*). The books were chosen for their "lower profile," so that any change in sales would be the result of appearing in the *NYTSBR* and not from an expensive marketing campaign. In addition, the authors of these books were not famous publishing celebrities, whose names alone influence sales.

The first book featured increased sales by 78 percent in the week following the article, rising from 234 copies before the cover article to 417 after. The other two didn't fare as well. The second received a negative review, and its sales declined by 13 percent. The third book, with similar content, had the misfortune of being included in the same article as the negatively reviewed title. The third book's sales suffered for it, falling by 32 percent after appearing in the *NYTSBR* article, even though its review was favorable. In light of this result, with no other apparent cause, the decline in sales was attributed to the book's unfortunate placement in the article. Two weeks after appearing in the *NYTSBR*, sales of all three titles dipped below their pre-article levels.

A second trio of books was chosen from the May 27, 2012, issue of the *NYTSBR*, using the same parameters as for the first group. These titles were all written on the subject of economics. They all received positive reviews, and each increased in sales in the week following the reviews. One of the titles saw phenomenal growth, a whopping 324 percent the first week after the review and 156 percent during the second week. The title with the next most significant gain increased sales by 82 percent the first week after the review and 155 percent the second week. The third title saw an increase of 158 percent the week after the review, but its sales cooled the second week, declining by 21 percent from its prereview level.

The results of the study indicate that the *NYTSBR* continues to influence readers, though perhaps not to the extent of making or breaking new releases. Still, four of the six titles included in the study saw significant increases in sales the week after their cover appearance, having no other apparent advantage. Two of them enjoyed triple-digit growth even after the second week. That's the power of a positive, high-profile review.

The resources cited in this chapter include industry powerhouses like Kirkus, *Publishers Weekly*, *Library Journal*, and *Booklist*, along with a sampling of highly respected publications and popular websites that feature book reviews. With so many reputable sources, it's easy for readers to find reliable information on their next great read.

Sandra Van Winkle

Further Reading

Booklist. www.ala.org/offices/publishing/booklist. Accessed May 5, 2017.

Booklistonline.com. www.booklistonline.com. Accessed May 5, 2017.

Clare, Pamela. *Breaking Point*. New York: Berkley, 2011.

Habash, Gabe. "How Much Does the Times Book Review Matter?" *Publishers Weekly*, July 6, 2012. http://www.publishersweekly.com/pw/by-topic/industry-news/bookselling/article/52907-how-much-does-the-times-book-review-matter.html. Accessed May 7, 2017.

Kirkus Reviews. www.kirkusreviews.com. Accessed May 5, 2017.

Library Journal. lj.libraryjournal.com. Accessed May 6, 2017.

Milliot, Jim, and Clive Chiu. *2010–11 U.S. Book Consumer Demographics and Buying Behaviors Annual Review*. Providence, NJ: Bowker, 2011.

NetGalley. https://s2.netgalley.com/. Accessed May 6, 2017.

New York Times: Book Reviews. https://www.nytimes.com/section/books. Accessed May 6, 2017.

"Reviews." *Publishers Weekly*. http://www.publishersweekly.com/pw/reviews/index.html. Accessed May 5, 2017.

RTBook Reviews. https://www.rtbookreviews.com/. Accessed May 5, 2017.

Richardson, Samuel (1689–1761)

When we think of romance writers, images of women immediately come to mind. But many claim the mother of the genre was not a woman at all but a 50-year-old man: the 18th-century English printer Samuel Richardson.

Richardson was born in Derbyshire in 1689 to a father who worked as a joiner (a skilled carpenter). His father intended him for the church, but due to financial difficulties he could not afford educating his son beyond grammar school. At the age of 17, Richardson had to choose a trade; he decided upon "printer," hoping it would "gratify my Thirst after Reading" (Rivero, xxxv). After serving an apprenticeship, Richardson opened his own successful printing shop in 1721. Throughout his life, he played an active role in London's book trade, typesetting, proofreading, writing indexes and prefaces, and abridging, abstracting, and compiling others' works.

Richardson did not begin his career as novelist until 1739, when two bookseller friends asked him to create an advice manual for uneducated country readers. While drafting instructions for girls sent out to service in "how to avoid the Snares that might be laid against their Virtue" (Rivero, xxxiii), Richardson recalled a story he had heard many years earlier. This story, that of a maidservant importuned by the son of the house whose "noble resistance, watchfulness, and excellent qualities, subdued him, and he thought fit to make her his wife" (Rivero, xxxiv), inspired Richardson to set aside his conduct book and write *Pamela, or Virtue Rewarded*.

Published in November 1740, Richardson's epistolary novel became the best seller of its day. Nearly everyone who read it, from Alexander Pope, the leading man of letters in mid-18th-century England, to those far less educated (upon hearing of the heroine's wedding, the villagers of Slough reportedly rang their church bells in celebration), sang its praises. Still, *Pamela* had its detractors, who took exception to the book's "low" style and its almost pornographic scenes of virtue in distress. The book was pirated or satirized at least 16 times during 1741, most famously by Richardson's rival novelist, Henry Fielding, in *Shamela*.

Richardson's sympathetic portrayals of women show him to be a man ahead of his time. He believed women just as capable of education as men; represented women as individuals, not simply appendages of their male relatives; and often put antifemale opinions in the mouths of his villains and fools. Richardson maintained an extensive correspondence with many of the educated women of his day and supported their literary aspirations. In turn, their opinions and ideas influenced his later novels, *Clarissa* (1748) and *Sir Charles Grandison* (1753).

In his later life, Richardson suffered from what was likely Parkinson's disease. He died of apoplexy in 1761.

Jackie Horne

See also: *Pamela*

Further Reading

Dobson, Austin. *Samuel Richardson*. Honolulu: University Press of the Pacific, 2003.

Flynn, Carol. *Samuel Richardson: A Man of Letters*. Princeton, NJ: Princeton University Press, 1982.

Rivero, Albert J. "Introduction." In *Pamela, or Virtue Rewarded* (1740), by Samuel Richardson, xxxi–lxxvi. Cambridge, UK: Cambridge University Press, 2011.

Roberts, Nora (1950–)

Nora Roberts is the single most successful romance writer of our time. She is the author of more than 200 popular romance novels in a wide variety of formats (category, single-title, novella) and subgenres (Contemporary, Suspense, Paranormal, Western). Writing an average of five novels every year, Roberts is known as a disciplined and prolific writer who has mastered the romance form like no other. Though Romance is her main genre, as J. D. Robb she also writes a genre-bending futuristic romantic suspense series. Roberts's work is exceptionally popular. With over 400 million copies of her books in print and a staggering 176 *New York Times* best sellers to her name—together her novels have spent more than 910 weeks (or 17 consecutive years) on this coveted list—Roberts is one of the best-selling authors on the planet as well as a trailblazer in the Romance genre.

Roberts's early life hardly predicted the stardom that would follow. Born Eleanor Marie "Elly" Robertson on October 10, 1950, in Silver Spring, Maryland, Roberts grew up as the youngest of five children in a Roman Catholic family. Surrounded by books from early childhood, she turned to romance writing when she found herself a stay-at-home mom without a formal higher education at the end of the 1970s. Though Harlequin repeatedly rejected Roberts's early submissions in what is now commonly regarded as one of the most short-sighted editorial decisions in romance-publishing history, Roberts had more success with Silhouette, the newly founded romance division at Simon & Schuster. *Irish Thoroughbred*, Roberts's first novel, was published in the Silhouette Romance line in May 1981 and signaled the beginning of Roberts's record-breaking career.

During the first six years of her career, Roberts wrote category romance novels exclusively. Part of an early cohort of American romance authors at Silhouette, she contributed to the Americanization and modernization of the category romance in the early 1980s. Many of her early novels supplant the traditional naïve, virginal heroine with a stronger, often career-minded female protagonist, use the hero's point of view (still novel at that time), and replace the old-fashioned big misunderstanding with a more substantial kind of conflict. In these early years of her career, Roberts's work already exhibited many of the core characteristics that would continue to define it during the next decades. From the start, Roberts was an exceptionally prolific writer, penning more than 40 category romances in just six years. She developed a predilection for serial narratives, writing multiple family series that continue to be among her most popular works. Early on in her career, Roberts also started experimenting with mixing Romance with other genres, in particular Suspense. Novels such as *Storm Warning* (1984), *A Matter of Choice* (1984), and *Playing the Odds* (1985) represent some of Roberts's earliest attempts at writing Romantic Suspense, a subgenre in which she would soon come to excel. In these first six years, Roberts developed a solid fan base in the romance community. She won numerous Rita Awards and in 1987 became the first inductee in the Romance Writers of America's (RWA) Hall of Fame.

Also in 1987, Roberts's first single title was published. *Hot Ice* is an action-filled romantic suspense story in which a Washington socialite and a down-on-his-luck jewel thief find true love while searching for a priceless treasure. The novel signals the start of Roberts's more thorough exploration of the Romantic Suspense subgenre. In the years that followed, she produced numerous single titles that seamlessly blended romance with mystery and suspense. Mainstream success soon followed; in 1991, Roberts scored her first *New York Times* best seller with the single title *Genuine Lies*. By the beginning of the 1990s, Roberts published one romantic suspense single title a year—a publishing schedule she maintains to this day—while also remaining very productive as a category romance author. Roberts's category romances from this period increasingly focused on the family series—popular series such as the Stanislaskis, Night Tales, and Calhouns series stem from this period—and gained her much acclaim in the romance community. She continues to win Rita Awards and received RWA's Lifetime Achievement Award in 1997.

In the mid-1990s, Roberts added two new types of novels to her expanding oeuvre. In 1994, *Born in Fire* was published. It was the first installment in a new contemporary romance trilogy published by Jove. These single-title romances differ from Roberts's earlier single titles in that they are straight romance. The trilogy expands on Roberts's prior experience with the narrative serial format and offers three full-fledged romance narratives (one per installment) as well as a series-wide story line. The Born In series was a massive success, and Roberts started writing single-title trilogies regularly. Between 1994 and 2012, she completed nine trilogies (including Born In, Dream, and Gallaghers of Ardmore) and two quartets (among them the hugely popular Chesapeake Bay series). By the end of the 1990s, these series increasingly included paranormal elements, a subgenre Roberts had previously touched on briefly in some category romances (for example, *Night Shadow* [1991] and the Donovan trilogy [1992]). In series such as Three Sisters Island, Keys, In the Garden, Circle, and Sign of Seven, the paranormal element is significantly expanded, and many of these novels are driven by their series-wide magical plotlines. By 2009, Roberts bid the Paranormal subgenre a temporary farewell and revisited contemporary romance with the Brides quartet (2009–2010) and Inn Boonsboro trilogy (2011–2012). She later returned to the paranormals with the Cousins O'Dwyer (2013–2014) and Guardians (2015–2016) trilogies, and an apocalyptic series, Chronicles of the One (2017–).

Roberts published *Naked in Death* in 1995. It is the first installment in the genre-bending In Death series Roberts wrote under the pseudonym J. D. Robb.

While the use of the pseudonym originated as a marketing gimmick to accommodate Roberts's naturally rapid writing pace without flooding the market with Nora Roberts books, the series also offered the author new creative possibilities. Written in a decidedly grittier tone than most of her more light-hearted romances, the In Death novels offer a blend of suspense, police procedural, futuristic science fiction, and romance. The open-ended series, which currently consists of 35 novels and a handful of novellas, follows the adventures of a single couple, New York City homicide cop Lieutenant Eve Dallas and her tycoon billionaire lover and later husband, Roarke. Eve and Roarke meet in the series's first installment and are happily married by the beginning of the fourth In Death novel—a plot development that has led some people to question the series's continued status as romance novels. Although the ties between Nora Roberts and J. D. Robb were officially kept under wraps until 2001 (when Roberts publicly "came out" as Robb), the series soon proved very popular in its own right and scored its first *New York Times* best seller listing with *Loyalty in Death* in 1999.

In the second half of the 1990s and first decade of the 21st century, Roberts's popularity soared. Transcending the commercial confines traditionally associated with genre fiction, Roberts gained increasing success in mainstream (American) culture. Since 1999 every new novel she has written has become a *New York Times* best seller; 52 of her novels have debuted on the list's coveted number-one spot. Roberts has repeatedly been included on *Forbes*'s and *Time*'s lists of most powerful celebrities and was recently named "America's favorite novelist" by *The New Yorker*. A number of her novels have been turned into successful made-for-TV movies by Lifetime Television. In 2011, Roberts became only the third author ever to sell more than one million Kindle e-books. While she frequently releases new work, her backlist remains very active as well. Silhouette, which Roberts left in 2001, regularly reissues the author's old category romances, and new editions of her single titles are frequently released as well. Her novels are, moreover, translated into 34 different languages and available all over the world.

Nora Roberts's significance to the Contemporary Popular Romance genre can hardly be overstated. Her work helped modernize and Americanize the genre, played a pivotal role in popularizing the now ubiquitous narrative series format, illustrated the creative possibilities and appeal of genre mixing, and revolutionized some of the genre's publishing and reissuing practices. In this process, Roberts managed to transform herself from a semi-invisible, dime-a-dozen category-romance writer into one of the best-selling authors in the world. Although Roberts's rise to stardom is part of the more general emancipation of the author in the Romance genre over the last few decades, very few stars in the romance sky shine as brightly as hers.

An Goris

Further Reading

Collins, Lauren. "Real Romance. How Nora Roberts Became America's Most Popular Novelist." *The New Yorker*, June 22, 2006: 60–69.

Little, Denis, and Laura Hayden, eds. *The Official Nora Roberts Companion*. New York: Berkley Books, 2003.

Mussell, Kay. "*Paradoxa* Interview with Nora Roberts." *Paradoxa: Studies in World Literary Genres* 3, 1–2 (1997): 155–63.

Regis, Pamela. "One Man, One Woman: Nora Roberts." In *A Natural History of the Romance Novel*, 183–204. Philadelphia: University of Pennsylvania Press, 2003.

Snodgrass, Mary Ellen. *Reading Nora Roberts*. Santa Barbara, CA: ABC-CLIO, 2010.

Romance, Definition of

As a term for literary classification, "romance" comes to us from the early 12th-century word *ronmanz*, for the emerging French vernacular languages derived from Latin. By the late 12th century, "romance" (*romanz, roman, romant*) referred to the books written in or translated to the vernacular. It then evolved not just to name the vernacular books themselves but also to evoke the characteristics and qualities of the popular literature of the time. The concept of "courtly love" originates in these medieval tales of adventure and chivalry—most famously the Arthurian verse romances by the French poet Chrétien de Troyes. "Courtly love" describes a highly conventionalized set of codes for love between aristocratic men and women (knights and damsels, heroes and heroines), which was established and followed in European literature of the 12th century, rather than in the real world of its audiences. Thus, for more than eight centuries, "romance" has been associated with tales of love and adventure that have enormous popular appeal despite (or because of) depicting worlds and characters far removed from the everyday lives of their audiences. This etymology is important to understanding the term's meaning today because it shows us that romance has never been a neutral or straightforward label.

"Romance" is a difficult, if not impossible, term to define in a way that would satisfy everyone. There is no singular, uncomplicated definition encompassing the myriad literary forms, texts, and textual elements that have attracted the label over the centuries. "Romance is a notoriously slippery category" (Fuchs, 1). This rings true whether we consider its long and complex history as a name for diverse types of literature or take a more narrow focus on Romance as a genre of popular fiction, whether we examine it as a critical and theoretical term in literary scholarship or think about its role in the commercial context for publishers, booksellers, writers, and readers, and, finally, whether we recognize the plethora of cultural contexts beyond the literary sphere in which the term resonates or limit our attention to the romance novel. In fact, the most common meaning of "romance" in its current everyday usage is to describe "a love affair" (Fuchs, 4); similarly, in relation to fiction, the term is now mostly used to mean "a love story."

In short, a romance tells a love story about one or more couples. There are romances in every storytelling medium, ranging from films to pop songs, from television series to comic books. This encyclopedia focuses on the most culturally significant branch of the broader narrative genre: the romance novel. In this context, *romance* refers to an immense category of fiction and embraces an enormous variety of subgenres. The protagonists of a romance novel can be young or old, human or supernatural, heterosexual or otherwise; they can live anywhere in the present-day world, in the past, or in another realm altogether; their relationships can be intensely sexual from the novel's first few pages or never consummated; but it is almost universally agreed that their story must have a "happily ever after" ending (or "HEA").

The term "romance" is "confusingly inclusive, meaning one thing in a survey of medieval literature and another, not entirely distinct, in a contemporary bookstore" (Regis, 19). Despite this bewildering diversity, however broadly it is defined, the "imaginative functions" of romance "remain constant": "romance can be distinguished from other forms of fiction by the relationship it imposes between reader and romance-world" (Beer, 8). Readers who accept the ideal fantasy world romance offers "are transported" (8) beyond their everyday reality. This means that romance is *both* escapist and a form of instruction, as readers compare their own lives and realities with those of the characters in the ideal "romance-world" (8).

The idea of "romance" as a designation for *popular* modes of storytelling, in contrast to more learned or refined modes, has persisted from the term's medieval origins to the present day; writers, critics, and fans of 20th- and 21st-century romance novels often complain that their genre is disparaged and dismissed as escapist entertainment. The idea that Romance is frivolous or vulgar is related both to its long history as a mass form of entertainment and to the sense that the genre values convention over originality. The American novelist Diana Gabaldon prefers not to describe her bestselling Outlander series as "romances" for this reason: "The romance genre has very specific expectations, and this leads to a great deal of predictability" (Perry). In contrast, Stephanie Laurens—the author of more than 40 popular romance novels—sees this predictability as both a defining feature and a strength of the genre: "[it] is all about telling a really good story and doing it again, and again, and again" (Sansevieri). For Laurens, the success of the romance writer depends on recognizing that the genre is governed by readers' expectations; in particular, she explains, romance readers want to be transported to "that other world" (Sansevieri) in which achieving a happy ending for love is the ruling principle. She insists, however, that the "essence of romance" is not the happy ending itself but the "hurdles along the journey from first meeting to forever-and-always commitment" (Clare). The phenomenally successful romance novelist Nora Roberts shares this view (Wendell). When asked, "Why should people read romance novels?" she responded, "They are a celebration of relations, finding love, overcoming obstacles and making commitments" (*Time*).

Pamela Regis, in her book *A Natural History of the Romance Novel*, offers a concise definition of the romance novel: "a work of prose fiction that tells the story of the courtship and betrothal of one or more heroines" (19). She goes on to argue that a novel *must* have "eight essential elements" to count as a romance:

> Eight narrative events take a heroine in a romance novel from encumbered to free. In one or more scenes, romance novels always depict the following: the initial state of society in which heroine and hero must court, the meeting between heroine and hero, the barrier to the union of heroine and hero, the attraction between the heroine and hero, the declaration of love between heroine and hero, the point of ritual death, the recognition by heroine and hero of the means to overcome the barrier, and the betrothal. These elements are essential. (30)

Regis expressly rejects the idea that romance novels follow a "formula." The problem with her definition is that these "eight essential elements" come very close to sounding like a formula for fiction. The most useful definitions are less prescriptive; they identify the genre's core or defining features but remain flexible enough to accommodate its essential diversity and to allow for development and change. Romance is not a static form governed by a set of unbending rules but an evolving and dynamic genre; any definition must consider its history and anticipate its future.

The novelist Jennifer Crusie was involved in writing a new definition of romance for the Romance Writers of America (RWA), which would govern the organization's activities into the 21st century. After much deliberation, she says, those involved in this process ("not even close to unanimously") agreed that the RWA definition must include the two aspects of romance that are "inviolable": "The story and the ending" (Crusie). The RWA definition does not include the requirement that a romance novel must focus on a heroine (although the vast majority of romances have a female protagonist at their center):

> Two basic elements comprise every romance novel: a central love story and an emotionally-satisfying and optimistic ending.
> **A Central Love Story**: The main plot centers around individuals falling in love and struggling to make the relationship work. A writer can include as many subplots as he/she wants as long as the love story is the main focus of the novel.

An Emotionally-Satisfying and Optimistic Ending: In a romance, the lovers who risk and struggle for each other and their relationship are rewarded with emotional justice and unconditional love. (Romance Writers of America)

These two basic elements are tied together by three words that are at the heart of every romance: "Thinking romance is a questioning of how it is that one may say 'I love you'" (Elam, 27). One of the best places to look for definitions of romance is, it almost goes without saying, in the novels themselves. Romance is a highly self-referential genre in which narrators and characters frequently draw attention to the meaning and significance of the kind of story in which they feature. For instance, Lucy Marinn, the heroine of Lisa Kleypas's *Rainshadow Road*, falls in love with a local vineyard owner, Sam Nolan, but despairs that they will never have a happy ending: "Sam and I both know that he'll hurt me. He'll never be able to say 'I love you' and surrender his heart to someone" (270). Sam is eventually able to say these all-important words because his relationship with Lucy shows him that "Love was the secret behind everything" (297). Roland Michell, the hero of A. S. Byatt's novel *Possession*, comes to a similar conclusion when he recognizes that he is *in* a romance with the novel's heroine, Maud Bailey; his moving declaration of love invites readers to think about what his words mean and why they are so central to the genre: " I love you. . . . In the worst way. All the things we—we grew up not believing in. Total obsession, night and day. When I see you, you look *alive* and everything else—fades. All that" (506).

Sarah Wendell, in her book *Everything I Know about Love I Learned from Romance Novels*, writes that romance novels are "complex and emotionally driven tales of courtship" (n.p.). She insists that a romance must have a happy ending if readers are to feel rewarded by and learn from their emotional engagement in the story. "Happiness," for Wendell, "is serious business." The editors of the recent academic book *New Approaches to Popular Fiction* agree and add that Romance should be defined not just by the stories it tells but by the "remarkable range of pleasures" it offers readers. Romances "offer encouragement and optimism in the name of love . . . *predictably*, novel after novel, with the lovers' Happily Ever After (HEA) never in doubt" (Selinger and Frantz, n.p.).

Lisa Fletcher

Further Reading

Beer, Gillian. *The Romance*. London: Methuen, 1970.

Byatt, A. S. *Possession: A Romance*. London: Vintage, 1991.

Clare, Pamela. "Interview with Stephanie Laurens." *USA Today*, October 18, 2012. https://web.archive.org/web/20120217130647/http://books.usatoday.com/happyeverafter

/post/2012-02-09/interview-stephanie-laurens-author-of-the-capture-of-the-earl-of
-glencrae/623426/1. Accessed June 3, 2017.

Crusie, Jennifer. "I Know What It Is When I Read It: Defining the Romance Genre." http://
www.jennycrusie.com/for-writers/essays/i-know-what-it-is-when-i-read-it-defining
-the-romance-genre/#container. Accessed May 31, 2017.

Elam, Diane. *Romancing the Postmodern*. New York: Routledge, 1992.

Fuchs, Barbara. *Romance*. New York: Routledge, 2004.

Kleypas, Lisa. *Rainshadow Road*. New York: St. Martin's Griffin, 2012.

Perry, Susan K. "Interview with Diana Gabaldon." *Writing World*. http://www.writing
-world.com/romance/gabaldon.shtml. Accessed May 31, 2017.

Regis, Pamela. *A Natural History of the Romance Novel*. Philadelphia: University of
Pennsylvania Press, 2007.

Romance Writers of America, "About the Romance Genre." http://www.rwa.org/p/cm/ld
/fid=578. Accessed May 31, 2017.

Sansevieri, Penny C. "An Interview with Stephanie Laurens." *Huffington Post*, July 16,
2012; updated September 15, 2012. http://www.huffingtonpost.com/penny-c-sansevieri
/bestseller-series-an-inte_2_b_1666896.html. Accessed May 31, 2017.

Selinger, Eric Murphy, and Sarah S. G. Frantz. "Introduction: New Approaches to Popular
Romance Fiction." In *New Approaches to Popular Romance Fiction*, edited by Sarah
S. G. Frantz and Eric Murphy Selinger, 1–19. Jefferson, NC: McFarland, 2012.

"10 Questions for Nora Roberts." *Time*, December 10, 2007, 6. http://web.b.ebscohost
.com.ezproxy.sfpl.org/ehost/detail/detail?vid=0&sid=845d9346-54e6-458a-a67f-54c57
24de6aa%40sessionmgr120&bdata=#AN=27711620&db=voh. Accessed June 3, 2017.

Wendell, Sarah. *Everything I Know about Love I Learned from Romance Novels*.
Naperville, IL: Sourcebooks, 2011.

Romance Blogs, Wikis, and Websites

Overview

Blogs, wikis, and websites are all forms of electronic information sharing that have become prevalent in the past decade due to the mass adoption of computers and the ease of accessibility to the Internet. While all three are commonly found formats for organizing and presenting information on the Internet, there are recognizable distinctions among them. The most general of the three is the website; the term *website* simply denotes any collection of related electronic pages on the Internet. Websites are created by individuals, institutions, or interest groups working together to share information on a specified topic or to express the enjoyment of the featured content. Blogs and wikis are two specific types of websites, each with a different particular purpose and method, and have become extremely popular within the last decade. Blogs, short for "web logs," primarily contain personal entries showing an individual's or core group's thoughts and opinions on a topic, such as their criticism and evaluation of the romance stories they have read. As a personal log, blogs tend to follow the structure and character of a journal or diary, with dated posts intended to be read in chronological order and with frequent reference to older posts. Wikis are a type of website that allows people to collaboratively add, modify, or delete content on varied topics. Wikis are created to be a reference resource and generally resemble an encyclopedia in their organization and layout. They exist to provide a place where people can come to read about a unique topic and learn from the collective knowledge of others who contributed to the writing and research of a topic. Additionally, users are encouraged to enrich the collective understanding of a topic by adding their own expertise to the existing articles. This article will cover the current state of blogs, wikis, and websites for the Romance genre.

History

The presence of the Romance genre on the Internet is closely tied to the development of the Web itself and the timeframe in which it became widespread. According to PewResearch Internet Project, the creation of the World Wide Web portion of the Internet was brought about by Sir Tim Berners-Lee's release of an information-management-system code in 1990 (Fox and Rainie). Publication news and other information on romance novels became available online in the late 1990s, when Internet Web usage expanded rapidly and became part of American culture (Spiegel). Websites are considered the building blocks of the Web since they were the earliest and most prevalent format for organizing information on the Web. As it became more common for corporations and industries to have websites, publishers and booksellers began creating their own websites to reach out to readers. The bookseller giant Barnes & Noble, for example, has had a website running since 1997, and the famous romance publisher Harlequin has been online since 2000. These websites were primarily created for commercial reasons and served as methods of advertising to build awareness and anticipation for new releases among fans, as well as provide an online marketplace for users to purchase books from home.

Around the same time, individual fans of books and literature created websites to celebrate their enthusiasm for the books and to share their interests with other users across the Internet. Many of these early fan-built websites were constructed using Internet hosting services, such as Angelfire, Geocities, and Yahoo, which offered free Web space. Some of these hosts are now defunct as those Internet services have been supplanted by newer and more robust Web hosting sites, but some literary fan pages remain accessible (Delayne; Mollycoddles).

Numerous early fan pages were very popular with romance readers, but they required a high degree of technical skill in website design to operate effectively. More typical Internet users quickly found other ways to participate in the new Web-based culture of interest-sharing as well as add an interactive, community-driven element to their online activity. While fan communities had existed alongside the early websites in the form of e-mail newsgroups and Web forums, a major development came with the advent of online journals, such as *LiveJournal*, launched in 1999. *LiveJournal*, and other online journals, were also known as blogs. These blogs not only allowed for users to leave a comment and respond to comments on one another's journal pages, but also had interest-based community pages, which enabled community members to congregate to discuss, critique, and support their favorite books, TV shows, and movies. The permanence and personal quality of these journals allowed users to showcase their own writing and cultivate their own readership. The result was a flourishing world of fan-created works that placed characters from published stories into new situations, explored different love interests for them, or simply recreated their official love stories from a different angle. Even the best-selling Harry Potter series, in which romance was by no means a focus, quickly developed a fan base that thrived on placing different characters from the books into romantic situations (also called *shipping*, short for "relationships") and creating a love story around them, as the Harry Potter Fandom site on *LiveJournal*, although it is no longer being updated, shows (Newbieguide). Written fan works are now popularly known as fan fiction (or fanfiction or fanfic for short), and *LiveJournal* still contains many active fan-fiction communities.

Wikis were created about the same time as blogs but did not filter into the public consciousness until a bit later. To be more precise, while wikis can be dated from 1995 with the creation of the WikiWikiWeb knowledge base, they did not become a popular form of sharing collective knowledge until 2001, when Wikipedia was launched. Due to the popularity and mass use of Wikipedia, its article entries have set the standard format for other wiki-development endeavors. Wikipedia is currently the most popular wiki website on the Internet, and it contains some wiki pages on romance novels, as well as on nearly every other subject imaginable. Wikipedia's article on romance novels provides a definition, breaks down its various formats, subgenres, history, and the extent of its national and international markets.

Romance Blogs

The most popular way of sharing specific information about romance novels today is through highly developed fan blogs, which act as an online book club for readers. Elements of a romance blog can include book reviews by site owners or guest posts, giveaways of books (occasionally signed copies), author interviews, book chats or more formal book clubs, and blog tours. Blog tours are a relatively new concept in the blog sphere. Blog tours are set up like traditional bookstore tours, featuring a designated number of author visits to various locations (there can be 10 to 20 different blog stops, depending on how many blogs the author can schedule a visit with), and can roll out over the course of a week, a month, or longer. The author's blog visit can consist of a book discussion or review, a question-and-answer session, and/or a book giveaway. Some of the most popular romance blogs currently on the Internet are *Smart Bitches Trashy Books*, *Schmexy Girl Book Blog*, *Romance Junkies*, *Smexybooks.com*, and *Not Another Romance Blog*.

The *Smart Bitches Trashy Books* blog is predominantly focused on romance novel reviews, delivered in a funny, witty, and honest style by two avid romance readers. As the creators phrase it, their page "is a website that reviews romance novels from a couple of smart bitches who will always give it to you straight" (*Smart Bitches Trashy Books*). The blog was originally created by two fans of the Romance genre in 2005 and is currently still run by one of them with the occasional guest posts. The blog also comes out with weekly podcasts, which contain discussions of various aspects of romance stories, interviews with romance writers, or responses to reader e-mails. The romance stories that are reviewed can include historical, modern, paranormal, erotic, and urban fantasy romances.

The *Schmexy Girl Book Blog* was created by four avid readers of romance novels and features book reviews, new-release information, and giveaways in which followers of the blog are eligible to win free copies of books. Giveaways are very common on blog sites, as they are a means of increasing a blog's popularity, as well as promoting word-of-mouth advertising for the free book. Generally, giveaway book prizes are provided by publishers to advertise and get feedback on their new releases.

Romance Junkies is a review blog created and maintained by a wife-and-husband team. In addition to reviews of old and current romance novels, this blog routinely features giveaways of books in both print and digital formats, the former often signed by the author. It also features an annual writing contest and on occasion gives readers the opportunity to interview visiting authors, who sometimes appear *in persona* of the main characters of their own works. This type of interview is called the Speed Date Interview on this blog.

Smexybooks.com was created in 2009 by a devoted fan of romance books, who in addition to offering her own reviews of new books also collects and publishes reader recommendations on the blog. This blog focuses on both romance and urban-fantasy books and frequently provides giveaways of recently released books in those genres. Eligibility to win a giveaway book on this blog is based on user participation rather than simply entering one's name. Any user who comments on the blog page becomes eligible to win. The books usually come from sponsors of the blog (typically publishers, though there are occasionally booksellers), who are also highlighted on the blog page. Other notable features of this blog include lists of highly recommended books (for example, top ten favorites of the month, top ten favorites of the year, and other variations), a weekly wrap-up list (for example, a recap list of books read that week and the enjoyment grade for the book), and end-of-the-week excerpts of titillating scenes from a book (called "Smex Scene Sunday").

Not Another Romance Blog was started by a lover of historical romances with the intent to provide the romance-novel-reading community with honest reviews, interesting dialogue, guest posts, and interviews with established and debuting authors. According to the blog owner, the "goal was to make each unique click on the site like walking into my home, sitting down on a settee, and settling in for some good book chat with a fellow addict" (*Not Another Romance Blog*). Many romance blogs are similarly run by ardent romance fans who desire to share and discuss romance novels through this type of personal online medium.

Romance Wikis

There are only a few Romance-genre specific wikis present on the Web currently. One attempt at the creation of a wiki of sorts for the Romance Novel genre is the RomanceWiki website. However, at present, this wiki is not well maintained, with parts of it untouched for several years while certain pages are extensively updated. This site is poorly organized, making it not only difficult to navigate but also to determine where changes were made. This uneven editing and development reveals some of the limitations of the wiki model, especially in cases in which the editing community is small and participates only irregularly in making improvements to the site.

Another wiki website that is widely used for topics of popular interest, including popular romance novels, is Wikia. Wikia is a wiki farm that hosts thousands of wikis using open-source software and was founded by members of the foundation known for operating Wikipedia. In the realm of literature, there are wikis in the genres of Science Fiction, Mystery, Fantasy, Young Adult, Children's Books, and more, as well as more specific wikis for particular series. Essentially, any authors, individual books, or book series that have an ardent and technologically inclined fan base have wiki sites created for them. The immensely popular romance series The Twilight Saga, for example, has a large and active wiki site dedicated to it, comprising 985 distinct articles. Articles include in-depth character summaries, information about the derivative movie series, any news published about the series, even a blog section to give site visitors the opportunity to share thoughts on the Twilight series. Other vampire romance series such as Blue Bloods and The Vampire Diaries have similarly organized wiki sites devoted to them.

Nonparanormal love stories set in modern times such as *A Walk to Remember, Fifty Shades of Grey*, or *Beautiful Disaster* also have featured wiki pages. Popular romance authors, ranging from historical to contemporary, also have their own wiki pages. Jane Austen, for example, has a wiki devoted to her life and works, with particular attention paid to her most beloved novel, *Pride and Prejudice*. Meg Cabot also has a wiki for her many works, including a wiki article for each tween, teen, and adult novel she has ever written. In general, for wikis, the range of content is potentially infinite, with the only limiting factors being the size and activity of the user community.

The fact that there is a much smaller number of wiki sites devoted to romance stories than there are blogs and personal websites indicates that wikis are not the preferred format for romance readers to share romance-specific information. Rather, blogs appear to be the predominant forum in which romance readers and fans prefer to interact and engage in Romance-genre news.

Romance Websites

Romance-related websites can take the form of any of the following types: fan sites, discussion forums, book-review sites, author sites, publisher sites, and self-publishing sites. Book-review sites are very popular with avid readers of the Romance genre, as it helps them to filter through the sheer number of romance novels produced (whether published as a print book, electronic book, or in chapters on a website for self-publishing writers) to find what they might like to read. These sites differ from the blogs previously mentioned in that they are usually staffed by a wide range of writers coordinated by dedicated editors, functioning similarly to a published magazine. This section will discuss some of the most popular websites currently found on the Internet for romance readers.

One extremely popular book-recommendation and discussion-forum website used primarily by English readers on the Internet is Goodreads. Goodreads launched in January 2007 with the mission of helping readers find and share books they love. It currently has 25 million members, 750 million books referenced, and 29 million reviews. This makes it one of the most widely used and well-populated websites in the world. In Goodreads, romance novels can fall under the categories of "chick lit" or "romance." The distinction between the two is that chick lit places a greater emphasis on female character development, or in the site's own words, "addresses issues of modern womanhood, often humorously and lightheartedly.

Although it sometimes includes romantic elements, chick lit is generally not considered a direct subcategory of the romance novel genre, because the heroine's relationship with her family or friends is often just as important as her romantic relationships" (Goodreads). Stories labeled "romance" adhere to the more traditional tropes of the genre.

Paranormal romance, as popularized by the Twilight series, falls under the category of "paranormal" rather than any dedicated romance subject heading. Paranormal stories are any that involve characters' experiences that lack a scientific explanation. Popular subjects in paranormal books are supernatural creatures, extrasensory perception (such as clairvoyance, telepathy, and other psychic abilities), ghosts, and UFOs. To help users navigate the massive selection available, Goodreads collects and publishes readers' choice statistics, wherein readers vote for the books they like best in various genres, and new books are suggested based on comparison to other readers' responses.

Websites more closely aligned to the publishers include those of the Romance Writers of America, HarperCollins (Avon and Harlequin), and Kensington Publishing Corporation websites. The Romance Writers of America site provides the most comprehensive data on the romance-publishing industry, including industry statistics, reader statistics, romance authors, and best-selling romances. Its romance authors section is very useful for finding the independent websites of individual authors. Harlequin/Avon and Kensington are two long-established and well-known romance-novel publishers, and their websites catalog their publications as well as providing updates on upcoming titles. Apart from these two, smaller publishers all have their own websites that list romance publications.

Trends for the Romance Genre on the Internet

Blogs continue to be popular with romance readers looking for the next interesting romance story, and their focus on presenting book reviews in an engaging manner helps readers navigate the sheer quantity of romance titles produced by publishers. This can make them the objects of fan-following as much as the books they discuss. Wikis are less popular, and while there are relatively active wikis for especially popular series like Twilight, there remains no thriving and comprehensive wiki dedicated to Romance as a genre. These and other romance websites continue to crop up, though it can be noted that the most dynamic growth in recent years has been on social media sites such as Tumblr, Facebook, and Twitter, where readers can even more readily access and share book or author information.

Writers themselves are joining this trend and make great use of social media to reach out to their readership, especially on Tumblr. Authors' Tumblrs, such as that of a famous writer like Cassandra Clare of the Mortal Instrument series, can elicit thousands of responses and comments within days of posting, depending on their popularity and number of followers. The growth of the Internet fan community is continually tied to the technological development of the Internet itself. Just as the first websites, message boards, and blogs were enabled by the popularization of Internet usage in the late 1990s, the social media boom of the early 21st century is allowing users an additional means beyond traditional organized forums to interact with one another, and even authors directly, on a person-to-person basis.

Lena Pham

Further Reading

Delayne, Elizabeth. "More Than Novellas." http://www.angelfire.com/ga3/delayne/main.html. Accessed May 7, 2017.

Fox, Susannah, and Lee Rainie. "The Web at 25 in the U.S." *Pew Research Internet Project*, February 27, 2014. http://www.pewinternet.org/2014/02/27/the-web-at-25-in-the-u-s/. Accessed May 7, 2017.

Goodreads. "Chick Lit." https://www.goodreads.com/genres/chick-lit. Accessed May 7, 2017.

Kachka, Boris. "Book Publishing's Big Gamble." *New York Times*, July 9, 2013. http://www.nytimes.com/2013/07/10/opinion/book-publishings-big-gamble.html?_r=1&. Accessed May 7, 2017.

LiveJournal. "Results for Communities Interested in 'Fanfiction.'" http://www.livejournal.com/interests.bml?int=fanfiction. Accessed May 7, 2017.

Mollycoddles. "Other People's Stories." http://www.angelfire.com/weird2/mcoddles/otherstories.html. Accessed May 7, 2017.

Newbieguide. "Fandom: Harry Potter." http://newbieguide.livejournal.com/1327.html. Accessed May 7, 2017.

Not Another Romance Blog. "Not Another Romance Blog." http://notanotherromanceblog.blogspot.com/p/about.html. Accessed May 7, 2017.

Romance Junkies. "Romance Junkies." http://www.romancejunkies.com. Accessed May 7, 2017.

RomanceWiki. "Main Page." http://www.romancewiki.com/Main_Page. Accessed May 7, 2017.

Romance Writers of America. "RWA Author Websites." https://www.rwa.org/p/cm/ld/fid=2013. Accessed May 7, 2017.

Schmexy Girl Book Blog. "Schmexy Girl Book Blog." http://www.schmexygirlbookblog.com/. Accessed May 7, 2017.

Smart Bitches Trashy Books. "Smart Bitches Trashy Books." http://www.smartbitchestrashybooks.com/. Accessed May 7, 2017.

Smexy Books. "Smexy Books." http://smexybooks.com. Accessed May 7, 2017.

Spiegel, Rob. "When Did the Internet Become Mainstream?" *E-Commerce Times*, September 12, 1999. http://www.ecommercetimes.com/story/1731.html. Accessed May 7, 2017.

Tumblr. "Lord of Shadows." http://cassandraclare.tumblr.com/. Accessed May 7, 2017.
Wikia. "About." http://www.wikia.com/About. Accessed May 7, 2017.
Wikia. "Twilight Wiki." http://twilightsaga.wikia.com/wiki/Twilight_Saga_Wiki. Accessed May 7, 2017.

See also: "Social Media and Romance" and "Romance Listservs"

Romance Listservs

As one of the first ways of communicating shared interests with other individuals online, listservs or electronic mailing lists were developed in the 1980s. An interest in Popular Romance Fiction spurred the development of numerous such lists devoted to the topic. In recent years the proliferation of blogs and websites devoted to Romance Fiction has diminished the use of such listservs, although there are still a number of active lists. Traffic on the lists is not as high as it was in the years before the development of other options for sharing interests. Many websites have message boards where their readers post comments and have discussions, thus serving the same function as a listserv. In addition, the use of Twitter and Facebook has changed the way readers and writers interact.

One of the main hosts for listservs today is YahooGroups. A search on this site will yield a list of many different listservs covering the Romance genre. Lists can be found for Regency romance, paranormal romance, multicultural romance, science fiction romance, romance writers, or specific authors such as Georgette Heyer or Nora Roberts. Activity and size of the lists vary widely. There is significant duplication in YahooGroups, and it is possible to find many groups with a similar focus. Many of the larger lists are focused on specific authors.

The following are examples of some of the larger, currently active romance listservs:

- **RRA-L**—Romance Readers Anonymous-L is one of the oldest in existence. It was started in 1992 by Leslie Haas and Kara Robinson of Kent State University. After they retired from the list, it moved to YahooGroups. All topics related to romance fiction are discussed with participation from both authors and readers. At its height, annual romance awards were voted on by the subscribers. This list was recognized as one of the more influential lists in the romance-reading community although the use of the list has decreased considerably in recent years.
- **RomanceScholar**—This list is dedicated to the academic study and teaching of romance and is run by Eric Murphy Selinger at DePaul University. Participants in this list tend to be academics discussing romance scholarship and the teaching of romance fiction.

- **RW-L**—Romance Writers List is one of the earliest lists for romance writers dating back to 1994.
- **Regency**—Founded in 1998, this is for readers of romances set in the Georgian or Regency historical periods.
- **Fiction-L**—Originally established in 1995 by the Readers' Service staff of the Morton Grove Public Library and now hosted by Cuyahoga Public Library, this general-interest list often includes discussion of popular romance fiction.
- **Indie Romance Ink**—One of the newer, quite active lists, this is for independently published or "indie-curious" romance writers.

Christina Martínez

Further Reading

Fiction-L. https://listserver.cuyahogalibrary.net/scripts/wa.exe?A0=FICTION_L. Accessed May 9, 2017.

Indie Romance Ink. https://groups.yahoo.com/neo/groups/Regency/info. Accessed May 9, 2017.

Regency. https://groups.yahoo.com/neo/groups/Regency/info. Accessed May 9, 2017.

RomanceScholar. https://mailman.depaul.edu/mailman/listinfo/romancescholar. Accessed May 9, 2017.

RRA-L Romance Readers Anonymous-L. http://groups.yahoo.com/group/rra-l/. Accessed May 9, 2017.

RW-L Romance Writers List. http:/dir.groups.yahoo.com/group/RWL/. Accessed May 9, 2017.

Romance Readers

Assumptions about romance readers, and why they read Romance, abound not only in popular common wisdom but also in writing that analyzes Romance with a more intellectual lens. Romance readers are lonely, sexless, and live with lots of cats. They're undereducated. They're sexually repressed, using romance novels as a substitute for lackluster love lives. Or they're stay-at-home moms, using fiction instead of narcotics to get them through the tedium of their days. Or they're overworked and overstressed, relying on Romance to escape endless hours of underappreciated family caretaking. As Glen Thomas ironically concludes after his review of decades of writing on the topic, "In sum, readers are morons, unhappy, or unhappy morons" (210).

One common belief about romance readers is true: the majority (at least in the United States) are middle-aged women. According to market research conducted for the Romance Writers of America (RWA) in 2011 and 2012, American romance readers are most likely to be women between the ages of 30 and 54. Thirty-nine percent of romance readers have a household income between $50,000 and $99,900. Intriguingly, although previous RWA surveys assumed an all-female readership, the 2009 survey discovered that almost 10 percent are male, a finding confirmed in the 2012 survey.

The 2012 RWA survey found that slightly more than half of romance readers report living with a spouse or significant other, suggesting that most are not reading romance as a substitute for a romantic partner in their day-to-day lives. But studies of the sex lives of romance readers have yielded mixed results. A 1984 study suggested a correlation between romance reading and sexual activity: "readers [older than college-age] reported having sexual intercourse twice as much as did nonreaders and, indeed, more frequently than the national average for all women. . . . In addition, housewife readers reported being more satisfied with sex than nonreaders" (Coles and Shamp, 206). Huei-Hsia Wu's 2006 study of 770 white American college students, however, found that while romance readers "self-reported greater sex addiction, greater sex drive and greater number of orgasms required for sexual satisfaction than female non-readers," they also "had fewer sex partners, a lower level of self-assessed femininity than non-readers, and were older when they had their first thoughts about sex and had their first sexual intercourse" (131). Wu theorizes that "the *Harlequin* stereotype of nourishing a satisfying sex life in the context of romantic monogamous fidelity while at the same time vicariously fulfilling sexual desires through fictitious characters in romance novels" accounts for the contradiction (131). But Gretchen T. Anderton's 2009 doctoral thesis, based upon an online survey completed by 53 women, found that more than three quarters of study participants (75.5 percent) reported that reading romance novels made them more likely to engage in sex, and more likely to try new sexual experiences.

Geography appears to have the most influence on whether or not a reader is likely to embrace Romance. Americans who live in the South form the highest percentage of romance readers (at 39 percent), while those in the Northeast take up only 17 percent of the market. The Northeast also has the highest number of high school and college graduates, while the South has the lowest (U.S. Census), suggesting a possible correlation between educational attainment and romance reading. Yet the RWA Market survey of 2005 states that 42 percent of romance readers hold a bachelor's degree or higher, and several informal polls (on amazon.com and on romance review blogs such as *Heroes and Heartbreakers*) show that readers who read Romance also read many other genres of literature, both popular and literary.

Given the above (admittedly somewhat ambiguous) facts, why do so many myths about romance readers, and about the evil influence romance reading might have upon them, abound? Such myths have a long history, dating back to the rise of the novel (initially called "romance") itself. Before the Early Modern Period, reading was considered a male activity, reserved for the educated elite training for religious or political work. By the 18th century, however, women in England had become active participants in the literary marketplace, both as authors and as readers. As literary historian Jacqueline Pearson explains, this "feminization of the reading public" led not only to pride in the superiority of modern British culture, but also to anxieties about the dangers of the woman as reader, particularly as a reader of novels. Warnings came from defenders of elite androcentric culture; from moralists fearful of novels' corrupting influence on girls; and even from champions of women's education.

What did such writers fear would happen if women read romances (or, as many described them, "horrid trash")? On the cusp of an age of great social mobility, many social elites expressed their anxieties about losing their class privilege through arguments about women's reading. Novels were dangerous because they raised "false expectations," especially about social mobility. Encouraging readers to believe that they, like Richardson's eponymous Pamela, could "marry up" could only lead to social unrest.

Worries about gender roles were also at play. Novel reading was "utterly unfit" for young women because romances' focus on "passion and pleasure" would inevitably lead to corruption of "both the head and the heart," critics contended (Pearson, 83). Many 18th-century feminists had argued long and hard that women could be just as rational as men, and few wished to see their fellow sisters undermining their arguments by embracing a genre devoted to emotional tumult. The more conventional worried that romances would distract women from their true duties to house and family or, worse, would make them susceptible to the blandishments of seducers. While contemporary critics often point to television or the Internet as the embodiment of "low," corrupting culture, in the 18th and early 19th centuries, it was the novel or romance that held the lowest position in the English cultural hierarchy.

Even as the novel gained status during the 19th and early 20th centuries, women readers continued to fill critics with dismay. Henry James and other champions of the novel advocated for the novel's prestige by bifurcating the genre: "literature," or novels with cultural worth, and "genre fiction," novels with little to no aesthetic or intellectual value. The "romance," a term that became reserved for novels that focused primarily on love and romantic relationships, was placed firmly amongst the latter, lesser group, along with its primarily female readership.

With the rise of second-wave feminism, a new worry arose: would romances give readers unrealistic expectations about real-life romantic relationships? Despite being a genre written primarily by women and for women, would romances enforce female readers' dependence on men and acceptance of the repressive ideology purveyed by popular culture? In one of the key works of the feminist movement, *The Female Eunuch* (1970), Germaine Greer ridiculed the perfect male common in popular romance: "This is the hero that women have chosen for themselves. The traits invented for him have been invented by women cherishing the chains of their bondage" (176). Ten years later, literary scholar Ann Douglas pointed to female masochism to explain women's attraction to texts with dominating heroes and submissive heroines: "women who couldn't thrill to male nudity in *Playgirl* are enjoying the titillation of seeing themselves, not necessarily as they are, but as some men would like to see them: illogical, innocent, magnetized by male sexuality and brutality" (28).

Writers attempting to study or analyze the Romance in the wake of such denigration often found themselves forced to defend romance's readers. They did so primarily by taking a psychological approach, suggesting different reasons why reading romances might meet or at least assuage readers' psychological problems, especially the problem of being women living under the restrictions of patriarchy. The work of three scholars set the tone for much Romance literature analysis that followed: Ann Snitow's essay "Mass Market Romance: Pornography for Women is Different" (1979); Tania Modleski's *Loving with a Vengeance: Mass-Produced Fantasies for Women* (1982); and Janice Radway's *Reading the Romance: Women, Patriarchy, and Popular Literature* (1984). Although Radway was the only one of the three to ask women readers why they read Romance, each sympathizes with, rather than casts aspersions on, romance's readers.

Snitow suggests that Harlequin romances might be considered pornography for women. Her use of the word "pornography" here is not negative, but rather in recognition of how few works of literature, high or low, address women's sexuality and desire. The formula Harlequins set forth for how women can get their sexual desires met, however, she finds less encouraging; their pattern—"converting rape into love making"—insists that women must remain passive and unthreatening even while somehow teaching men how to feel emotional intimacy. While such a "regressive" model may reflect readers' very real fears about expressing their own sexuality in a patriarchal culture, Snitow mourns the necessity of women's (both heroines' and readers') sexual double bind: "both the desire to be ravished" and "the desire to be spiritually adored, saved from the humiliation of dependence and sexual passivity through the agency of a protective male who will somehow make reparation to the woman he loves for her powerlessness" (320).

Modleski's work also focuses on Harlequin romances and points to the complexity of the ideological positions they ask their readers to inhabit. Modleski argues that "the so-called masochism pervading these texts is a 'cover' for anxieties, desires, and wishes which if openly expressed would challenge the psychological and social order of things. For that very reason, of course, they must be kept hidden; the texts, after arousing them, must . . . work to neutralize them" (20). Championing female selflessness, the novels ask their heroines to subvert their aggressive tendencies. But because readers are put into a superior position, knowing more than the heroines do (in particular, that the hero is treating the heroine poorly out of his fear of emotional intimacy), Harlequins simultaneously allow readers to experience vicarious vengeance against men: "all the while he is being so hateful, he is internally grovelling, grovelling, grovelling" (37). They also point to the double bind society imposes on women: "their most important achievement is supposed to be finding a husband, their greatest fault is attempting to do so" (40). Modleski, like Snitow before her, concludes by denouncing not the books or the women who read them but "the conditions which have made them necessary" (49). But she sees reason for optimism: "the energy women now use to belittle and defeat themselves can be rechanneled into efforts to grow and to explore ways of affirming and asserting the self" (49).

Like Modleski and Snitow, Radway focuses solely on Harlequin romances, using them as representative of the entire romance field. But her methodology differs: in addition to analyzing how texts construct readers, Radway interviews actual female romance readers in a Midwestern American community, asking them why they read the books they do, and what they gain from their reading. Much of the satisfaction readers take from Romance stems from its depiction of the hero, a man "capable of the same attentive observation and intuitive 'understanding' that they believe women regularly accord to men" but rarely receive in their own lives, devoted as they are to other-focused caretaking (83). Romance reading is an act of protest to these women because it allows them to reject, albeit temporarily, their self-abnegating social roles. But romance reading simultaneously works to contain and defuse any impulse to change those social roles in the real world, Radway fears: "despite the utopian force of the romance's projection, that projection actually leaves unchallenged the very system of social relations whose faults and imperfections gave rise to the romance and which the romance is trying to perfect" (215).

Radway cautions that the small sample size of her study, as well as the self-selected nature of its participants, makes her conclusions more hypotheses than definitive statements. She also states that ideological norms put forth in popular culture, such as Harlequin romances are powerful, are never "all-pervasive, totally vigilant, or complete" (222). The elision Radway, Modleski, and Snitow make between Harlequin romances and romance in general, assuming that all Romance follows the same patterns as single-title category romance does, is also problematic. Yet much subsequent academic investigation of Romance and its effects on readers did not stop to investigate the broader validity of their claims.

In response to what they felt was uninformed criticism of their genre, many romance writers came to romance's defense. In interviews, stand-alone articles, and essay collections, Jayne Ann Krentz, Susan Elizabeth Phillips, Candace Camp, and other romance authors vehemently protested scholars' depiction of romance readers as dupes of patriarchal culture. Academics failed to trust the intelligence of romance readers, they argued; readers knew perfectly well that their romances were expressions of fantasy and did not reflect what they wanted in their everyday lives. Writers also argued that much academic criticism saw the romance reader as a lesser "other," an "us/them" distinction that set scholars up as superior to the reader in ways that inevitably colored their analyses.

Glen Thomas has recently argued that both critics who denigrate romance's effects on readers and proponents who hold up its benefits take a far too simplistic view. Both groups view romance reading as "a symptom of an internal psychological problem (if not a crisis) that manifests itself in reading" romance (208); readers are either duped and/or oppressed by patriarchy, or they're "tired and overworked but made happier by romance" (210). In contrast, Thomas argues in favor of using a "creative industries framework" to analyze romance, assuming producers will produce what consumers want, rather than what producers *think* consumers want. Thomas challenges those who study Romance to move beyond "the circularity of the debate over a fantasy reader who is oppressed and relieved by turns, be that oppression by the heavy hand of patriarchy, or the relief that stems from feeling happier or enjoying enhanced sexual relations with a significant other. Rather than focus on the unitary fantasy reader of romance fiction, it's time to talk of readers in the plural, and how these readers' choices are one element in constructing and shaping a complex reading position and identity" (213).

Some scholars have begun to take tentative steps in this direction. For example, psychologist Amanda Diekman and her colleagues wondered whether women who read romances, which rarely featured discussions of safe sex at the time of their study (2000), would be less likely to engage in "precautionary sexual health behaviors" in their own lives than romance nonreaders. They discovered that "high levels of romance reading were associated with negative attitudes toward condoms and reduced intent to use condoms in the future," but also, more hearteningly, that the addition of safe-sex discussions or scenes in romances "increased positive attitudes toward condoms and marginally increased intent to use condoms in the future" (179). Intriguingly, a 2011 study of RITA Award–winning romances from 1989 to 2009 showed an increase in depictions of contraceptive use (18.5 percent in books published between 1989 and 1999, 57.9 percent in those published between 2000 and 2009), suggesting that romance authors have taken Diekman's study to heart (Ménard and Cabrera).

The study of Romance's effects on readers is still in its infancy. Ménard and Cabrera suggest that future researchers use a mix of qualitative and quantitative approaches "to determine how romance novel readers understand and interact with the material as well as how they are impacted by it." Researchers might explore whether romance novel readers are more or less likely to endorse stereotypic gender roles and sex myths than romance nonreaders, or whether their sexual beliefs and behaviors differ. Only after these and other questions about romance readers have been studied will we be able to say with any degree of certainty whether romances "constitute sex education, sex entertainment, or both" (253).

Jackie Horne

Further Reading

Coles, Claire, and M. Johanna Shamp. "Some Sexual, Personality, and Demographic Characteristics of Women Readers of Erotic Romances." *Archives of Sexual Behavior* 13 (1984): 187–209.

Diekman, Amanda B., Wendi L. Gardner, and Mary McDonald. "Love Means Never Having to Be Careful: The Relationship Between Reading Romance Novels and Safer Sex Behavior." *Psychology of Women Quarterly* 24 (2000): 179–88.

Douglas, Ann. "Soft-Porn Culture." *New Republic*, August 30, 1980, 25–29.

Frampton, Megan. "Genre Reading: Is Romance All There Is?" *Heroes and Heartbreakers.* http://www.heroesandheartbreakers.com/blogs/2011/12/genre-reading-is-romance-all-there-is. Accessed May 9, 2017.

Greer, Germaine. *The Female Eunuch.* New York: McGraw-Hill, 1971.

Krentz, Jayne Ann, ed. *Dangerous Men and Adventurous Women: Romance Writers on the Appeal of the Romance.* Philadelphia: University of Pennsylvania Press, 1992.

Ménard, A. Dana, and Christine Cabrera. "'Whatever the Approach, Tab B Still Fits into Slot A': Twenty Years of Sex Scripts in Romance Novels." *Sexuality and Culture* 15 (2001): 240–55.

Modleski, Tania. *Loving with a Vengeance: Mass-Produced Fantasies for Women*, 2nd ed. New York: Routledge, 2008.

Pearson, Jacqueline. *Women's Reading in Britain 1750–1835: A Dangerous Recreation.* Cambridge, UK: Cambridge University Press, 1999.

Radway, Janice. *Reading the Romance: Women, Patriarchy, and Popular Literature.* Chapel Hill: University of North Carolina Press, 1984.

Romance Writers of America. "Reader Statistics." https://www.rwa.org/p/cm/ld/fid=582. Accessed May 9, 2017.

Romance Writers of America. "RWA [2011] Romance Book Consumer Survey." https://www.rwa.org/p/do/sd/topic=1356&sid=2084. Accessed May 7, 2017.

Snitow, Ann. "Mass Market Romance: Pornography for Women Is Different." In *Women and Romance: A Reader*, edited by Susan Ostrov Weisser, 307–22. New York: New York University Press, 2001.

Thomas, Glen. "Happy Readers or Sad Ones? Romance Fiction and the Problems of the Media Effects Model." In *New Approaches to Popular Romance Fiction: Critical Essays*, edited by Sarah S. G. Frantz and Eric Murphy Selinger, 206–17. Jefferson, NC: McFarlane, 2012.

U.S. Census Bureau. *Report on Educational Attainment in the United States*, 2003. http://www.census.gov/prod/2004pubs/p20-550.pdf. Accessed May 9, 2017.

Wu, Huei-Hsia. "Gender, Romance Novels, and Plastic Sexuality in the United States: A Focus on Female College Students." *Journal of International Women's Studies* 8, 1 (2006): 125–34.

Romance Research Collections

The academic study of contemporary Romance Fiction is a relatively recent field of study. The earliest citations listed on the Romance Scholarship section of the RomanceWiki date to the 1970s. Each subsequent decade shows an increase in the critical writing on the genre. Most of the bibliography in the RomanceWiki focuses on critical writing about Romance Fiction from the latter part of the 20th century into the 21st century. Research resources will vary considerably for earlier, historical authors of the genre compared to more contemporary authors.

Public libraries have purchased romance fiction to satisfy the demands from their readers for current popular fiction, but they have not built historical, research collections over time. A few academic libraries have made an effort to collect in this area, but the number is small. The ephemeral nature of romance publishing has also made it more difficult for libraries to build collections in this area. The short publication lifespan of many titles along with the high percentage of paperback publications are also challenges to libraries building collections in this area. Another difficulty for the researcher is that even libraries with extensive collections do not always catalog titles individually, often choosing to lump category romances together under one entry in the catalog.

The online RomanceWiki is the most up-to-date source that identifies academic libraries with romance collections suitable for research purposes. The types of collections range from the papers and publications of an individual author to collections with a wide-ranging selection of romance fiction. A relatively recent source that includes information about library collections in romance is Ramsdell's

Romance Fiction: A Guide to the Genre. Older sources include the chapter on "Romantic Fiction" by Kay Mussell in Inge's *Handbook of American Popular Literature*, and Mussell's *Women's Gothic and Romantic Fiction*. A more general source, *Subject Collections* by Ash, provides extensive information on special collections in libraries, although there is no specific entry for Popular Romance. A researcher would need to look at a variety of subject headings to cull the needed information. These older sources might be particularly useful for the researcher looking for material on earlier writers or types of writing of more historical significance. For example, Stanford University has an extensive collection of dime novels that would include examples of early romances.

Significant collections of romance fiction in English can be found in the national libraries of the United States (Library of Congress), the legal deposit libraries of the United Kingdom and Ireland, the National Library of Australia, and Library and Archives Canada. None of these libraries actually have all romance books published in their respective countries. Access to holdings in the libraries is through the various online catalogs of the different institutions.

The largest and most diverse collection of contemporary popular romance in the United States can be found at the Browne Popular Culture Library at Bowling Green State University in Ohio. The romance fiction collection includes more than 10,000 volumes of romance fiction including category, historical, and contemporary romances. The library also has manuscript collections including fan mail, correspondence, manuscripts, and galleys from a number of different romance writers. Information about the contents of the collection can be found on the library's website. The archives of the Romance Writers of America are also a part of the library's collection. These archives document the establishment and growth of the organization, which was founded in 1980.

Another significant collection of contemporary romance fiction can be found at Michigan State University in the Russell B. Nye Popular Culture Collection. The collection includes about 5,000 titles, many of them category romances, but not exclusively. The collection was built up over a period of about 20 years, but items have not been actively added since about 1990.

The Schlesinger Library at the Radcliffe Institute for Advanced Study, Harvard University, houses a medical romance collection of works by Missouri writer Elizabeth Seifert, 1897–1983, along with some collections of nurse romances. The library actively collects currently published romances, and holdings may be identified in the Harvard University online catalog. Another nurse romance collection of over 400 items can be found in the special collections of the library at the University of Wisconsin-Milwaukee.

The Fales Library and Special Collections, Elmer Holmes Bobst Library, New York University houses the Harlequin Romance Collection of Treva M. Taylor, which consists of 1,671 books, mostly Harlequin romances published in the 1970s through the 1990s.

The University of Rochester has a collection of about 1,400 books in the Silhouette Desire and Silhouette Romance category lines. They are not cataloged individually, but they are listed under "Love stories-Periodicals" in their catalog.

The National Library of Australia has a large collection of romance fiction published and distributed in Australia, particularly those books published by Mills & Boon, Silhouette, and Harlequin. Titles published prior to 1990 have individual records in the catalog, but after 1990 only collective records may be found for romance fiction (for example, Mills & Boon romance novels) in the catalog. The Fryer Library at the University of Queensland houses the Australian Romance Fiction Collection built primarily from the collection of Dr. Juliet Flesch, author of *From Australia with Love: A History of Modern Australian Popular Romance Novels*. The University of Melbourne also has a Romance Fiction Collection located in its special collections. The collection focuses on Australian and New Zealand authors or romance books relating to Australia published since 1960. Although titles prior to 1980 are not listed online, the library does provide access to a printed list of titles. At the time this collection was started it was the only collection of its type.

The University of Calgary Library special collections include early Harlequin novels in their Canadian Collection and have a manuscript collection of material from Paul Grescoe in connection with material used for his book *The Merchants of Venus: Inside Harlequin and the Empire of Romance*.

Finally, the papers and/or collected works of various individual authors are located in a number of libraries around the world.

Christina Martínez

Further Reading

Ash, Lee, and William G. Miller. *Subject Collections*, 7th ed. New Providence, NJ: R. R. Bowker, 1993.

Flesch, Juliet. "Not Just Housewives and Old Maids." *Collection Building* 16, no. 3 (1997): 119–24.

Mussell, Kay. "Romantic Fiction." In *Handbook of American Popular Culture*, edited by Thomas Inge, 251–72. New York: Greenwood Press, 1988.

Mussell, Kay. *Women's Gothic and Romantic Fiction: A Reference Guide*. Westport, CT: Greenwood Press, 1981.

Ramsdell, Kristin. "Collections." In *Romance Fiction: A Guide to the Genre*, 2nd ed. Santa Barbara, CA: ABC-CLIO, 2012.

RomanceWiki. "Romance Resources for Academics." http://www.romancewiki.com /Romance_Resources_for_Academics. Accessed May 9, 2017.

Romance Writers of America (RWA)

History

The Romance Writers of America (RWA) was founded in 1980 by editor Vivian Stephens and 37 romance authors, including notable writers such as Nora Roberts, Rita Clay Estrada, Linda Howard, and Linda Randall Wisdom. RWA was chartered as a nonprofit trade association in 1981. Its mission is to "advance the professional interests of career-focused romance writers through networking and advocacy. RWA works to support the efforts of its members to earn a living, to make a full-time career out of writing romance—or a part-time one that generously supplements his/her main income" ("About RWA," 2017).

Membership

Membership in RWA falls into three categories: general, associate, and affiliate. General membership is open to individuals seriously pursuing a career in romance fiction writing, which they must verify in several ways. These members have the right to vote and hold elected office in RWA. Associate membership is open to all other members who do not qualify for general membership, including writers pursuing a career in a genre other than Romance, RWA employees, and industry professionals involved in the manuscript-acquisition process, such as agents, publishers, and acquiring editors. Affiliate membership is open only to librarians and booksellers. Neither associate nor affiliate members have the right to vote or hold elected office in the organization.

There is no citizenship or residency requirement for membership in the Romance Writers of America. Of its 10,000 members, approximately 900 of them reside outside of the United States.

Organization

RWA offers two tracks—called Communities of Practice (CoP)—for its active membership, PRO and PAN. Members become eligible to join the PRO CoP when they provide evidence to RWA that they have completed a romance manuscript of at least 20,000 words or several romances that add up to that length. PRO members are not required to have published a book. PRO is a CoP that focuses on the business side of romance and promotes and protects the interests of romance writers as they work toward becoming published.

Conversely, members in the Published Authors Network (PAN) must prove not only that they have published or contracted a book for publication, but that they have made at least US$1,000 in the form of an advance or royalties. Active RWA members who have self-published a book must prove that they have made at least US$1,000 in royalties on a single romance novel or novella to be eligible for PAN. RWA provides listservs for both PAN and PRO members to network, discuss issues, ask questions, and communicate concerns within and about the publishing industry. Note: See the RWA Communities of Practice website for specific, current information on PAN and PRO membership requirements.

Furthermore, there are local, online, and special-interest chapters affiliated with RWA. These can also offer the opportunity for networking and holding discussions between members, for hosting events, and for sponsoring writing and service awards. Chapter membership is usually limited to those who are also members of the national RWA organization.

Advocacy

One of the functions of RWA is to serve as an advocacy group for romance authors. By leveraging its position as the largest nonprofit genre-writing organization in the world, RWA has managed to convince Harlequin to register the copyright for authors' works as well as persuade publishers to allow authors to own their pen names if they move to a different publishing house. Previously, authors had had to change their pseudonyms—and thus lose a portion of their established readership—when they changed publishers.

Additionally, in 2011, Harlequin changed the royalties rate for its e-books, which led to many questions from authors who worked with this publisher. While RWA remained neutral in the dispute, it hired an independent law firm to review the legality of the letter sent to Harlequin authors regarding royalties, allowing RWA members to become better educated on their rights in the matter.

RWA also is focusing its advocacy efforts on increasing awareness and prevention of Internet piracy. In a "bid to combat the increasing problem of the online piracy of romance novels, the Romance Writers of America (RWA) has created a database on its Web site that lists sites where romance novels are available for illegal downloading. The database also features information for copyright holders, the authors, about how to protect their works" (Andriani, 15). RWA also offers authors information and sample takedown letters to use to demand Internet pirate sites remove files that infringe upon authors' copyright.

Controversy

Like many large organizations, RWA is not without internal conflicts and controversy. For example, in 1998–1999 the Board of Directors revoked PAN status from authors who had gained that status through an electronic publisher (e-publisher), igniting several years of debate between traditionally published and e-published authors. In 2007, RWA changed the PAN rules again to extend PAN status to authors who had earned US$1,000 on an advance or royalties from one title; however, the rules specified that the book must have been published by a recognized "non-subsidy, non-vanity publisher." RWA labeled publishers whose primary "means of offering books for sale is through a publisher-generated Web site" (Krozser) as vanity or subsidy publishers, which at the time included most e-publishers and again excluded many e-published authors as well as authors who had self-published their work. The PAN status guidelines were revised to their current state in 2012.

In 2009, members of RWA hosted their own Rogue Digital Conference before the start of the regular RWA annual conference as a protest of the lack of programming RWA offered that focused on digital publishing. The RWA chapter Electronic and Small Press Authors' Network published an essay on its website by agent and author Diedre Knight criticizing RWA's attitude toward e-publishing, and a rebuttal essay was issued by the then-president of RWA, Diane Pershing, stating that there was not enough interest in e-publishing to warrant programming for it. Much of the controversy was discussed on social media websites, especially Twitter, under the hashtag #RWAChange. This issue has since been resolved, and the annual RWA conferences now include a number of sessions and/or tracks focused on these topics.

Additionally, there have been several controversies surrounding the issue of sexually explicit, erotic, same-sex, or alternative lifestyle romances. In 2000, Jenny Crusie wrote an article in the RWA monthly magazine, *Romance Writers Report*, that discussed the process of redefining what constituted Romance and how there were those who wanted to insert morality caveats into the definition or limit it to relationships that involved only one man and one woman. In the end, the definition agreed upon was a "romance is a love story that has an emotionally satisfying, optimistic ending" (Crusie). However, the controversy reignited in 2006 when the *Romance Writers Report* published a letter to the editor written by Jan W. Butler, who expressed the opinion that RWA should change its definition to state that romance can only exist between one man and one woman, equating the recognition of relationships outside of this dynamic with a slippery slope of immorality that could lead to organizations that promoted man-boy pedophilic love stories as being included in Romance.

Much of this debate came to the fore with the rise of erotic romance, which was more likely to feature same-sex and alternative-lifestyle love stories. Erotic romance saw a surge in popularity with e-publishers beginning in the late 1990s and early 2000s, leading to speculation that the disenfranchisement of e-published authors from PAN had as much to do with the sexual content featured in their work as it did with the amount of money they made from advances and royalties. In 2005, the then-president of RWA, Tara Taylor Quinn, introduced the concept of "graphical standards" for romance novels, which banned the RWA national and chapter websites from displaying or linking to author or publisher websites that featured covers that contained sexually graphic scenarios or partial-nudity or had book excerpts that included sexually explicit language. These standards were later repealed.

Annual Conference

In the summer of each year, most typically in July, RWA hosts its annual conference. The first such event was held near Houston, Texas, in 1981. More than 600 authors attended, which was four times the expected turnout. The conference is held in a different U.S. city each year but has returned several times to cities in New York, Georgia, California, and Texas. An effort is made to hold the conference in New York City every three years because of access to the large number of romance publishers.

The conference typically follows a Wednesday-through-Saturday schedule. Wednesday begins with Librarians Day, which includes workshops and programming for librarians, a Librarians Day Luncheon, and a Librarian/Bookseller Networking Event, which PAN members are encouraged to attend. On Wednesday evening, there is the "Readers for Life" Literacy Autographing, wherein authors registered for the conference may elect to participate by signing their works. Books for the event are typically donated by the publishers, and all proceeds from book sales go to ProLiteracy Worldwide and other local literacy organizations within the conference city.

Over 100 workshop sessions are held on Thursday, Friday, and Saturday. These sessions, presented by authors and industry professionals, are categorized by predetermined tracks set forth by RWA, including Career, Craft, Industry, Research, Self-Publishing, and Writer's Life. Thursday and Friday are also when the Keynote Luncheon and Awards Luncheon are held. The conference culminates with the RITA and Golden Heart Awards Ceremony on Saturday evening.

Throughout the conference, RWA chapters and publishers may choose to hold events of their own. Often these will include breakfasts or evening cocktail parties to minimize overlap with the conference program. Publishers may also participate in informational sessions in which they can report any updates and provide details on the types of manuscripts their editors wish to acquire from romance authors. Additionally, publishers can hold promotional signings for their authors during the conference; unlike the Literacy Autographing, which is open to the public, these publisher signings provide free books only to registered conference attendees.

Editors and agents can take appointments with authors who would like to work with them. The authors may present or "pitch" their manuscripts to the editor or agent, who will ask to see the partial or full manuscript after the conference, if interested. Golden Heart and RITA Award finalists receive first priority for scheduling editor and agent appointments.

It is worth noting that while the above has been the conference pattern for a number of years, the 2017 RWA Conference experimented with a different schedule. Most of the same elements were included, but the order was different. Of particular importance: the Rita Awards ceremony was held on Thursday night instead of Saturday, and the Literacy Autographing was held on Saturday night instead of Wednesday. The 2018 conference will use a similar schedule, and RWA will continue to assess the results.

Contests and Awards

The most recognizable awards offered by RWA are for its romance writing contests. These include recognition for both published and unpublished works—the RITA Award for published stories and the Golden Heart Award for unpublished stories. The RITA Award was originally called the Golden Medallion and was renamed in 1989 to honor RWA's first president and founding member Rita Clay Estrada. The first awards were given in 1982, and in 1984 the contests were divided into six subgenre categories. Several categories have been added, redacted, or combined since then. Currently, there are 13 categories for the RITAs, including Best First Book, Contemporary Romance: Long, Contemporary Romance: Mid-Length, Contemporary Romance: Short, Erotic Romance, Historical Romance: Long, Historical Romance: Short, Mainstream Fiction with a Central Romance, Paranormal Romance, Romance Novella, Romance with Religious or Spiritual Elements, Romantic Suspense, and Young Adult Romance. For the Golden Heart contest, there are seven categories: Contemporary Romance, Contemporary Romance: Short, Historical Romance, Paranormal Romance, Romance with Religious or Spiritual Elements, Romantic Suspense, and Young Adult Romance.

The Centennial, Hall of Fame, and Lifetime Achievement Awards all recognize RWA members with significant, long-term achievements and publications in the Romance genre. The Centennial Award is awarded to authors upon the publication of their 100th romance novel; the Hall of Fame Award is given to authors who have won three RITAs in the same category; and the Lifetime Achievement Award is awarded each year at RWA's annual conference to a living author whose career has spanned 15 years or more, who has been a continuing member of RWA, and who has contributed significantly to the Romance genre.

The organization offers additional, nonwriting awards, such as the Cathie Linz Librarian of the Year, Steffie Walker Bookseller of the Year, Vivian Stephens Industry Award, Veritas Media Award, and several service awards, including the

Emma Merritt Award. Some of the awards have been renamed over the years to honor individuals who exemplify the values of the awards. RWA also gives an annual Research Grant to support the development of academic research pertaining to romance novels, writers, and readers. Two of the earliest grants were given to scholars who were responsible for founding the International Association for the Study of Popular Romance (IASPR) and establishing the *Journal of Popular Romance Studies* (*JPRS*).

Many RWA chapters hold contests as well, and several chapters host award ceremonies during the national conference each year. Notable examples include the Greater Detroit RWA chapter's Booksellers Best Awards, the Oklahoma RWA chapter's National Readers Choice Award, The Royal Ascot from the Beau Monde chapter (Regency Romance), the Prism Award from the Fantasy, Futuristic, and Paranormal chapter, and the Daphne du Maurier Award from the Kiss of Death chapter (Romantic Suspense).

Crystal Goldman

Further Reading

Andriani, Lynn. "RWA Fights Illegal Downloads of Romance Novels." *Publishers Weekly* 255, 13 (2008): 15. http://web.a.ebscohost.com.proxylib.csueastbay.edu/ehost/pdf viewer/pdfviewer?vid=3&sid=67866d08-e18a-4224-bfed-c6b7aa54c9c7%40sessionm gr4009&hid=4201. Accessed May 10, 2017.

Crusie, Jenny. "I Know What It Is When I Read It: Defining the Romance Genre." *Romance Writers Report* (2000). http://jennycrusie.com/non-fiction/essays/i-know -what-it-is-when-i-read-it-defining-the-romance-genre/. Accessed May 10, 2017.

Danford, Natalie. "Embraced by Romance." *Publishers Weekly* 252, 46 (2005): 16–21. http://www.publishersweekly.com/pw/print/20051121/21816-embraced-by-romance .html. Accessed May 10, 2017.

Hogan, Ron. "A Beginner's Guide to #RWAChange." MediaBistro, 2009. http://www .adweek.com/galleycat/a-beginners-guide-to-rwachange/10465?red=as. Accessed May 10, 2017.

Krozser, Kassia. "Rogue Digital Conference at RWA Conference." BookSquared, 2009. http://booksquare.com/rogue-digital-conference-at-rwa-conference/. Accessed May 10, 2017.

Krozser, Kassia. "RWA Gets It (Almost) Right." BookSquared, 2007. http://booksquare .com/rwa-gets-it-almost-right/. Accessed May 10, 2017.

"Librarians' Day at RWA." *Library Journal* 137, 7 (2012): 72. http://reviews.library journal.com/2012/08/books/genre-fiction/romance/romance-writers-of-america-rwa -2012-librarians-days/. Accessed May 10, 2017.

Lynch, Katherine E., Ruth E. Sternglantz, and Len Barot. "Queering the Romantic Heroine: Where Her Power Lies." *Journal of Popular Romance Studies* 3, 1 (2012).

http://jprstudies.org/2012/10/queering-the-romantic-heroine-where-her-power-lies-by
-katherine-e-lynch-ruth-e-sternglantz-and-len-barot/. Accessed May 10, 2017.

Romance Writers of America. 2017. https://www.rwa.org/p/cm/ld/fid=1. Accessed May 10, 2017.

Romance Writers of America. "About RWA." 2017. https://www.rwa.org/p/cm/ld/fid=504. Accessed May 9, 2017.

Romance Writers of America. "About RWA: Our History." 2017. https://www.rwa.org/p/cm/ld/fid=519. Accessed May 9, 2017.

Romance Writers of America. "Become a Member Overview." 2017. https://www.rwa.org/p/cm/ld/fid=521. Accessed May 9, 2017.

RomanceWiki. "RWA Controversy." 2008. http://www.romancewiki.com/RWA_Controversy. Accessed May 10, 2017.

Rothwell, Kate. "What I'm Talking about Above—The Letter in *RWR*." 2006. http://katerothwell.blogspot.com/2006/07/what-im-talking-about-above-letter-in.html. Accessed May 10, 2017.

Scott, Judith. "Update: Harlequin Digital Royalty Changes." *RWA Alert*. Message to Romance Writers of America Members. July 13, 2011. E-mail.

Viles, Peter. "The Dream of Romance-Novel Greatness." CNN, 2000. http://www.cnn.com/2000/books/news/05/30/romance.writing/index.html. Accessed May 10, 2017.

Romance Writers of Australia

The Romance Writers of Australia promotes excellence in romance writing in Australia and supports both published and unpublished authors with their romance fiction careers.

Formed in 1991 with seven founding members, by 2017 the organization had over 1,000 members. Although most members live in Australia, membership also includes writers from Fiji, New Zealand, Singapore, Switzerland, the United States, and the United Kingdom. Membership for all includes the monthly newsletter *Hearts Talk*, access to writers' groups or critique partners, and an annual conference. Additional services exist to specifically serve the published authors, such as a published authors' loop and a Professional Development for Authors Scheme.

The key founding member and first president was the late romance novelist Lynne Wilding (1941–2007). Wilding faced isolation on her own long path to publication especially since most, if not all, romance publishers then were based overseas in the Northern Hemisphere. Before the ubiquity of Internet use for business contact, Australia, with its large land mass and small population, was very isolated from the publishing industry. Wilding vowed to set up a support system of local writing groups so that others like her would not flounder through lack of romance-publishing knowledge. Soon after her first novel, *The Sheik*, was published by Silhouette, she was approached by six women who sought her help as a published author to assist other writers with their own publication processes, and in August 1991, the Romance Writers of Australia was formed. By February 1992, the first issue of *Hearts Talk*, the newsletter for the organization, was produced.

Along with Wilding, the founding members were Enisa Hasic, Dale Hoffman, Ann Kelleher, Margaret Morton, Mary Ann Stresau, and Hilary Weiser. A number of other published Australian authors such as Emma Darcy, Lynsey Stevens, Helen Bianchin, and Valerie Parv also helped to establish Romance Writers of Australia. The core support of the association has always been its volunteers, and in 2012 more than 180 volunteers helped Romance Writers of Australia to flourish.

However, even the most dedicated volunteers can reach a breaking point, and in 2002 the organization almost folded. Burnt-out executive members could not continue in their roles, and no new members had then stepped forward to replace them. An extraordinary general meeting of members was to be held to close down the organization. Based in Singapore at the time, Alison Brideson and a group of concerned members, however, began to network online. Romance Writers of Australia was reinvigorated by Brideson and her team, who restructured the organization and established a Published Author Liaison to make the association as useful to published authors as well as to unpublished writers.

From 2002, committee members were able to meet online, which eased some of the logistics of running the organization. It also meant that committee members were not drawn only from the eastern states of Australia but could be part of a wider Australian and even an overseas pool. Brideson was so instrumental in pulling back the association from the brink that she won the Lynne Wilding Meritorious Award in 2004. This annual award was established in 1996, named after the inaugural president, and designed to honor outstanding contributions and support to Romance Writers of Australia. Winners like Brideson have enabled the organization to keep afloat and to endure. The award of a clock symbolizes the time given by the volunteer to the association.

Writing contests for members are run throughout the year. Most are for unpublished authors, although the Little Gems short story contest accepts both published and unpublished submissions, and the R*BY (Romantic Book of the Year) is for the best published book in a series of romantic fiction categories. The R*BY, pronounced ruby, is a prestigious award judged by readers.

The Emerald Award is a full-manuscript award for unpublished Romance Writers of Australia members. The Emerald Award started as the Emma Darcy Award in 1994/1995 and continued under that name until 2004/2005. Darcy lent her name to the award because as a popular international author with sales in the multimillions, she provided significant clout in drawing editorial attention to winners. She also provided half of the $2,000 prize money, while the Romance Writers of Australia provided the other half. Over time, however, with more Australian romance authors being successful, she felt the award no longer needed her name attached to it. From 2006 the Romance Writers of Australia took on full sponsorship and renamed the award the Emerald. Darcy saw a need for writers to complete a full-manuscript competition instead of a partial-chapter contest because if a novel is slated for publication, a full manuscript is required, not merely the opening chapters. The Emerald Award is prestigious, with a significant proportion of winners and finalists continuing to publish their novels.

Just as the Romance Writers of Australia saved itself from collapse because executive volunteers were able to communicate and hold meetings online, the organization continues to attract new members thanks to various social media and Internet initiatives such as online registration. Given that romance readers and publishers were early adopters of electronic books, this seems only fitting, especially with the distance from U.S. and U.K. publishers being not such a concern now. The association has a Digital-first Published Author Liaison to help members navigate concerns specific to the electronic environment.

Romance Writers of Australia continues to help its writers with all aspects of writing and publication, as well as dealing with a number of romance publishers both large and small, including stalwarts such as Avon and Harlequin/Mills & Boon.

Doreen Sullivan

Further Reading

Bailey, Rachel. "President's Report." *Annual Report*. Neutral Bay, NSW: Romance Writers of Australia Inc., 2012, 1–6.

Brideson, Alison. "The Writer's Twelve (or How RWA Re-Invented Itself)." In *A Fine Romance: Celebrating 20 Years of Romance Writers of Australia 1991–2011*, edited by Bridget Ransome. Neutral Bay, NSW: Romance Writers of Australia, Inc., 2011.

Darcy, Emma. "A Letter from Emma Darcy." In *A Fine Romance: Celebrating 20 Years of Romance Writers of Australia 1991–2011*, edited by Bridget Ransome. Neutral Bay, NSW: Romance Writers of Australia, Inc., 2011.

Gumbley, John. "How It All Began . . . A Letter from John Gumbley (Lynne Wilding's husband)." In *A Fine Romance: Celebrating 20 Years of Romance Writers of Australia 1991–2011*, edited by Bridget Ransome. Neutral Bay, NSW: Romance Writers of Australia Inc., 2011.

Romance Writers of Australia, Inc. "About RWA. " http://romanceaustralia.com/about-rwa/. Accessed May 10, 2017.

Romance Writers of Australia, Inc. "Conference." http://romanceaustralia.com/events/conference/. Accessed May 10, 2017.

Romance Writers Report (RWR)

Romance Writers Report (RWR) is a magazine published by Romance Writers of America (RWA), a nonprofit association dedicated to advancing the professional interests of career-focused romance writers through networking and advocacy.

The purpose of the *Romance Writers Report* is to advance the professional interests of career-focused romance writers through a print and online magazine that educates and informs the members of Romance Writers of America. The *RWR* mails out monthly to RWA's membership (around 10,500 members) and contains articles and columns on the craft and career aspects of writing romance fiction, as well as informing members about association news. A typical issue of the magazine runs between 48 and 64 pages.

From Newsletter to Magazine

The first edition of what would become the *RWR* was published on February 15, 1981, as "the newsletter of Romance Writers of America." The cover story featured an interview with one of RWA's founders, Vivian Stephens, then the editor-in-chief of Dell Candlelight and Candlelight Ecstasy books.

The name of the publication evolved throughout the first few issues: it went from "the newsletter of Romance Writers of America" to *RWA Report* and finally to *Romance Report* (alternatively, *Romance Writers Report*) by October 1981.

RWA had volunteer members act as the publication's editor for approximately the first 10 years and then hired an editor for the *RWR* in 1992. At first, the editor position was awarded to a freelancer as a contract job, but the first RWA-employee editor was hired in 1996—and every editor since has been an RWA employee.

The *Romance Writers Report* was published bimonthly in February, April, June, August, October, and December from 1981 to 1984; the October/November 1984 issue was the last *RWR* produced in newsletter format. The *RWR* launched in magazine format with the November/December 1984 issue. (The *RWR* changed its bimonthly delivery schedule to January, March, May, July, September, and November at this time.) The magazine continued to be produced on a bimonthly basis until March 1996, when the *RWR* launched as a monthly publication (and it continues to be published on a monthly basis to this date).

Changing Technology

When the *RWR* first began publishing, volunteers put it together by typing and printing the newsletter (or sometimes photocopying a master copy) before mailing it out. The design of the publication changed frequently as the editors and producers tried to find the right look for the newsletter. Sometime within the first few years, RWA hired a graphic design/production company to create a professional publication for the association. For a period in the 1990s, an RWA staff member did the magazine design and production in-house, but it was later outsourced to a graphic designer.

It's interesting to note the change in technology used to work on the *RWR* throughout the past 30-plus years. The *RWR* editor in 1992, Renée Zemanski, requested articles be submitted on floppy disk so she could "start automating the magazine." Editor Pat Walker mentioned (in the May/June 1993 *RWR*) acquiring a new scanner that would allow her to scan a letter into her computer and "modem it . . . for production" to save time.

Now, all magazine production is conducted electronically: articles are e-mailed to the editor in a Word document or text file format; items are edited on a computer's word-processing program; files are sent between the editor and graphic designer via e-mail or uploaded to an FTP site; the graphic designer and editor communicate via e-mail, telephone, and even the occasional text message; and final copies of the magazine pages get uploaded to the printer's website for online review and approval. RWA even posts an electronic copy of the *RWR* on the association's website for members to read.

Not only has technology changed how the *RWR* is produced, but it's also changed the type of content included in the magazine. With the ability to send e-newsletters and post content online on social media and websites, RWA members don't have to wait for a magazine to come in the mail to receive industry news, discuss current trends, and so on. This means some content has moved from the magazine to the website or e-newsletter—or has been dropped completely.

What hasn't changed, however, is the magazine's never-ending effort to provide quality content to published and unpublished romance writers. As interim *RWR* editor Debbie Hancock said, "I suspect this magazine will always be a work-in-progress. And that's how it should be" (*RWR*, March 1996).

Erin Fry

Further Reading

Romance Writers of America. www.rwa.org. Accessed June 6, 2017.

Romances Written by Men: A Writer's Voice

Although the vast majority of popular romances are written by women, it is not a totally feminine arena. A small number of men have successfully written romances over the years, often, but not always, using pseudonyms. Several of the better known early examples are Roger Erskine Longrigg, who wrote historical romantic adventures as Laura Black; Tom Huff, who wrote romances under several pseudonyms, most famously Jennifer Wilde; and Peter O'Donnel, who wrote as Madeleine Brent. Prominent current male romance authors include Harold Lowry, who writes western romances as Leigh Greenwood; M. (Matthew) L. (Lieber) Buchman, who writes adrenaline-laced romantic suspense, contemporary, and military romance under his own name; and Ezra Barany, who writes erotic romance as Liz Addams.

Of the men writing romances today, Harold Lowry (aka Leigh Greenwood) is one of the best known. For more than 30 years, he has entertained readers with action-packed, realistic, often family-focused historical western romances. In the essay that follows, he discusses the genre and a man's place in it.

A Man in a Woman's World

When you think of romance writers, you invariably think of women like Kathleen Woodiwiss, Rosemary Rogers, Nora Roberts, Debbie Macomber, and hundreds of others. Although none has achieved the success of the authors mentioned above, a few men have managed to invade the field. As a veteran of 30 years and 50 published romances, I'm proud to be one of them. However, we make up only a fraction of 1 percent. The question might be asked: Why?

With the broadening of the Romance genre and the proliferation of subgenres, I need to make it clear that I'm using the traditional definition of romance, in which the love story is the central element of the book, and it ends with a happy ending.

I don't have the answer, but I believe there are two major obstacles. First, romances are written primarily for women. They focus on a woman's perception of love and the kind of man she wants for a husband, lover, and father of her children. Since the love scenes are nearly always from the woman's point of view, who is better able to understand and express what a woman wants than another woman? (I've written only one love scene from the man's point of view and then because he was a virgin and the woman a widow.)

Then there's the financial side. For most people, writing is a full-time job with a part-time income. Since a man is most often the major breadwinner—the salary that brings with it medical insurance and retirement benefits—it's not an easy decision to give up the regular income for royalty checks that may never come. It is estimated that only 15 percent of writers actually make a living at writing. I've never seen an estimate of how many writers never sell that first book, or the third, fifth, or eighth. In my case, I sold the third book I wrote in 1986. It was 10 years before I made more from my writing than I had as a teacher. For eight of those years I held a part-time job while my wife's job provided the medical insurance. I've always told anyone who asked that you should write because you can't *not* write. That way you take your enjoyment from the work itself, not the potential reward.

A few men have worked as coauthors with their wives, but there are several who worked alone. Undoubtedly, one of the most successful was the late Tom Huff. Written under the pen name Jennifer Wilde, his first release, *Love's Tender Fury*, had 41 printings in its first five years, and his second historical romance, *Dare to Love*, spent 11 weeks on the *New York Times* paperback best-seller list. Roger Sanderson writes as Gill Sanderson for Harlequin/Mills & Boon. Gordon Aalberg writes as Victoria Gordon for Five Star. Michael Hinkemeyer used to write as Vanessa Royall. Wayne Jordan and E. Barri Flowers (aka Devon Vaughn Archer) write for Harlequin's Kimani line. Dan Walsh, Murray Pura, M. K. (Mark) Gilroy, and John Campbell Clark write for spiritual lines. I've written for Dorchester, Kensington, Sourcebooks, Silhouette, and Harlequin.

I write as Leigh Greenwood, which is a pseudonym. You might ask why I don't write under my own name? Because my first editor told me I had to choose a female-sounding pen name. The thinking was, and still is as far as I know, that Romance is women's fiction. Thus a woman is less likely to buy a book written by a man merely because of the belief that a man can't know what a woman wants or how she feels. There are hundreds of books written on the differences, real and imagined, between men and women. Couples, whether married or not, deal with them every day. Many hold that the differences are impossible to bridge, so it's logical that a woman would believe another woman would be the best author to realize her fantasies in print. Except for Tom Huff, who wrote a very different kind of romance in the 1970s and 1980s, no male author has come close to the success of the four women I mentioned at the beginning of this essay.

In my case, my editors didn't want my readers to know I was a man. Even after I had an article in *Romantic Times* exposing my gender, I had to write about 20 more books before my editor would put my picture in the back of my books. My sales didn't go down, and I've never gotten a letter from a reader who stopped buying my books because I was a man. On the contrary, I got many letters from readers excited and pleased that I was male. Still, I'm positive many first-time readers put my book down when they saw my picture. I expect the same would happen if a man wanting to buy an action-adventure book discovered it was written by a frilly blond named Tiffany.

I've often been asked what it's like to be a man in a woman's field. I'm not sure people believe me when I say I've been accepted from the very beginning. I attended my first Romance Writers of America conference in 1985. Although I was unpublished, didn't have an agent, and was remarkably ignorant, I was welcomed by everyone I met and had my questions answered so well I went home and wrote a book that sold. I have formed many friendships that have lasted over the years, even when the friends ascended to the *New York Times* and *Publishers Weekly* best-seller lists and I remained in my comfortable niche. As a sign of wider acceptance, I served two terms as president for my local Romance Writers of America chapter and spent six years on the national board of RWA, two years as president. I was the first man to be a chapter president and am still the only man to have served on the national board. Although I'm sure some editors looked askance at a man in his forties and fifties writing romance for modern women, I know of only one instance when an editor rejected my book because I was male. Ironically, the same woman later referred to me in the foreword to one of my books as the "legendary Leigh Greenwood."

Except for Tom Huff, I haven't read the work of the men mentioned above, so I can't say if there's an across-the-board difference between romances written by women and those written by men. I can tell you some of the differences in my work. A reader wrote to say she had always known I was a man because I wrote men as they were, not as women wanted them to be. My long-term editor said I never avoided or underplayed a confrontation, that if guns or fists were involved, I let them go at it. I write mostly westerns, and let's face it, a cowboy who backs away from a fight simply isn't a hero. And if he doesn't get into at least one fight, he's not much of a cowboy.

I believe another difference is that there's more action in my books and less internalization. Though I do have long sections of internal dialogue and always include a love scene in which I concentrate on the emotions rather than the physical, I prefer action to talking about it. I believe westerns require that. I recall reading a western by a best-selling author in which there would be five pages of internal dialogue and one or two lines of spoken dialogue followed by five more pages of internal dialogue. I couldn't finish that book, so how could I write one like it?

I like to make my stories as real as possible. I once had another author tell me she stopped reading my books when I had a miner have a steady supply of eggs. I research the background of every book as carefully as possible. Many times I've traveled to the setting of a book to get a feel for the land, know what it looks like, and visit any surviving structures from the past. From lists of items that were available in army supply stores as well as what was in individual homes, I found you could get virtually anything in the West as long as you could pay for it. That included caviar in cans and a grand piano delivered by oxcart. However, money couldn't alter certain conditions. In another book by a best-selling author, the heroine was trapped in a Colorado mountain valley during the winter. With temperatures below freezing, this woman washed her hair in a mountain stream. If she's blocked in by a wall of snow, the stream is probably frozen. If not, the air temperature would have to be below freezing, so her hair would freeze rather than dry. I know romances are part fantasy, but I like to keep everything as real as possible because it makes the fantasy easier to believe.

I'm particularly fond of relatives and children, something many editors say to avoid so the emphasis can remain on the main couple. I find including family and friends gives the couple grounding, a feeling of being real, of not living in a vacuum. In a series like The Seven Brides or The Cowboys, it provides continuity. Some of us like to know what happens to our heroes and heroines after they fall in love. Including children, especially those abandoned or abused, brings to the fore a side of men that is seldom portrayed in romances. Men have very strong protective instincts. With children it can be seen in its purest form, unalloyed by love and sex.

I believe choice of words is determined more by the kind of books authors choose to write than by their gender. I've read books by women who employ language I would never use and plots involving a level of brutality I find difficult to read. But these women weren't writing romance. They were writing suspense, thrillers, or hard-boiled action. On the other hand, Nicholas Sparks—not a traditional romance writer—writes books that make women weep.

When all is said and done, there simply aren't enough male romance writers to make a meaningful comparison. As to why there aren't more, no one really knows.

Harold Lowry (aka Leigh Greenwood)

Further Reading

Leigh Greenwood Website. May 10, 2017. http://leigh-greenwood.com/. Accessed June 1, 2017.

"Men Writing Romance: A Chat with Historical Romance Author Leigh Greenwood." *RTBook Reviews*. February 28, 2011. https://www.rtbookreviews.com/rt-daily-blog/men-writing-romance-chat-historical-romance-author-leigh-greenwood. Accessed June 1, 2017.

"The Secret Lives of Male Romance Novelists." *The Airship*. http://airshipdaily.com/blog/the-secret-lives-of-male-romance-novelists. Accessed June 1, 2017.

Romantic Novelists' Association (RNA)

Origins

The Romantic Novelists' Association (RNA) was set up in the United Kingdom in 1960 by 115 members engaged in the Romance genre. It was headed by a triumvirate: the hugely successful Denise Robins, then dubbed Queen of Romance by the press, as the first president; her great friend and successor to the title, Barbara Cartland, as the vice president; and the redoubtable Alex (sometimes Vivian) Stuart, then writing romance primarily for Mills & Boon, as the first chairman.

Their objective was to restore attention and respect to the genre. Alex Stuart said she had found enthusiastic reviews for romantic novelists like Maud Driver in prestige titles such as *The Sunday Times* and *The Scotsman*, and even the august *Times Literary Supplement*, as recently as 1938. By 1960, however, the genre received no reviews and was generally looked down upon. Denise Robins opened the first meeting with a fiery speech declaring that although, according to the libraries, romantic novels gave the most pleasure to the most people, writers of romance almost had to apologize for what they did. This had to stop.

They proposed to run an annual award to recognize excellence in published novels and to introduce a critique scheme to encourage excellence in aspiring romance writers. Within a year, Alex Stuart and the new committee had set up a series of awards, run a celebratory dinner to present them, initiated the New Writers' Scheme, organized several meetings for members with speakers in Central London, and produced a bimonthly *Newsletter*. This was all achieved by volunteers, without an office or any administrative help, except for the professional typist who produced the *Newsletter*—prepared on a typewriter by removing the ribbon so that the typist impressed characters onto a wax sheet, which was then used to duplicate as many copies as required. It was a substantial achievement. But the tide of history was flowing in the opposite direction.

In January 1960 the RNA held its inaugural meeting in London; in October Penguin published the full (banned) text of *Lady Chatterley's Lover*, resulting in a headline-grabbing six-day trial for obscenity. The jury cleared the publishers, and when Foyle's Bookshop opened on November 10, it sold out of copies in 15 minutes, taking orders for a further 3,000. In the United States, Grove Press went to the Supreme Court to defend *Lady C* in 1960, but Australia held out until 1963, prohibiting it as an import, along with two other racy tales, *Lolita* and *Peyton Place*. Successful novels, both literary and commercial, now became not only more sexually explicit but also seriously unromantic. Romantic novelists were old hat.

RNA founding member Mike Legat, author, teacher, and sometime editorial director of Corgi Books, recalled those early days during the 50th-anniversary celebrations in 2010: "The Association came in for a lot of mickey-taking [making fun of]. The press and the BBC sent it up something rotten, doing their utmost to make the members look ridiculous."

Fashion was changing too. The media particularly laughed at the hats worn to meetings by the older (and mega-successful) generation. By the end of the decade, not a hat was to be seen.

Miss Cartland, a woman who developed a unique, instantly recognizable image while everyone else in the industry still thought branding was only for soap powders, *insisted* on hats. But by the mid-1960s Miss Cartland, and even Miss Robins, along with Alex Stuart and other founding members, had resigned. Dismayed by the media's reaction, they had proposed changing the RNA's name to The British Women's Fiction Writers Association, or something similar. And the membership had voted down the change.

Members generally felt that they wrote romantic fiction and weren't going to let mockery stop them from saying so. They regretted that their two biggest names had quit, but the RNA already had an identity that was wider than that of a few authors, however starry. Among the members who remained were Evadne Price, a TV playwright as well as a novelist, and who, as a journalist, was the first woman into the Belsen concentration camp; veteran Berta Ruck, a big name in the 1920s, who survived a spat with Virginia Woolf; Mills & Boon star-in-the-making Anne Weale; gentle Carnegie Medal–winner Elizabeth Goudge, now promoted to vice president; and the new president, Mary Burchell.

Evolution

President Mary Burchell (1966–1986)

The RNA was amazingly lucky that the presidential baton passed to Mary Burchell. While by no means a household name, she was a much-loved author of category romance, a hard-working professional with decided views and firm principles. But she was also a natural diplomat, charming, generous, just sufficiently loopy to be interesting, and above all, sensible.

On her accession to the presidency, she told the *Newsletter* frankly, "I passionately enjoy writing romantic novels, but I am not a compulsive writer. I adore my work, but I do it for a living and have made a good one out of it for more than 30 years. I understand and hope I've given a lot of pleasure to many nice people and find no necessity to apologise to anybody about it. The fact is, I have other interests of equal intensity: refugee work, opera and raising funds for leukaemia research."

As she later revealed in her autobiography (*Safe Passage*, republished by Mira in 2008 under her real name Ida Cook), both opera and refugees were indeed of huge importance. Before the start of World War II, through her friendship with the Austrian conductor Clemens Kraus and his wife, Burchell and her sister Louise helped Jews to escape from Nazi Germany and to come to the United Kingdom. She writes movingly of the responsibility, the anxiety, and sometimes the heartbreak of the work. But characteristically, she also cherished the ridiculous where she found it.

On one occasion, Burchell was asked to bring out of Germany a very expensive brooch that represented someone's entire capital. She was appalled to discover it was a great oblong of blazing diamonds. So she pinned it onto her inexpensive Marks and Spencer jumper (jacquard satin with glass buttons down the front) and trusted that the suspicious train guards and customs officials would assume the brooch came from Woolworths. It worked.

She agreed to be president as an emergency stopgap, but in the end she stayed in office until she died, 20 years later. She was clearly a party girl, hosting what became the RNA's traditional summer party in the three-and-a-half-acre gardens of the prestige block where she owned an apartment—and where she had put up so many of those poor refugees—in Dolphin Square. After her unexpected death in 1986, then-Chairman Dorothy Mackie Lowe recalled, "None of us who enjoyed her hospitality at a Mary Burchell party will ever forget her beaming smile after being thanked, as she flung her arms wide and said, 'Darling, *I* enjoy it too. I love talking and I love you all!'"

President Diane Pearson (1986–2011)

Another stroke of luck for the RNA was in having a member with Diane Pearson's unique combination of experience. Her day job was in publishing. She started at age 16 at Jonathan Cape, worked her way through magazines, and eventually came back as a steadily promoted editor, until she was running the fiction's list at Corgi, which then metamorphosed into Transworld, now a wholly owned subsidiary of Random House. But by night she was a novelist, and a best-selling novelist at that. Her *Csardas* (1975) is a classic, hailed on first publication as the European *Gone with the Wind*. It is set in Hungary, a saga of two families over 40 years and two world wars; reprinted most recently in 2014, it is now available in e-book form as well.

For most of her tenure as RNA president, Pearson was a hugely respected editor at Transworld, where she worked with household names like Terry Pratchett, Joanna Trollope, Jilly Cooper, and Kate Atkinson. In 1994 she was the British Book Awards Editor of the Year. She brought a wealth of publishing experience, know-how, and gossip to inform the deliberations of the RNA committee. Like her predecessor, a born diplomat, she helped negotiate sometimes choppy waters while meticulously reminding everyone of her nonexecutive and neutral role.

She was also endlessly generous with time, consideration, contacts, and more. She endowed a prize for the shorter, category romance—now known as the RoNA Rose—feeling that no matter how good individual books might be, the conventional shorter length meant that judges struggled to appreciate their merits when comparing them with the mainstream novels they were up against in the main prize.

She coauthored the RNA's 50th-anniversary memoir, *Fabulous at Fifty*, which is still available from the RNA.

President Katie Fforde (2011–)

Katie Fforde took over in 2011 when Pearson retired after 24 years on the job. Fforde is the first president to have gone through all the stages of RNA membership: first before she was published, on the New Writer's scheme, and then, after the publication of *Living Dangerously* in 1995. She did more than one job as a committee member for many years, while producing international best sellers. She was elected chairman for 2009–2011.

She has endowed the RNA with the Katie Fforde Bursary because, as she says herself, "I was a 'nearly there' writer for a long time. I found it a bit of a struggle to pay my annual subscription to the Romantic Novelists' Association, so when I finally became published, I wanted to give something back. That's the bursary, a year's subscription and a place at the conference. It does seem to give people a valuable boost to their confidence."

Publishing Landscape

When the RNA started, U.K. fiction publishing mainly produced hardback books. Paperback houses, like Corgi, bought their titles from the grand main houses—which split the subsequent royalties 50–50 with the authors, in most cases. Cheaper editions were created for libraries, but these too were hardback. During the 1960s, private commercial libraries closed down at an increasing rate. They had always been great purchasers of books for recreational reading, especially romance and crime, areas in which public libraries were very patchy. Publishers and lines that relied mainly on library sales struggled, unless they could forge a link with one of the new paperback houses. Publishers started to close their romance lists. Many RNA members found themselves orphaned.

All but one dedicated romance publisher was gone by 1978, leaving only Mills & Boon and its newly forged link with Harlequin of Canada.

Types of Romantic Fiction

The founders never tried to define the romantic novel, either for the purposes of membership or as a qualification for entering the main award. They seemed to have taken the view that it was self-evident. In 1973 the president, Mary Burchell, debated with founding member and first Main Award winner Mary Howard the merits of traditional *versus* modern romance. The definitions that the advocates offered were that "traditional romance relied on feelings and fact rather than realism" and "modern romance was summed up in 'the world well lost for love,' as in the final scenes of *Wuthering Heights*." As an example, Howard was particularly keen on *Love Story* by Erich Segal, that year's blockbuster from the United States, whose plot was essentially *The Lady of the Camellias*—that is, the relationship fractures, and the heroine dies.

Over the years a number of subgenres emerged that have been embraced by the RNA without quibble. Some of the most notable are Medical Romance, Gothic, Romantic Suspense/Women-in-jeopardy, Hot Historicals, Regency and Georgian Romances, Regional Sagas (crisply called "clogs 'n' shawls" by the trade), Middle-class Relationship Novels, Romantic Comedy in all its aspects from farce to fairy-story, the Giant Epic, and, most recently, Paranormal.

The Present

The objectives of RNA have remained constant: (1) to raise the prestige of romantic authorship, and (2) generally to encourage and foster the writing of romantic works.

Services to Members

Raising prestige is an ongoing activity, of which the flagship is the Main Award, but it is also supported by various social, networking events and, for the last four or five years, by coordinated activities on social media.

The RNA undertakes education partly by means of the New Writers Scheme and partly through the annual conference, as well as other ad hoc talks and workshops that may be arranged from time to time.

Regional chapters, which first emerged in the 1960s as members complained about the cost and inconvenience of having to come to London for every meeting, continue to multiply. At the last count there were 24, where members meet regularly, offering a chance to network and share news and issues and, from time to time, talks and workshops.

Membership benefits include the following:

1. Membership in the RNA's online discussion e-group, where people may seek advice, report writing news, post chapter and other events, and, once a week, promote their work. Available as a daily digest or as individual messages.
2. Monthly announcements on social media and to libraries of new releases by members.
3. Facebook pages for the Association and various chapters and Twitter at @RNATweets.

4. Access to the official website, including news of upcoming events and photographs of past ones, and a database of individual author members at www.romanticnovelistsassociation.org.

Who Can Join

The original three types of membership envisaged by the founders have been augmented by the addition of a category covering professional self-publishing.

- **Full Members**—traditionally published writers of romantic novels or serials of at least 30,000 words.
- **Independent Author Members**—self-published writers of romantic novels, novellas, and full-length serials of at least 30,000 words, subject to certain minimum annual sales/income criteria.
- **Associate Members**—publishers, editors, literary agents, booksellers, book reviewers, publishers' readers, librarians, and other book-industry professionals.
- **New Writers**—writers who have written but not yet sold at least one full-length romantic novel, which they may submit for critique by a member of the RNA.

There are currently around 900 members, of whom more than 20 are independent author members, 250 are new writers, and 40 or so are associates.

Awards

Over the years a number of different awards have been offered, but the *primus inter pares* has been the Romantic Novel of the Year. It has always been presented at a function in London that aims for glamour, flair, and general rejoicing. Barbara Cartland wanted it to compare with the Oscar ceremony. In the early years it was a formal dinner, for which the dress code was long frocks and furs; official gentlemen guests, like Ian Fleming, wore dinner jackets. It was so expensive that the husband of four-time winner Margaret Maddocks told her not to be shortlisted again because they couldn't afford it.

That dinner morphed into a luncheon, still grand, but at least visitors didn't have to spend a night in London. At the time of this writing, it has been replaced for the last few years by a cocktail-hour reception (so it doesn't eat into the publishers' working day) in the historic Gladstone Library, with guests sitting at dedicated tables for "bubbles and bites" during a lively but brisk presentation. As of this writing, the awards ceremony is held in March each year and is where the RoNAs (Romantic Novel Awards) are announced. Currently, they are awarded to the winners of seven specific categories of romantic novel: Contemporary, Epic,

Historical, Paranormal and Speculative, Romantic Comedy, Young Adult, and the RoNA Rose (for shorter/category romance). The winning books will have gone forward to a panel of industry-expert judges who select an overall winner who receives the Romantic Novel of the Year Award and the trophy. The winner of the RoNA Rose category also receives the Betty Neels Rose Bowl.

New Writers' Scheme

From its first year, the RNA instituted a program under which writers who were generally already working as journalists, or perhaps wrote short stories, might submit draft romantic novels for advice and criticism. They were called probationers. (RNA member Mary Howard, who turned out to be the first winner of the Romantic Novel of the Year, initially ran the scheme.) It has remained an intrinsic part of the RNA ever since. Today it has become so popular that in the last dozen years the RNA has had to institute a cap of 250 on the number of participants. The scheme opens in January each year, and take-up is such that it is generally full within days.

The organizer has a team of more than 60 readers who are authors with extensive publishing histories in various types of romantic novels. The scripts are sent to an appropriate reader who provides a report that may include, for example, comments on plotting, characterization, and structure. The reports are intended to be honest and constructive suggestions from published novelists—they point out flaws but also offer advice based on experience.

The organizer will advise and support authors whose reports indicates that their novels are ready, or almost ready, to be submitted to a publisher and agent. Manuscripts that have been entered into the NWS and subsequently published as a debut novel are eligible for the Joan Hessayon New Writers' Scheme Award, which is sponsored by Dr. David Hessayon, botanist and author of the famous Expert series of books on gardening, in memory of his late wife, a much-loved RNA member.

Annual Conference

Unlike the New Writers' Scheme and the Major Award, which have been part of the RNA since the very beginning, the conference is a more recent innovation, beginning in 1998. In the ensuing years a program has emerged with something for everyone, from the newest new writer to the best of best sellers. The conferences have proven very popular, especially as the venue changes from year to year, with the objective of covering the widest possible area of the country.

Each year the annual conference offers a wide variety of talks, seminars, and workshops by top authors and by publishing professionals with a wide range of interests. RNA members can network with the editors, agents, and publishers who frequently drop in on the conference, as well as learn from experts in other areas such as social media, technology, and business. Each conference also includes opportunities for readers to meet and chat with their favorite writers.

Attending for the first time can be daunting, so new attendees are welcomed and mentored until they get their bearings. The venues, hitherto, have been university campuses, and the resulting kitchen parties in student flats have become not only a great source of support and togetherness but also a major reason why some people come.

Instructive, inspiring, and the best networking event of the year, the RNA's annual conference is a key event that writers look forward to and treasure.

Jenny Haddon

Further Reading

Romantic Novelists' Association (RNA). http://rna-uk.org/. Accessed April 12, 2107.

Romantic Suspense

Romantic Suspense novels are just what they sound like: love stories with suspenseful plots. Done well, the two elements mix together and balance each other, making for an engrossing reading experience. Notably, the suspense side of the genre uses obstacles and external forces to heighten the challenges the potential lovers must overcome before they can ultimately emerge safely (Cawelti, 41). Simply put, Romantic Suspense novels are exciting, often adrenaline-soaked love stories.

Back in the Romantic Suspense heyday of the 1960s, the story would be told from the heroine's point of view, the danger would be implied rather than graphic, the story fast-paced, and the suspense built steadily; and there were often two romantic heroes—thus providing a conflict because one of them was probably a villain (Saricks, 243). Now, contemporary Romantic Suspense reflects a changing world with the genre exhibiting a grittier, sexier, and more realistic set of circumstances; a heroine quite independent and probably well versed in weaponry or self-defense; a variety of points of view might be expressed (including the villain's); and the love story could be more shrouded (Ramsdell, 132–33). What remains the same is that by the conclusion, the heroine will be safe, and she will have found a happy and romantic relationship.

Romantic Suspense is a descendent of Gothic romance (see separate entry). But while Gothic fiction typically involves a narrator who has found herself in an inhospitable environment (haunted castle, spooky mansion), romantic suspense doesn't necessarily have that contained quality. Traditional romantic suspense often involves exotic locations where the heroine is not particularly comfortable. She must adapt and perhaps trust quickly, and this might backfire on her. More-contemporary romantic suspense might not be so glamorous with its settings, but the heroine will still be confronting something out of the ordinary, be it a new job or the aftermath of an accident.

Historically, romantic suspense traces its origins to two Gothic-toned books: Horace Walpole's *The Castle of Otranto* (1765) and Ann Radcliffe's *The Mysteries of Udolpho* (1794). The next nods usually go to the Brontë sisters: Charlotte Brontë's *Jane Eyre* (1847) and Emily Brontë's *Wuthering Heights* (1847). The Victorian Era's sensation novels by Wilkie Collins (*The Woman in White*, 1860) also weigh in as influential. Building on these models, Mary Roberts Rinehart made her mark as a significant influence, particularly with *The Circular Staircase* (1908). Smith posits that Rinehart's "Had-I-But-Known" school of writing allowed the heroine to both experience regret and learn things about herself, in plot devices that were appropriate to the cultural norms of that era (Smith, 1184–87).

Most credit Daphne du Maurier's *Rebecca* (1938) for jumpstarting the 20th century's fascination with romantic suspense. Purists will put *Rebecca* into Gothic, but the book defies easy categorization, consistently being voted onto favorite lists and winning the mystery community's Anthony Award for Best Novel of the Century.

But when Victoria Holt's *Mistress of Mellyn* (1960) came out, the romantic suspense and Gothic revival went wild. In the 1960s, the romantic suspense boom revolved around best sellers from Holt, Phyllis A. Whitney (see separate entry), and the standard-bearer for the genre, Mary Stewart (see separate entry). With her finely crafted and well-researched stories, populated by memorable characters, Stewart's model is tough to beat. Just one example: *This Rough Magic* (1964), set on the island of Corfu, puts a vacationing actress into an unexpected drama off-stage, a wonderful takeoff on Shakespeare's *The Tempest*.

Influenced by Stewart, Barbara Michaels (pen name for Barbara Mertz) is another talented writer who graced the romantic suspense field during this period and who also writes mysteries as Elizabeth Peters. Her titles—complicated, elaborate with Gothic overtones, and gracefully written—include her memorable *Wait for What Will Come* (1978).

While romantic suspense might have fallen out of favor in the 1980s, it never disappeared. It's a dangerous world out there, and romance authors have found myriad ways of commenting on how hard it is to be an independent female today. An interesting migration by contemporary romance writers toward romantic suspense—and usually centered around topical issues—led by such leaders as Nora Roberts, Jane Ann Krentz, and Linda Howard, has opened up the genre once more. For the most part, as mentioned before, authors writing romantic suspense today will bring an edgier tone with more danger, violence, and explicit sex than the traditional favorites of the 1960s.

Sandra Brown emerged in the 1990s as a force to be reckoned with; her *Witness* (1996) is frequently cited as a "classic" already. She uses her setting as a character, carefully crafts twisty plots, and ramps up the adventure and violence to grab her readers' attention. Similarly, longtime romantic suspense author Heather Graham continues to experiment; she is known for atmospheric novels (*Picture Me Dead*, 2003), sometimes tossing in quite a bit of the paranormal, which hearkens back to the subgenre's Gothic roots (*Ghost Moon*, 2010). Karen Robards, known for her strong women (*Shattered*, 2010), consistently keeps her readers up all night with her nail-biters. She partners well with Iris Johansen (her *Face of Deception* [1998] launched the hugely successful Eve Duncan series).

Luscious settings make the difference for go-to romantic suspense authors such as Elizabeth Adler, who has created a romantic duo with her private eyes Mac Reilly and Sunny Alvarez (*From Barcelona, With Love*, 2011). Adler once wrote more of the "rich and famous" type of romance, and the move to romantic suspense has kept her up to date. Stella Cameron, known for her historicals, has shifted to romantic suspense, writing steamy titles set in the South (*French Quarter*, 1998).

Mary Higgins Clark, well-known suspense writer, does not technically write romantic suspense. However, her seminal works (*Where Are the Children?* [1992] is often cited) involving women and endangered children have opened up a whole new line of storytelling possibilities. Several romantic suspense writers are pushing the envelope even more so with darker tales that are ultimately redeeming, but the heroines definitely have seen hard times. Those addressing difficult themes and using the antihero in their titles include Anne Stuart (*Ice Blue*, 2007), Eileen Dreyer (*A Man to Die For*, 1991), Lisa Gardner (*The Perfect Husband*, 1998), and Tami Hoag (*Night Sins*, 1995).

Today, after the United States has been at war for more than a decade, the Romantic Suspense genre leans heavily on the military and law enforcement. Honor and patriotism, physical agility and smarts—what differs now is that the heroine is also a soldier or an officer who takes a more active role in her own safety. Look to Carla Neggers for heroines who meet their challenges head-on and always find love in unexpected places (*Cold Pursuit* [2008] is book one of a trilogy), such as her Secret Service agent who meets resistance in Vermont. Nora Roberts also lets her heroine wear the uniform, in this case as a smoke jumper, in *Chasing Fire* (2011).

Sometimes, girls just want to have fun, and humor permeates a number of romantic suspense novels, particularly those that are exploring other genres such as Mystery and Adventure. Call them romps or capers, perhaps, but the romantic suspense tone still rings true. Consider Jennifer Crusie (*Welcome to Temptation*, 2000), who excels at this by herself and who teams up with other authors to add to the appeal, for example, with Bob Mayer (*Agnes and the Hitman*, 2007). Janet Evanovich, with her deep roots in romance, is best known for her madcap Stephanie Plum mystery series. Consider her Full series, since reissued, for a generous dose of romantic suspense. She, too, collaborates with other authors so that she can mix it up. Stephanie Bond is another humorous romantic suspense author whose Atlanta-based series might get classified as mystery (*Body Movers*, 2006), but it's comic romantic suspense.

Not everyone wants to read gritty and edgy, however, and consequently a demand for reissues continues, with Sourcebooks and Severn House, in particular, both bringing back classic titles. Other traditional romantic suspense authors from the 1960s and 1970s are still sought by readers, including Evelyn Anthony, whose 1970 title *The Assassin* inspired Sandra Brown; Catherine Gaskin, with her historical romantic suspense *The Tilsit Inheritance* (1963); Susan Howatch, with *Call in the Night* (1973); and Anna Gilbert, with *The Look of Innocence* (1975) (Ramsdell, 135).

Additionally, in line with those looking for a gentler read, a huge growth in inspirational or Christian romantic suspense can be seen with best-selling authors such as Dee Henderson (*Before I Wake*, 2006) and Irene Hannon (*Lethal Legacy*, 2012).

Romantic suspense continues to update itself while adjusting to current reader demands and exploring topical themes in the popular culture at large. The flexibility of the genre coupled with talented writers assures a long future for this captivating and always evolving genre hybrid.

Teresa L. Jacobsen

See also: Du Maurier, Daphne; Gothic Romance; Hibbert, Eleanor Burford; Mystery/Suspense/Thriller and Romance; *Rebecca;* Roberts, Nora; Stewart, Mary; Whitney, Phyllis A.

Further Reading

Cawelti, John G. *Adventure, Mystery, and Romance: Formula Stories as Art and Popular Culture*. Chicago: University of Chicago Press, 1976.

Ramsdell, Kristin. *Romance Fiction: A Guide to the Genre*, 2nd ed. Santa Barbara, CA: ABC-CLIO, 2012.

Regis, Pamela. *A Natural History of the Romance Novel*. Philadelphia: University of Pennsylvania Press, 2003.

Saricks, Joyce G. *The Readers' Advisory Guide to Genre Fiction*. Chicago: American Library Association, 2001.

Smith, Jennifer Crusie. "The Romantic Suspense Mystery." In *Mystery and Suspense Writers: The Literature of Crime, Detection, and Espionage*, edited by Robin W. Winks and Maureen Corrigan, 1183–97. New York: Scribner's, 1998.

Royal Ascot Awards

The Royal Ascot is the annual contest of the Beau Monde chapter of the Romance Writers of America (RWA), a group devoted to the promotion of romance fiction set during the Regency Period. The award was established in 1994 to promote Regency romances by encouraging the development of authors of historical romance set between 1780 and 1840.

Soon after its founding, Beau Monde chapter leaders decided to launch a contest. As then-Secretary Jo Ann Ferguson notes, "It was obvious to the founders of the Beau Monde right from the beginning that a contest would be a great way to raise awareness of Regency writers and their work. . . . [W]e wanted to get our members' works in front of editors and agents who could help our members' careers" (King, part 1).

The first contest, held in 1994, took place in the fall so entrants would be able to use judges' feedback to revise their manuscripts before entering RWA's contest for unpublished writers, the Golden Heart. The Royal Ascot was later moved to the spring so that awards could be given at the annual Beau Monde conference, held the day before the annual RWA conference. The second Royal Ascot contest took place in 1996, and the contest has been held each year since.

Changes in the submission categories for the contest mirror changes in the Regency romance market. In 1994, writers could submit in one of two categories: "Traditional Regencies" or "Non-Traditional Regencies," the latter of which were gaining an increased share of the romance market during the 1990s. The collapse of the market for traditional Regencies led to multiple changes in category names: in 2006, "Traditional/Short Regency-set Historical" and "Long Regency-set Historical"; in 2007, "Traditional Regency," "Regency Historical," and "Paranormal Regency Romance"; and in 2008, "Hot and Wild Regency," rather than "Paranormal," with Regency-set erotica now qualifying for the contest. Also in 2008, "Traditional Regency" became "Sweet and Mild Regency."

Since 2011, "Regency Historical" (Longer Regency or Mainstream Regency-set), "Hot Regency" (Very Sensual to Erotic Regency), "Wild Regency" (Paranormal,

Time Travel, other similar Regency), and "Sweet and Mild Regency" (Traditional, Inspirational, Young Adult, or other without explicit sex) have been the contest's categories, reflecting the multiple subgenres in which Regency-set romances can be found today. Categories are used only for assigning entries to first-round judges. The contest no longer awards prizes in each category; submissions with the highest scores during the preliminary judging round are awarded a place on the finalists' list, with the overall winner selected by authors, agents, and editors experienced in judging Regency romance.

Recently, the Royal Ascot Contest has added the Royal Ascot Reader's Choice Category Awards, which allow authors to introduce new readers to their works and have them judged by potential consumers. This contest is open to writers who have submitted an eligible entry in the Royal Ascot Contest, and the judging will be done by reader-judges who are subscribers to the Beau Monde's blog, *The Regency Reader*. Entries will be judged in the same four categories included in the main Royal Ascot Contest, and awards will be given in each category.

Past finalists and winners of the Royal Ascot Award include well-known historical romance authors Jennifer Ashley, Jacquie D'Alessandro, Shannon Donnelly, Diane Gaston, Karen Hawkins, Victoria Hinshaw, Janet Mullany, and Tracy Anne Warren.

Jackie Horne

See also: Romance Writers of America (RWA) Regency Romance, Traditional

Further Reading

The Beau Monde. "About Us." http://main.thebeaumonde.com/about-us. Accessed June 3, 2107.

The Beau Monde. "The Royal Ascot Contest." http://thebeaumonde.com/resources/the-royal-ascot-contest/. Accessed June 3, 2107.

The Beau Monde. "Royal Ascot Reader's Choice Category Awards." http://thebeaumonde.com/resources/the-royal-ascot-contest/royal-ascot-readers-choice-awards/. Accessed June 3, 2017.

King, Cara. "From the Annals of the Beau Monde, Part 1." *The Quizzing Glass*, March 2002.

King, Cara. "From the Annals of the Beau Monde, Part 2." *The Quizzing Glass*, April 2002.

RT (Romantic Times) Book Reviews: The Founder's Voice

I established *RT Book Reviews* in 1981; it is now a monthly magazine reviewing over 200 books in 14 genres for women readers.

When I announced that I wanted to publish a romance newsletter, people thought I was crazy. No one took romances seriously back then nor imagined the genre could become a billion-dollar industry. After all, barely 30 percent of paperback sales in America were romances (many with limited print runs)—just a mix of Gothics, sagas, contemporary and historical novels, some even written by men. Graphic sex scenes were taboo, and lovemaking usually took place behind closed doors. The usual ending included wedding bells for a virginal heroine and an older male with resources and status.

An avid reader, I grew up devouring Nancy Drew mysteries and every historical biography and historical novel in the local library. After college, I moved from Michigan to Greenwich Village at a time when the feminist movement and free love were on the rise. I walked beside Susan Brownmiller, a leader of the Redstockings, in the Second Women's Liberation Parade, joining over a thousand women marching up Fifth Avenue to hear Bella Abzug in Central Park. It was definitely the Age of Aquarius, and we all felt liberated.

At the core of the women's sexual revolution was the concept—radical at the time—that women, just like men, enjoyed sex and had sexual needs. This marked a shift in thinking about sexuality, as well as a growing acceptance of premarital sex and birth control. Romantic fiction has always reflected women's fantasies, going as far back as the Brontë sisters and Jane Austen. Fantasies were aflame as never before. And as another Village bohemian, Bob Dylan, wrote, "The Times They Are A-Changin.'"

I was in the right place at the right time, even though I didn't know the first thing about publishing. I had been a history major in college and wrote two nonfiction books on dollhouses and miniatures. My primary qualification to this day is that I was an avid reader. I never had to do research on the subject, and at that time there were no courses or books on the subject. But I had an original idea and felt there was a niche market for it.

I really enjoyed the new sensual historical romances that appeared in the mid-1970s, and when I learned they had sold a million copies and, shockingly, jumped on the best-seller lists, I figured there must be other readers like me—women who wanted information on all aspects of romance. I was sure they would appreciate a newsletter, and I knew exactly what it should contain.

It was Nancy Coffey, the brilliant Avon editor who found *The Flame and the Flower* by Kathleen Woodiwiss on her slush pile in the early 1970s. This was the book that revolutionized paperback publishing (not unlike a similar phenomenon with *Fifty Shades of Grey* decades later). In the early stages of development, historical settings made the sex scenes less threatening, establishing a necessary distance for the readers unaccustomed to such plots. Critics scoffed and called them "soft-core porn" until the day that sales figures doubled and tripled and all the publishers woke up. Sex sells. Money talks.

Coffey discovered the two writers who started the craze: Woodiwiss, the Minnesota military wife, whose style was exclusive sensuality and sex between one man and one woman, and Rosemary Rogers, a single mother in California, who favored the other end of the spectrum—her heroines took on entire continents, in a manner of speaking. To this day, the sensuality levels in romance range from sweet or mild to scorching, and this is why the books at *RT Book Reviews* are rated by adding various labels to help readers make appropriate choices.

By the end of the 1970s, Nancy Coffey had a best-selling group known as the Avon Ladies. In addition to Woodiwiss and Rogers, her stable included Bertrice Small, Johanna Lindsay, Shirley Busbee, and Virginia Henley. The luscious, illustrated Avon covers made the novels so enticing, with bigger-than-life handsome heroes, such as the shirtless cover model Fabio. Female models wore long period dresses and displayed a luscious bosom. The New York publishers and journalists, male of course, called these historicals "bodice rippers." If the hero's hands were above the waist, that signaled moderate sensuality. If his hands were below the waist, the reader knew it was going to be a hotter read. And be he pirate, king, Viking, or Scottish laird, he'd better be excellent under the covers and between the sheets.

The first issue of *Romantic Times* was published in June 1981 in Brooklyn, New York. Distributed in the Waldenbooks chain, it appeared in newsprint tabloid-style (glossy paper and color was beyond the budget back then) and proved that readers wanted to know everything about the books: the authors, calendar of forthcoming titles, illustrators, male cover models, pseudonyms, recommended reads, and information about how to write a romance novel and get it published. Paperback romances were distributed primarily to supermarkets, drugstores, and used bookstores and were sold from wire racks, preferably near the cashier line. Sales were spurred by three things—the beautiful covers, the back-cover copy, and the opening pages. These paperbacks were usually priced under $3.99.

More publishers copied the success of Avon Books and discovered their own popular historical romance authors, such as Jennifer Wilde, aka Tom Huff. Contemporary lines with more sensual plots were created by several publishing houses and often featured heroines who were professional women rising to the top of the corporate ladder (reflecting the readers' fantasies). This was fodder for *Romantic Times* readers.

By *Romantic Times*'s fifth year in business, we could afford white glossy paper and color pages. The advent of the Apple Macintosh Desktop publishing system made the company grow even faster. We could send the files directly to the printer in Maine, which saved an enormous amount of production and distribution time, and we soon expanded beyond reviewing only historicals and category romances as authors dabbled in other genres and characters. Readers also liked mysteries, vampires, paranormal, Regencies, sci-fi, inspirationals, and so on. When the magazine eventually covered 14 different fiction genres, we changed the publication's name to *RT Book Reviews* to reflect what we were actually doing. We were now reviewing around 250 books a month. The staff included 50 reviewers and a coterie of editors, plus an art director and an advertising manager. It was a long way from a walk-in closet and a 24-page tabloid newspaper. *RT* was now a genuine hobby magazine, and its readers were buying 20 to 40 books a month.

Along the way, I wrote *Love's Leading Ladies* (1982) and *How to Write a Romance and Get It Published* (1983). *RT* also started a manuscript service to help new writers. The annual Booklovers Conventions held workshops for writers and readers, and for about a year, we held Saturday Romance Writing Seminars in Manhattan. Independent booksellers were great supporters, and *RT* created a newsletter for them, "Bookstores That Care," and distributed bookmarks from authors with their shipments. For several years, the magazine sponsored tours to Europe, visiting castles and historical sites and having tea with Barbara Cartland.

Publishers were receiving hundreds of manuscripts a month from writers and accepting only a handful of submissions. Editors often became agents as advances went into the four figures. But all the while, publishing was owned and managed by men, and the women were editors who did the work. Illustrators made more money than most of the authors, and Fabio became a household word. Through it all, *RT* kept up with all the news and gossip and relayed it to readers.

Today, the world of romance publishing has again changed drastically. Expansion and globalism are the keywords. The first development took place at the turn of the century when Ellora's Cave began publishing erotica in digital format for readers who preferred reading on computers and handheld devices. These readers purchased millions of stories as e-books. Next came Amazon's success, which, unfortunately, shut down many independent (indie) bookstores. Waldenbooks/Borders departed the scene. New categories arrived and had big sales—YA, fantasy, military romances, S & M, plus a variety of LGBTQ romances and diversity lines. New York publishers were slow to enter the e-book business but have done their best to catch up. Finally, in an interesting change from tradition, most of the e-book companies and indie publishers, as well as my *Romantic Times*, are owned and operated by women.

The advent and evolution of self-publishing is one of the most important changes in romance publishing in this century. The Internet connects authors, readers, and the newly arrived bloggers around the world. Many authors, particularly those with strong followings, prefer to control their own careers rather than remain with New York publishers. It is a toss-up, and some authors are doing both. *Romantic Times* was the first to recognize and welcome this "new blood" because the staff knew that romances are like fashion—they change every year.

Hardcover books and trade paperbacks are still preferred by many readers, but romance readers utilize a higher percentage of handheld devices than other types of readers. It is likely due to the fact that they read 20 to 40 books a month, and e-books (and Amazon) keep their costs down. The sales of audiobooks and films based on romance books are also growing.

The future of romance publishing will continue to go through changes as women (and some men) writers reflect the current culture in their stories. But one fact still remains. If an author writes a great book, it will be recognized. Pushing the envelope on plots and characters, and getting a sexy alpha male to commit, is still a sure-fire way to hit the best-seller lists.

After 35 years of publication, in June 2016, *RT* went digital with the magazine and ceased to offer a print version. This is especially helpful to international readers, and while some readers may still wish for print, the online version has much to offer and appeals to the increasingly digitally oriented community. I have retired, and I live part of the year on my organic farm in Texas. However, many of the original employees are still in charge, managing the office in Brooklyn and planning and hosting the annual convention that brings together readers and authors. Over the years *RT* has archived all its reviews, and it is possible to go to the website (RTBookreviews.com) and look up thousands of romance authors and read the reviews of their books. At last count there were over 80,000.

Editor's Note: In May 2018 *RT Book Reviews* announced that it was ceasing publication. The website would be available for a year, although no new content would be added, and after that, the website would go dark.

Kathryn Falk

Further Reading

Falk, Kathryn. *How to Write a Romance and Get It Published: With Intimate Advice from the World's Most Popular Romantic Writers*. New York: Crown, 1983.
Falk, Kathryn. *Love's Leading Ladies*. New York: Pinnacle, 1982.
RT Book Reviews. www.rtbookreviews.com. Accessed August 1, 2017.
RT Booklovers Convention. www.RTConvention.com. Accessed August 1, 2017.

RT (Romantic Times) **Booklovers Convention**

One year after launching the *Romantic Times Book Reviews* in 1981, the publication's founder and CEO, Kathryn Falk, hosted the first *RT* Booklovers Conference at the St. Moritz Hotel in New York City. The first of its kind, it was a relatively small event because the professional romance community was limited in numbers, but the romance-reading community was not, and it was considered important to bring all the players to the table so they could network. The inaugural conference was scheduled as a three-day weekend in 1982 and was broadly advertised in *Romantic Times (RT)*. It was promoted as an opportunity to meet face-to-face with agents and publishers and to attend publishing workshops. It was a novel experience, and the networking paid off amazingly well, creating friendships and relationships that lasted for decades and even lifetimes. Booklovers are a special tribe and treat their addiction as a serious hobby!

The handful of existing publishers rented hotel suites on Friday to entertain their authors and hold discussions with unpublished writers. Saturday morning featured writers' workshops with emphasis on writing sensually, finding an agent, and learning to query publishers. After lunch, the first awards ceremony took place. The three recipients were a shy Rosemary Rogers, the amusing Jennifer Wilde (aka Tom Huff), and the extraordinary Regency author Elsie Lee. It was a far cry from today, when more than 50 authors receive awards in various categories. The Sunday bookfair at the conference was another small, but successful, first. It was held in the gymnasium of a nearby school, and more than 200 hundred readers lined up to buy autographed copies an hour before starting time. Over the years, the bookfair has grown along with the conference, and the 2017 convention attracted 1,200 authors for signings and some 3,000 readers.

As the subscription base for *RT Book Reviews* grew and increasing numbers of bookstores and librarians carried copies, so did interest grow for *RT*'s second convention in 1983. By then, nearly every publisher in New York was starting a romance line due to the success of Avon Books, Zebra Romances, and Harlequin. As a promotional stunt, Falk made an arrangement with Amtrak to create a "Love Train" that went from Los Angeles to New York City. Along the way, it stopped at dozens of train stations to pick up authors heading for the Big Apple and to greet groups of readers who waited on the platforms, wearing pink outfits to show their support for the Romance genre. *RT* gave away 500 gift bags at these railroad stops.

Waiting at New York's Penn Station was the Queen of Romance, Barbara Cartland, and a phalanx of 50 reporters and television news cameras from the United States and England. After four days on the rails, the travelers managed to march into the station singing, "Hello, Barbara" to the tune of "Hello, Dolly!" Dame Barbara was delighted, and the journalists were overjoyed.

Among the authors on the train were Jude Deveraux and the world's best-selling author, Janet Dailey, and the Love Train event made every news outlet, including the prestigious *New York Times*. The crowning touch was having the authors travel by horse-and-carriage to the Roosevelt Hotel, waving at hundreds of waiting fans. Dame Barbara appeared on all the popular television shows that week, including Johnny Carson, to publicize the event.

These events were the talk of the town, and it was the Second Booklovers Convention that put romance novels on the map of America. Romance was finally on its way to the hearts and hands of millions of readers. This was also the year that Falk wrote *How to Write a Romance and Get It Published* in both hardcover and paperback. Known by some as the "Bible of Romance," it sold more than 100,000 copies and inspired thousands of women and a few men to become romance writers. To this day, someone will occasionally pop up and tell Falk that the book meant the world to them. Usually, it is a best-selling author whose mother was a subscriber to *RT* when she was growing up.

Over the decades, the romance community has grown from a handful of American authors to many thousands, in part due to the self-published authors who started arriving on the scene after 2013. *RT*'s original three-day event has blossomed into a week-long extravaganza. A full-time staff works the entire year to bring together all aspects of the romance industry: authors, readers, aspiring writers, agents, editors, book publishers, cover models and photographers, audio publishers and narrators, bloggers, publicists, Internet services, e-book distributors, booksellers, and librarians. There are even special seminars for the Husbands of Romance.

More than 200 workshops provide updates on the ever-changing and expanding billion-dollar book business. Even foreign publishers attend, hoping to meet writers and purchase translation rights. Authors, as well as publishers, create parties and pop-up signings, eager to give out excerpts and reading copies to avid fans. The right promotion and advance orders can land a book on the various best-seller lists. Attendees know they will go home with souvenirs, tote bags, and over $200 worth of free books, enough to fill the extra suitcase they know to bring along.

The conventions are attracting a growing number of international authors and readers. In addition to neighboring Canada, they arrive from such distant places as Australia, New Zealand, Great Britain, France, Germany, Thailand, Siberia, Brazil, and Azerbaijan, to name only a few.

By the late 1980s, the conference began traveling to various cities. Readers informed *RT* that they took their vacation time to attend year after year, inspiring the staff to seek out interesting cities with large enough hotel ballrooms and plenty of workshop space and sleeping rooms to accommodate the crowd. Destinations have included Savannah, San Diego, Orlando, Chicago, Las Vegas, Toronto, Daytona Beach, Nashville, New Orleans, Houston, Atlanta, Dallas, Los Angeles, and Reno.

Over the years, *RT*'s staff of editors and 60 reviewers (who read everything!) have decided on the best books in 14 broad categories—historical, contemporary,

Regency, paranormal, YA, mystery, inspirational, urban fantasy, and so forth—with a variety of awards given in each. *RT* prides itself on an excellent reputation for honest and accurate reviews and has heralded some of the most gifted newcomers. A few years ago, *RT* added coverage and awards for self-published books, erotica, diversity, and LGBTQ romances. The formal award ceremony takes place on Friday night, and readers savor the opportunity to see the outstanding authors, listen to their acceptance speeches, and attend a champagne reception afterward for more networking.

The convention also includes sponsored mixers, costume balls, YA Day, and various theme nights. Complete information, including the weeklong schedule that lists tours of the city, appointments with editors and agents, and a pre-convention Boot Camp for beginning writers, can be found at the convention's website (www.RTConvention.com). This conference is considered by attendees to be an exhausting, but memorable, experience and often concludes with a slumber party and movie on the final night.

To this day the conference's mottos appropriately remain "May you always have Romantic Times" and "You Can Sleep When You're Dead!"

Kathryn Falk

Further Reading

RT Book Reviews. www.rtbookreviews.com. Accessed August 1, 2017.
RT Booklovers Convention. www.RTConvention.com. Accessed August 1, 2017.

RUSA-CODES Reading List Awards

Chosen annually by the Reference and User Association's (RUSA) Reading List Council, a committee of experienced collection-development and readers' advisory librarians, the Reading List "seeks to highlight outstanding genre fiction that merit special attention by general adult readers and the librarians that work with them" (RUSA Book and Media Awards). Books in eight different adult fiction genres are considered, with one winner being chosen and up to four runner-up "short-listed" titles included for each genre. "Read-alikes," similar titles that may also appeal to readers, are sometimes listed for each genre as well. The format has evolved over the years, and although the genres included may change with reading tastes and interests, the Reading List generally includes the following genres: Adrenaline, Fantasy, Historical Fiction, Horror, Mystery, Romance, Science Fiction, and Women's Fiction.

This award was established in 2007 by the Collection Development and Evaluation Section (CODES) of RUSA, a division of the American Library Association (ALA). The selections are usually announced at ALA's annual Midwinter Meeting in January or February.

Kristin Ramsdell

Further Reading

RUSA. "The Reading List" RUSA Update. http://rusa.ala.org/update/awards/the-reading-list/. Accessed April 12, 2017.

RUSA. "RUSA Book and Media Awards." http://www.ala.org/rusa/awards/media. Accessed April 12, 2017.

RWR

See Romance Writers Report (RWR)

S

Science Fiction Romance

See Futuristic (or Science Fiction) Romance

Second Chance at Love/Reunion Plot

The second chances plotline is one of the most widely appreciated in the Romance genre, and for good reason. Readers relate to these stories on a very personal level, empathizing with characters' emotions from their own experiences. Many of these stories involve old hometowns and first loves, both popular themes.

A study on the subject of romantic reunions, "Guess Who's Back," published in *Psychology Today* magazine (Weintraub, 78–84), found that the deep emotional bonds forged in first or early love relationships never truly end. Even after the study's participants had married their spouses, raised families, and built successful careers, the tender feelings for their first loves lingered on, for some, well into their senior years. In fact, the study showed separation, like adversity, intensifies these feelings.

The reasons for their breakups will sound familiar to second chances romance readers: their parents disapproved; he was drafted or enlisted in the military; she went off to college or a professional career. Some of them were too young to understand their relationship at the time, and they let it slip away. Years later, things that had seemed so important in their restless teens and early twenties no longer mattered. Their lives changed with maturity, leaving them wondering, "What if?"

Like real-life lost-and-found love stories, second chance romances contain emotional turmoil for the reunited lovers to overcome. The characters are often wary, afraid of another crushing rejection. There may be resentment over how their relationship had ended, lost trust, and hurt feelings. These hurdles complicate the story for the hero and heroine as they come to terms with their past. It isn't until these issues are resolved that the couple is able to forge their new relationship and move forward.

An example of this is Kat Martin's 2010 romantic suspense *Against the Wind*. The hero and heroine began as high school classmates. She was his first love, but she rejected him and humiliated him to impress her highborn friends. Years later, he's a successful rancher, and she's the widow of a conman, a down-and-out single mom. When they reunite, her rejection is still fresh in his mind, but he hasn't gotten over his love for her. She regrets her behavior, realizing now how cruel she'd been, but she doesn't know how to make it up to him. In truth, she'd had a bit of a crush on him too. As the story progresses, adversity brings them together, they reconcile their past, and fall in love all over again.

The *Psychology Today* article "Rekindling Old Flames" (Gabe, 32) profiles an earlier study on rekindled romances. The author, a psychiatrist, has a unique perspective, both through her practice and in her personal life. Her lost love contacted her 30 years after he'd ended their engagement within days of their wedding. Conflicting career paths had cooled their relationship and jeopardized any hope of a happy marriage, at least at that time. Decades later, with their ambitious career aspirations behind them, they were able to focus on their true hearts' desires.

In Peter Golden's 2012 reunion romance *Come Back Love*, the hero and heroine have a similar experience. They were college soul mates in the 1960s with a tumultuous relationship. Their career paths sent them in different directions, and although he was willing to compromise, she was not. Decades later, he's in town on business and decides to drop in on her, his first and only love. Showing up in her office unannounced is risky. He wonders if she'll even want to see him. Will those old feelings still be there? What if she's married? Plus, the last time she'd seen him, he was a much younger man. His angst is both troubling and tantalizing. This inner turmoil—driven by both hope and fear—is part of what makes these stories so irresistible and satisfying when two people who belong together finally find each other.

Second chances plotlines often take advantage of small, intimate settings, like ranches or small towns where everyone knows everybody else's business. Outside interference from family and friends complicates the relationship, creating that wonderful sense of adversity. The more interference the hero and heroine encounter, the greater the tension—and romance is all about the tension.

Historical second chance romances are often complicated by the rigid, puritanical rules of society. A woman caught alone with a man is scandalous, and her reputation is ruined. Brenda Joyce's 2010 romance *An Impossible Attraction* takes this scenario a step further by adding an unplanned pregnancy. Even though the heroine's intentions are noble, she is outcast for agreeing to be the hero's mistress, for a price. When the hero realizes he's falling in love with her, he panics, calls off the arrangement, and sends her home. Except by now, everyone knows she's a ruined woman. Her father kicks her out, leaving her to fend for herself in a London slum, pregnant and disgraced. When the hero finally comes to his senses, he seeks her out and offers to care for her and his heir. Of course, he's kidding himself with this practical offer. She's the love of his life.

There are many more examples, too numerous to include here. Each subgenre has second chances stories that invoke a nostalgia only the reader can understand. A 1996 study covered in *Health* magazine, "Rekindling an Old Flame" (Laskas, 46), found it was usually men who attempted the first contact with past loves. They tended to be men of action with optimistic outlooks, risk-takers with romantic souls. If these traits sound familiar to you, expect a call, because an estimated 10 percent of the population reconnects with a love from their past.

Sandra Van Winkle

Further Reading

Gabe, Grace. "Rekindling Old Flames." *Psychology Today* 26 (September/October, 1993): 32.

Golden, Peter. *Come Back Love*. New York: Atria, 2012.

Joyce, Brenda. *An Impossible Attraction*. Don Mills, Ontario: HQN, 2010.

Laskas, Jeanne Marie. "Rekindling an Old Flame." *Health* 10 (January/February, 1996): 46.

Martin, Kat. *Against the Wind*. New York: MIRA, 2010.

Weintraub, Pamela. "Guess Who's Back." *Psychology Today* 39 (July/August, 2006): 78–84.

Secret Baby Plot

The secret baby plot is a commonly used theme or trope in romance novels that has proven enduringly popular with readers. At its simplest, a secret baby plot is one in which the mother of a baby conceals that baby's true paternity from its biological father, usually by concealing from him that she is pregnant or by claiming that someone else is the father of the child. During the course of the story, which may take place several years later, the father, who is invariably the hero of the novel, becomes aware of the deception. It is the ensuing conflict and resolution that provides the framework for the novel.

Secret baby plots, while a stalwart of the contemporary Romance genre, were not invented by it. This trope can be traced back to Greek and Roman mythology. Mythology is rife with mothers who are placed in danger after being ravaged or seduced by gods. This danger—whether it is jealousy from another god, a bid to protect a birthright, or an attempt to thwart a prophecy—leads the mother to hide or abandon her offspring. In some cases, she may be banished with her offspring, or her child may be thought dead. In these stories, the babies act as the agents of fate. One need only look to the stories of Romulus and Remus, Perseus or Theseus, and Oedipus or Paris for examples. In these tales, secret babies have the power to topple the status quo and to wreak ruin and infamy on their communities. These are stories that tap into our most basic fears and desires surrounding betrayal, truth, and our lineage. These are stories that have been retold in many variations throughout the generations in many different cultures.

Unlike Greek and Roman myths, however, romance novels demand a happy ending. Rather than ending in tragedy, a romance novel must end in triumphant union. Secret baby plots in the Romance genre, therefore, have evolved to ensure that the parents of the child—the heroine and hero—are forced into close proximity throughout the course of the story. This enforced proximity ensures that the heroine and hero must work through the resentments and conflicts created by the secret, leading to an outcome of understanding, forgiveness, and ultimately, love.

It should be noted, however, that while the most common form that the secret baby plot takes is the one in which the mother conceals the truth from the father, there are many variations on this theme. In some cases, the child's mother may be unaware of the child's existence. For example, she may have been led to believe that her baby died during childbirth, as is the case for Lady Dedlock in Dickens's *Bleak House*. Alternatively, the child's heritage may be kept a secret from others whom one or both of the child's parents may see as a threat, such as grandparents or other extended family who would seek to claim the child or wish the child harm. One example of this is Anne Gracie's *The Stolen Princess*. The widowed mother of a seven-year-old heir to the throne flees to protect her son from the murderous intentions of a pretender to the throne. In these stories the romantic conflict does not occur between the child's biological parents. Usually, one of those parents is dead. The romantic conflict is engendered by the secrets of the past impacting the present or the continued need for secrecy to ensure the child's safety. The story questions that a secret baby plot generates are:

- To whom does the baby belong?
- From whom is it being kept a secret?
- Why is it being kept a secret?

It is these questions that are at the heart of the romantic conflict. It is only by unraveling them that peace and resolution can be found.

Secret baby plots continue to be popular since they play upon our deepest fears and give rise to a host of intense emotions—emotions primarily of fear, guilt, and the desire for retribution. It is the secret baby plot's very purpose for the secret to be discovered and, therefore, for the ensuing conflict to play out. At the heart of this trope is a mother's fear for the safety and well-being of her child and her desire to do all she can to keep that child safe. For the father, it is outrage that his child and heir has been kept from him, a determination to become a part of the child's life, and often a desire for vengeance upon the woman who has kept this secret from him. These stories play upon the very human and very real fear of whether or not it's possible to know one's true parentage and whether or not it is possible to know one's true offspring.

It is in subsuming their individual resentments and fears to undertake what is best for the child that the seeds for reconciliation and union are planted. During the course of these stories, the heroine and hero learn to appreciate each other's strengths and to recognize the other's genuine love for the child. The child, of course, is a symbol of innocence, of all that is good and precious in the world; and when the heroine and hero acknowledge that the other is a worthy parent, it paves the way for forgiveness. This in turn lays the groundwork for a loving relationship to develop, leading to a declaration of love. Hence, the uncovering of the secret, followed by a working out of the conflict, with its ensuing sacrifices and period of growth for the heroine and hero, is rewarded with the attainment of true love.

These romances begin with what Pamela Regis refers to as a flawed society, but it is a society that is transmuted and remade by story's end. Society is symbolically redefined and made whole when the hero and heroine overcome their discord and find the path to true love. While the secret baby plot may come in many shapes and guises, these stories tap into archetypal fears and concerns and continue to be popular with readers today.

Therese Dryden

Further Reading

Bulfinch, Thomas. *Bulfinch's Complete Mythology*. London: Spring Books, 1989.

Dickens, Charles. *Bleak House*. London: Penguin Books Ltd., 2003.

Gracie, Anne. *The Stolen Princess*. New York: Berkley Sensation, 2008.

Leland, Christopher T. *The Art of Compelling Fiction: How to Write a Page-Turner*. Cincinnati: Story Press, 1998.

Regis, Pamela. *A Natural History of the Romance Novel*. Philadelphia: University of Pennsylvania Press, 2003.

Self-Publishing and Self-Published Romances

Although it has long been possible for authors to publish without going through the traditional method of having their books acquired, edited, and marketed by an established publishing house, until relatively recently this has usually involved using a vanity or subsidy press, a publisher that charges authors to have their books published. However, technology has altered the landscape; and with the rise of the Internet, the commercialization of the Web, the development of the e-book, and the explosion of social media, the publishing arena has changed dramatically, allowing more and more writers to explore other, sometimes more profitable, options—in particular, self-publishing.

Not only has technology created tools that allow authors to take on many of the actual publication tasks themselves, but social media has enabled authors to connect directly with readers, forming relationships and marketing their books in ways that bypass the traditional author/publisher/reader cycle completely. A number of companies have sprung up to help with this process, providing a variety of online print-on-demand, self-publishing, and distribution services. Lulu Press, founded in 2002, and Smashwords, launched in 2008, and the various Amazon options made available to consumers at various times—KDP-Kindle Direct Publishing (e-books), in 2007; CreateSpace (print books), blended from two earlier companies and launched in 2009; and ACX-Audiobook Creation Exchange (audio books), in 2011—are some of the better-known companies and services.

The appeal for authors to "go indie" is twofold: (1) having total control over the book's content, presentation, and marketing; and (2) receiving a greater percentage of royalties earned. Both are important considerations, especially for writers who are writing for a living. On the other hand, having a publishing company acquire (essentially validate) your work and then take on the task of editing, publicizing, and distributing the novel is a definite attraction. There are advantages and disadvantages to both sides, and ultimately, it's up to the individual author. In a stunning, articulate keynote address at the 2012 Romance Writers of America annual conference, "Weathering the Transition—Keeping the Faith," longtime best-selling romance author Stephanie Laurens rattled a few cages but laid out the facts in a way that clearly explained the current situation and the pathways ahead. As Laurens stated, "In the offline industry—author sells her work to publisher. In the online industry, publisher sells its services to author. That is a 180-degree turn around in relationship." It's not an easy transition to make, but it is happening.

As more and more romance authors have joined the self-publishing ranks, a number of services have arisen to support them. While traditionally published writers can rely on their publishers to take care of editorial, artistic, formatting, and distribution issues, indie authors must either do this themselves or hire it done.

Freelance editors of various kinds, cover artists, book designers, and technology experts versed in a wide range of online formatting and distribution techniques are all part of this growing industry and only a few examples of the services that self-published authors may need.

With the growing importance of the online self-publishing market, traditional publishers have added their own online imprints, as well as releasing their print titles in electronic format. Current data indicate that the overall market seems to be stabilizing (Milliot), but most of the figures reported by traditional services don't include self-publishing information, and according to Data Guy at Author Earnings, self-published romance fiction accounts for 55 percent of that market, compared with 11 percent for Amazon's imprint and 34 percent for traditional publishers. Needless to say, romance is a major player in the self-publishing market, and as the 2016 statistics show, self-published ISBNs (unique numbers assigned to every book published) increased by 8.2 percent over 2015, with the print titles increasing by 11.3 percent but the e-books falling by 3.2 percent (Milliot).

While some authors go the traditional route, many writers choose to be totally self-published. Some, however, take the middle ground and go hybrid (some books traditionally published, others self-published), keeping a foot in both camps. This is especially true of writers who have been traditionally published and have built up name recognition. Often these writers are also able to get their rights back to their earlier books, freeing them to release these titles independently, usually online as e-books. In an interesting twist, the big publishing houses have begun to take note of the self-published authors who have large followings, offering them traditional contracts to sign with them. This makes sense from the publisher's point of view because an author with a large group of readers will often guarantee good sales without a lot of marketing costs. E. L. James of *Fifty Shades of Grey* fame and Meredith Wild (Hacker series) are only two of the many examples. On the other hand, there are authors like two-time Rita Award–winner Barbara Freethy who were originally traditionally published but have discovered success in the self-publishing arena and aren't about to go back.

As of this writing, the traditional publishers and indie authors are holding their own, and things may be coming into balance as everyone realizes there is room for both. Traditional publishing definitely has a large part to play, but as Data Guy says, "Indie authors can sell competitively in (almost) any genre . . . but huge opportunities exist for indies in genres underserved by traditional publishers" ("Print vs Digital. . ."). It's still a bit like the Wild West in the self-publishing arena, and while the future, as always, is uncertain, it is an exciting, dynamic world and definitely bears watching.

Kristin Ramsdell

Further Reading

Amazon.com. https://www.amazon.com/gp/seller-account/mm-summary-page.html?topic =200260520. Accessed October 22, 2017.

Chloe. "Ten Top Trends in Publishing Every Author Needs to Know in 2017." *The Written Word*, January 4, 2017. https://www.writtenwordmedia.com/2017/01/04/top-ten-trends -in-publishing-every-author-needs-to-know-in-2017/. Accessed October 29, 2017.

Cocozza, Paula. "How eBooks Lost Their Shine: 'Kindle's Now Look Clunky and Unhip.'" *The Guardian*, April 27, 2017. https://www.theguardian.com/books/2017/apr/27/how -ebooks-lost-their-shine-kindles-look-clunky-unhip-. Accessed April 27, 2017.

Data Guy. "Print vs Digital, Traditional vs Non-Traditional, Bookstore vs Online: 2016 Trade Publishing by the Numbers." *Author Earnings*. http://authorearnings.com/report /dbw2017/. Accessed October 22, 2017.

Laurens, Stephanie. "Weathering the Transition . . . Keeping the Faith." 2012 Romance Writers of America Conference Keynote Address, July 26, 2012. http://www.stephanie laurens.com/weathering-the-transition-keeping-the-faith/. Accessed October 8, 2107.

Lulu Press, Inc. www.lulu.com. Accessed October 22, 2017.

Milliot, Jim. "Self-Published ISBNs Hit 786,935 in 2016." *Publishers Weekly*, October 20, 2017. https://www.publishersweekly.com/pw/by-topic/industry-news/manufacturing /article/75139-self-published-isbns-hit-786-935-in-2016.html. Accessed October 21, 2017.

Peterson, Valerie. "Vanity Presses and Self-Publishing Today." *The Balance*, October 18, 2016. https://www.thebalance.com/vanity-presses-and-self-publishing-today-2800262. Accessed October 21, 2017.

Sargent, Betty Kelly. "Surprising Self-Publishing Statistics." *Publishers Weekly*, July 28, 2014. https://www.publishersweekly.com/pw/by-topic/authors/pw-select/article/63455 -surprising-self-publishing-statistics.html. Accessed October 22, 2017.

Smashwords. https://www.smashwords.com/. Accessed October 22, 2017.

Sensuality Levels in Popular Romance Fiction

The way in which the romantic relationships, including the sex scenes, are handled in popular romances varies from book to book and author to author and is often one of the key criteria for readers when it comes to choosing and evaluating a book. Just as fans of sassy, upbeat contemporary romances might not find dark, gritty paranormals to their taste, a reader who enjoys romances on the steamy side might find sweeter, less-explicit romances too tame. Although the romances of the early to mid-20th century (a number of which were mass-market series titles from Harlequin/Mills & Boon) were primarily sweet or innocent, with the 1972 publication of Kathleen E. Woodiwiss's ground-breaking historical *The Flame and the*

Flower, a new, elevated level of sensuality was ushered in. By the 1980s, contemporary romances were adding sexier lines, and other subgenres soon followed suit. With the advent and rapid growth of e-publishing (and new online publishers such as Ellora's Cave), erotica added its influence to the mix, and currently the heat levels of romance fiction run the gamut from the super sweet to the incendiary erotic and include everything in between.

Terms and definitions for the various sensuality levels have varied over the years, and there are no hard and fast rules. Nevertheless, the list below offers a few broad guidelines and may be helpful:

- **Sweet or Innocent**—Although the sexual tension in these romances can be high, the bedroom door is firmly closed, and there is no physical intimacy described other than hand-holding or chaste kissing. Traditional Regency romances, inspirational romances, and the original Harlequin or Silhouette romance lines are examples.
- **Warm or Sensual**—The sensual level of these stories rises, and there may be one or more love scenes, but these are not necessarily explicitly described. Rather, the emphasis is on the emotional reactions of the characters and the effect of their lovemaking on their relationship.
- **Hot or Spicy**—The sex in these romances is graphic, more sensually explicit, often creative, and there may be multiple love scenes. However, the primary focus is still on the way the lovemaking makes the characters feel and how it affects their relationship.
- **Erotic Romance**—These stories are extremely sexually explicit, include numerous detailed sex scenes, and use graphic, realistic, noneuphemistic language. Few holds are barred in the erotic romance, and in some cases, the only thing that keeps them from being pure erotica is the emotional connection between the protagonists and the requisite HEA (Happily Ever After) ending.

Kristin Ramsdell

See also: Sweet Romance

Further Reading

Christiansen, Cindy A. "Romance Heat Level Ratings: Sweet, Spicy and Hot!" August 28, 2013. https://www.goodreads.com/author_blog_posts/4776761-romance-heat-level -ratings-sweet-spicy-and-hot. Accessed July 2, 2017.

Morris, Linda. "Rating Gauges the Raunch in Romance Novels." *The Sunday Morning Herald*, September 15, 2013. http://www.smh.com.au/entertainment/books/rating-gauges -the-raunch-in-romance-novels-20130914-2treu.html. Accessed July 2, 2017.

"Sensuality Ratings Guide" *AAR Is All About Romance.* https://allaboutromance.com
/sensuality-rating-system/. Accessed July 2, 2017.

Sequels and Spin-offs

Many romance novels are contained within a single book—a story with a beginning, middle, and end. This is the case when there is enough material and closure
for the story so that an author does not feel the need to continue the romance beyond the one volume. However, sometimes there are stories that a single book
cannot contain. Sequels and spin-offs are a way of continuing a story that doesn't
stop with a single book.

A sequel answers the question "What happens after?" The purpose is to continue a story that already began in the hopes of defining and developing a couple's
romance. There are authors, such as Nicolas Sparks, who are able to tell the beginning, middle, and end of a love story in its entirety without the need to follow up
any further. More often than not, one story is enough to tell the entire tale of two
people who fall in love. However, sometimes there are reasons to expand the story
of a couple's romance, either before or after the events of the initial book.

Chronologically speaking, the first kind of sequel does not take place *after* the
main text but rather *before* in the form of a prequel. Prequels explore how the
events or key persons of the main story came into being. According to literary
critical author Maria Nikolajeva, the primary assumption on the part of the reader
when reading a prequel is that he or she already knows the outcome (Nikolajeva,
201). This being the case, the appeal in reading prequels is finding out what happened to bring about the events that occur in the main text. Additionally, prequels
essentially create a new beginning for a saga. For example, after the success of the
first two books in the Guardians of Vesturon series, A. M. Hargrove went back in
time and wrote out the lives of the parents of one of the protagonists, showing the
inevitable direction of the series while creating a new beginning from which the
series originates. Other examples include Dee Henderson's *Danger in the Shadows*
(The O'Malley series), Isaac Marion's *The New Hunger* (prequel to *Warm Bodies*),
and Jennifer Armentrout's *Daimon* (Covenant series).

Interquels occur *during* the timeline of a series of works, but there are two
distinct types: *interquels* and *intraquels*. Interquel (with an "e") stories occur between two novels while intraquels (with an "a") occur within a single novel (Wolf,
207). These in-between types of stories are typical when authors compile an anthology or write a single short story. With the increasing prevalence of e-books
and other electronic forms of media distribution, authors are able to make use of

shorter interquels and intraquels in lieu of lengthier stories to act as a bridge, elaborate current story lines, or provide a diversion for readers between works by the author. For example, one of the most prolific romance authors, Nora Roberts, has a highly popular series—her In Death series. Under the pen name J. D. Robb, Roberts has written over three dozen novels in this series and has added to it with a number of shorter interquel stories, either as stand-alone novellas or as contributions to various anthologies. These interquel novellas do little to help with the progress of the main story line but act as mini-novels or vignettes that add to the overall series.

Intraquels are much different from interquels because they occur *during* an already existing story. Intraquels are similar to parallel stories (see below), but one famous example of an intraquel is related to *Gone with the Wind*. First written by Margaret Mitchell in 1936, *Gone with the Wind* is a historical romance set during and after the American Civil War and focuses on the life of Scarlett O'Hara. On the other hand, *The Wind Done Gone* (2001) by Alice Randall is a "what happened to" kind of novel that takes place during the timeline of *Gone with the Wind* but from the perspective of a mixed-race slave, Cynara (unnamed in the original *Gone with the Wind*). Even though the two novels occupy the same universe of the American Civil War and share the same timeline presented in *Gone with the Wind*, the difference is that *The Wind Done Gone* is not only a parody of the original, but describes some of the same events from a different point of view. That is to say, Randall's novel is a commentary from a different perspective on Mitchell's 1936 novel (see *Suntrust* for more details on the legal case that resulted). Another example is Jane Austen's *Emma* and Joan Aiken's *Jane Fairfax*. *Emma* and *Jane Fairfax* each focus on its own respective titular character, Jane Fairfax being a contemporary, friend, and rival of Emma Woodhouse. Both *The Wind Done Gone* and *Jane Fairfax* occur within the same timeline within the original book but are separate, but related, stories.

Parallel novels are the next kind of sequel, but there is some contradiction as to what this term means. Think of parallel lines on a piece of paper: two sets of lines both occupying different spaces but existing together on the same piece of paper. One type of parallel novel occurs when these two story lines exist in the same universe. Intraquels like the ones listed above are examples of parallel works in which the non-main texts are parallel story lines. In other words, *The Wind Done Gone* exists alongside *Gone with the Wind*, and *Jane Fairfax* alongside *Emma*. Historical romances are also possible examples of the parallel novel. There already exists an established story line, but one based on history. Therefore, the novels that historical romance authors write have a basis in reality but tell the parallel romance of individuals occupying it. Several prolific authors in the Historical Romance genre include Georgette Heyer, Cheryl Bolen, and Sarah Lark.

Another kind of parallel would be one in which there are two different universes existing at the same time; in other words, a parallel universe. These types of parallel novels are often present in contemporary fantasy romance. Contemporary fantasy is just that: a story that takes place in modern times but has an added fantasy element. These can be classified as parallel because the parallel universe to these types of novels is the contemporary, nonfantasy romance. J. R. Ward's Black Dagger Brotherhood series, Stephanie Meyer's Twilight series, and Sherrilyn Kenyon's Dark-Hunter series are all examples of novels in which the settings can occur contemporarily except for some magical element of werewolves, vampires, or other supernatural elements. Of course, adding a fantasy element to the contemporary universe is not the only type of parallel novel. Other examples of parallel novel authors are Gail Carriger (steampunk), Bryan Lee O'Malley (superpower), and Veronica Roth (science fiction/dystopia).

Spin-offs are novels that take place in the same world as the main text and may often share many of the same characters. While some subgenres of sequels, such as interquels, intraquels, and parallels, can be a type of spin-off, the main difference between a sequel and a spin-off by-and-large is that there is a new protagonist or protagonists. Taking the example of *Gone with the Wind* and *The Wind Done Gone*, the protagonist for the original text was Scarlett O'Hara, while the protagonist for the latter was one of the unnamed slaves. This is an example of both an intraquel *and* a spin-off text. Another example includes Gena Showalter's Lords of the Underworld series, featuring 12 immortal warriors carrying the demons of Pandora's Box within. Showalter also started the Angels of the Dark series, complementing the original series to explore the angelic side of the Lords of the Underworld world. While both occupy the same world of angels and demons with the same mechanics ruling them, the difference shifts from demons (in Lords of the Underworld) to angels (in Angels of the Dark).

Lynn Kurland is different and quite interesting in terms of spin-off romances. In contrast to Showalter, who created an entirely new series based on a preexisting series, Kurland's de Piaget and MacLeod series are spin-offs within the series and of themselves. Kurland is able to achieve this effect by creating different romances for different persons within a single family line, along with several of the family's friends and acquaintances. As the current family hierarchy exists, there are romance novels for the grandparents, parents, all of the children, grandchildren, and many others. The reason this is not a sequel is because sequels imply a chronological sequence of events. Instead, the de Piaget series began with the grandparents' and parents' romances, but the third publication happens further down in time. Subsequent publications are also written out of sequence; in other words, the stories' chronology and the publication schedule differ. Because of the difference, most of Kurland's romances are spin-offs and not sequels.

The benefit of these kinds of romances is the ability to offer readers more: more stories, more possibilities, more romance. Sometimes a single story is not enough, either for the author or the reader, so sequels and spin-offs provide the means of continuing a story. However, the benefit is not only to continue a story, but to provide a resting point between stories. If, for instance, an author committed to telling a romance from beginning to end, but the story was long and would take thousands of pages to complete, splitting the story into smaller stories would not only allow the author more creative freedom but would give readers a welcome break between stories.

Finally, sequels and spin-offs allow writers the opportunity to continue exploring and expanding a favorite world they have created (or one created by another author that they have permission to write about) and give readers the chance to revisit it and learn more about it with each new book. In any case, there is little doubt that given the chance, most people would want to revisit especially good romances—and the worlds they are set in—again and again. Sequels and spin-offs let them do just that.

Hannah Lee

Further Reading

Aiken, Joan. *Jane Fairfax*. New York: St. Martin's Press, 1991.

Austen, Jane. *Emma*. New York: Knopf, 1991.

Mitchell, Margaret. *Gone with the Wind*. New York: Macmillan, 1936.

Nikolajeva, Maria. "Beyond Happily Ever After: The Aesthetic Dilemma of Multivolume Fiction for Children." In *Textual Transformations in Children's Literature: Adaptations, Translations, Reconsiderations*, edited by Benjamin Lefebvre, 197–213. New York and London: Routledge, 2013.

Randall, Alice. *The Wind Done Gone*. Boston: Houghton Mifflin, 2001.

Suntrust Bank v. Houghton Mifflin Co., 275 F.3d 58 (2001). FindLaw. http://caselaw.find law.com/us-11th-circuit/1332488.html. Accessed June 7, 2017.

Wolf, Mark J. P. *Building Imaginary Worlds: The Theory and History of Subcreation*. New York: Routledge, 2012.

Setting, Importance of

Setting is one of the essential building blocks of narrative fiction and can be defined as the "where" of a story. It is the location of the story action. A setting can be a city or a building within that city, a country town or country estate, a castle, a workplace, a ranch, a single room within a house, or the seaside. A setting may also encompass a time period, such as 1890s France, Ancient Rome, 1980s New York, or London during World War I. The setting also encompasses the time of day of the story action. A story that takes place at midday will be very different from one that takes place at midnight. In a science fiction or paranormal romance, the setting may even be a spaceship, an imaginary planet, or a parallel universe. The setting is the locale—including its weather, the time period, and time of day where the romantic couple find themselves together during the course of their story. The setting is important as it has a twofold significance upon a romance novel. First, it affects an individual novel's mood and tone, reflects the characters' emotions and values, and foreshadows and heightens the drama of the story. However, it may also define the romantic subgenre to which that individual novel belongs.

Importance in Individual Romance Novels

Authors use the details of a setting to bring scenes to life. These details not only provide the reader with clues and insights into the world of the protagonists but influence the mood and tone of the story as well. Consider the differences between a story set at a glamorous 1920s party with a heroine dressed as a flapper in a silver lamé fringed dress sporting a strand of waist-length pearls who is the archetypal convivial hostess, and a story set in a London slum with a heroine dressed in rags attempting to make dinner from a few meager scraps. Both stories may contain a sweeping romance, but the individual details signal to the reader the atmosphere of the story, the tone in which the story will be told, and the types of protagonists in whose company they will be spending the rest of the book.

When the details of a setting are filtered through a particular character's viewpoint, it not only provides the reader with an awareness of that character's emotions, it can also indicate the character's set of values. If, for example, the reader sees the heroine from the slum put a fresh daisy in a glass of water and place it on the dinner table, she can surmise that our heroine has hope, can recognize beauty even amidst the poverty that surrounds her, and values it. If our 1920s party hostess's focus is engaged mostly upon her faded curtains and chipped china, we can identify her anxiety and fear of reduced circumstances while recognizing how important it is to her to maintain appearances.

The romantic relationship that develops between the heroine and hero of a romance novel is impacted and influenced by the very environment in which it is played out. The setting is so important because it influences the direction that the romance can take. Consider three different scenarios. In the first, the romantic couple is stranded on a windswept moor; in the second, they are singles holidaying in the Bahamas; and in the third, they are colleagues working side-by-side in a high-powered office environment. Each of these settings impacts the speed and manner in which the relationship can develop, not to mention how it is developed. For example, the couple stranded on the moor may loathe each other and under normal circumstances would simply walk away and never see each other again, but that becomes impossible when they are reliant on each other for their survival. Of course, being forced into such proximity will then encourage the couple to recognize each other's strengths, paving the way for a greater understanding that will lead to love.

Additionally, elements of the setting may mirror, contrast, or otherwise indicate the level of conflict or tranquility that exists between the heroine and hero at different times, foreshadowing events to come. A storm followed by a rainbow may symbolize a breakthrough for our couple stranded on the moor, indicating the prospect of a happy ending. Fluctuations in the stock exchange may mirror a setback in our office romance, while an unending party atmosphere may provide an ironic, even humorous contrast to the antagonistic romance of our holidaying singles.

Importance in Defining Subgenres of Romance

Readers select romance novels based on the tropes or fantasies that appeal to them. Certain settings become so heavily invested with reader expectations that over time they break away to create a subgenre of their own. Historical Romance, Medical Romance, and small-town Contemporary Romance are all such examples. One need only look to the Gothic romances that Daphne du Maurier made so popular in the 1930s with their brooding country houses and sense of isolation and menace to perceive how a subgenre may form. Du Maurier followed in the tradition of the Brontës, but the popularity of her novels created a fresh demand from the public, which led to the whole new subgenre of Gothic Romance.

A host of historical romance novels are defined by their settings and time periods. Georgette Heyer created a pattern and a standard for the traditional Regency romance that subsequent writers have followed. Writers do not comply with these standards blindly. They adhere to them because of reader demand. Readers clamored for romances set in the domestic world of gently bred heroines, among the well-to-do of the *ton*, and usually located in London or Bath. The very definition of a Regency romance ensures that drawing rooms, ballrooms, and walks in the park abound. That is, it defines the arena in which the romance can develop. If one turns one's attention, however, to a different historical subgenre such as the Medieval Scottish Romance, a vastly different setting—reflecting a different kind of action and a different kind of heroine and hero—is immediately signaled. Castle keeps, the Highlands, and rugged terrain bring to mind strong Highland warriors, bloody battles, and plucky heroines. The focus of both the Regency romance and the medieval Scottish romance will center on the developing romantic relationship, but the situations in which the stories play out will be very different. The same reader may in fact enjoy both types of historical story but will bring a different set of reader expectations to each of them.

As it is for historical romance novels, the same holds true for contemporary romance novels. A city romp will establish different reader expectations than a small-town contemporary set in Middle America. Readers will expect the two to have differences in tone and for the protagonists to hold different values, which results in different kinds of action. While a comedic city-girl heroine might hold liberal views about sex, a small-town American heroine would be expected to have more conservative views that would be in tune with her background. In large part, it is the values the characters hold that determine the actions they will take.

Many of the category lines of Harlequin Mills & Boon are also defined by their settings. Western romances with their ranches and/or small country towns are a staple of Harlequin's American line. Medical settings, be they hospitals, doctor surgeries, or medical clinics, define the Medical line. The Presents line thrives on glamorous and sophisticated locations. This is not a new innovation. From the very first, Mills & Boon romance novels could be divided according to their setting. jay Dixon in *The Romance Fiction of Mills & Boon 1909–1990s* details four types of these earliest Mills & Boon romances—exotic, society, city, and country. The first two were set among the English upper classes, with society novels set in southern England and exotic novels usually set somewhere within the British Empire. The city and country novels featured middle-class heroes and heroines and were usually set in London and southern England, respectively. These four categories were not only differentiated by their locations but in the values the protagonists could be expected to hold. Each of them reflects different aspects of society at that time. Hence, a reader of society novels may not enjoy country novels, and vice versa. By the 1920s the differences between the categories had blurred and merged, though elements of them are still popular today, like wealthy heroes and exotic locations.

Setting is one of the essential building blocks of fiction. A setting is important in grounding a romance novel in its particular reality and in ensuring that reality is believable, while signposting to the reader the kind of story they can expect. The setting plays an important role in determining the tone and mood of a novel while adding depth to the developing romance within the novel's pages.

Therese Dryden

Further Reading

Bickham, Jack. *Setting: How to Create and Sustain a Sharp Sense of Time and Place in Your Fiction*. Cincinnati: Writers Digest Books, 1994.

Burroway, Janet, Elizabeth Stuckey-French, and Ned Stuckey-French. *Writing Fiction: A Guide to Narrative Craft*. Boston: Longman, 2011.

Dixon, jay. *The Romance Fiction of Mills & Boon 1909–1990s*. London: Routledge, 2003.

Gardner, John. *The Art of Fiction: Notes on Craft for Young Writers*. New York: Vintage Books, 1983.

Setting as Character

The setting for any romance story is vitally important and is usually expressed in terms of location or time period—for example, a small town, the Regency Period, or a medieval castle. These generalized elements can be a kind of literary short-hand that clues readers in and sets expectations for how characters will behave and the plot will develop. Setting may be confined to this kind of shorthand, sticking to lush descriptions of landscape or clothing. But setting can go much further to enrich a romance novel by encompassing historical background, cultural attitudes, regional traditions, and even speech patterns. These details merge with the book's characters, plot, theme, and tone to tell an emotionally satisfying story.

In *Story*, Robert McKee says that setting has four elements: time period, duration, location, and level of conflict. These elements work together to establish mood and evoke emotion, enhance story unity, intensify suspense, motivate or explain character, and clarify the novel's theme (Bickham).

These elements are important for any novel, but the setting's ability to establish mood and evoke emotion is especially crucial in a romance novel, in which the themes of love, family, relationships, and community are the central focus. Indeed, romance has always been different from other genres because it's not based on geography or locale (westerns), time and place (fantasy), or technology (science fiction), but on an emotion. The failure to create an atmosphere, mood, or narrative tone in any novel leaves readers bored or confused, according to Janet Burroway in *Writing Fiction*. However, the failure to create atmosphere, establish mood, or evoke emotion is fatal in romance novels because romance readers want, need, and expect the emotional response the romance novel provides.

Much as a character in the plot shapes the narrative, a setting can both evoke emotion and strengthen conflict to a degree that it, too, significantly shapes the narrative. When this happens, the setting takes an active role in the development of the novel—it assumes the role of character. Essentially, the setting *becomes* a character—sometimes even an *uber*-character, the reason a story achieves immortality. Michael Walsh, writing about *The Phantom of the Opera*, asks why this story by Gaston Leroux, published in 1909, still resonates. "Surely not for its creaky plot, its standard-issue heroine, its wooden swain, its Svengali-like villain," he writes. "No, the reason we still read and watch *Phantom* is its setting: the Opéra itself. Above all, *Phantom* is a story of place. . . . [T]he building is as much a player—and is more lovingly observed—than any of the humans who live and love in its dark embrace."

This evocation of feeling that Walsh describes moves the romance novel's setting beyond simple set decoration; it *defines* the story and, to a certain extent, also circumscribes it. The setting shapes characters by forming their histories and cultural attitudes and limiting their options. For example, in *Montana Sky* (Nora Roberts), three sisters who barely know one another are compelled by their deceased father's will to live together for one year on the family ranch. Readers can tell immediately by the novel's title—*Montana Sky*—how important the setting will be to the story. Indeed, the setting of the Montana ranch works as a unifying theme for the individual plotlines of the sisters, each of whom also has her own love story with men who have their own relationships to the ranch. As the novel unfolds, the sisters work together to battle bad weather and outside predators to save the ranch and their inheritance. Their short-term options are confined to the ranch and its survival; and while each sister brings a different outlook to that isolated, rural life, by novel's end, they have come to know and love one another and the ranch as well.

In *Jane Eyre* (Charlotte Brontë), an impoverished, orphaned governess falls in love with the master of Thornfield Hall. While the manor offers Jane Eyre her first taste of comfort, acceptance, independence, and happiness, its suggestive name also hints of trouble, anguish, and pain. Indeed, the atmosphere of Thornfield Hall is dark and disturbing, even frightening. Inexplicable events amplify the manor's mystery and the notion that it conceals secrets, creating a Gothic atmosphere of suspense. Rochester's eccentric behavior, which is motivated at least in part by these secrets and, in time, explained by them, increases this suspense. In addition, horror is awakened when the mad wife is revealed in the attic and culminates when she sets Thornfield on fire, burning it to the ground, and then commits suicide by plunging from the roof. Only when Jane Eyre learns of these events does she return to the scene—but to Ferndean, not Thornfield—to marry Rochester and start a new life. By providing the basis for events as compelling as these—with the house itself serving as human prison and protector of secrets—the Thornhill setting essentially advances the plot. It first provides Jane Eyre with a refuge, then it torments her with its past, and finally it combusts, destroying the chains that bound Rochester to its walls and his past life, freeing Jane to return.

While setting often includes geography, time period, and other carefully depicted details, even in fantasy or paranormal plots, a setting can also encompass abstractions. In *Indigo* by Beverly Jenkins, Hester is a freed slave and a conductor on the Underground Railroad who helps runaways cross the border into Canada. She conceals Galen, another conductor, after a proslavery gang surprises him on the road with a fugitive slave family and beats him to unconsciousness. While these characters move physically between towns, visiting friends and relatives and conducting business, and ultimately fall in love, the force and tension of the romance derive from the safety issues involved in keeping a station on the Railroad. However, the Underground Railroad has no actual physical presence. When one hiding spot is revealed, the conductors move elsewhere. No room, attic, or basement is constant. No route is predetermined. The Railroad helps people get to freedom, but it has no fixed physical location or even consistent conductors. However, it represents constant danger. No house, store, or even wagon is safe as long as bounty hunters are legally permitted to search for and recapture runaway slaves, and it is this historical fact that pits characters against one another and powers the suspense and conflict of the novel.

These examples demonstrate how settings can be crucial to the development of the romance novel. These books—from their tone and mood to characterization and even plot—are defined or refined by their settings. The characters face their specific problems because of the settings they are in. Their actions are motivated and influenced by the setting in which they find themselves. For example, in *Indigo*, Hester, a woman living alone, rejects the idea that her reputation will be sullied because she protects the injured conductor Galen. "I don't know where you're from originally Galen, but on the Road here, we women don't always have the luxury of worrying about our reputations when there's work to be done" (Jenkins). In addition, characters' feelings are determined, at least in part, by their settings. "To pass [Thornfield's] threshold was to return to stagnation" (Brontë), Jane Eyre thinks. Specific settings define stories and limit their characters' possible actions. While rural adventures, Gothic romances, and morality tales can be told with various geographies, time periods, or characters, the setting of a specific tale can determine how that romance will play out.

Setting can be so important that often characters come into conflict with one another not only *in* the setting but *because* of the setting—to gain an inheritance, fight for territory, retreat to personal space, or other reasons. In *Montana Sky*, the sisters come *to* the ranch, where their conflicts *about* the ranch play out. In *Jane Eyre*, the new governess finds a home and love at Thornfield Hall, but she is driven from it by a dark presence in the attic. Only when the house burns down can she find the love and security she deserves in Rochester's arms. In *Indigo*, Galen both admires Hester's work on the Underground Railroad and becomes angry when she persists in conducting travelers on it, fearing for her safety. The Underground Railroad is the place where Hester dwells every day, but is also the place from which danger threatens. In *The Phantom of the Opera*, Christine wants to learn more about the "Angel of Music," whom she finds at the Opéra, although that fascination ultimately leads to her kidnapping.

Just as characters influence one another in the romance novel, setting also influences characters. In *Montana Sky*, Willa, who grew up on the ranch, is fiercely independent, but when change comes to the ranch, she learns how to share responsibility. Lily, who comes to the ranch to fulfill the terms of her father's will, is timid and fearful, but by undertaking some of the responsibilities the ranch requires, she loses her fear and gains self-reliance. In *Indigo*, Hester's experiences on the Underground Railroad force her to be circumspect with her neighbors and camouflage her true self. In *Jane Eyre*, Jane finds her first happiness—and true despair—while living at Thornfield Hall.

Some settings enhance characters' inherent qualities or shape them to such extent that they seem all but foreordained. In *The Phantom of the Opera*, Eric, the villain, lives in the cellars of the Opéra, beneath the sparkle and lights of the stage where Christine, the heroine, shines. Just as the singers and actors wear makeup and costumes to conceal their true identities, Eric wears a mask to cover his distorted face. But the performers' masks are only artifice. Eric truly lives in the dark, terrorizing performers and managers and extorting money from them. As he grows closer to Christine, he kidnaps her, tries to force her into marriage, and threatens to blow up the theater to keep her from her lover. She wins her freedom by giving him a kiss, and Eric dies of a broken heart.

Likewise, in *Montana Sky*, Willa, who's grown up on the ranch, is hardworking, independent, and authoritative at a young age. She manages the land and animals and hires the crews who work there, and she's learned to account for human frailties and the vagaries of weather. But when her authority is tested by the arrival of her sisters, she adjusts, however reluctantly, to new circumstances. This flexibility, born of necessity, is a quality she learned from living on a ranch that required its caretakers to be practical and self-reliant.

Setting is only one aspect that makes a romance novel come to life, but it can be a powerful force, defining and structuring critical moments and evoking powerful feelings. When setting reaches this level of importance in the romance novel—when it acts upon characters to heighten tensions or enhance emotions, or when characters respond to the setting as they would to other characters—the inanimate setting achieves the status of human character in the novel. Because as Walsh wrote about *The Phantom of the Opera*, although "we may forget the characters, it is the places that haunt our dreams."

Kay Keppler

Further Reading

Bickham, Jack M. *Setting*. Cincinnati: Writers Digest Books, 1994.
Brontë, Charlotte (as Currer Bell). *Jane Eyre*. London: Smith, Elder & Co., 1847.
Burroway, Janet. *Writing Fiction*, 6th ed. New York: Longman, 2003.
Jenkins, Beverly. *Indigo*. New York: Avon, 1996.
McKee, Robert. *Story*. New York: HarperEntertainment, 1997.
Roberts, Nora. *Montana Sky*. New York: Putnam, 1996.
Walsh, Michael. "A Record Find." *Smithsonian*, March 2008. www.smithsonianmag.com/arts-culture/preseence-200803.html?c=y&page=1). Accessed June 7, 2017.

The Sheik (1919)

E. M. Hull's *The Sheik* is arguably the most famous sheikh romance of them all. Pamela Regis even calls *The Sheik* the "ur-romance novel of the twentieth century" (115). While not the first romance set in the East, as Rachel Anderson points out, "it was *The Sheik* which firmly established the convention of a desert passion and sparked off a whole train of sandy romances" (189), introducing many of the features of the modern sheikh romances—the forceful hero, abduction, the desert.

First published in 1919, *The Sheik* tells the story of Diana Mayo, a headstrong young heiress, who decides, against advice, to travel into the Sahara Desert, where she is abducted by Sheikh Ahmed Ben Hassan, who is later revealed to be an Englishman. Trapped in his desert camp, Diana is raped and forced into submission by Ahmed and, eventually, finds herself falling in love with him. When Diana is kidnapped by a rival sheikh while out riding, Ahmed realizes he loves Diana and rescues her, sending her away shortly afterward to return to England. Diana refuses to leave, insisting that she would rather die than be without Ahmed. Eventually, Ahmed relents, and the couple declares their love, resolving to live in the desert.

The Sheik's author, E. M. Hull, was the pseudonym of Edith Maude Winstanley, famously the wife of a "dull pig-breeder called Percy" (Anderson, 185) and who had, at the time of writing *The Sheik*, never left England. Hull's novel was an instant best seller, selling more copies than all other best sellers in the interwar period (Melman, 90). The novel's popularity was boosted with the novel's adaptation into film in 1921, famously starring Rudolph Valentino, which cemented Valentino's status as an exotic heartthrob. In fact, Billie Melman points out how the word "sheik" became a byword in the early 1920s for a virile, sensual male lover, a significance no doubt enhanced by the "Valentino effect." The film was phenomenally successful, seen by 125 million people (Melman, 89–90).

While it might have been popular with the reading public, *The Sheik* was not well received by Hull's literary peers, who were disparaging of the novel: a January 1922 article in the *New York Tribune* writes that *The Sheik* "has been called indecent, immoral and degenerate" (Putnam). Modern readers have been critical of the novel's gender politics, in particular Diana's rape into submission by the hero, Ahmed. Commentaries have also pointed to the treatment of miscegenation and the novel's insistence on European heritage for Ahmed to dispel fears of interracial sexual contact (see Teo; Gargano). Yet the influence of *The Sheik* continues to resonate as subsequent romance authors continue to echo Hull's story in their own works, for example, Violet Winspear's *Blue Jasmine* (1969) and Morey's *The Sheikh's Convenient Virgin* (2008).

Amy Burge

See also: Sheik Romance

Further Reading

Gargano, Elizabeth. "'English Sheikhs' and Arab Stereotypes: E. M. Hull, T. E. Lawrence, and the Imperial Masquerade." *Texas Studies in Literature and Language* 48, 2: 171–86.

Melman, Billie. *Women and the Popular Imagination in the Twenties: Flappers and Nymphs*. Basingstoke, UK: Macmillan, 1988.

Morey, Trish. *The Sheikh's Convenient Virgin*. Richmond: Harlequin Mills & Boon, 2008.

Putnam, Sidney Haven. "Ben Hecht and E. M. Hull, *Erik Dorn* and *The Sheik*: Peculiar Merits of Two Best Sellers Weighed in the Balance of Critical Readers." *New York Tribune*, January 15, 1922.

Regis, Pamela. *A Natural History of the Romance Novel*. Philadelphia: University of Pennsylvania Press, 2003.

Teo, Hsu-Ming. "Orientalism and Mass Market Romance Novels in the Twentieth Century." In *Edward Said: The Legacy of a Public Intellectual*, edited by Ned Curthoys and Debjani Ganguly, 241–62. Carlton, Victoria, Australia: Melbourne University Press, 2007.

Winspear, Violet. *Blue Jasmine*. London: Mills & Boon, 1969.

Sheikh Romance

"Magical, timeless and [. . .] *indefinable*": this is how Rachel Anderson, writing in 1974, describes the sheikh romance (180). And indeed, many of the features that make up a sheikh romance—the desert, the harem, abduction—have been consistent since the start of the consistently popular genre. The so-called sheikh romance is a love story set in the deserts of North Africa or the Middle East, featuring an erotic relationship between a Western heroine and an Eastern sheikh or sultan hero: Jessica Taylor argues that the sheikh romance is "one of the few occasions where the color line is broken in [. . .] category romance" (1036). Generally accepted as the prototype for the modern sheikh novel is E. M. Hull's *The Sheik* (1919), which established many of the motifs of later novels.

Juliet Flesch points out that "the Arab is the earliest and most enduring exotic figure of romance" (213). The sheikh hero has always been an alpha male, routinely likened to a bird of prey whose sexual appetite accords with the harem, who wears desert robes and asserts his (often royal) dominance: all factors that serve to simultaneously eroticize and exoticize him. However, in early romances, including Hull's novel, the sheikh was not Arabian at all but what can be termed a "pseudo-sheikh" (Burge): a Western man posing as an Arabian sheikh. It was not until the 1970s that sheikhs with some Eastern ethnic heritage became predominant: Violet Winspear's *Palace of the Pomegranate* (1974) was among the first to feature a hero with Arabian parentage.

While the pseudo-sheikh was all but obsolete by the 1990s, the sheikh hero whose ethnicity is drawn from a mix of East and West remains common. Equally, while a number of sheikhs in romances published from the 1990s onward are fully ethnically Eastern, they are made palatably Western in other ways: they are educated in the West; wear Western-style clothing; travel regularly to the West; speak fluent English; and are not practicing Muslims.

Sheikh romances liberally draw on 18th- and 19th-century Orientalist imagery to characterize their (fictional) Eastern world. Thus, heroines are languorously bathed in milk, massaged with oils, and dressed in silk embroidered with gold thread while housed in desert tents furnished with cushions, rugs, and lamps. The couple eats exotic fruit, rides in the desert, and enjoys traditional veiled dances by the fire. However, more recent sheikh romances also acknowledge contemporary views of the Middle East, with nods to oil companies, nationalist rebels, environmental conservation, and the luxurious modernity of the United Arab Emirates (UAE).

The Eastern world of the sheikh romance is both desirous and abhorrent for the Western heroine, echoing the cultural conflict between hero and heroine that provides much of the substance of the plot. She rejects certain aspects of the East—in particular, those that relate to women, such as veiling, women's lack of public freedom and education, and the fetishizing of female virginity—while simultaneously celebrating other aspects of Eastern culture, such as family bonds, which stand in contrast to her own orphan status or estrangement from her own family, the mythologizing of the desert landscape, and the luxury of Eastern textiles, food, and entertainment. Her engagement with the sheikh's Eastern world thus mirrors the readers' own engagement, as Westerners, with the reality and fantasy of the Middle East.

In fact, as products of contemporary Western popular culture, the sheikh romances can be revealing of popular attitudes toward the Middle East. Several scholars have considered sheikh romances in light of global politics (see Burge; Haddad; Jarmakani, "Desiring" and "'The Sheikh Who Loved Me'"; Teo, *Desert Passions* and "Orientalism"), exploring ways in which the genre's motifs have altered in relation to current affairs. For example, Amira Jarmakani notes that sheikh romances "conflate [. . .] ethnic/religious/geographic identities while blurring any direct reference to the Middle East or Islam," ensuring that religion, so much a part of Western political discourse on the Middle East, does not overtly characterize these romances ("Desiring," 922), which tend to elide overt reference to Islam. The hybridity of the sheikh equally speaks to contemporary concerns about otherness. Such changes indicate how the Sheikh genre continues to develop and point to the future evolution of the sheikh romance.

Amy Burge

See also: *The Sheik* (1919)

Further Reading

Anderson, Rachel. *The Purple Heart Throbs: The Sub-Literature of Love*. London: Hodder and Stoughton, 1974.

Burge, Amy. "Desiring the East: A Comparative Study of Middle English and Modern Popular Romance." PhD thesis, University of York, 2012.

Flesch, Juliet. *From Australia with Love: A History of Modern Australian Popular Romance Novels*. Fremantle, Australia: Curtin University Books, 2004.

Graham, Lynne. *The Arabian Mistress*. London: Harlequin Mills & Boon, 2001.

Haddad, Emily A. "Bound to Love: Captivity in Harlequin Sheikh Novels." In *Empowerment versus Oppression: Twenty-first Century Views of Popular Romance Novels*, edited by Sally Goade, 42–64. Newcastle: Cambridge Scholars Publishing, 2007.

Hull, E. M. *The Sheik*. London: E. Nash and Grayson, 1919.

Jarmakani, Amira. "Desiring the Big Bad Blade: Racing the Sheikh in Desert Romances." *American Quarterly* 63, 4 (2011): 895–928.

Jarmakani, Amira. "The Sheikh Who Loved Me': Romancing the War on Terror." *Signs* 35, 4 (2010): 993–1017.

Taylor, Jessica. "And You Can Be My Sheikh: Gender, Race, and Orientalism in Contemporary Romance Novels." *Journal of Popular Culture* 40, 6 (2007): 1032–51.

Teo, Hsu-Ming. *Desert Passions: Orientalism and Romance Novels*. Austin: University of Texas Press, 2013.

Teo, Hsu-Ming. "Orientalism and Mass Market Romance Novels in the Twentieth Century." In *Edward Said: The Legacy of a Public Intellectual*, edited by Ned Curthoys and Debjani Ganguly, 241–62. Carlton, Victoria: Melbourne University Press, 2007.

Winspear, Violet. *Palace of the Pomegranate*. London: Mills & Boon, 1974.

Shoujo Manga in Romance

Manga is the Japanese term for comics, graphic novels, and cartoon illustrations. In Japan, manga is a commonly found medium of literature that can have readers of all ages and genders. In fact, 35 to 40 percent of Japan's total print output is comprised of manga (Gravett). *Shoujo (*or *shojo*) manga specifically refers to Japanese romance graphic novels aimed at the 10 to 18-year-old female demographic. The word *shoujo* itself means "little girl" in Japanese, and the main characters in these romance stories tend to be young teenage girls. A primary theme of shoujo manga features the teenage protagonist's falling in love or experiencing love for the first time, and her experiences are often expressed through intense narratives of self-realization.

Shoujo Manga Popularization in the United States

While graphic novels have been an integral part of the Japanese culture and literature from early on, the development of certain manga styles did not appear until the late 19th century. In fact, the modern manga style has been attributed to Japan's involvement in World War I, a period that saw a rise in Japan's efforts to use comics as propaganda and satire to advance its war agenda.

Manga was later introduced to the United States through association with anime (that is, Japanese animated productions or cartoons) in the post–World War II era. Early accounts of American awareness of Japanese anime occurred as early as the 1970s and 1980s at fantasy and comics conventions. As anime fans learned more about Japanese entertainment, they became exposed to manga series, which in many cases are the original format for related anime series. In the same way that many movies in the United States are based upon novels, in Japan a manga series that enjoys widespread popularity could eventually be selected by an animation studio to be made into an anime for television or home-video release.

During the 1990s Japanese manga made notable headway into the European and North American markets, though initially through unofficial channels. Avid manga fans in the United States would purchase manga series from Japan, scan the images, translate the manga's Japanese text into English (the end products are known as *scanlations*), and upload the digital images to the Internet to share with other fans. As the readership for manga grew due to the propagation of *scanlations*, publishing companies entered the market and began licensing and publishing popular manga titles in English, in print form comparable to the Japanese originals and with the work of professional translators. One of the pioneers in the American market was TOKYOPOP, founded in 1997 as Mixx, which became one of the dominant manga publishers in the United States until suspending its activities in 2011. VIZ Media (founded in 1986, but not popular until it merged with Japanese heavyweight publisher Shueisha in 2002) and Kodansha Comics (a preexisting Japanese firm that established an office in New York in 2008) are two other large manga production companies still actively publishing English-translated manga in the United States.

Themes in Shoujo Manga

Within shoujo manga there are several well-known subgenres and themes of teenage romance stories, including the transformative power of love, magical girls, competition-turned-love, and class disparity. The common thread in these themes is the coming-of-age of the main character and her development into young, but matured, womanhood. Through the progression of shoujo stories, the many phases of a romantic relationship are explored: a surprising or embarrassing first meeting, the thrilling expectations of a first date, the misunderstandings and trust issues that crop up when a third person or old friend enters the picture, and even the trepidation and novelty of losing one's virginity. Many slice-of-life romance stories feature these significant stages of a relationship, and this subgenre also emphasizes the everyday experience of Japanese teenage life through the seasonal holidays and the academic calendar. Common to these stories are school spirit competitions among the different grade levels, Bon festivals (to honor ancestral spirits) or Gion festivals in July (originally a festival to appease the gods), Christmas, cherry blossom festivals, a beach outing, school camping trips, chocolate gift-giving on Valentine's Day by females, and reciprocal gift-giving on White Day (March 14) by males.

The theme of love being a critical catalyst for character development is seen in many shoujo series. In shoujo manga, a character's first love experience typically occurs in a school setting. The protagonist is generally a female student in either middle or high school, and she falls in love with one of the school's most popular male students. *Kyou, Koi o Hajimemasu* (or *Today, We Begin Our Love*) is one such story. Typically, through the trials of a new and deep love, a shoujo manga heroine will experience some heartaches and undergo a change in perspective. This change can be seen in the way the heroine grows to understand the importance of selflessness and the pursuit of her own goals. This theme of independence through a secure love can be seen in manga endings in which the heroine is able to make difficult decisions, such as living apart from her love so they can each chase after their dreams or careers, albeit with the confidence that they can maintain their relationship despite the distance (seen in *Hana Yori Dango, Hanazakari no Kimitachi e*, and others). Through reliance on the strength and trust of their bond, we see the main characters, especially the heroine, develop a sense of individuality and independence.

Another, more literal, type of character transformation in shoujo manga pertains to the subgenre of Magical Girls. Magical Girls can also be considered a subgenre of Japanese fantasy stories that feature young girls using magic. One of the most famous magical-girl romances is the shoujo series Pretty Soldier Sailor Moon, which features five high school girls who fight evil intergalactic enemies by transforming into sailor-suit-wearing guardians with magical powers. The anime adaptation of the series was broadcast in Japan in 1992 and spread to American television in 1995. It was an instant hit, and the later sales of the English-translated manga made *New York Times* and *Time* news. The Sailor Moon series was different from more adventure-oriented magical-girl stories in that in addition to fighting evil forces using a masked identity, the young heroines still go through the trials and heartaches of typical teenage life. The main character Usagi, for example, has to juggle getting her homework done and finding time to pursue her love interest in between the periods of fighting to save Earth from evil creatures.

Fushigi Yuugi (or *Mysterious Play*) and *Sora wa Akai Kawa no Hotori* (or *Red River*) are two other shoujo series with magical-girl elements. There is a difference, however, as both of these series feature a middle school heroine who gets transported from modern-day reality to a (fantasy) semihistorical past. In *Fushigi Yuugi*, the main character finds out she is the Priestess of Suzaku, tasked with the duty of gathering seven celestial warriors to obtain three wishes. She falls in love with one of the warriors and faces the dilemma of returning to her own time period or remaining in ancient China to fulfill her duty. Similarly, in *Red River*, the heroine is transported back in time and discovers herself to be the incarnation of the goddess Ishtar. She falls in love with a Hittite prince and must choose between returning to her own time and staying in the past to help save and rule the Hittite Empire. In each of these stories, the heroine may have some magical powers, but it is demonstrated that the real power of the character lies in her decision to take on the responsibility of the tasks set before her.

Competition romance involves the two main characters in a rivalry with each other and their developing feelings for each other through competing against each other. They often intensely dislike each other at the beginning because they view each other as rivals in the arenas of academics or athletics. Several popular manga share this theme of rivalry-turned-romance, depicting how through their obsessive rivalry the main characters come to understand, respect, and eventually love each other. For example, in the manga *Kare Kano* (or *His and Her Circumstances*) published from 1996 to 2005, the main character projects the image of being a perfect girl at school with her excellent grades and impeccable demeanor. However, in the privacy of her home, she is revealed to be a selfish slob, bent on studying to achieve high grades to attain the praise of others. Upon entering high school, she meets a boy who displaces her from the top position in academics, finds out the truth about her secretly being a slovenly person, and actually likes her in spite of (or because of) her imperfections.

The manga *Last Game* is very similar to this, but with a bit of role reversal between the two main characters. In *Last Game*, the male hero is a character who is perceived as perfect and enjoys the admiration of his female classmates until the heroine appears and shows him how a girl could be better than him in areas such as academics and sports. Another manga that epitomizes love blossoming through competition is *Special A*. In this manga, the heroine is nearly the best at her school and in everything she does but is always "Miss Second Place." The one person she cannot seem to defeat in any subject or activity is her rival. Little does she realize that it is her struggle to best him that has gained his admiration and that becomes the catalyst for their love story.

The class-disparity theme involves romantic conflict stemming from differences in social and economic status between the two main characters. Many times the female character comes from a financially poor background, and she meets and falls in love with a male character who appears to have it all: popularity among his peers, wealth, and social status due to a prominent family background. *Hana Yori Dango* (or *Boys over Flowers*) is one the most famous manga in recent times that embodies all of the elements of this theme. This romance story features a poor heroine whose family worked hard to pay for her tuition to a prestigious private academy where generally only the rich can afford to send their children. At this upscale preparatory school the heroine meets the school's four most wealthy and handsome boys, and by standing up to the leader of the group in a protest against his mistreatment of other classmates, she wins his admiration and love. This story has such mass appeal that not only has it been made into an anime, but it also generated live-action television shows in Taiwan (called *Meteor Garden*, 2001), Japan (*Hana Yori Dango*, 2005), Korea (*Boys over Flowers*, 2009), China (*Meteor Shower*, 2009), and even the United States (*Boys over Friends*, 2013). Class disparity is also explored in several other popular shoujo series, such as *Kaichou Wa Maid-sama!* (or *The Student Council President Is a Maid!*) and *Ookami Heika no Hanayome* (or *Wolf King's Bride*).

Conclusion

Shoujo Manga as a genre enjoys wide readership in Japan and increasing attention in the United States. Many shoujo titles have been translated into English, especially by publishing companies such as VIZ Media, Kodansha, and TOKYOPOP. In fact, romance graphic novels have become so popular and widespread that they have attracted the attention of the American graphic novel and comics company Dark Horse. In 2005, Dark Horse collaborated with Harlequin Books to publish a number of its traditional romance novels in graphic novel form. Asian artists who draw in the style of Japanese manga were selected to provide the art for these romance stories.

Other popular American romance stories have also been turned into manga, such as *Twilight* (young adult paranormal romance), *Infernal Devices* (young adult fantasy romance with historical backdrop), *Beautiful Creatures* (young adult fantasy romance), *Gossip Girls* (high school romance), and *The Clique* (middle school romance). These romance series, published by Yen Press in the United States, are essentially the American equivalent of Japanese shoujo manga as their target audience is female teenagers.

Lena Pham

Further Reading

Cornog, Martha, and Timothy Perper. "Non-Western Sexuality Comes to the U.S.: A Crash Course in Manga and Anime for Sexologists." *Contemporary Sexuality* 39, no. 3 (2005): 1–6. http://corneredangel.com/amwess/papers/non_western_sexuality.pdf. Accessed June 19, 2017.

Dark Horse. "The Romance of Harlequin Manga Continues!" http://www.darkhorse.com/Press-Releases/1225/The-romance-of-Harlequin-manga-continues. Accessed June 19, 2017.

Gravett, Paul. *Manga: Sixty Years of Japanese Comics*. New York: Harper Design, 2004.

Grigsby, Mary. "Sailormoon: Manga (Comics) and Anime (Cartoon) Superheroine Meets Barbie: Global Entertainment Commodity Comes to the United States." *Journal of Popular Culture* 32, no. 1 (1998): 59–80. http://web.archive.org/web/20120617030124/http:/www.yorku.ca/jjenson/4303/readings/comics/sailormoon.pdf. Accessed June 19, 2017.

Patten, Fred. *Watching Anime, Reading Manga: 25 Years of Essays and Reviews*. Berkeley, CA: Stone Bridge Press, 2004.

Sanchez, Frank. "Hist 102: History of Manga." AnimeInfo.org. http://web.archive.org/web/20080205123443/http://www.animeinfo.org/animeu/hist102.html. Accessed June 19, 2017.

Thorn, Matt. "Shôjo Manga—Something for the Girls." *The Japan Quarterly* 48, no. 3 (2001): 43–51. https://www.academia.edu/12110561/Sh%C3%B4jo_Manga_Something _for_the_Girls. Accessed May 25, 2018.

Wong, Wendy. "The Presence of Manga in Europe and North America." *Media Digest*, September 2007. http://www.rthk.org.hk/mediadigest/20070913_76_121564.html. Accessed June 19, 2017.

Yen Press. "Graphic Novels, Manga, and More." http://www.yenpress.com/series/. Accessed June 19, 2017.

Skye O'Malley (1980)

She is the quintessential historical heroine, strikingly beautiful, brave, and smart, able to extricate herself by wile or guile from any situation. She has conquered kings and continents. She has been kidnapped and forced into a sultan's harem. She has lost husbands and lovers and enemies. She has suffered rape and torture and had really hot sex. Her hair is raven's wing black in riotous curls, her eyes sky blue, her skin gardenia fair. She is Skye O'Malley, beautiful, brave, and unconventional, the head of a dynasty. Desired by all men, from kings to rogues, Skye is the creation of Bertrice Small, an author who, along with her fellow "Avon Ladies" authors Rosemary Rogers and Kathleen Woodiwiss, forever changed the Romance genre by throwing open the bedroom door to readers and including sensually detailed loved scenes in their books.

Published in 1980, *Skye O'Malley* was Small's third novel, and it clearly demonstrated this author's willingness to break rules when it came to the Romance genre since Skye was not the typical romance heroine of the time. Forced into marriage at 15 (considered old in that time) to a depraved but well-off man, Skye meets the true love of her life, Niall Burke, before the wedding and falls in love with him. He demands *Droit du Seigneur*, the right to take the bride's virginity. Thus starts the love story of Niall and Skye, separated by her family and destined to search for each other around the world.

Rather than ending up being romantically involved with just one man, Skye, over the course of her long literary career, marries six different men, as well as engaging in relationships (some consensual, some not) with such a considerable number of lovers that readers almost need a scorecard to keep everything straight. However, what set Skye even more apart from other female protagonists in the Romance genre of the time was her bold spirit and her willingness to take charge of her own destiny, be it in the bedroom, on the deck of a ship, or while engaged in a dangerous duel of wits with wily Queen Elizabeth I.

Readers could not get enough of Skye O'Malley, and Small would go on to write five more volumes detailing Skye's adventures in and out of the bedroom in her O'Malley Saga series before turning to Skye's immediate and extended family to write another six books in her Skye's Legacy series. *Vixens*, which introduced readers to the great-great granddaughters of Skye, became the final chapter in the Skye O'Malley family saga and was published in 2003.

While Skye's fans were legion, not every romance reader was enamored with the series. Small's willingness not only to include sensually descriptive love scenes but also her distinctively extravagant, lush prose style—some critics went so far as to call it "purple"—meant that her books were not for every reader. However, whether one is a fan or not of Small's books, there is no denying her extraordinary contribution to the Romance genre.

Small said, "I do not write weak women" (Wendell). With her creation of proud, unconventional Skye O'Malley, as well as the many other fictional heroines she dreamed up over the years, Small proved this point time and time again to the delight of satisfied romance readers around the world.

Joanne Hamilton-Selway

Further Reading

Roberts, Sam. "Bertrice Small, 77, Writer of Risqué Romance Novels, Dies." *New York Times*, March 5, 2015. https://www.nytimes.com/2015/03/06/books/bertrice-small-novelist-of-risque-romances-dies-at-77.html?_r=0. Accessed June 19, 2017.

Small, Bertrice. *Skye O'Malley*. New York: Avon, 1980.

Veronica Asks: Author Interviews. "Bertrice Small." September 30, 2009. https://veronicaasks.wordpress.com/2009/09/30/bertrice-small/. Accessed June 19, 2017.

Wendell, Sarah. "Bertrice Small: 1937–2015." *Smart Bitches Trashy Books*. February 25, 2015. http://smartbitchestrashybooks.com/2015/02/bertrice-small-1937-2015/. Accessed June 19, 2017.

Small, Bertrice (1937–2015)

Born Bertrice Williams on December 9, 1937, in New York City, Bertrice Small, the daughter of David R. and Doris S. Williams, both of whom worked in the television business, was educated at St. Mary's School for Girls. Small credits two of her teachers at the school—Sister Mercedes and Miss Frances Andersen—with encouraging her early attempts at writing. Many years later, after her fame grew, reporters got a kick out of mentioning that Small was educated in a school run by

Anglican nuns, feeling that the contrast between her demure education and her passionate prose and erotic story lines was somehow amusing. After St. Mary's, Small attended Western College for Women (1955–1958) but left college to enroll at the Katherine Gibb Secretarial School. She then worked in advertising and the business side of radio, as well as in retail sales. She married George Small in 1963, and the couple had one child.

It was while she was recovering from agoraphobia that Small wrote her first novel, *The Kadin*. She spent two years researching every detail—from what her characters would eat to what they would wear—to give her story the historical verisimilitude she thought readers deserved. As she once stated, "If you're going to undress a heroine, you'd better damn well know what she's got on underneath" (Allen). Small has said that she was inspired to write *The Kadin* by the family stories told by a schoolmate at St. Mary's who was from Turkey, an exotic locale that intrigued Small, and a possible reason that the harem leitmotif later became a prominent trope in so many of her novels. Small was 41 when *The Kadin* was published in 1978, and the book quickly became a favorite with romance readers, who enjoyed the unusual setting, the vivid characters, and the unrestrained sexuality of Small's debut novel. *The Kadin* was soon followed by a sequel, *Love Wild and Fair*.

Small would go on to pen almost 60 novels, including historical romances, contemporary erotic romances, romantic novellas, and fantasy-infused romances. Her vividly written, boldly sensual, and lushly detailed books have been set in a variety of locales and time periods, including Elizabethan England, the Middle Ages, ancient Constantinople, the merry court of Charles II, and the world of Hetar. But of all her books, Small is best known (and perhaps best loved) for her novel *Skye O'Malley*. The eponymous book that introduces Skye and her legacy was published in 1980 and launched a series that would eventually envelope almost all of Skye's extended family. Cousins and in-laws, brothers, half-brothers, children and grandchildren, all the members of the O'Malley clan were given their own stories over the next few decades by Small. Small died on February 24, 2015, in Southold, New York, and her last novel, *Serena*, which was part of her Silk Merchants series, was published later that same year.

Over the course of her writing career, not only did Small's books appear on a number of best-seller lists, including *Publishers Weekly* and the *New York Times*, but she also garnered a plethora of awards, including the Silver Pen from *Affaire de Coeur*, a Lifetime Achievement Award from the Romance Writers of America, and a Lifetime Achievement Award from *Romantic Times*. However, the title, also given to her by *Romantic Times*, that gave her the most pleasure was "Lust's Leading Lady." It was a sobriquet Small wore with great pride.

Joanne Hamilton-Selway

Further Reading

Allen, Jennifer. "Eight Who Write of Love for Money: Reaping the Wild Rewards of Romance." *Life*, November 1981. http://www.maryellenmark.com/text/magazines /life/905W-000-015.html. Accessed June 20, 2017.

Roberts, Sam. "Bertrice Small, 77, Writer of Risqué Romance Novels, Dies." *New York Times*, March 5, 2015. https://www.nytimes.com/2015/03/06/books/bertrice-small -novelist-of-risque-romances-dies-at-77.html?_r=0. Accessed June 19, 2017.

Small, Bertrice. *The Kadin*. New York: Avon, 1978.

Small, Bertrice. *Love Wild and Fair*. New York: Avon, 1978.

Small, Bertrice. *Skye O'Malley*. New York: Avon, 1980.

Tan, Cecilia. "Bertrice Small at IASPR, Interviewed by Sarah Franz & the Audience." June 30, 2011. blog.ceciliatan.com/archives/791. Accessed June 20, 2017.

Soap Opera and Romance

Soap operas and Romance Fiction are arguably the two biggest genres of storytelling aimed primarily at a female audience. It is not a coincidence, then, that neither genre has been given the respect it deserves. This is true regardless of the fact that each genre comes from a well-established tradition and has left a cultural impact that has influenced other, more critically acclaimed forms of television and novels.

American daytime soap operas come from a long line of serialized storytelling. Laurence Sterne's novel *Tristam Shandy* was published in Great Britain over the course of seven years (Rouveral, 4). The tradition was continued across the Western world by authors such as Henry James, Harriet Beecher Stowe, Balzac, and, in the 20th century, Armistead Maupin and Helen Fielding.

Soap operas began in the United States as serialized radio dramas. The "soap" part of the moniker refers to the advertisers that sponsored the programs (Allen). Irma Philips could be called the founding writer of the genre. She began with writing radio soaps in the early 1930s. In 1952, she transitioned her soap opera *Guiding Light* to television. The show ran until 2009, making it the second-longest-running show in history.

Like Romance Fiction, soaps became a cultural phenomenon in the 1980s. As a result, prime-time television began to adopt characteristics from the daytime shows. Dramas such as *Dallas, Dynasty*, and, in more recent years, *Grey's Anatomy, Desperate Housewives*, and *Ugly Betty*, adopted both serialized storytelling and "the structuring device of the extended family . . . and kinship and romance plots" (Allen). The serialized structure of storytelling also became popular in Romance Fiction as both trilogies (with a closed ending) and ongoing series (with an open ending) have become common. Readers of romance know that the story in each book will end with a Happily Ever After. However, it is different for soap fans. The nature of ongoing storytelling demands that drama and conflict be continually introduced. This is something romance novelist Nora Roberts clearly understands. In her book *Convincing Alex*, the heroine (a soap opera writer) explains that soap opera viewers crave, and are rewarded with, ongoing conflicts:

> In soaps, a character loses the edge if he or she isn't dealing with some crisis or tragedy. . . . That's why Elana's been married twice, had amnesia, was sexually assaulted, had two miscarriages and a nervous breakdown, went temporarily blind, shot a former lover in self-defense, overcame a gambling addiction, had twins who were kidnapped by a psychotic nurse—and recovered them only after a long, heartrending and perilous search through the South American jungles. (289)

Roberts herself has written many trilogies, family sagas, and an ongoing mystery romance series, so she is obviously aware of the similarities her genre has with daytime drama.

However, the main difference with ongoing stories in soaps is that they occur in real time. Fans of *All My Children*, for instance, followed the life of Erica Kane for decades, growing older with the character. And on *General Hospital*, fans watched Robin Scorpio (as portrayed by Kimberly McCullough) from her first appearance on the show as a child in 1985, through her recent exit from the show's canvas in 2012. That sort of phenomenon builds a bond with loyal fans who have followed the shows for decades and who know the stories even better than the often changing writers.

Along with telling love stories (once dubbed "Love in the Afternoon" on soap operas), Romance Fiction and daytime dramas both depict female stories and sexuality in a way that is hard to find in other genres. In most film and television, women characters are sexual objects—styled and written to be appealing to men. Although there have been some improvements, it is still hard to find women characters who are more than just love interests or sounding boards for the men driving the stories, and who have their own points of view.

However, when romances and soaps are at their best, they are stories about women. And when sex is involved, the focus isn't a female character's body, but her desires and emotions. Also, both genres represent the rare occurrence when men are the subject of the female gaze—a well-deserved quid pro quo from most women's points of view. Just as Romance Fiction became known for its steamy passages, soap operas had their own version of eroticism with carefully lit and choreographed love scenes and montages. Both offer fantasies for women to enjoy, but also the opportunity for women to be curious and think about what they want in their own lives.

One difference between these sex scenes is that in a romance novel, the detailed scenes will almost always be between the heroine and her true love. In a soap, a woman (especially if she has been on a show for years, like the aforementioned Erica Kane) will have many such scenes with various good-looking men—sometimes within a monogamous relationship, sometimes not. Because of this, "the stereotype of women as having low libidos or being interested in romance and intimacy at the expense of lust and erotic desire is debunked. . . . They demonstrate the third-wave 'rebellion against the false impression that since women don't want to be sexually exploited, they don't want to be sexual'" (Goren, 108).

One thing found in soap operas, and not so much in Romance Fiction, is the transgressive woman: Reva Shane on *Guiding Light*, Sami Brady on *Days of Our Lives*, Dorian Lord on *One Life to Live*, and more. Only in soaps can a female character evolve from being the heroine to a villain and then back. These women are allowed to go after what they want, make mistakes, do bad things, and yet they are still shown to deserve happiness. Some of the most interesting relationships on soaps are long and complicated ones between women: Dorian and Vicki (rivals, frenemies, family), Blair and Tea (taking turns pushing each other out of windows and looking after each other's children), Reva and Cassie (long-lost half-sisters), and more.

Also unique to soaps is their record of telling social issues story lines. Back in 1969, *One Life to Live* had a character who was a black woman passing as white who later learned to reclaim her identity (Allen). Erica Kane had an abortion in the 1970s. (Illegal at the time and before easy birth control had been widely available.) Robin Scorpio contracted HIV as a teenager, and learning to have a full, happy life with the disease has been a part of her character arc ever since. Other social issues explored on soaps include class, race, homophobia, war, adoption, and violence against women.

Unlike romance novels, which are more popular than ever, American soaps are in trouble. Due to low ratings and slashed budgets, several once-popular and beloved soaps have been canceled in the past several years (*Guiding Light, As the World Turns, All My Children*, and *One Life to Live*). They have been replaced by unremarkable, yet cheap to produce, talk shows that are unlikely to inspire the kind of loyal audience that will follow a program for decades.

There are still a handful of soaps representing the genre, but if it is going to survive, then the powers that be are going to have to be creative and proactive about saving it. There are some ideas that could be taken from the romance industry, and others that will need to be unique to television.

Romance Fiction has thrived in e-books, but soaps haven't figured out how to utilize technology yet. In some ways it has even been a hindrance. Fans can skip entire episodes of a soap and just watch clips of their favorite characters spliced together online. And instead of watching a show live or even recording it, they can read recaps on message boards and decide that they'll skip that day (or week or month or year).

Soaps could make use of technology by taking charge of Internet viewing. A few soaps are available on official sites, but the networks could go even further: have subscription services to stream canceled shows and old episodes, put out DVD collections that chronicle popular story lines, and create content for the Internet. Soaps were the first format of drama to move successfully from radio to television. Perhaps they can be at the forefront of figuring out how to use new technologies. There was an attempt to move canceled shows to the Internet through a production company called Prospect Park. That deal fell through, but the shows that are still alive and kicking should begin exploring new avenues (James).

The good news is that with good writing, audiences will come back. Many fans are just waiting for their shows to get good again. Soap fans are loyal and are checking out message boards and blogs to see if there is a reason to tune back in. Just as popular romance has done so well, the soaps need to pay attention to what fans want (romance, adventure, intrigue, diversity, and current events). If they tell a good story, the viewers will come back.

Natalie McCall

Further Reading

Allen, Robert C. "Afternoon, 1966 NBC Had a Creditable Line-Up Across the Key." *The Museum of Broadcast Communications*. 5 August 2012. http://www.museum.tv/eotv /soapopera.htm. Accessed June 20, 2017.

Ford, Sam. *The Survival of Soap Opera Transformations for a New Media Era*. Jackson: University Press of Mississippi, 2011.

Goren, Lilly J. *You've Come a Long Way, Baby: Women, Politics, and Popular Culture*. Lexington: University Press of Kentucky, 2009.

James, Meg. "Plan to Continue ABC Soap Operas Online Falls Through." *The Los Angeles Times*, November 23, 2011. http://articles.latimes.com/2011/nov/23/business/la-fi-1124 -ct-soaps-20111124. Accessed June 20, 2017.

Peretti, Katie, and Alina Adams. *Oakdale Confidential: Secrets Revealed*. New York: Pocket Books, 2006.

Roberts, Nora. *The Stanislaski Brothers: Mikhail and Alex*. New York: Silhouette Books, 2000.

Romance Writers of America. "Reader Statistics." https://www.rwa.org/p/cm/ld/fid=582. Accessed June 20, 2017.

Rouverol, Jean. *Writing for the Soaps*. Cincinnati: Writer's Digest Books, 1984.

Social Media and Romance

Romantic fiction publishers have long had a close relationship with their readers and authors, and romance publishers were at the forefront of producing e-books. The erotica publisher Ellora's Cave started publishing online in 1997. Harlequin Enterprises has also been online since 1997 with its online community for readers and writers, offering the chance to chat with Harlequin employees, such as editors. The interlinked relationships between romance publishers, readers, and authors are often blurred, and social media plays a considerable role in the development of the romance community.

Social media encompasses online sites and tools that allow users to connect, discuss, and engage with one another. Common examples include Facebook, Twitter, book recommendation portals such as Goodreads, blogs, and various virtual forums. LinkedIn is another resource, although romance members are more likely to be published authors who use LinkedIn to connect with peers and other industry professionals than to use it to connect with romance fans. Each medium differs in how it works and what its benefits and drawbacks are. Key to social media is the ability to socialize with other participants, whether that communication is synchronous, using tools such as Skype or the various chat options, or asynchronous, such as posting comments on a blog.

As to the interactivity among writers, publishers, and readers, Avon publicity director Pam Jaffe discovered that not only were romance fans finding new novels and preferred authors to read, but readers who followed Avon editors online were beginning to select books based on who edited them (L. D.).

Authors of romance are often avid readers of the genre. In his business history of Mills & Boon, Joseph McAleer reveals that many of the writers for this imprint had much in common with the readers for whom they wrote. Mills & Boon began in 1908. Harlequin was founded in 1949 in Winnipeg, Manitoba, Canada. In addition to some business reports, the company reprinted British fiction, including romances from Mills & Boon, until 1970 when Harlequin bought Mills & Boon, merging both companies (Charles and Mosley). The reader-writer-publisher relationship that developed among these groups is shown by the company's relatively recent online writing competitions. Harlequin's Mills & Boon division initiated a contest known as New Voices that ran in 2010 and 2011. Harlequin launched a similar competition in North America named So You Think You Can Write. In 2012 the New Voices competition merged with Harlequin's, and the combined competition became So You Think You Can Write, or SYTYCW. Previously, New Voices was operated from London, and then the United States ran the SYTYCW a few months later. Merging the competitions, both of which were open to most countries and used similar Harlequin employees to establish and run, made sense.

For the New Voices competition, which ran in 2010 and 2011, entries from around the globe were submitted and uploaded to the *Romance Is Not Dead* blog (www.romanceisnotdead.com). Readers and writers could comment on entries and perhaps gain an idea of what a typical editor's slushpile might contain. Readers, as well as writers, were interested in the competition and could read all of the entries if they chose. The competition was deliberately designed to engage with and increase the company's reader base, a goal it achieved during its first competition with more than 1.2 million page views and 822 entries, which added 5,000 additional addresses to its e-mail database and increased the use of the company's Facebook site by 36 percent (Marketing). Authors such as Leah Ashton, Lucy Ellis, and Charlotte Phillips are among those who received contracts with Harlequin and have now published romance novels with the company.

The So You Think You Can Write competition used social media to promote itself and also included an online conference where entrants and others could liaise with and learn from more than 50 Harlequin Mills & Boon editors. Social media included podcasts and videos, live chats, and Twitter events (Williams).

In an in-depth look at the Covers Gone Wild section of the Smart Bitches Trashy Books romance review site, academic Miriam Greenfeld-Benowitz confessed that she stopped talking about reading romances with some of her friends because she felt the stigmatization of the genre. However, she acknowledged that the Internet had relieved some of the risk of derision because people can seek out like-minded others in various romance forums and sites. Readers, authors, and industry professionals, such as publishers and editors, are all part of this romance community, a broadly based group linked by an interest in popular romance fiction. Social media helps to cement this community, though each segment might interact with social media in different ways and use different media.

Authors

Obviously, without the authors there would be no romance novels to read. Social media has affected how authors conduct themselves online. Now authors, including romance novelists, are often required to have a platform, defined as an online or social media presence, so that readers can interact with them (Clifton). Most editors and publishers expect their authors to have at least a minimal online presence.

Novelists who are not published, especially in Romance genres such as women's fiction, have been encouraged to be visible online and to establish an audience before submission, though opinions may be beginning to change a little. Now, blogs for fiction writers are no longer seen as *de rigueur*, for either potential or published authors. Perhaps group or publisher blogs, such as the ones run by

Harlequin for its various lines like medical romance, are more common. As an author has a new release, she or he will write and answer comments on group blogs, but the responsibility of coming up with material over an extended period for an individual blog is lessened. Organizations such as Romance Writers of Australia also provide an umbrella blog where authors can write about various issues or announce new ventures. Not forgetting the social aspect of social media, many authors work alone and can appreciate the "water cooler" break effect of participating at times during their day. Of course, many romance authors do maintain individual professional websites as a means of connecting with their readers, especially if they are independently or self-published, as many currently are.

As for prospective romance writers learning how to write for the genre specifically, few college-level courses exist. Numerous classes are available for fiction in general. However, recently Pam Regis and Jennifer Crusie designed and delivered an online romantic fiction creative-writing program for McDaniel College. Crusie stresses that romantic fiction has additional requirements to the general plot and structure that need to be learned yet are seldom taught. Delivered forum-style, the classes, though formal, echo many romance community forums and workshops in style (Crusie).

Aspiring romance authors can also train themselves, especially about romance-industry mores and trends, when they participate in social media even if that participation is limited to reading, though many outlets do incorporate discussion. Romance University is one example. Designed to help writers learn about romance writing, the site delivers posts on the technique of writing and the business of publishing; it also provides labs, which are critiques given by romance-industry editors of submitted manuscript excerpts. Agents of agencies representing romantic fiction also give advice on submission and rejection etiquette, and how to recognize an effective literary agent. The Romance Writers of America (RWA) also offers a number of educational options for its members through various workshops, conferences, and its wide-ranging online Romance University program.

The So You Think You Can Write competition ran several online and Twitter chats led by senior editors at Harlequin Mills & Boon on topics such as the difference between their Intrigue and Romantic Suspense lines, romantic tension in wholesome romances, and tips for submitting specifically to the London office. Editors from the lines Harlequin Presents, Harlequin KISS, and Harlequin Medical answered questions including what each specific category wanted from a writer, submission response times, feedback, and secondary characters (2012). The use of Twitter in this instance gave contestants access to Harlequin editors that outside of a conference or workshop or Harlequin online would be comparatively rare.

Harlequin has long had discussion boards on its website (https://www.har lequin.com/community.html) divided into writing discussions, chats about books and authors, and a social section. The writing section is further divided into conversations about writing techniques, emotional support, and talking to the editors.

Once authors are contracted, Harlequin provides virtual training sessions on how to use social media for romance writers (L. D.). Organizations like Romance Writers of America offer social media training to members through online classes, articles in the association magazine *Romance Writers Report*, and various chapter and conference workshops.

Authors use social media to learn about upcoming submission opportunities, new romance publishing lines, news about the industry; published and unpublished writers use social media to learn about the craft of writing romance and the business side of the profession; and published authors, in particular, participate to engage with their readers. If novels are subsequently sold or read as a result, then almost all members of the author-reader-publisher triangle are satisfied.

Readers

Readers find out about and discuss romance novels through social media. This readership includes fans of specific subgenres such as historical or medical romances, and academic readers interested in deep readings and analysis of the genre. Writers are often readers too, whether unabashed fans or reading closely for research or professional reasons (Crusie). For example, although people might assume novelist Emma Darcy, first published in 1983 and with over 95 romance novels to her name, has no need or time to read new fiction, in a 2008 interview she noted that she will always read debut authors to determine the writer's appeal and see why the author was accepted for publication (Thomas). She reads selected current releases for research and professional-development reasons. As far back as 1990 Emma Darcy would read the six titles released each month in the Harlequin Presents series, since most of her novels fit into this category, and new authors from the now-defunct Romance series. In fact, before she wrote her first novel, having decided on crafting a Mills & Boon romance, she bought 100 second-hand romances and analyzed them, and then used that synthesis to create her first published novel (Moran). As an author, this type of reading is part of her research of the romance industry. Editors often suggest that to understand a particular type of romance, especially a category romance such as those published by Harlequin Mills & Boon, writers should read recently published novels.

Romance readers and writers tend to have blurred lines, where readers and authors can interact directly with one another instead of through an intermediary such as a publisher. This interaction has been made much easier with the wide adoption of social-networking tools and e-books by members of the romance community.

Review and discussion websites such as All about Romance (AAR) and Dear Author have very engaged communities to help readers find novels, but more importantly to encourage discussion. All about Romance was launched in 1998 (with some 1996 and 1997 reviews) by Laurie Gold and since 2008 has been run by then-new publishers. There are thousands of reviews of various romance novels on the site and an active forum to discuss romance fiction. The site reviewers and editors have compiled lists of novels by themes, character types, and settings. On some sites, authors are considered conversation inhibitors, even when not referring to their own books. All about Books welcomes authors, athough two discussion boards are specifically for either writers or readers.

DearAuthor.com also has an active reviewing community and offers recommendations for themes or characteristics in romances that would otherwise be difficult to find in their "I need a rec!" section. Novels set in Southeast Asia or with Southeast Asian characters, and characters with disabilities are two examples. Reviews are written in the form of letters to the authors, but the reviews are designed for the readers. DearAuthor.com provides publishing industry news, e-book news, and gives authors a once-per-month "Author Promo" discussion thread where authors can promote their new releases; but most of all this site focuses on the reader.

Social reading communities such as Goodreads (acquired by Amazon in 2013 and now merged with the online reading community Shelfari) contain niche communities of romance readers to discuss and discover romantic fiction.

Romance Industry

The romance industry here is defined as publishers, publicists, agents, and editors of romantic fiction, as well as associated roles, such as booksellers. The social aspect remains important for industry professionals, especially when liaising with readers. An entire conversational feed from an editor, for example, that deals only with business aspects can be off-putting. Also, one of the greatest frustrations for those who engage in social media is the pressure to buy, whether a novel or a critique service, especially when no connection has been formed beyond one Tweet or "like" on a Facebook page.

Nonetheless, business issues form the basis of most romance industry use of social media. Literary agents, editors and, by extension, publishing houses, and potential authors are the primary users of social media for this purpose. Editors and agents often inform writers interested in writing for them about their likes and dislikes for a particular line and whether an imprint is open or closed to submissions, and to solicit other material for publication.

In recent years, editors and agents have at times held online competitions that include pitch sessions, where writers present their story concepts in a very brief form, generally no more than two sentences or so. (In the trade this is known as the "elevator pitch.") Harlequin also introduced a fast-track competition in 2010, beginning with their medical romance line. The fast-track competition was open for one month in August 2010. The writers could submit one chapter of the full manuscript to the editors with the promise that all entrants would have a response by the end of that month. The competition received 174 submissions and discovered new author Annie Claydon (Hodgson and Nicoll). Since the first Harlequin fast-track, other competitions have been introduced for various lines, such as Love Inspired, Harlequin Special Edition, and Harlequin Presents.

In October 2012 Carina Press offered responses to submissions within six weeks, as well as a few lines of feedback to all participants. The company noted that writers who receive a contract receive significant feedback as a matter of course.

Back in 1990, Emma Darcy commented that she found the feedback given to authors from Mills & Boon terrible because it was essentially nonexistent. Based on her premise that the most important person in the romance community is the reader, she created her own reader feedback panel, although she noted some readers were hesitant to give responses for fear of being unkind (Moran). With the rapid uptake of social media by the romance community, Emma Darcy may now have access to this deep feedback she wanted, especially directly from readers, and also from editors who do know what their readers want. More than 20 years on, the sheer volume of online discussion about most books is overwhelming. Previously, most reviews and feedback postpublication were delivered via newspaper or magazine; therefore, public commentary was in the hands of the few. At times, readers might also write a letter to an author if a novel moved or incensed them. Now, online commentary is almost instantaneous and easy to discover. The value of the feedback depends on who is giving it and how it is delivered. Yet before the ubiquity of the Internet in everyday life as well as in the romance community, authors probably would not have been aware of how some readers felt or if there were particular groups of readers that had specific opinions and expectations, such as Emma Darcy was able to do with her readers who were already fans of Mills & Boon romances.

Based on the premise that Harlequin romances have always been available where their readers are, Harlequin participates extensively in social media. In fact, Harlequin scaled back on some of its social media tools in 2012 because the resources were distracting from the core discussions (Morgan). For example, Harlequin used to successfully hold book launches in Second Life, an online three-dimensional world popular at the time, where avatars of people hold discussions either through text chat or audio (Jacobs). Harlequin (now a part of Harper Collins) and many other romance publishers provide platforms for reader-writer-publisher interaction and produce content for their sites as well as moderating some discussion forums.

Romance publishers build online communities that promote not only their novels with their own imprints, but those of others as well. For example, the Tor.com site includes science fiction and fantasy from various publishers and has included Avon authors for an urban-fantasy and paranormal romances promotion in the past. Macmillan also has a community site known as Heroes and Heartbreakers that focuses on romance fiction from a variety of publishers, not just Macmillan.

Publishers source and promote authors via social media as another point of contact. Through social media potential authors have at times had more immediate access to those in the industry with the power to publish them than they have traditionally had in the past.

Technology is fluid, and social media, in particular, rapidly adopts promising tools, but just as quickly discards them when they are considered outmoded—such as the older social media site MySpace. The romance fiction community has long embraced social media to discover new books and to engage with others who appreciate or critique romances. While Facebook, Twitter, SnapChat, Instagram, and various blogs and chat-sites may be popular social communication resources today, this will likely change as tastes and society evolve. What has always remained constant, however, is the close interaction of readers, authors, and publishers within the romance community. At times this very interaction changes the types of romances produced, as authors and publishers adapt to reader tastes. This adaptation has always been true for romances, regardless of social media use. Social media, however, enables readers, authors, and publishers to interact with one another with ease and speed. While the tools might change, the interlinked relationships in the romance community will remain.

Doreen Sullivan

See also: "Romance Blogs, Wikis, and Websites" and "Romance Listservs"

Further Reading

All about Romance. https://allaboutromance.com/. Accessed June 21, 2017.

Charles, John, and Shelley Mosley. "Bookmakers: Harlequin Turns 60." *The Booklist* 106, no. 2 (September 15, 2009): 42. https://www.booklistonline.com/Bookmakers-Harlequin -Turns-60-John-Charles/pid=3715689. Accessed June 21, 2017.

Clifton, P. "Teach Them to Fish: Empowering Authors to Market Themselves Online." *Publishing Research Quarterly* 26, 2 (2010): 106–9.

Crusie, Jennifer. "Majoring in Romance: The Romance Novel and Academe." *Romance Writers Report* 32, 11 (2012): 18–20.

Dear Author. dearauthor.com. Accessed June 2017.

"Enhance Your Romance Writing Career." Romance Writers of America. https://www.rwa.org/p/cm/ld/fid=2101. Accessed June 21, 2017.

Gold, Laurie. "Laurie Gold." LinkedIn. https://www.linkedin.com/in/laurie-gold-544bb73/. Accessed June 21, 2017.

Goodreads. https://www.goodreads.com/. Accessed June 21, 2017.

Greenfeld-Benowitz, Miriam. "The Interactive Romance Community: The Case of 'Covers Gone Wild'." In *New Approaches to Popular Romance Fiction: Critical Essays*, edited by Sarah S. G. Frantz and Eric Murphy Selinger, 195–205. Jefferson, NC: McFarland, 2012.

Hodgson, Sheila, and Flo Nicoll. "Announcement: Medical Romance Submission Fast-Track Acquisition!" http://www.iheartpresents.com/2011/03/announcement-medical-romance-submission-fast-track-acquisition/. Accessed June 21, 2017.

Jacobs, Holly. "A Writer's Net." *Romance Writers Report* 29, 1 (2009): 20–23.

L. D. "Branding and Promotion, 2010-Style." *Publishers Weekly* 257, no. 21 (May 24, 2010): 22. Business Source Premier, EBSCOhost. Accessed June 21, 2017.

"Marketing Campaign of the Year." *Bookseller* no. 5481 (May 20, 2011): 29. Business Source Premier, EBSCOhost. Accessed June 21, 2017.

McAleer, Joseph. *Passion's Fortune: The Story of Mills and Boon*. Oxford: Oxford University Press, 1999.

Moran, Albert. "'No More Virgins': Writing Romance—an Interview with Emma Darcy." *Continuum: Journal of Media & Cultural Studies* 4, no. 1 (January 1, 1990): 37–53. E-Journals, EBSCOhost. Accessed June 21, 2017.

Morgan, Nick. "What Do Harvard Business Publishing and Harlequin Have in Common?" *Forbes.com*, September 25, 2012. https://www.forbes.com/sites/nickmorgan/2012/09/25/what-do-harvard-business-publishing-and-harlequin-have-in-common/#555e1d3858e8. Accessed June 21, 2017.

Romance University. http://romanceuniversity.org/. Accessed June 21, 2017.

Romance Writers of America. https://www.rwa.org/. Accessed June 21, 2017.

So You Think You Can Write. "Twitter Chat: From London with Love: Top Tips for Submitting." http://www.soyouthinkyoucanwrite.com/wp-content/uploads/2012/11/FromLondonWithLove-chat_11122012.pdf. Accessed June 21, 2017.

"So You Think You Can Write Contest & Events." Harlequin SYTYCW—So You Think You Can Write; Finding New Voices in Romantic Fiction. http://www.soyouthinkyoucanwrite.com/events/. Accessed June 21, 2017.

Thomas, Glen. "'And I Deliver': An Interview with Emma Darcy." *Continuum: Journal of Media & Cultural Studies* 22, no. 1 (February 2008): 113–26. Communication & Mass Media Complete, EBSCOhost. Accessed June 21, 2017.

Williams, Charlotte. "Mills & Boon Launches Writing Comp." *The Bookseller*, June 26, 2012. http://www.thebookseller.com/news/mills-boon-launches-writing-comp.html. Accessed June 21, 2017.

Statistics for the Genre

Skeptics who snicker at romance novels may be surprised to learn that Romances lead all other adult fiction genres when it comes to the numbers. Recent market research conducted on publishing and consumer trends bears this out. R. R. Bowker, the publishing industry's leading source of bibliographic services and information, released the results of their latest comprehensive, consumer-based study in June, 2011.

Bowker's 2010–2011 Book Consumer Demographics and Buying Behaviors Annual Review provides an in-depth analysis of who American book buyers are, what they're buying, and why. The data for this study, gathered via consumer surveys submitted by 40,000 book buyers, profile their reading preferences and purchasing habits.

Bowker's study is a valuable tool for publishers and booksellers who are attempting to navigate the turbulent waters of an increasingly dynamic and rapidly evolving market. Economic conditions, coupled with the emerging demand for e-books, make it difficult to determine which is having the greater impact on the industry. The consumer feedback provided in the report takes the mystery out of what buyers are thinking, what's truly behind current market changes, and what direction the readers' preferences are likely to take in the future. For the Romance genre, it's all good.

Of all book categories, Adult Fiction continues to be the foundation of the publishing industry. The Romance genre, in particular, leads all Adult Fiction genres. Romances claimed 13.4 percent of market category sales, outpacing its nearest competition, espionage/thriller and mystery/detective novels. In 2010, publishers increased production of romances by 1 percent and generated sales of $1.358 billion. This reversed a downward trend that began in 2008. Sales continued to rise in 2011 with Romance projected to reach $1.368 billion in sales, a 0.7 percent increase over 2010.

According to 2010 Adult Fiction sales figures, Romance outsold religion/inspirational novels by 44 percent; mystery by 50 percent; science fiction/fantasy by 59 percent; and classic literary fiction by 66 percent.

The study revealed women purchased far more books overall than did men. In fact, women bought 67 percent of all mass-market paperbacks in print, an important but waning medium among romance publishers. Sixty-two percent of women surveyed said they bought at least one book during the past year, compared to only 44 percent of men. In addition, nearly 10 percent of women were repeat customers, buying 10 or more titles per year. The largest book-buying demographic is Baby Boomers, who claimed a third of all sales.

In terms of readership, the Southern region of the United State leads the nation in Romance sales, at 38 percent. This is twice as many as either the Northeastern or the Western regions, which posted sales of 17 percent and 19 percent, respectively. The Midwest region came in a strong second, accounting for 26 percent of romance purchased. Historicals were the most frequently purchased Romance subgenre. Other reader favorites included Romantic Suspense, Fantasy, novels with television and film connections, Paranormals, and Christmas holiday novels.

Romance novels made frequent appearances on national best-seller lists. In 2010, 469 titles by 239 romance writers, including 77 new authors, made their way to the bestseller lists. Harlequin MIRA topped the list of romance publishers who produced bestsellers. Rounding out the top 10 were Grand Central Publishing, HQN, Jove, Berkley, Avon, Pocket, Signet, St. Martin's Press, and Silhouette.

Interestingly, not all of the books appearing on these lists are the top sellers. Obviously, veteran authors, such as Nora Roberts, with well-established marketability among romance buyers, are fast-tracked to the best-seller lists. For the rest, list-makers use carefully guarded formulas to select titles for their lists. It's a sure bet, if an item isn't a top seller before making the list, it will be after. Attention-grabbers such as garnering rave reviews, winning RITA Awards, or attracting the interest of the entertainment industry certainly improve the odds, as does releasing a book at the optimal time of year. For example, releasing Christmas books in the fall or summer love stories in the spring generates greater sales.

According to the survey respondents, the typical romance reader is female, between the ages of 30 and 54, and over half of them report they live with a spouse or significant other. Women purchased 91 percent of all romances. Although men reportedly bought the remaining 9 percent, with so many women buying and bringing new romance novels home, it's likely the number of men who secretly *read* romances far exceeds the number who buy them.

Consumer book-purchasing habits are changing. In the first half of 2011, Internet booksellers outperformed traditional bookstores for the first time in history. The shift from print to e-books is having a profound impact on the rapidly changing publishing industry. Print books in all categories experienced modest declines in sales during 2010 and 2011, but that trend appeared to be reversing in 2012.

February and March 2012 data from the Association of American Book Publishers indicated sales of adult print books were on the rise, increasing by 6.9 percent from a year earlier. While paperback sales continued to lose ground to e-books, adult fiction in hardcover jumped 24.4 percent. Plus, there was growing interest in self-publishing, once dismissed as "vanity press." In 2011, self-publishing contributed 6 percent to print book production, as more authors explored this option.

Of course, not all readers are rushing to make the transition to e-books. Fifty-one percent of romance consumers who don't currently own an e-reader don't intend to get one. They don't believe they need one while there are still plenty of print books to go around. Conversely, 41 percent of respondents reported they are open to the idea of buying an e-reader, although 19 percent consider the cost of the readers prohibitive.

Print romance buyers in this study reported an average age of 49 years, with a weighted mean annual income of $58,000. Using the same criteria, e-reader romance buyers were slightly younger, 42 years old, and their annual income was $70,000. Ninety percent of book buyers who use e-readers use their devices specifically for romance novels. This is particularly true for erotic romance, where the sales of the e-book format topped print erotica by a ratio of 2 to 1.

In the trend toward e-books, romances are increasingly going digital. During the first half of 2011, while the overall sales of adult fiction actually increased, sales of adult fiction print books declined by over 25 percent, and mass-market paperbacks dropped by over 26 percent from January to July. The increase in adult fiction sales was attributed mostly to the surge in e-books, which represented 29 percent of romances purchased in the first half of 2011.

However, the initial rush toward e-readers appeared to be leveling off. The March 2012 AAP Monthly Book Sales Report (*RT Book Reviews*, June 21, 2012, http:/www.rtbookreviews.march-aap-book-sales-report) indicated e-book sales were stabilizing. Though robust sales continued into 2012, the format gained only 9.9 percent from the previous year. While this appears to be a significant drop compared to the double-digit growth in 2011, current analysis indicates the 2011 sales figures were abnormally high. This gives the appearance that 2012's performance was sluggish in comparison, when in fact, as of March 2012, e-book sales were $21.4 million ahead of where they were the year before. Don't you just love statistics?

Bowker's study revealed some interesting insights into romance readers and their activities. Forty-six percent of women surveyed said they buy romance novels for the story and the happily-ever-after ending. Twenty-three percent are loyal readers who base their purchases on their favorite authors, or on a new book in a series they're reading. Other reader activities include the following:

- 60 percent of romance buyers either visit author websites or are interested in doing so.
- 49 percent bought a book, or would be motivated to buy it, after viewing a promotional trailer on it.
- 44 percent have gone or would consider going to a live author event, such as a book signing.
- 38 percent follow or would consider following author blogs.
- 35 percent have entered or would enter into a contest related to a book they're reading.

- 31 percent have attended or would attend an online author event.
- 30 percent have watched or would consider watching a YouTube video on an author or book.
- 30 percent either follow or are interested in following an author on Facebook.
- 29 percent read or would like to read a blog by a group of authors.
- 25 percent follow or would consider following an author on a reader community site.
- 19 percent follow or would be interested in following an author on Twitter.

With so many interesting ways to research and plan a book purchase, nearly one in three romances purchased were motivated entirely by impulse. The majority of these impulse buys were paperbacks purchased by consumers who had no prior plan to buy a book. This is understandable considering the easy access to tempting paperback displays in just about every retailer from Albertsons to Walmart. Bookstore promotions and displays also entice impulse buyers. By comparison, e-book buyers tend to be more deliberate about their purchases. No surprise there, but they were also found to buy more books and to buy books more often.

While it is true paperbacks are struggling, there is still a market for them. The buying preferences of paperback versus e-book readers vary by subgenre. Romantic suspense, contemporary romance, and christian romance paperbacks actually outsold e-books by a combined 12 percent. Historical romance sales were split equally between paper and digital formats. More than twice as many erotic romances were purchased in e-book format than paperback, and paranormals and young adult romance e-books outsold print by a combined margin of 13 percent.

The majority of romance readers either bought their books at stores, 54 percent, or online, 26 percent, than borrowed them from libraries. However, libraries were an important factor in exposing readers to new authors. The study revealed over half of library users who find an author they like in the collection will later shop for and buy that author's books.

Twenty-two percent of romance readers get their novels from family or friends. In fact, word-of-mouth recommendation from friends is the number one means for finding new romance authors. Other popular sources include browsing store book displays or visiting online bookseller websites.

Where are book buyers shopping? Barnes & Noble leads the list with 28 percent of sales, followed by Amazon.com with 24 percent. Other bookstores, which at the time of the study included Borders, performed on a par with department stores, like Target and Walmart. However, brick-and-mortar book retailers are finding it increasingly difficult to compete with the burgeoning trend of online book buying. Rounding out the list of popular booksellers are discount stores, warehouse clubs, and direct Kindle downloads

It's been estimated that more than 100 million adults didn't buy books in 2010. The industry is challenged with enticing new readers into the market when there are so many other entertainment options competing for people's time. In fact, reading as a leisure activity is steadily declining in popularity. This is a significant concern to an industry that relies heavily on Adult Fiction leisure reading, particularly Romance, to pay the bills.

The world of publishing is experiencing unprecedented and dramatic changes, but this much is certain: the happily-ever-after ending of a good romance never loses its appeal. As long as there are romantic storytellers, there will be romance readers and buyers looking for their next great love story.

Sandra Van Winkle

Further Reading

Milliot, Jim. "Print Units Drop 10 Percent in First Half of 2011: Adult Fiction, Mass Market Paperback Hardest Hit." *Publishers Weekly*, July 8, 2011. https://www.publishersweekly.com/pw/by-topic/industry-news/financial-reporting/article/47932-print-units-drop-10-in-first-half-of-2011.html. Accessed August 25, 2017.

Milliot, Jim, and Clive Chiu. *2010–11 U.S. Book Consumer Demographics and Buying Behaviors Annual Review*. Providence, NJ: Bowker, 2011.

Pierleoni, Allen. "Best-sellers Lists: How They Work and Who They (Mostly) Work For." *The Sacramento Bee*, January 22, 2012: 10AANDE.

RT Book Reviews. "AAP Book Sales Report: March 2012." June 21, 2012. https://www.rtbookreviews.com/rt-daily-blog/aap-book-sales-report-march-2012. Accessed August 25, 2017.

RT Book Reviews. "February AAP Book Sales Report." May 7, 2012. https://www.rtbookreviews.com/rt-daily-blog/february-aap-book-sales-report. Accessed August 25, 2017.

Stewart, Mary (1916–2014)

The modern-day Romantic Suspense genre owes everything to Mary Stewart. Over the course of her literary career, Stewart wrote more than a dozen novels that managed to strike the perfect balance between suspense and Romance. The proof of Stewart's skill at blurring the line between Romance Fiction and mystery novels lies in the fact that not only have Stewart's romantic suspense books received acclaim from critics in both genres, but also that these titles are eagerly embraced by both romance and mystery readers alike.

Stewart was born Mary Florence Elinor Rainbow on September 17, 1916, in Sunderland, County Durham, England. Stewart's father, Frederick Rainbow, was an Anglican clergyman who met her mother, Mary Edith, while sailing around Cape Horn on a trip to New Zealand. Stewart grew up in County Durham and attended schools there before enrolling at Durham University, where she received her BA in English in 1938. After receiving her teaching certificate in 1939, Stewart taught at several local schools. Stewart then went on to earn her MA from Durham University in 1941 and then became an associate lecturer in English at her alma mater while also serving part time in the Royal Observer Corps during World War II.

Stewart met her husband, Frederick Henry Stewart, at a VE party at the university, and they were married three months later in 1945. While her husband lectured in Geology at Durham, Stewart continued to serve as an English lecturer at the university while also teaching at St. Hild's Teacher Training College. When Stewart began writing her first novel, which would become *Madam, Will You Talk?*, publication was the last thing on her mind. Stewart's husband, however, convinced her to submit the manuscript to a publisher, who quickly offered Stewart a contract. Even though her publishers were thrilled with her book, Stewart herself continued to have serious doubts about seeing her work in print. In fact, after receiving the galleys of the manuscript, Stewart frantically tried to convince her publishers to return the manuscript and cancel its forthcoming publication. Fortunately, the publisher refused to listen to Stewart and went ahead with publishing the novel. *Madam, Will You Talk?* debuted to both critical and popular acclaim, and Stewart soon retired from teaching to concentrate on her writing career.

When it was published in 1954, *Madam, Will You Talk?* was an immediate hit with readers. The novel is the story of two Englishwomen vacationing in Provence who stumble into danger and romance, and Stewart's first book set the template for the next nine books she would write. With her first three books, Stewart tried her hand at writing different kinds of suspense. As Charity Selborne and her friend Louise Cray, the heroines of *Madam, Will You Talk?*, try to help a teenaged David Bryon stay one step ahead of the dangerous people on his trail, the story becomes a quintessential chase-driven suspense novel. *Wildfire at Midnight*, Stewart's next novel, is essentially a classic closed-room mystery as the heroine Gianetta Brooke and her ex-husband Nicholas Drury try to discern who is the real murderer hiding among the guests at a small inn in the Scottish Hebrides. With *Thunder on the Right*, Stewart flirted with using a third-person narrative style instead of her traditional first-person method.

By the time it came to write her fourth novel, *Nine Coaches Waiting*, Stewart had perfected her recipe for romantic suspense. After *Jane Eyre, Nine Coaches Waiting* is the quintessential "governess" romance, and the book whisks readers to the south of France, where Englishwoman Linda Martin has taken a job as the new governess for nine-year-old Comte Philippe de Valmy. As Linda settles into her new job, she discovers Philippe seems unusually terrified of his guardian, Leon Valmy. At first Linda begins to wonder if Leon might be plotting against the heir to the Valmy estate, but Linda gradually begins to suspect that Philippe's cousin Raol, with whom Linda is rapidly falling in love, may be the person responsible for a series of "accidents" that befall Philippe.

After the publication of *The Gabriel Hounds* in 1967 and the novella *The Wind off the Small Isles* in 1968, Stewart switched literary gears. Beginning with *The Crystal Cave* published in 1970, Stewart wrote a series of historical fantasy novels featuring Merlin and King Arthur in addition to several fantasy novels for children. *Touch Not the Cat*, published in 1976, was Stewart's return to the Romantic Suspense genre. As she wrapped up her Merlin books, Stewart would also write three more novels—*Thornyhold, Stormy Petrel*, and *The Rose Cottage*—that featured a softer mix of suspense and romance.

From *Madam, Will You Talk?* to *The Rose Cottage*, Stewart delivered the perfect synthesis of romance and danger her readers craved, but each of these books also contained three things that came to define Stewart's romantic suspense novels. The first is a courageous, smart heroine, who is willing to face danger to see to it that wrongs are righted and justice is served. The second is a strong sense of place. Whether it is Corfu in *This Rough Magic*, Lebanon in *The Gabriel Hounds*, or England in *The Ivy Tree*, Stewart had the ability to transport readers to those places with her beautifully evoked settings. The last is an elegant writing style that is deftly infused with a subtle sense of wit.

When asked to define her novels during one interview, Stewart hesitated to stick them with a specific genre label but instead replied, "I'd rather just say that I write novels, fast-moving stories that entertain. To my mind there are really only two kinds of novels: badly written and well written. Beyond that you cannot characterize—can't I just say I write stories? 'Story-teller' is an old and honorable title, and I'd like to lay claim to it" (Flood). Stewart's readers would most certainly agree with her on this score. Call Stewart's books whatever you may like, be it romance, thrillers, or romantic suspense. In the end they are simply the best kind of literary entertainment a reader could ever want.

John Charles

Further Reading

Flood, Alison. "Mary Stewart's Forgotten Novella Is the Perfect Celebration of Her Centenary Year." *The Guardian*, September 17, 2016. https://www.theguardian.com /global/2016/sep/17/mary-stewarts-forgotten-novella-is-the-perfect-celebration-of -her-centenary-year. Accessed June 22, 2017.

Friedman, Lenemaja. *Mary Stewart*. Boston: Twayne, 1990.

Hore, Rachel. "Mary Stewart Obituary." *The Guardian*, May 15, 2014. https://www.the
guardian.com/books/2014/may/15/mary-stewart. Accessed June 22, 2017.

Thompson, Raymond. H. "Interview with Mary Stewart." *The Camelot Project*. http://d
.lib.rochester.edu/camelot/text/interview-with-mary-stewart. Accessed June 22, 2017.

Suspense

See Mystery/Suspense/Thriller and Romance

Sweet Romance

The term "sweet romance" is a designation applied originally by publishers to
describe a romance novel that either does not contain sex scenes or does not overtly
describe them in the pages of the novel. This designation applies to both single-
title and category romance novels. In the romance publishing industry, sweet romances are also known as traditional or classic romances.

In the 1970s, as societal norms changed and romance novels became more
erotically charged, they were divided into two different categories—sweet romance and its sexier, more explicit counterpart. This division allowed readers to
identify the kinds of romance novels they preferred to read. As genre fiction is
concerned with meeting reader expectations, this division exemplifies how publishers and the genre does its best to fulfill and satisfy these reader expectations.

There are, in effect, two types of sweet romance. In the first type, the lead
characters do not make love prior to marriage. Inspirational and Christian romances fall into this category. Harlequin's Heartsong Presents, Love Inspired, and
Heartwarming lines, along with the romances from Avalon Books (bought by
Amazon in 2012) are examples of this kind of sweet romance. These stories are
often described as tender and have low levels of sexual tension. In the second type
of sweet romance, the bedroom door is firmly closed. Characters may make love,
but these scenes are not depicted in any detail on the page. Examples include
Harlequin's original Romance line and Entangled's Bliss line. Debbie Macomber's
single-title romances fit here as well. These stories, while described as sweet, may
have high levels of sexual tension.

Sweet Romances tend to focus on the emotional issues and conflicts that occur
between the lead characters, tracing the emotional journey rather than the sexual

journey. They revolve around classic home-and-hearth themes like family, babies, brides, and cowboys. However, this does not mean they are old-fashioned. They may also address contemporary issues like infertility, divorce, infidelity, and single parenthood.

In a sweet romance the heroes may be less alpha than heroes of sexier books. Rather than billionaire businessmen (although these are common too), heroes may be small-business owners, police officers, doctors, farmers, and university lecturers. Likewise, heroines are not Cinderellas waiting to be rescued but modern women forging their own destinies—modern women with modern jobs that, like the hero's, can range from small-business owner to police officer, doctor, farmer, and university lecturer. It is vital, however, that these characters be likable. A term often used to describe them is aspirational—that is, characters readers could aspire to become and characters they'd choose to have as friends. This may be why many readers describe sweet romances as more realistic and stories they believe could happen in real life.

The sweet romance novel can range in tone from tender and gentle through to dramatic and intense. The designation "sweet" only prescribes the amount of sexual content, not the theme, subject matter, or tone of a story. While sweet romances are not sexually explicit, with their focus on the characters' inner journeys, they can wield a powerful emotional punch.

Therese Dryden

Further Reading

Dixon, jay. *The Romance Fiction of Mills & Boon 1909–1990s*. London: Routledge, 2003.

Pepitone, Julianne. "Amazon Buys 62-Year-Old Publisher Avalon Books." *CNN Money*, June 4, 2012. http://money.cnn.com/2012/06/04/technology/amazon-avalon-books/index.htm. Accessed June 22, 2017.

Regis, Pamela. *A Natural History of the Romance Novel*. Philadelphia: University of Pennsylvania Press, 2003.

T

Teaching Popular Romance

Since the 1960s, popular fiction has found an increasingly welcoming home at every level of the academy. Works of fantasy, science fiction, and mystery/detective fiction are routinely included in K–12 curricula, and many colleges and universities offer courses on individual genres, on genre fiction in general, and on best-seller fiction (whatever its genre) as an index of cultural change. Until the early 2000s, however, with a few exceptions, such courses routinely excluded popular romance novels. When romance novels did appear on syllabi, as we see in Sarah Webster Goodwin's landmark 1997 essay "Romance and Change: Teaching the Romance to Undergraduates," they were mostly treated as an undifferentiated set of texts rather than as individual artworks. "I open the course with Holland and Eisenhart's sociological study, *Educated in Romance: Women, Achievement and College Culture*," Goodwin explains of her course on "Romance and Gender in the United States," taught in the mid-1990s. "From there we go to Lawrence Stone's *The Family, Sex, and Marriage in England 1500–1800*. Finally, before we crack open a Harlequin, we read Janice Radway's *Reading the Romance: Women, Patriarchy, and Popular Literature*" (Goodwin, 234). No particular Harlequin novel is ever named, nor is any difference noted between Harlequin's shorter, contemporary category romances and the longer, historical romances favored by Radway's readers. ("Neither Dot nor many of her customers are Harlequin fans," Radway notes early in the study [56]). For the purposes of this course—to give students a "critical purchase" on romance fantasies in Anglo-American culture (Goodwin, 233)—every romance novel might as well have been a Harlequin, and any Harlequin would do.

Goodwin's essay, though dated, illuminates the three overlapping challenges that continue to face anyone who wants to teach a course on or including Popular Romance. First, there is the *moral/political reputation* of the genre, which can make teachers and faculty reluctant to associate themselves, even for the sake of critique, with works that are said to be antifeminist or even pornographic, albeit lacking the radical cachet (at least in academic settings) of actual pornography. These associations would not pose such a challenge, however, were it not for the *aesthetic disdain* that surrounds the genre, specifically the assumption that romance novels are formulaic and essentially interchangeable artifacts, so that whatever is said about one—from either a literary or a political standpoint—will be true for them all. Other popular fiction genres are commonly taught as evolving from pulp or mass-culture roots into instances of greater literary achievement or cultural impact. Because it is seen to lack such instances, the Romance genre can be a hard sell to department chairs, except perhaps in the case of an historically distant novel such as E. M. Hull's *The Sheik* (1919) or a recent blockbuster phenomenon such as the Twilight saga by Stephanie Meyer or E. L. James's *Fifty Shades of Grey*. (In fairness, even the genre's defenders sometimes insist that the romance novel's commitment to inspiring an affective, even visceral response in the reader puts it off the table for academic analysis. "To enter the world of the romance," British scholar jay Dixon thus insists, "the method of analyzing literature which is taught in schools and higher education must be abandoned" [10].) Finally, Goodwin's decision not to name the "Harlequins" she assigns highlights the third enduring barrier to teaching Popular Romance: the *institutional occlusion* of the genre, which has long made it difficult for those who wish to teach romance to find syllabi to study, supplementary materials to deploy, and pedagogical discussions to learn from and join.

Much has changed on each of these three fronts, thanks both to the publication of new scholarship on the genre and to the academic infrastructure offered by the International Association for the Study of Popular Romance (IASPR), the online Romance Scholarship Wiki Bibliography, the lively Romance Area of the Popular Culture Association, and the presence of romance scholars and teachers on social media (notably Twitter, Facebook, the *Teach Me Tonight* academic romance blog, and the RomanceScholar listserv). Indeed, the first decades of the 21st century have been a time of public experimentation and international dialogue about the teaching of popular romance fiction, and anyone now wishing to teach a course on Popular Romance or to add Romance to an existing course has access to a lively range of course models and materials, as well as to peer-reviewed essays specifically focused on Popular Romance pedagogy, notably those tagged as "Teaching and Learning" pieces in the online *Journal of Popular Romance Studies*. (A list of courses taught in the United States, Europe, the Philippines, Australia, and elsewhere, most with links to syllabi or course descriptions, is available at the *Teach Me Tonight* blog's "Teaching Popular Romance" page.) Based on these materials, one can see that courses on, or including, popular romance fiction are currently being taught in a variety of institutional and disciplinary contexts, and popular romance novels can be put to a variety of pedagogical uses, ranging from the historical and political aims pioneered by Goodwin to the teaching of literary close reading and instruction in the entrepreneurial practices of romance writing and publishing (the subject of courses at Duke University in the United States and at Queensland University of Technology in Australia).

Perhaps the first decision an instructor needs to make in teaching Popular Romance is whether to include popular romance fiction in a course on something broader, as Goodwin did, or to focus exclusively on the genre. In her 2014 essay "Genre, Author, Text, Reader: Teaching Nora Roberts's *Spellbound*," Australian scholar Beth Driscoll describes the advantages of including Romance in a course on various popular literary genres, including classic detective fiction, science fiction, fantasy, espionage and legal thrillers, and antiromantic "sex-and-shopping" women's fiction, with most genres represented by at least two different texts. This "genre-based approach," she argues, invites students to "think reflexively about what textual qualities they have been taught to value. When they say a book is 'good' or 'bad,' what criteria are they using and what assumptions are they making?" (Driscoll, unpaginated). It also allows the instructor to bring multiple perspectives to each text, including a "publishing studies" angle that explores "romance's place at the cutting-edge of digital- and self-publishing developments," and it encourages students to attend both to commonalities (for example, what makes genre fiction different from capital-L Literature) and to differences (not only what makes one genre different from another, but what makes one *instance* of a given genre distinctive) (Driscoll, unpaginated). Driscoll offers an extraordinarily useful summary of a lecture designed "to introduce the genre of romance fiction, to describe the career of Roberts, and to model some close reading of *Spellbound*'s setting and its depiction of gender roles" followed by an analysis of student reactions to the book and the romance unit (Driscoll, unpaginated). (Their general "antipathy" to Romance marks a sharp contrast to the embrace of the genre among Goodwin's students two decades before and a continent away.)

A contrasting model of inclusion is offered by the coauthored "Pedagogy Report: Embedding Popular Romance Studies in Undergraduate English Units: Teaching Georgette Heyer's *Sylvester*" by Lisa Fletcher, Rosemary Gaby, and Jennifer Kloester. They dispute the idea—articulated most forcefully by Ken Gelder—that "popular fiction and Literature are antagonistic fields; they each define themselves against the other." The idea of genre, they contend, "cuts through the curtain he brings down between, to use different terms, 'lowbrow' and 'highbrow' texts" (Fletcher et al., unpaginated). The unit they describe on "Fictions of History" places Georgette Heyer's Regency romance in a context that includes canonical drama (Shakespeare's *Henry V*), a foundational text of historical romance (Sir Walter Scott's *Ivanhoe*), and two acclaimed works of literary historical fiction (J. G. Farrell's Booker-prize-winning *The Siege of Krishnapur* and Beryl

Bainbridge's *The Birthday Boys*). A pair of lectures, summarized in the essay, frames the text first as a work of historical fiction—one that draws on 19th-century historiography and on Heyer's meticulous research in primary documents from the period—and then as a highly self-conscious metafictional "romance," a love story about love stories: their readership, their authorship, and their reputation.

The strategy of "embedding" romance novels in courses on multiple popular genres, on genres that cut across the high art/pop culture divide, or on other topics (for example, women's writing, as described in Julie Dugger's "'I'm a Feminist, But . . .' Popular Romance in the Women's Literature Classroom," or American best sellers, as in a longstanding course offered by William Gleason at Princeton, or the "Reading and Screening Desire" and "Bad Romance" media studies classes taught by Katie Morrissey at the University of Rochester) allows the instructor to sidestep institutional skepticism about the Romance genre and to address student antipathy or ambivalence head-on. Indeed, Joanna Gregson's upper-division Sociology seminar "Gender and Society," taught at Pacific Lutheran University, frames its romance unit with the idea of Romance as a stigmatized genre. The co-author (with Jennifer Lois of Western Washington University) of "Sneers and Leers: Romance Writers and Gendered Sexual Stigma," a four-year ethnographic study of how this stigma is applied (by outsiders) and managed (by romance authors), Gregson asks students to choose a RITA-award-winning novel alongside the coauthored study; their goal is not to analyze the novel per se, but rather their own reaction to being required to purchase, read, and discuss it. The award-winning documentary film *Love Between the Covers*, which explores romance authorship, readers, and publishing, offers an accessible and engaging introduction to the stigma surrounding the genre, as well as to its history and to the ongoing revolution in publishing that romance has pioneered. The film's online resource guide houses supplementary materials on topics such as "The Happily Ever After—and the Tragic Ending," "Race and Romance," and "Romance in the Digital Age" to facilitate teaching with the film. (In addition, a handout of study questions and sample paper topics based on the film, "Teaching with Love Between the Covers," is available from the film's distributor, Women Make Movies: http://www.wmm.com/film catalog/study/LBTC_study.pdf.)

There is, of course, one significant drawback to "embedding" popular romance fiction in a course on some broader topic. A single unit on Popular Romance cannot explore in any detail the internal diversity of the Romance genre, either in terms of its changes over time or in terms of the proliferation of Romance subgenres at any given moment. To give students even a preliminary introduction to that diversity, a full-length course on Popular Romance may be necessary, just as it would be to teach the diversity of detective or science fiction. Although such courses remain rare, they do exist in several countries, and many have been made available to potential instructors, either as course materials or as the topic of a blog post, video interview, or essay by the instructor. German scholar Karin Heiss's essay "14 Weeks of Love and Labour: Teaching Regency and Desert Romance to Undergraduate Students," for example, details a semester-long unit that included both extensive contextual study of the publishing, marketing, author-presentation, and material culture of popular romance novels and an intensive exploration of three British books: Georgette Heyer's *Bath Tangle* (1955), E. M. Hull's *The Sheik* (1919), and Marguerite Kaye's *The Governess and the Sheikh* (2011), a Mills & Boon category romance in which the Regency and Desert subgenres intersect. Jessie Matthews has documented the thinking and corpus selection behind her George Mason University course "Why Women Read Romance" in a series of video interviews at the Popular Romance Project; the novels for this course all included Byronic "alpha" heroes, but they ranged in subgenre from Historical Fiction to Contemporary BDSM and Paranormal Romance. (Included topics: "Teaching Fifty Shades of Grey," "Busting Stereotypes," "Roots of Romance," "Tyranny of Choice," and "Teaching the Romance.") Duke University's popular romance courses, taught through its program on Creative Entrepreneurship, are aligned with a speaker series that brings romance authors, publishers, bloggers, and other industry professionals to campus. The course and series are amply documented online, with contributions from students and faculty appearing at the course blog, "Unsuitable: Conversations about Women, History & Popular Fiction" (https://sites.duke.edu/unsuitable; the course and lecture series can be followed at https://twitter.com/unsuitableduke).

Perhaps the most elaborate and varied set of romance-only courses has been taught at DePaul University in Chicago, where one to four such courses have been offered every year since 2005. They range in structure from historical surveys of the genre, beginning with *The Sheik*, to samplings of seven or eight subgenres (regularly including LGBTQIA romances), to courses on African American and/or Asian American romance, to single-author courses and 10-week senior seminars focused on individual romance novels (Laura Kinsale's *Flowers from the Storm* and Susan Elizabeth Phillips's *Natural Born Charmer*). Taught mostly by Eric Murphy Selinger in the English Department—and, more recently, by Julie Moody-Freeman of African and Black Diaspora Studies as well—these courses draw extensively on the models of literary "close reading" of romance fiction available in *JPRS*, in the essays collected in such volumes as *New Approaches to Popular Romance Fiction: Critical Essays* and *Romance Fiction and American Culture: Love as the Practice of Freedom?*, and in Laura Vivanco's accessible, student-friendly monograph *For Love and Money: The Literary Art of the Harlequin Mills & Boon Romance*. Vivanco's chapters on the "Modes" of romance, its retellings of "Mythoi" (including classical mythology and fairy tales), its frequent generic self-consciousness as "Metafiction," and its use of both local and overarching "Metaphors" frequently serve as the scaffolding for Selinger's courses, each paired with a novel or two; other courses have drawn on the "eight elements" of the romance novel detailed by literary historian Pamela Regis; have used sociologist Eva Illouz (*Consuming the Romantic Utopia*) and theorist Thomas J. Roberts (*An Aesthetics of Junk Fiction*) to frame the reading of particular texts; or have assigned a range of queer romances to explore how the conventions of popular romance do and do not change as the genre expands to include same-sex couples, polyamorous relationships, and asexual characters.

Because Popular Romance pedagogy is still a new thing in the academy, there is no consensus on a "teaching canon" for the genre. Some books and authors do seem to be iconic and get taught in multiple venues: Hull's *The Sheik* and Katherine Woodiwiss's *The Flame and the Flower* (1972) show up on multiple syllabi, as do texts by Georgette Heyer and African American novelist Beverly Jenkins, both of whom have a secure place as innovators in the genre. (Rita Dandridge's interview of Jenkins in a *JPRS* article and one in *Romance Fiction and American Culture* mentioned above are especially useful when teaching her works.) Other novels and authors, however, seem to have only a local or time-bound appeal. J. R. Ward's Black Dagger Brotherhood vampire romances, for example, were popular with instructors in the mid-2000s but seem to be taught less frequently as the ongoing series has shifted from romance into urban fantasy; Jennifer Crusie's *Bet Me* is a staple of American courses on Popular Romance, and Crusie's essays on the genre, available at her website, as well as several articles in the 2.2 issue of the *Journal of Popular Romance Studies*, supplement the novel nicely for American readers; but Australian scholar Lisa Fletcher has spoken of her difficulty in teaching the novel to students at the University of Tasmania. (They responded much better to a novel by the acclaimed Australian author Anne Gracie, whom Fletcher has interviewed at length in *JPRS*.) The increased visibility of queer romance and romance fiction by authors of color—each of which has its own substantial history—has brought these into romance teaching, and the availability of peer-reviewed scholarship on these aspects of the genre makes it possible to pair, for example, an article on "Queering the Romantic Heroine" with a novel by one of this essay's coauthors (Len Barot, who writes as Radclyffe, and Katherine E. Lynch, who writes as Nell Stark), or to match up Ann Herendeen's polyamorous (m/m/f) Regency romance *Phyllida and the Brotherhood of Philander* with one of Herendeen's several essays on writing a bisexual "alpha" hero.

An introductory bibliography of scholarship on queer romance is appended to Andrea Wood and Jonathan A. Allan's "Editor's Introduction" to the *JPRS* special issue "Queering Popular Romance" (2016), and the critical anthology *Romance Fiction and American Culture: Love as the Practice of Freedom?*

includes several essays on Romance and race, including African American and Asian American–authored romance. (The *lack* of scholarship on excellent, highly teachable romance novels can also be a spur to including them in courses, since upper-division and graduate students can then be the first to publish on them.)

Because romance novels appeal to a wide range of readers, including those who find literary fiction challenging or simply "unrelatable," the genre offers instructors an ideal opportunity to teach academic skills such as close reading and contextual analysis. The genre also offers students the opportunity to reflect on issues and choices that have an immediate bearing on their own individual and political lives. As Kecia Ali demonstrates in her recent monograph on the J. D. Robb (Nora Roberts) In Death novels, *Human in Death* (2016), romance novels can be read as novels of ideas, including ideas about vocation, friendship, violence, and political morality.

And, of course, romance novels are novels of ideas about love and relationships. Jayashree Kamblé notes that romance novels must meet "a set of conditions that allow the story to be 'romantic'" to appeal to their audience: "conditions that are constantly changing, because what is 'romantic' is always changing" (Kamble, 20). The advent of digital publishing may have led to a proliferation of popular romance authors and subgenres, but all romance novels—from the most conservative to the most radical—aim to capture and articulate what some imagined reader will find "romantic," making the genre a useful archive for tracking the multiple, often contradictory attitudes, fantasies, and social norms that make up any given moment's thought about love. Although few courses so far seem to have taken up the challenge of bringing together individual, deliberately selected romance novels—romance novels-of-ideas, in effect—with the array of philosophical, sociological, or other theoretical accounts of love that are emerging from Critical Love Studies and queer theory, this juxtaposition is quite promising, not least because romance novels so vividly capture and promulgate what Elizabeth Blake calls "amatonormativity": that is, "the assumption that a central, exclusive, amorous relationship is normal for humans, in that it is a universally shared goal, and that such a relationship is normative, in the sense that it should be aimed at in preference to other relationship types" (Blake, 88). (As Kim Castillo says in a telling moment in the *Love Between the Covers* documentary, "These novels taught me what normalcy was.") As skeptical students learn to see the interest and appeal of Romance fiction as an art form and a commercial medium, and as student fans learn to ask more skeptical questions both *of* and *with* the novels they study, popular romance courses offer instructors a valuable opportunity to change not only hearts and minds but—sometimes—lives.

Eric Murphy Selinger

Further Reading

Ali, Kecia. *Human in Death: Morality and Mortality in J. D. Robb's Novels*. Waco, TX: Baylor University Press, 2017.

Blake, Elizabeth. *Minimizing Marriage: Marriage, Morality, and the Law*. Oxford: Oxford University Press, 2012.

Crusie, Jennifer. *Essays*. http://jennycrusie.com/non-fiction/essays. Accessed June 23, 2017.

Dandridge, Rita. "Interview: Beverly Jenkins." *Journal of Popular Romance Studies* 1, 1 (2010): unpaginated. http://jprstudies.org/2010/08/interview-beverly-jenkins-by-rita-b-dandridge/. Accessed June 24, 2017.

Dixon, jay. *The Romance Fiction of Mills & Boon 1909–1990s*. Philadelphia: UCL Press, 1999.

Driscoll, Beth. "Genre, Author, Text, Reader: Teaching Nora Roberts's *Spellbound*." *Journal of Popular Romance Studies* 4, 2 (2014): unpaginated. http://jprstudies.org/2014/10/genre-author-text-reader-teaching-nora-robertss-spellboundby-beth-driscoll/. Accessed June 24, 2017.

Dugger, Julie M. "'I'm a Feminist, But . . .' Popular Romance in the Women's Literature Classroom." *Journal of Popular Romance Studies* 4, 2 (2014): unpaginated. http://jprstudies.org/2014/10/im-a-feminist-but-popular-romance-in-the-womens-literature-classroom-by-julie-m-dugger/. Accessed June 24, 2017.

Fletcher, Lisa. "Love-O-Meter." Podcast BT007. January 11, 2015. http://bookthingo.com.au/bt007-love-o-meter. Accessed June 23, 2017.

Fletcher, Lisa, Rosemary Gaby, and Jennifer Kloester. "Pedagogy Report: Embedding Popular Romance Studies in Undergraduate English Units: Teaching Georgette Heyer's *Sylvester*." *Journal of Popular Romance Studies* 1, 2 (2011): unpaginated. http://jprstudies.org/2011/03/pedagogy-report-embedding-popular-romance-studies-in-undergraduate-english/. Accessed June 24, 2017.

Frantz, Sarah S. G., and Eric Murphy Selinger, eds. *New Approaches to Popular Romance Fiction: Critical Essays*. Jefferson, NC: McFarland & Co., 2012.

Gleason, William A., and Eric Murphy Selinger, eds. *Romance Fiction and American Culture: Love as the Practice of Freedom?* Farnham, UK: Ashgate Publishing, 2016.

Goodwin, Sarah Webster. "Romance and Change: Teaching the Romance to Undergraduates." *Paradoxa: Studies in World Literary Genres* 3, nos. 1 and 2 (1997): 233–41.

Heiss, Karin. "14 Weeks of Love and Labour: Teaching Regency and Desert Romance to Undergraduate Students." *Journal of Popular Romance Studies* 5, 1 (2015): unpaginated. http://jprstudies.org/2015/08/14-weeks-of-love-and-labour-teaching-regency-and-desert-romance-to-undergraduate-students-by-karin-heiss/. Accessed June 24, 2017.

Herendeen, Ann. "The Upper-Class Bisexual Top as Romantic Hero: (Pre)dominant in the Social Structure and in the Bedroom." *Journal of Popular Romance Studies* 3, 1 (2012): unpaginated. http://jprstudies.org/2012/10/the-upper-class-bisexual-top-as-romantic-hero-predominant-in-the-social-structure-and-in-the-bedroom-by-ann-herendeen/. Accessed June 24, 2017.

Illouz, Eva. *Consuming the Romantic Utopia*. Berkeley: University of California Press, 1997.

Kahn-Leavitt, Laurie. *Love Between the Covers*. New York: Women Make Movies, 2015. (DVD video).

Kamble, Jayashree. *Making Meaning in Popular Romance Fiction: An Epistemology*. New York: Palgrave Macmillan, 2014.

Lois, Jennifer, and Joanna Gregson. "Sneers and Leers: Romance Writers and Gendered Sexual Stigma." *Gender & Society* 29, 4 (August 2015): 459–83.

Love Between the Covers: Multimedia Resource Guide. http://www.lovebetweenthecov ers.com/resource-guide-intro. Accessed June 23, 2017. (A handout of study questions and sample paper topics based on the film, "Teaching with Love Between the Covers," is available from the film's distributor, Women Make Movies: http://www.wmm.com /filmcatalog/study/LBTC_study.pdf.)

Lynch, Katherine E., Ruth E. Sternglantz, and Len Barot. "Queering the Romantic Heroine: Where Her Power Lies." *Journal of Popular Romance Studies* 3, 1 (2012): unpaginated. http://jprstudies.org/2012/10/queering-the-romantic-heroine-where-her-power-lies-by -katherine-e-lynch-ruth-e-sternglantz-and-len-barot/. Accessed June 24, 2017.

Matthews, Jessie. "Teaching the Romance." http://popularromanceproject.org/topics/teach ing-romance/. Accessed June 23, 2017.

Radway, Janice. *Reading the Romance: Women, Patriarchy, and Popular Literature*. Chapel Hill: University of North Carolina Press, 1991.

Regis, Pamela. *A Natural History of the Romance Novel*. Philadelphia: University of Pennsylvania Press, 2003.

Roberts, Thomas J. *An Aesthetics of Junk Fiction*. Athens: University of Georgia Press, 1990.

"Teaching Popular Romance." http://teachmetonight.blogspot.com/p/teaching-popular -romance.html. Accessed June 23, 2017.

Vivanco, Laura. *For Love and Money: The Literary Art of the Harlequin Mills & Boon Romance*. Tirril, UK: Humanities-Ebooks, LLP, 2011.

Themes in Popular Romance Fiction

In literary works, the theme is the underlying message or idea that the author is trying to convey to the reader. It is what the story means on a deep level. Normally these themes are universal in nature, explore human experience, and transcend cultural barriers. In other words, they are basic concepts that should resonate with readers whatever their race, ethnicity, religion, gender identification, political leaning, or social persuasion.

Not surprisingly, the overarching theme in most Romance fiction is the conviction that love conquers all. Whatever the problem, love has the answer and will help the characters resolve or deal with whatever difficulties and issues come their way. This doesn't necessarily mean that everything will be all sweetness and light or rainbows and roses, but it does mean that love will give the characters the strength to overcome all obstacles and endure. Even when there are other themes in the story, this fundamental idea almost always underlies the plot.

Closely tied to the above is another common theme, the healing power of love. Often found in romances in which the protagonists have been separated or estranged through some kind of tragedy, betrayal, or deep misunderstanding, this theme focuses on mending the relationships that were broken, aided by the power of love. This theme also is common in romances featuring individual characters wounded or damaged emotionally, and sometimes physically, by events that have nothing to do with their ultimate partners (for example, war, tragic accidents, abuse) but need healing just the same.

Because at their core premise romances are essentially stories about relationships, the importance and value of human relationships is another key theme that is completely at home in the Romance genre. Of course, the primary focus is almost always on the romantic relationship between the protagonists, but the way in which family, friends, and even strangers interact with one another and the importance of these interactions to the well-being and happiness of the characters is important to the overall tone and mood of the novel and often critical to the outcome of the story.

Although the idea that opposites attract is certainly common in the Romance genre, the broader, but closely linked, theme of differences-that-divide, and overcoming them, is much more prevalent. A classic example is the fierce enmity between the Montagues and the Capulets in *Romeo and Juliet* (not a romance, of course, but it illustrates the point); however, family feuds are only one of the many issues that can keep the lovers apart. Class, race, culture, social status, and economic differences are usually at the root of most of these problems, but the ways in which they are dealt with in the various Romance subgenres may vary. For example, social-class differences are far more common in historical romances (for example, titled hero/commoner heroine, and vice versa), while economic differences (for example, poor boy/rich girl, or vice versa) are more often found in the contemporary subgenre. By their nature, paranormal and futuristic romances often deal with race and cultural clashes (for example, human/vampire, werewolf/werecat, alien/human), and the logistical problems for characters in time travel romances are obvious. There are, of course, numerous exceptions.

While the themes above are common to the Romance genre, they aren't the only ones the genre uses. Many of the themes found in the other fiction genres are equally at home in Romance, including such classics as revenge, justice/fairness, betrayal, courage, honesty, honor, hope/optimism, persistence, loyalty, insecurity, fear, repentance, forgiveness, and guilt, to name only a few.

Some romances will have one key theme that overrides all others, and some stories will have several. But if it's a romance, the belief that love has the power to make everything better will be there in some form.

Kristin Ramsdell

Further Reading

Chelton, Mary K. "Unrestricted Body Parts and Predictable Bliss: The Audience Appeal of Formula Romances." *Library Journal* 116 (12): 44–49.

Krentz, Jayne Ann, ed. *Dangerous Men and Adventurous Women: Romance Writers on the Appeal of the Romance*. Philadelphia: University of Pennsylvania Press, 1992.

York, Rebecca. "Romance Writing 101: A Master of the Genre Takes You through the Essentials of This Popular Form of Storytelling." *Writer* 124 (12): 34–36.

Three Weeks (1907)

Three Weeks, published in England in 1907 by Gerald Duckworth, launched Elinor Glyn's career as an international celebrity and established her as the early 20th century's arbiter of romance and female sexuality. Often described as the first erotic novel written for women, *Three Weeks* outraged public opinion and became a best seller throughout Europe and the United States.

Previously popular as a writer of society novels, Glyn, in her autobiography, *Romantic Adventure*, ascribed the inception of *Three Weeks* to her husband's neglect and her own loneliness in marriage. The plot concerns the adulterous love affair between an aristocratic young Englishman and a Balkan queen who is married to a cruel king. Far from condemning adultery, the novel makes the relationship its moral compass, questioning both the sexual and moral mores of the era, particularly those associated with women and marriage.

Narrated exclusively from the hero's viewpoint, the novel begins when Paul Verdayne, the son of an English nobleman, is sent to Switzerland by his parents to forget an unsuitable young woman. Ironically, and in a complete sexual role reversal, he meets and is seduced by the older married Lady, who remains both nameless and essentially mysterious throughout the novel. The sexual imagery associated with the heroine throughout the erotic encounter is predatory, either as a snakelike being or a tiger. She begins her seduction of the virginal Paul when he discovers her reclining on a tiger skin with a rose between her teeth, an image much replicated in romance novels and films of the 1910s and 1920s. It also lent itself to much parody in popular culture references of the day, including the now-famous anonymous doggerel that asked, "Would you like to sin/With Elinor Glyn/On a tiger skin?/Or would you prefer/To err /With her/On some other fur?"

Despite the Lady's aggressive sexuality, the two lovers are established as the novel's emotional force. However, Glyn's single acquiescence to conventional Edwardian morality does not allow the heroine's sexual freedom to go unpunished. The wages of passion are death at the instigation of her tyrannical husband, although the son conceived during the three-week idyll ascends to the throne, forging a dynastic link between the lovers and celebrating the triumph of class, British imperial influence, and true love.

Despite universal condemnation of the novel, poor reviews, and a ban in some parts of England and the United States, *Three Weeks* became an international best seller, reviving the Glyn family fortunes, which had gradually been dissipated by Glyn's husband. Allied to a flair for self-promotion and a strong business acumen, it also led to Elinor Glyn's career as a commentator on all things pertaining to love and sex, which continued to flourish during the postwar world of the 1920s. The story was filmed twice during the silent era, once in 1914 and again in 1924, when Glyn was firmly established in Hollywood as both a consultant and, later, a screenwriter.

While *Three Weeks* was born out of disappointment in marriage, its importance as one of the first romance novels of the 20th century to challenge contemporary attitudes toward female sexuality makes it a landmark novel both in its own time and for the contemporary era.

Heather Cleary

Further Reading

Etherington-Smith, Meredith, and Jeremy Pilcher. *The "It" Girls: Lucy, Lady Duff Gordon, the Couturière "Lucile," and Elinor Glyn, Romantic Novelist*. London: Hamish Hamilton, 1986.

Glyn, Anthony. *Elinor Glyn: A Biography*. London: Hutchinson, 1955.

Glyn, Elinor. *Romantic Adventure*. London: Nicholson and Watson, 1936.

Glyn, Elinor. *Three Weeks*. 1907. Reprint ed. introduction by Sally Beauman. London: Virago, 1996.

Hardwick, Joan. *Addicted to Romance: The Life and Adventures of Elinor Glyn*. London: Andre Deutsch, 1994.

Thriller

See Mystery/Suspense/Thriller and Romance

Time Travel Romance

Time Travel romance is just that—romance that sweeps its characters between one time period and another and forces them to deal with the realities of living in totally unfamiliar cultures and times. In the Romance genre, this often happens through some version of the "time slip," with the characters accidentally ending up in another time with little idea of how it happened. Portals of various kinds (for example, ancient stone rings, sacred groves/wells/caves, other "places of power") and magically endowed artifacts (for example, jewelry; music boxes, snow globes, statuettes, and other *objets d'art;* books and manuscripts; swords, daggers, or other weapons) are common triggering mechanisms, and in some cases, once the characters have figured out how it all happened, they may be able to use the same means to return to their own times. As expected, adaptation to different cultures and customs is a large part of the conflict between the protagonists (imagine a contemporary woman dropped into a society where she has no rights of her own and is considered the property of her father, brother, or husband), but in romance there is the added issue of the two protagonists' being from different times and the sacrifices they must make if they are to stay together. Travel between the past and the present (in either or both directions) is most common, but characters have also moved between the present and the future, or even between multiple past or future times as well.

Some romance readers may trace the Time Travel genre from best-selling author Jude Deveraux's *A Knight in Shining Armor* (1989) or Diana Gabaldon's debut novel, *The Outlander* (1991), but time travel is not a new idea. Mark Twain took a humorous, although a not necessarily romantic, crack at it in 1889 with his classic *A Connecticut Yankee in King Arthur's Court* (originally *A Yankee in King Arthur's Court*), and H. G. Wells sent his hero into a dystopian future in *The Time Machine* (1895). Most of these early time-travel stories, and indeed much of the broader fantastic fiction scene, were dominated by male authors. However, as women joined the ranks, contributing stories that reflected a distinct "feminine perspective on plot, character, theme, structure, and imagery" (Spivak, 8–9), personal relationships, including romantic ones, gradually assumed more importance in these stories, even though they would not be considered romances. However, although she was not writing romance or time travel per se, Anne McCaffrey comes close in her Dragonriders of Pern books (beginning with *Dragonflight*, 1968*)* when she creates dragons who, with their mentally linked riders, can teleport not only between places but between times as well.

Then in 1979, June Lund Shiplett penned what is considered by many to be one of the earliest romances with a time-travel theme, *Journey to Yesterday*, and others soon followed suit. Constance O'Day-Flannery's *Timeless Passion* (1986) and its successors kept the ball gently rolling, and when best-selling historical author Jude Deveraux caught romance fans' attention with her now-classic *A Knight in Shining Armor* in 1989, Pamela Simpson added a Wild West flair with *Partners in Time* in 1990, and Diana Gabaldon launched her ongoing Outlander series with *The Outlander* in 1991 (entitled *Cross Stitch* in the United Kingdom), the subgenre took off.

The 1990s abounded with time-crossing romances, and titles like *Knight of a Trillion Stars* (1995) and *Rejar* (1997) by Dara Joy, *Memories of You* (1997) by Jane Goodger, and *After the Storm* (1996) by Susan Sizemore soon filled the shelves. The decade also saw the launch of continuing series with paranormal twists, including Sandra Hill's classic Viking series with *The Reluctant Viking* in 1994 and Lynn Kurland's enduring Macleod Family books with *A Dance through Time* in 1996. Karen Marie Moning's popular Highlander series also was inaugurated in the 1990s with her debut title, *Beyond the Mist*, published in 1999.

The subgenre continued to evolve, and some of the more recent titles were experimenting with including elements from other fiction genres—for example, *Time for Eternity* (2009) by Susan Squires includes a vampire heroine who loses her memory; *No Proper Lady* (2011) by Isabel Cooper features a fierce warrior heroine who is sent from a demon-ridden future into a Victorian steampunk world to change the past; and Melissa Mayhew's *Warrior Reborn* (2012) sends a former special ops agent with a Fae heritage back to medieval Scotland.

Unarguably, time travel romances are a niche market, but their appeal to their readers is strong and, as of this writing, shows no signs of abating.

Kristin Ramsdell

See also: Alternative Reality Romance Subgenres

Further Reading

"The Best Time-Travel Romance Novels." *Goodreads*. https://www.goodreads.com/list/show/421.The_Best_Time_Travel_Romance_Novels. Accessed May 3, 2017.

Calhoun-French, Diane M. "Time Travel and Related Phenomena in Contemporary Popular Romance Fiction." In *Romantic Conventions*, edited by Anne K. Kaler and Diane M. Calhoun-French, 100–112. Bowling Green, OH: Bowling Green State University Popular Press, 1999.

Fantasy, Futuristic, and Paranormal Romance Writers. http://romance-ffp.com/. Accessed May 5, 2017.

"Special Issue Call for Papers: The Romance of Science Fiction/Fantasy." *Journal of Popular Romance Studies*, September 30, 2016. http://jprstudies.org/submissions/special-issue-call-for-papers/. Accessed April 9, 2017.

Spivak, Charlotte. *Merlin's Daughters: Contemporary Women Writers of Fantasy*. New York: Greenwood Press, 1987.

Translations (English to Other Languages)

The increase of literacy, mostly during the 20th century, gradually turned book production into one of the most profitable contemporary industries, an industry that, as Worpole (2) characteristically notes, has since been "multi-nationalized in the process." The globalization of book markets has considerably altered book production and distribution as it changed the profile of, at least, a core agent of each literary polysystem: the readership. Before the globalization of the book markets, each book was mainly addressing a rather limited reading public, consisting mostly of readers sharing a similar linguistic and cultural background. Nevertheless, the scene dramatically changed with the continuous expansion of the books markets leading to literary books addressing a multicultural heterogeneous audience instead. This essential change highlighted the need for mediation not only between languages but also between cultures—in other words, the need for translation.

Translation is a process that encompasses much more than semantic decisions, as a translator has to take into consideration not only possible language differences and restraints between the source and the target community but also recurring clashes in terms of cultural norms, as well as power differentials between widespread and less-popular cultural groups. This is why many scholars such as Lefevre and Bassnett and Snell-Hornby have stressed the link between translation and culture, and this is also one of the two reasons why this paper adopts a cultural approach to the translation of romances. The second reason for this decision is that romances themselves are cultural products that cannot be studied in a vacuum; they need to be approached in relation to a specific cultural and historical context, without ignoring the mutual influence between the two.

In an effort to paint a comprehensive yet concise picture of the translation of romances in the 20th and 21st century, this article will try to address the translation of both category and single-title romances, including their textual and paratextual aspects, while focusing on the translational challenges presented when introducing such books into both Western and non-Western cultures.

Starting with category romance, it has to be stressed that the translation process in this case not only greatly differs from that of single-title romances but is also not translation in the strict sense of the term: the "translation'" of category romances, according to both Wirtén and Badr Al-Bataineh, is mostly adaptation, rewriting, and editing of the original text to suit the needs of a target audience. The translators are usually not only expected to reduce the length of the text by 10 percent through the elimination of selected passages, but it is left to their discretion to considerably distance themselves from the source text to produce a text that reads smoothly, fits properly into the intended sociocultural context, and, more importantly, pleases the target readership. Adopting the words of

Ewa Högberg, editor in the Swedish Harlequin offices, translation in this case can "make or break" the book (personal online communication with Wirtén).

To better explain the translator's contribution in the global distribution of category romances, it would be useful to take a closer look at the example of Harlequin romances. Harlequin's global distribution can be organized into three steps: first, Harlequin romances are produced in the English language by mostly American, British, and fewer Australian authors; second, these books are published worldwide and start catching the attention of "local Harlequin offices and/ or business with which Harlequin has a licensing agreement" (Goris, 60); the third and final stage entails the "translation" of the selected texts, which is a combination of elimination of the 10–15 percent of the original text; neutralization or, occasionally, substitution of most English cultural elements that may cause comprehension problems to the intended readership; and, in extreme cases, rewriting of certain passages. Harlequin produces only one translation per language and distributes it to all interested communities speaking the language even if there are considerable cultural differences among them; for example, a French translation is prepared in Paris and addresses both the French and Québécois audiences. For this reason, this translation has to be as culturally neutral as possible, while the various Harlequin offices will have the chance to better target their local readerships through changes in the paratextual elements of the books.

As Paizis ("Category Romances," 5), Wirtén, and Goris (60) all maintain, the shortening of the translated texts by approximately 10 percent is an editorial decision that is imposed on the translators of category romances. Goris (60) explains that what are usually cut or summarized are descriptive passages or characters' introspections. However, it could be argued that most passages that are sacrificed aim to improve the flow of the text and sustain the target readers' interest.

The same aims also motivate the elimination or substitution of culture-specific elements. As Wirtén characteristically writes for the translation of Harlequins from English into Swedish, the important thing is for the text to be "vibrant and alive, to feel 'Swedish.'" One of those cultural elements that creates the most problems is sexual scenes: following Santaemilia (119), translating sex is a highly sensitive area as it is associated with taboos, prejudices, and questions of power and authority; and thus, the explicitness of the scenes will depend on cultural preferences and/or tolerance. In Western cultures, the explicitness of the scenes depends on the editor's decisions based on his/her guess of what readers expect; in the Swedish translations, many sex scenes are shortened and made more romantic. In the French translations, Paizis ("Category Romances," 9) argues that the sexuality of the heroine is often suppressed together with any mentions of oral sex, while the Greek Harlequins have a tendency to slightly shorten, but yet remain close to, the content of the original text. However, if we examine the translations of non-Western cultures, the treatment of love scenes may be more radical, as well as radically different from culture to culture. Focusing on the Arabic translations of Mills & Boon, Badr Al-Bataineh (193) explains that the conservativeness of the Arabic culture dictates the elimination of all sexual themes, often at the expense of the narrative, as translators omit entire paragraphs without compensating for the loss. On the contrary, Shibamoto Smith's (99) analysis of Harlequins translated into Japanese, although it does not focus on love scenes per se, suggests that the translators remain relatively close to the original texts. As Shibamoto Smith stresses, the lovers portrayed in such romances are quite different from those found in Japanese books: Harlequin heroes and heroines are passionate, intense, and openly express their feelings, while Japanese society favors a moderate expressivity of emotions with a short or no declaration of love.

Nevertheless, sex scenes are only one of the cultural elements that may prove to be a minefield for translators and editors alike. Customs and conventions, food and alcohol consumption, religious connotations may all be eliminated in the translation. Badr Al-Bataineh (123) even adds dialogue to the list since translating dialogues into Arabic poses the problem of using either classical or vernacular Arabic, with the first sounding possibly unnatural and the second raising criticism from literary circles.

While the role of the text is, of course, undeniable in a novel, it is important not to forget all the paratextual elements that surround it, such as the title, book cover, introductory pages, and blurbs, which in their own way raise reader expectations and promote the book. Focusing on book covers, Paizis (*Love and the Novel*, 51) explains that they have "a double aspect—to include and exclude, to identify and differentiate," meaning that they signal what the book has to offer and what readership it addresses, a point that can be generalized to summarize the role of many paratextual elements. When a text travels from one culture to another, all these elements may be either reproduced or significantly altered, based on both cultural norms and the decisions of individual editors. For instance, Flesch (52) explains that while most of the times Greek, Korean, and French romance covers are reproductions of the English ones, occasionally they are "startlingly different." In her turn, Capelle (97) maintains that while the Dutch Harlequin editors reproduce rather faithfully the novels' introductory pages providing a short biography of the author, this element is omitted in the French translations.

Having summarized and discussed some core aspects in the translation of category romances, the rest of the paper will briefly refer to the translation of single-title romances, a subject area that appears slightly more neglected in the literature. Based on Lamprinou's work, the translation process of single-title romances differs significantly from that of category romances because the translators are not necessarily asked to eliminate 10 percent of the text. As a matter of fact, half of the translations studied present an approximately 10 percent reduction in the number of words, while the other half present a 9–10 percent increase. Focusing on the translation of emotional intensity from English into Greek, Lamprinou (227) argues that the influence of cultural norms on the translators resulted in translational shifts that bring the English texts closer to the expectations of the Greek readership: the frequent intensification of anger (for example, from "anger" in the source text into "rage" in the Greek translation) and the reduction of the emotional intensity of instances of fear reflect the way Greek romance authors present the emotional reactions of their heroes and heroines. Interestingly, even though there is a considerable power differential between the widespread English language and the less popular modern Greek, it is the Greek norms that dominate, probably because of the translators' consideration of their readership and the potential (negative) effect that too many foreign elements could have on book sales. However, this cannot be taken for granted as, based on the well-established Polysystem Theory, in such cases it would be reasonable to expect the prevalence of the cultural norms of the more "dominant" language and literature, that is, English in this case.

Regarding the translation of paratextual elements in single-title romances, Lamprinou's Greek covers are occasionally exactly the same as those of her British originals, especially when a novel has been turned into a film (for example, McEwan's [2007] *Atonement*, DeBernières's [2001] *Captain Corelli's Mandolin*), as the editors probably see it as a good advertisement for the book. In the rest of the cases, the book jackets may be completely different, while arguably still communicating the genre of the text through the choice of romantic images and pale colors.

To sum up, rendering romances from English into a plethora of other languages and cultures is not only a common and necessary practice nowadays, but it also has implications that are perhaps hard to imagine. Badr Al-Bataineh (216) argues that due to translation, the romantic novel has been imported into the Arabic culture as a new literary genre. Shibamoto Smith's (97–98) study reveals that Harlequin translations have "transformed the Japanese 'romance fiction' market," product, and reader as they introduce cultural norms that are dissimilar to these of the Japanese culture (for example, the expectation of a happy ending). Consequently, romances in translation are indeed multidimensional entities of sociocultural importance. However, surprisingly perhaps, translated romances have only recently attracted scholarly attention, with the result being relatively limited literature available on the subject. Therefore, it would be appropriate to conclude by stressing that translated romances still constitute a rich and promising academic subject that would greatly benefit from further research.

Artemis Lamprinou

Further Reading

Badr Al-Bataineh, A. "The Modern Arabic Novel: A Literary and Linguistic Analysis of the Genre of Popular Fiction, with Special Reference to Translation from English." PhD diss., Heriot-Watt University, 1998.

Benson, S. "Stories of Love and Death: Reading and Writing the Fairy Tale Romance." In *Image and Power: Women in Fiction in the Twentieth Century*, edited by S. Sceats and G. Cunningham, 103–13. London: Longman, 1996.

Capelle, A. "Harlequin Romances in Western Europe: The Cultural Interactions of Romantic Literature." In *European Readings of American Popular Culture*, edited by J. Dean and J. P. Gabilliet, 91–100. Westport, CT: Greenwood Press, 1996.

De Bernières, L. *Captain Corelli's Mandolin*. London: Vintage Books, 2001.

Flesch, J. *From Australia with Love. A History of Modern Australian Popular Romance Novels*. Fremantle, Australia: Curtin University Books, 2004.

Goris, A. "Romance the World Over." In *Global Cultures*, edited by F.A. Salamone, 59–72. Newcastle upon Tyne, UK: Cambridge Scholars, 2009.

Lamprinou, A. "A Study on the Cultural Variations in the Verbalisation of Near-Universal Emotions: Translating Emotions from British English into Greek in Popular Bestseller Romances." PhD diss., University of Surrey, 2010.

Lefevere, A., and S. Bassnett. "Introduction: Where Are We in Translation Studies?" In *Constructing Cultures: Essays on Literary Translation*, edited by S. Bassnett and A. Lefevere, 1–11. Clevedon: Multilingual Matters, 1998.

McEwan, I. *Atonement*. London: Vintage Books, 2007.

Paizis, G. "Category Romances. Translation, Realism and Myth." *The Translator: Studies in Intercultural Communication* 4, 1 (1998): 1–24.

Paizis, G. *Love and the Novel: The Poetics and Politics of Romantic Fiction*. Basingstoke, UK: Macmillan, 1998.

Romance Writers of America (RWA). https://www.rwa.org/. Accessed May 8, 2017.

Santaemilia, J. "The Translation of Sex/The Sex of Translation." In *Gender, Sex and Translation. The Manipulation of Identities*, edited by J. Santaemilia, 117–36. Manchester: St. Jerome Publishing, 2005.

Shibamoto Smith, J. S. "Translating True Love: Japanese Romance Fiction, Harlequin-Style." In *Gender, Sex and Translation. The Manipulation of Identities*, edited by J. Santaemilia, 97–116. Manchester: St. Jerome Publishing, 2005.

Snell-Hornby, M. *The Turns of Translation Studies: New Paradigms or Shifting Viewpoints?* Amsterdam: John Benjamins, 2006.

Wirtén, Eva Hemmungs. "They Seek It Here, They Seek It There, They Seek It Everywhere: Looking for the 'Global' Book." *Canadian Journal of Communication* 23, 2 (1998). http://www.cjc-online.ca/index.php/journal/article/viewArticle/1034/940. Accessed May 8, 2017.

Worpole, K. *Reading by Numbers: Contemporary Publishing and Popular Fiction*. London: Comedia, 1984.

V

Veryan, Patricia (1923–2009)

Patricia Veryan was a 20th-century author of 36 romantic adventure and mystery novels. Born Patricia Valeria Bannister on November 21, 1923, in London, she attended secretarial school and then worked for the war effort with the British military. Reportedly, she worked with David Niven in the so-called Phantom Unit, which maintained wireless contact with advance troops on the continent. She also worked for the London-based division of Columbia Pictures, as well as the U.S. Army in London, Paris, and Frankfurt. In 1946 she married Allan Berg, and they moved to the United States. They lived in California while raising a son and daughter, and Veryan worked at the University of California-Riverside while also writing her novels. Her husband died in 1980, and she later moved to Bellevue, Washington, and lived there until her own death on November 18, 2009.

While Veryan never achieved best-seller status, she was regarded by many Georgian/Regency readers as an heir to the Georgette Heyer tradition. But Veryan's novels were more adventure than romance, and more mystery than social comedy, and she herself always credited historical adventure novelist Jeffrey Farnol as the major influence on her works. Other writers whom she felt influenced her work were Heyer, Jane Austen, Eva Ibbotson, and Miss Read. In turn, a number of recent romance authors consider Veryan an influence on them, including Edith Layton, Lynn Kerstan, and Eileen Dryer.

Veryan's Four Series of Novels

According to her "unofficial" webpage (http://www.mandry.net/veryan/), Veryan was best known for four series of novels, which use 18th- and 19th-century British events as the springboards for rollicking adventure novels.

The Sanguinet Saga

In these six books set in the Regency era, the three French Sanguinet brothers seek to destabilize Great Britain by assassinating the Prince Regent. The young couples featured in each book contribute to the prevention of this plot and in the final book ally to conquer the Sanguinet brothers. These were published 1981–1987, mostly by St. Martin's Press.

The Golden Chronicles

These six books track the heroes and heroines in their quests to gather, preserve, or steal the legendary war chest that Bonnie Prince Charlie acquired for his attempt to take the throne of Great Britain. These books were published in 1985–1989 by St. Martin's Press.

The Tales of the Jewelled Men

These six books set after the Jacobite rebellion show the growing rapacity of a small group of wealthy men, allying to seek greater power through the ruination of old aristocratic families. The young couples featured in the Jewelled Men novels are engaged in foiling this conspiracy and discovering the hidden identities of the conspirators. These were published from 1991 to 1995 by St. Martin's Press.

The Riddle Series

This series of five historical mysteries features characters and stories linked to her other series. The Riddle books were published by St. Martin's Press from 1997 to 2002.

Veryan also wrote historical mystery novels under the Veryan name and romance novels as Gwyneth Moore. Her World War II novel, *Poor Splendid Wings* (1992), was, Veryan said on her fan-club page, "written out of affectionate memory for my first fiancé, an American bomber pilot killed over Germany."

Veryan's novels are known for their adventurous plots, "clean" romances, interlocking series story lines, and what Kemp called "the gradual forging of complete social worlds." Her books frequently offered glimpses of her personal preoccupations: cats, sword fighting, and classical music. The stories are generally authentic to their settings; however, she frequently featured unconventional characters, such as working women, a mixed-race heroine and hero, and several heroes with disabilities.

Alicia Rasley

Further Reading

Kemp, Barbara E., ed. "Veryan, Patricia." In *Twentieth-Century Romance and Historical Writers*, 3rd ed. London: St. James Press. 1994.

Patricia Veryan Fan Club. https://patriciaveryanfanclub.wordpress.com/. Accessed June 24, 2017. Maintained by Nancy Eads, this site includes an archive of fan-club newsletters, with personal letters from Veryan, as well as scans of Veryan's character charts and scrapbooks.

The Unofficial Patricia Veryan Website. http://www.mandry.net/veryan/. Accessed June 24, 2017. This website includes lists and reviews of Veryan's books and character trees.

Virgin Heroines

The virgin heroine is a figure closely associated with the Romance genre. She is a recognizable figure, to the extent that we might consider her an archetype. The virgin heroine is certainly not mandatory in romance fiction, and her presence has perhaps been overstated, particularly in early criticism of the Romance genre—for instance, in 1985, Juliette Woodruff wrote that in Harlequin romances, "there must be no explicit sex: the heroine must remain chaste," and quoted from a columnist who called Harlequin "virginity merchants" (Woodruff, 28), which is not especially accurate. However, it is fair to say that virgins have been historically overrepresented among the ranks of romance heroines, and the drama of defloration has been a popular plot trope.

If we trace the literary history of the virgin heroine, we can see her ancestors in figures like Samuel Richardson's *Pamela* (1740), a novel that many scholars, including Pamela Regis, see as a direct predecessor of the romance novel (Regis, 63). In this novel, the eponymous heroine has no treasure but her virginity. In a world where she might trade it for significant financial gain (which she has ample opportunity to do), Pamela maintains her virginity and does not surrender it until the correct price is paid: marriage. Her master, Mr B, realizes, after several failed attempts to rape her, that she is a "sound investment" (Dijkstra, 65–66), as her estimation of her virginity's worth signals the promise of postmarital chastity. Thus, despite the fact that she is "closer to a dairymaid than to a princess" (Harol, 11), Pamela becomes marriageable.

Other literary ancestors of the modern virgin heroine include figures like Elizabeth Bennet (particularly in contrast to her sister Lydia, who loses her virginity outside wedlock, which then has to be hastily recuperated in her marriage to Wickham) and Jane Eyre (who refuses to become Mr. Rochester's mistress after he fails to bigamously marry her). We can see here the way that notions of virginity, morality, and worth—social worth, but perhaps especially self-worth—are bound together, and this is a link that continues to be seen in more recent romance fiction. However, if we turn to the 20th century, another plot trope begins to intrude on the virgin in romance: rape.

This is, of course, not a new trope: for instance, Richardson's follow-up to *Pamela, Clarissa* (1748), dealt with the rape of the title character. But there is a key difference. Clarissa could not reconcile her virginal mind with her violated body and so died: a common fate for raped virgins in literature. But in 20th-century romance fiction, this pattern shifted, and the raped virgin became a romantic heroine. One such heroine was Diana of E. M. Hull's *The Sheik* (1919), who is kidnapped and repeatedly raped by hero Ahmed ben Hassan before they eventually fall in love. Another is Heather of Kathleen Woodiwiss's *The Flame and the Flower* (1972), who, fleeing one rapist, immediately meets another in hero Brandon. She falls pregnant and is compelled to marry him, and like Diana and Ahmed, Heather and Brandon too eventually fall in love. Both these novels were highly influential. Hull's work gave rise to a whole genre of romance novels with aggressive foreign heroes, including some of the early romances published by Mills & Boon: as jay Dixon notes, the hero of the Mills & Boon romance in the 1920s was "more likely to be an expressively passionate Latin lover than an English gentleman" (Dixon, 6). Woodiwiss's novel is widely recognized as the first erotic historical romance novel, laying the foundations for a genre that would become very popular in the 1970s and 1980s, almost always featuring virgin heroines (or, to be more accurate, heroines who were virgins at the beginning of the novel). Hsu-Ming Teo writes of such heroines that "if her virginity is forcibly taken from her, the experience is traumatic but it does not signify the end of the world for her" (Teo, 155). What this also shows is the way in which the defloration of the romance heroine had begun to be located within the narrative, as sex became increasingly important in the portrayal of love.

This is a trend that has continued in representations of virgin heroines and virginity loss into the 21st century. The rapist hero has fallen dramatically out of fashion, which means that virginity loss has increasingly become eroticized in the romance novel. The virgin does not exist in all romance novels; indeed, while she was once virtually de rigueur, this is no longer the case. She is still fairly popular in historical romances, but because her virginity is assumed by virtue of societal constraints (it is effectively the social default), it is not quite as prominent a plot point as it is in contemporary romances (McAlister). In contemporary romances, the virgin heroine has almost always chosen her virginity, and so surrendering it to the hero is an important beat in the narrative arc of their romance. This does not necessarily mean that she waits until a romantic relationship is established before she sleeps with him (although some heroines do)—for instance, in Lynne

Graham's 2009 book *Desert Prince, Bride of Innocence*, virgin heroine Elinor sleeps with hero Jasim within hours of meeting him, despite having "standards" that, for her, link sex to love (Graham, 106). However, the virgin heroine's desire (so overwhelming it causes her to forget her "standards") becomes an infallible prophet of future romantic attachment, and couples like Elinor and Jasim invariably live happily ever after.

It is sometimes assumed that virgin heroines are mandatory in the Romance genre, particularly with the widespread visibility of virgin heroine texts like E. L. James's *Fifty Shades of Grey* (2012). This is not the case. However, virgins remain popular heroines, and we might contend that the virgin heroine became an unofficial subgenre, especially of category romance, in the 21st century. We can see this in Harlequin Mills & Boon's use of "keyword titles" in the 2000s. One thing often highlighted in these titles was the heroine's virginity, using the word "virgin" as well as more euphemistic words such as "innocent," "inexperienced," "untouched," and "unworldly." (Titles like *The Italian Millionaire's Virgin Wife, His Virgin Secretary, The Tycoon's Virgin Bride, One Night with His Virgin Mistress, The Sheriff and the Innocent Housekeeper, Innocent Secretary . . . Accidentally Pregnant!, The Billionaire Boss's Innocent Bride, The Sicilian's Innocent Mistress, The Ruthless Italian's Inexperienced Wife, The Italian's Inexperienced Mistress, Untouched until Marriage*, and *Unworldly Secretary, Untamed Greek* are classic examples.) This seems to signal a market interested specifically in virgin heroines. Indeed, if we look at online reader communities, it is clear this market exists. As one commenter on website I Heart Presents (referring to Harlequin Presents) suggests, books should carry a V-mark, "not for Vegetarian but for Virgin!!" (James).

Jodi McAlister

Further Reading

Austen, Jane. *Pride and Prejudice*. 1813. Reprint ed. Ware, UK: Wordsworth Editions, 1993.

Brontë, Charlotte. *Jane Eyre*. 1847. Reprint ed. London: Penguin, 2008.

Dijkstra, Bram. "The Androgyne in Nineteenth-Century Art and Literature." *Comparative Literature* 26, 1 (1974): 62–73.

Dixon, jay. *The Romance Fiction of Mills & Boon, 1909–1990s*. London: UCL Press, 1999.

Graham, Lynne. *Desert Prince, Bride of Innocence*. London and Toronto: Harlequin, 2009.

Harol, Corrinne. *Enlightened Virginity in Eighteenth-Century Literature*. New York: Palgrave Macmillan, 2006.

Hull, E. M. *The Sheik*. 1919. Reprint ed. Sydney, Australia: Read HowYouWant, 2008.

James, Julia. Comment on "Harlequin Presents Code 5: Virgin." I Heart Presents, May 28, 2007. http://www.iheartpresents.com/2007/05/harlequin-presents-code-5-virgin/comment-page-1/#comment-1007. Accessed June 24, 2017.

McAlister, Jodi. "Romancing the Virgin: Female Virginity Loss and Love in Popular Literatures in the West." PhD thesis, Macquarie University, 2015.

Regis, Pamela. *A Natural History of the Romance Novel.* Philadelphia: University of Pennsylvania Press, 2003.

Richardson, Samuel. *Clarissa, or the History of a Young Lady.* 1748. Reprint ed. Buffalo, NY: Broadview Editions, 2011.

Richardson, Samuel. *Pamela, or Virtue Rewarded.* 1740. Reprint ed. Oxford: Oxford University Press, 2001.

Teo, Hsu-Ming. *Desert Passions: Orientalism and Romance Novels.* Austin: University of Texas Press, 2012.

Woodiwiss, Kathleen. *The Flame and the Flower.* New York: Avon, 1972.

Woodruff, Juliette. "A Spate of Words, Full of Sound and Fury, Signifying Nothing: Or, How to Read in Harlequin." *The Journal of Popular Culture* 19, 2 (1985): 25–32.

W

Websites, Romance

See Romance Blogs, Wikis, and Websites

Western Romance

The definition of what makes a western romance is not as clear and concise as it would seem. As a subset of historical romance, western romances are primarily set in the western half the United States during the 19th century. However, while post–Civil War settings do tend to dominate the subgenre, stories set during earlier, and later, periods can be included under the western umbrella.

Colonial-era stories set in what was considered the frontier of that time, such as Ohio and Kentucky, often have trademarks of 19th-century– era westerns. Likewise, Americana-style stories, such as those written by Pamela Morsi, that take place in rural, 20th-century America can also feature popular western themes and elements.

All of which begs the question, "What makes a western romance a western?" The answer is not so simple, as westerns can vary in tone, writing style, and setting. Western romances are also no longer relegated to just the historical subgenre, and westerns can include stories focused on everything from darker themes, like vigilante justice, to lighter tales centered on established, small-town life.

While frontier settings like Canada and Australia can find their way on to the western landscape, the subgenre is still primarily an American-set one. Historical western romance themes often deal with westward expansion, and stories featuring characters traveling west toward a new future, and presumably a better life, are common. This theme tends to be employed equally among heroes and heroines, ranging from heroes looking for a fresh start after the Civil War to heroines traveling west as mail-order brides.

What tends to attract romance readers to historical western settings is the potential for story conflict. Given the lack of civilization, the frontier lifestyle, and nature's elements, characters have to be strong and resilient. Heroes making their way out west naturally tend to have alpha characteristics, and likewise, heroines need to have gumption if they have any hope of living past winter. Not only do these character traits feed into the potential for internal struggle and conflict, the unpredictability of living in an environment where civilization is at a premium means that external conflict is fairly easy to come by as well.

This lack of civilization, of hero and heroine finding each other in the frontier, also means that certain societal mores and norms of the time can be bent more easily by writers. A heroine inadvertently showing her ankle is not seen as a total scandal when she needs to know how to shoot wild game to avoid starving to death during winter. Likewise, with fewer people around, with established settlements being miles away, it means a lot of forced proximity for the romantic couple. In many historical western romances, where the closest neighbor is often many miles away (and modern motor vehicles are not an option), it means plenty of alone time for the romantic couple to spend together. These forced-proximity romances are often referred to as either "road" or "cabin" romances, depending on whether the couple is traveling together or seeking shelter together. These themes lend themselves readily to western settings, and fans of both themes tend to be, in turn, fans of western romance.

Historical western romances are also ideal settings for traditional outsider heroes—heroes who skirt the edge of propriety and build upon the bad-boy mystique that intrigues so many romance readers. Native American heroes and heroes with mixed heritages are popular staples with the subgenre, and their personal experiences tend to provide plenty of potential conflict, both internal and external, for writers to explore.

However, that is not to say that all western romances employ harsh frontier settings, isolation, or outsider heroes. Established small towns also play sizeable roles within the subgenre. Heroes can often be local law enforcement—sheriffs are always popular—and heroines may have actually been born and raised out west by parents who settled in the area years earlier. This allows authors to more rigidly explore the social mores and norms of the time. Behavior that may have once been tolerated in a more life-or-death environment would be seen as unacceptable once civilization is established. Historically, this was done by women, who would naturally want to settle an area not only for their own safety but also for that of their children. As the American West was settled, it was women who established community groups, looked toward building schools, securing teachers, and bringing in permanent law enforcement, as well as building churches hopefully for permanent ministers and preachers.

This history of the establishment and civilization of the American West has also led to the natural progression and relative dominance of the western within inspirational romance. Established towns meant established meeting and community centers, which at the time meant building churches. Women worked just as hard in the home and in the fields as their husbands did, which meant there was little time for socializing. Church on Sunday would have been the only time people could not only reinforce their faith but also congregate together as a community. The sheer strength of pioneers and the drive to travel and settle the West naturally lends itself to characters with a strong core of faith.

While it is easy to think of western romances as being the sole jurisdiction of historical romance, that is no longer the case. Strong, alpha heroes have always been a staple of the Romance genre, and over the years certain archetypes have naturally risen to the forefront. This includes wealthy business magnates, sheikhs, doctors, and cowboys. The modern western romance is often referred to as "cowboy romance" because many of these contemporary stories feature modern-day cowboys and ranchers.

Cowboy heroes continue to enjoy a place in the realm of category romance, being especially popular in lines that feature strong American ties, such as Harlequin American Romance. Cowboys are also extremely popular in category suspense lines, like Harlequin Intrigue, which often features popular iconic images of western lawmen updated for modern sensibilities. There is possibly nothing manlier, more heroic, and more alpha than a hero who is not only in law enforcement but also a cowboy.

As modern conveniences have made the world a smaller place, contemporary western romances no longer mean isolation. The rise in popularity of small-town romances has naturally fed into the demand for western settings, with authors like Linda Lael Miller, Diana Palmer, and Carolyn Brown succeeding in single-title contemporaries. This has naturally led to increased reader demand for connected books and series, and the authors and publishers are only too happy to oblige. The exploration of small-town life and the endless cast of potential characters, along with common western themes, give writers plenty of terrain to explore and create.

Ultimately, the appeal of the western romance rests on the very archetypes that the Romance genre has used successfully for years. History is written by the winners, and over the course of that history, cowboys and western settlers have been viewed as strong-minded, strong-willed people. Men had to be men, or they were doomed for failure. Women had to be intelligent, strong, and resilient, or it could very well mean death. It was also an environment that meant sometimes bad things happened to good people, not necessarily through fault of their own, but because the lifestyle was that unpredictable. Along with these elements, the story of the forging of a new life and ultimately being rewarded with the genre's required happy ending make for a satisfying romantic read for the romance-reading audience.

Just as the image of a strong western hero is a given, the idea of a weak-willed cowboy is absurd. As readers, it is inconceivable to wrap our minds around such a possibility. Likewise, while countless pioneers failed to tame the wild, harsh western landscape, the idea that a romance hero will ultimately fail is not in the genre's lexicon. Despite the elements, the outlaws, and the dangerous work, romance readers know that in the end the hero will succeed. He will not only realize his ambition, but he will fall hopelessly in love with the heroine in the process.

Their sacrifices, their hard work, and the determination it requires to survive in such elements are rewarded, which at the end of the day is what the Romance genre is all about. It is about being rewarded with the greatest gift life can give you: that one person who loves and understands you, who accepts you for who you are. In western romances, that also means finding that person who shares your ambition and admires you for your strength and resilience.

Wendy Crutcher

Further Reading

Mort, John. *Read the High Country: A Guide to Western Books and Films*. Westport, CT: Libraries Unlimited, 2006.

Mosley, Shelley. "The Many Sides of Western Romances." *NoveList*. https://www.ebsco host.com/novelist/novelist-special/the-many-sides-of-western-romances. Accessed June 25, 2017.

Westerns and Romance

The two genres of Western and Romance are presented as oppositional male or female fantasies; however, even a modest comparison reveals that the two genres are nearly identical in terms of structure, characterization and theme. The Western is considered "the man's adventure" and the most "manly" of the popular genres, written about men, for men, by men. The Romance is considered "the woman's adventure," written about, by, and for women. Yet the primary distinction between the two genres is that the Western is determined by a particular time or setting whereas the Romance is driven by plot.

Both genres are supportive and subversive of the status quo. Both genres depend on a strong plot, intriguing characters, innovative ideas, a sense of discovery and wonder, and a new way to understand the human struggle.

Romance

In the Romance, the plot is fairly simple. The organizing action is the development of a love relationship. Two individuals meet and are confronted by a series of physical, social, or psychological obstacles or barriers. The conflict can be external (Saxon v. Norman, Western v. Eastern) or internal (security v. adventure, past abuse/scarring). The more difficult and intense the conflict, the more satisfying the resolution.

There may be instant attraction or instant dislike. There may be secondary elements of mystery and adventure that serve to disrupt and cement the relationship. Other characters and the setting serve to facilitate the conflict. There may be interim relationships and rivals, often more suspected than actual.

The primary action is the gradual removal of emotional barriers. As the plot progresses, the heroine comes to depend on the hero, whether wishing to or not; however, she remains free to voice her will. Convention determines that the woman eventually takes charge of domestic and purely personal spheres of human endeavor; the male's sphere is more world/business/action. He will—must—save her from physical "worldly" danger; she "saves" his soul and humanity.

In the resolution love is triumphant and permanent. The story ends with marriage or the promise of marriage, validating the whole person: female sexuality and male sentimentalism as well as domesticity and power.

The Romance novel can begin with the heroine's ambivalent feelings about her femaleness/womanhood. During the story the heroine learns to love being a woman as she experiences her journey to selfhood. This also happens in a Western as she is initially unable to adapt or defend the Western world, but learns.

The most salient characteristic in a Romance is the development of the characters and the growth of their relationship. The characters must be flawed yet sympathetic, and their flaws can be healed or dealt with. Both heroes—male and female—are equally developed in importance; men have a place in a woman's life and world, and vice versa.

Typically, Romance can incorporate a variety of issues beyond love and marriage. A variety of social issues and debates are interwoven with the basic plot: women's sexuality and eroticism, nurture versus seduction, economic and social unrest, class mobility, alcoholism, spouse abuse, terminal illnesses, physical handicaps, illiteracy, miscegenation, fidelity, and religion versus morality, to name a few.

Western

The first encounter between the hero and heroine is often fretful but establishes an awareness of the potential of each other. As the formula continues, they encounter and must overcome barriers both as individuals and as a couple. To become a couple requires the development of trust in each other and in the world (civilization) around them. The female finds strength; the male finds compassion.

The formulaic plot must pose some basic challenge to the hero and work toward his ultimate confrontation with the antagonist, usually a fistfight or shoot-out between "equals" in which the fastest, strongest man wins. The hero is able to demonstrate his superiority, and the challenge to American values is extinguished. The formula resolves into an HEA as the hero commits to civilization; he loves a girl and chooses the ideals of settled life.

Each Western ends its own story. The very location of the Western in the frontier of the 1870s–1880s is a mythic setting; it is every bit as idealistic as the literature it was to refute. The Western is mythical; it's not so much about the time and place of action as it is about the time, issues, and biases of the writer's era. The myth provides for escapism; as historical forces have moved into myth and legend, edges have become softened, transforming the Western into the stuff of romance.

The Western hero may be a cowboy, rancher, gunfighter, or marshal. He is the archetypal individualist, self-reliant, controlled, hard, silent, resourceful, intelligent, supreme in fighting skills and sexual attractiveness. The heroine is equally strong. She must be worthy of the hero. She accepts the hero's use of violence as necessary. When the hero gets the girl, it reassures the importance of the individual. *He* becomes civilized and accepts the responsibilities and limitations of a wife and family. *She* learns Western ways and values and accepts that Western ways and violence clear the way for civilization.

For the Western, the setting is the defining element: The West must be west of the Mississippi River. Usually, the timing for the Historical Western is the idealized 1870s–1880s. The most American of any setting is the West—a direction, a location, the Frontier, of which there were several—but the one most frequently identified with the typical Western is the Cattleman's or Ranching West. The broad Romance genre is not dependent upon setting, although it is important to certain Romance subgenres. For example, just as the landscape of the Western influences the characters and actions, so too does society influence the actions of the Romance, particularly in the Traditional Regency romance.

As with the structural elements, the dominant themes are also similar. Prominent themes in the Western involve the rule of law, justice, equality, and individualism. The development and significance of trust, honor, and individual integrity are essential for the character arc. The individual growth of these elements reinforces the morals and values of the dominant U.S. culture—for example, the importance of family and monogamous marriage to ensure future generations, and the necessity of providing security and safety.

The Western "began" with Owen Wister's *The Virginian*, was codified by Zane Grey, and made iconic by Louis L'Amour. Each step makes the Western more stylized and romanticized. Cowboys were chivalric, and Westerns acquired a high moral tone. "Historically, the Western represents a moment when the forces of civilization and wilderness life are in balance, the epic moment at which the old life and the new confront each other and individual actions may tip the balance one way or another, thus shaping the future history of the whole settlement" (Cawelti, *Adventure*, 192). Thus, an integral part of the Western formula is the "showdown" between villain and hero in which good will out, the threat is removed, and the tension between the savage/wilderness versus U.S. settlement/civilization is resolved. Finally, to build and continue the "new nation," the cowboy hero gets the girl and settles into honest farming or ranching.

According to Cawelti, the "real" Western must be set in a particular place during a particular historical period: "A Western must have a certain kind of setting, a particular cast of characters, and follow a limited number of lines of actions" (Cawelti, *The Six-Gun Mystique*, 2nd ed, 58). What defines the Western is not so much the plot of action or the characters but the setting: the American frontier and how that symbolic landscape influences the character and actions of the hero and heroine.

The Western is all about United States nation building. The Western hero/cowboy embodies the morals and politics on which Americans pride themselves: responsibility, duty, friendship, loyalty, courage, bravery, equality, honesty, power—and raw sexuality. The "code of the West" contains and promotes American individualism and the merits of individual freedom, self-help, private property, and democracy; the hero is a force of progress and "the people." The Western hero is violent when he needs to be but knows when to be; he doesn't seek fights, but he resorts to violence when he must. But violence is never the point; it's a ritual violence, a good or moral violence. The hero will defeat the corrupt banker or cattle baron, unite the workers, tame the land, and win the girl, giving up his guns, wandering, and philandering to settle down and begin a family. While a loner and "savage," he favors the coming of schools and churches, regulations and taxes. The hero of the ending is not the hard-bitten loner of the beginning.

Relevant Issues of Masculinity and Masculine Mythology

There's no doubt that the Western is a "man's adventure." It is made for, by, and about men, advocating and defining manhood and masculinity. Some cultural critics argue its very beginnings occurred because of the need for virility and the remasculanization of American fiction. Realist critics of the late 19th century attacked the "female sensibilities" of literature as the enemy of realism. (for example, the broad and emotional sympathy, excessive "refinement," and moral idealism common to sentimental/women's fiction.) After all, life is a struggle between differently "gifted" individuals and groups for social mastery and (limited) control over the amoral force of natural law. Heroic virtue is in the men who do the work. Violence is used to correct moral degeneration.

In the 1970s–1980s, revisionist historians redefined and reinterpreted the relationship with the West from one of "settlement" to one of "conquest." This paradigm shift is reflected in a shift in the context of the Western.

In Westerns like L'Amour's *Dark Canyon, Tall Stranger, Utah Blaine*, set in Utah, Arizona, and so forth, a drifting, lone gunman (hero) encounters "civilization" (wagon train of settlers/farmers, small rancher versus greedy banker). The hero desires only to establish his own home/ranch, but forced into defending town, he uses violence/gunplay when necessary to resolve the crisis and destroy the villain. Always a woman/heroine is involved, who trusts him and "earns" him by proving herself worthy (and Western) of him. The adventure ends with all conflicts resolved and the romantic relationship and new home established. Hope is undimmed; this is a land of new beginnings, and optimism reigns. L'Amour novels are considered the most classic of Westerns.

The iconic American characteristics so glorified in L'Amour's Westerns are every bit as integral to the popular Romance novel. Linda Lael Miller, Jodi Thomas, Kate Bridges, Joan Johnston, and a host of others who create what are, in effect, "traditional Westerns"—loner cowboy hero (bad at communicating), an honest, courageous, benevolent rancher struggling against the corrupt banker or tycoon, striving to tame the land—will eventually win the girl and settle down to begin a family. The Western Romance easily accommodates the characters, themes, action, and setting, which is usually the frontier between 1865 and 1890, although there are also many contemporary Western Romances with modern settings.

The Changing Landscape

Based on plot, action, setting, themes, and values, we can claim crossover between the two genres. While the Western tells the "man's story," the Western Romance tells essentially the same story, allowing women to participate in the "heroic struggle" of the settling of the West and extending the same mythos of the West to women. The revisionist history and moral ambiguity about sexism, racism, and the level and type of violence of the 1970s forced a sea change in attitudes about the American West from which the Western never really recovered. There was much weeping, wailing, and angst in the late 1980s and 1990s about the impending demise of the Western. (Ironically, in a little known article published in 1978, Cawelti predicted that because of the new feminisms, the popular Romance would go "the way of the Norse saga or the nickelodeon" (109).)

But Romance is much less monolithic than the Western. Joan Johnston's Romances prove the power and value of one individual's actions (cowboy as legendary guardian) and validate the American West as the land of new beginnings and regeneration. Peter Brandvold's Westerns resolve the barrier/conflict that separates the couple in an HEA. After a century of opposition, in very many ways, the distinction between the genres is disappearing. In fact, it can be easily argued that the Western Romance writers of the past three decades have assumed the mantle of the classic Westerns of Grey and L'Amour, whereas the "traditional Western" has all but disappeared. So, when is a Western not a Western? Apparently, when it's written by a woman.

Maryan Wherry

Further Reading

Cawelti, John G. *Adventure, Mystery, and Romance*. Chicago: University of Chicago Press, 1976.

Cawelti, John G. *The Six-Gun Mystique*, 2nd ed. Bowling Green, OH: Bowling Green State University Popular Press, 1984.

Cawelti, John G. *The Six-Gun Mystique Sequel*. Bowling Green, OH: Bowling Green State University Popular Press, 1999.

Frye, Northrop. *Anatomy of Criticism: Four Essays*. Princeton, NJ: Princeton University Press, 1957.

Frye, Northrop. "The Archetypes of Literature." *The Kenyon Review* 13, 1 (Winter 1951). http://www.kenyonreview.org/kr-online-issue/kenyon-review-credos/selections /northrop-frye-656342/. Accessed June 25, 2017.

Kaler, Anne K., and Rosemary Johnson-Kureck, eds. *Romantic Conventions*. Bowling Green, OH: Bowling Green State University Popular Press, 1999.

Pilkington, William T., ed. *Critical Essays on the Western Novel*. Boston: G. K. Hall, 1980.

Regis, Pamela. *A Natural History of the Romance Novel*. Philadelphia: University of Pennsylvania Press, 2003.

Tompkins, Jane. *West of Everything*. New York: Oxford University Press, 1992.

Whitney, Phyllis A. (1903–2008)

Real estate is all about location, location, location. The same thing is true with the novels of Phyllis A. Whitney. Not only do geographic settings play a key role in Whitney's books, but in many cases they also have provided a primary source of inspiration for the author. As Whitney herself states in the introduction to her last book *Amethyst Dreams*, "I have sometimes thought that if I spread a map of the

United States, blindfolded myself, and took a pin to pick out any spot on the map, I would find a wonderful place to write about" (vii).

Phyllis Ayame Whitney was born in Yokohama on September 9, 1903, to Charles Joseph and Mary Lillian (Mandeville) Whitney, Americans living in Japan. The Whitney family traveled and lived in various parts of Asia (including the Philippines), but after her father's death in 1918, Phyllis and her mother returned to the United States. In 1925, Whitney married George A. Garner. The couple would go on to have one daughter (Georgia), but in 1950, Whitney divorced Garner and married Lovell F. Jahnke.

Initially, Whitney planned on becoming a professional dancer, but after a couple of years spent unsuccessfully trying to break into the field, Whitney shifted career gears and returned to her first creative love: writing. Whitney sold her first short story after graduating from high school in Illinois, and she would eventually sell more than 100 stories to various publications. However, supporting herself as a writer wasn't easy. Whitney also worked in bookstores and libraries (including the Chicago Public Library), worked as the Children's Book Editor for the *Chicago Sun Book Week* and the *Philadelphia Inquirer* before her first book, *A Place for Anne*, was published. After writing two more books for children, Whitney turned in her first adult novel, *Red Is for Murder*, which was published in 1943. More books for children followed before Whitney returned to adult fiction with the publication of *The Quicksilver Pool* in 1955.

For the next two decades, Whitney alternated between writing one adult novel and one children's book, often setting both titles in the same geographic locale. For example, Whitney's 1958 romantic suspense novel, *The Moonflower*, is set in Japan, as is her children's book *The Secret of the Samurai Sword*, also published that year. The same thing is true with Whitney's 1964 book, *Black Amber*, and her 1957 children's novel, *Mystery of the Golden Horn*, both of which are set in Istanbul. At this point in her career, Whitney actually was better known for her children's mysteries, two of which won Edgar awards from the Mystery Writers of America. However, once Gothic novels became the new craze in publishing in the late 1960s and 1970s, Whitney began focusing on writing adult novels of romantic suspense. For the next three decades, Whitney turned out more than 20 romantic suspense novels. Whitney's last book, *Amethyst Dreams*, was published in 1997, and Whitney died on February 8, 2008.

All of Whitney's novels of romantic suspense exude a strong sense of place. Over the course of her literary career, Whitney took readers on a journey around the globe from Norway in *Listen to the Whisperer* to South Africa in *Blue Fire*. Whitney was known for extensively researching her books' settings, and the information she gathered on local customs and culture on these trips always found its way into her stories. Even when Whitney began to exclusively focus on the United

States as a setting in the latter part of her writing career, she still managed to find something unique and fascinating about each locale, be it Florida in *Dream of Orchids* or Arizona in *Vermillion*, that gave her stories their vivid sense of place.

One of the beloved literary tropes of the Gothic novel is that the heroine almost always finds herself trapped in an isolated setting, such as a castle or an estate, and Whitney used this romantic convention to great effect in many of her books. In *The Winter People*, Dina Chandler finds herself fighting for her life at High Towers, the brooding Victorian mansion on the edge of the lake where her mother-in-law drowned. When governess Camilla King receives a summons from her grandfather to return to the ancestral home in *Thunder Heights*, she realizes the gloomy mansion on the Hudson River is a place of dark shadows and dangerous secrets. In *The Turquoise Mask*, Whitney uses a hacienda in Santa Fe as the setting for her tale of Amanda Austin, who must untangle a deadly web of lies to uncover the truth about her mother's mysterious death.

The past plays a prominent role in many of Whitney's romantic suspense novels. As the author herself states in an article she wrote for *Writer* magazine, "Look into your characters' pasts. Since none of our characters leap into existence full blown but grow out of events that have shaped them, it pays to look into the past" (2008). Thus some prior event, such as a long-standing family feud, an unexpected death or disappearance, or an unresolved mystery, becomes the catalyst that sets many a Whitney plot into motion. For example, in *Spindrift*, the book's heroine, Christy Moreland, returns to the Newport estate where she grew up to find out the truth about her father's death years earlier. In *Rainsong*, Hollis Sands knows her husband, Ricky, is dead, but somehow she keeps hearing someone who sounds exactly like Ricky singing the song she wrote exclusively for him. Carol Hamilton, the heroine in *Emerald*, discovers a long-ago affair between her great-aunt Monica Arlen and movie star Saxon Scott that has repercussions in her own life in Palm Springs. Hallie Knight is summoned to Topsail Island in North Carolina by Captain Nicholas Trench, who wants Hallie to look into the mysterious disappearance of his granddaughter (and Hallie's old college friend) Susan in Whitney's *Amethyst Dreams*. It is only by solving these old mysteries that the heroines in Whitney's novels can ensure a happy romantic ending for themselves.

Whitney's literary career spanned five decades, and in that time she wrote 76 novels, as well as several books and numerous articles on the art and craft of writing. Whitney's romantic suspense books were published in 24 different languages, and many secured a place on the *New York Times* best-seller list upon publication. Whitney's novels were read and loved by both mystery fans and romance readers, as is evidenced by her securing a spot in the Romance Writers of America's Hall of Fame, as well as being awarded the title of Grandmaster by the Mystery Writers of America. Those searching for the key to Whitney's success with readers will find that it is really quite simple: Whitney knew the power of a good story, and she consistently delivered captivating tales of danger and desire.

John A. Charles

Further Reading

Macdonald, Gina. "Phyllis A. Whitney." In *Contemporary Popular Writers*, edited by Dave Mote. Detroit: St. James Press, 1997.

Mussell, Kay. "Phyllis A. Whitney." In *St. James Guide to Crime and Mystery Writers*, 4th ed, edited by Jay P. Pederson 1051–3. Detroit: St. James Press, 1996.

Phyllis A. Whitney: The Web Site. http://www.phyllisawhitney.com. Accessed June 25, 2017.

Stevenson, Nancy. "Phyllis A. Whitney." In *Twentieth-Century Romance and Historical Writers*, 3rd ed, edited by Aruna Vasudevan, 712–13. New York: St. James Press, 1994.

Whitney, Phyllis A. *Amethyst Dreams*. 1997. New York: Fawcett, 1998.

Whitney, Phyllis A. " Ten Ways to Cure the Midnovel Blues." *The Writer*, October 2008, 22–23.

Wikis, Romance

See Romance Blogs, Wikis, and Websites

Winsor, Kathleen (1919–2003)

The daughter of Harold Lee and Myrtle Belle (Crowder), Kathleen Winsor was born on October 16, 1919, in Olivia, Minnesota. Winsor grew up in Berkeley, California, and later attended the University of California at Berkeley, where she met and married UC football star Robert John Herwig. While pursuing her degree, Winsor also worked part-time as a sports journalist for the *Oakland Tribune* and later as a receptionist for the same newspaper. Winsor completed her BA in 1938, the same year that she lost her job at the newspaper due to staff cuts.

Winsor was inspired to begin writing *Forever Amber* while her husband was working on his senior thesis on Charles II. Herwig joined the U.S. Marine Corps when World War II began, and while he was off in the Pacific fighting the enemy, Winsor was back home, reading every book she could find on the Restoration era. Ultimately, Winsor spent five years poring over a vast array of fiction and nonfiction books—Winsor later claimed to have read at least 356 books during her years of research, including Daniel Defoe's *Journal of the Plague Year*—before writing her first draft of *Forever Amber*. Successive drafts that ran close to 2,500 pages were eventually whittled down into the 972-page book published by Macmillan in 1944.

Forever Amber is the tempestuous tale of orphaned Amber St. Clare, who uses her wits and beauty to survive and thrive in Restoration England. While Amber enjoys her many, many romantic liaisons during her long run as actress-turned-mistress, including a romp with King Charles II, her heart remains true to nobleman Bruce Carlton. Sixteen-year-old Amber first meets Bruce when he rides through the small village of Marygreen where she lives. After he enjoys her considerable charms and claims her virtue, she convinces him to take her with him to London; but once there, Bruce abandons now-pregnant Amber, who must survive by using the only tools at her disposal: her wits, her body, and her considerable skill at using both. Those gifts will eventually take her from being a prisoner in Newgate to nobility. Obstacles, both man-made and natural, keep Amber from ever being with Bruce, though she does nurse him when he is struck down during the Great Plague. The book ends with Amber's sailing off from England to Virginia in the mistaken hope of being reunited with Bruce.

Forever Amber was an immediate literary sensation, selling 100,000 copies in the first week it was published, and going on to sell more than 3 million copies over the following decades. The book's vividly detailed setting, as well as Winsor's skillful integration of real historical personages such as Charles II and Nell Gwyn into the plot, brought the story of Amber to life. However, it was the soap-opera and sexually promiscuous plight of the novel's impetuous, ambitious, and cunning heroine (whom some critics compared to another popular but less morally loose literary protagonist of the time, Margaret Mitchell's Scarlet O'Hara) that kept millions of readers racing through the pages of the doorstop-sized novel.

"Adultery is not a crime, it is an amusement," Amber confides to another character in *Forever Amber*, thus clearly demonstrating she is a gal who is willing to do whatever it takes to succeed in life. Amber's willingness to continually trade her body for material gain did not go unnoticed by many readers, and *Forever Amber* was banned in Boston for being "obscene, indecent, and impure" in 1945, despite the fact that the descriptions of the love scenes were really not explicit. However, it was not so much what Amber did in bed but rather the number of people with whom she did it that stirred up the wrath of those with delicate literary sensibilities. The novel was eventually censored in 14 different states, ironically creating even more of a demand from readers for the "naughty" novel. Legal battles over the "bawdy" book ended on March 10, 1947, when a judge ruled that *Forever Amber* was not obscene, stating "the book by its very repetitions of Amber's adventures in sex acts as a soporific rather than an aphrodisiac." In October 1948 the Massachusetts Court of Appeals upheld the Superior Court's ruling, thus effectively putting the issue of *Forever Amber*'s immorality to bed permanently. However, the United States was not the only country to take exception to *Forever Amber*. Australia had issues with it as well, and from 1945 to 1958 the book was prohibited from being imported into the country.

Of course, the popularity of *Forever Amber*, which would spend 75 weeks on the *New York Times* best-seller list, attracted the attention of Hollywood even before the first copy of the book arrived in bookstores, creating a bidding war among the studios, with the screen rights ultimately going to 20th Century Fox for a record $200,000. As written, the story would never get past the censors, so the screenplay whittled down the multitude of Amber's lovers to the more respectable but still shocking (for the times) figure of four. The studio added a prologue to the movie that informed viewers "the wages of sin were death," and an epilogue in which Bruce lamented to Amber that they had caused enough unhappiness and begged God for forgiveness for their sins. Despite some early cast changes—English actress Peggy Cummins was dumped in favor of Linda Darnell, and director John Stahl was replaced by Otto Preminger—as well as the vociferous objections by groups such as the National League of Decency, the movie version was a success.

Winsor, whose own beauty—much to the consternation of some jealous, less pulchritudinously endowed fellow authors—was said to rival that of her heroine Amber, divorced Herwig in 1946. Following in the footsteps of Hollywood beauties Lana Turner and Ava Gardiner, Winsor became the fourth wife of bandleader Artie Shaw, whom she divorced less than two years later. Another marriage would follow, with Winsor eventually ending up wed to lawyer and politician Paul A. Porter. After the publication of *Forever Amber*, Winsor went on to write seven more books, including *Star Money* published in 1950, an apparent roman à clef about a beautiful author whose first novel, an 18th-century-set historical novel featuring an independent heroine, becomes an overnight best seller. More novels, including *The Lovers, America with Love, Wanderers Eastward, Wanderers West, Calais*, and *Jacintha*, followed. Winsor's final book, *Robert and Arabella*, was published in 1986. Unfortunately, none of Winsor's successive literary efforts ever matched the success—both financial and critical—Winsor received for *Forever Amber*. Winsor died on May 26, 2003, in New York City.

John Charles

Further Reading

Clarke, Tracey. "Forever Amber." *Banned*. November 7, 2013. http://blog.naa.gov.au /banned/2013/11/07/forever-amber/. Accessed April 12, 2017.

Homberger, Eric. "Kathleen Winsor." *The Guardian*, June 3, 2003.

Rourke, Mary. "Kathleen Winsor, 83: Wrote Bestseller *Forever Amber.*" *Los Angeles Times*, May 31, 2003: B23.

Women's Fiction and Romance

Women's fiction is a catchall term for fiction that specifically appeals to female readers. "Women's fiction," as a category or genre, reaches into all the genres of fiction, overlapping many genres and encompassing many time periods. It also does not hold to just one style—the books can be funny, tragic, literary, or gritty. There are several factors that make a book women's fiction rather than general fiction, as well as some key differences between women's fiction and Romance.

The common thread in women's fiction is that the central character (or characters) is female, and the main thrust of the story is something happening in the life of that woman—as opposed to the overarching theme being a romance, for example. These are novels that explore the lives of female protagonists, with a focus on their many-layered relationships with spouses, parents, children, friends, and community. Overall, emotions and relationships are the common thread among books that can be classified in this genre. The woman is the star of the story, and her emotional development and journey drive the plot.

The primary appeal elements of women's fiction are character and story line. Because women's fiction novels focus on relationships, characters are of the utmost importance in these novels. Character is a huge appeal element because readers identify with women's fiction characters. When a reader picks up a women's fiction novel, she is looking for a sense of recognition—feeling as though she is that character, she knows that character, or she understands just what that character is going through.

Story line is hard to pin down, since there is a wealth of different stories and plots that women's fiction takes on. For example, many women's fiction novels revolve around friendships and other important relationships, and those relationships play out over many different plot lines. Other novels may concentrate on a woman's work or career, so the story is very focused on the details of work life. Many women's fiction novels are family stories, with myriad plots that can go along with the personalities that make up various families. Other novels still fall under the classic term "domestic fiction," concentrating on a woman's place in her surroundings, although the range of those surroundings is certainly quite broad in women's fiction—from East Coast skyscrapers to West Coast beaches and all points in between.

Finally, mood/tone cannot be discounted, although it is not usually the main appeal factor, and it's very hard to pigeonhole women's fiction by mood. These novels can be laugh-out-loud funny or desperately sad, and they can be sentimental or soap-opera dramatic. But when discussing mood/tone as it relates to women's fiction, it's interesting to note that there is a very strong emotional appeal in women's fiction. In addition, pacing varies widely from book to book, as do language and setting. It's very hard to pin down a women's fiction book based on these elements alone.

To understand the variety of books that fall under women's fiction, the following is a short list of styles that are found under the women's fiction umbrella:

Chick Lit: Distinguished by its humor—wisecracking characters or ridiculous situations, usually involving work or dating—Chick Lit offers fun, entertaining reading. This type of book's aim of eliciting a response of "I'm exactly like that" or "That just happened to me!" strikes a chord with women in their twenties and thirties who want to be reassured that they are not alone in screwing up their lives—or that screwing up doesn't preclude a happy ending. These funny, light, romantic novels appeal to women readers of all ages and life stages, even though they tend to feature young working women making their way in a big city. Chick Lit took the world by storm in the late 1990s. Partially due to oversaturation, and partly due to a maturing readership, the trend started to fade a bit by the mid-2000s. However, the natural progression of being single in the big city is to be married in the suburbs, then trying your best as a working mom and wife, and so on. Thanks to this progression, Chick Lit has matured, and to most readers the term now means any light, romantic contemporary women's fiction novel.

Ensemble Fiction: These stories feature a cast of characters—there may or may not be one "main" character because sisters, friends, coworkers, and the like all share starring roles in the story. Readers enjoy these ensemble stories because they can easily find a character within the group that they identify with, or they can see their friends in the cast of characters.

Gentle: Many readers appreciate gentle fiction, those stories that contain little strong language, explicit sex, or violence and have happy, satisfactory endings. A fair amount of women's fiction meets these criteria.

Humor: Humorous contemporary women's fiction appeals to readers looking for something light and entertaining. Humor in women's fiction runs the gamut from adorable Southern wit to goofy British froth. A large number of Chick Lit novels also qualify as humorous.

Issue-Driven Fiction: These are heavy books about heavy issues. Full of drama, they often feel like "ripped-from-the-headlines" stories. Issue-driven novels have always been with us, across many genres and often found in general fiction. The continued popularity of book clubs, in general, keeps the demand high for issue-driven fiction, particularly issue-driven women's fiction. Typical family problems will seem like *nothing* after reading these books, which is what a large part of the appeal is. Controversial issues abound, and the authors tend to pull no punches. Readers looking for issue-driven women's fiction are often looking for something that packs an emotional wallop, something that they can sink into and find themselves absorbed in.

Another good way to understand the breadth of women's fiction is by taking a look at some of the benchmark authors and their writing styles.

- **Elizabeth Berg**—classic, general women's fiction
- **Barbara Taylor Bradford**—classic, sagas
- **Barbara Delinsky**—started out writing romance, now writes more issue-driven women's fiction
- **Emily Giffin**—contemporary women's fiction, featuring modern relationships
- **Jane Green**—contemporary women's fiction, modern relationships, her early books are fun and frothy British chick lit
- **Kristin Hannah**—started in romance and is now a grand master of the tear-jerker, romantic storylines
- **Jodi Picoult**—queen of the issue-driven novel
- **Nora Roberts** (also writes romance and mystery)—a prolific writer of many books under many styles
- **Danielle Steel**—another prolific grand dame
- **Jennifer Weiner**—character-driven, contemporary women's fiction

Because love and romance may be present in women's fiction, what makes this genre different from romance? Characters do fall in love in a large percentage of women's fiction novels, and boyfriends, husbands, and lovers show up as main characters as well. Here are some key elements that differ between women's fiction and romances:

- In women's fiction, a lover may be waiting for the heroine of these novels at the end of her journey, but that person does not usually get equal time or equal depth to (usually) his internal journey during the course of a book.
- In romance fiction, there is the expectation of a "happily-ever-after" ending. That expectation does not exist for women's fiction.
- In a romance novel, a happy ending generally means that the love relationship is a success; in women's fiction, a happy ending might mean something entirely different—the protagonist escapes a bad relationship, mends fences with a dysfunctional family, or starts a successful business, for example.

In short, while women's fiction often incorporates romantic elements, there is more to the story than the love interest or sexual relationship. Not to put too fine a point on it, every single romance novel contains a romance, but there are many women's fiction titles that do not have any romantic piece at all. Yet there is a great deal of crossover appeal between the two genres. Readers are looking for a good story, one that they can relate to or get lost in, and both genres fill the bill.

Rebecca Vnuk

Further Reading

Craig, Lisa. "Women's Fiction vs. Romance: A Tale of Two Genres." *Writing-World.com.* http://www.writing-world.com/romance/craig.shtml. Accessed June 25, 2017.

Sambuchino, Chuck. "Agent Scott Eagan On: Romance vs. Women's Fiction." *Writer's Digest,* January 5, 2010. http://www.writersdigest.com/editor-blogs/guide-to-literary -agents/agent-scott-eagan-on-romance-vs-womens-fiction. Accessed June 25, 2017.

Vnuk, Rebecca, and Nanette Donohue. *Women's Fiction: A Guide to Popular Reading Interests.* Santa Barbara, CA: Libraries Unlimited, 2013.

Woodiwiss, Kathleen E. (1939–2007)

Kathleen E. Woodiwiss was born Kathleen Erin Hogg in Alexandria, Louisiana, on June 3, 1939. Woodiwiss was the youngest of eight children. At the age of 17, she married Ross Eugene Woodiwiss in 1956 and had three sons. She died of cancer on July 6, 2007, in Princeton, Minnesota.

Woodiwiss met her husband at a sock hop at age 16 while he was serving in the Air Force. Once they married, his Air Force career took them overseas to Japan. While living in Japan, Woodiwiss tried a career as a model in Tokyo. After Japan, the Air Force moved the family to Topeka, Kansas; the family eventually settled down onto the 100-acre farm, Tanglewood Manor, in Princeton, Minnesota. Ross Woodiwiss died in 1996.

While Woodiwiss may have been the godmother of the modern historical romance novel, she lived a very normal life in Minnesota. Woodiwiss was considered a very private person and was modest about her literary life and, in fact, considered herself a born-again Christian. She was more likely to be found at her sons' high school football games than at social engagements.

While living in Kansas, Woodiwiss began writing her first novel and sent it out to established hardcover publishers in 1968. Many rejection letters soon followed. Next she tried the paperback publishers, and working in alphabetical order, sent her novel to Avon. Nancy Coffey, a senior editor at Avon, looking for something to read over a long weekend, pulled Woodiwiss's novel from the slush pile. Coffey later said that "I couldn't stop reading it. She was such a natural storyteller. In this business you very rarely come across someone who keeps you turning the pages"

(Falk, 330). Because it was published in paperback format, Woodiwiss's novel was available in drugstores and supermarkets, places where women shopped. Additionally, Avon gave Woodiwiss the full promotional treatment for *The Flame and the Flower*, which was unheard of at the time for a new writer.

Her first novel, *The Flame and The Flower*, was published in 1972, a time when shorter category or Gothic novels were what was mostly available. Woodiwiss's first novel is credited with starting the subgenre of historical romance novels that were lush, sweeping sagas set in exotic locations. Dashing heroes, beautiful heroines, excitement, adventure, and sex were a hallmark of Woodiwiss's books. Woodiwiss didn't limit herself to just one period in history; her novels featured settings from the Norman Conquest through the American Civil War.

In *The Flame and the Flower*, the focus of the story was on the two main characters, Heather and Brandon, with one main plot, the romance between them. Of her 13 novels, three focus on the Birmingham family, first introduced in *The Flame and the Flower*. The novels included in the Birmingham family series are *The Elusive Flame*, featuring Heather and Brandon's son Beauregard with the heroine Cerynise, and *A Season Beyond a Kiss*, featuring Heather and Brandon's son Jeffery, the brother to Beauregard, with the heroine Raelynn.

Woodiwiss's books involve a strong heroine placed in difficult circumstances and forced to make difficult choices. The hero is the prototypical alpha male who knows he's always right and often makes bad choices toward the heroine due to his stubborn nature. While the "happily ever after" is never in doubt, the journey is often complicated by the decisions made by both the hero and the heroine. It's the bad decisions, usually a "big misunderstanding," that create the tension in the book.

One of the most revolutionary elements of *The Flame and the Flower* and all her novels that followed was Woodiwiss's detail in describing sex scenes. In the Gothics and category novels of the time, if sex was included at all it was "sweet" or referred to in obscure ways. In many of the early Harlequin and Mills & Boon works, the heroine was a virgin and stayed that way throughout the story. If the heroine had sexual experience, it was very limited and usually considered unsatisfying. Woodiwiss began the trend of graphic and flowery descriptions of sex. Her descriptions of sex seemed to inflame the critics of romance novels who often called her work pornographic. Woodiwiss herself was annoyed when confronted with the pornography label. In a 1977 interview with *Publishers Weekly*, Woodiwiss stated, "I'm insulted when my books are called erotic. . . . I believe I write love stories. With a little spice" (Stuttaford).

Controversy over her sex scenes, as well as her characters, has plagued Woodiwiss and the larger Historical Romance subgenre for decades. Depending on who was reviewing her novels, the female characters were either strong and powerful or embodied the female stereotype of submissiveness. Many critics overlooked the fact that the heroines were often considered the intelligent equal of the hero and were much more emotionally evolved. It is the love of the heroine for the hero that eventually turns him from a brooding scoundrel into a man worthy of the heroine's love.

The most controversial of Woodiwiss's elements is her use of rape. In many of her earlier works the heroine is raped by the hero, occasionally repeatedly. In the 30 years after the publication of *The Flame and the Flower* there has been much literary criticism and theoretical work regarding rape in historical romance novels. Some argue that a female character who survives and thrives regardless of circumstances and goes on to win the hero is a fighter; that she "becomes a fully developed sense of herself as an individual, not defined by sex, marriage, or family lineage" (Thurston). In turn, other critics argue that the romance novel continues to celebrate the patriarchal society ruled by men.

Reviews of Woodiwiss's books are split. At the time of initial publication, most reviewers mentioned the author's extreme popularity and large fan base and then focused on the detailed descriptions of both characters and action found in her books. Some of her books do not stand the test of time for a modern reader. The "purple prose," the long descriptions, and the uber-alpha hero may not be welcome to the modern romance reader. For every positive review of her works, there can be found an equally negative review. The online romance website All About Romance (http://www.likesbooks.com/) provides a wonderful example of conflicting reviews. Two online reviewers read *The Flame and the Flower* in 1998, the 25th anniversary of its publication, with one reviewer giving the book an A rating and the second reviewer giving the book a D.

In 1988, the Romance Writers of America awarded Woodiwiss the Lifetime Achievement Award, then called the Golden Treasure Award, "presented to a living author in recognition of significant contributions to the romance genre" (RWA Nora Roberts Lifetime Achieve Award). Over her lifetime, over 36 million copies of Woodiwiss's books found their way into the hands of readers. All her works were listed on the *New York Times* best-seller list, and all of her novels still remain available in print.

Novels

Everlasting, 2007
The Reluctant Suitor, 2003
A Season Beyond a Kiss, 2000
The Elusive Flame, 1998
Petals on the River, 1997
Forever in Your Embrace, 1992
So Worthy My Love, 1989

Come Love a Stranger, 1984
A Rose in Winter, 1982
Ashes in the Wind, 1979
Shanna, 1977
The Wolf and the Dove, 1974
The Flame and the Flower, 1972

Sarah Sheehan

Further Reading

Breu, Giovanna. "Romance Writer Kathleen Woodiwiss Is Passionate about Horses—and Happy Endings." *People Magazine*, February 7, 1983, 75.

Falk, Kathryn. "Kathleen Woodiwiss." *Love's Leading Ladies*. New York: Pinnacle Books, 1982.

Fox, Margalit. "Kathleen Woodiwiss: Novelist, Dies at 68." *New York Times*, 12 July 2007, B7.

Hinnant, Charles H. "Desire and the Marketplace: A Reading of Kathleen Woodiwiss's The Flame and the Flower." In *Doubled Plots: Romance and History*, edited by Susan Strehle and Mary Paniccia, 147–64. Jackson: Mississippi University Press, 2003.

"Kathleen E. Woodiwiss." *Fantastic Fiction*. https://www.fantasticfiction.com/w/kathleen-woodiwiss/. Accessed June 25, 2017.

"Kathleen E. Woodiwiss." *HarperCollins Publishers*. https://www.harpercollins.com/cr-103847/kathleen-e-woodiwiss. Accessed June 25, 2017.

Klemesrud, Judy. "Behind the Best Sellers." *The New York Times Book Review* vol. 84, 4 (November 1979): 52.

Petersen, Clarence. "A Tender, Wicked, Sweet, Savage Saga of Money and Romance." *Book World*, July 9, 1978.

Radway, Janice. "Kathleen E. Woodiwiss." In *Twentieth-Century Romance and Historical Writers*, edited by Aruna Vasudevan, 729–30. London: St. James Press, 1994.

"RWA Nora Roberts Lifetime Achievement Award." *Romance Writers of America*. https://www.rwa.org/p/cm/ld/fid=543. Accessed June 25, 2017.

Stuttaford, Genevieve. "PW Interviews." *Publishers Weekly* vol. 211 (30 May 1977): 6–7.

Thurston, Carol. *Romance Revolution: Erotic Novels for Women and the Quest for a New Sexual Identity*. Urbana: University of Illinois Press, 1987.

Wuthering Heights (1847)

Written by Emily Jane Brontë and published in December 1847 under the pseudonym Ellis Bell, *Wuthering Heights* is a classic Gothic novel of love, loss, and revenge that still fascinates readers today. Troubled, conflicted characters struggle with themselves and one another in a dark, intensely compelling story that is as stark and haunted as the isolated, windswept moors on which it is set.

The story begins when Mr. Lockwood, a wealthy man who has rented Thrushcross Grange, a house on the moors, goes to nearby Wuthering Heights to call on the landlord, Heathcliff, only to be snowed in and forced to the spend the night. But an eerie, frightening dream alarms him, and when he returns to the Grange, he asks Nelly, the housekeeper, to tell him more about the unusual people at Wuthering Heights, which she does in great detail.

Heathcliff, an orphan on the streets of Liverpool, was adopted as a young boy by the Earnshaws, the family that owned Wuthering Heights, and was raised with the family's two children. He and the daughter, Catherine, bonded and became fast friends, but the son, Hindley, was resentful.

Things become more difficult for Heathcliff when Mr. Earnshaw dies and Hindley, now married, inherits the manor and relegates him to the role of servant; the situation gets even worse when Heathcliff and Catherine become involved with the neighboring Linton family, who live at the Grange. Their acceptance of Catherine and rejection of him further enhances Heathcliff's feeling of isolation and nonbelonging. Catherine's engagement to Edgar Linton and a partially over-heard conversation send Heathcliff packing, and when he returns three years later, now a wealthy gentleman, he finds Catherine in an unhappy marriage.

Complications mount as Heathcliff moves in with Hindley and his son, Hareton, and he soon marries Isabella Linton, Edgar's sister. Then Catherine dies while giving birth to a daughter, Cathy; and torn by hatred and grief, Heathcliff sets out to destroy Edgar and anyone else who gets in his way.

After Catherine's funeral, Heathcliff and Hindley fight viciously, and es-tranged from her brother, Edgar, and angry with Heathcliff, Isabella leaves for London, where she gives birth to a son, Linton. Hindley, a serious drinker, dies soon after, leaving Heathcliff and Hareton at Wuthering Heights and Edgar and Cathy at the Grange with no communication between the two families.

Thirteen years later, Edgar is called to London by the dying Isabella to bring her son, Linton, back to the Grange. While he is gone, Cathy, who has been re-stricted to the Grange grounds all her life, meets her cousin Hareton while on a forbidden excursion in search of a legendary fairy cave, and Nelly, who is in charge of her while Edgar is gone, finds her at Wuthering Heights. When Edgar returns with Linton, a weak, sickly child, Heathcliff claims Linton and insists he live at Wuthering Heights, primarily as a means of revenge against Edgar.

Three years later, Cathy meets Heathcliff and Hareton on the moors and goes to Wuthering Heights where she meets Linton, taller but still a whiney, unpleasant boy, again. When Cathy tells her father, Edgar, about the meeting, he forbids her to see Linton again; she doesn't understand and begins a secret correspondence with him, which Nelly secretly disrupts. Some months later, Cathy meets Heathcliff, who secretly wants Linton and Cathy to marry to further his revenge, so encourages her to visit Linton, which she does out of guilt. Cathy soon ends up nursing her ailing father during the day and sneaking out to Wuthering Heights to nurse the sickly Linton at night. Eventually, Nelly finds out and tells Edgar, who forbids Cathy to go to Wuthering Heights. He does, however, agree that Cathy and Linton can meet on the moors—with Nelly in attendance—but Cathy worries about Linton's health, which seems to be declining.

Heathcliff, concerned that Linton will die before he and Cathy can be married and thus foil his plans to further ruin Edgar, lures her and Nelly back to Wuthering Heights and imprisons her until she and Linton are wed. With Linton's help she escapes and returns home to be with her father as he dies. Eventually, Heathcliff, as her father-in-law, requires Cathy to return to Wuthering Heights, and she cares for Linton until he dies.

As the story winds down, Cathy and Hareton draw closer, and their future together seems assured. Heathcliff realizes that his plans for revenge are no longer important. He only wants to be with Catherine, who has been haunting him throughout the story. In the end, Heathcliff dies peacefully, although there are rumors that he and Catherine haunt the moors.

Clearly, *Wuthering Heights* is not a romance by today's definition; but just as *Gone with the Wind*, another classic that fails the "happy ending" test, gives us the fiery, independent, strong-willed, but not necessarily "good" heroine, so *Wuthering Heights* provides the dark, inwardly tormented, and brooding (although cruel and heartless, in this case) hero so common to the modern Gothic—and occasionally historical—romances. This, in addition to the windswept moors, the isolated estates, and the other mysterious, ominous, haunting elements—supernatural and otherwise—are classic components of today's Gothic romances, making *Wuthering Heights* an important novel with strong ties to the Romance genre.

Kristin Ramsdell

Further Reading

Dunn, Richard J., ed. *Wuthering Heights: The 1847 Text, Backgrounds and Contexts, Criticism*, 4th ed. New York: Norton, 2003.

Fegan, Melissa. *Wuthering Heights*. New York: Continuum, 2008.

Wuthering Heights. https://archive.org/stream/wutheringheights01bron#page/n5/mode/2up. Accessed July 2, 2017.

Y

Young Adult (YA) Romance

The young adult years, typically defined as between the ages of 12 and 18, witness the transition between childhood and adulthood. Two major components of that transition are negotiating romantic relationships and dealing with the emergence (or reemergence) of sexuality. It is somewhat surprising, then, to discover that it was not until the 1980s that books specifically marketed as "romances" were published for teens. But romance has often been a key component of novels published for adolescents, whether they were labeled "romance" or not. To discover the history of young adult romance, then, requires expanding the definitions of romance, taking into consideration the different needs of the young adult audience.

As Carolyn Carpan suggests, while adult readers often turn to romance as a refuge or diversion from everyday life, romance for teens is often a far more serious business. For many adolescents, real-life romance is *terra incognita;* fictions that feature romantic relationships can act not just as escape but also as guide (xv). In recognition of this difference, Carpan argues that young adult romance should not just be defined by its central love story but should also focus on the new or emergent experience of love and/or sex. Kristin Ramsdell suggests that a definition should also include YA's emphasis on coming-of-age, a characteristic not found in other genres of Romance (208).

Novels written during the 19th and early 20th centuries that featured adolescent protagonists, such as Charlotte Mary Yonge's *The Daisy Chain*, Louisa May Alcott's *Little Men*, and the later volumes in L. M. Montgomery's Anne of Green Gables series, often included plotlines of love and courtship. Such books were intended for mixed audiences of children and adults, or for children alone, not for adolescents exclusively. The idea that a distinct developmental stage between childhood and adulthood existed, never mind needed a separate literature of its own, made little sense to societies in which the majority of children entered the workforce during their early teen years.

Psychologist G. Stanley Hall is often credited with the "invention" of adolescence as a separate life stage. His 1904 book *Adolescence: Its Psychology and Its Relations to Physiology, Anthropology, Sociology, Sex, Crime, Religion, and Education* influenced a generation of educators and youth workers in arguing that the storm and stress common to the teen years required active intervention and guidance from adults. However, it was not until the Great Depression of the 1930s, which pushed teens out of the workforce and into full-time schooling, that a separate teen culture began to emerge. Spending days together in the new four-year high school, largely separate from adults, adolescents began to develop a new culture based on high school social life. The year 1941 marked the first appearance of the word "teenager"; 1957, the creation of a guiding body to judge the literature published for said teenager, the American Library Association's Young Adult Services Division.

The first young adult novel is also the first young adult romance. Maureen Daly's *Seventeenth Summer*, published in 1942, signaled a clear shift away from the career-oriented books that had up until then served as literature for the 20th-century adolescent. Daly drew upon her own experience growing up in small-town Wisconsin to depict the budding romance between 17-year-old middle-class Angie and not-quite-middle-class Jack. Daly's use of a first-person narrator, her inclusion of teen smoking and drinking, and her own young age (only 21 at the time of the book's appearance) gave *Seventeenth Summer* a sense of immediacy that appealed to thousands. Other publishers soon attempted to capitalize on the popular new trend with their own teen romances. Authors such as Betty Cavanna (*Going on Sixteen*, 1946), Janet Lambert (*Practically Perfect*, 1947), Rosamund du Jardin (*Practically Seventeen*, 1949), Anne Emery (*Senior Year*, 1949), and others continued the romance trend well into the 1950s.

These early books prove strikingly innocent by today's standards; Daly's smoking and drinking rarely appear, and kisses, not sex, preoccupy their teen protagonists. Dating, going steady, or finding a date for the prom were the typical problems their characters faced. As Michael Cart argues, like the category "teenager" itself, these books focused on white, middle- and upper-class teens living in small cities or towns. Black, Latino, and ethnic-minority teens, and those who lived in the city and on farms, often still had to work, and thus didn't have the leisure that defined "teenager."

By the late 1960s, both writers and critics began to call for a new type of literature for young adults, literature that reflected the lives teens currently lived rather than nostalgically evoking a romanticized adolescent past. Though not a romance, S. E. Hinton's *The Outsiders* paved the way for a new type of teen novel, one seen at the time as far more realistic than its postwar romance-novel counterpart.

During this same period, sex emerged as an important topic in the young adult novel. Paul Zindel's *My Darling, My Hamburger* (1969) and Norma Fox Mazer's

Up in Seth's Room (1979) portrayed adolescent girls' struggles to decide whether or not to have sex with their boyfriends, both of whom seemed as focused on their entitlement to "score" as on creating caring relationships. Only with the publication of Judy Blume's 1975 book *Forever* could teens read a book in which the protagonists have sex by mutual choice, enjoy it, and aren't forced to suffer any negative consequences. Though Blume's novel often reads more like a sex manual than a work of fiction, to teen readers who had never seen sex and sexuality portrayed as a positive development in their literature, *Forever* proved a revelation.

The early 1980s witnessed the renaissance of formulaic stories far more similar to the romances published in the 1940s and 1950s than to the realistic novels that emerged in the 1960s and 1970s. Noting the popularity of several light paperback romances offered via its Teenage Book Club, publisher Scholastic developed a new marketing strategy aimed not at the adults (librarians and teachers) who worked with teens and until that time had been the main purchasers (and arbiters) of YA books, but at teens directly, via the new chain bookstores found in local malls. Rather than publish in hardcover, Scholastic decided to issue its new teen romances in paperback, at a price point that adolescents could afford. Scholastic's *Wildfire* romance line debuted in January 1980, succeeding far beyond the publisher's dreams: 1.8 million copies of 15 *Wildfire* titles were sold during the line's first year. The economic recession of the early 1980s meant that the budgets of the youth-serving institutions that once purchased the majority of books for teens were being slashed; publishers eagerly sought to recoup their institutional market losses by selling directly to teenagers themselves.

Scholastic quickly developed additional teen romance lines: *Wishing Star*, whose protagonists faced physical, emotional, and social problems in addition to falling in love, in 1980; *Windswept*, Gothic romances, in 1981; and *Sunfire*, historical romances, in 1984. Eager to win a piece of this lucrative new market, other publishers soon followed suit: Dell's *Young Love*, Harlequin/Silhouette's *First Love*, and Bantam's *Sweet Dreams* in 1981; Simon & Schuster's *First Love* in 1982; Tempo's *Caprice* in 1984; and more. Readers could even vicariously choose their own guy by choosing the path of the heroine in such series as Pocket's *Follow Your Heart* and Wanderer's *Dream Your Own Romance*.

Unlike the romances of the 1940s and 1950s, the 1980s series romances asked readers to be loyal to a publishing imprint, rather than to an author. Publishers' marketing research showed that teen girls wanted what their mothers had in the category romances of Harlequin, Silhouette, and their like; publishers proved eager to sate such desires. With print runs as large as 25 times those of the typical young adult hardcover, teen paperback romances made publishers sit up and take notice as profits from their once sleepy children's book departments began to make significant contributions to their bottom lines. Million-dollar marketing campaigns, previously unheard of, signaled a shift in children's book publishing away from printing books because of their literary or educative value, and toward printing books that would earn the highest profits.

Teen romance moved from trend to phenomenon with the appearance of Francine Pascal's *Sweet Valley High* series in 1983. Unlike previous lines, which featured stand-alone titles, Pascal proposed to write romances with a central cast of unchanging characters. Similar to a soap opera, each novel would end with a cliff-hanger, leaving readers primed to devour each subsequent book in the series. Publisher Bantam, which had experience with series romance through its *Sweet Dreams* line, eagerly snapped up Pascal's proposal. Book packager Cloverdale Press and Daniel Weiss Associates gave book outlines prepared by Pascal to a stable of ghostwriters, allowing the series at its height to issue a new book each month (with a printing of 350,000 copies).

In 1985, *Perfect Summer*, a Sweet Valley High "super edition," became the first YA novel ever to reach the *New York Times* paperback best-seller list. The popularity of the brand led to massive proliferation: super editions, super thrillers, super stars, and manga editions, all versions of the "core" series, and nine different spin-off series, including *Sweet Valley Kids*, *Sweet Valley University*, and more. By the end of the 1980s, 34 million Sweet Valley books were in print; by 1994, 81 million.

While some argue that the 1980s romance boom stemmed from young readers tired of the social problems that appeared in the realistic novels of the 1970s, others suggest that adults—parents, teachers, booksellers, publishers, and librarians—were the true cause of the shift in the market. Whatever its source, this backlash against realism found its justification in a discourse emerging in both the social and political realms: a fear of "disappearing childhood." The more socially conservative political climate of the Reagan years also aligned with the romances' generally conservative themes.

From their first appearance, 1980s YA mass-market romance series were roundly criticized, by the literarily inclined for their dull prose and formulaic plots, and by the ideologically minded for their largely homogenous portrait of contemporary American life and their limiting visions of female identity. The *Council on Interracial Books for Children* protested against Scholastic's Wildfire series for teaching girls that boys' interests should be put above their own; that girls are not allies, but competition; and that no life exists beyond the suburban white middle-class nuclear family. Linda K. Christian-Smith extended that argument to the entire 1980s market, arguing that young readers "become part of a fictional world where men give meaning and completeness to women's lives and women's destinies are to tend heart and hearth. If girls have interests other than boys in these books, the interests are subordinated to the important task of getting and keeping a boyfriend. . . . Girls are constructed as objects of others' desires with few desires of their own (1993, 46).

Some publishers sought to address such criticisms. In 1992, Bantam contracted with noted African American children's book author Walter Dean Myers for a romance series featuring African American teens. Writing under the name "Stacie Johnson," Myers penned 12 books between 1992 and 1994. But by the mid-1990s, the market for romance (with the notable exception of *SVH*) began to dwindle, overtaken by a new fascination with horror novels. Less-popular lines gradually ceased publication: *Windswept* in 1984, *Caprice* in 1985, *Wildfire* in 1986, and *Sunfire* in 1989. *Sweet Dreams*, perhaps Sweet Valley High's biggest competitor, closed up shop in 1995, after publishing 232 titles; and in 1999, *Sweet Valley High* followed.

During the 1990s, the market for all YA fiction, not just romance, seemed in danger of disappearing. Schools and libraries needed to devote larger and larger chunks of their budgets to purchasing technology rather than books. Among librarians, those trained in service to young adults were often cut first when budgets grew tight. The typical age of YA protagonists moved lower and lower, from 16 and 17 to 12–14, and the new chain "superstores" typically shelved YA not in a separate section but scattered within the children's fiction section. The year 1991 marked the 15th year of decline in America's teen population. Publishers were issuing fewer and fewer books for the YA market; some even predicted that in the near future, no such market would exist.

But YA books made a comeback during the late 1990s. As the number of adolescents once again began to grow (16.6 percent from 1990 to 2000), authors began to call once again for hard-hitting literary fiction for older teens; literary critics began to discuss YA as a genre separate from children's literature; and bookseller Barnes & Noble announced it would create stand-alone YA sections in all of its stores. In 1996, the National Book Foundation reestablished a prize for the most distinguished book of the year for young readers; four out of its first six years, the award was given to a YA title. And in 1999, the Young Adult Library Services Division established the Printz Award, an award comparable to the American Library Association's Caldecott Award for picture books and Newbery Award for children's literature.

Although children's publishers continued to issue literary fiction that often contained romance plotlines, Teen Romance as a genre did not reemerge until the turn of the century, with the migration of adult "chick lit" to the adolescent market. Louise Rennison's *Angus, Thongs, and Full-Frontal Snogging* (published in the United States in 2000) signaled the beginning of this new look for YA romance. But Cecilie von Ziegesar's Gossip Girl series (2002) led the field in the direction of "mean girl" books, sometimes known as "privileged chick lit." Series such as *The*

A List, The Clique, and *Pretty Little Liars* feature wealthy teens enjoying sex, shopping, and the worship of high-end consumer brands—a far cry from the romance books of the 1980s. Indeed, a *New York Times* article describing the phenomenon is titled "In Novels for Girls, Fashion Trumps Romance."

Teenagers have always read books intended for an adult audience, but with the Gossip Girl series, the crossover went in the opposite direction, with many grown women (and many gay men) in their twenties and thirties also purchasing the books. And since the late 1990s, all types of romances intended for the older end of the teen market are increasingly being purchased, and enjoyed, by grown-ups. The biggest YA romance of the 21st century, Stephenie Meyer's Twilight series, climbed the best-seller charts in part due to its adult readers. Adult readers who would once have been embarrassed to admit to reading a "kid's book" are now buying them in droves.

The same period has witnessed the blurring of lines between Romance and other subgenres. In addition to YA "chick lit" and "soap opera," Romance has been combined with fantasy and the paranormal (Melissa Marr's Wicked Lovely books, 2007–2011; Kristin Cashore's Graceling Realm books, 2008–2012); historical fiction (Libba Bray's Gemma Doyle trilogy, 2005–2007); mystery and suspense (myriad novels by Joan Lowry Nixon); and speculative fiction (Suzanne Collins's Hunger Games trilogy, 2008–2010).

Contemporary romance continues to be most popular, though, with books about first love (many of Sarah Dessen's novels), romances with humor (Meg Cabot's *Princess Diaries*), romances with protagonists of color (Jacqueline Woodson's *If You Come Softly*, 1998), and stories that combine social or personal problems (such as sex, rape, grief, and abuse) with romance. Paperback original series romance has also reemerged; Bantam updated and reissued the Sweet Valley High series in 2008, while other publishers have created new lines, many of them based on characters from popular television shows. Christian publisher Bethany House began to explore the YA market with Robin Jones Gunn's Christy Miller series and continues to be the dominant player in inspirational romance for teens today.

Graphic novels have also joined the YA romance mix, with manga first published in Japan (such as Miwa Ueda's Peach Girl: Change of Heart series, 2003–present) then translated for an American audience. And romances with gay and lesbian characters have finally stopped ending with breakups or tragic unwanted outings, pointing to the possibilities of happy adolescent homosexual love (David Levithan's *Boy Meets Boy*, 2003; Lauren Myracle's *Kissing Kate*, 2003).

The Romance Writers of America (RWA) began awarding a Golden Medallion (later renamed the RITA Award) to the "Best Young Adult Romance" in 1983. The first award was given to Jo Stewart for *Andrea;* other early winners include Lurlene McDaniel and Cheryl Zach. The weakened market for YA fiction in the 1990s, however, led to the suspension of the award in 1996. It was reinstituted in 2008, awarded to Melissa Marr for her fantasy romance *Wicked Lovely*, and has been awarded each year since. In 2009, Rosemary Clement-Moore and other authors worked to create their own subchapter of RWA, the Young Adult Special Interest Chapter, testifying to the increasing interest in romance fiction in the 21st century.

Jackie Horne

Further Reading

Carpan, Carolyn. *Rocked by Romance: A Guide to Teen Romance Fiction*. Westport, CT: Libraries Unlimited, 2004.

Cart, Michael. *Young Adult Literature: From Romance to Realism*. Chicago: ALA, 2010.

Christian-Smith, Linda K. *Becoming a Woman through Romance*. London: Routledge, 1990.

Christian-Smith, Linda K., ed. *Texts of Desire: Essays on Fiction, Femininity, and Schooling*. London: Falmer Press, 1993.

Harvey, B. "*Wildfire*: Tame but Deadly." *Interracial Books for Children Bulletin* 12: 8–10.

Herald, Diana Tixier. "Romance." *Teen Genreflecting 3: A Guide to Reading Interests*. Santa Barbara, CA: Libraries Unlimited, 2011.

Pattee, Amy. *Reading the Adolescent Romance: Sweet Valley High and the Popular Young Adult Romance Novel*. New York: Routledge, 2011.

Pecora, N. "Identity by Design: The Corporate Construction of Teen Romance Novels." In *Growing Up Girls: Popular Culture and the Construction of Identity*, edited by S. R. Mazzarella and N. O. Pecora, 49–86. New York: Peter Lang, 1999.

Pollack, Pamela D. "The Business of Popularity: The Surge of Teenage Paperbacks." *School Library Journal* 28 (1981): 25.

Ramsdell, Kristin. *Happily Ever After: A Guide to Reading Interests in Romance Fiction*. Santa Barbra, CA: Libraries Unlimited, 1987.

Willinsky, J., and R. M. Hunniford. "Reading the Romance Younger: The Mirrors and Fears of a Preparatory Literature." In *Texts of Desire: Essays on Fiction, Femininity, and Schooling*, edited by Linda K. Christian-Smith, 87–105. London and Washington, D.C.: Falmer Press, 1993.

Appendix 1: Rita Award Winners

The Rita Award (called the Medallion Award prior to 1990) is the premier award for excellence in romance fiction and is presented by the Romance Writers of America (RWA). Named for the organization's first president, Rita Clay Estrada, it has become what some consider to be the Oscar of popular romance fiction. The awards are presented at the annual RWA conference each year in July for books published in the previous year. The first awards were given in 1982 and have been given each year since. As the romance genre has evolved, the categories have changed over the years.

Golden Medallion Winners

1982

Category Contemporary Romance
Winner Take All by Brooke Hastings
Mainstream Contemporary Romance
The Sun Dancers by Barbara Faith
Category Historical Romance
Rendezvous at Gramercy by Constance Ravenlock
Mainstream Historical Romance
Day beyond Destiny by Anna James

1983

Contemporary Mainstream Romance
Opal Fires by Lynda Trent
Contemporary Sensual Romance
Heart's Victory by Nora Roberts
Contemporary Sweet Romance
Renegade Player by Dixie Browning

Category Historical Romance
Defiant Love by Mara Seger
Mainstream Historical Romance
The Endearment by LaVyrle Spencer
Young Adult Romance
Andrea by Jo Stewart

1984

Contemporary Romance under 65,000 Words
Memory and Desire by Eileen Bryan
Contemporary Romance between 65,000 and 80,000 Words
This Magic Moment by Nora Roberts and *Destiny's Sweet Errand* by Deirdre
Mardon
Traditional Romance
Untamed by Nora Roberts
Category Historical Romance
The Clergyman's Daughter by Julie Jeffries
Historical Romance
Hummingbird by LaVyrle Spencer
Young Adult Romance
Julie's Magic Moment by Barbara Bartholomew

1985

Long Contemporary Series Romance
A Matter of Choice by Nora Roberts
Short Contemporary Romance
Opposite's Attract by Nora Roberts
Mainstream Romance
After All These Years by Kathleen Gilles Seidel
Traditional Romance
The Karas Cup by Brittany Young
Historical Romance
Twice Loved by LaVyrle Spencer
Regency Romance
The Lurid Lady Lockport by Kasey Michaels
Inspirational Romance
For the Love of Mike by Charlotte Nichols
Young Adult Romance
The Frog Princess by Cheryl Zach

1986

Long Contemporary Series Romance
  Today, Tomorrow, and Always by Georgia Bockoven
Short Contemporary Romance
  Much Needed Holiday by Joan Hohl
Single Title Romance
  Banish Misfortune by Anne Stuart
Traditional Romance
  The Crystal Unicorn by Doreen Owens Malek
Historical Romance
  Not So Wild a Dream by Francine Rivers
Regency Romance
  The Beauty's Daughter by Monette Cummings
Inspirational Romance
  From This Day Forward by Kathleen Karr
Young Adult Romance
  Waiting by Amanda by Cheryl Zach

1987

Long Contemporary Series Romance
  One Summer by Nora Roberts
Short Contemporary Romance
  Still Waters by Kathleen Creighton
Single Title Romance
  Sunshine and Shadow by Tom and Sharon Curtis
Traditional Romance
  Opal Fire by Sandy Dengler
Historical Romance
  By Right of Arms by Robyn Carr
Regency Romance
  Lord Abberley's Nemesis by Amanda Scott
Young Adult Romance
  Video Fever by Kathleen Garvey

1988

Long Contemporary Series Romance
  In Defense of Love by Kathleen Creighton

Short Contemporary Romance
> *Stolen Moments* by Terri Herrington

Single Title Romance
> *Twilight Whispers* by Barbara Delinsky

Traditional Romance
> *It Takes a Thief* by Rita Rainville

Historical Romance
> *The Gamble* by LaVyrle Spencer

Regency Romance
> *Sugar Rose* by Susan Carroll

Young Adult Romance
> *Does Your Nose Get in the Way, Too?* by Arlene Erlbach

1989

Long Contemporary Series Romance
> *A Crime of the Heart* by Cheryl Reavis

Short Contemporary Romance
> *Winter's Daughter* by Kathleen Creighton

Single Title Romance
> *Leaves of Fortune* by Linda Barlow

Traditional Romance
> *Flirtation River* by Bethany Campbell

Historical Romance
> *Sunflower* by Jill Marie Landis

Regency Romance
> *Brighton Road* by Susan Carroll

Suspense Romance
> *Brazen Virtue* by Nora Roberts

Young Adult Romance
> *The Ghosts of Stony Cove* by Eileen Charbonneau

Rita Awards

1990

Long Contemporary Series Romance
> *The Ice Cream Man* by Kathleen Korbel

Short Contemporary Series Romance
> *Night of the Hunter* by Jennifer Greene

Single Title Contemporary Romance
Private Relations by Diane Chamberlain
Traditional Romance
Rhapsody in Bloom by Mona Van Wieren
Series Historical Romance
Silver Noose by Patricia Gardner Evans
Single Title Historical Romance
The Bride by Julie Garwood
Regency Romance
The Rake and the Reformer by Mary Jo Putney
Romantic Suspense
Perchance to Dream by Kathleen Korbel
Young Adult Romance
Renée by Vivian Schurfranz
Best First Book
Out of the Blue by Alaina Hawthorne
Best Romance of 1989 (Golden Choice Award)
Morning Glory by LaVyrle Spencer

1991

Long Contemporary Series Romance
Patrick Gallagher's Widow by Cheryl Reavis
Short Contemporary Series Romance
Step into My Parlor by Jan Hudson
Single Title Contemporary Romance
Public Secrets by Nora Roberts
Traditional Romance
Song of the Lorelie by Lucy Gordon
Series Historical Romance
A Wild Yearning by Penelope Williamson
Single Title Historical Romance
Where Love Dwells by Elizabeth Stuart
Regency Romance
The Sandalwood Princess by Loretta Chase
Romantic Suspense
Night Spice by Karen Keast
Best First Book
Black Horse Island by Dee Holmes

Best Romance of 1990 (Golden Choice Award)
The Prince of Midnight by Laura Kinsale

1992

Long Contemporary Series Romance
A Rose for Maggie by Kathleen Korbel
Short Contemporary Series Romance
A Human Touch by Glenda Sanders
Single Title Contemporary Romance
A Man to Die For by Eileen Dreyer
Traditional Romance
Every Kind of Heaven by Bethany Campbell
Series Historical Romance
The Tender Texan by Jodi Thomas
Single Title Historical Romance
Courting Miss Hattie by Pamela Morsi
Regency Romance
Emily and the Dark Angel by Jo Beverley
Romantic Suspense
Night Shift by Nora Roberts
Young Adult Romance
Now I Lay Me Down to Sleep by Lurlene McDaniel
Futuristic/Fantasy/Paranormal Romance
Angel for Hire by Justine Davis
Best First Book
Candle in the Wind by Christina Dodd
Best Romance of 1991 (Golden Choice Award)
Outlander by Diana Gabaldon

1993

Long Contemporary Series Romance
The Silence of Midnight by Karen Young
Short Contemporary Series Romance
Navarrone by Helen R. Myers
Single Title Contemporary Romance
This Time Forever by Kathleen Eagle
Traditional Romance
Father Goose by Maria Ferrarella

Series Historical Romance
The Prisoner by Cheryl Reavis
Single Title Historical Romance
Keeper of the Dream by Penelope Williamson
Regency Romance
An Unwilling Bride by Jo Beverley
Romantic Suspense
Divine Evil by Nora Roberts
Young Adult Romance
Song of the Buffalo Boy by Sherry Garland
Futuristic/Fantasy/Paranormal Romance
Emily's Ghost by Antoinette Stockenberg
Best First Book
Trust Me by Jeane Renick
Best Romance of 1992 (Golden Choice Award)
Come Spring by Jill Marie Landis

1994

Long Contemporary Series Romance
Dragonslayer by Emilie Richards
Short Contemporary Series Romance
Avenging Angel by Glenna McReynolds
Single Title Contemporary Romance
Private Scandals by Nora Roberts
Traditional Romance
Annie and the Wise Men by Lindsay Longford
Series Historical Romance
Untamed by Elizabeth Lowell
Single Title Historical Romance
My Lady Notorious by Jo Beverley
Regency Romance
Deirdre and Don Juan by Jo Beverley
Romantic Suspense
Nightshade by Nora Roberts
Young Adult Romance
Summer Lightning by Wendy Corsi Staub
Futuristic/Fantasy/Paranormal Romance
Falling Angel by Anne Stuart

Best First Book
> *A Candle in the Dark* by Megan Chance

Best Romance of 1993 (Golden Choice Award)
> *Lord of the Night* by Susan Wiggs

1995

Long Contemporary Series Romance
> *A Soldier's Heart* by Kathleen Korbel

Short Contemporary Series Romance
> *Getting Rid of Bradley* by Jennifer Crusie

Single Title Contemporary Romance
> *Again* by Kathleen Gilles Seidel

Traditional Romance
> *Oh, Baby!* by Lauryn Chandler

Historical Romance
> *To Tame a Texan's Heart* by Jodi Thomas

Long Title Historical Romance
> *Dancing in the Wind* by Mary Jo Putney

Regency Romance
> *Mrs. Drew Plays Her Hand* by Carla Kelly

Romantic Suspense
> *Hidden Riches* by Nora Roberts

Young Adult Romance
> *Second to None* by ArLynn Presser

Paranormal/Fantasy/Time Travel Romance
> *Lord of the Storm* by Justine Davis

Inspirational Romance
> *An Echo in the Darkness* by Francine Rivers

Best First Book
> *Ghostly Enchantment* by Angie Ray

Best Romance of 1994 (Golden Choice Award)
> *It Had to Be You* by Susan Elizabeth Phillips

1996

Long Contemporary Series Romance
> *Morning Side of Dawn* by Justine Davis

Short Contemporary Series Romance
> *Single Dad* by Jennifer Greene

Single Title Contemporary Romance
> *Born in Ice* by Nora Roberts

Traditional Romance
Stranger in Her Arms by Elizabeth Sites
Short Historical Romance
Lord of Scoundrels by Loretta Chase
Long Title Historical Romance
Something Shady by Pamela Morsi
Regency Romance
Gwen's Christmas Ghost by Lynn Kerstan and Alicia Rasley
Romantic Suspense
Winter's Edge by Anne Stuart
Young Adult Romance
Runaway by Cheryl Zach
Paranormal Romance
The Covenant by Modean Moon
Inspirational Romance
As Sure as the Dawn by Francine Rivers
Best First Book
The Warlord by Elizabeth Elliott
Best/Favorite Romance of 1995
Born in Ice by Nora Roberts

1997

Long Contemporary Series Romance
Wild Blood by Naomi Horton
Short Contemporary Series Romance
Cowboy Pride by Anne McAllister
Single Title Contemporary Romance
Daniel's Gift by Barbara Freethy
Traditional Romance
Her Very Own Husband by Lauryn Chandler
Short Historical Romance
Always to Remember by Lorraine Heath
Long Historical Romance
Conor's Way by Laura Lee Guhrke
Regency Romance
The Lady's Companion by Carla Kelly
Romantic Suspense
See How They Run by Bethany Campbell
Paranormal/Fantasy/Time Travel Romance
Stardust of Yesterday by Lynn Kurland

Inspirational Romance
> *The Scarlet Thread* by Francine Rivers

Best First Book
> *Stardust of Yesterday* by Lynn Kurland

Favorite Romance/Book of 1996
> Not given because of lack of member participation in voting for the award. (This award is based on a popular vote of the RWA membership.)

1998

Long Contemporary Series Romance
> *Reckless* by Ruth Wind

Short Contemporary Series Romance
> *Nobody's Princess* by Jennifer Greene

Single Title Contemporary Romance
> *Nobody's Baby but Mine* by Susan Elizabeth Phillips

Traditional Romance
> *His Brother's Child* by Lucy Gordon

Short Historical Romance
> *Heart of a Knight* by Barbara Samuel

Long Historical Romance
> *The Promise of Jennie Jones* by Maggie Osborne

Regency Romance
> *Love's Reward* by Jean R. Ewing

Romantic Suspense
> *On the Way to a Wedding* by Ingrid Weaver

Paranormal Romance
> *Fire Hawk* by Justine Dare

Inspirational Romance
> *Homeward* by Melody Carlson

Best First Book
> *Brazen Angel* by Elizabeth Boyle

Favorite Romance/Book of 1997
> *Nobody's Baby but Mine* by Susan Elizabeth Phillips

1999

Long Contemporary Romance
> *Meant to Be Married* by Ruth Wind

Short Contemporary Romance
> *The Notorious Groom* by Caroline Cross

Single Title Contemporary Romance
> *Dream a Little Dream* by Susan Elizabeth Phillips

Traditional Romance
> *Monday Man* by Kristin Gabriel

Short Historical Romance
> *Merely Married* by Patricia Coughlin

Long Historical Romance
> *My Dearest Enemy* by Connie Brockway

Regency Romance
> *His Grace Endures* by Emma Jensen

Romantic Suspense
> *Cool Shade* by Theresa Weir

Paranormal Romance
> *The Bride Finder* by Susan Carroll

Inspirational Romance
> *Patterns of Love* by Robin Lee Hatcher

Best First Book
> *My Darling Caroline* by Adele Ashworth

Favorite Romance/Book of the Year
> This award has been changed to Ten Favorite Books of the Year (chosen by popular vote of the RWA membership), and Rita's are no longer presented for them.

2000

Long Contemporary Romance
> *Undercover Princess* by Suzanne Brockmann

Short Contemporary Romance
> *The Stardust Cowboy* by Anne McAllister

Single Title Contemporary Romance
> *Body Guard* by Suzanne Brockmann

Traditional Romance
> *Annie, Get Your Groom* by Kristin Gabriel

Short Historical Romance
> *The Proposition* by Judith Ivory

Long Historical Romance
> *Silken Threads* by Patricia Ryan

Regency Romance
> *The Rake's Retreat* by Nancy Butler

Romantic Suspense
> *The Bride's Protector* by Gayle Wilson

Paranormal Romance
> *Nell* by Jeanette Baker

Inspirational Romance
> *Danger in the Shadows* by Dee Henderson

Best First Book
> *The Maiden and the Unicorn* by Isolde Martyn

Novella
> "Starry, Starry Night" by Marianne Willman (included in the anthology *Once upon a Star*)

2001

Long Contemporary Romance
> *Rogue's Reform* by Marilyn Pappano

Short Contemporary Romance
> *It Takes a Rebel* by Stephanie Bond

Single Title Contemporary Romance
> *First Lady* by Susan Elizabeth Phillips

Traditional Romance
> *The Best Man and the Bridesmaid* by Liz Fielding

Short Historical Romance
> *The Mistress* by Susan Wiggs

Long Historical Romance
> *Devilish* by Jo Beverley

Regency Romance
> *A Grand Design* by Emma Jensen

Romantic Suspense
> *Carolina Moon* by Nora Roberts

Paranormal Romance
> *The Highlander's Touch* by Karen Marie Moning

Inspirational Romance
> *The Shepherd's Voice* by Robin Lee Hatcher

Best First Book
> *A Man Like Mac* by Fay Robinson

Novella
> "Final Approach to Forever" by Merline Lovelace (included in the anthology *Special Report*)

2002

Long Contemporary Romance
   Coming Home to You by Fay Robinson
Short Contemporary Romance
   A Long Hot Christmas by Barbara Daly
Single Title Contemporary Romance
   True Confessions by Rachel Gibson
Traditional Romance
   Quinn's Complete Seduction by Sandra Steffen
Short Historical Romance
   Tempt Me Once by Barbara Dawson Smith
Long Historical Romance
   The Bridal Season by Connie Brockway
Regency Romance
   Much Obliged by Jessica Benson
Romantic Suspense
   The Surgeon by Tess Gerritsen
Paranormal Romance
   Heart Mate by Robin D. Owens
Inspirational Romance
   Beneath a Southern Sky by Deborah Raney
Best First Book
   The Border Bride by Elizabeth English
Novella
   "I Will" by Linda Kleypas (included in the anthology *Wish List*)

2003

Long Contemporary Romance
   Taking Cover by Catherine Mann
Short Contemporary Romance
   Taming the Outlaw by Cindy Gerard
Single Title Contemporary Romance
   No Place Like Home by Barbara Samuel
Traditional Romance
   The Christmas Basket by Debbie Macomber
Short Historical Romance
   The Bride Fair by Cheryl Reavis
Long Historical Romance
   Stealing Heaven by Madeline Hunter

Regency Romance
    A Debt to Delia by Barbara Metzger
Romantic Suspense
    Three Fates by Nora Roberts
Paranormal Romance
    Contact by Susan Grant
Inspirational Romance
    Never Say Goodbye by Irene Hannon
Best First Book
    Shades of Honor by Wendy Lindstrom
Novella
    "To Kiss in the Shadows" by Lynn Kerstan (included in the anthology *Tapestry*)

2004

Long Contemporary Romance
    The Top Gun's Return by Kathleen Creighton
Short Contemporary Romance
    The Knight's Kiss by Nicole Burnham
Single Title Contemporary Romance
    Birthright by Nora Roberts
Traditional Romance
    Her Royal Baby by Marion Lennox
Short Historical Romance
    Worth Any Price by Lisa Kleypas
Long Historical Romance
    The Destiny by Kathleen Givens
Regency Romance
    Prospero's Daughter by Nancy Butler
Romantic Suspense
    Remember When: Part One by Nora Roberts
Paranormal Romance
    Shades of Midnight by Linda Fallon
Inspirational Romance
    Autumn Dreams by Gayle Roper
Best First Book
    Back Roads by Susan Crandall
Novella
    "Prisoner of the Tower" by Gayle Wilson (included in the anthology *The Wedding Chase*)

Novel with Strong Romantic Elements
Between Sisters by Kristin Hannah

2005

Long Contemporary Romance
John Riley's Girl by Inglath Cooper
Short Contemporary Romance
Miss Pruitt's Private Life by Barbara McCauley
Single Title Contemporary Romance
Bet Me by Jennifer Crusie
Traditional Romance
Christmas Eve Marriage by Jessica Hart
Short Historical Romance
A Wanted Man by Susan Kay Law
Long Historical Romance
Shadowheart by Laura Kinsale
Regency Romance
A Passionate Endeavor by Sophia Nash
Romantic Suspense
I'm Watching You by Karen Rose
Paranormal Romance
Blue Moon by Lori Handeland
Inspirational Romance
Grounds to Believe by Shelley Bates
Best First Book
Time Off for Good Behavior by Lani Diane Rich
Novella
"Her Best Enemy" by Maggie Shayne (included in the anthology *Night's Edge*)
Novel with Strong Romantic Elements
A.K.A. Goddess by Evelyn Vaughn

2006

Long Contemporary Romance
Worth Every Risk by Dianna Love Snell
Short Contemporary Romance
The Marriage Miracle by Liz Fielding
Single Title Contemporary Romance
Lakeside Cottage by Susan Wiggs

Traditional Romance
> *Princess of Convenience* by Marion Lennox

Short Historical Romance
> *The Texan's Reward* by Jodi Thomas

Long Historical Romance
> *The Devil to Pay* by Liz Carlyle

Regency Romance
> *A Reputable Rake* by Diane Gaston

Romantic Suspense
> *Survivor in Death* by J. D. Robb

Paranormal Romance
> *Gabriel's Ghost* by Linnea Sinclair

Inspirational Romance
> *Heavens to Betsy* by Beth Pattillo

Best First Book
> *Show Her the Money* by Stephanie Feagan

Novella
> "The Naked Truth about Guys" by Maggie Shayne (included in the anthology *The Naked Truth*)

Novel with Strong Romantic Elements
> *Lady Luck's Map of Vegas* by Barbara Samuel

2007

Long Contemporary
> *The Mommy Quest* by Lori Handeland

Short Contemporary
> *From the First* by Jessica Bird

Single Title Contemporary
> *Adios to My Old Life* by Caridad Ferrer

Traditional
> *Claiming His Family* by Barbara Hannay

Short Historical
> *The Book of True Desires* by Betina Krahn

Long Historical
> *On the Way to the Wedding* by Julia Quinn

Romantic Suspense
> *Blackout* by Annie Solomon

Paranormal
> *A Hunger Like No Other* by Kresley Cole

Inspirational
> *Revealed* by Tamera Alexander

First Book
> *The Husband Trap* by Tracy Anne Warren

Novella
> "'Tis the Silly Season" by Roxanne St. Claire (included in the anthology *A NASCAR Holiday*)

Novel with Strong Romantic Elements
> *Lady Raised High* by Laurien Gardner

2008

Contemporary Series Romance
> *Snowbound* by Janice Kay Johnson

Contemporary Series Romance: Suspense/Adventure
> *Treasure* by Helen Brenna

Single Title Contemporary Romance
> *Catch of the Day* by Kristan Higgins

Regency Historical Romance
> *The Secret Diaries of Miss Miranda Cheever* by Julia Quinn

Historical Romance
> *Lessons of Desire* by Madeline Hunter

Romantic Suspense
> *Ice Blue* by Anne Stuart

Paranormal Romance
> *Lover Revealed* by J. R. Ward

Inspirational Romance
> *A Touch of Grace* by Linda Goodnight

Best First Book
> *Dead Girls Are Easy* by Terri Garey

Novella
> "Born in My Heart" by Jennifer Greene (included in the anthology *Like Mother, Like Daughter*)

Novel with Strong Romantic Elements
> *Silent in the Grave* by Deanna Raybourn

Young Adult Romance
> *Wicked Lovely* by Melissa Marr

2009

Contemporary Series Romance
   A Mother's Wish by Karen Templeton
Contemporary Series Romance: Suspense/Adventure
   Danger Signals by Kathleen Creighton
Contemporary Single Title
   Not Another Bad Date by Rachel Gibson
Regency Historical Romance
   My Lord and Spymaster by Joanna Bourne
Historical Romance
   The Edge of Impropriety by Pam Rosenthal
Romantic Suspense
   Take No Prisoners by Cindy Gerard
Paranormal Romance
   Seducing Mr. Darcy by Gwyn Cready
Inspirational
   Finding Stephanie by Susan May Warren
First Book
   Oh. My. Gods by Tera Lynn Childs
Novella
   "The Fall of Rogue Gerard" by Stephanie Laurens (included in the anthology
   It Happened One Night)
Novel with Strong Romantic Elements
   Tribute by Nora Roberts
Young Adult Romance
   Hell Week by Rosemary Clement-Moore

2010

Contemporary Series Romance
   A Not-So-Perfect Past by Beth Andrews
Contemporary Series Romance: Suspense/Adventure
   The Soldier's Secret Daughter by Cindy Dees
Contemporary Single Title
   Too Good to Be True by Kristan Higgins
Regency Historical Romance
   What Happens in London by Julia Quinn
Historical Romance
   Not Quite a Husband by Sherry Thomas

Romantic Suspense
> *Whisper of Warning* by Laura Griffin

Paranormal Romance
> *Kiss of a Demon King* by Kresley Cole

Inspirational
> *The Inheritance* by Tamera Alexander

First Book
> *One Scream Away* by Kate Brady

Novella
> "The Christmas Eve Promise" by Molly O'Keefe (included in the anthology *The Night Before Christmas*)

Novel with Strong Romantic Elements
> *The Lost Recipe for Happiness* by Barbara O'Neal

Young Adult Romance
> *Perfect Chemisry* by Simone Elkeles

2011

Contemporary Series Romance
> *Welcome Home, Cowboy* by Karen Templeton

Contemporary Series Romance: Suspense/Adventure
> *The Moon That Night* by Helen Brenna

Contemporary Single Title
> *Simply Irresistible* by Jill Shalvis

Regency Historical Romance
> *The Mischief of the Mistletoe* by Lauren Willig

Historical Romance
> *His at Night* by Sherry Thomas

Romantic Suspense
> *Silent Scream* by Karen Rose

Paranormal Romance
> *Unchained: The Dark Forgotten* by Sharon Ashwood

Inspirational
> *In Harm's Way* by Irene Hannon

First Book
> *Pieces of Sky* by Kaki Warner

Novella
> "Shifting Sea" by Virginia Kantra (included in the anthology *Burning Up*)

Novel with Strong Romantic Elements
> *Welcome to Harmony* by Jodi Thomas

Young Adult Romance
  The Iron King by Julie Kagawa

2012

Contemporary Series Romance
  Doukakis's Apprentice by Sarah Morgan
Contemporary Series Romance: Suspense/Adventure
  Soldier's Last Stand by Cindy Dees
Contemporary Single Title
  Boomerang Bride by Fiona Lowe
Regency Historical Romance
  A Night to Surrender by Tessa Dare
Historical Romance
  The Black Hawk by Joanna Bourne
Romantic Suspense
  New York to Dallas by J. D. Robb
Paranormal Romance
  Dragon Bound by Thea Harrison
Inspirational
  The Measure of Katie Calloway by Serena Miller
First Book
  First Grave on the Right by Darynda Jones
Novella
  I Love the Earl by Caroline Linden
Novel with Strong Romantic Elements
  How to Bake a Perfect Life by Barbara O'Neal
Young Adult Romance
  Enclave by Ann Aguirre

2013

Long Contemporary Series Romance
  A Gift for All Seasons by Karen Templeton
Short Contemporary Series Romance
  Night of No Return by Sarah Morgan
Contemporary Single Title
  The Way Back Home by Barbara Freethy
Historical Romance
  A Rogue by Any Other Name by Sarah MacLean

Romantic Suspense
Scorched by Laura Griffin
Paranormal Romance
Shadow's Claim by Kresley Cole
Inspirational
Against the Tide by Elizabeth Camden
First Book
The Haunting of Maddy Clare by Simone St. James
Novella
Seduced by a Pirate by Eloisa James
Novel with Strong Romantic Elements
The Haunting of Maddy Clare by Simone St. James
Young Adult Romance
The Farm by Emily McKay

2014

Contemporary Romance
Crazy Thing Called Love by Molly O'Keefe
Short Contemporary Romance
Why Resist a Rebel? by Leah Ashton
Historical Romance
No Good Duke Goes Unpunished by Sarah MacLean
Romantic Suspense
Off the Edge by Carolyn Crane
Paranormal Romance
The Firebird by Susanna Kearsley
Erotic Romance
Claim Me by J. Kenner
Inspirational Romance
Five Days in Skye by Carla Laureano
First Book
The Sweet Spot by Laura Drake
Novella
Take Me, Cowboy by Jane Porter

2015

Contemporary Romance: Long
Baby, It's You by Jane Graves

Contemporary Romance: Mid-Length
  One in a Million by Jill Shalvis
Contemporary Romance: Short
  A Texas Rescue Christmas by Caro Carson
Historical Romance: Long
  Fool Me Twice by Meredith Duran
Historical Romance: Short
  Romancing the Duke by Tessa Dare
Romantic Suspense
  Concealed in Death by J. D. Robb
Paranormal Romance
  Evernight by Kristen Callihan
Erotic Romance
  The Saint by Tiffany Reisz
Inspirational Romance
  Deceived by Irene Hannon
First Book
  Run to You by Clara Kensie
Novella
  His Road Home by Anna Richland
Young Adult Romance
  Boys Like You by Juliana Stone

2016

Contemporary Romance: Long
  Brokedown Cowboy by Maisey Yates
Contemporary Romance: Mid-Length
  Him by Sarina Bowen and Elle Kennedy
Contemporary Romance: Short
  The Nanny Plan by Sarah M. Anderson
Historical Romance: Long
  Tiffany Girl by Deeanne Gist
Historical Romance: Short
  It Started with a Scandal by Julie Anne Long
Romantic Suspense
  Flash Fire by Dana Marton
Paranormal Romance
  Must Love Chainmail by Angela Quarles
Erotic Romance
  For Real: A Spires Story by Alexis Hall

Inspirational Romance
> *A Noble Masquerade* by Kristi Ann Hunter

First Book
> *Forget Tomorrow* by Pintip Dunn

Novella
> *Nice Girls Don't Ride* by Roni Loren

Young Adult Romance
> *The Anatomical Shape of a Heart* by Jenn Bennett

2017

Contemporary Romance: Long
> *Miracle on 5th Avenue* by Sarah Morgan

Contemporary Romance: Mid-Length
> *Carolina Dreaming* by Virginia Kantra

Contemporary Romance: Short
> *Christmas on Crimson Mountain* by Michelle Major

Historical Romance: Long
> *No Mistress of Mine* by Laura Lee Guhrke

Historical Romance: Short
> *A Duke to Remember* by Kelly Bowen

Romantic Suspense
> *Repressed* by Elisabeth Naughton

Paranormal Romance
> *Pages of the Mind* by Jeffe Kennedy

Erotic Romance
> *Off the Clock* by Roni Loren

Romance with Religious or Spiritual Elements
> *My Hope Next Door* by Tammy L. Gray

First Book
> *Once and For All: An American Valor Novel* by Cheryl Etchison

Novella
> *Her Every Wish* by Courtney Milan

Mainstream Fiction with a Central Romance
> *The Moon in the Palace* by Weina Dai Randel

Young Adult Romance
> *The Problem with Forever* by Jennifer L Armentrout

Sources: Romance Writers of America (https://www.rwa.org/p/cm/ld/fid=535) and *What Do I Read Next?: A Readers' Guide to Current Genre Fiction, 1990–2015* (Gale). For recent information, check Romance Writers of America (www.rwa.org).

Appendix 2: Testing the Waters: A Brief Core List of Suggested Romance Titles

This brief list is by no means comprehensive. There are hundreds, maybe thousands, of excellent romances out there waiting to be read; but if you're unfamiliar with the genre, where do you start? The authors and titles listed below are a diverse group and some to consider. Granted, they are only the tip of the proverbial iceberg, but they're a good place to start.

Please note that some of the titles listed below are parts of series, and most of these authors have written other books that are worth checking out. In addition, the various entries on the subgenres in the *Encyclopedia of Romance Fiction* might offer a few more suggestions, as would the list of Rita Award winners in Appendix 1.

Contemporary

Carr, Robyn. *Any Day Now*. Don Mills, Ontario, Canada: Mira, 2017.
Freethy, Barbara. *Tender Is the Night*. Burlingame, CA: Hyde Street Press, 2016.
Morgan, Sarah. *Moonlight over Manhattan*. Don Mills, Ontario, Canada: HQN, 2017.
Novak, Brenda. *Discovering You*. Don Mills, Ontario, Canada: Mira, 2016.
Phillips, Susan Elizabeth. *Heroes Are My Weakness*. New York: William Morrow, 2014.
Shalvis, Jill. *Then Came You*. New York: Berkley, 2014.

Erotic Romance

Dane, Loren. *Falling Under*. New York: Forever, 2015.
Kenner, J. The Stark Trilogy (*Claim Me, Release Me, Complete Me*). New York: Bantam, 2013.
Loren, Roni. *Off the Clock*. New York: Berkley, 2016.
Rai, Alisha. *Hate to Want You*. New York: Avon, 2017.

Reisz, Tiffany. *The Saint*. Don Mills, Ontario, Canada: Mira, 2014.

Rosenthal, Pam. *The Edge of Impropriety,* New York: Signet Eclipse, 2008.

Historical

Balogh, Mary. *Someone to Wed*. New York: Jove, 2017.

Bourne, Joanna. *My Lord and Spymaster*. New York: Berkley Sensation, 2008.

Burrowes, Grace. *Too Scot to Handle*. New York: Forever, 2017

Chase, Loretta. *Lord of Scoundrels*. New York: Avon, 1995.

Chase, Loretta. *Silk Is for Seduction*. New York: Avon, 2011.

Dreyer, Eileen. *Barely a Lady*. New York: Forever, 2010.

Gracie, Anne. *The Autumn Bride*. New York: Berkley Sensation, 2013.

James, Eloisa. *Once Upon a Kiss*. New York: Avon, 2010.

Jeffries, Sabrina. *The Danger of Desire*. New York: Pocket Books, 2016.

Kinsale, Laura. *Flowers from the Storm*. New York: Avon, 1992.

MacLean, Sarah. *A Rogue by Any Other Name*. New York: Avon, 2012.

Putney, Mary Jo. *Nowhere Near Respectable*. New York: Zebra, 2011.

Inspirational Romance

Alexander, Tamera. *To Wager Her Heart*. Grand Rapids, MI: Zondervan, 2017.

Gist, DeeAnne. *Tiffany Girl*. New York: Howard, 2015.

Henderson, Dee. *Full Disclosure*. Bloomington, MN: Bethany House, 2012.

Lewis, Beverly. *The Proving*. Bloomington, MN: Bethany House, 2017.

Rivers, Francine. *The Scarlet Thread*. Wheaton, IL: Tyndale House, 1996.

Scott, Regina. *The Husband Campaign*. New York: Love Inspired Historical, 2014.

LGBTQ Romances

Beecroft, Alex. *False Colors*. Philadelphia: Running Press, 2009.

Brockmann, Suzanne. *All Through the Night: A Troubleshooter Christmas*. New York: Ballantine, 2007.

Herendeen, Ann. *Phyllida and the Brotherhood of Philander: A Bisexual Regency Romance*. New York: Harper, 2008.

Lane, Amy. *The Bells of Times Square*. Burnsville, NC: Riptide, 2014.

Ripper, Kris. Queers of La Vista Series (*Gays of Our Lives, The Butch and the Beautiful, The Queer and the Restless, One Life to Lose, As La Vista Turns*). Burnsville, NC: RipTide Publishing, 2016–2017.

Multicultural

Alers, Rochelle. *The Inheritance*. New York: Dafina, 2017.
Cole, Alyssa. *An Extraordinary Union*. New York: Kensington, 2017.
Eagle, Kathleen. *Mystic Horseman*. Don Mills, Ontario, Canada: Mira, 2008.
Jenkins, Beverly. *Forbidden*. New York: Avon, 2016.
Lin, Jeannie. *Butterfly Swords*. Don Mills, Ontario, Canada: Harlequin Historical, 2010.

Paranormal

Castle, Jayne. *Illusion Town*. New York: Jove, 2016.
Feehan, Christine. *Shadow Rider*. New York: Jove, 2017.
Gabaldon, Diana. *Outlander*. New York: Delacorte, 1991.
Owens, Robin D. *HeartMate*. New York: Berkley Sensation, 2001.
Singh, Nalini. *Slave to Sensation*. New York: Berkley Sensation, 2006.
Ward, J. R. *Dark Lover*. New York: Signet Eclipse, 2005.

Romantic Suspense/Gothic

Brockmann, Suzanne. *Breaking the Rules*. New York: Ballantine, 2011.
Diamond, Tess. *Dangerous Games*. New York: Avon, 2017.
Dodd, Christina. *Virtue Falls*. New York: St. Martin's Press, 2014.
Krentz, Jayne Ann. *Secret Sisters*. New York: Berkley Books, 2015.
Roberts, Nora. *Come Sundown*. New York: St. Martin's Press, 2017.
Rose, Karen. *Every Dark Corner*. New York: Berkley, 2017.

Women's Fiction with Strong Romance Elements

Hannah, Kristin. *Summer Island*. New York: Crown, 2001.
Mallery, Susan. *Daughters of the Bride*. Don Mills, Ontario, Canada: HQN, 2016.
O'Neal, Barbara. *How to Bake a Perfect Life*. New York: Bantam, 2010.
O'Neal, Barbara. *The Lost Recipe for Happiness*. New York: Bantam, 2008.
Thomas, Jodi. *Welcome to Harmony*. New York: Berkley, 2010.
Wiggs, Susan. *The Apple Orchard*. Don Mills, Ontario, Canada: Mira, 2013.

Young Adult Romance

Bennett, Jenn. *The Anatomical Shape of a Heart*. New York: Feiwel and Friends, 2015.

Elkeles, Simone. *Perfect Chemistry*. New York: Walker, 2009.
Kagawa, Julie. *The Iron King*. Richmond: Mira, 2011.
McKay, Emily. *The Farm*. New York: Berkley, 2012.
Stone, Juliana. *Boys Like You*. Naperville, IL: Sourcebooks Fire, 2014.

A Handful of Older Classics Still Read Today

Not all of these are true romances, but they all had an impact on the popular romances of today. Many of these authors also wrote other books that may be of interest.

Austen, Jane. *Sense and Sensibility* (1811)
> Two sisters learn that happiness and social survival take both sense and sensibility.

Austen, Jane. *Pride and Prejudice* (1813)
> A couple learns the foolishness of pride, prejudging someone based on rumors and first impressions in Austen's most popular comedy of manners.

Austen, Jane. *Mansfield Park* (1814)
> An impoverished girl, raised with her wealthy cousins, has concerns about their new flashy neighbors and their London values and ways.

Austen, Jane. *Emma* (1814)
> A meddling heroine learns the folly of interfering in other people's love lives in an elegant story that served as the basis for the film *Clueless*.

Austen, Jane. *Northanger Abbey* (1818)
> A parody of the popular sensational sentimental Gothic romances of the day.

Austen, Jane. *Persuasion* (1818)
> A young woman reconnects with her former fiancé in a classic reunion story.

Brontë, Charlotte. *Jane Eyre* (1847)
> An orphaned governess finds danger and love on the English moors.

Bujold, Lois McMaster. *Shards of Honor* (1986)
> Two enemies fall in love as they work together to survive in a classic sci-fi novel that is part of Bujold's Vorkosigan series.

Du Maurier, Daphne. *Rebecca* (1938)
> An atmospheric contemporary Gothic romance that became the model for the modern Gothic.

Holt, Victoria. *Mistress of Mellyn* (1960)
> Danger and romance on the windswept cliffs of Cornwall during Victorian England.

Mitchell, Margaret. *Gone with the Wind* (1936)
> Love, loss, and survival in the Civil War South.

Scott, Sir Walter. *Ivanhoe* (1819)
> A 12th-century romantic adventure.

Seton, Anya. *Dragonwyck* (1944)

An American Victorian Gothic.

Seton, Anya. *Katherine* (1954)

The love story of Katherine Swynford and John of Gaunt, Duke of Lancaster, in 14th-century England.

Spencer, LaVyrle. *Morning Glory* (1989)

A World War II–era romance.

Spencer, LaVyrle. *The Gamble* (1987)

An historical romance with an 1880s Western setting.

Stewart, Mary. *Nine Coaches Waiting* (1958)

A brilliant contemporary Gothic.

Stewart, Mary. *My Brother Michael* (1960)

A favorite contemporary romantic suspense with a Greek setting.

Bibliography

Charles, John, and Shelley Mosley. *Romance Today: An A-to-Z Guide to Contemporary American Romance Writers*. Westport, CT: Greenwood Press, 2007.

Chelton, Mary K. "Unrestricted Body Parts and Predictable Bliss: The Audience Appeal of Formula Romances." *Library Journal* 116 (12): 44, 49.

Franz, Sarah S. G., and Eric Murphy Selinger, eds. *New Approaches to Popular Romance Fiction: Critical Essays*. Jefferson, NC: McFarland, 2012.

Henderson, Lesley, and D. L. Kirkpatrick, eds. *Twentieth-Century Romance and Historical Writers*. Chicago: St. James, 1990.

Krentz, Jayne Ann, ed. *Dangerous Men and Adventurous Women: Romance Writers on the Appeal of the Romance*. Philadelphia: University of Pennsylvania Press, 1992.

Markert, John. *Publishing Romance: The History of an Industry, 1940s to the Present*. Jefferson, NC: McFarland, 2016.

Mussell, Kay, and Johanna Tuñon, eds. *North American Romance Writers*. Metuchen, NJ: Scarecrow, 1999.

Ramsdell, Kristin. *Happily Ever After: A Guide to Reading Interests in Romance Fiction*. Littleton, CO: Libraries Unlimited, 1987.

Ramsdell, Kristin. *Romance Fiction: A Guide to the Genre*. Englewood, CO: Libraries Unlimited, 1999.

Ramsdell, Kristin. *Romance Fiction: A Guide to the Genre,* 2nd ed. Santa Barbara, CA: Libraries Unlimited, 2012.

Regis, Pamela. *A Natural History of the Romance Novel*. Philadelphia: University of Pennsylvania Press, 2003.

Rodale, Maya. *Dangerous Books for Girls: The Bad Reputation of Romance Novels Explained*. New York: Maya Rodale, 2015.

Romance Wiki, The. http://www.romancewiki.com/Main_Page.

Romance Writers of America. www.rwa.org.

RT Book Reviews. www.rtbookreviews.com/.

Teach Me Tonight: *Musings on Romance Fiction from an Academic Perspective*. http://teachmetonight.blogspot.com/.

Vasudevan, Aruna, and Lesley Henderson, eds. *Twentieth-Century Romance and Historical Writers,* 3rd ed. London: St. James, 1994.

Vinson, James, and D. L. Kirkpatrick, eds. *Twentieth-Century Romance and Gothic Writers*. Detroit: Gale, 1982.

Vivanco, Laura. *For Love and Money: The Literary Art of the Harlequin Mills & Boon Romance*. Tirril, Penrith, UK: Humanities-EBooks, 2011.

Vivanco, Laura. *Pursuing Happiness: Reading American Romance as Political Fiction*. Tirril, Penrith, UK: Humanities-EBooks, 2016.

Wendell, Sarah, and Candy Tan. *Beyond Heaving Bosoms: The Smart Bitches' Guide to Romance Novels*. New York: Simon & Schuster, 2009.

About the Editor and Contributors

Editor

KRISTIN RAMSDELL has been a romance reader since she discovered Betty Cavanna and Maureen Daly in her junior high library and a science fiction fan since she discovered Robert Heinlein and Ray Bradbury in the same place. She is also the author of the first and second editions of *Romance Fiction: A Guide to the Genre* (1999, 2012) and its predecessor, *Happily Ever After;* the Romance columnist for *Library Journal;* the editor of the Romance fiction section of the readers' advisory reference source, *What Do I Read Next?;* a regular contributor to Gale's Books and Authors; and a librarian emerita at California State University, East Bay. She received the Romance Writers of America Librarian of the Year Award in 1996 and the Melinda Helfer Fairy Godmother Award from *Romantic Times* in 2007.

Contributors

Elizabeth Reid Boyd
Edith Cowan University
Perth, Western Australia, Australia

Amy Burge
Lecturer in Popular Fiction
University of Birmingham
United Kingdom

John Charles
Adult Services Librarian, Retired
Scottsdale Public Library & The Poison Pen Bookstore
Scottsdale, Arizona

Erin Christmas
Interim Library Director
Riverside Public Library
Riverside, California

Heather Cleary
Newcastle, New South Wales, Australia

Wendy Crutcher
LA County Library
Los Angeles, California

Emily E. Direen
University of Melbourne
Melbourne, Victoria, Australia

jay Dixon
Freelance Editor and Independent Scholar
United Kingdom

Beth Driscoll
Senior Lecturer
University of Melbourne
Parkville, Victoria, Australia

Therese Dryden
Author
University of Newcastle
Newcastle, New South Wales, Australia

Kathryn Falk, Lady of Barrow
Founder and CEO
RT Book Reviews
Alvin, Texas

Lisa Fletcher
Associate Professor
University of Tasmania
Hobart, Tasmania, Australia

Erin Fry
Editor and Publications Manager
Romance Writers of America
Houston, Texas

Rosemary Gaby
Adjunct Senior Lecturer
University of Tasmania
Hobart, Tasmania, Australia

Crystal Goldman
Library Instruction Coordinator
University of California, San Diego
La Jolla, California

An Goris
Independent Scholar
Belgium

Jenny Haddon
Vice President
Romantic Novelists' Association
London, United Kingdom

Joanne Hamilton-Selway
Collection Development Coordinator, Retired
Scottsdale Public Library
Scottsdale, Arizona

Doug Highsmith
Librarian Emeritus
California State University, East Bay
Hayward, California

Jackie Horne
Writer and Independent Scholar
Cambridge, Massachusetts

Teresa L. Jacobsen
Librarian, Retired
Davis, California

Lisa Jass
Middle Tennessee State University
Murfreesboro, Tennessee

Laurie Kahn
Filmmaker and Resident Scholar
Brandeis Women's Studies Research Center
Watertown, Massachusetts

Kay Keppler
Author and Editor
Oakland, California

Tammi Kim
Special Collections and Archives
University of Nevada, Las Vegas
Las Vegas, Nevada

Jennifer Kloester
University of Melbourne
Melbourne, Victoria, Australia

Claire Knowles
Senior Lecturer in English
La Trobe University
Melbourne, Australia

Artemis Lamprinou
Associate Lecturer in Translation
The Open University
United Kingdom

Hannah Lee
Librarian
Beverly Hills, California

Harold Lowry
(AKA Leigh Greenwood)
Author
Charlotte, North Carolina

John Markert
Associate Professor of Sociology
Cumberland University
Lebanon, Tennessee

Christina Martínez
Associate Dean
Kraemer Family Library
University of Colorado, Colorado Springs
Colorado Springs, Colorado

Jodi McAlister
Deakin University
Melbourne, Victoria, Australia

Natalie McCall
Branch Manager
Albany Branch
Alameda County Library
Albany, California

Hannah McCann
University of Melbourne, Australia

Cindy Mediavilla
Library Consultant
Culver City, California

Shelley Mosley
Librarian, Retired
Glendale, Arizona

Lena Pham
Library Programs Consultant
California State Library
Sacramento, California

Alicia Rasley
Writing Advisor and Lecturer
University of Maryland University College
Indianapolis, Indiana

Joanna Schreck
TheBookTrailer.org
Founder and Administrator
Indianapolis, Indiana
and
Member and Contributing Author
Catholic Library Association

Eric Murphy Selinger
Professor of English
DePaul University
Chicago, Illinois

Sarah Sheehan
Assistant Director for Reference and Instruction
O'Malley Library, Manhattan College
Riverdale, New York

Louise Snead
Affaire de Coeur Magazine
Oakland, California

Doreen Sullivan
Librarian
RMIT University
Melbourne, Australia

Sandra Van Winkle
Glendale, Arizona

Rebecca Vnuk
Executive Director
LibraryReads
Forest Park, Illinois

Wendy Wagner
Professor
Johnson & Wales University
Providence, Rhode Island

Maryan Wherry
Independent Scholar

Index

Note: Page numbers in **bold** indicate main entries in the encyclopedia.